Advanced Principles for Improving Database Design, Systems Modeling, and Software Development

Keng Siau
University of Nebraska-Lincoln, USA

John Erickson
University of Nebraska-Omaha, USA

Information Science REFERENCE

INFORMATION SCIENCE REFERENCE
Hershey · New York

Director of Editorial Content:	Kristin Klinger
Assistant Development Editor:	Deborah Yahnke
Director of Production:	Jennifer Neidig
Managing Editor:	Jamie Snavely
Assistant Managing Editor:	Carole Coulson
Typesetter:	Larissa Vinci
Cover Design:	Lisa Tosheff
Printed at:	Yurchak Printing Inc.

Published in the United States of America by
Information Science Reference (an imprint of IGI Global)
701 E. Chocolate Avenue, Suite 200
Hershey PA 17033
Tel: 717-533-8845
Fax: 717-533-8661
E-mail: cust@igi-global.com
Web site: http://www.igi-global.com

and in the United Kingdom by
Information Science Reference (an imprint of IGI Global)
3 Henrietta Street
Covent Garden
London WC2E 8LU
Tel: 44 20 7240 0856
Fax: 44 20 7379 0609
Web site: http://www.eurospanbookstore.com

Library of Congress Cataloging-in-Publication Data

Advanced principles for improving database design, systems modeling and software development / Keng Siau and John Erickson, editors.

p. cm.

Includes bibliographical references and index.

Summary: "This book presents cutting-edge research and analysis of the most recent advancements in the fields of database systems and software development"--Provided by publisher.

ISBN 978-1-60566-172-8 (hardcover) -- ISBN 978-1-60566-173-5 (ebook)

1. Database design. 2. Computer software--Development. 3. System design. I. Siau, Keng, 1964- II. Erickson, John, 1956-

QA76.9.D26A385 2009

005.74--dc22

2008040207

British Cataloguing in Publication Data
A Cataloguing in Publication record for this book is available from the British Library.

All work contributed to this book is original material. The views expressed in this book are those of the authors, but not necessarily of the publisher.

Advanced Principles for Improving Database Design, Systems Modeling, and Software Development is part of the IGI Global series named *Advances in Database Research (ADR) Series*, ISBN: 1537-9299

Editorial Advisory Board

Table of Contents

Section II
Systems Building

Chapter IV
Towards Code Reuse and Refactoring as a Practice within Extreme Programming 63
Vijayan Sugumaran, Oakland University, USA
Gerald DeHondt, Grand Valley State University, USA

Chapter V
Requirements Elicitation Technique Selection: A Theory-Based Contingency Model 79
Miguel I. Aguirre-Urreta, DePaul University, USA
George M. Marakas, University of Kansas, USA

Chapter VI
IT Value of Software Development: A Multi-Theoretic Perspective 96
VenuGopal Balijepally, Prairie View A&M University, USA
Sridhar Nerur, University of Texas at Arlington, USA
RadhaKanta Mahapatra, University of Texas at Arlington, USA

Chapter VII
UB2SQL: A Tool for Building Database Applications Using UML and B Formal Method 111
Amel Mammar, University of Paris, France
Régine Laleau, University of Paris, France

Section III
Queries and Data Analysis

Chapter VIII
Using Decision Trees to Predict Crime Reporting 132
Juliette Gutierrez, Claremont Graduate University, USA
Gondy Leroy, Claremont Graduate University, USA

Chapter IX
A Model for Estimating the Savings from Dimensional vs. Keyword Search 146
Karen Corral, Boise State University, USA
David Schuff, Temple University, USA
Robert D. St. Louis, Arizona State University, USA
Ozgur Turetken, Ryerson University, Canada

Section V
Organizations and Structures

Detailed Table of Contents

Chapter III
Semantic Integration and Knowledge Discovery for Environmental Research 39
Zhiyuan Chen, University of Maryland, Baltimore County (UMBC), USA
Aryya Gangopadhyay, University of Maryland, Baltimore County (UMBC), USA
George Karabatis, University of Maryland, Baltimore County (UMBC), USA
Michael McGuire, University of Maryland, Baltimore County (UMBC), USA
Claire Welty, University of Maryland, Baltimore County (UMBC), USA

Environmental research and knowledge discovery both require extensive use of data stored in various sources and created in different ways for diverse purposes. We describe a new metadata approach to elicit semantic information from environmental data and implement semantics-based techniques to assist users in integrating, navigating, and mining multiple environmental data sources. Our system contains specifications of various environmental data sources and the relationships that are formed among them. User requests are augmented with semantically related data sources and automatically presented as a visual semantic network. In addition, we present a methodology for data navigation and pattern discovery using multi-resolution browsing and data mining. The data semantics are captured and utilized in terms of their patterns and trends at multiple levels of resolution. We present the efficacy of our methodology through experimental results.

Section II
Systems Building

Chapter IV
Towards Code Reuse and Refactoring as a Practice within Extreme Programming 63
Vijayan Sugumaran, Oakland University, USA
Gerald DeHondt, Grand Valley State University, USA

The authors of this chapter propose a framework that incorporates the practice of code reuse into the Extreme Programming methodology. As an Agile development technique Extreme Programming is a methodology that emphasizes an accelerated programming process. The chapter proposes that incorporating code reuse into extreme programming will increase the efficiency of systems development.

Chapter V
Requirements Elicitation Technique Selection: A Theory-Based Contingency Model 79
Miguel I. Aguirre-Urreta, DePaul University, USA
George M. Marakas, University of Kansas, USA

This chapter develops one of the first theory-based models to assist with selecting the appropriate requirements elicitation technique. The authors argue that their biggest contribution lies in providing a theory to help the understanding of why some elicitation techniques work better than others in specific implementation instances.

Chapter VI
IT Value of Software Development: A Multi-Theoretic Perspective 96
VenuGopal Balijepally, Prairie View A&M University, USA
Sridhar Nerur, University of Texas at Arlington, USA
RadhaKanta Mahapatra, University of Texas at Arlington, USA

This selection demonstrates a research model that combines social capital, organizational learning and knowledge based views of organizations. The idea they develop is to use the resultant model to assess the IT value of systems created by systems development teams using different systems development methodologies.

Chapter VII
UB2SQL: A Tool for Building Database Applications Using UML and B Formal Method 111
Amel Mammar, University of Paris, France
Régine Laleau, University of Paris, France

This chapter describes creation of a tool that was created to aid in design and development of database applications. The tool defines rules and tactics, along with a means of proofing the correctness of the specification and process, and has been integrated into a plug-in for the Rational Rose software development application.

Section III
Queries and Data Analysis

Chapter VIII
Using Decision Trees to Predict Crime Reporting 132
Juliette Gutierrez, Claremont Graduate University, USA
Gondy Leroy, Claremont Graduate University, USA

In this selection, the authors develop an approach to identify the variables and predict crime reporting rates using decision trees. The approach contrasts sharply with the traditional practice of using only descriptive statistics to determine the crime reporting rates.

Chapter IX
A Model for Estimating the Savings from Dimensional vs. Keyword Search 146
Karen Corral, Boise State University, USA
David Schuff, Temple University, USA
Robert D. St. Louis, Arizona State University, USA
Ozgur Turetken, Ryerson University, Canada

This chapter develops a model that can be used to approximate the cost to a business for using keywords searches as its primary means of searching. The authors go on to illustrate how the model shows that a dimensional search approach can reduce costs for almost all businesses.

The authors of this chapter present a middleware solution that provides a means of designing and structuring a dynamic architecture for web-based database applications. The resulting system called WEBFINDIT represents a scalable infrastructure for heterogeneous data sources, making it especially relevant to web databases and web commerce applications.

Chapter XIV
Retrieval Optimization for Server-Based Repositories in Location-Based Mobile Commerce 255
James E. Wyse, Memorial University of Newfoundland, Canada

This chapter provides an evaluation and extension of the author's location-aware method of resolving location-referent transaction-related queries. The determination methods developed resulted in a "useful linkcell size determination heuristic" for optimizing queries in this environment.

Chapter XV
Migrating Legacy Information Systems to Web Services Architecture.. 282
Shing-Han Li, Tatung University, Taiwan
Shi-Ming Huang, National Chung Cheng University, Taiwan
David C. Yen, Miami University, USA
Cheng-Chun Chang, National Chung Cheng University, Taiwan

This selection describes a means to convert a legacy system architecture into a Service-oriented Architecture. The authors propose that their solution differs from similar approaches in that their solution includes specific object-oriented and functional-oriented features.

Section V
Organizations and Structures

Chapter XVI
A Socio-Technical Interpretation of IT Convergence Services: Applying a Perspective from Actor Network Theory and Complex Adaptive Systems.. 308
Myeong Ho Lee, Yonsei University, Korea
Lee Jung-hoon, Yonsei University, Korea
Kwak Jeong Ho, Yonsei University, Korea

This chapter uses an interpretive case study to explore and provide possible explanations of the effect of convergence of digital services. Complexity Adaptive Systems Theory and Actor Network Theory represent the theoretical basis for the research, and the resulting new framework proposes a means to connect the two theories and finally presenting possible ways to explain the underlying behaviors.

Chapter XVII
Understanding Organizational Transformation from IT Implementations: A Look at Structuration Theory 329
T. Ariyachandra, Xavier University, USA
L. Dong, Ryerson University, Canada

This chapter uses Adaptive Structuration Theory (AST) to examine variables in a data warehouse environment that imply how organizations are changed or transformed by the implementation effort. The authors propose that through use of AST, three key aspects of organizations, technology structure, other sources of technology, and group internal system, can be identified and that likely have an impact on how organizational transformations happen.

Chapter XVIII
Social Network Structures in Open Source Software Development Teams 346
Yuan Long, Colorado State University–Pueblo, USA
Keng Siau, University of Nebraska–Lincoln, USA

This selection takes the perspective of an open source software (OSS) team in examining how the dynamics of social network structures affect team performance. Results show that at the beginning of an OSS-based project, there is generally a single hub social structure that moves toward a core/periphery model at later stages of such projects.

Chapter XIX
Design of a Data Model for Social Network Applications 360
Susanta Mitra, International Institute of Information Technology, Kolkata, India
Aditya Bagchi, Indian Statistical Institute, Kolkata, India
A.K. Bandyopadhyay, Jadavpur University, Kolkata, India

This chapter proposes that an object-relational graph data model can be used to represent a social network. The authors indicate that this model can be used to represent the node-based properties common to social network theory-based structures.

Compilation of References 386

About the Contributors 423

Index 429

Preface

Databases and database technologies have thoroughly permeated the business and consumer world, and represent the most common and accepted means of data storage and processing in use today. In such an environment development and enhancement of database technologies provide vital support for businesses in their drive to achieve higher performance, efficiency, and customer satisfaction goals. Creating reusable code modules and moving legacy systems to a web environment represent two ongoing trends that are very relevant to database developers and administrators. This volume, *Advanced Principles for Improving Database Design, Systems Modeling, and Software Development* presents nineteen chapters that represent top research in the areas of database theory, systems building, data analysis techniques, web/mobile commerce and middleware, and organization and structures.

Maintaining the high quality of previous volumes in the Advances in Database Research Series the editors have selected research from acknowledged experts in the area of database and systems development and compiled them into this volume. The following sections present a brief synopsis of each chapter.

Chapter I, "*Semantics of the MibML Conceptual Modeling Grammar: An Ontological Analysis Using the Bunge-Wang-Weber Framework*" conducts an ontological analysis of the MibML conceptual modeling grammar. The authors propose that their approach represents a starting point for continuing ontological development.

Chapter II, "*A Measurement Ontology Generalizable for Emerging Domain Applications on the Semantic Web*" provides an ontology for measuring Semantic web application programs. The authors provide details on the creation of the ontology, how it can be used in analysis and how the ontology was validated.

Chapter III, "*Semantic Integration and Knowledge Discovery for Environmental Research*" provides an approach to obtain semantic information from environmental data. The approach details a metadata semantic integration approach to help users integrate, move around in, and query multiple data sources, and the benefits of the approach are indicated in the experimental results.

Chapter IV, "*Towards Code Reuse and Refactoring as a Practice within Extreme Programming*" proposes a framework that incorporates the practice of code reuse into the Extreme Programming methodology. As an Agile development technique Extreme Programming is a methodology that emphasizes an accelerated programming process. The chapter proposes that incorporating code reuse into extreme programming will increase the efficiency of systems development.

Chapter V, "*Requirements Elicitation Technique Selection: A Theory-Based Contingency Model*" develops one of the first theory-based models to assist with selecting the appropriate requirements elicitation technique. The authors argue that their biggest contribution lies in providing a theory to help the understanding of why some elicitation techniques work better than others in specific implementation instances.

Chapter VI, "*IT Value of Software Development: A Multi-Theoretic Perspective*" demonstrates a research model that combines social capital, organizational learning and knowledge based views of organizations. The idea they develop is to use the resultant model to assess the IT value of systems created by systems development teams using different systems development methodologies.

Chapter VII, "*UB2SQL: A Tool for Building Database Applications Using UML and B Formal Method*" describes development of a tool that was created to aid in design and development of database applications. The tool defines rules and tactics, along with a means of proofing the correctness of the specification and process, and has been integrated into a plug-in for the Rational Rose software development application.

Chapter VIII, "*Using Decision Trees to Predict Crime Reporting*" develops an approach to identify the variables and predict crime reporting rates using decision trees. The approach contrasts sharply with the traditional practice of using only descriptive statistics to determine the crime reporting rates.

Chapter IX, "*A Model for Estimating the Savings from Dimensional Versus Keyword Search*," develops a model that can be used to approximate the cost to a business for using keywords searches as its primary means of searching. The authors go on to illustrate how the model shows that a dimensional search approach can reduce costs for almost all businesses.

Chapter X, "*Integrity Constraint Checking for Multiple XML Databases*" develops a new technique that allows semantic integrity constraints to be checked for XML-based databases. The authors' *XConstraint Checker* includes an efficient algorithm optimized for semantic integrity constraints and is installed on a prototype system to demonstrate its utility.

Chapter XI, "*Accelerating Multi Dimensional Queries in Data Warehouses*" details the creation of a data compression method that allows quicker query returns in a data warehouse. In laboratory and real-world conditions, the method outperformed other leading schemes in both decoding time and error rates.

Chapter XII, "*View Materialization in a Data Cube: Optimization Models and Heuristics*" provides a materialization scheme for determining the correct number of views to create for a data warehousing application. Their design provides a number of heuristics that the authors examine for accuracy and timeliness in a performance guarantee scenario.

Chapter XIII, "*WebFINDIT: Providing Data and Service-Centric Access through a Scalable Middleware*" presents a middleware solution that provides a means of designing and structuring a dynamic architecture for web-based database applications. The resulting system called WEBFINDIT represents a scalable infrastructure for heterogeneous data sources, making it especially relevant to web databases and web commerce applications.

Chapter XIV, "*Retrieval Optimization for Server-Based Repositories in Location-Based Mobile Commerce*" provides an evaluation and extension of the author's location-aware method of resolving location-referent transaction-related queries. The determination methods developed resulted in a "useful linkcell size determination heuristic" for optimizing queries in this environment.

Chapter XV, "*Migrating Legacy Information Systems to Web Services Architecture*" describes a means to convert a legacy system architecture into a Service-oriented Architecture. The authors propose that their solution differs from similar approaches in that their solution includes specific object-oriented and functional-oriented features.

Chapter XVI, "*A Socio-Technical Interpretation of IT Convergence Services: Applying a Perspective from Actor Network Theory and Complex Adaptive Systems*" uses an interpretive case study to explore and provide possible explanations of the effect of convergence of digital services. Complexity Adaptive Systems Theory and Actor Network Theory represent the theoretical basis for the research, and the resulting new framework proposes a means to connect the two theories and finally presenting possible ways to explain the underlying behaviors.

Chapter XVII, "*Understanding Organizational Transformation From IT Implementations: A Look at Structuration Theory*" uses Adaptive Structuration Theory (AST) to examine variables in a data warehouse environment that imply how organizations are changed or transformed by the implementation effort. The authors propose that through use of AST, three key aspects of organizations, technology structure, other sources of technology, and group internal system, can be identified and that likely have an impact on how organizational transformations happen.

Chapter XVIII, "*Social Network Structures in Open Source Software Development Teams*" takes the perspective of an open source software (OSS) team in examining how the dynamics of social network structures affect team performance. Results show that at the beginning of an OSS-based project, there is generally a single hub social structure that moves toward a core/periphery model at later stages of such projects.

Chapter XIX, "*Design of a Data Model for Social Network Applications*" proposes that an object-relational graph data model can be used to represent a social network. The authors indicate that this model can be used to represent the node-based properties common to social network theory-based structures.

Section I
Ontologies and Semantics

Chapter I
Semantics of the MibML Conceptual Modeling Grammar: An Ontological Analysis Using the Bunge-Wand-Weber Framework

Hong Zhang
Missouri State University, USA

Rajiv Kishore
State University of New York at Buffalo, USA

Ram Ramesh
State University of New York at Buffalo, USA

ABSTRACT

A conceptual modeling grammar should be based on the theory of ontology and possess clear ontological semantics to represent problem domain knowledge in a precise and consistent manner. In this paper, we follow the notion of ontological expressiveness and conduct an ontological analysis of a newly-developed conceptual modeling grammar termed MibML (Multiagent-based Integrative Business Modeling Language). The grammar is developed to respond to the emerging needs for a special-purpose conceptual modeling grammar for the MIBIS (Multiagent-based Integrative Business Information Systems) universe. We assign ontological semantics to the MibML constructs and their relationship using the BWW (Bunge-Wand-Weber) model. This paper provides a starting point to further develop ontological principles and step-by-step guidelines to ensure the straightforward mapping from domain knowledge into MibML modeling constructs.

INTRODUCTION

Conceptual modeling is the activity of formally describing some aspects of the physical and social world around us for purposes of understanding and communication (Mylopoulos, 1992). It is the first step for system developers to understand and describe the conceived or the real world system in information system (IS) analysis and design. A conceptual-modeling grammar is the language used to generate conceptual models. It provides a set of constructs and rules that show how to combine the constructs to model real-world domains (Wand & Weber, 2002). A conceptual modeling grammar should be based on a theory of ontology—a theory that articulates those constructs needed to describe the structure and behavior of the world in general (Wand & Weber, 1993; Weber, 2003). Upper-level Ontologies help clarify the semantics of a conceptual modeling grammar and enhance its expressive power to capture problem domain knowledge precisely and unambiguously.

The precision, unambiguity, coherence, and expressive power of conceptual grammars broadly address two fundamental requirements in conceptual grammar development: soundness and completeness. While precision, unambiguity, and coherence address the soundness issue, the expressive power of a conceptual grammar is a measure of completeness of the grammar. Soundness of a grammar can be ensured by its careful design, but universal completeness is generally not attainable. Conceptual modeling grammars may only be boundedly complete in the sense that their expressive strength is adequate to satisfy most requirements within a bounded universe of discourse (Kishore, Sharman, & Ramesh, 2004). The notion of ontological expressiveness and a formal approach to assess ontological expressiveness of conceptual modeling grammars have been proposed by Wand and Weber (1993, 2004), and have been used by several researchers in the past (e.g., Milton, 2004; Green & Rosemann, 2000, 2004; Wand, Storey, & Weber, 2000).

The goal of this article is to elaborate the semantics of a recently developed conceptual modeling grammar from an ontological expressiveness perspective. The grammar, termed MibML (*M*ultiagent-based *I*ntegrative *B*usiness *M*odeling *L*anguage), provides fundamental constructs, relationships, and axioms specially developed for systems analysis and design in the MIBIS (multi-agent-based integrative business information system) universe (Zhang, Kishore, Sharman, & Ramesh, 2004, 2005). Nevertheless, there is a need to understand the clear ontological semantics of the MibML grammar in order to apply it for conceptual modeling in a problem domain. As stated above, conceptual precision, unambiguous definitions, coherence of conceptual structures, and expressive power of the semantics are central to capturing problem domain knowledge correctly into MibML conceptual models. Otherwise, conceptual modeling could become arbitrary and the mapping of domain knowledge into modeling constructs could become highly dependent upon the beliefs, knowledge, and prior experience of system analysts. For example, the MibML grammar includes both *goal* and *task* as foundation constructs. Without a precise, unambiguous, and coherent denotation of these constructs, it may be difficult to model an instance such as "order inventory" as a goal or as a task. This problem of semantic ambiguity (clarity) is common in many conceptual grammars including the ER modeling formalism, which has recently been addressed by Wand et al. (2000). We believe such difficulties can be overcome by providing ontological semantics of the MibML constructs and their relationships via ontological analysis of the grammar.

In this article, we follow recent work in this area and apply the upper-level ontology of the Bunge-Wand-Weber (BWW) model (Wand, 1996) to interpreting the ontological expressiveness (Wand,

1996; Wand & Weber, 1993) of the MibML grammar. The proposed semantic mapping between the MibML grammar and the BWW model will help: (1) overcome difficulties and confusion for system analysts in selecting correct grammatical constructs to represent real-world phenomena; (2) facilitate knowledge sharing and reuse, and thus make it easy to integrate conceptual models from different developers; and 3) improve communication between system analysts and other stakeholders such as users.

The remainder of this article proceeds as follows. First, we discuss the MIBIS universe and the MibML meta-model. Next, we describe the Bunge-Wand-Weber (BWW) model. We then explain the ontological approach of analyzing IS modeling grammars and how it is applied in our analysis of MibML. Following this we discuss the ontological analysis of MibML in the context of the BWW model. Finally, we conclude the paper and discuss future directions.

THE MIBIS UNIVERSE AND THE MIBML META-MODEL

Multiagent technology is being widely utilized for developing enterprise integration applications, such as in the areas of business process management (Blake & Gomaa, 2005; Huhns & Singh, 1998; Jennings et al., 1996; Jennings, Norman, Faratin, O'Brien, & Odgers, 2000), supply chain management (Huhns & Stephens, 2001; Salam, Singh, & Iyer, 2005; Smith, & Sadeh, 1998; Swaminathan, Smith, & Sadeh, 1998), and enterprise modeling (Lin, Tan, & Shaw, 1999; Pan & Tenenbaum, 1991; Sikora & Shaw, 2002). This phenomenon is partly driven by the fact that coordination is at the heart of both business integration applications and multiagent systems. While one of the fundamental requirements in business integration is that of coordination, multiagent systems are essentially coordination models and implement a number of coordination mechanisms (Kishore, Zhang, & Ramesh, Forthcoming). Such integrative application systems developed using multiagent technologies have been termed multi-agent-based integrative business information system (MIBIS) applications and they constitute a special class of information systems and a bounded universe of discourse (Kishore, Zhang, & Ramesh, 2004; Kishore et al., forthcoming).

A MIBIS system regards software agents as fundamental units to support integration of multiple distributed and decentralized work systems. Such a system is more flexible than a traditional workflow system in that it does not require all control flows to be specified at the system design time. Agents not only react to stimuli and changes in the system and the environment, but also adapt their behaviors and interactions with others based on their knowledge and information received at the run time in order to achieve their individual goals. Furthermore, a MIBIS system overcomes a workflow system's inability to control resources involved in business processes. For example, a task in a traditional workflow system may be delayed if the person supposed to perform the task is on vacation. In MIBIS, agents are defined by roles, and a task can be performed by any agent playing a similar role. In short, a MIBIS system is role-centric and goal-oriented, and exhibits autonomous behavior.

In order to fully understand the MIBIS universe, *Goal, Role, Interaction, Task, Information, Knowledge, Resource* and *Agent* need to be captured in MIBIS conceptual models (Kishore et al., Forthcoming). Unfortunately, the traditional general-purpose conceptual modeling grammars, such as ER, UML, and workflow modeling languages, lack enough expressive power to capture completely these unique characteristics of MIBIS systems at the systems analysis level. Entity-relationship (ER) modeling ignores behavioral perspectives of entities. Object orientation such as UML provides no explicit support for agent concepts such as autonomy, reactivity, and sociability (Franklin & Graesser, 1996; Odell, 2002;

Wooldridge, 2002) and it is, therefore, difficult to model agent knowledge and interactions within MIBIS systems using OO modeling formalisms. Most enterprise and workflow models lack the essential semantics to concisely represent specific activities, tasks, business processes, business goals, and organization structures of a business (Scheer, 1999; Weigand & Heuvel, 2002). To respond to such emerging needs, MibML is developed to refine and formally define the above constructs, their relationships and axioms (Zhang et al., 2004). While resource was identified as a foundational ontological construct for the MIBIS universe, the MibML grammar does not include this construct because in a system's modeling context, information about resources, rather than resources themselves, is a matter of concern.

A MIBIS is an organization of agents working together to accomplish business goals. As depicted in Figure 1, *agents* play *roles*. A *role* is essentially an abstraction for the *tasks* that are necessary to be performed and/or the *interactions* that need to occur to achieve individual agent *goals*, the *information* that needs to be accessed or will be generated during the course of performance of those tasks/interactions, and the *knowledge* that is needed for the successful execution of tasks and interactions and achievement of the goals.

THE BWW MODEL

The BWW model is an ontology of information systems proposed by Wand and Weber (1989, 1990, 1993) based on Bunge's philosophical ontology (Bunge, 1977, 1979). The BWW model can be used to analyze the meaning of grammatical modeling constructs and has been applied for evaluating and improving notations and semantics of various conceptual modeling grammars. Wand et al. (2000) apply the BWW model in analyzing ER modeling constructs. Their analysis not only provides precise definitions of ER modeling constructs, but also derives rules for the use of relationships in ER conceptual modeling. Weber and Zhang (1996) examine and indicate the ontological deficiencies of Nijssen information analysis method (NIAM) using the BWW model. Green and Rosemann (2000) use the BWW

Figure 1. The MibML meta-model

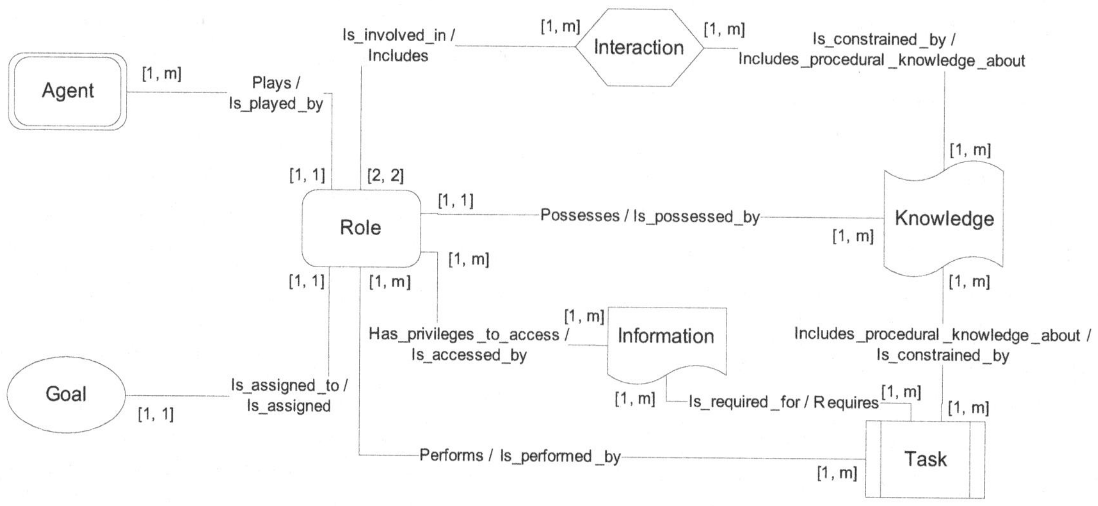

model to analyze the five views—process, data, function, organization and output—provided in the architecture of integrated information systems (ARIS). Their analysis indicates potential problems in representing all required business rules, specifying the scope and boundaries of the system, and employing a "top-down" approach to analysis and design. In addition, the BWW model is applied to examining Data Flow Diagrams (Wand & Weber,1989), object-oriented modeling (Evermann & Wand, 2001; Opdahl & Henderson-Sellers, 2004; Parsons & Wand, 1997; Takagaki & Wand, 1991), and reference models in information systems development (Fettke & Loos, 2003).

Table 1. Basic constructs in the BWW model (Adopted from Bunge, 1977 and Wand, Monarchi, Parsons, & Woo, 1995)

Ontological constructs	Explanation
BWW-thing	The elementary unit in the BWW model. The real world is made up of things. A composite thing may be made of other things.
BWW-properties	Things possess properties. A property is modeled via a function that maps the thing into some value. A property of a composite thing that belongs to a component thing is called a *hereditary property*. Otherwise it is called an *emergent property*. A property that is an inherent property of an individual thing is called an *intrinsic property*. A property that is an inherent property of two or more things is called a *mutual property*. A *complex* property comprises other properties, which may themselves be complex.
BWW-state	The vector of values for all property functions of a thing.
BWW-state law	A property that restricts the values of the properties of a thing to a subset that is deemed lawful because of natural or human laws.
BWW-event	A change of state of a thing. It is affected via a transformation.
BWW-transformation	A mapping from one state to another state.
BWW-transformation law	A property that defines the allowed changes of state.
BWW-history of a thing	The chronologically ordered states that a thing traverses in time.
BWW-coupling	A thing acts on another thing if its existence affects the history of the other thing. The two things are said to be coupled or interact.
BWW-system	A set of things is a system if, for any bi-partitioning of the set, couplings exist among things in the two subsets
BWW-system environment	Things that are not in the system but interact with things in the system
BWW-level structure	Defines a partial order over the subsystems in a decomposition to show which subsystems are components of other subsystems or the system itself.
BWW-stable state	A state in which a thing, subsystem or system will remain unless forced to change by virtue of the action of a thing in the environment.
BWW-unstable state	A state that will be changed into another state by virtue of the action of transformations in the system.
BWW-external event	An event that arises in a thing, subsystem or system by virtue of the action of some thing in the environment on the thing, subsystem or system.
BWW-internal event	An event that arises in a thing, subsystem, or system by virtue of lawful transformations in the system
BWW-class	A set of things that can be defined via their possessing a particular set of properties

Figure 2. Ontological deficiencies of a conceptual model grammar

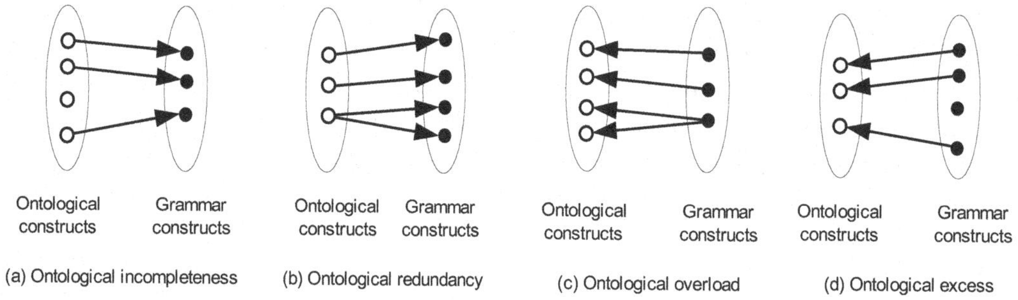

This article applies the BWW model to interpret the semantics of the MibML constructs. Table 1 explains the BWW constructs used in the rest of the article. We attach the prefix "BWW" to the BWW constructs to clearly distinguish them from the constructs in the MibML grammar.

ONTOLOGICAL ANALYSIS APPROACH FOR IS GRAMMARS

Ontological analysis of IS conceptual modeling grammars follows the notion of ontological expressiveness (Wand, 1996; Wand & Weber, 1993). Ontological expressiveness is based upon the view that an information system is a representation of the perceived real-world system. Therefore, a good modeling grammar must manifest the meaning of the real-world to be represented. Because ontology is traditionally studied as philosophical theory concerning the basic traits of the world (Bunge, 1974), the domain semantics of a conceptual modeling grammar can be further clarified and amplified via matching between modeling constructs and ontological constructs.

Ontological expressiveness includes two types of mappings: a *representation mapping* from real world concepts to the modeling constructs, and an *interpretation mapping* from a 'script' in the grammar, into ontological concepts (Wand & Weber, 1993). From these two mappings, four ontological deficiencies may be found in the grammar:

- *Ontological incompleteness* or *construct deficit* occurs when ontological constructs do not have equivalent constructs in the conceptual modeling grammar (Figure 2(a)). A modeling grammar is complete if all grammar constructs perfectly map to the ontological constructs.
- *Construct redundancy* is where several constructs from the conceptual-modeling grammar map onto a single ontological construct (Figure 2(b)).
- *Construct overload* is where several ontological constructs are mapped onto a single construct in the grammar (Figure 2(c)).
- *Construct excess* is where a grammatical construct might not map to any ontological construct (Figure 2(d)).

The semantics of the MibML grammar can be elaborated by assessing its ontological expressiveness. As depicted in Figure 3, we regard a MIBIS system as a model of the real world integrative business system. Accordingly, the MibML grammar should include necessary grammatical constructs to represent the ontological constructs that are used to describe the integrative business systems in the real world domain. In this article, we seek to identify ontological principles that will ensure that construct excess, construct overload and construct redundancy are avoided in the grammar. This will not only reduce the semantic ambiguity of MibML, it will also help amplify

Figure 3. The relationship between the MIBIS modeling and the real-world problem domain

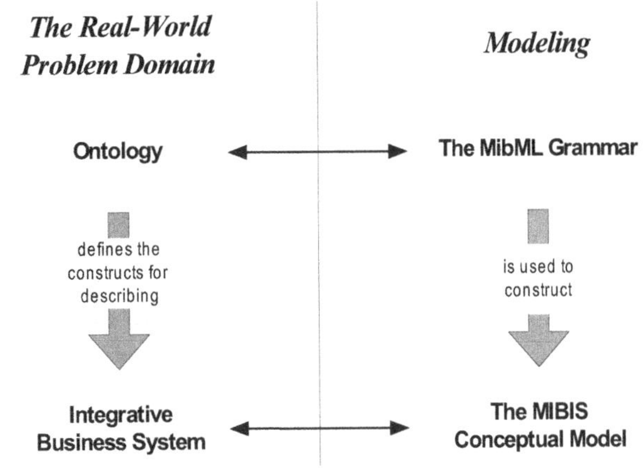

the semantics of the MibML grammar. We do not focus upon ontological incompleteness because while upper-level ontologies in the philosophy discipline are generally developed to embody concepts for the entire universe, MibML is a limited modeling grammar designed to model only certain necessary aspects of the MIBIS bounded universe of discourse. For this reason we do not expect all ontological constructs to be completely mapped onto MibML constructs and believe that the MibML grammar will exhibit ontological incompleteness or construct deficit. This is in consonance with recent findings in the literature which indicate that some of the constructs of the BWW model, such as conceivable state space, conceivable event space, and lawful event space, do not have equivalent representations in the modeling grammars examined so far (Green & Rosemann, 2000).

ONTOLOGICAL ANALYSIS OF THE MibML GRAMMAR

In this section, we map the MibML constructs into the BWW model and thereby the *meaning* of the MibML constructs is defined precisely in terms of what it presents in the problem domain. Table 2 summarizes the interpretation of the MibML constructs. In this section, we prefix "MibML" and "BWW" to the grammatical constructs and the ontological constructs, respectively, to distinguish them clearly. We also follow the notations in (Wand et al., 2000) to represent ontological semantics of the MibML constructs in either propositional forms or functional forms. Please note that propositional forms and functional forms can be mutually converted. For example, assume P is a set of persons and C is a set of companies. Employment E can then be represented as a propositional form:

E: $P \times C \rightarrow$ person p works for company c, where $p \in P$ and $c \in C$ or as a function form E: $P \rightarrow C$.

Agent, Role, and External Entity

A MIBIS system is composed of interacting MibML-agents that work together in order to achieve a common system goal. MibML-agents are independent problem-solving units. They are software programs that are capable of perceiving their environment and taking autonomous actions in order to meet their design objectives. In the real world, a business organization consists of things such as human actors, computer systems,

Table 2. Interpretation mapping of the MibML constructs

The MibML Construct	BWW Interpretation and Justification
MibML-agent	A BWW-thing within the scope of the application
MibML-external entity	A BWW-thing outside the scope of the application
MibML-role	A complex BWW-binding mutual property between a BWW-thing representing a MibML-agent and a BWW-system representing a MIBIS system
MibML-goal	A stable state of a BWW-thing representing a MibML-agent or a MIBIS system
MibML-goal tree	A level structure of BWW-stable states that represent MibML-goals
MibML-individual goal	A stable state of a BWW-thing representing a MibML-agent.
MibML-goal assignment to role	A kind of BWW-state law that constrains the assignment of MibML-goals to MibML-roles
MibML-knowledge	A kind of BWW-complex property that consists of MibML-facts, MibML-deduction rules, MibML-activity execution structure, and MibML-activity execution constraint
MibML-fact	A kind of intrinsic BWW-property that represents a MibML-agent's beliefs on other MibML-agents and the MIBIS environment
MibML-deduction rule	A kind of BWW-state law that governs the possible values of new MibML- facts (BWW-emergent properties) derived from existing MibML-facts (existing BWW-properties)
MibML-execution structure	A collection of BWW-transformation laws that constrain the order of performing MibML-tasks inside a MibML-agent
MibML-execution constraint	A collection of BWW-transformation laws that constrain how MibML-tasks between different MibML-agents should be performed
MibML-event	A BWW-event
MibML-external event	A kind of BWW-external event that emanates from the environment of a MibML-agent
MibML-temporal event	A kind of BWW-external event based on time passage consideration
MibML-state event	A BWW-internal event
MibML-interaction	A group of coupled BWW-events such that when a BWW-event in one thing changes a BWW-binding mutual property, it induces a BWW-event in another thing.
MibML-speech act	A BWW-event which is able to change a binding mutual property of a BWW-thing.
MibML-message	The BWW-binding mutual property that is changed when a MibML-interaction takes place.
MibML-task	A BWW-transformation of a BWW-thing
MibML-task input	A kind of BWW-transformation law to govern a MibML-agent's state before a MibML-task can be performed
MibML-task output	A kind of BWW-transformation law to govern a MibML-agent's state after a MibML-task is performed
MibML-task method	A kind of BWW-transformation law to specify how a MibML-task should be performed
MibML-partOf relationship between tasks	A BWW-transformation is a component of another BWW-transformation.
MibML-isa_typeof relationship between tasks	A BWW-transformation is a specialization of another BWW-transformation.

continued on following page

Table 2. continued

MibML-information entity	A BWW-thing that represents a passive business object
MibML-information flow	A BWW- transformation law that governs pre- or post-conditions of a MibML-task execution

and machines to process business transactions. Therefore, we propose that MibML-agents represent a kind of BWW-thing within the scope of the MIBIS application in the context of the BWW model.

Just like a human actor plays a role in a business organization, a MibML-agent plays a MibML-role in a MIBIS system. A MibML-role defines the responsibilities and the privileges of the MibML-agent. It determines what MibML-tasks and MibML-interactions should be performed and what MibML-information and MibML-knowledge are accessible for the MibML-agent. In the context of the BWW model, we therefore propose that a MibML-role represents a complex BWW-binding property between a MibML-agent and the MIBIS system. Since a MibML-role is used as a template to define MibML-agents in the grammar, the definition of MibML-roles can be represented as a functional schema:

$R : I \times T \times P \times K \rightarrow$ Functional schemata of MibML-roles

where I is a set of MibML-interactions $I = \{i_1, \ldots, i_s\}$; T is a set of MibML-tasks $T = \{t_1, \ldots, t_k\}$; P is a set of privileges to access necessary MibML-information $P = \{p_1, \ldots, p_n\}$; and K is a set of MibML-knowledge $K = \{k_1, \ldots, k_m\}$.

MibML-external entities are parties outside a MIBIS system but interact with the systems to receive services. These parties constitute the environment that defines the functions and the services of the system, and they may include employees, customers, suppliers, etc. Therefore, in the context of the BWW model, we propose that they represent BWW-things outside the scope of the MIBIS application.

Goal

MIBIS is a goal-oriented system. In the early stages of MIBIS development, a MibML-system goal is identified, decomposed iteratively, and structured into a MibML-goal tree to capture user requirements at different levels of details. The MibML-individual goals at the leaf level are then assigned to MibML-roles for MibML-agents playing these roles to accomplish.

In the context of the BWW model, a MibML-goal can be understood as a stable state which a MibML-agent or a MIBIS system tries to reach. For example, a goal "to create new customer order" indicates a state where the new customer information has been recorded and the new order has been created. Before a MibML-agent reaches its goal it will keep changing its state by performing necessary MibML-interactions and MibML-tasks. Correspondingly, a MibML-goal tree represents a level structure of BWW-stable states that represent MibML-goals.

Each MibML-role is assigned a MibML-individual goal. MibML-agents which play a certain MibML-role are responsible for accomplishing the MibML-goal assigned to the MibML-role. Such MibML-goal assignment constrains values of MibML-goals and MibML-roles for particular MibML-agents. For example, if a MibML-agent plays MibML-role "salesperson", then it must accomplish MibML-goal "to create new customer order." In this sense, MibML-goal assignment represents a BWW-state law of a BWW-thing that represents a MibML-agent. Correspondingly, MibML-agents can be represented as a functional schema:

$A : R \times G \rightarrow$ Functional schemata of MibML-agents

where R is a set of MibML-roles $R = \{r_1, \ldots, r_i\}$; and G is a set of MibML-goal $G = \{g_1, \ldots, g_j\}$.

Interaction

A MibML-interaction, as a coordination mechanism to resolve interdependencies among MibML-agents, is defined as a sequence of MibML-speech acts. MibML-speech acts are utterances that contain information needed to assert and perform actions and serve as building blocks of communication protocols. They are used to perform actions such as booking, complaining, forgiving, etc. Associated with MibML-speech acts, MibML-messages are used to pass information between MibML-agents.

In the context of BWW model, a direct coupling between two or more BWW-things is caused by one or more BWW-binding mutual properties that all the BWW-things possess. Whenever one BWW-thing changes a BWW-binding mutual property, a corresponding BWW-event is induced in each of the other BWW-things. In this sense, MibML-messages represent BWW-binding mutual properties to be changed. MibML-speech acts represent BWW-external events that change BWW-binding mutual properties of message-receiving MibML-agents. Correspondingly, a MibML-interaction represents a sequence of BWW-external events that change BWW-binding mutual properties of MibML-agents.

For example, in a supply chain system, a buyer agent can induce a BWW-external event (MibML-speech act "request") in a supplier agent by changing BWW-binding mutual property "price quote request" which is possessed by both MibML-agents. In response, the supplier agent can induce a BWW external event (MibML-speech act "assertion") in the buyer agent by changing BWW-binding mutual property "price quote." In MibML, both events of requesting price quote and returning price quote make up a MibML-interaction.

Interaction patterns in MibML are described in MibML-roles. Therefore, the above interpretation can be defined as follows.

Let *Msg* represent MibML-messages passed between MibML-agents playing different MibML-roles. *Msg* is a functional mapping from one MibML-role to another:

$Msg : R_1 \rightarrow R_2$

where R_i ($i = 1, 2$) represents a set of roles.

Let SA_i represent MibML-speech acts induced in MibML-agents playing role R_i. SA_i is a functional mapping of MibML-agents' states and MibML-messages passed between MibML-agents:

$SA_i : S_{i1} \times S_{i2} \times Msg \rightarrow$ Statements of SA_i

where S_{i1} and S_{i2} are states of MibML-agents playing role R_i ($i = 1, \ldots, n$).

The pattern of a MibML-interaction then is a functional mapping from a Cartesian product of MibML-roles into a Cartesian product of their MibML-speech acts:

$I : R_i \times R_j \rightarrow SA_j \text{ x } SA_i$

Task

A MibML-task is an activity performed solely by a MibML-agent. It is defined by MibML-input, MibML-output, and MibML-method. The MibML-inputs include facts from MibML-agents' declarative knowledge component and data flows from databases and external entities; the MibML-outputs are task generated, and could result in updates or may even cause data flows within the MIBIS application or to external users; the MibML-method embodies the procedural knowledge used, which specifies the detailed logic for execution of the MibML-task.

MibML-inputs and MibML-outputs describe the pre-conditions (the state before task execution) and the post-conditions (the state after task execution) of a MibML-agent. That is, execution of a MibML-task transforms a MibML-agent from an input state to an output state. In the context of the BWW model, a MibML-task represents an internal BWW-transformation within a MibML-agent. MibML-inputs, MibML-outputs, and MibML-method represent BWW-transformation laws because they put constraints on task execution. For example, before a MibML-agent playing a supplier role can perform "generate price quote" task, it must be in a state where "inventory" information is known. After the task is performed, the agent is transformed to a new state in which price quote is generated.

Let T be a set of MibML-tasks of a MibML-agent and S be a set of possible states of the agent. Then:

T: $S \times S \rightarrow s_j$ is transformed to s_k following a predefined method

where $s_j, s_k \in S$, and s_j and s_k represent the initial and the final state of task execution.

A MibML-task can be decomposed recursively into a task hierarchy along dimensions of subpart and subtype. A subpart of a MibML-task t is a constituent task of t, which reflects the composition relationship between MibML-tasks. A subtype of a MibML-task s is a specialization of the task s. The MibML-task hierarchy describes task interdependencies within a MIBIS application. For example, if MibML-task a_1, a_2, and a_3 are subparts of MibML-task a, then execution of MibML-task a requires MibML-task a_1, a_2, and a_3 all are executed. In this light, both task subpart and task subtype in MibML represent a kind of BWW-transformation laws.

Information

MibML-Information refers to data resources available within a MIBIS application. It consists of MibML-information entities and MibML-information flows.

MibML-information entities refer to internal data within the system that are part of data stores. They represent regular business objects (such as PRODUCT, CUSTOMER, etc.) and other materialized views of data. The schema of MibML-information entities includes the structure of tables, the relationships, entity integrity constraints, referential integrity constraints, cardinality constraints, etc. MibML-Information entities may be implemented using relational databases and the schema corresponds to items typically stored in database repositories. The above explanation indicates that MibML-information entity is a complex construct which covers most concepts in ER modeling such as entity, relationship, cardinality, etc.

In the context of the BWW model, there is not a single ontological construct that can be mapped to MibML-information entity. On the one hand, MibML-information entity represents BWW-things (e.g., PRODUCT, CUSTOMER); on the other hand, it is also used to represent BWW-mutual properties (e.g., the relationship between PRODUCT and CUSTOMER) and laws of BWW-things (e.g., cardinality constraints of PRODUCT and CUSTOMER). Therefore, MibML-information entity suffers construct overload. In addition, MibML-information entity also suffers construct redundancy when used as a representation of BWW-things. It has an overlap with the concept of MibML-external entity (e.g., both can be used to represent CUSTOMER). Construct overload and construct redundancy of MibML-information entity may result in confusion of developers whether a business domain phenomenon should be modeled as an external entity, as an information entity, or as a property.

It is a design consideration to include database-related aspects such as the table structure and cardinality as part of the MibML-information entity specification. Conceptual models should include only business-level entities to reflect the real-world business systems. In order to reduce semantic ambiguity, we want to confine the semantics of MibML-information entity to representing only business objects in business organizations. Such business objects can be physical business entities (e.g., inventory, machine, etc) or conceived business entities (e.g., bank account, order, etc). Therefore, we propose that MibML-information entities are mapped to BWW-things that represent passive business objects in the context of the BWW model. These business objects are passive in the sense that they do not initiate MibML-information flows.

MibML-Information flows represent data that are in transit; for example, they represent data moving between external users and MibML-agents, between MibML-information entities and MibML-agents, or between other external systems and MibML-agents. When MibML-information flows between a MibML-agent and an entity exist, it indicates that the MibML-agent requires data inputs to perform its tasks or it generates data outputs. Data inputs govern whether a MibML-task can be executed or not (e.g., task "create a new order" can only be executed when the specific customer data have already been transmitted to the MibML-agent.) On the other hand, data outputs govern which task or tasks should be executed (e.g., if data output "a new order" is required, only tasks necessary to create a new order should be executed.) In this sense, in the context of the BWW model, MibML-information flows represent BWW-transformation laws.

In addition, MibML-agents must possess necessary privileges (e.g., read, write, modify, delete, print, etc.) in order to send, receive, or process data. Such privileges are included in the MibML-role definition and represent mutual properties between a BWW-thing representing a MibML-agent and a BWW-thing representing a business object. Therefore, we have:

$P: R \times INF_e \rightarrow$ role r has privilege p to process information entity inf_e

where P is a set of information privileges, R is a set of roles, and INF_e is a set of information entities.

Knowledge

MibML-knowledge represents computational knowledge that describes MibML-agents' beliefs about their environment and the constraints that govern their behaviors. It consists of MibML-facts, MibML-deduction rules, MibML-activity execution structure, and MibML-activity execution constraints, and is conceptualized to exist within individual MibML-agents. In this sense, MibML-knowledge represents a complex property of the BWW-thing that represents a MibML-agent in the context of the BWW model. Therefore, MibML-knowledge is defined as a functional mapping from a MibML-role into a Cartesian product of value sets of MibML-facts, MibML-deduction rules, MibML-activity execution structure, and MibML-activity execution constraints:

$$K: R \rightarrow V_F \times V_L \times V_T \times V_X$$

where K is a set of MibML-knowledge, R is a set of MibML-roles, V_F is a value set of MibML-facts, V_L is a value set of MibML-deduction rules, V_T is a value set of MibML-activity execution structure, and V_X is a value set of MibML-activity execution constraints.

Both MibML-facts and MibML-deduction rules are declarative knowledge (know-that). MibML-facts are beliefs that a MibML-agent keeps about itself, about other MibML-agents in the system, and about the environment it resides in. Clearly, a MibML-fact is an intrinsic property of a MibML-agent. In general, MibML-facts are defined as:

$F : R \rightarrow V_F$

where R is a set of MibML-roles, and V_F is a value set of MibML-facts.

MibML-deduction rules empower MibML-agents to engage in deductive reasoning. They allow MibML-agents to use existing information and facts to form new facts. Since new facts are derived from existing facts and existing facts represent intrinsic properties of an agent, new facts represent emergent properties – properties whose values depend upon the values of other properties. Because MibML-deduction rules put constraints on values of new facts, they represent BWW-state laws in the context of the BWW model. In general, deduction rules can be represented as:

$L : R \times F_{new} \times INF_f \times F_{old\_1} \times \ldots \times F_{old\_n} \rightarrow$ Statement of the restrictions on deriving new facts from existing facts and information entities

where R is a set of roles, F_{new} is a set of new facts, INF_f is a set of information flows, and F_{old_i} $(i = 1, \ldots, n)$ is a set of existing facts.

MibML-activity execution structure and MibML-activity execution constraints represent procedural knowledge. MibML-Activity execution structure relates to knowing the order in which activities need to occur. It also includes information regarding how frequently activities have to be performed and whether certain activities are optional. In other words, it constrains how activities should proceed. In the context of the BWW model, we propose that MibML-activity execution structure represents BWW-transformation laws.

MibML-activity execution constraints determine the MibML-events that trigger activities. The MibML-event can be a MibML-external event, a MibML-temporal event, or a MibML-state event. MibML-external events emanate either from the environment including other MibML-agents or from end-users (such as a customer placing an order). MibML-temporal events are constraints placed on the execution of MibML-tasks or MibML-interactions based on some time consideration such as the lapse of some time period. A MibML-state event is an event

Figure 4. Ontological semantics of MibML

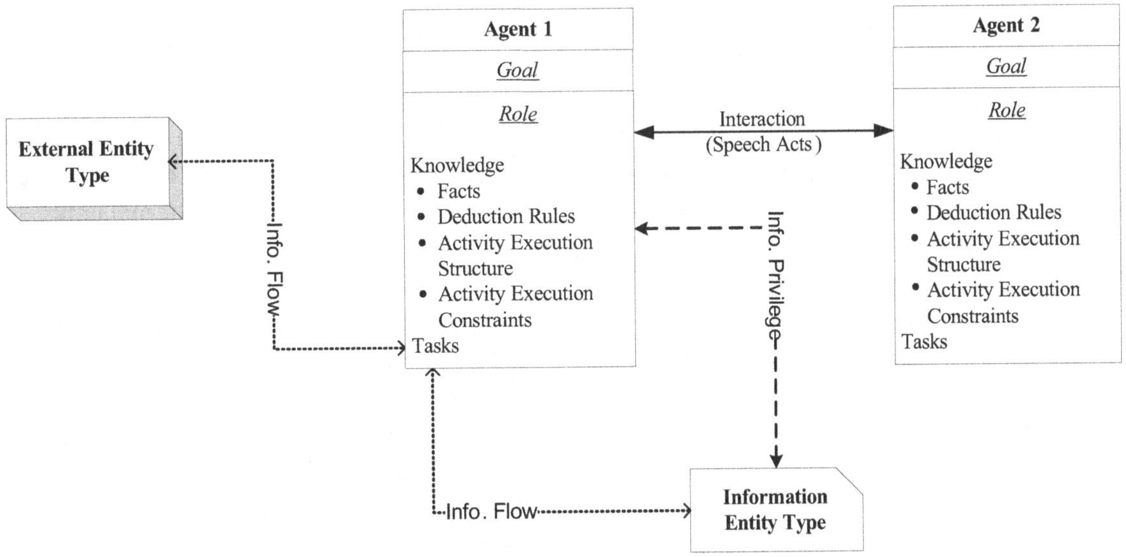

that occurs inside a MibML-agent, and changes the state of the MibML-agent, and accordingly triggers a MibML-task or a set of MibML-tasks. The mapping between MibML events and BWW constructs are straightforward. A MibML-event corresponds to a BWW-event. Both MibML-external event and MibML-temporal event represent the BWW-external event. MibML-state event represents the BWW-internal event.

Let *EV* be a set of MibML-events, *S* be a set of possible states of a MibML-agent and *C* be a set of causes that result in the MibML-agent state transitions. Then:

EV: $S \times S \times C \rightarrow c$ causes a state transition of the MibML-agent from s_j to s_k

where s_j, $s_k \in S$, and $c \in C$. *C* may be a set of actions of MibML-external entities and other MibML-agents in the system, a set of values of time passage, or a set of MibML-tasks performed by the MibML-agent itself. Correspondingly, these different types of causes result in MibML-external events, MibML-temporal events, and MibML-state events.

Discussion

This study is a further development of the MibML grammar to clarify its ontological semantics in the context of the BWW ontology. The clarification is summarized in Figure 4. The MibML grammar includes three types of things: *agents*, *information entities*, and *external entities*. *Agents* interact with each other via *interactions* defined in speech acts (represented as double-headed solid lines between agents to indicate that they change binding mutual properties of *agents*.) *Agents* also communicate with *external entities* and *information entities* via *information flows* for task execution (represented as double-headed dotted lines connecting to *tasks* to indicate that *information flows* either provide inputs to *tasks* or are generated as outputs of *tasks* and thus serve as transformation laws of *tasks*.) *Agents* require information privileges to communicate with *information entities* (represented as double-headed dashed lines between *agents* and *information entities* to indicate they are mutual properties.) The functional scheme of *agents* is determined by *goal* and *role*. A *goal* is a stable state an *agent* tries to reach. A *role* defines an *agent's* intrinsic properties (*knowledge* including facts, deduction rules, activity execution structure, and activity execution constraints), mutual properties (*interactions* and information privileges), and internal transformation (*tasks*).

The definitions of the ontological semantics of the MibML grammar given above are quite clear and they will enhance user communication, and will benefit MIBIS system developers greatly as they will be able to develop precise conceptual models for a MIBIS system. The clear semantics also make it easy for systems developers to identify correct MibML constructs to represent problem domain knowledge. Take *goal* and *task* for example. It is always difficult to differentiate a goal and a task. A real-world instance "order inventory" can either be modeled as a goal or as a task depending on the level of abstraction. With a goal clearly defined as a stable state of an agent and a task as an internal transformation, we understand that a task changes states of an agent. That is, if an instance generates data flows or modifies values of internal properties of an agent, it is modeled as a task. Therefore, if "order inventory" results in update or creation of inventory information, it is modeled as a task. Otherwise, it is modeled as a goal. Similarly, we can easily determine that a "customer" is modeled as an external entity, but a "product" is modeled as an information entity based on their ontological semantics.

Further, unambiguous ontological semantics will also help systems developers focus on business modeling without considering design and implementation details at the systems analysis stage. While the MibML grammar incorporates some design and implementation details in the construct specifications to facilitate MIBIS development during the design and implementation stages, these technical considerations result in complex conceptual models and make it increasingly difficult for users to understand the conceptual models. For example, the *information entity* specification in MibML includes table structure, referential constraints, etc. Therefore, these technical issues are not part of ontological semantics defined and it is not necessary for these details to be included in MIBIS conceptual models.

In summary, ontological analysis of the MibML grammar in this paper provides a starting point for developing ontological principles and step-by-step guidelines or a methodology for constructing MIBIS conceptual models.

CONCLUSION AND FUTURE WORK

MibML is a recently proposed conceptual-modeling grammar to respond to the emerging needs for a special-purpose conceptual-modeling grammar for developing multiagent-based integrative business information systems. To further develop the grammar, there is a need to amplify and clarify ontological semantics of the MibML constructs through ontological analysis. Such clarification not only provides a precise ontological definition for the MibML constructs, but also facilitates the mapping from business domain knowledge onto MibML constructs. In the paper, we have carefully examined the MibML constructs and clarified and amplified their ontological semantics in the context of the Bunge-Wand-Weber ontology.

Some future directions for development of the grammar includes the following areas: (1) further detailed ontological investigations of the MibML grammar which would lead to the identification and discovery of ontological principles for using MibML in conceptual modeling; (2) development of a systematic design methodology with step-by-step guidelines for MIBIS modeling (e.g. how to identify the scope of the model, how to identify relevant MIBIS entities, etc.) using MibML as the representation and analysis formalism; (3) experimental validation of the MibML rules through practical design evaluations; and (4) development of a CASE tool to enable automated MIBIS analysis and design and enforcement of MibML model consistency based on the ontological rules developed in this work. All these areas have strong research potential and significant practical value and we are currently investigating some of these areas.

ACKNOWLEDGMENT

The authors are grateful to Kaushal Chari, participants at the MSS Colloquim at SUNY Buffalo, anonymous reviewers at the AMCIS 2004 conference, and the guest editors and anonymous reviewers at the Journal of Database Management for providing their invaluable comments and suggestions during the course of development of this paper. The article has improved much as a result of their comments.

REFERENCES

Blake, M. B., & Gomaa, H. (2005). Agent-oriented compositional approaches to services-based cross-organizational workflow. *Decision Support Systems, 40*(1), 31-50.

Bunge, M. (1974). *Treatise on basic philosophy: Vol.1: Sense and reference.* Boston: D. Reidel Publishing.

Bunge, M. (1977). *Treatise on basic philosophy: Vol. 3: Ontology I: The furniture of the world.* Boston: D. Reidel Publishing.

Bunge, M. (1979). *Treatise on basic philosophy: Vol. 4: Ontology II: a world of systems.* Boston: D. Reidel Publishing.

Evermann, J., & Wand, Y. (2001, November 27-30). *Towards ontologically based semantics for UML constructs.* Paper presented at the 20th International Conference on Conceptual Modeling, Yokohama, Japan.

Fettke, P., & Loos, P. (2003). *Ontological evaluation of reference models using the Bunge-Wand-Weber model.* Paper presented at the Ninth Americas Conference on Information Systems, Tampa, FL.

Franklin, S., & Graesser, A. (1996). *Is it an agent, or just a program? A taxonomy for autonomous agents.* Paper presented at the Third International Workshop on Agent Theories, Architectures, and Languages.

Green, P., & Rosemann, M. (2000). Integrated process modeling: an ontological evaluation. *Information Systems, 25*(2), 73-87.

Green, P., & Rosemann, M. (2004). Applying ontologies to business and systems modelling techniques and perspectives: Lessons learned. *Journal of Database Management, 15*(2), 105-117.

Huhns, M. N., & Singh, M. P. (1998). Workflow agent. *IEEE Internet Computing, 2*(4), 94-96.

Huhns, M. N., & Stephens, L. M. (2001). Automating supply chains. *IEEE Internet Computing, 5*(4), 90 -93.

Jennings, N. R., Faratin, P., Johnson, M. J., Norman, T. J., O'Brien, P., & Wiegand, M. E. (1996). Agent-based business process management. *International Journal of Cooperative Information Systems, 2 & 3*, 105-130.

Jennings, N. R., Norman, T. J., Faratin, P., P. O'Brien, & Odgers, B. (2000). Autonomous agents for business process management. *Journal of Applied Artificial Intelligence, 14*(2), 145-189.

Kishore, R., Sharman, R., & Ramesh, R. (2004). Computational ontologies and information systems I: Foundations. *Communications of the Association for Information Systems, 14*(8), 158-183.

Kishore, R., Zhang, H., & Ramesh, R. (2004). A helix-spindle model for ontological engineering. *Communications of the ACM, 47*(2), 69-75.

Kishore, R., Zhang, H., & Ramesh, R. (Forthcoming). Enterprise integration using the agent paradigm: foundations of multiagent-based integrative business information systems. *Decision Support Systems.*

Lin, F. R., Tan, G. W., & Shaw, M. J. (1999). Multiagent enterprise modeling. *Journal of Organizational Computing and Electronic Commerce, 9*(1), 7-32.

Milton, K. S., & Kazmierczak, E. (2004). An ontology of data modelling languages: A study using a common-sense realistic ontology. *Journal of Database Management, 15*(2), 19-38.

Mylopoulos, J. (1992). Conceptual modeling and telos. In P. Locuopoulos & R. Zicari (Eds.), *Conceptual modeling, databases and cases.* New York: John Wiley & Sons.

Odell, J. (2002). Objects and agents compared. *Journal of Object Technology, 1*(1), 41-53.

Opdahl, A. L., & Henderson-Sellers, B. (2004). A Template for defining enterprise modelling constructs. *Journal of Database Management, 15*(2), 39-73.

Pan, J. Y. C., & Tenenbaum, J. M. (1991). An intelligent agent framework for enterprise integration. *IEEE Transactions on Systems, man, and cybernetics, 21*(6), 1391-1991.

Parsons, J., & Wand, Y. (1997). Using objects in system analysis. *Communications of the ACM, 40*(12), 104-110.

Salam, A. F., Singh, R., & Iyer, L. (2005). Intelligent infomediary-based eMarketplaces: agents in eSupply chains. *Communications of the ACM.*

Scheer, A. W. (1999). *ARIS-Business Process Modeling.* Berlin: Springer.

Sikora, R., & Shaw, M. (2002). Multi agent enterprise modeling. In C. Holsapple, V. Jacob & H. R. Rao (Eds.), *Business modeling: A multidisciplinary approach essays in honor of Andrew B. Whinston* (pp. 169-185). Kluwer Academic Press.

Swaminathan, J. M., Smith, S. F., & Sadeh, N. M. (1998). Modeling supply chain dynamics: a multiagent approach. *Decision Sciences, 29*(3), 607-632.

Takagaki, K., & Wand, Y. (1991). An object-oriented information systems model based on ontology. In F. V. Assche, B. Moulin & C. Rolland (Eds.), *Object oriented approach in information systems* (pp. 275-296). North, Holland: Elsevier Science.

Wand, Y. (1996). Ontology as a foundation for meta-modelling and method engineering. *Information and Software Technology, 38*, 281-287.

Wand, Y., Monarchi, D. E., Parsons, J., & Woo, C. C. (1995). Theoretical foundations for conceptual modeling in information systems development. *Decision Support Systems, 15*, 285-304.

Wand, Y., Storey, V. C., & Weber, R. (2000). An ontological analysis of the relationship construct in conceptual modeling. *ACM Transactions on Database Systems, 24*(4), 494-528.

Wand, Y., & Weber, R. (1989). An ontological evaluation of systems analysis and design methods. In E. D. Falkenberg & P. Lindgreen (Eds.), *Information system concepts: An in-depth analysis* (pp. 79-107). Amsterdam: North-Holland.

Wand, Y., & Weber, R. (1990). An ontological model of an information system. *IEEE Transactions on Software Engineering, 16*(11), 1282-1292.

Wand, Y., & Weber, R. (1993). On the ontological expressiveness of information systems analysis and design grammars. *Journal of Information Systems, 3*(4), 217-237.

Wand, Y., & Weber, R. (2002). Research commentary: information systems and conceptual modeling - a research agenda. *Information Systems Research, 13*(4), 363-376.

Wand, Y., & Weber, R. (2004). Reflection: ontology in information systems. *Journal of Database Management, 15*(2), iii-vi.

Weber, R. (2003). Conceptual modelling and ontology: Possibilities and pitfalls. *Journal of Database Management, 14*(3), 1-20.

Weber, R., & Zhang, Y. (1996). An analytical evaluation NIAM's grammar for conceptual schema diagrams. *Information Systems Journal, 6*(2), 147-170.

Weigand, H., & Heuvel, W. J. v. d. (2002). Cross-organizational workflow integration using contracts. *Decision Support Systems, 33*, 247-265.

Wooldridge, M. (2002). *An introduction to multiagent systems.* West Sussex, UK: John Wiley & Sons, Ltd.

Zhang, H., Kishore, R., Sharman, R., & Ramesh, R. (2004). *The GRITIKA ontology for modeling e-service applications: formal specification and illustration.* Paper presented at the 37th Hawaii International Conference on System Sciences (HICSS-37), Big Island, Hawaii.

Zhang, H., Kishore, R., Sharman, R., & Ramesh, R. (2005). MibML: A conceptual modeling grammar for integrative business information systems using the agent metaphor (Working Paper). New York: State University of New York at Buffalo, School of Management.

This work was previously published in Journal of Database Management, Vol. 18, Issue 1, edited by K. Siau, pp. 1-19, copyright 2007 by IGI Publishing, formerly known as Idea Group Publishing (an imprint of IGI Global).

Chapter II
A Measurement Ontology Generalizable for Emerging Domain Applications on the Semantic Web

Henry M. Kim
York University, Canada

Arijit Sengupta
Wright State University, USA

Mark S. Fox
University of Toronto, Canada

Mehmet Dalkilic
Indiana University, USA

ABSTRACT

This paper introduces a measurement ontology for applications to semantic Web applications, specifically for emerging domains such as microarray analysis. The semantic Web is the next-generation Web of structured data that are automatically shared by software agents, which apply definitions and constraints organized in ontologies to correctly process data from disparate sources. One facet needed to develop semantic Web ontologies of emerging domains is creating ontologies of concepts that are common to these domains. These general, "common-sense" ontologies can be used as building blocks to develop more domain-specific ontologies. However most measurement ontologies concentrate on representing units of measurement and quantities, and not on other measurement concepts such as sampling, mean values, and evaluations of quality based on measurements. In this paper, we elaborate on a measurement ontology that represents all these concepts. We present the generality of the ontology, and describe how it is developed, used for analysis and validated.

INTRODUCTION

According to Tim Berners-Lee, whom many attribute as the inventor of the World Wide Web, the Web will evolve into the *Semantic Web*, which relies upon using machine processable domain knowledge represented in *ontologies* to execute and compose automated *Web services* (Berners-Lee, Hendler, & Lassila, 2001; Chen, Zhou, & Zhang, 2006). An ontology is a data model that "consists of a representational vocabulary with precise definitions of the meanings of the terms of this vocabulary plus a set of formal axioms that constrain interpretation and well-formed use of these terms" (Campbell & Shapiro, 1995). Ontology use ensures that data instances are so precisely defined and constrained that the instances can be processed automatically and accurately by Web-based computer programs, or *software agents*. Berners-Lee's et. al (2001) vision of the Semantic Web is that "many software agents, accessing data instances and applying ontologies to the instances, execute Web services in concert, where agents, data instances, and ontologies are distributed all over the Web."

Ontologies for the Semantic Web represent an emerging method for modeling the semantics required to interpret data. In a similar vein, applications such as genomics and GIS's represent emerging domains represented for semantic modeling. There exist Semantic Web ontologies for traditional applications in computer science, and business (Davies, Duke, & Stonkus, 2002; Gandon & Sadeh, 2004; Klischewski & Jeenicke, 2004). There are also emerging domains modeled using traditional semantics modeling techniques (Khatri, Ram, & Snodgrass, 2004; Ram & Wei, 2004). There are even some ontologies of emerging domains such as representations of the Gene Ontology (Ashburner et al., 2000; Wroe, Stevens, Goble, & Ashburner, 2003) and a bioinformatics ontology (Stevens, Goble, Horrocks, & Bechhofer, 2002), which are represented in the de facto Semantic Web Ontology Language, OWL (McGuinness & van Harmelen, 2003), or its predecessor, DAML+OIL (Bechhofer, Goble, & Horrocks, 2001). Although one of the goals of ontology development is a generalization of terms in an application, it is possible to make intelligent choices when several ontologies are available for the same domain (Lozano-Tello & Gomez-Perez, 2004).

When contemplating the development of ontologies of any domain, it is instructive to state the following informal definition: "an ontology is an explicit representation of shared understanding" (Gruber, 1993). Gruber also outlines the conundrum of ontological commitment: the more one commits to represent a given domain in an ontology to make data more sharable for software applications closely associated with that domain's needs, the less sharable the data becomes for other applications. For example, commitments made to develop a gene ontology useful for genomics applications render the ontology to be less likely to be used to share medical records data. Yet data sharing between genomics and patient care applications is critical in many situations. The remedy to this seeming conundrum is to identify general concepts that cut across many domains—the domains' "common-sense"—and collect them in a common-sense ontology (Lenat, 1995; Milton & Kazmierczak, 2004). This ontology is separated from more domain-specific ones. In fact, terms in several domain-specific ontologies can be defined using terms from a common general ontology. For example, a molecular biological ontology may provide building block representations for a biomedical ontology, which in turn underpins both gene and health care ontologies. The general ontologies also underlie an ontology of a different perspective—that of costing (Fox & Gruninger, 1998).

Arguably the ontologies of *emerging domains*, to be discussed below, make ontological commitments to their respective domains. It is prudent to ask, however, what are the common-sense ontologies that underlie these emerging domains?

Can their representations serve as building blocks to define Semantic Web ontologies of different emerging domains? The attributes shared among common emerging domains, which sets them apart from traditional business and computer science domains, is their grounding in the physical sciences. The common-sense of emerging domains is the common-sense of our physical world. There are common-sense models of time (Allen, 1983), space (Retz-Schmidt, 1988), causality (Reiger & Grinberg, 1977), and physics (Hayes, 1985; Kuipers, 1986). So how do traditional and emerging domains differ? We set our sights on the life sciences, since it is here that the most significant number of emerging technologies have taken place.

The life sciences have relied on the so-called scientific method—discovery through a process of observation, hypothesis formulation and data generation. In these traditional domains, data play an ancillary role to the hypotheses (these domains are often referred to as "hypothesis driven"). For example, a scientist believes that two particular genes might have some kind of relationship in some stage of larval development in a *D. melanogaster.* Experiments are then conducted to validate this conjecture. The data are generally interesting only in the context of this experiment. There are long standing traditional as well as practical reasons (Attie, 2003) why data is put into this ancillary role, and we only present a few here: they need not be present during the observation and hypothesis formulation phases of discovery; furthermore, a surplus of data does usually little to enhance this process of discovery; data are often prohibitively expensive to produce or gather once, let alone many times. Emerging domains (Ronco, Grossel, Zimmer, & Socash, 2003), like bioinformatics (and particular areas of focus, for example, genomics, proteomics, metabolomics) through a direct consequence of recent and rapid advancements in technology, have taken the scientific method and made it, in a sense, stand on its head. There are also domains where data are generated and discoveries made without any preceding hypothesis (Attie, 2003) and are often referred to as "technologically driven." Technology in this case typically refers to high-throughput gene product data where tens of thousands of interactions are measured in unison. To motivate our article, we will focus on microarrays (Duggan, Chen, Meltzer, & Trent, 1999; Mount, 2004), the most well-known and ubiquitous of the technologically driven data tools. Numerous challenges are faced by these emerging disciplines. One critical problem is data quality—many of the high throughput techniques, microarrays included, suffer from a great deal of noise (Lesk, 2005). Furthermore, no formal ANSI standards exist for managing these data systematically though some informal standards have emerged. One such standard is the MIAME format for microarrays (Duggan, Chen, Meltzer, & Trent, 1999; Mount, 2004), though this format does not include quality control information. So, handling data quality is made even more difficult and can be cast into a more general framework of measurement.

There is the abstract and mathematical field of measurement theory (Roberts, 1979),which serves as a valuable reference for those works that represent measurement concepts in an ontology. Whether stated in formal data models (Goh, Bressan, Madnick, & Siegel, 1999; Novak, 1995), or as computational ontologies (Gruber & Olsen, 1994), works that can be considered ontologies of measurement are predominantly concerned with units of measurement, specifically using the ontology to accurately convert from one unit of measure to another. This holds for Semantic Web measurement ontologies for traditional domains; some examples are the measurement ontologies for KSL (Fikes & Farquhar, 1999), SHOE (Heflin, 2000), Cyc® (Lenat, 1995), SUMO (Pease & Niles, 2002) and GNU (Nozick, Turnquist, Jones, Davis, & Lawton, 2004) projects. The same can be said for emerging domains, and examples include the measurement units represented in

SEEK (ecology) (Bowers & Ludäscher, 2004), MGED (genomics) (Stoeckert Jr. & Parkinson, 2004), and PharmGKb (pharmacology) (Hewett et al., 2002) ontologies.

Measurement theory is certainly more than just measurement unit conversions and quantities. Therefore, regardless of whether it is for traditional or emerging domains, or whether it is for the Semantic Web or closed networks, there is a definite research opportunity in developing an ontology that represents additional measurement common-sense. With such an ontology in tow, developers of Semantic Web ontologies of emerging domains as diverse as biology and geography have a reference for ensuring that important and subtle measurement concepts are diligently represented in their ontologies and not ignored. *Ecolingua* is an ontology for modeling ecological metadata (Brilhante & Robertson, 2001) and represents the important measurement notion of sampling. What is needed is a measurement ontology that, like *Ecolingua*, can be used for developing Semantic Web ontologies of emerging domains, but represents even more.

We believe that the TOVE measurement ontology (Fox, 1992) is one of the most extensive ontologies for enterprise modeling (Noy & Hafner, 1997). This article elaborates on what had previously been written about this measurement ontology. We first provide two scenarios for ontology use: one for the emerging domain of genomics using microarrays and the other for the traditional domain of enterprise applications. We then present a demonstration of how the ontology can be used for this scenario. The demonstration has two parallel audiences. We show how the ontology can be used by a scientist who is working in one of these emerging domains, e.g., a bioinformatician who seeks to discover significant gene-gene interactions in the presence of noise, missing data, and conflicting data. We further demonstrate that this can transparently be cast in terms of an enterprise domain. We present arguments on generalizablity of the ontology.

Figure 1. TOVE ontological engineering methodology

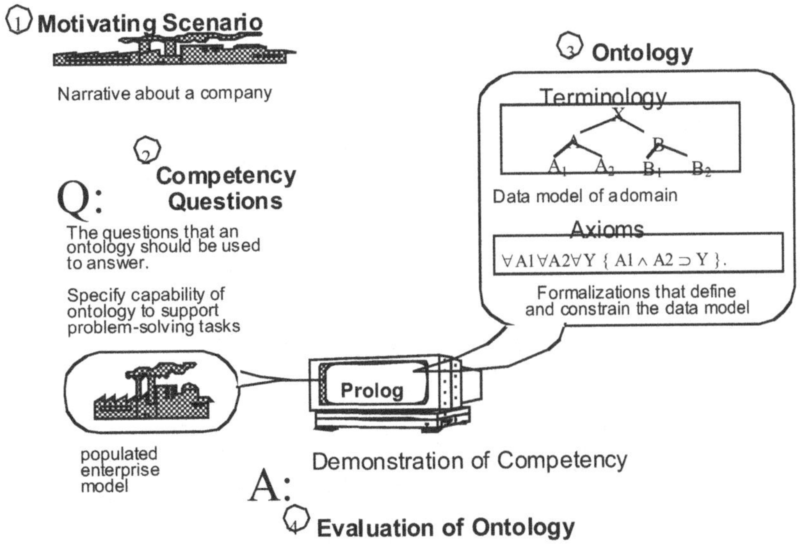

Figure 2. This graph depicts gene/gene relationships that have been experimentally determined (lines—thickness is strength). The two circles are uncharacterized genes. The small shapes are further annotations of information to help the emerging domain scientist explore possible characterizations of the two uncharacterized ones.

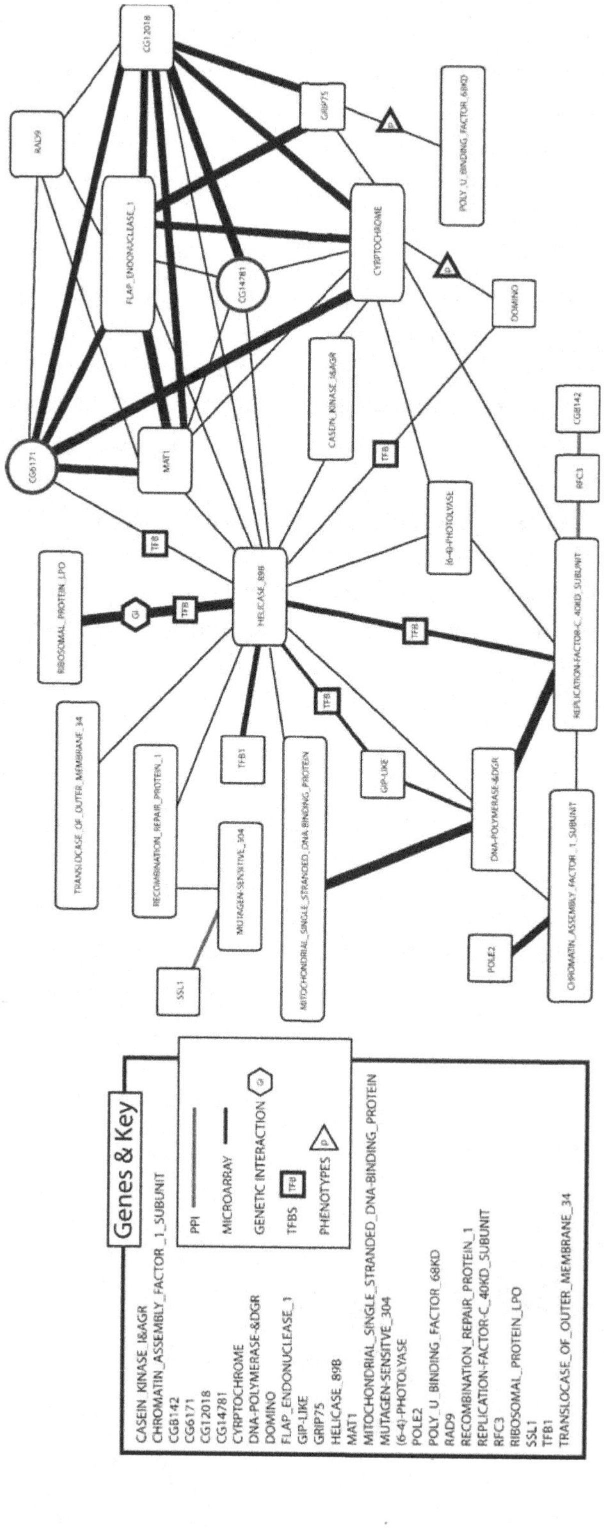

Finally, we make concluding remarks and state our intentions for future work.

MEASUREMENT ONTOLOGY

Finkelstein (1984) defines measurement as the process by which numbers or symbols are assigned to attributes of entities in the real world in such a way as to describe them according to clearly defined rules. In a philosophical discussion of an ontology of measurement units, Mars (1993) summarizes the modern axiomatic treatment of the theory of mathematics (Massey, 1971; Narens, 1985) as the problem of finding an axiomatic introduction of a function φ that assigns a numerical value to an object. Axioms of (1) ordering ($a \gtrsim b \leftrightarrow \varphi(a) \geq \varphi(b)$, where $\gtrsim$ denotes an empirical ordering of objects), and (2) extension ($\varphi(a)+\varphi(b) = \varphi(a \bullet b)$, where $\bullet$ denotes an empirical combination of two objects) are central. These axioms are formal and sharable, since they are expressed in mathematics, and represent fundamental measurement concepts. Fenton (1994) relates measurement as fundamental for ensuring software quality, and gives practical guidance in delineating the fundamentals of measurement into "what is measurement" (e.g., types: direct vs. indirect) and "issues for measurement" (e.g., which type of attributes can and cannot be measured, and on what kinds of scales). We synthesize these concepts using the motivation of a real-life enterprise application to transform abstract concepts to explicit ontology terms, definitions, and constraints.

A graphical overview of the ontology development steps in the methodology that Gruninger and Fox (1995) used to engineer the TOVE Measurement Ontology representations is shown in Figure 1. These steps involve (1) developing a *motivating scenario*, (2) designing *informal competency questions* to capture the scenario, (3) formalizing them to more *formal competency questions*, and (4) logically deducing the competency questions as a *demonstration of competency.*

A *motivating scenario* is a detailed narrative about a specific enterprise, where emphasis is placed on problems or tasks it faces. When the scenario is analyzed, enterprise-independent, generic concepts are abstracted to state *informal competency questions* in natural language *that bind the query capability or competency of the ontology.* Terms with which such queries can be composed comprise the *terminology* or data model of the ontology. Queries re-stated using the terminology and restrictive syntax of the ontology are called *formal competency questions.* Answers to these questions can be logically deduced if *axioms* that define and constrain the terminology are developed as restrictive semantics. These deductions constitute a *demonstration of competency.*

This methodology, which has posing and answering of informal and formal competency questions as its basis, is arguably the most popular ontology development methodology. According to a search via Google Scholar™ (www.scholar.google.com) in July 2005, Uschold and Gruninger's (1996) paper on ontological engineering is the fifth most cited paper on computational ontologies, and by far the most popular paper on ontology development methodology. This methodology has been applied to develop ontologies for fields as diverse as knowledge management (Gandon, 2001; Kim, 2002), bioinformatics (Stevens, Goble, & Bechhofer, 2000) and transportation engineering (Schlenoff, Balakirsky, Uschold, Provine, & Smith, 2003). These examples provide ample evidence that the methodology used to develop the measurement ontology can be used to develop ontologies of a wide variety of domains beyond enterprise modeling, the domain from which the ontology originates.

Motivating Scenario 1: Gene Expression Microarrays

Functional genomics is the study of gene function and their respective relationships among each other. A multitude of perspectives exist as to the kinds of relationships—phenotypic expression, protein-protein interaction, but microarrays measuring gene expression levels are most commonly used. A number of promising and potential discoveries in functional genomics can be made that include drug discovery, biomarker determination, and biodiversity. We will present a high level description of microarrays, though a detailed description can be found in Mount (2004).

To identify the primary concepts for the measurement aspects of microarrays, we consider some of the details of microarray analysis:

Microarrays measure levels of associated substrate: one chemical species is fixed to a medium—a slide—and collections of other chemical species, that are fluorescently labeled, are brought into contact with the first. Those most strongly attracted adhere—called hybridization—and are then examined to provide some kind of degree of affinity by measuring the light intensities. Controls are added to give baseline indications of affinity and trials are repeated to help establish the quality of results. Recent technological advances have made it possible to measure thousands of these relationships on a single slide.

The key concept (C-1) abstracted from this excerpt is the following:

C-1: There must be a systematic way of describing how a particular physical characteristic is to be measured and this description must be used to meet the quality expectations of the scientists.

To obtain the next concept, we now consider some of the activities that are involved in microarray analysis.

There are a number of standard activities that take place when conducting microarray experiments. The substrates must be decided upon and procured, then fixed to the slides. The possible other substrates must be prepared by fluorescent labeling before hybridization. After exposure the slides must be washed of unbound substrates, scanned, and intensities displayed numerically.

The concept that can be derived from the above excerpt is the following:

C-2: Quality assessment is made through a system of activities, which perform measurement; this is a view of measurement as an activity.

Finally, we consider the decision process using the measurements:

Used cleverly, many kinds of relationships can be discovered. For example, given a set of genes, we may want to decide if significant interactions exist among them. In the case of functional genomics, gene-gene interactions can be indirectly observed by measuring the amounts of RNA that bind to DNA fragments. Gene expression can be identified with one of four states: up-regulated (enhanced production), equally expressed, no observable change, and down-regulated (inhibited production). Historically, green, black, yellow, and red have been used, respectively, with these four states where various intermediary colors represent a degree of mixing of these states. The final product then is a slide of a rectangular collection of tiny dots of color. These dots of color are actually of ratio of probes labeled with two fluorophores, commonly cyanine 3 (Cy3) peak absorption at 550 nm and emission at 570 nm and cyanine 5 (Cy5) with peak absorption at 649 and emission at 670 nm. The ratio is Cy5:Cy3, where equal intensities of both shows yellow, Cy5 > Cy3 shows red, Cy5 < Cy3 shows green, and black means neither is expressed. Microarrays are subject to numerous statistical variations brought about not only by the complex nature of the technology itself, but also by the sheer number of things being measured. To compare multiple run values must be further processed by, for ex-

ample, normalization and include dimensions of time, light intensity, treatments, etc. To be at all useful, the quality of output must be well-known. Several methods are applied for improving quality, including sampling and repeated measurement of the same cell (repeat runs).

The concept embedded in the decision making process can be simply stated as:

C-3: Every quality assessment is a decision that begins with a value of measurement at a given point in time.

Motivating Scenario 2: BHP Steel

To show the applicability of the concepts, we take an alternative scenario from a more traditional standpoint of enterprise measurement.

BHP Steel is an industrial collaborator for TOVE Measurement Ontology development. The following excerpt describes its losses with respect to cost, time, and revenue when products of unacceptable quality (called non-prime products) are produced.

As raw materials are transformed by the different production units of BHP Steel's supply chain, non-prime products may be produced. These are the products whose physical properties do not satisfy necessary tolerance specifications. Non-prime products lead to lost revenue due to re-grading and scrapping, increased costs due to additional rework, carrying of excess inventory to meet delivery promises, and increased variability of leadtime performance.

The same key concept (C-1) can be abstracted from this excerpt:

C-4: There must be a systematic way of describing how a particular physical characteristic is to be measured and this description must be used to meet the customer expectations of quality.

The next excerpt describes BHP Steel's need to understand and improve its inspection processes, the collection of activities that assesses whether a product is non-prime.

If the products are consistently found to be non-prime, this is an indication that there is something faulty in the production unit. A cause for this occurrence is suspected to be an inadequate inspection processes.

C-5: Quality assessment is made through a system of activities, which perform measurement.

The following excerpt specifies what is entailed in determining a product as non-prime.

Especially when the product is shipped to the customer, it is essential that the product satisfies the tolerance specifications of the customer. Therefore, the product's physical characteristics are measured, compared against tolerance specifications and a decision about whether the product is non-prime is made.

C-6: Every quality assessment uses a decision process that begins with a value of measurement at a given point in time.

Informal Competency Questions

Not only are the informal competency questions developed to elaborate concepts, they are also designed from the findings of the measurement models' review.

Measurement Description System: To elaborate C-1, the transformation of the relationship between an entity and its attributes into the more tractable domain of term, numbers, and operators must be modeled (Grady, 1993). The following then are informal competency questions (e.g., ICQ-1) about requirements:

Example 1.

Core-1 *holds(f,s)*	*Fluent f is true (i.e., holds) in situation s*
Core-2 $occurs_T(f,T)$	*Fluent f occurs in time period T*

Example 2.

Core-3 organization_agent(Oa) *Oa is an organization_agent*

<Oa> an individual or group of individuals

Core-4 agent_constraint(A,c($\underline{X}$))

holds(agent_constraint(Oa,c($\underline{X}$)),s) ↔ Φ(Oa,$\underline{X}$,s).

<s> a given situation

<Oa> an organization agent which seeks to achieve a goal in situation s

<$\underline{X}$> entities that must be represented in order to represent the constraints on Oa; $\underline{X}$ is a vector with none, one, or more entities

<c($\underline{X}$)> predicate name for the agent constraint

<Φ(Oa,$\underline{X}$,s)> a first-order logic expression for the constraint described as c($\underline{X}$)

Core-5 organizational_constraint(C)

<C> unique identifier for each instance of c($\underline{X}$)

- **ICQ-1:** Is this a quality requirement?
- **ICQ-2:** What are the physical characteristics that are measured?

In measuring physical characteristics, one important aspect is sampling, which occurs when a subset of a population of an evaluated entity is measured, rather than the whole (Scheaffer & McClave, 1982). The following are some questions for representing sampling.

- **ICQ-3:** Is every entity that is produced measured?
- **ICQ-4:** If the product is a batch, is a sample taken from that batch and measured?
- **ICQ-5:** If a sample is taken and measured, is the value for the measurement some aggregate (e.g. average) of the measurement upon individual units of that sample?
- **ICQ-6:** Or, is the value of the measurement a measure of whether or not individual units of the sample passed or failed a certain threshold (e.g., does the sample in well 34 show up-regulation)?
- **ICQ-7:** What ought to be the measured value; that is, what is the expected value for that physical characteristic?
- **ICQ-8:** What are the tolerance specifications for a physical characteristic that is measured?
- **ICQ-9:** What is the unit of measurement for a physical characteristic of an entity?

Measurement Activities: In order to elaborate C-2, the following questions about measurement and inspection can be asked.

- **ICQ-10:** Is this an activity that performs measurement?
- **ICQ-11:** Is this an inspection activity?

Measurement Points: In order to elaborate C-3, the elemental piece of information needed to make a quality assessment can be represented

Example 3.

Core-6	resource(R)	*R is a resource*
Core-7	ru(Rt)	*Rt is a traceable resource unit*
Core-8	has_tru(R,Rt)	*Rt is an individual unit within R*
Core-9	activity(A)	*A is an activity*
Core-10	primitive_activity(A)	*A is a primitive activity*
Core-11	has_subactivity(A,Ao)	*Ao is a subactivity in activity A*
Core-12	consume_res_tru(A,Rt); consume_res_tru(A,R)	
Core-13	produce_res_tru(A,Rt); produce_res_tru(A,R)	
Core-14	use_res_tru(A,Rt); use_res_tru(A,R)	

Example 4.

Core-15	activity_duration(A,T)	*Activity A is performed within time T*
Core-16	has_point(T,Tp)	*Tp is a time point in T*

Example 5.

Core-17	has_subclass(X,X_o)	*Class X has a subclass Xo*
Core-18	has_attribute(X,Ch)	*X has an attribute Ch*
Core-19	has_attribute_value(X,Ch,V)	*Attribute Ch of Object X has value V*
<X>	an object	
<X_o>	a subclass of X	
<Ch>	an attribute of X	
<V>	value of Atr for X	

Example 6.

Term-1	quality_requirement(Qr)	Qr is a quality requirement
Term-2	measured_attribute(At)	At is a measured attribute
Term-3	samples_attribute(Ch,At)	At is a measured attribute sample of Ch.

Example 7.

Term-4	has_sample_sizing(At,Sz)	*Measured Attribute At has sample size Sz*
Term-5	has_sampling_plan(At,Sp)	*At has type of sampling plan Sp*

Example 8.

Term-6	has_standard_value(At,Mu)	*Mu is a standard value of At*
Term-7	has_specification_set(At,SL)	*SL is a specification set of At*
Term-8	has_unit_of_measurement(At,U)	At is measured using unit U

Figure 3. Measurement description system data model

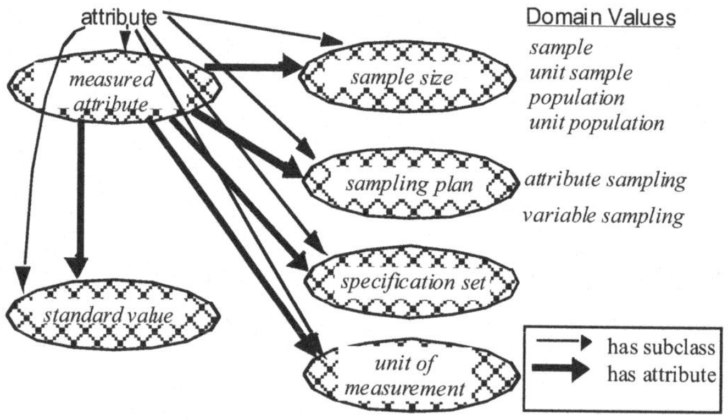

Example 9.

Term-9	measuring_resource(R)
Term-10	primitive_measure(A)
Term-11	measure(A)
Term-12	inspect_and_test(A)

as the value of a measurement taken at a point in time. Following are questions about quality that build on this.

- **ICQ-12:** What is the measured value for a physical characteristic at a given *point* in time?
- **ICQ-13:** What are the measured values for a physical characteristic during a given *period* of time?
- **ICQ-14:** Is an entity of "good" quality at a given point in time?
- **ICQ-15:** Is an entity of "bad" quality at a given point in time?
- **ICQ-16:** Is an entity of conforming quality over a given period of time?

The terminology with which these questions can be more formally posed is developed next.

Terminology & Formal Competency Questions

TOVE Core Ontologies: TOVE measurement ontology terms are defined with propositions (or Boolean terms) from the TOVE Core Ontologies, which are founded upon a first-order language for representing dynamically changing worlds. This first-order language is called the situation calculus (McCarthy & Hayes, 1969). In situation calculus, each perturbation to the modeled world changes the world from one *situation* <s> to another. If the truth value of a term, which describes an entity in this world or a relationship between entities, varies from situation to situation, then the term is a *fluent* <f>. A fluent *holds* in a given situation, if the term is true in that situation. A fluent *occurs in*

Example 10.

Term-13	measurement_pt(Rt,At,Mp,Tp)	*tru Rt of Attribute At measured using measurement point Mp at time point Tp*
Term-14	conformance_pt(Q,Rt,At,Tp)	*Q is a conformance/non-conformance point*
Term-15	nonconformance_pt(Q,Rt,At,Tp)	*with related tru Rt, attribute At at time Tp.*

Example 11.

Term-16 conforming_quality(X,Qr)

Example 12.

CQ-1 Does there exist a quality requirement 'θρ'[1] in a situation 'σ'?

holds(quality_requirement('θρ'),σ).

CQ-2 Does there exist a measured attribute <At> for a tru 'κ' in a situation 'σ'?

∃At [*holds*(tru('κ'),σ) ∧ *holds*(has_attribute('κ',At),σ) ∧ *holds*(measured_attribute(At),σ)].

∃At [*holds*(tru('κ') ∧ has_attribute('κ',At)∧measured_attribute(At),σ)].

CQ-4 For a measured attribute 'α' of a tru 'κ' in a given situation 'σ', does it have a 'unit_sample' or 'sample' sample sizing plan?

holds(tru(κ),σ) ∧ *holds*(has_attribute(κ,α),σ) ∧ *holds*(measured_attribute(α),σ) ∧

(*holds*(has_sample_sizing(α,unit_sample),σ) ∨ *holds*(has_sample_sizing(α,sample),σ)).

CQ-8 For a measured attribute 'α' in a given situation 'σ', does it have a specification set (expressed as an interval set [<T_1>,<T_2>] or a list [<W_i>]?

$\exists T_1 \exists T_2 \exists \{W_i\}$ [*holds*(measured_attribute('α'),σ) ∧

(*holds*(has_specification_set('α',[T_1,T_2]),σ) ∨ *holds*(has_specification_set(α,{W_i}),σ))].

a given time period <T>, if for all situations which occur during that period, the fluent holds. Note that unless otherwise stated, all predicates of the ontology are fluents, e.g., the predicate presented as organization_agent(Oa) is actually expressed in the ontology as holds(organization_agent(Oa),s). Also, a variable or parameter of a term is denoted within <> brackets when the term is defined. <R> denotes that 'R' is one of the variables of the term *resource*, e.g. if R='chair' for the expression resource(R) then this is read as 'a chair is a resource.' See Example 1.

An *agent constraint* is a special fluent representing a constraint upon an *organization agent* that must be satisfied in order for that agent to achieve some goal. See Example 2.

Some agent constraints refer to use of *resource* <R>—a conceptual or prototypical entity such as arm assembly—and *tru* (traceable resource unit) <Rt>—a physical set of individual units of a resource, such as 'lot#123 of arm assemblies' (Kim, Fox, & Grüninger, 1999), or a microarray assay plate or reagents. An *activity* <A> may *consume trus* of one resource to *produce trus* of another resource, and may *use trus* of yet another resource; if a tru is used, individual units of the resource that comprise it are not consumed so they are available for use after an activity's execution. Activities can be hierarchically modeled as comprised of *subactivities* <Ao>; a *primitive activity* has no sub-activities. **Core-12** can be

Example 13.

Cons-1 A measured attribute must be an attribute of a tru.

Cons-2 measured attribute must be sampled from an attribute of a resource

∀At∀s [*holds*(measured_attribute(At),s) →

∃Atr∃R (*holds*(samples_attribute(Atr,At),s) ∧

holds(has_attribute(R,Atr),s) ∧ *holds*(resource(R),s))].

<At> measured attribute

<Atr> attribute sampled for At

<Rt> tru for which At is an attribute

<R> resource for which Atr is an attribute

<s> an extant or hypothetical situation

Example 14.

Cons-3 All measured attributes must have a specification set, and the standard value for that measured attribute must be an element of the specification set.

∀At∀Mu∀s [*holds*(has_standard_value(At,Mu),s) →

$\exists T_1 \exists T_2$(*holds*(has_specification_set(At,[T_1,T_2]),s) ∧ $T_1 \leq Mu \leq T_2$) ∨

$\exists \{W_i\}$ (*holds*(has_specification_set(At,$\{W_i\}$),s) ∧ $Mu \in \{W_i\}$)]

<At> a measured attribute

[<T_1>,<T_2>] upper and lower bounds of a specification set for a measured attribute of ratio scale

$\{W_i\}$ a set of "acceptable" values for the measured attribute

<Mu> the standard value for At

<s> an extant or hypothetical situation

interpreted as "consume resource or tru." This interpretation also holds for "produce" and "use." See Example 3.

The time duration <T> within which an activity <A> is performed can be represented as a sequential list of discrete time points <Tp>. See Example 4.

Finally, general object-oriented constructs are represented as seen in Example 5.

Measurement Description System: A *quality requirement* <Qr> specifies physical characteristics <Ch> of a resource—e.g., "the number of genes examined or the number of probes used per gene"—that has a bearing on quality, as well as constraints that define acceptable quality. A *measured attribute* <At> of a sample of a tru—e.g., "average light intensity and color"—is the explicit, exact descriptor of what is measured. So, the following are used to formally express ICQ-1 to ICQ-3. See Example 6.

There are two additional issues regarding sampling:

- **Sample Size:** How many individuals in a set are measured to model the characteristics of the set?
- **Sampling Plan:** When determining an aggregate value from the sample, does it refer directly to the actual attribute that is physically measured or is the reference indirect?

Table 1. Steps for using an advisor for demonstrating competency

Step #	**Bioinformatician View**: Using the Advisor to Analyze Specific Enterprise		**Ontology Builder View**: Using the Advisor to Evaluate Competency of Ontology
1	Stating facts about experimental conditions	⇔	Representing populated enterprise model
2	Stating explicit gene-gene relationships	⇔	Representing formal competency questions
3	Stating data dictionary of experimental terms	⇔	Representing ontology terminology and axioms
4	Answering queries	⇔	Deducing answers to formal competency questions

⇔ denotes translation between knowledge about an enterprise and how that knowledge is represented using an ontology

Therefore, the terms in Example 7 are used to express ICQ-4 to ICQ-6.

To express ICQ-7 to ICQ-9, a *standard value* μ <Mu> for what the value of a measured attribute <At> ought to be is represented, as well as a function of μ and σ^2 ($f(\mu,\sigma^2)$) and an operator (⊗). *Unit of measurement* <U> is also represented. For a measured attribute <At>, a subset $[\mu-k\sigma^2, \mu+k\sigma^2]$, a generic term called a *specification set* <SL> is represented, where elements of this subset denote acceptable measurement values. See Example 8.

Measurement Activities: The simplest measurement action is the measurement of one measured attribute of one tru at one point in time. When this measurement is performed using a special resource <R> called a *measuring resource*, this activity <A> is a *primitive measure* activity. A primitive measure activity or an aggregation of primitive measure activities is a *measure* activity. An *inspection and test* activity is a form of a measure activity. The following terms then are used to formally express ICQ-10 and ICQ-11. See Example 9.

Measurement Point: To formally express ICQ-12 and ICQ-13, the result of a measurement activity is represented using a *measurement point* <Mp>, relating the value of the measurement, and concomitantly the measured attribute <At>, the time of measurement <Tp>, and tru measured <Rt>. See Example 10.

The following term then represents the concept that "quality is conformance to requirements." See Example 11.

Using these terms, ICQ-14 to ICQ-16 are expressed. Informal competency questions are stated formally next.

Formal Competency Questions

For brevity, only the competency questions for the measurement description system are presented. The informal competency question is re-stated in English using the terminology developed from the ontology, then expressed formally in First-Order Logic.

Measurement Description System: See Example 12.

Axioms

The axioms in the ontology are presented next. Once again, we only describe the axioms for the measurement description system for lack of space.

Measurement Description System: A categorical characterization of the content of all quality requirements is difficult; axioms about quality requirements true for all enterprises in all industries are not likely to exist. Rather, quality requirement is stated as a *primitive term* (PT)—a term that is instantiated and stated as a fact in

Table 2.

#1	Stating facts about the process	⇔	Representing populated model
Emerging	"collections are fluorescently labeled"	⇔	*holds(*activity(process_fl_label), sw_actual)
Traditional	"There are many activities…" from Motivating Scenario	⇔	*holds*(activity(process_wp_hcpf_260_1) , sv_actual).
#2	Stating queries for analyzing process	⇔	Representing formal competency questions
Emerging	"Is this an activity in which a specific gene is determined to be under-expressed?"	⇔	*holds(*inspect_and_test(α),σ).
Traditional	"Is this an activity in which products are determined to be non-prime?"	⇔	*holds*(inspect_and_test(α),σ).
#3	Stating data dictionary of actual process's terms	⇔	Representing ontology terminology and axioms
Emerging	"An activity where a gene is determined to be unexpressed is an inspect and test activity according to the TOVE Measurement Ontology"	⇔	*holds(measure(inspect_and_test_exp_gene1), sv_actual)*
Traditional	"An activity where products are determined to be non-prime is an inspect and test activity according to the TOVE Measurement Ontology."	⇔	*holds*(measure(inspect_and_test_wp_hcpf_1),sv_actual).
#4	Answering queries	⇔	Deducing answers to formal competency questions
Emerging	"The inspections are done through an activity which measures the average light intensity for a specific cell using a light sensor"	⇔	*holds(*inspect_and_test(C_{ij}), s)
Traditional	"The inspections are done through an activity which measures the average coil length using a sensor."	⇔	*holds*(inspect_and_test(A),s) ≡ …

the populated enterprise model—in the TOVE measurement ontology. That is, the enterprise modeler determines that a given agent constraint is a quality requirement and states this as a fact. All *definition* (Defn) axioms are ultimately formally defined in terms of primitive terms. By applying *constraint* **(Cons)** axioms, proper use of primitive terms is enforced. Primitive terms are populated (instantiated) as *ground terms*; e.g. a fact that 'widget' is a resource is represented as a ground term, resource (widget), which is an instance of the primitive term, resource(R). Measured attribute and samples attribute are also primitive terms.

The quality of an activity is evaluated by the quality of resources associated with that activity; and the quality of a resource (prototypical product) is gauged by the quality of trus comprised of individual units of that resource. The constraint axioms in Example 13 express this.

These axioms ensure valid answers for ICQ-2. Additional such constraints constrain the use of the primitive terms has_sample_sizing, has_sampling_plan, has_standard_value, has_specifica-

Table 3.

Manufacturing (Basis for Measurement Ontology)	Measuring QoS for Web services	Tracking cattle via RFID
ICQ-2: What is the physical characteristic that is measured?	What is the QoS metric that is measured? Answer could be mean response time, and facts could be represented using the ontology as has_attribute(message121,response_time) measured_attribute(mean_response_time)	Which data about beef quality needs to be collected? Answers could be fat thickness, and facts could be represented using the ontology as has_attribute(cowcarcass1871,fat_thickness).
ICQ-3: Is every entity that is produced measured?	Is the response time for every message measured? Answer would be yes and represented as Has_sample_sizing(mean_response_time,sample_population) to signify that the population is sampled—i.e. response times for all packets that comprise a message are calculated. If only some packets were sampled then this would be represented as has_sample_sizing(mean_response_time,sample).	Is every carcass measured? Answer would be yes and represented as has_sample_sizing(fat_thickness,unit_sample) to signify that each unit is sampled.
ICQ-5: If a sample is taken and measured, is the value for the measurement some aggregate (e.g. average) of the measurement upon individual units of that sample?	Are the response times for a message averaged? Answer is yes, since the mean response time for a message is the average of the response times of all packets that comprise that message. This would be represented as samples_attribute(mean_response_time,response_time) and has_sampling_plan(mean_response_time,attribute_sampling).	Is the mean fat thickness of each carcass from a lot averaged? Answer is no, since fat thickness is tracked individually and not associated with the lots that identify the herd of origin.

tion_set, and has_unit_of_measurement. The axiom in Example 14 ensures valid answers for ICQ-8.

DEMONSTRATION OF COMPETENCY

A demonstration of competency entails using the TOVE ontological engineering methodology for the following:

- **Microarray Analysis:** Does an ontology support problem-solving tasks for a specific pathway—wing development in *Drosophila melanogaster*?
- **Ontology Development:** Are ontology competency questions—which by design do not refer to any specific domain—answered, thus demonstrating that the ontology can be used to support similar problem-solving tasks for other domains?

The first question characterizes requirements for an analyst familiar with the domain, not the ontology's language or representations; the second question is relevant for an engineer with expertise in ontology-based enterprise modeling who is unfamiliar with details of the specific domain modeled. An *advisor* is a user interface and access routines front-end software to an ontology-based enterprise model. Table 1 lists how an advisor answers the two different questions.

We now provide the actual process in which each of the steps in Table 1 manifests in the ontology by identifying parts of the motivating scenario that correspond to the ontology predicates (see Table 2). This can be demonstrated computationally using the ISO 9000 Quality Advisor (Kim & Fox, 2002), a tool for evaluating ISO 9000 compliance of an enterprise modeled using ontologies. Evaluation entails answering questions about an enterprise's inspection and measurement system, so it can be used for enterprise analysis, as well as for assessing the competency of the measurement ontology.

A complete demonstration of competency using all of the components of the ontology is beyond the scope of this article because of length restrictions. A full demonstration is shown in (Kim, 1999), which also includes a demonstration of generalizability of the measurement ontology.

COMMENTARY ON GENERALIZABILITY

In our full demonstration of generalizability (Kim, 1999), we show that the measurement ontology's representations could be used to perform similar tasks as a related application. Specifically, it is shown that parts of SAP's quality control management model (SAP-AG, 1995) could be reasonably "reduced" or represented using only ontology representations. The implication then is that a query answerable using the SAP™ data model is answerable as a competency question posed and answered using the ontology. That is, the ontology is as "competent" as SAP™ with respect to the reduced set of competency questions.

Whereas that demonstration provides evidence of intra-domain, inter-application (using different models [or ontologies] in a similar domain) generalizability of the ontology, what we have shown in Table 2 provides evidence of inter-domain, intra-application (using same model [ontology] for different domains) generalizability. That is, we show that same set of general measurement representations can be used to pose and answer competency questions from two different domains.

We cannot claim that the measurement ontology can be a "plug-and-play" ontology for all other domains. Rather, we can claim that the ontology's representations can be used to define terms and express axioms for more domain-specific ontologies. The basis of this claim is the core of the methodology used: competency questions. If informal competency questions associated with a specific domain can be reasonably posed as formal competency questions represented using measurement ontology representations, we can make an inductive argument that the measurement ontology is generalizable to that domain. To that end, we show in Table 3 how the informal competency questions from measuring the quality of service (QoS) of Web services and agriculture (tracking cattle) domains relate to the informal competency questions that motivated this ontology. It is evident then that the measurement ontology can serve as a very re-usable, generalizable basis to develop more committed ontologies of highly diverse fields, from measuring QoS to tracking cattle.

CONCLUDING REMARKS

There is clearly a need for an ontology that represents both the obvious and more subtle fundamental concepts in measurement. This is certainly true in emerging domains like bioinformatics where quality plays such a vital and critical role in discovery. A measurement ontology is particularly useful for builders of Semantic Web ontologies of emerging domains because of the importance of measurement in these domains, which are firmly grounded in the physical sciences. The measurement concepts represented in this article are summarized as follows:

- A system for assessing measurements includes the appropriate *measured attribute*, as well as its *standard value* (μ), *sampling plan* and *size*, *specification set* of "acceptable values" of $f(\mu,\sigma^2)$, and *unit of measurement*. Measurements of attributes are recorded as *measurement points* in time that are assigned a value as a result of some *measurement activity*. These representations are the basic ones necessary to model any form of measurement.
- Quality can be represented as some composition of *conformance points*, which are "conforming" measurement points with respect to some *quality requirement*. Representing quality requirements, measurement points, and conformance points makes it possible to model and assess any entity within an enterprise as of *conforming quality*.

These concepts are formally represented by posing competency questions, analyzing the domain of measurement, stating assumptions, and developing terminology and axioms. Then, the competency of the ontology and its capability for use to gain insights about an enterprise are demonstrated by automatically deducing answers to questions such as:

- **Quality Assessment System Competency Questions:** What is the standard value for a given measured attribute of an entity? What is its specification set? How is the measured attribute sampled?
- **Measurement and Conformance Points Competency Questions:** What is the measurement point for a measured attribute? Is it a conformance point? Over a period of time, is an entity of conforming quality?

Measurement theory is more than just measurement unit conversions and quantities. The root of our contribution is that we present an ontology that represents more concepts than other ontologies. This general ontology is then a useful reference regardless of whether it serves as a building block for traditional or emerging domains, or for the Semantic Web or closed networks. With such an ontology in tow, developers of Semantic Web ontologies of emerging domains as diverse as biology and geography have a reference for ensuring that important and subtle measurement concepts are diligently represented in their ontologies and not ignored.

The clear future direction for this work is to (1) transform this ontology so that its representations are more general, and that ontological commitment made towards enterprise applications is further abstracted out; (2) develop separate domain specific ontologies of emerging domains that actually define and restrict their terms using the general ontology developed in (1) (as opposed to the realistic use of this ontology, which is to serve as inspiration and reference); and (3) implement both the general and the domain specific ontologies in the *de facto* ontology language of the Semantic Web, OWL.

Overall we believe that we have inspired builders of emerging domain ontologies to incorporate important common-sense of their domains—that of obvious and subtle measurement concepts—in their ontologies, so that their ontologies will be more robust and sharable for functioning on the Semantic Web.

REFERENCES

Allen, J. F. (1983). Maintaining knowledge about temporal intervals. *Communications of the ACM, 26*(11), 832-843.

Ashburner, M., Ball, C., Blake, J., Botstein, D., Butler, H., Cherry, J., et al. (2000). Gene ontology: Tool for the unification of biology. *National Genetics, 25*, 25-29.

Attie, A. D. (2003). The new industrialized approach to biology. *Cell Biology Education, 2*, 150-151.

Bechhofer, S., Goble, C., & Horrocks, I. (2001, July 30-August 1). *DAML+OIL Is not Enough*. Paper presented at the First Semantic Web Working Symposium (SWWS-01), Stanford, CA.

Berners-Lee, T., Hendler, J., & Lassila, O. (2001). The Semantic Web. *Scientific American, 284*(5), 34-43.

Bowers, S., & Ludäscher, B. (2004). *An ontology-driven framework for data transformation in scientific workflows*. Paper presented at the International Workshop on Data Integration in the Life Sciences (DILS'04), Leipzig, Germany.

Brilhante, V., & Robertson, D. (2001). Metadata-Supported Automated Ecological Modelling. In C. Rautenstrauch (Ed.), *Environmental information systems in industry and public administration*. Hershey, PA: Idea Group Publishing.

Campbell, A. E., & Shapiro, S. C. (1995). *Ontological mediation: An overview*. Paper presented at the IJCAI Workshop on Basic Ontological Issues in Knowledge Sharing.

Chen, Y., Zhou, L., & Zhang, D. (2006). Ontology-supported Web service composition: An approach to service-oriented knowledge management in corporate services. *Journal of Database Management, 17*(1), 67-84.

Davies, J., Duke, A., & Stonkus, A. (2002). *OntoShare: Using ontologies for knowledge sharing*. Paper presented at the Semantic Web Workshop of the WWW Conference, Hawaii, HI.

Duggan, D. J., Chen, M., Meltzer, P., & Trent, J. (1999). Expression profiling using cDNA microarrays. *Nature Genetics, 21*, 10-14.

Fenton, N. E. (1994). Software measurement: a necessary scientific basis. *IEEE Transactions on Software Engineering, 20*(3), 199-206.

Fikes, R., & Farquhar, A. (1999). Distributed repositories of highly expressive reusable ontologies. *IEEE Intelligent Systems, 14*(2), 73-79.

Finkelstein, L. (1984). A review of the fundamental concepts of measurement. *Measurement, 2*(1), 25-34.

Fox, M. S. (1992). The TOVE project, towards a common sense model of the enterprise. In C. Petrie (Ed.), *Enterprise integration*. Cambridge, MA: MIT Press.

Fox, M. S., & Gruninger, M. (1998). Enterprise modelling. *AI Magazine, 19*(3), 109-121.

Gandon, F. (2001, October 22-24). *Engineering an ontology for a multi-agents corporate memory system*. Paper presented at the ISMICK 2001 Eighth International Symposium on the Management of Industrial and Corporate Knowledge, Université de Technologie de Compiègne, France.

Gandon, F. L., & Sadeh, N. M. (2004). Semantic Web technologies to reconcile privacy and context awareness. *Journal of Web Semantics, 1*(3), 241-260.

Goh, C. H., Bressan, S., Madnick, S., & Siegel, M. (1999). Context interchange: New features and formalisms for the intelligent integration of information. *ACM Transactions on Information Systems, 17*(3), 270-293.

Grady, J. O. (1993). *System requirements analysis*: McGraw-Hill Inc.

Gruber, T. R. (1993, March). *Towards principles for the design of pntologies used for knowledge sharing*. Paper presented at the International Workshop on Formal Ontology, Padova, Italy.

Gruber, T. R., & Olsen, G. R. (1994). *An ontology for engineering mathematics*. Paper presented at the Fourth International Conference on Principles of Knowledge Representation and Reasoning, Bonn, Germany.

Gruninger, M., & Fox, M. S. (1995). *Methodology for the design and evaluation of ontologies*. Paper presented at the Workshop on Basic Ontological Issues in Knowledge Sharing, IJCAI-95, Montreal, Canada.

Hayes, P. J. (1985). Naive physics I: Ontology for liquids. In J. Hobbs & B. Moore (Eds.), *Theories of the commonsense world* (pp. 71-89). Ablex Publishing Corp.

Heflin, J. (2000, April 3, 2000). Measurement ontology 1.0 (draft). Retrieved August 15, 2004, from http://www.cs.umd.edu/projects/plus/SHOE/onts/measure1.0.html

Hewett, M., Oliver, D. E., Rubin, D. L., Easton, K. L., Stuart, J. M., Altman, R. B., *et al.* (2002). PharmGKB: the pharmaco-genetics knowledge base. *Nucleic Acids Research, 30*(1), 163-165.

Khatri, V., Ram, S., & Snodgrass, R. T. (2004). Augmenting a conceptual model with geospatiotemporal annotations. *IEEE Transactions on Knowledge and Data Engineering, 16*(11), 1324-1338.

Kim, H. M. (1999). *Representing and reasoning about quality using enterprise models.* Unpublished PhD thesis, Department of Industrial Engineering, University of Toronto, Toronto, Ontario, Canada.

Kim, H. M. (2002, January 7-10). *XML-hoo!: A prototype application for intelligent query of XML documents using domain-specific ontologies.* Paper presented at the 35th Annual Hawaii International Conference on Systems Science (HICSS-35), Hawaii, HI.

Kim, H. M., & Fox, M. S. (2002, January 4-7). *Using enterprise reference models for automated ISO 9000 compliance evaluation.* Paper presented at the 35th Hawaii International Conference on Systems Science (HICSS), Big Island, HI.

Kim, H. M., Fox, M. S., & Grüninger, M. (1999). An ontology for quality management: Enabling quality problem identification and tracing. *BT Technology Journal, 17*(4), 131-139.

Klischewski, A. R., & Jeenicke, M. (2004). *Semantic Web technologies for information management within e-government services.* Paper presented at the 37th Annual Hawaii International Conference on System Sciences (HICSS'04), Big Island, HI.

Kuipers, B. J. (1986). Qualitative simulation. *Artificial Intelligence, 29*(3), 289-338.

Lenat, D. B. (1995). CYC: A large-scale investment in knowledge infrastructure. *Communications of the ACM, 38*(11), 33-38.

Lesk, A. M. (2005). *Databasse annotation in molecular biology, principles and practice*: John Wiley & Sons Ltd.

Lozano-Tello, A., & Gomez-Perez, A. (2004). ONTOMETRIC: A method to choose the appropriate ontology. *Journal of Database Management, 15*(2), 1-18.

Mars, N. J. I. (1993, March 10-13). *An ontology of measurement units.* Paper presented at the International Workshop on Formal Ontologies in Conceptual Analysis and Knowledge Representation, Padova, Italy.

Massey, B. S. (1971). *Units, dimensional analysis, and physical similarity.* London: Van Nostrom Reinhold.

McCarthy, J., & Hayes, P. J. (1969). Some philosophical problems from the standpoint of AI. In B. Meltzer & D. Michie (Eds.), *Machine intelligence* (Vol. 4, pp. 463-501). Edinburgh, UK: Edinburgh University Press.

McGuinness, D. L., & van Harmelen, F. (2003). *OWL Web Ontology Language overview* (No. CR-owl-features-20030818). W3C.

Milton, S. K., & Kazmierczak, E. (2004). An ontology of data modelling languages: A study using a common-sense realistic ontology. *Journal of Database Management, 15*(2), 19-38.

Mount, D. W. (2004). *Bioinformatics sequence and genome analysis.* Cold Spring Harbor, New York: Cold Spring Harbor Laboratory Press.

Narens, L. (1985). *Abstract measurement theory.* Cambridge, MA: MIT Press.

Novak, G. S., Jr. (1995). Conversion of units of measurement. *IEEE Transactions on Software Engineering, 21*(8), 651-661.

Noy, N. F., & Hafner, C. D. (1997). The state of the art in ontology sesign: A survey and comparative review. *AI Magazine, 18*(3), 53-74.

Nozick, L. K., Turnquist, M. A., Jones, D. A., Davis, J. R., & Lawton, C. R. (2004). *Assessing the Performance of Interdependent Infrastructures and Optimizing Investments.* Paper presented at the 37th Annual Hawaii International Conference on System Sciences, Big Island, HI.

Pease, A., & Niles, I. (2002). IEEE standard upper ontology: A progress report. *Knowledge Engineering Review, 17,* 65-70.

Ram, S., & Wei, W. (2004). *Modeling the semantics of 3D protein structures.* Paper presented at the ER 2004, Shanghai, China.

Reiger, C., & Grinberg, M. (1977). *The declarative representation and procedural simulations of causality in physical mechanisms.* Paper presented at the Joint Conference on Artificial Intelligence.

Retz-Schmidt, G. (1988). Various views on spatial prepositions. *AI Magazine, 9*(2), 95-105.

Roberts, F. (1979). *Measurement theory with applications to decision making, utility and the social sciences.* Reading, MA: Addison-Wesley.

Ronco, L., Grossel, M., Zimmer, M., & Socash, T. (2003). *Modules in emerging fields. Vol 4: Genomics and proteomics.*

SAP-AG. (1995). *SAP R/3 system: Quality management* (No. 4.6). Neurottstrasse 16, 69190 Walldorf, Germany: SAP AG.

Scheaffer, R. L., & McClave, J. T. (1982). *Statistics for engineers.* Boston, MA: PWS Publishers.

Schlenoff, C., Balakirsky, S., Uschold, M., Provine, R., & Smith, S. (2003). Using ontologies to aid navigation planning in autonomous vehicles. *The knowledge engineering review, 18,* 243-255.

Stevens, R., Goble, C., Horrocks, I., & Bechhofer, S. (2002). Building a bioinformatics ontology using OIL. *IEEE Transactions on Information Technology in Biomedicine, 6*(2), 135-141.

Stevens, R., Goble, C. A., & Bechhofer, S. (2000). Ontology-based knowledge representation for bioinformatics. *Briefings in Bioinformatics, 1*(4), 398-414.

Stoeckert Jr., C. J., & Parkinson, H. (2004). The MGED ontology: A framework for describing functional genomics experiments. *Comparative and Functional Genomics, 4*(1), 127-132.

Uschold, M., & Gruninger, M. (1996). Ontologies: Principles, methods and applications. *Knowledge Engineering Review, 11*(2), 93-136.

Wroe, C., Stevens, R., Goble, C., & Ashburner, M. (2003). A methodology to migrate the gene ontology to a description logic environment using DAML+OIL. *Pacific Symposium on Biocomputing, 8,* 624-635.

ENDNOTE

1 Facts or constants (as opposed to variables) expressed in competency questions are denoted in Greek letters within single quotes.

This work was previously published in Journal of Database Management, Vol. 18, Issue 1, edited by K. Siau, pp. 20-42, copyright 2007 by IGI Publishing, formerly known as Idea Group Publishing (an imprint of IGI Global).

Chapter III
Semantic Integration and Knowledge Discovery for Environmental Research

Zhiyuan Chen
University of Maryland, Baltimore County (UMBC), USA

Aryya Gangopadhyay
University of Maryland, Baltimore County (UMBC), USA

George Karabatis
University of Maryland, Baltimore County (UMBC), USA

Michael McGuire
University of Maryland, Baltimore County (UMBC), USA

Claire Welty
University of Maryland, Baltimore County (UMBC), USA

ABSTRACT

Environmental research and knowledge discovery both require extensive use of data stored in various sources and created in different ways for diverse purposes. We describe a new metadata approach to elicit semantic information from environmental data and implement semantics-based techniques to assist users in integrating, navigating, and mining multiple environmental data sources. Our system contains specifications of various environmental data sources and the relationships that are formed among them. User requests are augmented with semantically related data sources and automatically presented as a visual semantic network. In addition, we present a methodology for data navigation and pattern discovery using multi-resolution browsing and data mining. The data semantics are captured and utilized in terms of their patterns and trends at multiple levels of resolution. We present the efficacy of our methodology through experimental results.

INTRODUCTION

The urban environment is formed by complex interactions between natural and human systems. Studying the urban environment requires the collection and analysis of very large datasets that span many disciplines, have semantic (including spatial and temporal) differences and interdependencies, are collected and managed by multiple organizations, and are stored in varying formats. Scientific knowledge discovery is often hindered because of challenges in the integration and navigation of these disparate data. Furthermore, as the number of dimensions in the data increases, novel approaches for pattern discovery are needed.

Environmental data are collected in a variety of units (metric or SI), time increments (minutes, hours, or even days), map projections (e.g., UTM or State Plane) and spatial densities. The data are stored in numerous formats, multiple locations, and are not centralized into a single repository for easy access. To help users (mostly environmental researchers) identify data sets of interest, we use a metadata approach to extract semantically related data sources and present them to the researchers as a semantic network. Starting with an initial search (query) submitted by a researcher, we exploit stored relationships (metadata) among actual data sources to enhance the search result with additional semantically related information. Although domain experts need to manually construct the initial semantic network, which may only include a small number of sources, we introduce an algorithm to let the network expand and evolve automatically based on usage patterns. Then, we present the semantic network to the user as a visual display of a hyperbolic tree; we claim that semantic networks provide an elegant and compact technique to visualize considerable amounts of semantically relevant data sources in a simple yet powerful manner.

Once users have finalized a set of environmental data sources, based on semantic networks, they can access the actual sources to extract data and perform techniques for knowledge discovery. We introduce a new approach to integrate urban environmental data and provide scientists with semantic techniques to navigate and discover patterns in very large environmental datasets.

Our system provides access to a multitude of heterogeneous and autonomous data repositories and assists the user to navigate through the abundance of diverse data sources as if they were a single homogeneous source. More specifically, our contributions are:

1. **Recommendation of Additional and Relevant Data Sources:** We present our approach to recommend data sources that are potentially relevant to the user's search interests. Currently, it is tedious and impractical for users to locate relevant information sources by themselves. We provide a methodology that addresses this problem and automatically supplies users with additional and potentially relevant data sources that they might not be aware of. In order to discover these additional recommendations, we exploit semantic relationships between data sources. We define *semantic networks* for interrelated data sources and present an algorithm to automatically refine, augment, and expand an initial and relatively small semantic network with additional and relevant data sources; we also exploit *user profiles* to tailor resulting data sources to specific user preferences.
2. **Visualization and Navigation of Relevant Data Sources:** The semantic network with the additional sources is shown to the user as a visual hyperbolic tree improving usability by showing the semantic relationships among relevant data sources in a visual way. After the user has decided on the choice of relevant data sources of interest (based on our metadata approach) and has accessed the actual data, we also assist the user in navigating through the plethora of environmental

data using visualization and navigation techniques that describe data at multiple levels of resolution, enabling pattern and knowledge discovery at different semantic levels. We achieve that, using wavelet transformation techniques, and we demonstrate resilience of wavelet transformation to noisy data.

3. **Implementation of a Prototype System:** Finally, we have designed and implemented a prototype system as a proof of concept for our techniques. Using this system we have demonstrated the feasibility of our contributions and have conducted a set of experiments verifying and validating our approach.

This article is organized as follows. First, we present related work on data integration using semantics, and on exploration of multi-dimensional data. Next, we present our research methodology on semantic networks and pattern discovery with wavelet transformations. Then, we describe our prototype implementation and the experiments we conducted. Our conclusions are presented in the final section.

RELATED WORK

Data Integration

There is a rich body of existing work on data integration problems. The fundamental problem is to enable interoperation across different heterogeneous sources of information. In general, this problem manifests itself either as schema mismatches (schema integration) or data incompatibilities (data integration) while accessing disparate data sources. Several surveys identifying problems and proposed approaches on schema and data integration have been written over the years (Batini, Lenzerini, & Navathe, 1986; Ouksel & Sheth, 1999; Rahm & Bernstein, 2001). There has been a significant amount of work on data integration, especially on resolving discrepancies of different data schemas using a global (mediated) schema (Friedman, Levy, & Millstein, 1999; Levy, Rajaraman, & Ordille, 1996; Miller et al., 2001; Papakonstantinou, Garcia-Molina, & Ullman, 1996; Rahm & Bernstein, 2001; Ram, Park, & Hwang, 2002). More recently, there exists work on decentralized data sharing (Bowers, Lin, & Ludascher, 2004; Doan, Domingos, & Halevy, 2003; Halevy, Ives, Suciu, & Tatarinov, 2003; Rodriguez-Gianolli, Garzetti, Jiang, Kementsietsidis, Kiringa, Masud, Miller, and Mylopoulos, 2005; Tatarinov, & Halevy, 2004) and on integrating data in web-based databases (Bowers et al., 2004; Chang, He, & Zhang, 2005; Dispensa & Brulle, 2003). Clustering, classification and ontologies have also been extensively used as a tool to solve semantic heterogeneity problems (Jain & Zhao, 2004; Kalfoglou & Schorlemmer, 2003; Ram & Park, 2004; Sheth et al., 2004; Sheth, Arpinar, & Kashyap, 2003; Sheth et al., 2002; Zhao & Ram, 2002, 2004).

All the previously mentioned work takes a deep integration approach, where the data schemas (or query interface for integrating web databases) of all sources are integrated. However, this approach is often too restrictive for environmental research because: (1) there are so many different types of data collected by so many different groups that it is impractical for all of them to agree on a universal mediated schema; (2) unlike companies, environmental researchers often share data in an ad hoc way, e.g., a company may purchase products from several fixed suppliers while environmental researchers may use any dataset collected by other researchers but related to their current research task.

There has been much effort by the ecology research community to integrate its data (EML, ORS, SEEK). These systems take a *shallow integration* approach where only metadata is integrated; they allow researchers to store metadata in a centralized database and to select datasets by searching the metadata using keyword or SQL-based search. Such systems avoid the problem of defining a global-mediated data schema and allow researchers to share data in an ad hoc way. A semantics-based integration approach for geospatial data is presented in (Ram, Khatri, Zhang, & Zeng, 2001).

The main problem of existing systems for integrating environmental data is that they provide limited support to assist users in finding data sources semantically related to their research. Most existing systems assume researchers have full knowledge of what keywords to search and provide no assistance in selecting data sources based on relationships between them. However, unlike business applications, environmental research is more explorative and researchers are interested in searching semantically related datasets. Although experienced researchers may find all related keywords, inexperienced researchers such as graduate students may have trouble doing this. The only exception is the SEEK project (Bowers et al., 2004; Bowers & Ludascher, 2004), which uses an ontology for ecology concepts to find related datasets. However, SEEK assumes the ontology will be completely given by domain experts, while our approach augments such knowledge by incremental and automatic refinement of the semantic network.

There has also been work on discovering semantic similarity in (Fankhauser, Kracker, & Neuhold, 1991) based on generalization/specialization, and positive/negative association between classes; in our article, we do not restrict our work to these types of classes only, instead, we let the users identify the degree of relevance between data sources as their own semantic interpretation. Although our approach gives more emphasis on the user's semantics, it may require more manual work to calculate the semantic relationships in the semantic network, since it is user-based. To reduce the amount of manual work, we start with a small manually created semantic network, and then we apply an algorithm that we designed and implemented, to automatically expand, refine, and augment the semantic network by taking advantage of observed usage patterns. Another difference with (Fankhauser et al., 1991) is the way that the degree of relevance is calculated. They use triangular norms (T-norms) from fuzzy logic, while we use conditional probabilities. Relevant to our work is the topic of discovering and ranking semantic relationships for the Semantic Web (Aleman-Meza, Halaschek-Wiener, Arpinar, Ramakrishnan, & Sheth, 2005; Sheth et al., 2004). However, relationship ranking is not in the scope of this article.

Using Wavelets for Exploration of Multidimensional Data

In order to study long-term environmental factors, we need to evaluate measures across multiple dimensions such as time and geographic space at different dimensional hierarchies. An example of the type of queries that have to be answered is, "How do stream temperature and precipitation change over time and space?" In order to answer such queries, the system must integrate diverse sets of information, which is typically facilitated by dimensional modeling techniques (Kimball, 2002) and online analytical processing (OLAP). The challenge stems from the fact that such dimensional models grow exponentially in size with the number of dimensions and dimensional hierarchies. Current OLAP techniques, however, rely on the intuition of the decision maker in navigating through this lattice of cuboids and only provide navigation tools such as drill down and roll up. There have been very few attempts made to address this issue, most notably the work done by (Sarawagi, Agrawal, & Megiddo, 1998) and (Kumar, Gangopadhyay, & Karabatis, in press). However, the major deficiency of the existing work in this area is that the volume of data after a few drill-downs becomes prohibitively large, which hinders the effectiveness of the method. In order to help end users (scientists or engineers) discover and analyze patterns from large datasets, we have developed a methodology for visualization of data at multiple levels of dimensional hierarchy and pattern discovery through data mining techniques (Han & Kamber, 2000; Mitchell, 1997) at multiple levels of resolution.

The last decade has seen an explosion of interest in wavelets (Daubechies, 1992; Goswami & Chan, 1999), a subject area that has coalesced from roots in mathematics, physics, electrical engineering and other disciplines. Wavelets have been developed as a means to provide low-resolution views of data with the ability to reconstruct high-resolution views if necessary. Wavelet transformation has been applied in numerous disciplines such as compression and de-noising of audio signals and images, finger print compression, edge detection, object detection in two-dimensional images, and image retrieval (Stollnitz, Derose, & Salesin, 1996). There have been few studies on approximate query answering through lossy compression of multi-dimensional data cubes (Matias, Vitter, & Wang, 1998; Smith, Li, & Jhingran, 2004; Vitter & Wang, 1999; Vitter, Wang, & Iyer, 1998), data cleaning, and time-series data analysis (Percival & Walden, 2000). However, no study has been done on utilizing wavelet transformation to provide decision support. We use wavelets to provide coarse, low-resolution views to researchers with the capability of retrieving high-resolution data by zooming into selected areas.

Generally speaking, wavelet transformation is a tool that divides up data, functions, or operators into different frequency components and then studies each component with a resolution matched to its scale (Daubechies, 1992). A wavelet has many desirable properties such as compact support, vanishing moments and dilating relation and other preferred properties such as smoothness (Chui & Lian, 1996). The core idea behind a discrete wavelet transformation (DWT) is to progressively smooth the data using an iterative procedure and keep the detail along the way. The DWT is performed using the pyramid algorithm (Mallat, 1989) in $O(N)$ time.

RESEARCH DESIGN AND METHODS

Overview of the Architecture

The overall architecture of our system is shown in Figure 1. It consists of a data integration component, a data warehouse, and visualization, navigation, and pattern discovery component, all for the semantic utilization of heterogeneous data sources. The data integration component consists of a metadata repository, a semantic network, and a set of conversion functions. The metadata repository stores information about the source data including descriptions of each particular source along with information on its syntax and semantics. In our approach the metadata layer is not a global schema. Instead we collect various information artifacts about the sources to assist in finding relationships and correspondences among data in different sources. We also store information on how to access the data (including location identifier, access method, access rights, username, etc.) and how to transform the data to the canonical form if needed through conversion functions (on measurement units, formats, etc.), as explained in the following section.

The semantic network contains relationships between sources. Users request data sources by searching the metadata repository and our system will automatically use the semantic network to return not only the requested ones but also to recommend additional and related data sources that users might not know about. Once the users decide on the final selection of the sources they may download data directly to their local machines. Data being downloaded can be converted to canonical form for possible analysis. This is achieved by a set of conversion functions that are part of the integration component. Data that are integrated are stored in the data warehouse. The data warehouse is a multidimensional model of commonly used source data, which also stores wavelet coefficients. Once users have obtained

Figure 1. System architecture with data integration and knowledge discovery components

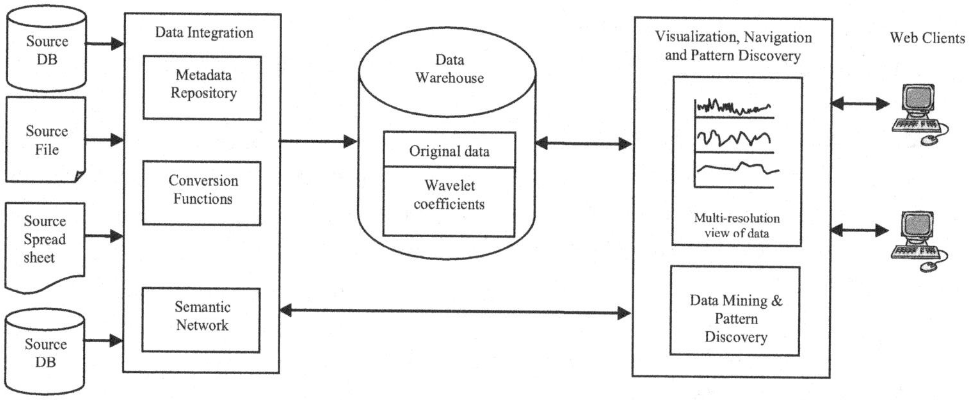

data, they can visualize, navigate, and discover patterns at different dimensions and resolutions to aid knowledge discovery.

Data Integration

In this section, we address issues related to (1) data sources and relationships that form among them, (2) semantic networks, for recommendation of additional and relevant data sources visualized as hyperbolic trees, and (3) automatic expansion and augmentation of the semantic network by observing user patterns.

Describing Data Sources and their Relationships

The plethora of diverse data in environmental research poses significant integration problems. Some data sources may be structured or semi-structured databases with varying data models (relational, object-oriented, object-relational, etc.); some may be available as spreadsheets, while others may be flat files. Data may also contain spatial information in raster or vector formats.

We take a metadata approach, in which we store information about the data, which is collected and stored in the metadata layer with details from both scientific and storage perspectives. For example, many ecosystem study projects collect data related to climate (e.g., precipitation depth, wind speed, wind velocity, air temperature, humidity), soils (e.g., temperature, water content, trace gases), and streams (e.g., depth, flow rate, temperature, nutrients, pathogens, toxics, biota). For each such category, we store its definition, measurement unit, collection frequency, and measurement location, to create an accurate description of what is being collected, how it is measured, where it is stored, and how it is accessed. Usually, this type of information is available from the data sources themselves. It is part of a routine process to specify specific metadata information when users submit data at the data sources. Additional information may also be stored from external sources (e.g., the Open Research System (ORS)). In general, information about data sources is not significantly large, especially when compared with the amount of actual data at the sources; metadata information can be collected from the sources either automatically (through an application programming interface (API) if available) or manually. All such information is kept in the metadata repository and it serves the purpose of a universal registry; similar but not identical to universal description, discovery and integration

(UDDI) for Web services. The metadata repository, stored in an object-relational database, is augmented with information on additional data sources as needed.

This work expands on the specification of relationships among database objects stored in heterogeneous database systems (Georgakopoulos, Karabatis, & Gantimahapatruni, 1997; Karabatis, Rusinkiewicz, & Sheth, 1999; Rusinkiewicz, Sheth, & Karabatis, 1991; Sheth & Karabatis, 1993). We have created a methodology allowing researchers to derive semantic relationships among data sources based on source descriptions in the metadata layer. These semantic relationships form a semantic network of related information, which assists users to discover additional information, relevant to their search but possibly unknown to them. We realize that some relationships may not be captured initially in the metadata repository, especially when semantic incompatibilities prevent direct identification of data (such as problems related to synonyms, homonyms, etc.). Nevertheless, missing relationships are captured and added to the metadata repository by observing researchers' usage patterns when they interact with the semantic network, as will be explained further in the current section. The notion of relationships between concepts is also related to the topic maps or concept maps (TopicMap), and Semantic Web (W3C) for XML and web documents containing metadata about concepts. However, our work does not limit itself only to XML or web data, but can be used to describe data in general.

Converting Data to a Canonical Form

Environmental data sources may have differences in formats, data units, spatial and temporal granularities, and may be collected at different time intervals. We have implemented methods and/or applications to convert between different units and formats. In addition, spatial and temporal disparities are resolved using spatial and temporal join/aggregation operations and integrating data at the appropriate level. As an example, suppose that we need to integrate stream chemical and biological data collected at each site with land use and land cover data. In our data warehouse model, each site belongs to a stream reach, and each stream reach belongs to a sub-watershed (the land area that drains to a particular point along a stream segment and is represented by a polygon feature). Land use/land cover data is also collected on areas represented by polygons (although these polygons are different and smaller than polygons for sub-watersheds). Thus, we aggregate stream data to sub-watershed level, and then aggregate land use/land cover data to areas represented by the same set of polygons for sub-watersheds using re-projection, spatial joins, or overlay functions provided by ArcObjects, the API included in the ESRI's ArcGIS software suite (www.esri.com/software/arcgis).

Using Semantic Networks to Expand User Queries

In this section, we provide details on the creation and utilization of semantic networks. We formally define semantic networks and we present techniques to extract information from semantic networks and recommend additional and relevant data sources to users in their search of related data sources. We also present an algorithm to automatically refine, and dynamically augment semantic networks; Semantic networks have long been used to represent relationships (Masterman, 1961). We take advantage of their structure to elicit additional semantic information for environmental data.

Definition 1: We formally define a semantic network G(V,E,W) as a graph G where:

- *V* is the set of nodes in the network. Each node represents a data source or data set. For convenience, we use data source and data set interchangeably in this article.

Figure 2. An example semantic network

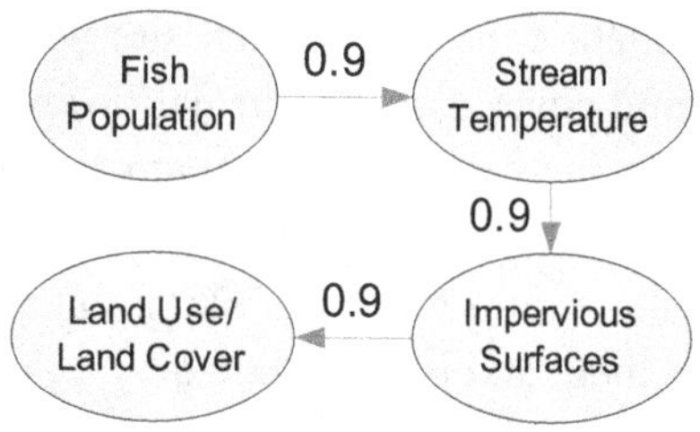

- E is the set of directed edges in the network. An edge (v_i, v_j) indicates that node v_i is semantically related to node v_j.
- W is a $|V| * |V|$ relevance score matrix, where $W(i,j)$ is a number in range of [0,1] and represents the degree of relevance (or relevance score) between nodes v_j and v_i.

Figure 2 depicts an example semantic network related to fish population. The number on each edge represents the relevance score associated with the two adjacent nodes. Based on these scores, we can infer the relevance between any two nodes in the network. We consider each relevance score as a conditional probability and assume they are independent of each other (Rice, 1994). For example, the relevance score between fish population and stream temperature can be considered as the conditional probability of a researcher interested in stream temperature given that he or she is interested in fish population.

Using the standard notation for conditional probability, we have:

P(surfaces | fish) = P(surfaces, stream temperature | fish) because the user will be interested in impervious surfaces, assuming the user is also interested in stream temperature.

Using chain rules and assuming all conditional probabilities are independent (Rice, 1994), we have:

*P(surfaces, temperature | fish) = P(temperature | fish) * P(surfaces | temperature) = 0.9 * 0.9 = 0.81.*

In general, if v_i and v_j are two nodes, there are k paths $p_1, \ldots, p_k$ between v_i and v_j, where path p_l $(1 <= l <=k)$ consists of nodes $v_{l1}, \ldots, v_{l|pl|+1}$ ($|p_l|$ is the length of path p_l).

The relevance score rs between v_i and v_j is

$$rs = \max_{\forall pl}\left(\prod_{1 \le i \le |pl|} w(l_i, l_{i+1})\right) \qquad (1)$$

The above formula computes the relevance score between v_i and v_j as the sum of relevance scores for all paths connecting v_i and v_j. For each such path, the relevance score between the two endpoints is computed as the product of relevance scores for all edges along the path. There can be more detailed types of semantic relationships (cause-effect, is-a, and is-part-of), or to use more advanced inference rules without the independent assumption on the conditional probabilities, but these extensions are beyond the scope of this article.

Construction of Semantic Network

We assume that domain experts have provided an initial semantic network, i.e., a set of edges and nodes with their relevance scores. Based on this initial semantic network, we compute the relevance scores between any pair of nodes in the network, and create the matrix W.

Let us consider the example in Figure 2. Suppose matrix R stores the relevance scores of all edges in the initial semantic network. The first, second, third, and fourth row (column) in the matrix corresponds to edges from (to) fish, temperature, surface data, and land data. R_{ij} stores the relevance score from node i to node j.

$$R = \begin{pmatrix} 0 & 0.9 & 0 & 0 \\ 0 & 0 & 0.9 & 0 \\ 0 & 0 & 0 & 0.9 \\ 0 & 0 & 0 & 0 \end{pmatrix}$$

Based on formula (1), the relevance score between any pair of nodes equals the sum of relevance scores of all paths between them. Using matrix multiplication rules, and for any given pair (i, j) with $i \neq j$, we calculate the sum of relevance scores of all paths between i and j with length k. It is equal to R^k_{ij} where R^k is the multiplication of k matrices R. For example, the relevance scores of all paths with length 2 is:

$$R^2 = R * R = \begin{pmatrix} 0 & 0 & 0.81 & 0 \\ 0 & 0 & 0 & 0.81 \\ 0 & 0 & 0 & 0 \\ 0 & 0 & 0 & 0 \end{pmatrix}$$

There are two non-zero entries: $R^2_{13} = 0.81$, identifying the relevance score between fish data to surface data, and $R^2_{24} = 0.81$ identifying the score between temperature and land data. Hence, the relevance score rs between any pair of nodes in the network can be computed using the following formula:

$$rs = \sum_{1 \le i \le N} R^i \qquad (2)$$

Using Semantic Networks to Elicit Additional Semantics

A user in search of ecosystem data sources may perform a keyword search or submit a regular SQL query to our system, which in turn will find data sources that directly satisfy the user's conditions. We call these data sources exact answers. In addition to the exact answers, we describe a novel approach to enhance and augment the result set with additional sources, semantically relevant to the exact answers, which the user might not be aware of. We achieve this goal by exploiting the semantic network, and returning all data sources whose relevance score with the exact answers is higher than a threshold. For simplicity, we have set the threshold in our system to 0.5 but a user can adjust it according to how closely additional data sources should be related to the exact answers.

For example, suppose a user wants to find all data sources related to 'fish population.' The exact answer contains only the fish population data set because only that data set contains the keyword 'fish population.' However, using the semantic network in Figure 2, our system will return all other three data sources in the figure because they are also related to the fish population according to the semantic network. Therefore, we can automatically recommend to the users additional semantic information (data sources) relevant to the exact answers.

Visualizing Semantic Networks

Most existing systems for ecological research (EML) return data sources as a list, and it is difficult for users to go through them when the list is long. Our system utilizes a hyperbolic tree technique (Lamping, Rao, & Pirolli, 1995) to visualize data sources and the semantic relationships they form. Figure 3 shows an example of such a tree. The main benefit of this technique is to show users the entire set of exact answers and additional related data sources at a glance, as a visualization of all relevant nodes and edges forming a semantic network. In addition, users can dynamically adjust the display size of a data source of their choice and automatically bring it to the foreground concentrating on a specific data source and all its edges connecting it to the relevant sources.

Dealing with Different User Preferences

We also consider the issue that different domain experts may not have the same interests; instead they may need to utilize different semantic networks (if available) pertaining to their own specialties. For example, a stream chemist may not be interested in land use/land cover, contrary to an urban developer who would certainly focus on it. We address this problem by creating different user profiles, each corresponding to a separate

Figure 3. Visualiing a semantic network as a hyperbolic tree

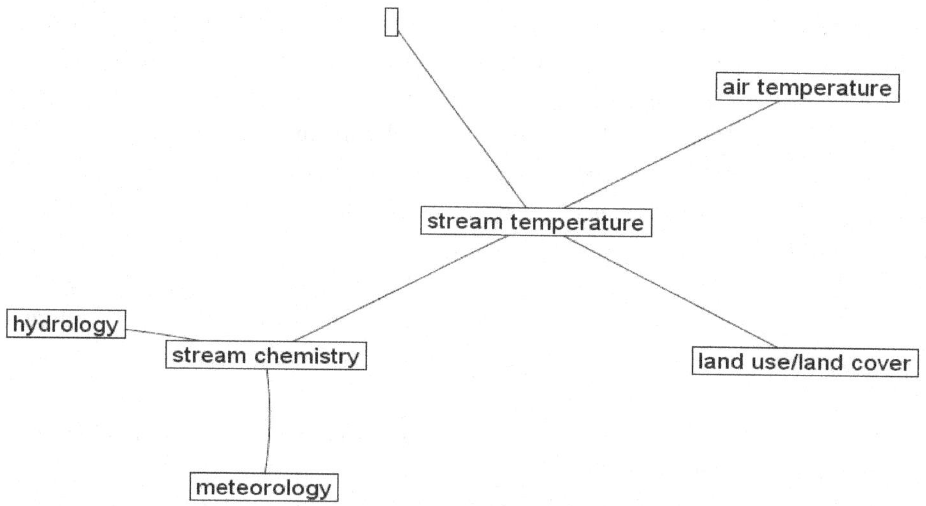

semantic network with its own bias towards a certain specialty. Initially, domain experts will define a set of profiles. A new user will select a profile before using our system, and can change this selection at any time. For each profile, we also track the usage patterns by users and collect information that is used to dynamically refine and augment the network based on these patterns. Therefore, although an initial profile may not completely satisfy every user, it will adapt to user preferences after some period of time.

Refining and Augmenting the Semantic Network

The key idea to automatically refine, evolve, and augment the semantic network is to monitor usage patterns. Once the initial semantic network (or a given profile) has been created by a domain expert, users can query the metadata repository for data sources. The system provides exact answers and recommends additional data sources (displayed visually as in Figure 3). Then, the users select (click on) those data sources potentially relevant to their research. They submit their queries to the data sources, while the metadata repository keeps copies of queries to identify query patterns. Based on the usage of these patterns by users, we can infer additional relationships that form between data sources. These relationships are used to automatically expand, enhance and refine the semantic network.

As an example, suppose two users have asked for data sources related to 'fish population.' *User1* selects all four data sources in Figure 2, while *User2* selects only fish, temperature, and land data. Let F, T, S, L represent fish, temperature, surfaces, and land, respectively. We assume that users agree to incorporate every edge connecting two sources that they selected in the network, but disagree with all other edges of sources they did not select. For example, *User1* agrees with the edges F-T, T- S, and S-L. However, *User2* agrees with the edge F-T, but not the other two. The issue is how *User2* selects the land data, which is only related to fish via surface data in the current network, and *User2* does not select surface. We assume the user agrees with relationship between fish and land, where fish is an exact answer and land is a selected source that is not covered by any existing edges that the user agrees with. Thus, we propose the Algorithm 1 to automatically augment and refine the network.

Algorithm 1. Automatic refinement of semantic network

Input: current network N, a set of usage patterns {Q1, ..., Qm}, where each Qi consists of a set of exact answers and a set of related answers selected by users.

Output: a refined network N'

1. *Create N' as exact copy of N*
2. *For each user query Qi,*
   a. *Identify all edges in the current network N that link two selected sources and add them to a multi-set S1.*
   b. *For any source selected by users but is not covered by an edge in N, generate an edge from the exact answer to that source and add it to a multi-set S2.*
3. *For each edge AB in existing network N*
   There are three possible cases:
   a. *AB appears in S1. The new relevance score r(AB) equals*
      *r(AB) * d + Occ(AB) / Occ(A) * (1-d)*
      where d is an aging factor ranging from 0 to 1, Occ(AB) is the number of times edge AB appears in S1, and Occ(A) is the number of times node A is selected in usage patterns.
   b. *AB does not appear in S1, and A is never selected. The score of AB remains unchanged.*
   c. *AB does not appear in S1, but A is selected. The new score equals r(AB) * d*
4. *For each edge AB in S2, add it to the new network N' with relevance score Occ(AB)/ Occ(A), where Occ(AB) is the number of times edge AB appears in S2, and Occ(A) is the number of times node A is selected in usage patterns.*

This algorithm first creates a copy of the current network at step 1. At step 2a) it identifies the edges that users agree on based on usage patterns. At step 2b), the algorithm identifies new edges not in the current network, but necessary for users to select those sources connected by these edges. For instance, in the above example, if the usage patterns consists of Q_1 = *{F, T, S, L}*, and Q_2 = *{F, T, L}*. At step 2a), the algorithm will add to S_1 edges F-T, T-S, S-L for Q_1, and F-T for Q_2. Thus, S_1 = {F-T, T-S, S-L, F-T}. At step 2b), the algorithm will add to S_2 edge F-L. Thus, S_2 = *{F-L}*. At step 3, the algorithm re-computes the relevance scores for the existing edges. The new score consists of two components, the first component is the current score, and the second component is the score based on usage patterns. These two components are combined using a weight *d,* which is also called an *aging factor* because it determines how quickly the new score converges to the usage patterns. We set the aging factor d = 0.5 in this article. In the above example, the new scores are:

*R(fish-temperature) = 0.9 * 0.5 + 1 * 0.5 = 0.95*

*R(temperature-surfaces) = 0.9 * 0.5 + 0.5 * 0.5 = 0.7*

*R(surfaces-land) = 0.9 * 0.5 + 0.5 * 0.5 = 0.7*

*R(fish-land) = 0.5 * 0.5 = 0.25.*

Data Navigation: A Visual Approach

Visualization of data can be proven to be a significant decision support tool. It can provide deep insights into data that are very difficult to capture by automatic means. Since environmental data often have different spatial and temporal granularities, environmental researchers are interested in viewing data at multiple resolutions. For example, a spike in stream flow, precipitation, and nitrogen content will tell a scientist that there is an influx of nitrogen in the stream due to a precipitation event. However, a steady increase or decrease in stream flow, precipitation, and nitrogen content for several years will indicate a possible change in the longer term. Furthermore, the recent development of wireless sensors and sensor networks has allowed for the collection of environmental data at high temporal resolution. In consequence, researchers often need to visualize this data for long time scales, that is, at lower resolutions.

Therefore, we present an effective multi-resolution visualization method using wavelets to help researchers discover patterns, trends, and surprises. The main benefit of using wavelets compared to using fixed levels of resolutions is that wavelets allow finer and more flexible levels of resolutions. For example, fixed levels allow users to view stream temperature at minutes, hours, and days, while wavelets allow users to view the temperature at one minute, two minute, or four minute spans, and so on.

In this article, we apply wavelet transformations—we used Haar wavelets (Goswami & Chan, 1999), and we are currently experimenting with other wavelet transforms—for numerical attributes. If the data contains spatial or temporal attributes (e.g., indicating the location or time the measurements were collected), we always sort the data records in the spatial or temporal order and apply wavelet transformations to the sequence of the measurement attributes in this order. Otherwise, we view the measurement attributes as a sequence in the order that records are stored in the database, and apply wavelet transformations. Of course, in the latter case, the different levels of resolutions do not have spatial or temporal meanings, and only provide a lower-resolution view of the data.

The generated wavelet coefficients are then stored in an Object-Relational database (Oracle 10g). We have developed an algorithm (see Goswami & Chan, 1999) to reconstruct not only the complete set of the original data but also a certain subset of it, at appropriate levels of resolutions. The utility of reconstructing a subset of the original dataset stems from the fact that a decision maker may want to find out only that part of the original dataset that was used to generate a particular coefficient.

We developed a visualization tool to help environmental scientists visually inspect temporal and spatial datasets for noticeable trends and relationships. Figure 4 depicts a prototype interface developed in Visual Basic which allows users to spatially locate and select data collection sites and visualize time-series data for the selected sites. The top pane connects to the ESRI's ArcSDE® Geodatabase system where the user can navigate spatially using zooming and panning tools. The bottom pane connects to a DBMS which stores raw data along with wavelet-transformed data at various levels of temporal resolution. The left side of the interface allows the user to (1) select the site or sites of interest spatially or from a list, (2) select the time period of the visualization, (3) select the dataset (4) select the type of visualization, and (5) interactively control the temporal resolution of the visualization. The user can select a site, or sites, either spatially by using the GIS interface, or by selecting specific sites based on the site name. Once a site is chosen, the user can select the time period of the visualization by providing the date and time. Then the user can select whether he or she may want to visualize the data using a line graph, bar graph, or scatter plot. The visualization is then displayed in the bottom pane of the interface. The slider below

Figure 4. Visual navigation of data

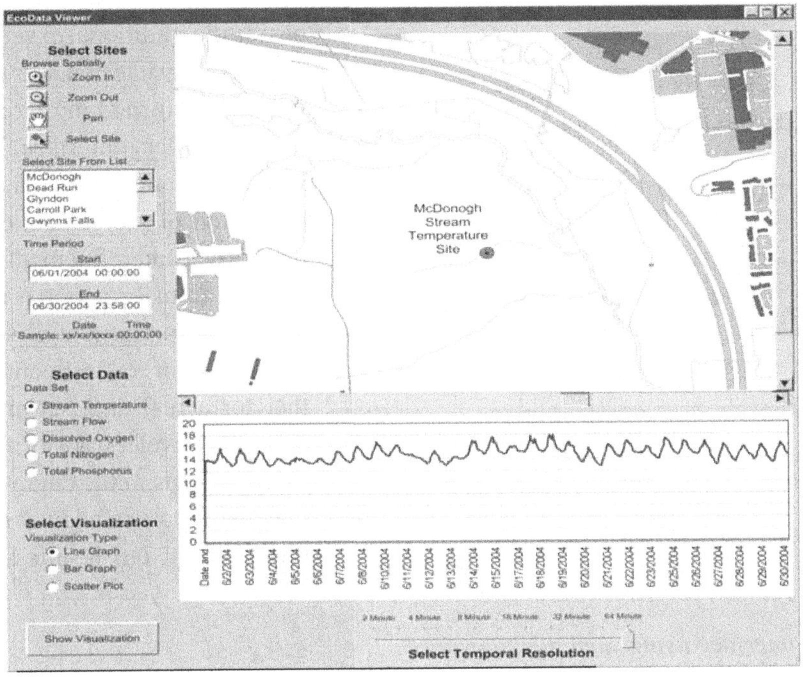

the displayed data allows the user to control the temporal resolution of the visualization. The slider goes from the resolution of the raw data on the left to the level *n* wavelet transformation on the right. The scale on the slider can change, based on a combination of the time period of the raw dataset and the level of wavelet transformations available. Data at the selected resolution will be reconstructed from the stored wavelet coefficients and shown to users. Figure 4 shows the McDonogh stream temperature site along with time series data at the 64 minute resolution for the month of June, 2004.

Pattern Discovery through Multi-Resolution Data Mining

Multi-resolution data mining is similar in concept to online analytical mining (OLAM) (Han, 1998; Han, Chee, & Chiang, 1998). Conceptually, it allows a user to mine the data at different levels of the dimension hierarchy. We propose to augment the dimensional hierarchies with wavelet coefficients at different levels of decomposition and provide mining capabilities including association rule mining, classification, and clustering. This approach provides the benefits of OLAM, but in addition, it enables users to select the appropriate levels of resolution that would be ideally suited for mining the data. If the data is noisy, wavelet decomposition could reduce noise in the data and would result in a better classifier. We illustrate the efficacy of using wavelet decomposition in classification and its resilience on noise in the following section.

IMPLEMENTATION AND EXPERIMENTAL RESULTS

We have conducted preliminary experiments to validate our approaches of using semantic networks to help environmental researchers find related data sources and using wavelets to identify

Figure 5. Database schema for the semantic network

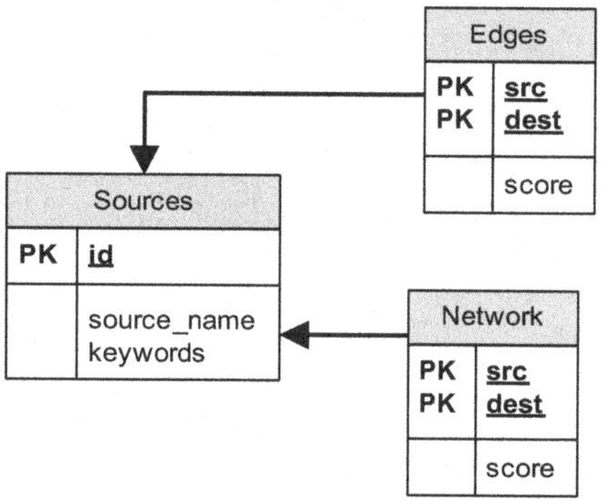

patterns in different data resolutions. Our major findings are:

- Users of our system concluded that our query expansion and visualization interface surpasses the traditional exact query interface. In all cases we tested, our query expansion interface returned more data sources than the exact query interface. They also found value in the automatic adaptation and augmentation of the semantic network based on profiles and refinement techniques.
- Wavelet transformation is a promising tool to discover patterns at different resolutions of data. Our experiments demonstrated that for a real data set and a benchmark data set, wavelet transformation preserved most patterns in the data while it was used to convert data to a lower resolution. More interestingly, our results also showed that

Figure 6. Query interface using semantic networks

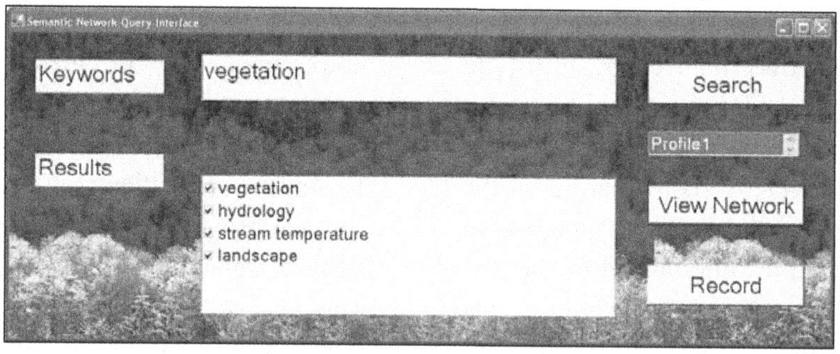

Figure 7. Visualization of results of Figure 6

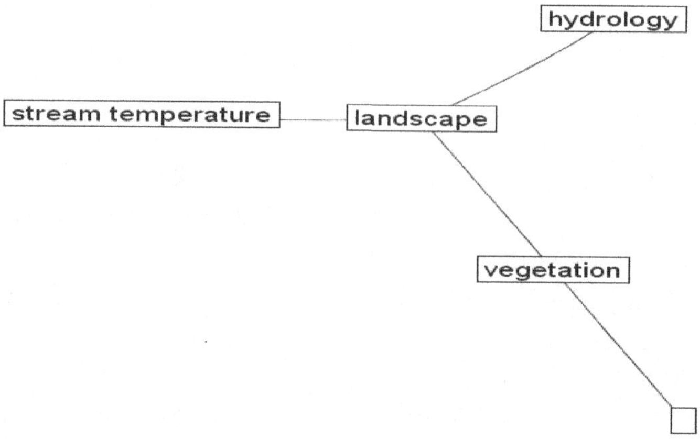

Table 1. Data sources used in semantic network experiments

Data Source Name	Description	Location
Vegetation	Riparian vegetation of the Gwynns Falls Watershed in Baltimore area	http://www.ecostudies.org/pub/besveg/riparian.zip
Hydrology	Streamflow data collected along the Gwynns Falls in Baltimore area	http://waterdata.usgs.gov/md/nwis/nwisman?site_no=01589352
Stream Temperature	Stream temperature of the Gwynns Falls Watershed	As an Excel file on local file server
Meteorology	Baltimore meteorological station data	http://www.ecostudies.org/pub/bes_206.zip
Stream Chemistry	Stream chemistry data of the Gwynns Falls Watershed	As a text file on local file server
Landscape	Satellite image data of Baltimore area landscape (forests, grass, crops, etc.)	As a text file on local file server

wavelet transformation is very robust to noise in data and in some cases even improved the quality of discovered patterns.

We first describe the implementation details, and then proceed to experimental results.

Implementation

We used Oracle 10g to store metadata of data sources and semantic networks using the database schema in Figure 5. We use three relational tables (sources, edges, network) to store information about data sources, keywords, and relevance scores. The Edges table stores the edges and their relevance scores in the semantic network. The Network table stores the relevance scores between any pair of nodes in the semantic network, which is computed from the Edge table. We implemented the algorithms described in the previous section as PL/SQL stored procedures for the construction, query expansion, and dynamic augmentation of the semantic network.

We implemented a semantic network query interface (written in Visual Basic) for researchers to search data sources with semantic terms related to their research; this interface is based on the semantic network and metadata repository and is shown in Figure 6. The user first needs to select a profile then provide keywords and finally submit the search to database. Our query expansion procedure will augment the query and return all sources related to the given keywords in the results window. The user can then visualize the relationships (as edges) between returned sources by clicking the 'view network' button. Figure 7 shows the hyperbolic visualization of the results obtained in Figure 6. We use a publicly available Hyperbolic Tree Java Library (http://sourceforge.net/projects/hypertree/) to display hyperbolic trees. Users can also record their selections by first checking the sources of interest and then clicking 'record.' Recorded selections are used as usage patterns to dynamically augment the network as described in the previous section. We have also implemented a Haar wavelet transformation as a stored procedure in an Oracle server and inserted the results into a table, which will be later used for pattern discovery.

Experiments with Semantic Networks

Setup: We evaluated our semantic network approach using data sets collected by the Baltimore Ecosystem Study (http://www.beslter.org/). Table 1 summarizes the details of these data sets.

Table 2. Adapted from A Primer on Landsat 7 (http://imaging,geocomm,com/features/sensor/landsat7)

Spectral Bandwidth Ranges for Landsat 7 ETM+ Sensor (μ)		
Band Number	**Wavelength Range**	**Recommended Application**
Band 1	0.45 - 0.52 (blue-green)	soil and vegetation discrimination and forest type mapping
Band 2	0.53 - 0.61 (green)	vegetation discrimination, plant vigor
Band 3	0.63 - 0.69 (red)	detection of roads, bare soil, and vegetation type
Band 4	0.78 - 0.90 (near-infrared)	biomass estimation, separation of water from vegetation, soil moisture discrimination
Band 5	1.55 - 1.75 (mid-infrared)	discrimination of roads, bare soils, and water
Band 6	10.4 - 12.5 (thermal infrared)	measuring plant heat stress and thermal mapping
Band 7	2.09 - 2.35 (mid-infrared)	discrimination of mineral and rock types, interpreting vegetation cover and soil moisture
Band 8	.52 - .90 (panchromatic)	for enhanced resolution and increased detection ability

We asked an environmental researcher to define the edges in the initial semantic network between these data sets. The researcher created three different semantic networks corresponding to three different profiles of users interested in vegetation, stream temperature, and stream chemistry respectively. Figure 8 shows the networks where *Pi* identifies the score in the ith profile. In this experiment, the researcher considered the relationships bidirectional.

We ran two experiments to test our search interface and the semantic network refinement algorithm. In the first experiment, we asked another researcher to use our search interface to find related data sources and asked him to give us feedback on the appropriateness of the results. Due to limited resources, we asked that researcher to take on alternate roles of three different types of users and then we selected one of the three profiles. The researcher posted three example queries as follows:

- **Query 1:** What data sets are related to riparian vegetation? The researcher selected profile 1 and searched the data sources with keyword 'vegetation.'
- **Query 2:** What factors contribute to the fluctuations in stream temperature? The researcher selected profile 2 and used 'stream temperature' as the keyword.
- **Query 3:** What factors may affect the stream chemistry? The researcher selected profile 3 and used 'stream chemistry' as the keyword.

In the second experiment, we asked the researcher to select a set of data sources in the results of Query 4 that he thought was most related to the question he asked. We then ran our algorithm to refine the semantic network based on his selection and compared the results for Query 4 with the results using the original network. Our search interface returned the following results:

- **Query 1:** Vegetation, hydrology, stream temperature, and landscape.
- **Query 2:** Stream temperature, meteorology, and landscape.

- **Query 3:** Hydrology, meteorology, stream chemistry, and landscape.

In all cases, the exact search interface only returned one data source with the search keyword, while our search interface returned multiple sources (4 for Query 1 and 3, and 3 for Query 2). We also asked the researcher to look at the results returned by our interface, and he found the answers returned by our search interface actually related to these research questions.

In the second experiment, the user selected only the first three data sources for Query 3. When the researcher ran Query 3 on the refined network, the 'landscape' data source is no longer in the search results due to the refinement. This reflected the user selection.

In summary, our experiments verified that our system exploits data source relationships that are maintained in semantic networks and supplies users with additional data sources that are relevant to their original search, but they might not be aware of.

Experiments for Knowledge Discovery using Wavelet Transformations

We conducted several experiments to test our hypothesis that wavelet transformation results in preserving patterns in data. In the first experiment, we used remote sensing data from the Landsat 7 ETM+ sensor. Data from the Landsat 7 ETM+ sensor is typically used by environmental scientists to characterize the landscape in terms of land cover. The Landsat 7 ETM+ sensor captures wavelength values for 8 spectral bands based on the reflectance of the earth's surface. Table 2 shows the range of wavelengths captured in each band and its recommended application.

We downloaded a Landsat 7 ETM+ scene from October 5, 2001, covering central Maryland (path 15/row 33), from the Global Land Cover Facility (http://glcf.umiacs.umd.edu/data/). We extracted spectral information from the Landsat image and a subset was evaluated for a 1.2 km^2 area in northern Baltimore County, Maryland. We then

Figure 9. Performance comparison

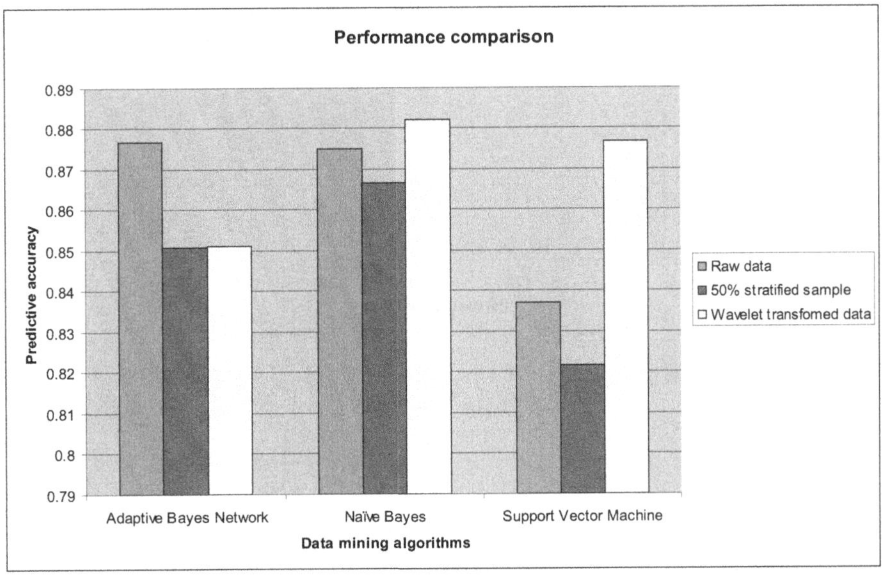

Figure 10. Performance comparison on noisy data

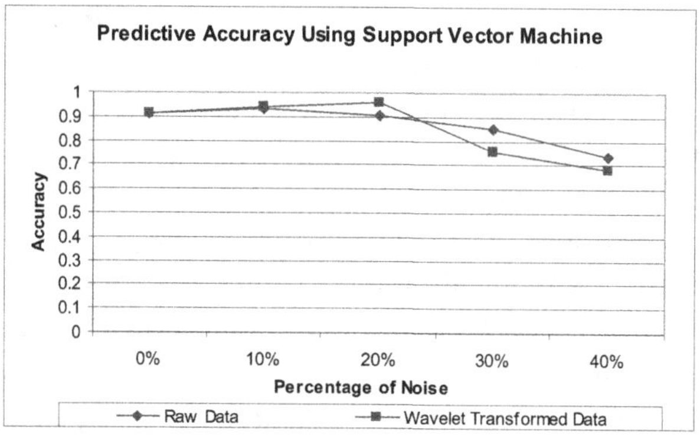

(a)

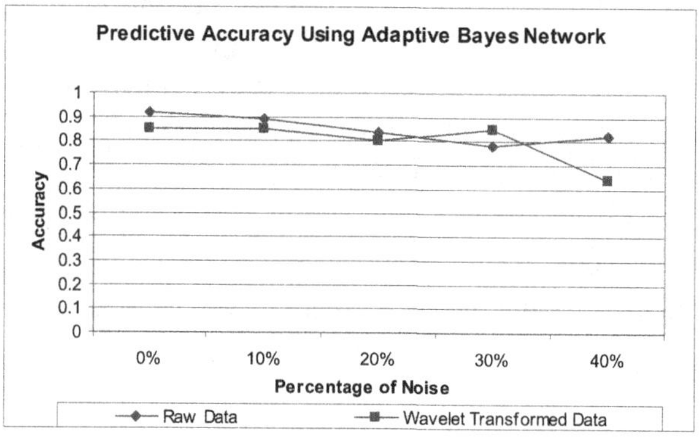

(b)

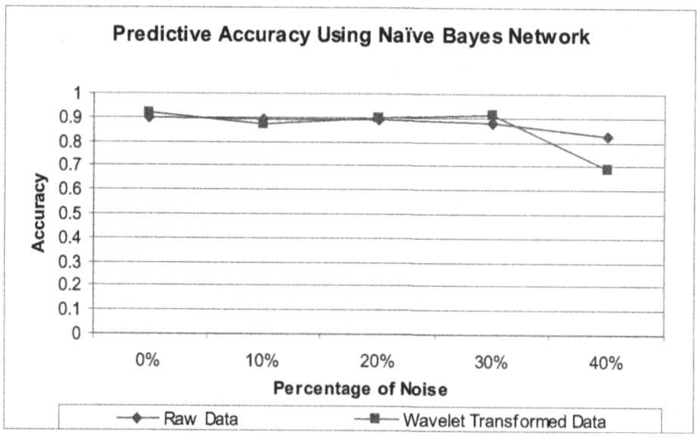

(c)

manually classified land cover values of crop, grass, forest, or water based on high resolution aerial photography.The resulting dataset consisted of eight attributes representing the spectral bands and one class attribute representing the four distinct land cover values. The spectral bands were used to identify whether the land cover is 'grass,' 'forest,' 'water,' or 'crops'.This yielded 1193 instances that were divided into two groups. Group 1 had 616 instances that were used for training and group 2 had 577 instances that were used for testing. We performed the following steps. We (1) divided the data into two disjoint sets — a test set and a training set; (2) performed first level of Haar wavelet transformation on the raw data; (3) created a 50% stratified sample of the training set of the raw data; (4) created three classifiers based on raw data, 50% stratified sample, and wavelet transformed data; and (5) compared the predictive accuracy on test data for the three classifiers. Two sets of three different classifiers were built using an adaptive Bayes network, a naïve Bayes method, and support vector machines (with linear kernel function) for the raw data and approximate coefficients from a Haar wavelet transformation of the raw data. We used Oracle 10g as the database and Oracle Data Miner for the mining functions. The reason for testing with a stratified sample is that the Haar wavelet transform reduces the data size by half. Hence the size of the training set for raw data is twice as large as that of the wavelet transformed data. As shown in Figure 9, in two out of three methods (naïve Bayes and support vector machine), the use of a Haar wavelet transform resulted in a better classifier than both (1) the raw data with twice the size of the training set and (2) a 50% stratified sample that had the same size of the training set. For the adaptive Bayes network, a wavelet transform resulted in 2% loss of predictive accuracy as compared with the raw data, but had a slightly higher predictive accuracy when tested with a training set of the same size.

In addition, we decided to test the sensitivity of classifier accuracy on a noisy dataset. For these experiments, we used the Iris plant dataset from the UCI machine learning repository (http://www.ics.uci.edu/~mlearn/MLSummary.html). The dataset contained 150 instances with four attributes and three class labels. The attributes represent sepal length, sepal height, petal length, and petal width and the class variable refers to one of three types of iris plant. Again, the same environment was used to test the predictive accuracy of three classifiers: an adaptive Bayes network, a naïve Bayes method, and support vector machine. In each case, we introduced random noise following standard normal distribution to 10%-40% of the instances. As shown in Figures 10a-c, use of the Haar wavelet transform resulted in a classifier with a comparable predictive accuracy to the raw data. It is evident that the raw data outperforms the wavelet transformed data with 40% noise with the disparity in performance being more pronounced in the adaptive Bayes and naïve Bayes methods. This indicates a threshold in the noise-to-signal ratio below which the benefit of wavelet transformation is lost. Wavelets can be applied to any numerical attributes assuming that the data is sorted in the order that they are stored in the database. This approach has also been used by many existing studies (Matias et al., 1998; Smith et al., 2004; Vitter & Wang, 1999; Vitter et al., 1998). The only difference is that the levels of resolutions do not have temporal or spatial meanings. While more research is needed to establish the efficacy of wavelet transformation, these preliminary experiments do indicate that wavelet transformation holds promise as a robust tool for pattern discovery at multiple levels of data and as a method for data reduction in very large datasets with little degradation in predictive accuracy.

CONCLUSION

In this article, we have described a methodology for data integration and pattern discovery for environmental research using data semantics. We used semantics to integrate multiple data sources to answer user queries for environmental research. Our methodology to describe the data sources is based on a metadata approach and takes advantage of data interrelationships represented as a semantic network. User queries are automatically expanded using a relevance score matrix and a semantic network, which can be visualized as a hyperbolic tree. We have utilized user profiles to capture diverse user preferences to precisely answer user queries, and have presented an algorithm to automatically expand, augment and refine the semantic network by observing usage patterns. We have demonstrated that our semantic integration techniques offer a powerful, straightforward and user-friendly approach for the visualization of significant amounts of environmental data sources.

In addition to enabling search for data in the integrated system described above, we also allow users to navigate through multi-dimensional data through visualization, implemented using wavelet transformation. We have used Haar wavelets that decompose data by averaging and differencing consecutive, non-overlapping pairs of data at each level of decomposition. Thus, users can visualize multiple levels of data and roll-up or drill down at different levels of hierarchy. They can also apply data mining techniques such as classification at different levels of resolution. We have illustrated that patterns in the data are well preserved at first level decomposition with 50% reduction in data size. We have also demonstrated the resilience of wavelet transformation to noisy data.

The research presented in this article is being enhanced by further development of the described methodologies and further experimentation with pattern discovery at multiple levels of resolution. We plan to incorporate data mining and machine learning techniques to aid in the enhancement and refinement of the semantic network. The methodology presented in this article can also be applied to other application areas where search, visualization, and pattern discovery of data from multiple sources are needed.

ACKNOWLEDGMENT

This material is based upon work partly supported by the National Science Foundation under Grant Nos. DEB-0423476 and BES-0414206 and by U.S. Environmental Protection Agency under grants R-82818201-0 and CR83105801. Although the research described in this article has been funded in part by the U.S. Environmental Protection Agency, it has not been subjected to the agency's required peer and policy review and therefore does not necessarily reflect the views of the agency and no official endorsement should be inferred.

REFERENCES

Aleman-Meza, B., Halaschek-Wiener, C., Arpinar, I. B., Ramakrishnan, C., & Sheth, A. P. (2005). Ranking complex relationships on the Semantic Web. *IEEE Internet Computing*, 37-44.

Batini, C., Lenzerini, M., & Navathe, S. (1986). A comparative analysis of methodologies for database schema integration. *ACM Computing Surveys, 18*(4), 323-364.

Bowers, S., Lin, K., & Ludascher, B. (2004). *On integrating scientific resources through semantic registration.* Paper presented at the Scientific and Statistical Database Management.

Bowers, S., & Ludascher, B. (2004). *An ontology-driven framework for data transformation in scientific workflows.* Paper presented at the International Workshop on Data Integration in the Life Sciences.

Chang, K. C.-C., He, B., & Zhang, Z. (2005). *Toward large scale integration: Building a MetaQuerier over databases on the Web.* Paper presented at the CIDR.

Chui, C. K., & Lian, J. (1996). A study of orthonormal multiwavelets. *Applied Numerical Mathematics: Transactions of IMACS, 20*(3), 273-298.

Daubechies, I. (1992). *Ten lectures on wavelets.* Capital City Press.

Dispensa, J. M., & Brulle, R. J. (2003). The Sprawling Frontier: Politics of Watershed Management. *Submitted to Rural Sociology.*

Doan, A., Domingos, P., & Halevy, A. Y. (2003). Learning to match the schemas of data sources: A multistrategy approach. *Machine Learning, 50*(3), 279-301.

EML. *Ecological Metadata Language.* http://knb.ecoinformatics.org/software/eml/

Fankhauser, P., Kracker, M., & Neuhold, E. J. (1991). Semantic vs. structural resemblance of classes. *SIGMOD Record, 20*(4), 59-63.

Friedman, M., Levy, A., & Millstein, T. (1999). *Navigational plans for data integration.* Paper presented at the AAAI/IAAI.

Georgakopoulos, D., Karabatis, G., & Gantimahapatruni, S. (1997). Specification and management of interdependent data in operational systems and data warehouses. *Distributed and Parallel Databases, An International Journal, 5*(2), 121-166.

Goswami, J. C., & Chan, A. K. (1999). *Fundamentals of wavelets: Theory, algorithms and applications*: John Wiley.

Halevy, A. Y., Ives, Z. G., Suciu, D., & Tatarinov, I. (2003). *Schema mediation in peer data management systems.* Paper presented at the ICDE.

Han, J. (1998). *Towards on-line analytical mining in large databases.* Paper presented at the ACM SIGMOD.

Han, J., Chee, S., & Chiang, J. (1998). *Issues for on-line analytical mining of data warehouses.* Paper presented at the Proceedings of 1998 SIGMOD'96 Workshop on Research Issues on Data Mining and Knowledge Discovery DMKD, Seattle, Washington.

Han, J., & Kamber, M. (2000). *Data Mining: Concepts and Techniques*: Morgan Kaufmann.

Hyperion. The Hyperion Project. http://www.cs.toronto.edu/db/hyperion/

Jain, H., & Zhao, H. (2004). *Federating heterogeneous information systems using Web services and ontologies.* Paper presented at the Tenth Americas Conference on Information Systems, New York.

Kalfoglou, Y., & Schorlemmer, M. (2003). Ontology mapping: The state of the art. *Knowledge Engineering Review, 18*(1), 1-31.

Karabatis, G., Rusinkiewicz, M., & Sheth, A. (1999). Interdependent database systems. In *Management of Heterogeneous and Autonomous Database Systems* (pp. 217-252). San Francisco, CA: Morgan-Kaufmann.

Kimball, R. (2002). *The data warehouse toolkit* (2nd ed.).

Kumar, N., Gangopadhyay, A., & Karabatis, G. (in press). Supporting mobile decision making with association rules and multi-layered caching. *Decision Support Systems.*

Lamping, J., Rao, R., & Pirolli, P. (1995). *A Focus+Context Technique Based on Hyperbolic Geometry for Visualizing Large Hierarchies.* Paper presented at the Proceedings ACM Conference Human Factors in Computing Systems.

Levy, A. Y., Rajaraman, A., & Ordille, J. J. (1996). *Querying heterogeneous information sources using source descriptions.* Paper presented at the VLDB.

Mallat, S. G. (1989). A theory for multiresolution signal decomposition: The wavelet representation. *IEEE Transactions on Pattern Analysis and Machine Intelligence, 11*, 674-693.

Masterman, M. (1961). Semantic message detection for machine translation, using an interlingua. *NPL*, pp. 438-475.

Matias, Y., Vitter, J. S., & Wang, M. (1998). *Wavelet-based histograms for selectivity estimation.* Paper presented at the ACM SIGMOD.

Miller, R. J., Hernandez, M. A., Haas, L. M., Yan, L., Ho, C. T. H., Fagin, R., et al. (2001). The clio project: managing heterogeneity. *SIGMOD Record, 30*(1).

Mitchell, T. M. (1997). *Machine learning*: Mc-Graw-Hill.

ORS. *Open Research System.* http://www.orspublic.org

Ouksel, A., & Sheth, A. P. (1999). Special issue on semantic interoperability in global information systems. *SIGMOD Record, 28*(1).

Papakonstantinou, Y., Garcia-Molina, H., & Ullman, J. (1996). *Medmaker: A mediation system based on declarative specifications.* Paper presented at the ICDE.

Percival, D. B., & Walden, A. T. (2000). *Wavelet methods for time series analysis.* Cambridge University Press.

Rahm, E., & Bernstein, P. A. (2001). A survey of approaches to automatic schema matching. *VLDB Journal, 10*(4).

Ram, S., Khatri, V., Zhang, L., & Zeng, D. (2001). *GeoCosm: A semantics-based approach for information integration of geospatial data.* Paper presented at the Proceedings of the Workshop on Data Semantics in Web Information Systems (DASWIS2001), Yokohama, Japan.

Ram, S., & Park, J. (2004). Semantic conflict resolution ontology (SCROL): An ontology for detecting and resolving data and schema-level semantic conflicts. *IEEE Transactions on Knowledge and Data Engineering, 16*(2), 189-202.

Ram, S., Park, J., & Hwang, Y. (2002). *CREAM: A mediator based environment for modeling and accessing distributed information on the Web.* Paper presented at the British National Conference on Databases (BNCOD).

Rice, J. A. (1994). *Mathematical statistics and data analysis.* Duxbury Press.

Rodriguez-Gianolli, P., Garzetti, M., Jiang, L., Kementsietsidis, A., Kiringa, I., Masud, M., Miller, R., & Mylopoulos, J. (2005). Data Sharing in the Hyperion Peer Database System. In *Proceedings of the International Conference on Very Large Databases (VLDB).*

Rusinkiewicz, M., Sheth, A., & Karabatis, G. (1991). Specifying interdatabase dependencies in a multidatabase environment. *IEEE Computer, 24*(12), 46-53.

Sarawagi, S., Agrawal, R., & Megiddo, N. (1998). *Discovery-driven exploration of OLAP data cubes.* Paper presented at the International Conference on Extending Database Technology.

SEEK. *The Science Environment for Ecological Knowledge.* http://seek.ecoinformatics.org

Sheth, A., Aleman-Meza, B., Arpinar, I. B., Bertram, C., Warke, Y., Ramakrishanan, C., et al. (2004). Semantic association identification and knowledge discovery for national security applications. *Journal of Database Management, 16*(1).

Sheth, A., Arpinar, I. B., & Kashyap, V. (2003). Relationships at the heart of Semantic Web: Modeling, discovering, and exploiting complex semantic relationships. In M. Nikravesh, B. Azvin, R. Yager & L. A. Zadeh (Eds.), *Enhancing the power of the Internet studies in fuzziness and soft computing.* Springer-Verlag.

Sheth, A., Bertram, C., Avant, D., Hammond, B., Kochut, K., & Warke, Y. (2002). Managing semantic content for the web. *IEEE Internet Computing, 6*(4), 80-87.

Sheth, A., & Karabatis, G. (1993, May). *Multidatabase Interdependencies in Industry.* Paper presented at the ACM SIGMOD, Washington DC.

Smith, J. R., Li, C.-S., & Jhingran, A. (2004). A wavelet framework for adapting data cube views for OLAP. *IEEE Transactions on Knowledge and Data Engineering, 16*(5), 552-565.

Stollnitz, E. J., Derose, T. D., & Salesin, D. H. (1996). *Wavelets for Computer Graphics Theory and Applications*: Morgan Kaufmann Publishers.

Tatarinov, I., & Halevy, A. Y. (2004). *Efficient Query Reformulation in Peer-Data Management Systems.* Paper presented at the SIGMOD.

TopicMap. *XML Topic Maps (XTM) 1.0* http://www.topicmaps.org/xtm/

UDDI. *Universal description, discovery and integration.* http://www.uddi.org

Vitter, J. S., & Wang, M. (1999). *Approximate computation of multidimensional aggregates of sparse data using wavelets.* Paper presented at the ACM SIGMOD.

Vitter, J. S., Wang, M., & Iyer, B. (1998). *Data Cube Approximation and Histograms via Wavelets.* Paper presented at the 7th CIKM.

W3C. Semantic Web. http://www.w3.org/2001/sw/

Zhao, H., & Ram, S. (2002). *Applying classification techniques in semantic integration of heterogeneous data sources.* Paper presented at the Eighth Americas Conference on Information Systems, Dallas, TX.

Zhao, H., & Ram, S. (2004). Clustering schema elements for semantic integration of heterogeneous data sources. *Journal of Database Management, 15*(4), 88-106.

This work was previously published in Journal of Database Management, Vol. 18, Issue 1, edited by K. Siau, pp. 43-68, copyright 2007 by IGI Publishing, formerly known as Idea Group Publishing (an imprint of IGI Global).

Section II
Systems Building

Chapter IV
Towards Code Reuse and Refactoring as a Practice within Extreme Programming

Vijayan Sugumaran
Oakland University, USA

Gerald DeHondt
Grand Valley State University, USA

ABSTRACT

Software reuse has been discussed in the literature for the past three decades and is widely seen as one of the major areas for improving productivity. Agile development techniques were first developed in the mid-1990s as a code-oriented method of software development that seeks to improve upon the traditional plan-based methodologies. Both approaches bring value to the software development process. The purpose of this chapter is to propose a framework that will integrate the strengths of code reuse into the Extreme Programming methodology. It is believed that this approach will lead to a more effective method of software development.

INTRODUCTION

Agile software development first began in the mid-1990s as an alternative to the traditional Systems Development Life Cycle or plan-based methodologies widely implemented at the time. These lifecycle methodologies take a phased approach to systems development, requiring that one phase be completed prior to beginning the next phase (Hoffer et al. 1998). Agile methods, on the other hand, focus on iterative software development, the continuous implementation of working code. From the beginning of the agile "revolution", specific methodologies have continued to refine these techniques, the most popular being Extreme Programming (XP). This approach was first implemented at Chrysler in 1996 (C3 Team 1998) as a way to accelerate development efforts while producing better software. XP is an implementation of Agile development techniques based upon twelve practices, one of which is refactoring. Specifically, refactoring involves modifying software to improve its internal structure in a way that does not alter the external behavior of the code (Fowler 1999).

At its core, Extreme Programming emphasizes rapid and frequent feedback to the customers and end users, unit testing, and continuous code reviews. By focusing on rapid iterations of simpler code, XP seeks to identify and resolve potential pitfalls in the development process early, leading to projects that remain focused on the ultimate goal – timely delivery of a well-designed and tested system that meets customer requirements. This methodology works by bringing the whole team together in the presence of simple practices, with enough feedback to enable the team to see where they are and tune the practices to their unique situation. It also seeks to implement the simplest design that will satisfy current user requirements (Lindstrom and Jeffries 2004) without attempting to anticipate future design or user requirements.

Nerur and Balijepally (2007) state that agile methods are people-centric, recognizing the value that competent people and their relationships bring to software development. In addition, it focuses on providing high customer satisfaction through three principles: quick delivery of quality software; active participation of concerned stakeholders; and creating and leveraging change (Highsmith 2002). Big upfront designs/plans and extensive documentation are of little value to practitioners of agile methods. Important features of this approach include evolutionary delivery through short iterative cycles — of planning, action, and reflection — intense collaboration, self-organizing teams, and a high degree of developer discretion (Nerur and Balijepally 2007). Organizations undertaking agile methodologies must invest in tools that support and facilitate rapid iterative development and versioning/configuration management (Nerur, Mahapatra, and Mangalaraj 2005). One way to achieve this is through investment in a suitable reuse strategy supporting agile development.

Reuse of existing software components has been an area of investigation since the early 1980's and is widely seen as one of the major areas for improving software productivity. By reusing previously tested and implemented code, it is hoped that developers will become more efficient by not having to solve the same problem twice. One of the key challenges with effectively implementing a program of software reuse is the identification of suitable components. If the identification process consumes more resources than saved in development time, these programs will not be undertaken by developers.

Additional challenges encountered in this approach include a lack of incentives, lack of available resources, suitable component identification, and necessary tools for customization and validation, among other items. In spite of this, appropriate component reuse can integrate previously implemented software into current development projects serving to propagate validated code within the application infrastructure (Ravichandran 2005).

Once the appropriate component has been detected, it is then up to the developers to refactor the software into a more suitable solution to the problem at hand. Both techniques, code reuse and refactoring, focus on efficiency in the systems development process. This research proposes an integrative framework that combines code reuse - for component identification - and refactoring - for improved software performance and maintainability - into an overriding process that will improve the efficiency and effectiveness of software development. This framework is also compatible with Extreme Programming, as it improves the refactoring practice or could be used as a method of integrating code reuse as an additional practice within XP.

The remainder of this chapter is organized as follows. The following section provides a brief review of the related literature, namely, software reuse, refactoring and the need for an integrative approach. The subsequent section describes the proposed framework and a potential application in the automotive industry. The advantages and limitations of the proposed approach are discussed in the fourth section, and finally the last section provides the conclusion and future work.

LITERATURE REVIEW

Software Reuse

It is widely believed that there is a direct relationship between software reuse and software productivity. Researchers are constantly exploring new methods and concepts to improve reuse - a problem that has been solved to a greater degree of success in the computer hardware field. Several models and frameworks have been proposed and discussed in Biggerstaff and Perlis (1989); however, the problem of reuse has not yet been solved satisfactorily. Understanding the application domain is a fundamental step towards reuse and is a key factor in the success of reusability. Higher level domain artifacts are more conducive to reuse because they capture the essential objects and functions that characterize the domain.

Software reuse has been an active area of research for nearly three decades. Reuse involves utilizing previously developed software artifacts or knowledge to create new software in new applications. Software reusability is widely seen as one of the major areas for improving software productivity (Sherif and Vinze 1999). A number of reusable artifacts have been developed such as class libraries, components (Szyperski 1998), frameworks, and patterns (Fowler 1997). Research has also been undertaken that attempts to realize the benefits of reuse for object-oriented conceptual design through the creation of tools to facilitate design and construction of new systems with reuse (Sugumaran et al. 2000). Higher-level design fragments and models are being developed (Nord and Tomayko 2006). Clayton et al. (1997) suggest that it would be useful to have a set of previously solved design problems, in the form of domain models that could serve as templates for future designs.

Systematic software reuse provides a promising means to reduce development cycle time, development cost, and improve software quality. Particularly, if reuse is materialized in the early stages of systems development by reusing requirement specifications, designs, and other higher level artifacts, the project team has a tremendous opportunity to drastically cut the overall development time and effort. However, many factors conspire to make systematic software reuse a non-trivial task. For example, contextual and behavioral issues such as management support and software developer's interest are seen to be more important than technical issues in determining the success or failure of a software reuse program (Kim and Stohr 1998).

In order to improve reuse, domain knowledge is essential. Domain modeling captures business domain knowledge at a higher level of abstraction (objectives, processes, actions, etc.), so the artifacts defined at this level can be used to define process requirements (Meekel et al. 1997). Prieto-Diaz (1991) presents a domain model that identifies various domain elements and their relationships, a domain taxonomy, a domain frame (architecture), and a domain language along with standards, templates, interface definitions and a thesaurus. Other research focuses on specific domain level artifacts and associated information for reuse, including processes (specifications, sequence and structure), data (attributes, relationships and structure), and entities (events, agents, and objects) (Chan et al. 1998).

Recently, component based development (CBD) is taking root in systems development. Numerous advantages of CBD are touted. An information system developed from reusable components is argued to be more reliable (Vitharana and Jain 2000), is believed to increase developer productivity (Lim 1994), reduce skills requirement (Kiely 1998), shorten the development life cycle (Due 2000), reduce time-to-market (Lim 1994), increase the quality of the developed system (Sprott 2000), and cut down the development cost (Due 2000). CBD also provides strategic benefits, such as the opportunity to enter new markets, or the flexibility to respond to competitive forces and changing market conditions (Lee 2006). Component providers have the opportunity to enter new markets because of the potential to cross sell components with associated functionalities.

Component based software development is changing the way applications are being developed and delivered to the end user. It is causing a shift in software development paradigms, particularly with the development of several component architecture standards such as CORBA, COM, and EJB (Szyperski 1998). A component is a well-defined unit of software that has a published interface and can be used in conjunction with other components to form larger units (Hopkins 2000). For example, in an auction application domain, one component captures the characteristics of a bid and its associated processes. Another component deals with transaction processing. These can be combined to form a larger component that would be a reusable artifact.

Previous work on CBD has led to the development of repositories for a number of different areas (Sugumaran et al. 2000; Mili et al. 1998). The storage and retrieval of artifacts from reusable repositories is still a challenge, especially when the repositories have many hundreds of components. Several factors impact the search and retrieval process including the scope of the repository, query representation, asset representation, storage structure, navigation scheme, relevance and matching criteria (Mili et al. 1998). Most retrieval methods focus on one or two of these factors to suit the specific domain they are working in. Furthermore, current repositories are limited in that they usually have one representation for each component. When a user searches for a component to satisfy his or her requirements, the user is required to be very specific about what he or she is looking for because some of the repositories do not contain information on how its components are related. Searching for appropriate artifacts does not usually take these relationships, or dependencies, into account and, therefore, limits the usability and consistency of the components returned to the user. Retrieved components are most useful if they respond directly to the user's needs. Although repositories provide artifacts that one could consider at a meta-data level, to be most useful, they need to be augmented with domain specific knowledge because this will provide a means to be able to go beyond a restricted query to identify additional, relevant components for the user. An overall schema of the component reuse process model is shown in Figure 1. As discussed above, the major activities within this process model include domain modeling, meta-data and repository management, conceptual component identification, and component searching and retrieval.

Refactoring

One of the most costly areas to maintain in today's corporations is the Information Technology function. A significant portion of this function is the development and maintenance of information systems, with the primary cost factor being the maintenance effort. As software continues along its lifecycle during the maintenance phase, it is modified, enhanced and adapted to new requirements. As this occurs, its complexity increases

Figure 1. Component reuse process model

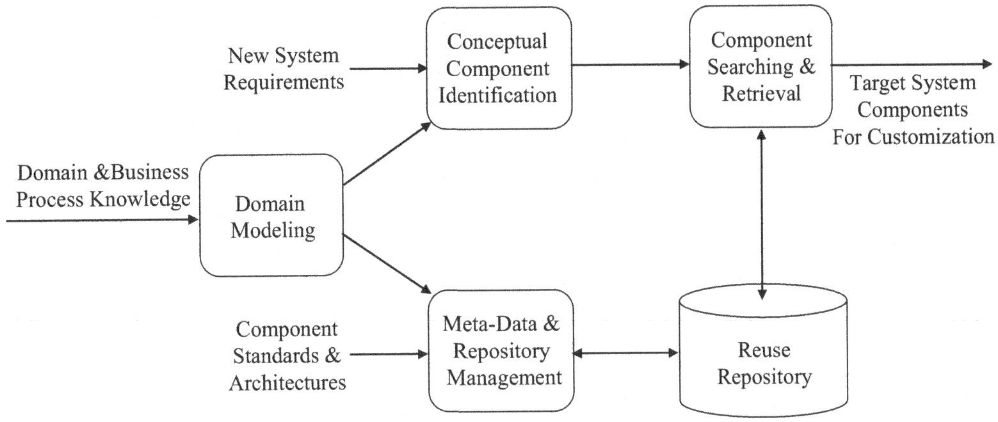

and it continues to drift further from its original design (Coleman 1994; Guimaraes 1983; Lientz and Swanson 1980). With this in mind, software development efforts and techniques continue to focus on the efficiency and simplicity of code design.

Refactoring, a term first introduced by Opdyke (1992) in his PhD dissertation, has been suggested as a method to help cope with the evolving complexity of these systems. This technique, articulated by Fowler (1999) as "the process of changing a [object-oriented] software system in such a way that it does not alter the external behavior of the code, yet improves its internal structure", seeks to restructure the code to improve the quality of the software (e.g., extensibility, modularity, reusability, complexity, maintainability, efficiency) (Mens and Tourwe 2004).

Viewed at its lowest level, refactoring is comprised of the following six activities, as articulated by Mens and Tourwe (2004):

1. Identify where the software should be refactored.
2. Determine which refactoring(s) should be applied to the identified places.
3. Guarantee that the applied refactoring preserves behavior.
4. Apply the refactoring.
5. Assess the effect of the refactoring on quality characteristics of the software (e.g., complexity, understandability, maintainability) or the process (e.g., productivity, cost, effort).
6. Maintain the consistency between the refactored program code and other software artifacts (such as documentation, design documents, requirements specifications, tests, etc.).

Typically, major refactoring efforts are only undertaken once the software has become nearly impossible to maintain (Mens and Tourwe 2004). However, this technique has received significant support from the Extreme Programming community, even going so far as to embed refactoring as one of it twelve principles (Beck 2000). This proactive use of refactoring helps enhance the quality of the delivered software and integrates well with the Test Driven Development (TDD) principle of XP. TDD uses its focus to help keep the code more understandable and maintainable (Nerur et al. 2005). Nerur et al. (2005) also state that TDD facilitates the continuous integration of new code and/or changes without adversely affecting the existing code base. Integrating refactoring into the development approach provides the development team with pre-existing test cases with which to benchmark their efforts.

At its core, XP is fundamentally the continuous delivery of incremental working software that is customer-driven and dependent on communication, incremental design, acceptance of changing requirements, and continuous testing (DeHondt and Brandyberry 2007). The customer-driven focus of refactoring helps integrate it into the XP methodology. Agile methods also emphasize delivering value to the customer early in the development process. This leads to the focus on highly valued features early on in the development cycle (Ramesh et al. 2006). Refactoring of reusable components can lead to shorter development cycles, as reusing components that support valuable features eliminates the effort of developing the component from scratch.

Based on our analysis of the refactoring literature, in particular, the work of Mens and Tourwe (2004), we have developed an overall refactoring process model, which is shown in Figure 2. The driver for this model is the need for quickly generating components by refactoring modules or code segments from prior projects or repositories which might be scattered across the organization. Thus, the main activities within this process model include identifying the sources to refactor, determining which refactoring method to apply, guaranteeing the behavior of resulting components, applying the refactoring method and assessing the refactored components, and storing the components in a reuse repository in a consistent manner for future use.

Overview of XP and the Need for Integration

Extreme Programming (XP) is an Agile development technique that emphasizes frequent feedback to the customers and end users, unit testing, and continuous code reviews. By focusing on rapid iterations of simpler code, XP seeks to identify and resolve potential pitfalls in the development process early, leading to projects that remain

Figure 2. Refactoring process model

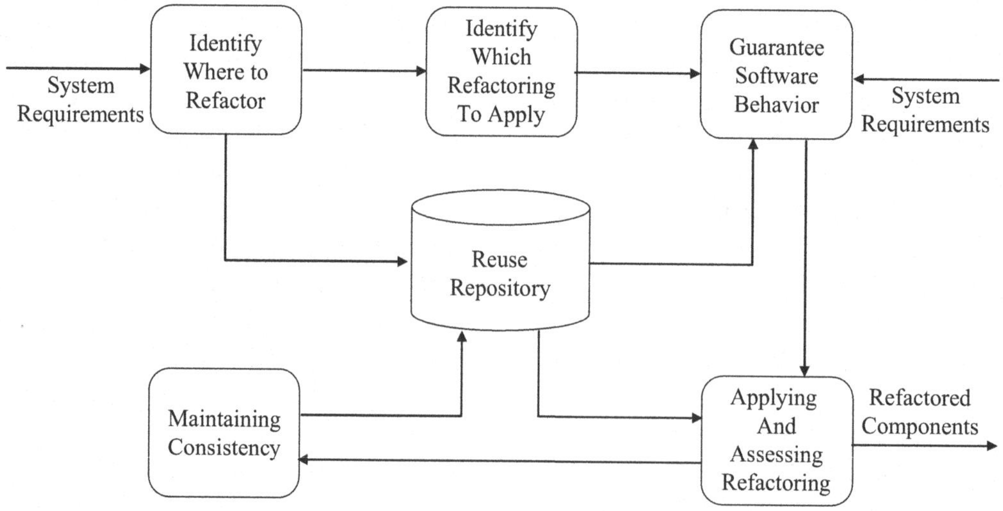

focused on the ultimate goal - timely delivery of a well-designed and tested system that meets customer requirements. It has also been described in terms of the values that support it: communication, feedback, simplicity, courage, and respect (Beck and Andres 2004).

XP utilizes an iterative approach that is helpful in developing, modifying, and maintaining systems more quickly and more successfully (Basili and Turner 1975; Boehm 1988). It is these short iterations that provide the flexibility to accommodate the changes requested by the customers and allows the customer to increase competitiveness in the market (Turk et al. 2005). This iterative approach also allows it to be tolerant of changes in requirements (Beck and Andres 2004).

Inherent practices also include continuous code integration and refactoring to improve the design and code (Nerur and Balijepally 2007). These two ideas form the basis of the integrative framework being proposed. One of the primary drivers of XP is the focus on delivering the features the customer wants. Previously implemented components represent customer requirements that have been sufficiently met. Refactoring and reuse of these components helps continue demonstrated understanding of customer requirements and places developers closer to a completed system. Not only is this explicit communication, but also delivering working code incrementally at frequent intervals. Ultimately, this is the best check to demonstrate understanding of customer requirements.

Integrating code reuse with refactoring increases the efficiency and effectiveness of the systems developers allowing them to continue to meet the needs of the business customer. The following section discusses our proposed framework, which does precisely that. Specifically, it combines the reuse process model and the refactoring process model discussed earlier to create the overall integrated model.

PROPOSED FRAMEWORK

While considerable research has been carried out independently in software reuse and agile software development, there has not been much synergy between these two areas. Since the underlying philosophy and goals of each of these fields of research are somewhat similar, namely, developing high quality software in a short duration of time, i.e., minimizing time to market, it is natural that there is cross pollination between these two streams of research. Results from each stream have the potential to significantly impact the other. Thus, in the context of Extreme Programming, developing an integrated approach for code reuse in terms of effectively identifying potential components to reuse and efficiently customizing them to meet the new requirements is crucial.

Domain and business knowledge is critical for systems design and implementation. The encapsulation of business knowledge has several benefits, even if a firm does not move from the analysis to the design phase. First, in today's process reengineering and redesign environments, accessing process knowledge from a repository, especially if it includes best practices, can be valuable for benchmarking and continuous improvement. Second, a firm can capture knowledge about its own business objectives, processes, etc. as part of a repository and continue to revise it, thus providing a source for training new employees. Lastly, if domain knowledge is captured independently of design considerations, design-induced, or representational bias (Buchanan et al. 1983) during requirement analysis will be reduced.

Our proposed integrated process model for reuse and refactoring is shown in Figure 3. It consists of the following steps: a) identifying initial components, b) knowledge-based component search & retrieval, c) identifying what to refactor & guaranteeing behavior, d) refactoring & customizing components, and e) consistency checking & repository management. Each of these steps is briefly described in the following sections.

Figure 3. Integrated framework for code reuse and refactoring in XP

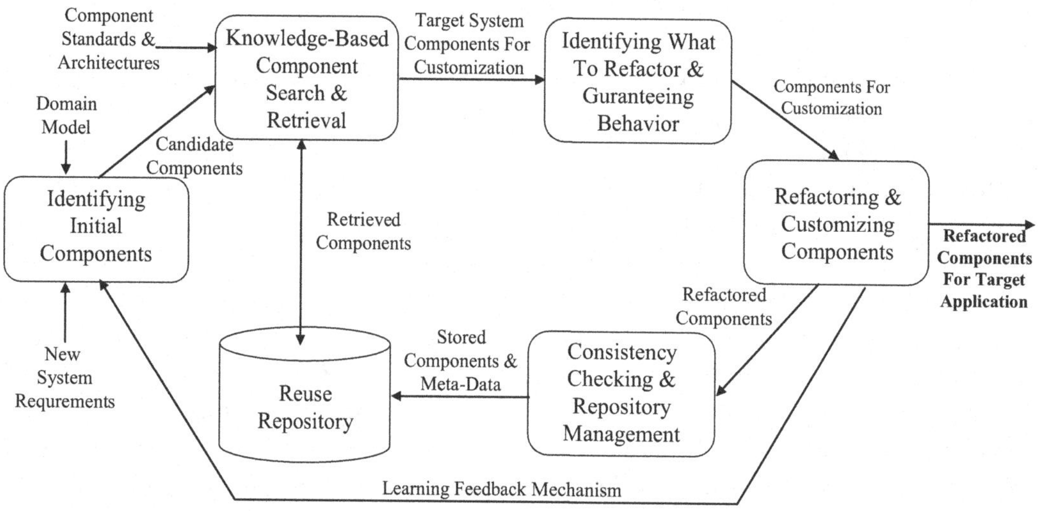

Identifying Initial Components

This step involves identifying "conceptual" objects that might be needed in order to support the functionalities specified for a new system. In domain modeling, the typical functionalities that are supported by a system in a particular application domain are modeled as features and appropriate "conceptual" component architectures are developed that specify the appropriate methods and properties for these components. Based on the requirements for the new system, one could begin to identify the types of components that are needed for the target system. Thus, in conjunction with a domain model, the developer can map out the types of components that are required for the target system. The domain model contains kernel objects that must be part of all systems in a particular domain as well as variations of objects that are specific to a particular feature or functionality. This approach is advantageous because the developer does not have to design classes from scratch, particularly, for those classes that already exist. The output of this step is the list of potential candidate classes or components that should be part of the target system to support the desired functionalities.

Knowledge-Based Component Search & Retrieval

This step focuses on retrieving the relevant components from the component repository, based on domain knowledge, component standards and architecture knowledge, and the requirements for the new system. The objective of this step is to move from the conceptual set of components identified in the previous step to a specific set of concrete components that implement the procedures/methods that support the functionalities desired in the target system. To search for components that are the most relevant, the operations of a component are compared to the desired functionalities expressed in the user's requirements. To assess how useful a component would be, we use the closeness measure proposed by Girardi et al. (1995). The closeness measure is the similarity value between requirement "q" and a software component "c", which is computed by comparing the frame structure associated with the representation of the requirement and of the software component operations. The output of this step is the set of components that may be relevant to the system requirements.

Identifying What to Refactor & Guaranteeing Behavior

The storage and retrieval of artifacts from reusable repositories is a challenge, especially when the repositories are disparate and contain hundreds of components. Hence, the components retrieved in the previous step may not all be directly usable in the new system. Some components may fully satisfy a requirement, however, they may not have been designed efficiently. Specifically, the components retrieved may only partially support the requirements. In this step, we focus on identifying which parts of the component are directly relevant and which parts need to be eliminated. Also, the parts that are useful, may not be highly structured or efficient. They may also contain duplicate code. Thus, these components are flagged as potential candidates for refactoring. In addition, to make these components more effective, their cohesiveness is also examined. If the components are not highly cohesive, they are also potential targets for refactoring. Another important aspect that needs to be enforced during refactoring is the fact that the behavior of the components should not be changed. This step also ensures that the pre-conditions, post-conditions, invariants and temporal constraints are preserved. In other words, the potential refactoring that would be applied to the component should preserve the semantics of the component.

Refactoring & Customizing Components

This step focuses on refactoring and customizing the components identified in the previous step by examining the sections of the components that have been flagged for potential changes. Several refactoring techniques exist that use invariants and constraints, graph transformation, program slicing, formal concept analysis, program refinement, software visualization, and dynamic program analysis etc. (Mens and Tourwe 2004). One or more of these techniques can be applied to perform refactoring and generate components that are efficient and meet the requirements for the target system. Some components that satisfy a particular requirement may also contain additional code that may not be necessary for the system under consideration. Such components have to be trimmed down to reduce the overhead of the system. Similarly, components that partially support a requirement may have to be extended or customized to meet the actual requirement. This could involve adding new properties or customizing an existing property. For example, methods within a component may be modified or new methods can be added to extend its functionality. The important point to note is that components may be refactored and customized to fully meet the criteria specified for this implementation, or refactored to more efficiently implement functionality for this scenario. In the former case, the functionality of the component will be efficiently brought in line with current needs. In the latter instance, developers may seek to improve the code while maintaining current functionality.

Traditionally, refactoring and customization are seen as cognitively intense activities. Thus, including them as part of the reuse process model might appear to increase the burden on the developers and prevent them from reusing and refactoring. However, we contend that the available business knowledge and the organizational learning and communication that take place within the organization would alleviate this problem to a large extent. In other words, having a formal learning mechanism and developers actively sharing their experiences and providing feedback would facilitate effective refactoring and reuse. This is an important aspect of the proposed framework. There is a feedback mechanism between this step and the initial step of component identification. As the refactoring step gets executed over a period of time, one can detect similarities and patterns in what and how components get customized and this knowledge could be used in the initial component identification. This learning component will help in better component design and identification. For example, methods unique to the higher level objects (which may not have been identified in the analysis phase) can be presented to the developer for review and possible inclusion.

Consistency Checking & Repository Management

The output of the previous step is a set of refactored and customized components that can be included in the target system. These components satisfy the requirements for the new system to a large extent. However, there may be a need for designing new components from scratch in order to satisfy the requirements that have not been previously encountered. All the components created at the end of the previous step can be stored in the repository for future use. However, we need to explicitly capture and represent the relationships between these components so that they can be better utilized in the future. Thus, consistency checking and repository management is an essential aspect of this approach. When a user searches for a component to satisfy his or her requirements, the searching process should take into account the relationships, or dependencies that exist between components. Or else, it will limit the usability and consistency of the components returned to the user. The retrieved components are most useful for the user if they directly meet the requirements and are consistent with each other. Storing the new components in the repository raises some issues. Version control of the components is critical. If a particular component is extended or customized, then its functionality changes to some extent. Should this component be treated as the next version or a different component? Similarly, when a component gets refactored, how do we manage the version control problem?

POTENTIAL APPLICATION

The proposed approach can be used in a number of application domains where there is considerable pressure to develop new components based on existing components in a relatively short period of time. Many organizations have evolved software development methodologies over a period of time that is specific to their environment and domain. Recently, the software product line (SPL) approach has received a lot of attention. SPL focuses on developing new software components from existing core assets (Sugumaran et al. 2006). For example, organizations such as Nokia, Phillips, Avaya, and GM have reported success in applying the SPL approach to their embedded control software development. One of the major issues faced in SPL is the identification of the most relevant existing components and then refactoring and customizing them to meet the new requirements. Our approach can be very useful in this context. Following is a description of a potential application of our approach in the automotive industry.

Over the years, software has become an integral part of automobiles. Modern cars often embody more than 50 electronic control units with several thousand lines of code running on them. More than 80 percent of automotive innovations are driven by electronics, and amongst them, 90 percent are supported by means of software. One of the key components within an automobile is the powertrain control system, which controls the engine and transmission. The engine control software coordinates fuel, spark and other subsystems to provide greater fuel economy. The transmission control software monitors engine and car speed as well as the loads on throttle, brake pedal, and engine to change gear ratios for an easier and smoother driving experience. The control system architecture comprises different parts related to base hardware, sensors and actuators, and other electronic devices. The controller software provides the interface between all these devices as well as the algorithms to control and coordinate the timing between them. There are a large number of these components (hardware and software) that have been developed over the years, which are stored in a huge reuse repository. For example, GM Powertrain maintains an extensive repository of design and code artifacts that it uses in designing new control systems.

As new engine types and different transmission requirements get introduced, they require appropriate embedded controls. Whenever a new feature is introduced into an automobile, software engineers have to design appropriate control software to support this feature. This is accomplished by extending existing software components as opposed to developing the component from scratch. In this context, the developer is faced with the task of selecting the most appropriate component from an enormous repository to support the specific requirement. Then, this component is customized and extended by adding additional algorithms or modifying the existing algorithm to meet the timing requirements, etc. The entire control system is tested using simulation. Once the controller meets the statement of requirements, it is then deployed to production control. In this scenario, our approach will be of great help to the software engineer in identifying appropriate components and refactoring them to meet new requirements. The new components developed are then stored in the repository for future use.

DISCUSSION

Improved Software Quality

One anticipated advantage of the proposed framework is the continuous improvement, or organizational learning that is a by-product of this approach to software development. Current refactoring efforts seek to improve the code developed for *the current project.* Code reuse seeks to match software that met user requirements *from previous projects* with similar user requirements from *the current project.* In this way, it is hoped that development efforts are more efficient in not having to re-develop an existing code base. The refactored components also become a part of the organization's reuse repository for potential future use. In line with traditional refactored components, these refactored components would be of higher quality, easier to understand, and improve maintainability. It is through this iterative process of continuous improvement that the organization is able to improve the quality of their components. This iterative process will also help improve the organization's efforts of "learning to learn" (Morgan 1998) and fits well with the emerging agile philosophy that values an organization's ability to nurture learning (Nerur and Balijepally 2007).

It is also theorized that this iterative refactoring of reusable components will continue to improve the quality of the components in the reuse repository. Providing an improving reuse repository to developers will also lead to improved software development efforts by the firm. The iterative nature of this approach allows the organization to continuously implement higher quality code in a more efficient manner. Refactoring of the components with each new project will allow the software to evolve and improve over time.

By integrating refactoring into the code reuse process, the organization is able to iteratively improve their software repository, and future development projects.

Accelerated Development Cycles

As an agile methodology, Extreme Programming seeks to improve communication with the user community and provide working code at more frequent intervals. It is believed that integrating software reuse into this Agile framework will save developers from "reinventing the wheel" and allow them to modify software that has proven effective for organizational needs. One requirement for appropriate integration is full documentation of the software and fully specified test cases and test results for each component. It is envisioned that by reusing a component, developers will have access to this information about the component to integrate into their development efforts. Disseminating the information about the component, how it works, and anticipated results will place developers that much further along the learning curve allowing more efficient software development. Access to fully specified test cases and test results will help validate the functionality of the component and add efficiency to the software development process and reuse efforts.

Software reuse also embodies collective code ownership, another XP practice. Making software components fully available to the organization, and implementing methods and techniques to speed identification of appropriate components, represents collective ownership of the code base. Any developer in the organization is encouraged to reuse and improve any component that meets their needs. Reusing previously effective solutions helps accelerate the development cycle. One of the challenges to reusing components is ensuring that they are easily identifiable, suit the task at hand, and can be easily refactored or extended to improve performance or more appropriately meet current needs. These efforts provide an evolving and improving code base from which to develop future software and satisfy customer requirements, further accelerating the development cycle.

A repository based reuse approach, as suggested, has several advantages. One advantage is that the reusable artifacts created by individual developers can be shared with others by storing them in the repository. Hence, everyone in the organization can contribute to the reuse effort. Another advantage is that the artifacts can be standardized to create an architectural framework that would use generic components that would be part of every system developed in a particular application domain. For example, in the domain of satellite control software, every ground control center should have a telemetry component for uploading commands and downloading data. Hence, the components that implement this functionality will be part of every ground control center software system.

Systematic software reuse provides a promising means to improve software quality, reduce development cycle time, and lower development costs. Particularly if reuse is materialized in the early stages of systems development by reusing requirement specifications, designs, and other higher level artifacts, the project team has a tremendous opportunity to drastically cut the overall development time and effort.

However, many factors conspire to make systematic software reuse a non-trivial task. For example, storage and retrieval of reusable components, and the tracking of features and functionality between each of the versions, can become an issue. Additionally, contextual and behavioral issues such as management support and the software developer's interest are seen to be more important than technical issues in determining the success or failure of software reuse programs (Kim and Stohr 1998).

Framework Caveats

While repositories of core reusable assets help operationalize software reuse, they can also present specific issues. The storage and retrieval of artifacts from reusable repositories is still a challenge, especially when the repositories have many hundreds of components. Several factors impact the search and retrieval process including scope of the repository, query representation, asset representation, storage structure, navigation scheme, relevance and matching criteria (Mili et al. 1998). Most retrieval methods focus on one or two of these factors to suit the specific domain they are working in. When a user searches for a component to satisfy his or her requirements, the user is required to be very specific about what he or she is looking for because some of the repositories may not contain information on how its components are related. Searching for appropriate artifacts does not usually take these relationships, or dependencies, into account and, therefore, limits the usability and consistency of the components returned to the user. Retrieved components are most useful if they respond directly to the user's needs. Thus, in order for reuse to be successful, the tools and techniques used should be flexible, agile and be able to support multiple systems development life cycle models. In particular, since agile development methodologies are gaining prominence, it is worthwhile to incorporate reuse practices in the context of agile development.

In addition to identifying the appropriate component comes the potential issue of version control, or in this instance, feature control. Once a refactored component is placed back into the reuse repository, it may contain more features than the original component. Identification of this second generation, enhanced component may cause difficulties with future component identification. Future efforts to identify appropriate components may become more challenging as later generations will have additional features not required by the current project. In these instances an earlier generation of the software may be required to meet the needs of the current project.

Version control in this scenario will require not only tracking between versions, but feature and functionality control as the component develops and improves over time. To effectively manage this process, a system will be required that not only manages each individual version of the software, but also the features added during each iterative generation of the component. This would require additional care in the version management process to adequately recognize the features added in each generation of the software.

As with any new idea, there will be an initial resource investment required to implement the process, train the developers, and identify the component identification ontology. Once the decision is made to enhance current organizational processes by integrating the code reuse strategy with a refactoring approach, the organization will begin climbing the learning curve to effectively implement this approach. With all new processes, there will be an adjustment and learning process to be able to fully utilize the new approach. Organizations will have to display the courage and fortitude to continue with the process even if initial expectations are unmet. These characteristics will be familiar to XP organizations as one of the values of this approach is courage (Beck 2000).

Another potential issue when implementing a new practice or process is organizational acceptance and buy-in. In order for new techniques to be accepted by the organization, those who will work closest with the process need to accept the process. One method used to obtain buy-in is to first educate developers in how this process will help them be more effective, efficient, and perform their job better. The next step is to provide incentives to the team to utilize this approach.

The belief is that developers will utilize a technique they believe will make them more efficient and effective. The proposed process will serve both purposes if utilized properly. A developer will invest time searching for a component if they believe the search process will be efficient (requiring less time searching for a component than developing from scratch) and effective (time invested searching will yield a better component than they could have developed on their own). An effective code reuse and identification process will allow the developer to readily detect components that will meet their criteria. These refactored components will provide more effective code than could potentially have been developed by the programmer. The efficiency aspect of the utilization model is addressed by the code reuse portion of the proposed framework and the effectiveness portion is addressed by the refactoring approach.

CONCLUSION

Software reuse has been discussed in the literature for the last three decades and it is still an active area of research within the software engineering community. Similarly, several agile software development methodologies have been proposed and practiced by organizations that develop commercial and non-commercial software. While considerable strides have been made in these two areas of research and practice, there seems to be a lack of synergy between these two streams of research. Much of the agile software development literature and methodologies do not explicitly discuss or incorporate research results from the software reuse literature. Similarly, the software reuse based development methodologies do not take into account some of the guiding principles from the agile development approaches. We have presented an integrated framework for code reuse within the context of Extreme Programming, an agile software development methodology. Our approach combines the salient features of component reuse and agile development and provides an integrated process model for refactoring and reuse within XP. We contend that this integrated approach will facilitate more efficient refactoring, thus improving the overall efficiency of XP. Our future work includes: a) further refinement of our overall framework, b) validating the framework through face validation as well as empirical validation by systems analysts and practitioners, c) applying it to a large scale projects and studying its effectiveness, d) investigating the factors that influence the adoption and diffusion of our approach in organizations, and e) generalizing our approach so that it can be used in conjunction with many agile development methodologies other than XP.

REFERENCES

Basili, V. and Turner, A. "Iterative Enhancement: A Practical Technique for Software Development," IEEE Transactions on Software Development (1:4), December 1975, pp. 390 – 396.

Beck, K. Extreme Programming Explained, Boston, Massachusetts: Addison-Wesley, 2000.

Beck, K. and Andres, C. Extreme Programming Explained: Embrace Change, Second Edition. Boston, Massachusetts: Addison-Wesley, 2004.

Biggerstaff, T.J, Perlis, A. J., (ed) (1989) *Software Reusability Concepts and Models, Volume I and II*, ACM Press Frontier Series, Addison Wesley.

Boehm, B. "A Spiral Model of Software Development and Enhancement," ACM SIGSOFT Software Engineering Notes (11:4), August 1986, pp. 14 – 24.

Buchanan, B.G. et al. Constructing an Expert System, in F. Hayes-Roth, D.A. Waterman, and D.B. Lenat, eds., Building Expert Systems, Reading, MA: Addison-Wesley, 1983.

C3 Team. Chrysler Goes to "Extremes". *Distributed Computing*, (October 1998), 24 – 28.

Chan, S. and Lammers, T. Reusing Distributed Object Domain Framework, 5th Intl. Conf. on Software Reuse, June 2-5, 1998, Victoria, BC, pp. 216-223.

Clayton, R., Rugaber, S., Taylor, L., and Wills, L. "A Case Study of Domain-Based Program Understanding" in Proceedings of the International Workshop on Program Comprehension, Dearborn, Michigan, May 1997.

Coleman, D.M., Ash, D., Lowther, B., and Oman, P.W. "Using Metrics to Evaluate Software System Maintainability," Computer (27:8), August 1994, pp. 44-49.

DeHondt, G. and Brandyberry, A. "Programming in the eXtreme: Critical Characteristics of Agile Implementations," e-Informatica Software Engineering Journal (1:1), February 2007, pp. 43-58.

Due, R. "The Economics of Component-Based Development," Information Systems Management (17:1), Winter 2000, pp. 92-95.

Fowler, M. Analysis Patterns: Reusable Object Models, Massachusetts, Addison-Wesley, 1997.

Fowler, M. Refactoring: Improving the Design of Existing Programs, Addison-Wesley, 1999.

Girardi, M.R. and Ibrahim, B. "Using English to Retrieve Software," Journal of Systems and Software (30:3), September 1995, pp. 249-270.

Guimaraes, T. "Managing Application Program Maintenance Expenditure," Communications of the ACM (26:10), October 1983, pp. 739-746.

Highsmith, Jim. Agile Software Development Ecosystems. Boston, Massachusetts: Addison-Wesley, 2002.

Hoffer, J., George, J., and Valacich, J. Modern Systems Analysis and Design. Boston, Massachusetts: Addison-Wesley, 1998.

Kiely, D. "The Component Edge," Information-week, No. 677, April 13, 1998, pp. 1A-6A.

Kim, Y. and Stohr, E.A. "Software Reuse: Survey and Research Directions," Journal of Management Information Systems: JMIS (14:4), Spring 1998, pp. 113-147.

Lee, J. C. "Embracing Agile Development of Usable Software Systems," CHI 2006, April 22 – 27, 2006, Montreal, Quebec, Canada, pp. 1767 – 1770.

Lientz, B.P. and Swanson, E.B. Software Maintenance Management: A Study of the Maintenance of Computer Application Software in 487 Data Processing Organizations. Addison-Wesley, 1980.

Lim, W.C. "Effects of Reuse on Quality, Productivity, and Economics," IEEE Software (11:5), September 1994, pp. 23-30.

Lindstrom, Lowell, Jeffries, Ron. "Extreme Programming and Agile Development Methodologies," Information Systems Management (21:3), Summer 2004, pp. 41 – 52.

Meekel, J., Horton, T., France, R., Mellone, C., and Dalvi, S. "From Domain Models to Architecture Frameworks," Software Engineering Notes (22:3), May 1997, pp. 75-80.

Mens, T. and Tourwe, T. "A Survey of Software Refactoring," IEEE Transactions on Software Engineering (30:2), February 2004, pp. 126-139.

Mili, A., Mili, R., and Mittermeir, R.T., "A Survey of Software Reuse Libraries," Annals of Software Engineering (5), January 1998, pp. 349-414.

Morgan, G. Images of Organization, San Francisco, California: Berrett-Koehler Publishers, Inc., 1998.

Nerur, S., Mahapatra, R. and Mangalaraj, G. "Challenges of Migrating to Agile Methodologies," Communications of the ACM (48:5), May 2005, pp. 73-78.

Nerur, S., and Balijepally, V. "Theoretical Reflections on Agile Development Methodologies," Communications of the ACM (50:3), March 2007, pp. 79 – 83.

Nord, R. L., and Tomayko, J. E. "Software Architecture-Centric Methods and Agile Development," IEEE Software (23:2), March/April 2006, pp. 47 – 53.

Opdyke, W.F. "Refactoring: A Program Restructuring Aid in Designing Object-Oriented Application Frameworks," PhD Thesis, Univ. of Illinois at Urbana-Champaign, 1992.

Prieto-Diaz, R. Domain Analysis for Reusability. In Domain Analysis and Software Systems Modeling, Prieto-Diaz, P., Arango, G. (eds), IEEE Computer Society Press, 1991, pp. 63-69.

Ramesh, B., Cao, L., Mohan, K. and Xu, P. "Can Distributed Software Development Be Agile ?,"

Communications of the ACM (49:10), October 2006, pp. 41 – 46.

Ravichandran, T. "Organizational Assimilation of Complex Technologies: An Empirical Study of Component-Based Software Development," IEEE Transaction on Engineering Management, (52:2), 2005, pp. 249 – 268.

Sherif, K. and Vinze, A. A Qualitative Model for Barriers to Software Reuse Adoption. In P. De and J.I. DeGross (Eds.), Proceedings of 20th Internal Conference on Information Systems, Charlotte, North Carolina, December 13-15, 1999.

Sprott, D. "Componentizing the Enterprise Application Packages," Communications of the ACM (43:4), April 2000, pp. 63-69.

Sugumaran, V., Tanniru, M., and Storey, V.C., "A Domain Model for Supporting Reuse in Systems Analysis," Communications of the ACM (43:11es), Nov. 2000, pp. 312 - 322.

Sugumaran, V., Park, S., and Kang, K., "Software Product Line Engineering," Communications of the ACM (49:12), December 2006, pp. 28 - 32.

Szyperski, C. Component Software: Beyond Object-Oriented Programming, Addison-Wesley, 1998.

Szyperski, C.A. "Emerging component software technologies - a strategic comparison," *Software - Concepts and Tools* (19:1) 1998, pp 2-10.

Turk, D., France, R., and Rumpe, B. "Assumptions Underlying Agile Software Development Processes," Journal of Database Management (16:4), October - December 2005, pp. 62 – 87.

Vitharana, P. and Jain, H. "Research Issues in Testing Business Components," Information & Management (37:6), September 2000, pp. 297-309.

ENDNOTE

1 An earlier version of this work appeared in the Proceedings of the 2007 Americas Conference on Information Systems (AMCIS).

Chapter V
Requirements Elicitation Technique Selection: A Theory-Based Contingency Model

Miguel I. Aguirre-Urreta
DePaul University, USA

George M. Marakas
University of Kansas, USA

ABSTRACT

Requirements elicitation has been recognized as a critical stage in system development projects, yet current models prescribing particular elicitation techniques are still limited in their development and application. This research reviews efforts aimed at addressing this issue, and synthesizes a common structure consisting of project contingencies, elicitation techniques, logic of fit, and a success construct, arguing for the need to more comprehensively study and organize each. As a first step in this research, models drawn from organizational literature are used to categorize project contingencies into dimensions dealing with their impact on the uncertainty and equivocality of the overall development project.

INTRODUCTION

Information requirements determination (IRD) has long been considered a critical stage in system development projects (Browne and Ramesh, 2002). The need for advancing our understanding in this area can be argued from four different perspectives. First, requirements determination is conducted early in the systems development lifecycle, and outcomes of this phase have a strong impact on project quality and outcomes. In addition, strong empirical evidence highlights the negative effects requirements uncertainty (Nidumolu, 1995) or requirements risk (Wallace, et al., 2004) have on development project performance. Third, issues related to requirements determination consistently top rankings of software development risks as perceived by project managers (Schmidt, et al., 2001). Finally, lack of understanding about users′ needs and expectations results in the failure of a significant proportion of development projects (Hickey and Davis, 2003). In summary, any improvement in the process of eliciting and understanding requirements holds significant promise for the improvement of development activities (Browne and Rogich, 2001).

Despite the importance for development success, and the significant amount of research studying the relative effectiveness of different elicitation techniques, the literature has yet to converge on a framework prescribing the most effective use of specific techniques in varying situations; although several have been proposed (Davis, 1982; Maiden and Rugg, 1996; Hickey and Davis, 2004; Tsumaki and Tamai, 2005). More than twenty years ago, Valusek and Fryback (1985) stated "*... we should soon be able to prescribe a strategy and tool for managing through the IRD portion of these problems...*" yet progress in this regard has been scant. While significant research has been conducted on the performance effects of specific elicitation techniques, we are no closer to prescription than before.

This work seeks to establish the foundations of a research program into the selection of requirements elicitation techniques. It does so by building on the contingency structure proposed by Hickey and Davis (2004), by providing the underlying logic, grounded on the information processing model proposed by Daft and Lengel (1986), for the increased effectiveness resulting from appropriately matching[2] elicitation techniques to project situations. The task for which the system is developed, users, stakeholders, and analysts, are characterized as sources of uncertainty and equivocality, and elicitation techniques as mechanisms with the capacity to reduce and resolve same. This framework offers a more detailed perspective by moving away from overall project levels of uncertainty and equivocality, and into the task, users and analysts, each with their own particular issues, as separate sources, potentially requiring different techniques for successful elicitation performance.

Literature Review

Most models of the IRD process distinguish between three different groups of activities: *elicitation, specification*, and *validation* (Browne and Ramesh, 2002). In the elicitation phase, functional requirements for the proposed system are obtained from all relevant users of the new application as well as interested stakeholders. This information can be obtained in a variety of ways and the selection of the most appropriate one, given project characteristics, is the main interest herein.

Elicited requirements form the input to the specification stage, in which a variety of modeling and representational techniques are employed to formalize and document said requirements, including process logic, data structure, and system behavior. These representations are then used in verifying that obtained requirements are correct, involving the selection of a validation or assurance strategy (Naumann, et al., 1980). The final output of IRD is a set of system diagrams, agreed upon by all involved parties, which can then be implemented into a new application. Although generally depicted as proceeding in a linear fashion, these activities are highly iterative in nature. Of the three phases, requirements elicitation is the most time and resource intensive one (Hickey and Davis, 2004).

Past research on IRD can be grouped into two different categories: that related to a specific technique or method, and that modeling the selection of elicitation techniques in general (Hickey and Davis, 2004). The first group of studies are empirical in nature and investigate the applicability of different elicitation techniques, without considering the situation in which such techniques would be most appropriate. This line of research compares the elicitation performance of an advocated approach against some baseline methodology. Examples include Montezemi and Conrath (1986) (cognitive mapping techniques), Marakas and Elam (1998) (semantic structuring), Zmud, Anthony and Stair (1993) (mental imagery), Browne and Rogich (2001) (prompting techniques) or Rockart (1979) (critical success factors). A more comprehensive review can be found in Byrd, Cossick and Zmud (1992).

The second category includes a number of conceptual models attempting to describe the elicitation process and model technique selection for a given project situation. This research can be traced back to the seminal work of Davis (1982), who proposed that different characteristics of the project, application, users, and analysts led to the formation of three process uncertainties: the existence and stability of a set of usable requirements, the ability of users to specify the requirements, and the ability of analysts to elicit and evaluate them. These process uncertainties in turn impacted an overall requirements process uncertainty. The level of this overall measure indicated which of the four elicitation strategies (asking, deriving, synthesizing or discovering) should be selected as a primary approach.

More recently, Hickey and Davis (2004) proposed a unified model of requirements elicitation that sought to improve on past conceptualizations by distinguishing between requirements already known and those remaining to be discovered, and among project situations (including characteristics of the problem domain, the solution domain, and the project). The authors developed a mathematical formulation of the model, where at each elicitation step, a technique is applied to the situation capturing some portion of the unknown requirements resulting in an improved state of knowledge about characteristics of the system under development.

While this model advanced the understanding of the elicitation process by clearly distinguishing and articulating its different components, it did not specify the underlying logic by which techniques should be matched to specific situations, nor did it provide organizing frameworks for the model components, limiting their research to examples of the elements found in each of them. This has also been a limitation of other models, such as those proposed by Maiden and Rugg (1996) and Tsumaki and Tamai (2005). In the first case, a sample of possible methods is provided along with heuristic guidelines as to their most appropriate use; however, their classification is only descriptive, and provides limited capabilities for comparing the methods. In addition, the distinction between elicitation and specification (or modeling) of the requirements is blurred. Tsumaki and Tamai (2005), on the other hand, did provide two different dimensions along which they organized a number of sample techniques, the first one related to the focus of the elicitation process (either static structures or dynamic behaviors), the second on the nature of the target space. Their logic for matching techniques to project characteristics was limited to recommendations along one dimension at a time, arguing away the relevancy of the other, depending on which contextual factor was being considered. While compatible with the Hickey and Davis (2004) model, the research model described in this paper delves deeper into each portion of that framework.

Recent work by Mathiassen, Saarinen, Tuunanen and Rossi (2007) provides a different perspective on the problem of matching requirement techniques to systems development projects. Taking a risk-oriented approach to the issue (Iversen, Mathiassen and Nielsen, 2004), the authors conducted an extensive literature review of past research dealing not only with technique selection models per se, but also with applications of particular techniques, which led to the development of a selection framework based on requirement development risks, techniques, and project-risk profiles as an approach to matching techniques to projects.

In the first case, risks were categorized into requirements identity (availability of requirements), volatility (stability of requirements), and complexity (understandability of requirements), which largely map to the categories developed later in this manuscript. Turning to the techniques themselves, Mathiassen et al (2007) grouped them into discovery, prioritization, experimentation, and specification methods. Finally, linking project risks to resolution techniques is achieved through the development of eight distinct archetypical risk profiles which are proposed to represent different stages a project will transition through as risks are reduced to an acceptable level. The interested reader is referred to their work for an alternative take on the same research problem as discussed in this paper.

RESEARCH MODEL DEVELOPMENT

Information Processing Theory

The review on this section is based largely on the works of Galbraith (1974), Tushman and Nadler (1978) and Egelhoff (2005). An early distinction should be made between the theoretical position reviewed here and other frameworks that emphasize cognitive views of organizational information processing (e.g. Daft and Weick, 1984). In those perspectives, while environmental conditions may still be the stimulus of information processing, the emphasis is placed on the influenced of what occurs within the individual (i.e. psychological determinants) and between individuals (social-psychological determinants). In contrast, information-processing theory is represented in terms of the capacities of different kinds of organizational structures and processes to transfer information within an organization. This perspective has also been referred to as the logistical view of organizational information processing. The cognitive perspective addresses how strategic decisions are made, while the logistical perspective tries to explain the information capacities inherent in the organizational design, and evaluate them against requirements for information processing.

The information-processing view of the organization rests on the basic premise that, the greater the uncertainty of the task, the greater the amount of information that has to be processed by decision makers. Although theorists viewing the organization from this perspective have traditionally considered environmental uncertainty to be the key contingency, later the list of factors has been expanded to include characteristics of the task, the relationship between subunits, and organizational strategy adopted by the organization. Later extensions to this perspective have incorporated the complementary notion of equivocality, which postulates that organizations also process information in order to resolve it. However, managers reduce equivocality by interpreting information rather than by collecting more of it (Weick, 1979).

Although all these are likely influenced by environmental uncertainty, they mediate the direct effect of the latter on the need to process information. The key intervening concept, information processing, can be defined as including the gathering of data, the transformation of data into information, and the communication and storage of information in the organization. It also relies on the basic contingency notion that the structure and processes of an organization should match or fit characteristics of certain variables both inside and outside the organizational system, and that those organizations that manage to accomplish this fit would be rewarded in performance as compared to those that do not. Finally, information-processing theory assumes that, as organizations grow, they differentiate to realize the benefits of economies of scale and specialization. At any

Figure 1. General information-processing approach (Egelhoff, 2005)

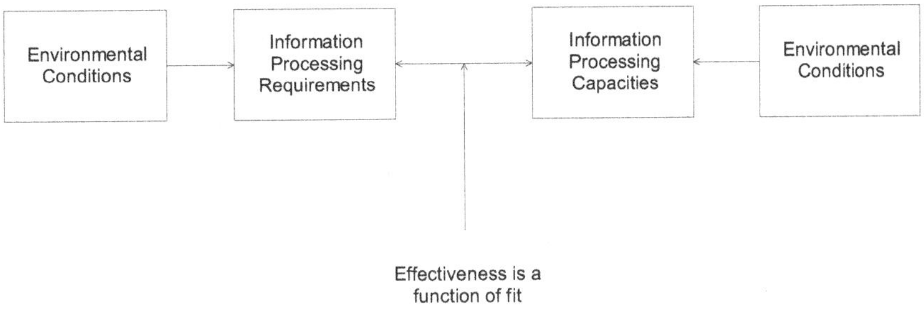

time, these subunits are interdependent in varying degrees and must share scarce resources. Thus, the basic unit of analysis is the subunit, and the basic structural problem is to design subunits and relations between subunits capable of dealing with information processing requirements faced during task execution. The general information-processing approach to organizational design is depicted in Figure 1.

On the one hand, the impact on an organization of its strategy and the environmental factors with which it chooses to deal can be expressed in terms of the *information-processing requirements* they create. On the other hand, the potential of the organization to cope with these requirements can be expressed in terms of the *information-processing capacities* furnished by its organizational design. Instead of attempting to measure information processing directly, macro-level studies must use information processing as an abstract intervening concept to aid in positing relationships between directly measured characteristics of an organization's design and its strategy and environment, both of which have identifiable information-processing implications.

Much of the research reviewed in the prior section has been based, although rather implicitly, on the information processing view of organizations, in particular with relationship to the idea of uncertainty; the models by Naumann et al (1980) and Davis (1982), and later derivations such as that from Fazlollahi and Tanniru (1991) or Burns and Dennis (1985) are examples of this. One important objective of this article is to take those past instantiations of the theory and formalize their relationship to it, and thus benefit from the explicit consideration of the logic behind the selection of techniques, how to analyze and understand the relevant contingencies and, perhaps most importantly, provide a theory-based argument for why some techniques would be more or less effective for different projects.

Research Model

The research model presented herein builds on a stream of literature applying contingency theory to specify the matching of particular techniques or methodologies to different project situations. Table 1 compares extant frameworks on their conceptualization of these components, as well as the logic employed to stipulate the fit between them. This paper draws upon the theoretical framework of information processing theory discussed above (Daft and Lengel, 1986) and synthesizes past research into the model depicted in Figure 2. Uncertainty is related to the absence of needed information, and was defined as such by Galbraith (1977): "*the difference between the amount of information required to perform the task and the amount of information already possessed by the organization*". Equivocality, on the other hand, is the existence of multiple and conflicting interpretations; where new informa-

Figure 2. Proposed research model

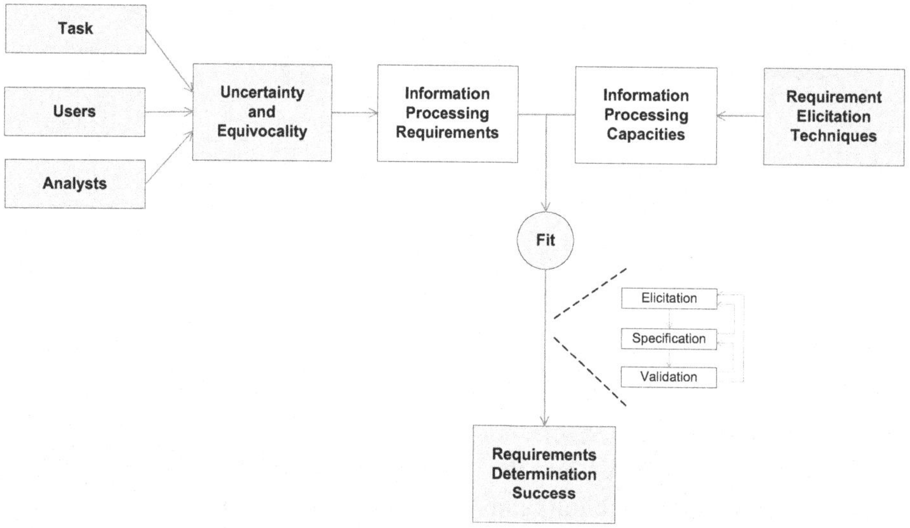

tion may reduce uncertainty, it may not resolve ambiguities when equivocality is high (Daft and Lengel, 1986).

The underlying assumption is that a first pass at a theory of requirements elicitation technique selection should be able to account for, organize, and relate at least four different components: the contingencies affecting the need for the elicitation process, the available techniques and their effects upon those contingencies, a logic of fit establishing the "why" behind matching techniques to contingencies, and a measure of requirements determination success to assess the performance effects of the matching described above (Premkumar, Ramamurthy and Saunders, 2003), and judge the degree to which the process has been completed and a new phase of the development lifecycle should begin. Each of these components is briefly described next, with the contingencies portion of the model being further developed, as the starting point of this research. Table 1 reviews and summarizes existing research in this area, categorized in terms of contingencies, techniques, and logic of fit. Requirements determination success, on the other hand, has not been explicitly discussed in the reviewed literature, and thus was not included in Table 1.

A Framework for Understanding Contingencies

Table 1 inventories a number of contingencies suggested as relevant to the selection of elicitation techniques. Some authors have attempted some degree of categorization of these contingencies, such as among the utilizing system, the application, users and analysts (Davis, 1982), or organization and project, customers and users, developers and analysts, and problem and solution domain (Hickey and Davis, 2004); in all cases, these efforts have been limited to grouping characteristics or examples around a common label (e.g. characteristics of users, of the utilizing system, of the analysts, etc.). However, an organizing framework, or a set of them, tying these lists of characteristics to their impact on the selection of techniques has not yet emerged.

This work applies models borrowed from the organizational literature to systematically understand the effects these issues have on uncertainty

Table 1. Reviewed contingency models

Model	Focus	Contingencies	Techniques	Fit Logic
Naumann et al (1980)	RV	Project size Degree of structuredness User task comprehension Developer task proficiency	Accept user statement Linear assurance process Iterative assurance process Experimental assurance process	Uncertainty level
Davis (1982)	RE	Utilizing system: Existence of a well-understood model of the system Stability of system structure Nonprogrammed versus programmed activity Stability in information use Application: High-level versus low-level application Complexity Number of users Users: Experience with utilizing system Experience with application Analysts: Experience with utilizing system Experience with application	Asking Deriving from an existing system Synthesizing from utilizing system Discovering from experimentation	Uncertainty level
Burns and Dennis (1985)	DM	Project uncertainty: Degree of structuredness User task comprehension Developer task proficiency Project complexity: Project Size Number of users Volume of new information Complexity of new information	System lifecycle Mixed methodology Prototyping	Uncertainty level Complexity level
Maiden and Rugg (1996)	RE	Purpose of requirements Internal filtering of knowledge Observable phenomena Acquisition context	Observation Interviews Protocol Analysis Card Sorting Laddering Repertory grids Brainstorming Rapid prototyping Scenario analysis RAD workshops Ethnographic methods	
Ratbe, King and Kim (2000)	DM	Project uncertainty: Level of application support Stability of user requirements Degree with which the application system is understood Degree of structure Developer's experience Top management support Project complexity: Size of the project Time constraint imposed Complexity of the application User's system experience	Systems development lifecycle Prototyping level I Prototyping level II Prototyping level III End-user development	Approaches prescribed in prior research

continued on following page

Table 1. continued

Model	Focus	Contingencies	Techniques	Fit Logic
Hickey and Davis (2004)	RE	Inherent characteristics of the organization and project: Specific methodology to be used Level of resources or time constraints Degree of personnel turnover Characteristics of customers and users: Number of different users Diversity of needs Level of experience Willingness to work together to reach consensus Ability to articulate requirements Characteristics of the developers: Experience with the problem and solution domain Experience with software development Characteristics of analysts: Leadership skills Communication skills Analytical skills Technical knowledge Problem domain: Problem understanding Problem complexity Application domain Importance of specific non-functional requirements Existing system (manual or automated) Solution domain: Type of solution anticipated Development strategy (in-house, outsourced, COTS)	Any technique that helps elicit requirements from stakeholders	Matching: Technique characteristics Situation characteristics State of requirements
Tsumaki and Tamai (2005)	RE	Application domain stability: Knowledge of target domain Experience developing similar systems Requirements engineers type: Logical and systematic vs. intuitive and imaginative Information resources: Abundance of information in documents or knowledge bases Investigation of existing systems User involvement: Needed or just collaboration (when formal sources available) Constraint on certain techniques (e.g. brainstorming) Non-functional requirements	Domain decomposition Goal-oriented approaches Scenario-based approaches Brainstorming	Elicitation operation types (static vs. dynamic) Target object types (closed vs. open)

RV = Selection of a requirements validation technique
RE = Selection of a requirements elicitation technique
DM = Selection of a development methodology

and equivocality, and thus on elicitation technique selection. Although some prior work was implicitly organized along those lines, this represents a first attempt to systematically apply information-processing theory to requirements elicitation technique selection. It should be noted many of the contingencies in the extant literature have not been included in the categorizations developed below: those concerning the proficiency of the analysts and developers, and those imposing constraints on the methodologies that could be employed. From a normative point of view, neither of these should influence the ideal pattern of alignment between contingencies and elicitation techniques. This could be incorporated into later versions of the framework as constraints on the availability of particular techniques.

Contingencies Related to the Task[3]

Characteristics of the task can be usefully conceptualized along the two dimensions of task variety and task analyzability (Daft and Macintosh, 1981). Central to this argument is the idea that tasks vary with respect to certain characteristics, and that those are valuable in distinguishing between the elicitation techniques that would be most appropriate to different projects. The first dimension relates to uncertainty and refers to the number of exceptions or novel events requiring different methods and procedures (Bensaou and Venkatraman, 1995). When task variety is low, little information is necessary to describe the new system. Conversely, high task variety requires a significant increase in the amount of information needed to fully describe the proposed system. Task analyzability, on the other hand, is closely tied to equivocality and depicts the extent to which there are known procedures specifying the sequence of steps to be performed in the completion of the task (Keller, 1994), affecting the extent to which activities can be structured in a routinized or systematized way (Van de Ven and Delbecq, 1974). Tasks on the unanalyzable end of the continuum require individuals to think about, create or find solutions to new problems (Rice, 1992). To some extent, this second dimension parallels Simon's (1965) distinction, made when dealing with decision situations, between programmed and nonprogrammed ones.

Another important distinction is between task-possessed (Chang, 2001) and non-possessed information prior to the start of the elicitation process. The idea behind task-possessed information (Chang, 2001; Chang and Tien, 2006), later extended to project-possessed information (Chang and Chiu, 2005; Chang and Ibbs, 2006), is that organizations do not begin projects anew every time, but rather they possess, stored in the form of experience, documentation, etc., prior information about the organization itself, previous similar projects, interactions among the same groups of stakeholders, to name a few. The underlying argument is that all this information is not discarded at the beginning of new projects, but rather serves to inform developers about which areas require more careful investigation and which ones benefit from knowledge reuse. Chang and colleagues (Chang, 2001; Chang and Chiu, 2005; Chang and Tien, 2006; Chang and Ibbs, 2006) have conducted extensive research supporting the notion of task-possessed information and its impact on the uncertainty and equivocality present in projects within the discipline of civil and infrastructure engineering.

Although not explicitly recognized in that form, we would argue past research in the area of requirements elicitation had already recognized the need to consider past experiences with development projects as important contingencies in the technique selection process. From this perspective, the characteristics of the task supported by the development project set an innate level of analyzability and variety needed to be addressed through appropriate gathering techniques. Prior research, however, has recognized the existence, in a variety of forms, of information about the task. These include past user and analyst experience with the task (Davis, 1982; Hickey and Davis, 2004; Ratbe, et al., 2000), or external sources such as documentation, knowledge bases, best practices, etc. (Tsumaki and Tamai, 2005). Maiden and Rugg (1996) make a similar distinction between eliciting information about the existing domain or requirements for the new system, and suggest that different methods are more effective in each case. Further research would be required to understand the extent to which the notion of task-possessed information may be a critical determinant suggesting the use of discovery (or experimental) elicitation methods.

Based on the discussion above, Table 2 groups proposed task-related contingencies (shown in Table 1) into three categories: those affecting task analyzability, those affecting task variety, and those affecting the nature and amount of task-possessed information. Ideally, the last category would also be split between factors influencing analyzability and variety, however, the very general expressions used to label these contingencies (e.g. user experience with the utilizing system) does not allow for such fine-grained distinctions at this stage.

Contingencies Related to Users and Analysts

Past research has emphasized communication-related issues when dealing with contingencies about users, stakeholders and analysts, including the perspective developed by Guinan and Bostrom (1986); within, among and between communication obstacles (Byrd, et al., 1992; Valusek and Fryback, 1985); and other cognitive limitations (Browne and Ramesh, 2002; Davis, 1982). However, an examination of Table 1 reveals few of the contingencies proposed in the literature address these issues, but for diversity of user needs and willingness to reach consensus (Hickey and Davis, 2004) and those related to project size (see Table 2), under the general assumption larger projects involve more disagreement among users. To the extent information-processing limitations (Davis, 1982) are present, to a greater or lesser degree, in all human beings, it seems appropriate the design of elicitation techniques take these issues, such as cognitive biases, satisficing, and recall problems, into account (Browne and Ramesh, 2002).

This research, however, challenges the notion communication obstacles between users and analysts and among different user groups are always present during elicitation. Rather, it proposes these need to be understood, measured, and incorporated as part of the contingencies dictating the optimal choice of elicitation technique. This includes both their existence and likely impact on the development project. For instance, although differences in the nature and stability of perceptual frameworks between users and analysts (Valusek and Fryback, 1985) may well exist, they may not be a major problem in a project where the large majority of the requirements may be derived from existing systems in the current or other organizations, industry studies and benchmarks, etc. (e.g. the deriving approach, Davis, 1982).

Similarly, communication obstacles among different user groups would only arise when there is more than one homogeneous group of users involved in the development effort. Although simplistic, these type of distinctions have not been considered in extant literature. To the extent that group techniques, such as those described by Duggan (2003) or Coughlan and Macredie (2002), are successful in addressing many of these issues but, at the same time, very costly to execute (in terms of the resource commitments necessary, both human and financial), improving our understanding of the most appropriate opportunities for their application becomes an important objective of this research. Other research has focused on developing a structure that can be imposed on requirements elicitation meetings with the objective of reducing the amount of time spent in the design process while simultaneously improve the effectiveness of users and analysts to develop shared system models (Bostrom and Thomas, 1983).

As far as the effects of these two communication obstacles on the proposed logic of fit, they appear to be most related to the notion of equivocality, particularly as it refers to the existence of multiple and conflicting interpretations about organizational situations (Daft and Lengel, 1986; Bostrom and Thomas, 1983). Differentiation between departments, which results from the adaptation efforts of units to better satisfy the demands of their own tasks and environments, leads to disparities in time horizons, goals, values and priorities (Lawrence and Lorsch, 1969; Daft and Lengel, 1986; Tushman, 1978). Equivocality is resolved by the exchange of views among participants to define problems and enact shared interpretations of the situation (Daft and Lengel, 1986). This closely resembles the objectives of group techniques such as those discussed above. Coughlan and Macredie (2002) noted that in order for a system to achieve its design objectives a comprehensive understanding of the problem area, which includes the users, the work context, and the organization into which the project is embedded, is needed. In this regard, the goal of the requirements stage of a development project is to achieve "*an understanding of the problem, and one that must be shared between disparate people ... an increased amount of communicative effort is required to surpass the semantic gap that estranged parties, such as users and designers, inevitably foster*" (Coughlan and Macredie, 2002).

Requirements Elicitation Techniques

As shown in Table 1, a wide variety of techniques have been proposed to deal with the project contingencies present in IRD. Extensive reviews of available techniques have been conducted by Taggart and Tharp (1977) and, more recently, by Byrd et al. (1992). The latter classified techniques according to communication obstacles (Valusek and Fryback, 1985) addressed by each (within, between, and among), problem domain categories emphasized, and locus of control of the elicitation process (analyst vs. user). Other researchers have attempted to construct an ontology of elicitation techniques by focusing on structural characteristics, such as physical and temporal co-location, analyst role, record-keeping, anonymity, stakeholder count, etc. (Hickey and Davis, 2003).

While useful for the purpose of describing different elicitation techniques, these frameworks are of limited value in distinguishing among them. For instance, of the eighteen techniques surveyed by Byrd et al., (1992), thirteen were classified as appropriate for addressing two or all three of the communication obstacles identified by Valusek and Fryback (1985). Similar issues arise with the ontological grouping devised by Hickey and Davis (2003) regarding technique characteristics. One possible explanation for this situation is there are a limited number of "archetypes" of which several techniques are relative variations, such as interviews: prompting (Browne and Rogich, 2001), semantic structuring (Marakas and Elam, 1998), teachback (Johnson and Johnson, 1987), closed and open (Davis, 1982), to name a few.

The development of appropriate dimensions to classify and distinguish elicitation techniques is beyond the scope of this manuscript. However, it is possible to envision some of the characteristics these dimensions should possess: some degree of independence or orthogonality, such that the addition of a dimension usefully discriminates among techniques; the possibility of judging elicitation techniques across a continuous scale anchored at extremes instead of classification via discrete categories; and finally, a mechanism making it possible to relate these dimensions to the logic of fit employed in the research model, in this case the reduction of uncertainty and resolution of equivocality. As an example of the first two issues, Tsumaki and Tamai (2005) grouped techniques along an open-closed axis (related to properties of the target space, such as stability) and a static-dynamic axis (whether techniques captured static structures or dynamic behaviors

Table 2. Grouping of task-related contingencies

Task Dimension	Factors	Sources
Task analyzability	Degree of structuredness	Degree of structuredness (Naumann, et al., 1980), stability of system structure (Davis, 1982), programmed vs. nonprogrammed activity (Davis, 1982), degree of structuredness (Burns and Dennis, 1985), degree of structure (Ratbe, et al., 2000).
	Application level	High-level vs. low-level application (Davis, 1982), application domain (Hickey and Davis, 2004), level of application support (Ratbe, et al., 2000).
	Complexity	Complexity (Davis, 1982), complexity of new information (Burns and Dennis, 1985), complexity of the application (Ratbe, et al., 2000), problem complexity (Hickey and Davis, 2004).
Task variety	Project size	Project size (Naumann, et al., 1980), number of users (Davis, 1982), project size and number of users (Burns and Dennis, 1985), size of the project (Ratbe, et al., 2000), number of different users (Hickey and Davis, 2004).
	Application level	High-level vs. low-level application (Davis, 1982), application domain (Hickey and Davis, 2004), level of application support (Ratbe, et al., 2000).
	Complexity	Complexity (Davis, 1982), complexity of new information (Burns and Dennis, 1985), complexity of the application (Ratbe, et al., 2000), problem complexity (Hickey and Davis, 2004).
	Volume of information	Volume and complexity of new information (Burns and Dennis, 1985).
Task-possessed information	Comprehension / understanding	User task comprehension (Naumann, et al., 1980), existence of a well-understood model of the system (Davis, 1982), user task comprehension (Burns and Dennis, 1985), degree with which the application system is understood (Ratbe, et al., 2000), problem understanding (Hickey and Davis, 2004), knowledge of target domain (Tsumaki and Tamai, 2005).
	Experience	Experience with utilizing system and application (Davis, 1982), developer experience and user system experience (Ratbe, et al., 2000), level of experience, experience with the problem and solution domain (Hickey and Davis, 2004), experience developing similar systems (Tsumaki and Tamai, 2005).
	Other sources of information	Observable phenomena (Maiden and Rugg, 1996), existing system (Hickey and Davis, 2004), abundance of information and investigation of existing systems (Tsumaki and Tamai, 2005).

of the target domain). The authors were then able to classify seventeen techniques which differed in varying degrees across these two dimensions.

Fit and Requirements Determination Success

Whereas earlier contingency models of elicitation drew on reduction of project uncertainty as the logic for their performance effects (Davis, 1982;

Naumann, et al., 1980), the iteration developed by Hickey and Davis (2004) is largely atheoretical. The main proposition of this research is that systems development projects can be usefully conceptualized as situations requiring the successful processing of information to achieve their stated objectives. This statement is fully in accordance with the seminal work of Davis (1982) and Naumann, et al. (1980). However, where extant literature has focused on overall project uncertainty, this research incorporates the notion of equivocality to provide a more comprehensive understanding of the dynamics of the elicitation process. Also, departing from past research, this model distinguishes between sources of uncertainty and equivocality instead of considering only overall levels of each for the project, with the intention of providing a more specific matching of techniques to contingencies.

The application of information processing theory to information systems research is not novel (Barki, Rivard and Talbot, 2001; Premkumar, et al., 2003), although it has not been extensively developed in the IRD literature. Although early formulations, as discussed above, employed uncertainty as the tying force behind their models, neither this concept nor equivocality, which was suggested for inclusion by Fazlollahi and Tanniru (1991), have been the subject of theorizing beyond providing a conceptual linkage between project contingencies and elicitation approaches.

The matching logic employed in any contingency model is by necessity closely tied to the conceptualization of performance or success expected from high levels of fit. The main argument of information processing theory is organizations process information in order to reduce uncertainty and resolve equivocality to levels acceptable for successful performance of the task of interest (Daft and Lengel, 1986). However, the IRD literature has not yet converged on a commonly accepted definition of success, although several and somewhat similar conceptualizations have been proposed: requirements need to be consistent, accurate, complete and agreed upon by users and developers (Naumann, et al., 1980); correct and complete (Davis, 1982); consistent, correct, and unambiguous (Yadav, 1983); stable, correct, clear, adequate, unambiguous, and usable (Wallace, et al., 2004).

Other authors, most notably Browne and Pitts (2004; Pitts and Browne, 2004) have focused on analyst stopping behavior by studying the different heuristics analysts employ to reach successful conclusion of the elicitation session. To our knowledge, no such work at the level of the determination process as a whole has been conducted. Several researchers have, however, offered lists of requirements categories that are applicable to information systems in general, such as goals, processes, tasks, and information (Browne and Rogich, 2001; Browne and Pitts, 2004; Pitts and Browne, 2004); information requirements, process, behavior and problem frame understanding (Byrd, et al., 1992); behavior, process and data (Maiden and Rugg, 1996); or the NATURE model of problem domains (Maiden and Hare, 1998).

To summarize, by integrating past research described in this section with the conceptual framework of information processing theory it is possible to state, albeit at a very abstract level, that requirements determination success occurs when each type or category of requirement that must be present to properly describe any information system has been completely specified (e.g. uncertainty has been reduced to an acceptable level; includes the notions of correctness, completeness, accuracy, etc. as discussed above) and agreed upon by all relevant stakeholders (e.g. equivocality has been resolved such that multiple and conflicting interpretations about the system no longer exist). The development of a comprehensive framework modeling requirements determination success represents one fruitful area of further research.

The actual nature of requirements presents researchers with another interesting dilemma. Whereas researchers in this area have provided definitions of requirements, the distinction between natural and design science (March and Smith, 1995; March and Allen, 2007) conceptualizations of system requirements has not been fully articulated. Whereas in the former the role of the systems analysts is to discover the appropriate (accurate, complete, and correct, as noted above) requirements for the system under consideration, in the latter the task is one of creation of an agreed-upon set of requirements that describe the artifact that is being designed (March and Allen, 2007). Elements of both conceptualizations are present in current characterizations of requirements, such as those noted in the preceding paragraph, and in the work of others such as Pohl (1994). In his framework of the requirements engineering process, the author identified three different dimensions: specification, representation, and agreement. From this perspective, Pohl (1994) argues the output of a requirements stage process should be a complete specification of the proposed system, in a formalized language, such that interpretational problems due to the use of natural language may be minimized, and on which all relevant parties agree.

CONCLUSION

The most important contribution of this work lies in the provision of a theoretically-grounded logic to understand why different techniques would perform better in specific project situations. A common underlying structure emerged from the synthesis of several conceptual models of the technique selection process. This research program seeks to provide organizing frameworks for each of the main components of the research framework thus developed.

In the past, different authors have limited the conceptualization of these components to lists of contributing factors, but no comprehensive models to organize and understand the effects these issues have been elaborated. As a starting point, a conceptualization of task-related contingencies, employing the analyzability-variety framework from the organizational literature, was developed. The research model described in this work sets the stage of further examination of its components (e.g. contingencies, techniques, logic of fit and performance measure), answering the call for research posed by Alter and Browne (2005). Further research into the nature and impacts of the different communication obstacles is needed before they can be meaningfully incorporated into the set of project contingencies.

REFERENCES

Alter, S., and Browne, G. "A Broad View of Systems Analysis and Design: Implications for Research," Communications of the Association for Information Systems (15), 2005, pp. 981-999.

Barki, H., Rivard, S., and Talbot, J. "An Integrative Contingency Model of Software Project Risk Management," Journal of Management Information Systems (17:4), 2001, pp. 37-69.

Bensaou, M., and Venkatraman, N. "Configurations of Interorganizational Relationships: A Comparison between US and Japanese Automakers," Management Science (41:9), 1995, pp. 1471-1492.

Bostrom, R. and Thomas, B. "Achieving Excellence in Communications: A Key to Developing Complete, Accurate, and Shared Information Requirements", Special Interest Group on Computer Personnel Research Annual Conference, Charlottesville, VA, 1983.

Browne, G., and Rogich, M. "An Empirical Investigation of User Requirements Elicitation: Comparing the Effectiveness of Prompting Techniques," Journal of Management Information Systems (17:4), 2001, pp. 223-249.

Browne, G., and Pitts, M. "Stopping Rule Use During Information Search in Design Problems,"

Organizational Behavior and Human Decision Processes (95:2), 2004, pp. 208–224.

Browne, G., and Ramesh, V. "Improving Information Requirements Determination: A Cognitive Perspective," Information and Management (39:8), 2002, pp. 625-645.

Burns, R., and Dennis, A. "Selecting the Appropriate Application Development Methodology," ACM SIGMIS Database (17:1), 1985, pp. 19-23.

Byrd, T., Cossick, K., and Zmud, R. "A Synthesis of Research on Requirements Analysis and Knowledge Acquisition Techniques," MIS Quarterly (16:1), 1992, pp. 117-138.

Chang, A. "Work Time Model for Engineers", Journal of Construction Engineering Management (127:2), 2001, pp. 163-172.

Chang, A. and Chiu, S-H. "Nature of Engineering Consulting Projects", Journal of Management in Engineering (21:4), 2005, pp. 179-188.

Chang, A. and Ibbs, W. "System Model for Analyzing Design Productivity", Journal of Management in Engineering (22:1), 2006, pp. 27-34.

Chang, A., and Tien, C. "Quantifying Uncertainty and Equivocality in Engineering Projects," Construction Management & Economics (24:2), 2006, pp. 171-184.

Coughlan, J., and Macredie, R. "Effective Communication in Requirements Elicitation: A Comparison of Methodologies," Requirements Engineering (7), 2002, pp. 47-60.

Daft, R., and Lengel, R. "Organizational Information Requirements, Media Richness and Structural Design," Management Science (32:5), 1986, pp. 554-571.

Daft, R., and Macintosh, N. "A Tentative Exploration into the Amount and Equivocality of Information Processing in Organizational Work Units," Administrative Science Quarterly (26:2), 1981, pp. 207-224.

Daft, R. and Weick, K. "Toward a model of organizations as interpretation systems", Academy of Management Review (9:2), 1984, pp. 284-295.

Davis, G. "Strategies for Information Requirements Determination," IBM Systems Journal (21:1), 1982, pp. 4-30.

Duggan, E. "Generating Systems Requirements with Facilitated Group Techniques," Human-Computer Interaction (18), 2003, pp. 373-394.

Egelhoff, W. "Information-processing theory and the multinational corporation", in *Organization Theory and the Multinational Corporation*, 2nd edition, Ghoshal, S. and Westney, E. editors, 2005.

Fazlollahi, B., and Tanniru, M. "Selecting a Requirement Determination Methodology-Contingency Approach Revisited," Information and Management (21:5), 1991, pp. 291-303.

Galbraith, J. "Organization design: an information processing view", Interfaces (4:3), 1974, pp. 28-36.

Galbraith, J. *Organization Design*. Addison-Wesley, Reading, MA, 1977.

Guinan, P., and Bostrom, R. "Development of Computer-Based Information Systems: A Communication Framework," The DATA BASE for Advances in Information Systems (17:3), 1986, pp. 3-16.

Hickey, A., and Davis, A. "A Tale of Two Ontologies: The Basis for Systems Analysis Technique Selection," Proceedings of the Ninth Americas Conference on Information Systems), 2003.

Hickey, A., and Davis, A. "A Unified Model of Requirements Elicitation," Journal of Management Information Systems (20:4), 2004, pp. 65-84.

Iversen, J., Mathiassen, L. and Nielsen. "Managing Risk in Software Process Improvement: An Action Research Approach", MIS Quarterly (28:3), 2004, pp. 395-433.

Johnson, L., and Johnson, N. "Knowledge Elicitation Involving Teachback Interviewing," In Knowledge Acquisition for Expert Systems, A. Kidd (ed.) Plenum Press, New York, NY, 1987, pp. 91-108.

Keller, R. "Technology-Information Processing Fit and the Performance of R&D Project Groups: A Test of Contingency Theory," The Academy of Management Journal (37:1), 1994, pp. 167-179.

Lawrence, P. and Lorsch, J. *Organization and Environment.* Irwin. Homewood, IL, 1969.

Maiden, N., and Hare, M. "Problem Domain Categories in Requirements Engineering," International Journal of Human-Computer Studies (49:3), 1998, pp. 281-304.

Maiden, N., and Rugg, G. "ACRE: Selecting Methods for Requirements Acquisition," Software Engineering Journal (11:3), 1996, pp. 183-192.

March, S. and Allen, G. "Challenges in Requirements Engineering: A Research Agenda for Conceptual Modeling", Science of Design – Design Requirements Workshop. Cleveland, OH, 2007.

March, S. and Smith, G. "Design and Natural Science Research on Information Technology", Decision Support Systems (15), 1995, pp. 251-266.

Marakas, G., and Elam, J. "Semantic Structuring in Analyst Acquisition and Representation of Facts in Requirements Analysis," Information Systems Research (9:1), 1998, pp. 37-63.

Mathiassen, L., Saarinen, T., Tuunanen, T. and Rossi, M. "A Contingency Model for Requirements Development", Journal of the Association of Information Systems (8:11), 2007, pp. 569-597.

Montezemi, A., and Conrath, D. "The Use of Cognitive Mapping for Information Requirement Analysis," MIS Quarterly (10:1), 1986, pp. 45-56.

Naumann, I., Davis, G., and McKeen, I. "Determining Information System Requirements: A Contingency Method for Selection of a Requirements Assurance Strategy," The Journal of Systems and Software (1), 1980, pp. 273-281.

Nidumolu, S. "The Effect of Coordination and Uncertainty on Software Project Performance: Residual Performance Risk as an Intervening Variable," Information Systems Research (6:3), 1995, pp. 191-219.

Pitts, M. and Browne, G. "Stopping Behavior of Systems Analysts During Information Requirements Elicitation", Journal of Management Information Systems (21:1), 2004, pp. 203-226.

Pohl, K. "The Three Dimensions of Requirements Engineering", Information Systems (19:3), 1994, pp. 243-258.

Premkumar, G., Ramamurthy, K., and Saunders, C. "Information Processing View of Organizations: An Exploratory Examination of Fit in the Context of Interorganizational Relationships," Journal of Management Information Systems (22:1), 2003, pp. 257-298.

Ratbe, D., King, W., and Kim, Y. "The Fit Between Project Characteristics and Application Development Methodologies: A Contingency Approach," Journal of Computer Information Systems, 2000, pp. 26-33.

Rice, R. "Task Analyzability, Use of New Media, and Effectiveness: A Multi-Site Exploration of Media Richness", Organization Science (3:4), 1992, pp. 475-500.

Rockart, J. "Chief Executives Define their Own Data Needs," Harvard Business Review (57:2), 1979, pp. 81-93.

Schmidt, R., Lyytinen, K., Keil, M., and Cule, P. "Identifying Software Project Risks: An International Delphi Study," Journal of Management Information Systems (17:4), 2001, pp. 5-36.

Simon, H. "The New Science of Management Decision", in *The Shape of Automation for Men and Management*, Harper & Row. New York, NY, 1965, pp. 57-79.

Taggart Jr, W., and Tharp, M. "A Survey of Information Requirements Analysis Techniques," ACM Computing Surveys (9:4), 1977, pp. 273-290.

Tsumaki, T., and Tamai, T. "A Framework for Matching Requirements Engineering Techniques to Project Characteristics and Situation Changes," Proceedings of SREP (5), 2005, pp. 44-58.

Tushman, M.L. "Technical Communication in R & D Laboratories: The Impact of Project Work Characteristics," The Academy of Management Journal (21:4), 1978, pp. 624-645.

Tushman, M. and Nadler, D. "Information processing as an integrating concept in organizational design", Academy of Management Review (3:3), 1978, pp. 613-624.

Valusek, J., and Fryback, D. "Information Requirements Determination: Obstacles Within, Among and Between Participants," Proceedings of the International Conference on Information Systems), 1985, pp. 103-111.

Van de Ven, A., and Delbecq, A. "A Task Contingent Model of Work-Unit Structure," Administrative Science Quarterly (19:2), 1974, pp. 183-197.

Wallace, L., Keil, M., and Rai, A. "How Software Project Risk Affects Project Performance: An Investigation of the Dimensions of Risk and an Exploratory Model," Decision Sciences (35:2), 2004, pp. 289-321.

Weick, K. *The Social Psychology of Organizing*, Addison-Wesley. Reading, MA, 1979.

Yadav, S. "Determining an Organization's Information Requirements: A State of the Art Survey," The DATA BASE for Advances in Information Systems (14:3), 1983, pp. 3-20.

Zmud, R., Anthony, W., and Stair, R. "The Use of Mental Imagery to Facilitate Information Identification in Requirements Analysis," Journal of Management Information Systems (9:4), 1993, pp. 175-191.

ENDNOTES

1. This chapter is a revised version of a paper originally presented at the *13th Americas Conference on Information Systems* held at Keystone, CO (2007).
2. The use of the term *matching* herein is intended to convey a high level of fit between two concepts and does not represent an argument for a particular conceptualization of fit.
3. Here *task* refers to the organizational task for which requirements are being gathered and a new system development proposed, and not to the task of developing the system itself.

Chapter VI
IT Value of Software Development:
A Multi-Theoretic Perspective

VenuGopal Balijepally
Prairie View A&M University, USA

Sridhar Nerur
University of Texas at Arlington, USA

RadhaKanta Mahapatra
University of Texas at Arlington, USA

ABSTRACT

Software development in organizations is evolving and increasingly taking a socio-technical hue. While empirical research guided by common sense reasoning has informed researchers and the software community in the past, the increasing social character of software development provides us with the context and the motivation to provide theoretical underpinnings to our empirical work. In this chapter we sample three theoretical domains that could serve our empirical research efforts: social capital, organizational learning and knowledge based view of the firm. We illustrate the utility of these theoretical perspectives by articulating a research model that captures the IT value created by software development teams practicing different methodologies.

INTRODUCTION

The field of software development has undergone significant changes in recent years. A hyper-competitive business environment characterized by change and uncertainty has prompted the software community to evolve new ways of building software. The emerging methodologies follow an evolutionary delivery model (Gilb, 1987) that allows developers to adapt to changing requirements. This is counter to the traditional plan-driven approach that uses a linear process in accomplishing the tasks involved in software development. In such an approach, an enormous amount of time and effort are spent in gathering requirements and evolving specifications with a view to preparing for all foreseeable changes during the lifecycle of the product. In contrast, emerging approaches such as agile methodologies rely on short iterative cycles with continuous stakeholder feedback and frequent planning to cope with and leverage change (Nerur, Mahapatra, and Mangalaraj, 2005).

Agile methodologies have attracted a lot of attention in the recent past. This new approach differs considerably from traditional software development in many ways. Foremost, there is an increased emphasis on self-organizing teams that enjoy greater latitude in goal-setting and decision-making with regard to setting priorities, deadlines, etc. Team members are encouraged to play multiple roles, such as developer, architect and analyst. A shared understanding and vision of the evolving product is facilitated by practices such as joint code ownership, role rotation and reflection workshops. This is in contrast to specialized roles assigned to developers in traditional methodologies. In the agile approach, specifications evolve through constant dialogue and feedback between developers and customers, while in the traditional approach, extensive specifications gathered up-front from customers guide the development process. Thus, there is a perceptible shift from a hierarchical, process driven, and command-and-control based approach to one that emphasizes people-orientation, collaboration, and leadership (Highsmith, 2003).

The changes in methodologies highlight the underlying transformation of software development from a technical enterprise to a more socio-technical endeavor. The lack of theory-driven empirical work in software development may be attributed to the emphasis that was placed on technical aspects of software development. Theoretical grounding of empirical research is still not considered an essential requirement, especially in the software engineering domain. Though there is some evidence of increasing awareness of theoretical issues (Hannay, Sjoberg, and Dyba, 2007; Nerur and Balijepally, 2007), the dominant thinking is predicated on the primacy of common sense reasoning over generalizable theory (Lindblom, 1987). While use of theory is taken for granted in various business disciplines, including several areas of IS research, software development research is still grappling with the issue of whether theory should be used (Hannay et al., 2007). The current social "makeover" of software development provides us with the context and the opportunity to refocus empirical research in software development towards theory building and testing. The centrality and importance accorded to teams and collaboration among team members by emerging methodologies affords an opportunity to draw on the extensive body of knowledge in organizational and management theory.

The primary objective of this chapter is to demonstrate the applicability of theoretical perspectives in software development research. One of the critical problems that confront software managers today is the choice of methodologies. This poses an interesting research problem that can be theoretically investigated. Keeping this in mind, we articulate three theoretical streams, namely social capital, knowledge-based view of the firm, and organizational learning. Traditionally, human capital is considered as the main resource of a software team that produces valued outcomes. While the resource value of relationships of members from within and across teams is understood by the software community at an intuitive level, the current trend towards increasing socialization of software development calls for capturing such resource value of social relationships in more explicit ways. We bring in social capital as a new explanatory factor to capture such social dynamics of software development in general and agile development in particular. Further, we propose a research model, informed by these theories, that explores the IT value created by software development teams. While many researchers have focused on the differences between agile and plan-driven approaches, or on the differences between pairs and individuals in software development, there has hardly been any effort to understand how these approaches create value by emphasizing different knowledge outcomes. Such an understanding should help software practice in making more informed methodological choices. The proposed model is a small step in this direction.

The next section describes the three theoretical perspectives that can potentially inform research on software development challenges. This is followed by an articulation of the research model and the propositions. Finally, conclusions are drawn.

THEORETICAL PERSPECTIVES

Three theoretical perspectives of potential interest to software development research are briefly described below.

Social Capital

Social capital is an interesting theoretical lens attracting increasing research attention in sociology and management literatures. Social capital is defined as "the sum of the actual and potential resources embedded within, available through, and derived from the network of relationships possessed by an individual or social unit" (Nahapiet and Ghoshal, 1998). Traditionally human capital embedded in the team in terms of skills and abilities of members is considered a critical success factor for software development teams. Social capital theory seeks to position network of relationships as another form of capital that provides significant benefits to the individual or the collectivity in the conduct of social affairs. Unlike human capital, which rests in the individuals, social capital is embedded in the networks of mutual acquaintances and relationships of the individual, group or the organization (Bourdieu, 1986; Coleman, 1988; Putnam, 1993). At the level of collectivity, group social capital is conceptualized as the resources available to a group through its "members' social relationships within the social structure of the group itself, as well as in the broader formal and informal structure of the organization" (Oh, Labianca, and Chung, 2006). As a meta-concept, social capital at the levels of both individual and the collectivity encompasses both the resources and the structure of the network conduits (Nahapiet and Ghoshal, 1998; Oh et al., 2006). Social capital lens could be very useful to explain several IS phenomena such as software development, IS outsourcing, organizational knowledge management, and IT-based inter-organizational networks (Balijepally, Mahapatra, and Nerur, 2004).

Organizational Learning

Organizational learning is a mature theoretical stream of enduring value used in several research domains. According to this view, learning is the process of acquiring, interpreting or distributing information, that changes the range of potential behaviors for the entity (Huber, 1991). For Argyris, learning is about detecting and correcting mismatches or errors. Learning occurs when a match is produced for the first time between intentions and actuality, that is genuinely new to the actors producing it (Argyris, 1996). In organizational learning, the entity involved is the organization as against the individual. Organization learning is "the process of improving actions through better knowledge and understanding." It leads to cognitive systems, associations and memories, developed and shared by organizational members (Fiol and Lyles, 1985). Learning in organizations may be conceptualized as adaptive learning and generative learning. Adaptive learning occurs when an organization seeks to accomplish performance requirements through active shaping of actions and responses based on feedback from previous actions. When the organization starts questioning its values and assumptions and seeks "new ways of looking at the world" in its actions and behaviors, the resulting learning is considered as generative learning. While adaptive learning underscores coping behaviors, generative learning is about creating (Senge, 1990). This has parallels to Argyris's single loop and double loop learning (Argyris, 1977, 1996) and Fiol and Lyles's low level and high level learning (Fiol and Lyles, 1985).

Deutero-learning, *meta-learning* and *planned learning* are other forms of organizational learning articulated in literature (Argyris and Schon, 1978). *Deutero-learning* is a largely unconscious continuous behavioral adaptation of relationships in organizational settings based primarily on communication patterns. Such learning could have both positive and negative effect on the relationships in organizations (Visser, 2007). *Meta-learning* on the other hand is considered as a deliberate cognitive reflection and inquiry into single-loop and double-loop learning processes, which could be at both individual and group levels in organizations. This is an intermittent activity in organizations which could largely be organized for yielding positive benefits (Argyris, 2003). *Planned learning* refers to this organization and institutionalization of meta-learning in organizations through creation and maintenance of appropriate structures, systems and routines (Visser, 2007).

Knowledge Based View of the Firm

Knowledge based view is based on the notion that knowledge is a valuable organizational resource, and the firm is a dynamic, evolving, quasi-autonomous system of knowledge and application (Spender, 1996a). Based on Polanyi, a distinction is made between two forms of organizational knowledge – explicit and tacit (Polanyi, 1966). Explicit knowledge is the codified knowledge that could be transmitted through formal systematic language. Tacit knowledge on the other hand is "deeply rooted in action, commitment, and involvement in a specific context" (Nonaka, 1994). It is therefore intangible and cannot easily be articulated. The tacit and explicit knowledge types could be at both individual and group levels, the aggregate of which constitutes the intellectual capital for the collectivity or the organization (Nahapiet and Ghoshal, 1998). Knowledge based view conceives organizations as innovating and knowledge creating entities where exchange, combination and dynamic interaction of explicit and tacit knowledge at both individual and aggregate level creates new knowledge. Innovation is typically viewed as "a process in which the organization creates and defines problems and then actively develops new knowledge to solve them" (Nonaka, 1994).

The epistemological dimensions of knowledge (tacit versus explicit) coupled with the ontological dimensions (individual versus collective) yield four types of knowledge: embrained (explicit knowledge at individual level), embodied (tacit knowledge at individual level), encoded (explicit knowledge at the collective level) and embedded (tacit knowledge at the collective level) (Collins, 1993; Lam, 2000). This has parallels to the four knowledge types articulated by Spender: conscious, automatic, objectified and collective (Spender, 1996b). Embrained (conscious) knowledge is the formal theoretical knowledge held by the individual which is highly dependent upon the individual's conceptual and cognitive abilities. Embodied (automatic) knowledge, on the other hand is the individual knowledge based on abstract theoretical reasoning. It is involuntary and is rooted in action. Its generation and use do not fit into any conscious decision-making processes (Spender, 1996b). Encoded (objectified) knowledge also called the "information" is the knowledge codified into manuals, recipes, blueprints and written procedures. As an enabler of centralization and control, this contributes to predictability of outputs and behaviors in organizations. Finally, embedded (collective) knowledge is based on shared beliefs and understanding (Lam, 2000). It is relation-specific, contextual, socially created, and shared by the "communities of practice" (Brown and Duguid, 1991).

THEORETICAL MODEL AND RESEARCH PROPOSITIONS

The focus of the theoretical model developed here is on the software development project team undertaking a software project using traditional plan-driven methodology or one of the agile methodologies. In case of large projects, this could be a project team working on an identifiable project subcomponent. We adopt social capital theory along with knowledge management and organizational learning perspectives to examine the IT value created by the software team. Figure 1 showcases the research model. We view the network of relationships among members of a software development team as a form of social capital for the team. This network of relationships could be from within the team or across project teams within the organization or even beyond the organization. This is in addition to the human capital available to the focal team in terms of skills and abilities of its members and captures the resources potentially available to the team and its members through the network of relationships.

We argue that software development is a knowledge creating activity, the knowledge outcomes of which are both tacit and explicit. IT artifacts such as plans and designs, test cases, data models, data flow diagrams, source code and documentation exemplify explicit knowledge created by the team (Boehm and Turner, 2004). The tacit knowledge generated could be in the form of mental schemas of the system and know-how regarding the technologies used and the business context. This tacit knowledge created could be at the level of both individual (embodied

Figure 1. Value creation in agile and plan-driven software development teams

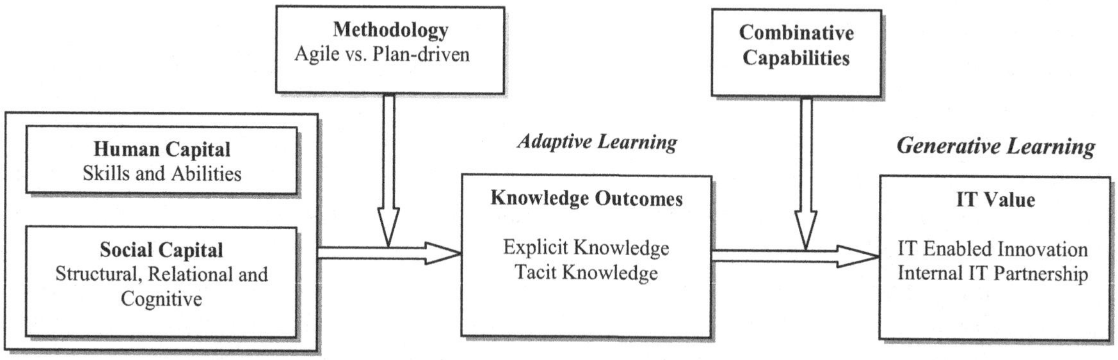

knowledge) and group (embedded knowledge). It is the combination of these knowledge types that exemplifies the knowledge outcomes of software development effort.

We consider the two-step process of organizational learning as underpinning the value derived from software development activity in project teams. In a recent article Ye and Agarwal adopted a similar two stage learning process to articulate the value derived from strategic outsourcing partnerships (Ye and Agarwal, 2003). The adaptive learning for the software development team involves intuition, interpretation, and integration (Crossan, Lane, and White, 1999) of team knowledge resources derived from human and social capital in creating the design artifacts, the software and the new knowledge that contributes to the knowledge stock of the team. The generative learning occurs when new ways of looking at things and recombining existing knowledge stock and capabilities take effect to create higher valued outcomes for the team and the organization. This is consistent with capabilities integration articulated by Grant (Grant, 1996b) and involves concepts such as information interpretation and distribution and organizational memory (Huber, 1991; Ye and Agarwal, 2003). Table 1 summarizes the theoretical perspectives underlying the IT value of software development. The next few sections showcase propositions related to the model.

Knowledge Creation in Software Teams

Software development is a dynamic knowledge creation endeavor wherein the business and technical knowledge of team members in both tacit and explicit forms is exchanged and combined in

Table 1. Summary of theoretical perspectives explaining IT value in software development

	Social Capital Theory	Organizational Learning	Knowledge-based View
Main idea	There is resource value to the network of relationships of individuals	Organizational learning is the process of improving actions through better knowledge and understanding.	Knowledge is a valuable organizational resource, and knowledge creation is a critical value adding activity in organizations
Core Constructs	Structural, relational and cognitive dimensions of network of relationships of individuals	Adaptive learning occurs through active shaping of actions and responses based on feedback from previous actions. Generative learning results from questioning existing values and assumptions and seeking new ways	Explicit knowledge is the codified knowledge that could be transmitted through formal systematic language. Tacit knowledge is "deeply rooted in action, commitment, and involvement in a specific context
Applicability to Software Development Context	The resource value of network of relationships of members of software development teams complement the human capital of project teams in creating knowledge outcomes	Adaptive learning during software development results in knowledge outcomes both explicit and tacit while generative learning contributes to higher knowledge outcomes such as IT enabled innovation and internal IT partnerships	Software development is a knowledge creation endeavor where the outcomes are both tacit and explicit The knowledge creation processes of socialization and internationalization are in greater play in agile methodologies leading to higher tacit knowledge outcomes while combination and externalization facilitated to a higher degree in plan-driven methodologies help create higher levels of explicit knowledge

complex ways to generate new knowledge some of which remains tacit within the team while the explicit form of the knowledge manifests in the software product and the documentation produced by the team. All knowledge creation occurs through the two generic processes of combination and exchange (Moran and Ghoshal, 1996). In a software development team, the knowledge resources of the individuals are combined to create the various IT artifacts and the software. There is exchange of information and knowledge between various members of the team such as between users and systems analysts, systems analysts and developers, developers and testers. The increased emphasis placed by agile methodologies on collaboration and self-organization among team members as well as on role rotation is likely to enhance the quality and intensity of knowledge exchanged.

Combination is the process of reconfiguring, sorting, adding, and conceptualizing existing explicit knowledge to create new explicit knowledge. It involves reconfiguring of existing information (explicit knowledge) through, adding, sorting, re-contextualizing and reappraising to provide new insights (Nonaka, 1994). In a software development team, explicit knowledge of analysts, developers and users is combined to produce new explicit knowledge through articulation to one self and to the team and applying to the problem context to create new explicit IT artifacts. Internalization is the process of converting explicit knowledge into tacit knowledge, which is akin to the conventional notion of 'learning.' Action or 'learning by doing' helps in the internalization process. Through trial and error, ideas and concepts are articulated and reconfigured till a more concrete form emerges (Nonaka, 1994). Internalization occurs at the individual level when explicit knowledge available such as user requirements and technical documentation and the resultant interactions during actual software development are absorbed as know-how.

Existing tacit knowledge of individuals and the team is converted into new explicit and tacit knowledge through the processes of externalization and socialization respectively Experience is considered critical to the transfer of tacit knowledge. The externalization mode triggers through a series of interactions and dialogue between software team members. Metaphors typically play an important role in articulating otherwise difficult to articulate individuals' perspectives and technical know-how. Being situated in practice, tacit knowledge of the software development team members is externalized while working on the problem at hand. Experienced programmers and systems analysts could externalize, through demonstration to other members of the team, tacit knowledge inherent in activities such as abstracting object designs, creating and using design patterns, identifying classes from the generic and organizational class libraries, using appropriate control structures and debugging techniques. Socialization is the process through which existing tacit knowledge of individuals is converted to new tacit knowledge. Socialization occurs through interaction between developers as in apprenticeship. Knowledge transfer by socialization could occur even without the help of language, through observation, imitation and practice. The shared experience during software development provides the context for people to transfer their thinking processes (Nonaka, 1994). The amount of knowledge creation through socialization in software development teams is however dependent upon the methodology used.

HUMAN CAPITAL AND TEAM KNOWLEDGE OUTCOMES

The human capital of the software development team, reflected in the skills and abilities of software developers, is an important factor determining the effectiveness of all aspects of software development irrespective of the methodology used. Skills and abilities reflect the existing knowledge resources inherent in the members of the team. These skills include programming ability and technical domain knowledge. For systems analysts, generalist skills (Benbasat, Dexter, and Mantha, 1980; Green, 1989) and technical skills that complement business skills (Todd, McKeen, and Gallupe, 1995) become important. For customers or users who may be part of systems development team either full time or part time, the ability to understand and articulate the business requirements becomes important. Unsuitable customer representation is a known project risk factor (Boehm and Turner, 2004). High ability developers, analysts and testers with higher levels of tacit skills are better equipped to work on the various explicit knowledge artifacts such as requirement specs, architecture plans and existing code artifacts in producing higher explicit and tacit outcomes by pooling their knowledge and skills through the four generic processes of knowledge conversion, that is combination, internalization, externalization and socialization.

We therefore argue that higher skills and abilities of software developers (human capital) in software development team contribute to higher knowledge outcomes, both tacit and explicit.

Proposition 1: The human capital embedded in a software development team is positively related to both explicit and tacit knowledge outcomes of the team

SOCIAL CAPITAL AND TEAM KNOWLEDGE CREATION

Social capital is a multidimensional construct with three analytically distinct but related facets: structural, relational and cognitive. Structural dimension of social capital refers to the overall pattern of connections between actors. In a software development team the networks of relationships could be both internal and external to the team. While ties between the members of the team capture the internal structure, the nature of relationships with other project teams within the organization or even external to the organization constitute external network structures. Strength/weakness of ties (both internal and external) and the resource content of these networks (e.g., network heterogeneity) are some structural aspects of social capital. (Nahapiet and Ghoshal, 1998). The relational dimension of social capital refers to personal relationships such as respect or friendship individuals develop among themselves through a history of interactions that help fulfill different social motives such as approval, sociability, and prestige. Trust and identification capture the relational aspects of social capital. The cognitive dimension refers to the resources that provide shared representations, interpretations, and systems of meanings among parties (Nahapiet and Ghoshal, 1998). Shared vision and transactive memory systems capture this dimension of social capital. Although individual dimensions of social capital are of immense research interest, in the interest of brevity, social capital is treated as an aggregated construct in deriving propositions in the rest of the chapter.

As conceptualized in Figure 1, we argue that the social and human capital embedded in a software development team yield knowledge outcomes and IT value through a combination of adaptive and generative learning. Social capital, conceptualized as the actual and potential resources available through the network of relationships of the focal actor, signifies the resource value of relationships. In software development project teams, we view the network of relationships of members of a software development team as a form of social capital for the team. This network of relationships enable access to potential resources that supplement the human capital available in the team and contribute to valued team outcomes by fostering adaptive and allocative efficiencies (Nahapiet and Ghoshal, 1998). Allocative efficiency results from improvement in information flow in the social network of the team members through reduction in structural redundancies in the network (Burt, 1997).

During software development, analysts and developers frequently look for advice and tips while working with new technologies. The non-redundant information available through their network contacts within and outside the team is a critical input to the software task at hand. Such information may provide opportunities to improvise during the software development process. Social capital facilitates such information flow by reducing the transaction costs for information retrieval (Putnam, 1993). Adaptive efficiencies result from the cooperative behavior encouraged by social capital that results in creativity and learning (Nahapiet and Ghoshal, 1998). The new information and knowledge available and accessed from the network of relationships of team members result in superior software products. Thus, social capital potentially facilitates creation of higher levels of both tacit and explicit knowledge.

Proposition 2 - The social capital embedded in a software development team is positively related to both explicit and tacit knowledge outcomes of the team

INTERACTION OF METHODOLOGY ON HUMAN CAPITAL AND SOCIAL CAPITAL

Software development teams using plan-driven methodologies perform elaborate requirements gathering to develop complete, consistent, traceable and testable specifications. Big upfront planning is used to control change. User involvement is mainly in the initial phases of development. While plans are evolved to guide development and control change, communication among developers is primarily through extensive documentation. Thus the traditional plan driven methodologies are predisposed to producing explicit knowledge artifacts such as designs, plans and documentation that serve as the means of communication. Creation of these artifacts results primarily from combination and externalization processes. The traceability and verifiability imperatives of plan-driven development entail externalization of tacit knowledge of the developers into explicit forms. Correspondingly, there is less emphasis on tacit knowledge with fewer opportunities for facilitating processes such as internalization and socialization that are essential for creation of new tacit knowledge.

Agile methodologies follow a minimalist approach to requirement gathering and documentation. Only some architectural designs and project vision documents are prepared in advance that guide developers. Participating users articulate the requirements in the form of user stories and prioritize them. The competence and knowledge of team members are used to cope with emergent problems (Highsmith, 2003). This is consistent with the idea that "communities of interaction contribute to the amplification and development of new knowledge" (Nonaka, 1994). With the primacy accorded to delivery of working code at frequent intervals, shared vision and shared understanding of project goals and objectives is emphasized to incorporate changes as they occur (Boehm and Turner, 2004). With collocated team members and a readily accessible user representative, the need for externalization processes to convert tacit knowledge into more explicit forms is reduced. Instead a climate for generating higher levels of tacit knowledge is fostered through processes such as socialization and internalization. There is thus substantially higher level of tacit knowledge (both embodied and embedded) generated in agile teams as compared to plan-driven software development teams. These arguments yield the following propositions.

Proposition 3a: The human capital and social capital embedded in a software development team produce higher levels of explicit knowledge when using plan-driven methodologies than when using agile methodologies

Proposition 3b: The human capital and social capital embedded in a software development team produce higher levels of tacit knowledge when using agile methodologies than when using plan-driven methodologies

IT VALUE CREATION THROUGH GENERATIVE LEARNING

The knowledge outcomes in the software development team underpin the organizational IT value created. The knowledge when it undergoes a process of recombination and integration with the existing knowledge and capabilities, leads to valued outcomes for the team and the organization (Grant, 1996a; Kogut and Zander, 1992). The IT value created may be conceptualized in terms of generative learning. Generative learning typically occurs when, based on exigencies, people start questioning the preset conditions and taken for granted assumptions. It involves changes in the underlying governing values or master programs that lead to changes in action (Argyris, 1977, 1996; Senge, 1990). Such learning outcomes enhance the human and social capital of the team and strengthen organizational capabilities for the future. We conceptualize that the generative learning for the team and the organization is reflected in the strengthened internal IT partnership and IT enabled innovation (Ye and Agarwal, 2003). We argue that knowledge outcomes interact with the combinative capabilities of the team in creating IT value through generative learning.

TEAM KNOWLEDGE OUTCOMES AND IT ENABLED INNOVATION

IT enabled innovation is the deployment of IT for the creation of new products and services, new forms of organization, or for exploring new market opportunities (Agarwal and Sambamurthy, 2002). Innovation, IT enabled or otherwise, is an important organizational capability that contributes to competitive advantage enjoyed by a firm. As any organizational innovation provides competitive advantage for a finite period before competitors catch up, continuous innovation through cannibalization of existing products and technologies is the mantra for organizations to survive and thrive in a competitive marketplace. Contribution of knowledge to creating and sustaining organizational innovation is well documented in knowledge management literature (Grant, 1996a, 1996b).

The knowledge outcomes of a software development team could spur IT-enabled innovation in complex ways. The IT artifact which personifies explicit knowledge may be used in novel ways not originally conceived by the software team. The knowledge gained during a systems development effort could help create new software products or services by the focal unit and the IT. For example, a software team based on its knowledge gained from a system development/implementation effort could provide consulting services on related matters to other teams within or even outside the organization. In the presence of generative learning, when a software team is able to come up with new ways of applying the knowledge gained to current or new problems, such efforts are expected to result in greater IT-enabled innovation. Thus,

Proposition 4: The knowledge outcomes of software development team are positively related to its IT enabled innovation

TEAM KNOWLEDGE OUTCOMES AND INTERNAL IT PARTNERSHIP

Having an effective relationship between IT and business in organizations is considered a key requirement for deriving IT value (Reich and Benbasat, 2000). Appreciating the complementarity of mutual contributions to the organizational value is a key to nurturing such partnerships. Internal partnership between line managers and IT managers and specialists helps an organization in deriving higher strategic benefits from IT resources and investments. Such partnerships foster harmonious relationships between IT and business which enhances mutual trust and confidence and even improves the overall standing of IT within the organization. Having internal IT-business partnership constitutes IT value as the success of any IT initiative is critically dependent upon the convergence of business and technology (Nambisan, Agarwal, and Tanniru, 1999).

Knowledge outcomes of software development contribute to fostering IT-business partnerships for the focal team in important ways. Higher levels of tacit and explicit knowledge outcomes enhance the visibility of the team and its contributions to the IT unit and the business. The explicit knowledge artifacts such as documentation help ease communication gaps between the team, IT unit and the business. The business customers carrying rich tacit knowledge from their involvement with the software development team become ambassadors of IT in nurturing and cementing the IT-business partnership. The boundary spanning activities of these business customers not only provides valuable resources to the focal unit and IT during the systems development effort, but also opens up innovative collaboration possibilities. The communication and interaction developed with business during the systems development effort also increases the responsiveness of focal unit and the IT to future business requirements. Thus,

Proposition 5: The knowledge outcomes of a software development team is positively related to its internal IT business partnership

INTERACTION OF TEAM KNOWLEDGE OUTCOMES AND COMBINATIVE CAPABILITIES

Argyris and Schon originally enunciated that a performance gap is a necessary condition for first and second order organizational learning (Argyris and Schon, 1978). Other researchers identified two additional necessary conditions (Duncan and Weiss, 1979; Huber, 1991). First, the organizational members should have the motivation, ability, and opportunity to resolve the perceived performance gap for the organization. Second the first and second order learning by individual members must be externalized or translated from the individuals' tacit knowledge into an appropriate useful form (Arthur and Aiman-Smith, 2001). Combinative capability of software development team is a factor that could potentially moderate the relationship between knowledge outcomes and IT value created by the team.

Combinative capability is the intersection of an entity's capability to exploit its current knowledge to create new opportunities (Kogut and Zander, 1992). Innovation and new learning are results of an entity's combinative capabilities to create new knowledge and applications from its existing pool of knowledge. Kogut and Zander provide illustrations of such abilities at the individual level and demonstrate its utility at the organizational level (Kogut and Zander, 1992). We conceptualize combinative capabilities in our model at the team level to show the generative learning outcomes of its interaction with knowledge outcomes of software team. The combinative capabilities comprise system capabilities, coordination capabilities, and socialization capabilities (Van Den Bosch, Volberda, and De Boer, 1999). System capabilities include the various explicitly laid down policies, procedures, manuals that provide direction in routine situations and help in the integration of explicit knowledge. They help in reducing the need for communication and coordination while tackling every day problem situations. Such system capabilities foster *meta-learning* (deliberate cognitive reflection and inquiry into adaptive and generative learning processes) through *planned learning* (institutionalization of meta-learning) initiatives (Visser, 2007). Creation of higher levels of new knowledge and innovation is determined by the combinative abilities of the focal unit and existing knowledge stock. In software development the combinative capability of the focal team include system capabilities to codify knowledge and experience to provide future direction, coordination capabilities to manage the project and socialization capabilities to interact with the stakeholders within and outside the focal unit. In software development teams high levels of this ability could determine whether the knowledge outcomes created by the team result in higher IT value for the team and by extension to the organization. This leads us to the last proposition:

Proposition 6: The strength of the positive relationship between knowledge outcomes of a software development team and IT value is positively moderated by the focal team's combinative capabilities[1]

FUTURE TRENDS

Among the contemporary issues in software development, agile methodologies have attracted significant interest from both practitioners and academics alike. For the field of software development, which has historically evolved under the paradigmatic spell of plan-driven approaches, agile methodologies represent a refreshingly new world view of things. Although there are striking differences in the philosophies underlying the two methodologies, software community is veering round to the view that each methodology has its unique strengths and could be more appropriate to certain contexts. The two approaches are therefore likely to coexist and benefit from the cross-pollination of ideas and best practices.

As software development research has long remained a-theoretical, especially in the software engineering domain, the current transformation of software development into a socio-technical endeavor offers a unique opportunity to develop sound theoretical underpinnings. For instance, several ad-hoc principles and practices enunciated in different methodologies need to be examined individually and in combination through theoretical lenses to identify the contexts and organizational settings which offer best fit for valued project outcomes. With offshoring of software development remaining a persistent trend, tailoring of methodologies for global software projects involving virtual teams separated by time and space, offers a wealth of issues begging for theory driven research inquiry. Examining the appropriateness of different methodologies and individual best practices based on project characteristics, organizational culture, personality and abilities of developers is another promising area which can benefit from theory driven research, especially with insights from management and other social disciplines. These are just a few exciting research opportunities waiting to be explored through theoretical lenses that could benefit future software practice in important ways. It is imperative that the academic community respond to the current social makeover of software development by resolving to undertake theoretical makeover of their research inquiry.

CONCLUSION

Theoretical foundations of empirical research in software development are not very robust. Given the changing nature of the field, there is ample opportunity to draw on the extensive corpus of knowledge in organizational and management theory to address myriad issues. This chapter examines the applicability of three very popular theoretical expositions to understand the benefits of social capital that accrue to software development teams using agile versus traditional plan-driven methodologies. We argue that software development is a knowledge creating activity where human capital and social capital embedded in a software team work to create knowledge outcomes, both tacit and explicit. The relative extent of knowledge outcomes is contingent upon the methodology used, with agile teams producing higher tacit knowledge and traditional plan-driven teams creating higher explicit knowledge outcomes. Drawing from the organizational learning literature, we argue that the adaptive learning of the software team results in knowledge outcomes, while generative learning leads to IT value for the team and the organization. By developing a robust model to investigate software development using different methodologies, we have demonstrated the value of applying widely accepted theories to software development. In addition we articulated a few research ideas on software development, which could benefit from such theory driven inquiry.

Note: An earlier version of this chapter appeared in the Proceedings of the Thirteenth Americas Conference on Information Systems, Key Stone, Colorado, 2007.

REFERENCES

Agarwal, R., & Sambamurthy, V. (2002). Principles and Models for Organizing IT Function. *MIS Quarterly Executive, 1*(1), 1-16.

Argyris, C. (1977). Double Loop Learning in Organizations. *Harvard Business Review, 55*(5), 115-125.

Argyris, C. (1996). Unrecognized Defenses of Scholars: Impact on Theory and Research. *Organization Science, 7*(1), 79-87.

Argyris, C. (2003). A Life Full of Learning. *Organization Studies, 24*(7), 1178-1192.

Argyris, C., & Schon, D. A. (1978). *Organizational Learning: A Theory of Action Perspective.* Reading, MA: Addison-Wesley.

Arthur, J. B., & Aiman-Smith, L. (2001). Gainsharing and Organizational Learning: An Analysis of Employee Suggestions Over Time. *Academy of Management Journal, 44*(4), 737-754.

Balijepally, V., Mahapatra, R., & Nerur, S. (2004). *Social Capital: A Theoretical Lens for IS Research.* Paper presented at the Tenth Americas Conference on Information Systems, New York, NY.

Benbasat, I., Dexter, A. S., & Mantha, R. W. (1980). Impact of Organizational Maturity on Information System Skill Needs. *MIS Quarterly, 4*(1), 21-34.

Boehm, B., & Turner, R. (2004). *Balancing Agility and Discipline: A Guide to the Perplexed.* Boston, MA: Addison-Wesley.

Bourdieu, P. (1986). The Forms of Capital. In J. G. Richardson (Ed.), *Handbook of Theory and Research for the Sociology of Education* (pp. 241-258). New York: Greenwood.

Brown, J. S., & Duguid, P. (1991). Organizational Learning and Communities-of-Practice: Toward a Unified View of Working, Learning, and Innovation. *Organization Science, 2*(1), 40-57.

Burt, R. S. (1997). The Contingent Value of Social Capital. *Administrative Science Quarterly, 42*(2), 339-365.

Coleman, J. S. (1988). Social Capital in the Creation of Human Capital. *American Journal of Sociology, 94*, S95-S120.

Collins, H. M. (1993). The Structure of Knowledge. *Social Research, 60*(1), 95-116.

Crossan, M. M., Lane, H. W., & White, R. E.

(1999). An Organization Learning Framework: From Intuition to Institution. *Academy of Management Review, 24*(3), 522-537.

Duncan, R. B., & Weiss, A. (1979). Organizational Learning: Implications for Organizational Design. In B. M. Staw (Ed.), *Research in Organizational Behavior* (Vol. 1, pp. 75-123). Greenwich, CT: JAI Press.

Fiol, C. M., & Lyles, M., A. (1985). Organizational Learning. *Academy of Management Review, 10*(4), 803-813.

Gilb, T. (1987). *Principles of Software Engineering Management*. Reading, MA: Addison-Wesley.

Grant, R. M. (1996a). Prospering in Dynamically-competitive Environments: Organizational Capability as Knowledge Integration. *Organization Science, 7*(4), 375.

Grant, R. M. (1996b). Toward a Knowledge-Based Theory of the Firm. *Strategic Management Journal, 17*, 109-122.

Green, G. I. (1989). Perceived Importance of Systems Analysts' Job Skills, Roles, and Non-Salary Incentives. *MIS Quarterly, 13*(13), 2.

Hannay, J. E., Sjoberg, D. I. K., & Dyba, T. (2007). A Systematic Review of Theory Use in Software Engineering Experiments. *IEEE Transactions on Software Engineering, 33*(2), 87-107.

Highsmith, J. (2003). Agile Project Management: Principles and Tools. *Agile Project Management Advisory Service, 4*(2), 37.

Huber, G. P. (1991). Organizational Learning: The Contributing Processes and the Literatures. *Organization Science, 2*(1), 88-115.

Kogut, B., & Zander, U. (1992). Knowledge of the Firm, Combinative Capabilities, and the Replication of Technology. *Organization Science, 3*(3), 383.

Lam, A. (2000). Tacit Knowledge, Organizational Learning and Societal Institutions: An Integrated Framework. *Organization Studies, 21*(3), 487.

Lindblom, C. E. (1987). Alternatives to Validity: Some Thoughts Suggested by Campbell's Guidelines. *Knowledge Creation, Diffusion, Utilization, 8*, 509-520.

Moran, P., & Ghoshal, S. (1996). Value Creation of Firms. In J. B. Keys & L. N. Dosier (Eds.), *Academy of Management Best Paper Proceedings* (pp. 41-45).

Nahapiet, J., & Ghoshal, S. (1998). Social Capital, Intellectual Capital, and the Organizational Advantage. *Academy of Management Review, 23*(2), 242-266.

Nambisan, S., Agarwal, R., & Tanniru, M. (1999). Organizational Mechanisms for Enhancing User Innovation in Information Technology. *MIS Quarterly, 23*(3), 365-395.

Nerur, S., & Balijepally, V. (2007). Theoretical Reflections on Agile Development Methodologies. *Communications of the ACM, 50*(3), 79-83.

Nerur, S., Mahapatra, R., & Mangalaraj, G. (2005). Challenges of Migrating to Agile Methodologies. *Communications of the ACM, 48*(5), 73-78.

Nonaka, I. (1994). Dynamic Theory of Organizational Knowledge Creation. *Organization Science, 5*(1), 14-37.

Oh, H., Labianca, G., & Chung, M.-H. (2006). A Multilevel Model of Group Social Capital. *Academy of Management Review, 31*(3), 569-582.

Polanyi, M. (1966). *The Tacit Dimension*. New York: Anchor Day Books.

Putnam, R. D. (1993). The Prosperous Community: Social Capital and Public Life. *American Prospect, 13*, 35-42.

Reich, B. H., & Benbasat, I. (2000). Factors that Influence the Social Dimension of Alignment between Business and Information Technology

Objectives. [Article]. *MIS Quarterly, 24*(1), 81.

Senge, P. M. (1990). The Leader's New Work: Building Learning Organizations. *Sloan Management Review, 32*(1), 7.

Spender, J. C. (1996a). Making Knowledge the Basis of a Dynamic Theory of the Firm. *Strategic Management Journal, 17*(S2), 45-62.

Spender, J. C. (1996b). Organizational knowledge, learning and memory: three concepts in search of a theory. *Journal of Organizational Change Management, 9*(1), 63.

Todd, P., McKeen, J. D., & Gallupe, R. B. (1995). The Evolution of IS Job Skills: A Content Analysis of IS Job Advertisements from 1970 to 1990. *MIS Quarterly, 19*(1), 1-27.

Van Den Bosch, F. A. J., Volberda, H. W., & De Boer, M. (1999). Coevolution of Firm Absorptive Capacity and Knowledge Environment: Organizational Forms and Combinative Capabilities. [Article]. *Organization Science, 10*(5), 551.

Visser, M. A. X. (2007). Duetero-Learning in Organizations: A Review and a Reformulation. *Academy of Management Review, 32*(2), 659-667.

Ye, F., & Agarwal, R. (2003). *Strategic Information Technology Partnerships in Outsourcing as a Distinctive Source of Information Technology Value: A Social Capital Perspective.* Paper presented at the Twenty-Fourth International Conference on Information Systems, Seattle, WA.

ENDNOTE

1 The propositions for moderating effect of combinative capabilities on the effect of knowledge outcomes on individual dimensions of IT value have not been shown for the sake of brevity.

Chapter VII
UB2SQL:
A Tool for Building Database Applications Using UML and B Formal Method

Amel Mammar
University of Paris, France

Régine Laleau
University of Paris, France

ABSTRACT

UB2SQL is a tool for designing and developing database applications using UML and B formal method. The approach supported by UB2SQL consists of two successive phases. In the first phase, with the design of applications using class, state and collaboration diagrams, B specifications are automatically generated from UML diagrams; the diagrams are then augmented with these B specifications in place. The second phase deals with the refinement of these B specifications into a relational database implementation, for which UML representation is constructed. In both phases, proofs are achieved to ensure correctness of the obtained B specification and correctness of the refinement process. To overcome the lack of rules and tactics in the B prover, UB2SQL defines specific rules and tactics making the proof task seem like a push-button activity. To increase the usability of UB2SQL in both academic and industrial contexts, the tool has been integrated as a plug-in to the Rational Rose CASE tool. Such integration allows users to develop and be able to visualize graphical UML diagrams and formal B notation in a single environment.

INTRODUCTION

In the area of database specification and design, most research work has been dedicated to data modeling through the definition of the Entity-Relationship (ER) model and its variants. Formal rules are designed to translate ER diagrams into database schemas and included as part of the functionality of existing industrial CASE tools. This principle has not yet been applied to database transaction design, even though some research work in that direction has been carried out (Barros, 1998; Edmond, 1995; Gunther, Schewe, and Wetzel, 1993). A couple of reasons for this should be mentioned. First, in this kind of application, data are the core component and their modeling requires much attention (since the quality of the built system mainly depends on this modeling). Second, specifying database transactions at the same abstraction level as the ER model requires the use of formal specification notations such as B (Abrial, 1996), VDM (Jones, 1990) or Z (Spivey, 1992); however, the use of formal methods raises some difficulties, as pointed out in a survey performed on experienced formal methods users (Snook and Butler, 2006). The survey observes that reading and understanding formal specifications is not a significant problem with suitable training; the main difficulty lies in creating formal specifications, and more precisely in finding useful abstractions like choosing the objects that make up the model. The authors conclude by recommending that formal methods should be more closely integrated with classical design methods, such as UML (OMG, 2003; Siau and Cao, 2001; Siau and Lee, 2004; Siau, Erickson, and Lee, 2005), which have been successfully used to design programs, and that graphical modeling tools supporting such integrations should be developed. Thus, a number of research projects (Bruel and France, 1996; Dupuy, Ledru, and Chabre-Peccoud, 2000; Ledang, Souquieres, and Charles, 2003; Marcano and Levy, 2002; Snook and Butler, 2006) have been devoted to such purpose. Formal proofs are another theme in formal methods. The objective is to increase the degree of proof-automation. A possible approach is to develop domain-dedicated provers and tools (Bernard, Legeard, Luck, and Peureux, 2004).

Our research work is at the junction of these themes and our aim is to define a method for the specification and design of database applications supported by a graphical modeling tool. In our proposal, data are first specified using UML class diagrams; transactions are then modeled with state and collaboration diagrams augmented with formal semantics. These adapted UML diagrams are converted into B specifications, which are then refined into a relational database implementation. The B method (Abrial, 1996) is a safe technique that covers the different phases of the software development life cycle: abstract specification, design by successive refinement steps and executable code generation. Using the B method, database engineers are able to check that transactions preserve integrity constraints expressed in the abstract specification. With the integration of UML+B, we can take advantage of the visual and structuring aspects of UML graphical notation, together with the rigorous reasoning possibilities of B formal notation. This paper focuses on the construction of the tool, *UB2SQL*, which supports our approach (UML+B). We highlight the main functionalities of *UB2SQL*, how it is integrated as a plug-in to the Rose CASE tool (Rational, 2003) and list the issues faced during its construction. Finally, we conclude by giving some quantitative elements and pointing out the advantages of such a tool. More details on the method itself can be found in our previous work (Laleau and Mammar, 2000a; 2000b, 2005; Mammar, 2002).

The paper is organized as follows. We start with a brief description of the B method, followed by an overview of our approach for the development of database applications and of the main functionalities of *UB2SQL*, which we describe in detail through a running example. After that, we discuss the benefits expected from such a tool, the main difficulties faced during its construction, and we compare it with other similar tools. Finally, we conclude and outline some future work.

OVERVIEW OF THE B METHOD

This section briefly presents the main concepts of the B formal method to help the reader understand our approach. Introduced by Jean-Raymond Abrial (Abrial, 1996), B is a formal method dedicated to developing safe systems. B specifications are organized in abstract machines. Each machine contains state variables on which operations act, and an invariant constraining them. The invariant is a predicate in a simplified version of ZF-set theory, augmented with relational operators. Operations are specified in the Generalized Substitution Language, which is a generalization of Dijkstra's guarded command notation. The *generalization* allows the definition of non-deterministic and preconditioned substitutions. A *substitution* is like an assignment statement. It allows us to identify which variables are modified by the operation without mentioning the variables not modified. A preconditioned substitution is the form (**PRE** *P* **THEN** *S* **END**) where *P* is a predicate, and *S* a substitution. When *P* holds, the substitution is executed, otherwise nothing can be ensured. For instance, the substitution *S* might not terminate or might violate the invariant. The B method is supported by commercial tools like AtelierB (Clearsy, 2003), BToolkit (B-core, 1996) and recently by a free tool called *B4free and Clik'n'prove* (Clearsy, 2004). The B refinement is the process of transforming a specification into a less abstract one. A refinement can operate on an abstract machine or on another refinement component. In B, we distinguish two kinds of refinement:

- Behavioral refinement: this refinement aims to eliminate nondeterminism and come close to control structures used in the chosen target programming language. Behavioral refinement includes, for example, weakening of preconditions, replacement of a parallel substitution by a sequence substitution, etc.
- Data structure refinement: an abstract data structure *D* is replaced by a concrete data structure *D'* which must be close to the data structure that is allowed in the target programming language. For example a set that is not available in standard programming languages, is often refined by a array structure that is available in most programming languages. In this kind of refinement, a predicate *J*, called the gluing invariant, must be defined. It states the existing relation between *D* and *D'*.

The last refinement step is called implementation, and the translation into the chosen target language of the data and control structures (used in this level) must be a straightforward task. Both specification and refinement steps give rise to proof obligations. At the abstract level, proof obligations ensure that each operation maintains the invariant of the system, whereas at the refinement level, they ensure that the transformation preserves the properties of the abstract level. To carry out these proofs, AtelierB includes two complementary provers. The first one is automatic, implementing a decision procedure that uses a set of deduction and rewriting rules; the second prover allows the users to enter into a dialogue with the automatic prover by defining their own deduction and/or rewriting rules that guide the prover to find the right way to discharge proofs. Each added rule must be proved by AtelierB before it can be used. AtelierB also provides users with the possibility of defining new tactics (proof scenarios) that may be missing in the prover.

OVERVIEW OF *UB2SQL*

Overview of the Approach

Our approach to develop database applications can be summarized by the following steps in Figure 1.

1. The data structure and the transactions are described using *IS-UML* diagrams. *IS-UML* notation is UML notation endowed with a formal semantics (Laleau and Polack, 2001a, 2001b) dedicated to the specification and design of database applications. Data structures are specified by class diagrams, while transactions are described by state and collaboration diagrams supplemented with precise annotations written in B.
2. According to translation rules we have defined (Laleau, 2000; Laleau and Mammar, 2000b), B specifications are generated from the previous *IS-UML* diagrams. Then, applying the generic refinement rules we have suggested (Laleau and Mammar, 2000a; Mammar, 2002), the B specifications are successively transformed until they become close enough to the B expression of a relational implementation. The last B specification, produced in the B implementation phase, reflects the architecture of the system, which consists of both a database schema and transactions.
3. From the final refinement step, the *SQL* definition of the database schema is automatically derived. Extending the derivation to the generation of programs representing transactions is also considered.

Unlike other similar approaches that are more general (Dupuy et al., 2000; Edmond, 1995; Gunther et al., 1993; Hall, 1990; Kim and Carrington, 1999; Ledang and Souquières, 2002; Marcano and Levy, 2002; Qian, 1993; Treharne, 2002), we completely focus on the development of database applications, enabling us to cover the entire development process from design to implementation. A detailed comparison of these approaches has already been established (Mammar, 2002).

Architecture of UB2SQL

UB2SQL denotes the tool we developed to support the approach described in the previous section.

*Figure 1. From **IS-UML** diagrams to a relational implementation*

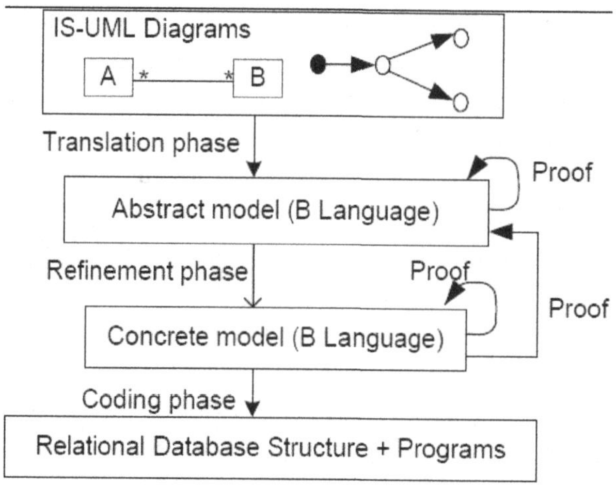

Figure 2. The functional architecture of the tool

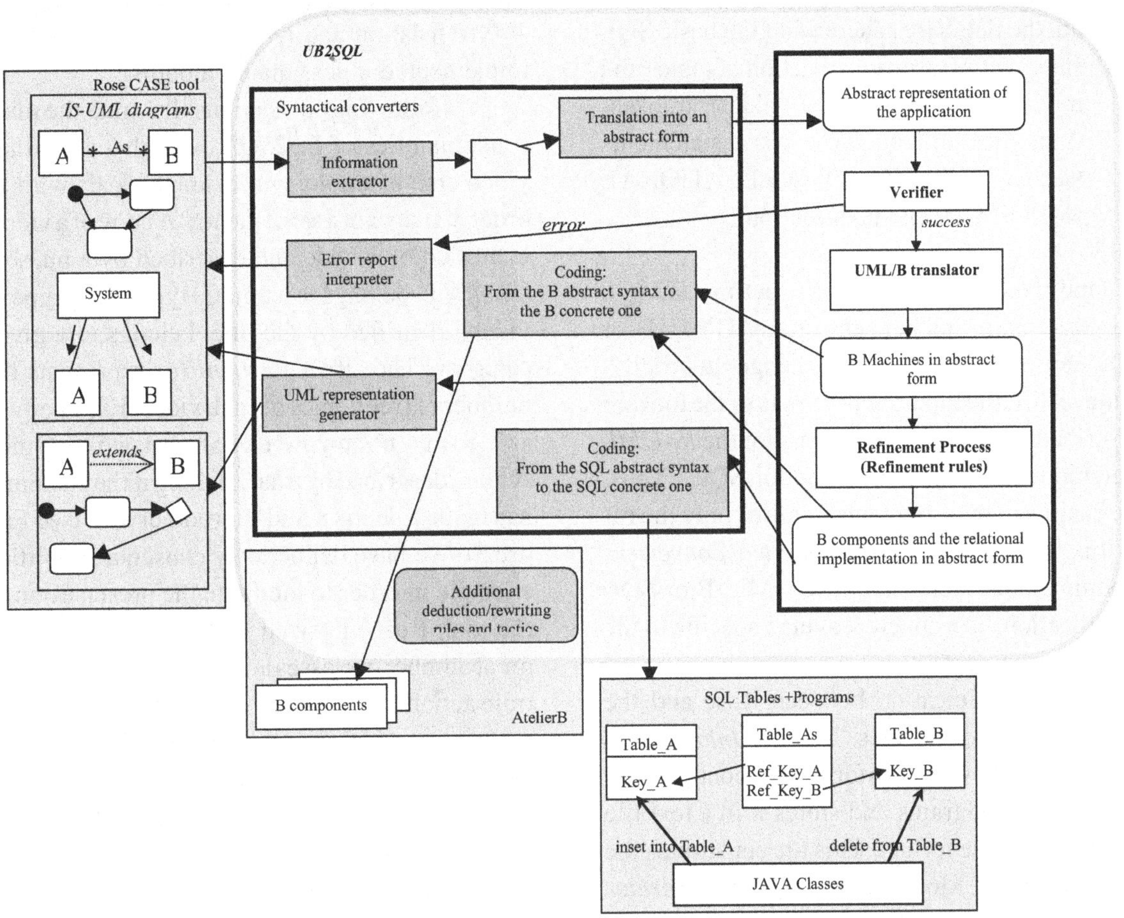

This tool, summarized in Figure 2, is accessible from the Rose CASE tool environment, which is one of the most user-friendly environments supporting UML notation. *UB2SQL* comprises two options. The first option produces B specifications that are directly useable in AtelierB for different tasks of type-checking and proof. The UML diagrams are then completed with these B specifications to have both formal and visual representations in the same environment. The second option goes further by refining the obtained B specification until a database schema and SQL code (transactions) embedded in JAVA language are generated. Both database schema and transactions are represented under Rose with graphical views. To achieve these two options, the tool operates following these steps:

1. Before performing the B translation, *UB2SQL* makes sure that the *IS-UML* diagrams satisfy some syntactical properties. For instance, it verifies that all classes and their attributes are named, and that the actions specified on a state diagram correspond to the operations expressed on the related class or association.
2. *UB2SQL* applies translation rules to derive B formal specifications. The obtained B specifications are successively refined until a relational implementation is obtained. The

refinement process comprises about 120 refinement rules. In this phase, we generate the database schema and the basic SQL statements (insertion, deletion of tuples and modification of attribute values); transactions are built on these basic statements (see GENERATION OF A RELATIONAL IMPLEMENTATION section).

One of the key points in constructing *UB2SQL* was to remain independent of any UML, B or SQL environments that may change. In order to achieve this, the inputs and outputs of the tool are described in abstract syntax: one for the *IS-UML* metamodel, one for B and one for SQL. Thus, the change of environments requires only the rewriting of the parts of the *Syntactical converters* module that act on or produce UML, B or SQL specifications in a concrete syntax specific to the used environments.

The communication between Rose and the tool is achieved via files. Module *Information extractor* retrieves all information contained in the *IS-UML* diagrams and stores it in a text file having a specific format. This file constitutes the input of the tool. Module *Error report interpreter* reads the error files generated by *UB2SQL* in order to point out the *IS-UML* element causing the syntactical error. Similarly, module *UML representation generator* reads the B files in order to complete back the *IS-UML* diagrams with the generated B specifications and also to give a UML representation of the database schema and transactions.

The three components on the left of module *Syntactical converters*, developed under Rose, are written in a script language based on the Visual BASIC syntax. This language defines a set of APIs allowing to extract from or add information to the *IS-UML* diagrams. All other components are written using the Ocaml functional language (a French variant of the ML language) (Chailloux, Manoury, and Pagano, 2000), which is particularly suitable for implementing transformational processes defined by a set of rules. *UB2SQL* has been developed in a reasonable time: more than 400 translation and refinement rules have been implemented in less than 3 months.

The following subsections illustrate the main functionalities of *UB2SQL* through a simplified video club example. Our example deals with an order manager of a set of videos. A copy of a video, identified by a code and described by a number (*ShelfNo*), belongs to a unique type. Each type of video, identified by the title, belongs to a given category. The attribute *NumFree* represents the number of free copies of each video. Each copy of a video may be borrowed by at most one customer. A loan, described by a date, is long if the customer has made a deposit, and short otherwise (see Figure 3). We have deliberately chosen a simplified example in order to facilitate the presentation of the tool. Real-life sized systems may contain a great number of classes and associations, whereas transactions, most often, involve few classes and associations. In this case, we would obtain a larger B specification, which implies a great number of refinement proofs. However, the skeleton of these refinement proofs remains the same. For the sake of brevity, we assume readers are familiar with the relational model.

FROM *IS-UML* DIAGRAMS TO A B SPECIFICATION

Elaboration of IS-UML Class Diagrams and their B Translation

The class diagram is the first to be edited. The other diagrams use information related not only to this diagram but also to its corresponding B specification. For example, we need to know the name of the operations derived for each class and association. Figure 3 shows how the class diagram of the running example is edited.

For each element of a UML diagram, a standard input form is provided to obtain specific informa-

Figure 3. Editing class and state diagrams under the Rose environment

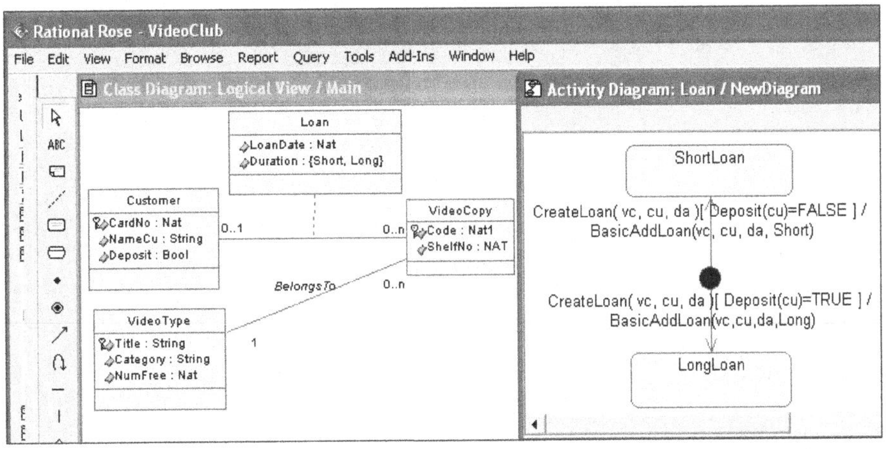

tion from users: association multiplicity, qualifier of an association end, etc. When a constraint we would like to express on a class diagram cannot be included in these input forms, we add it to the documentation fields of UML elements: class, attribute, association, etc. Once the class diagram has been edited, the *B Specification* entry added to Rose permits the execution of the program translating the *IS-UML* diagrams into B specifications. For each attribute or association, users are asked to add some details such as attribute multiplicities or the frozen characteristic of each association end. The main rules used for generating B specifications are summed up as follows. An abstract set of all the possible instances and a variable v_A representing the set of the existing ones are associated with each class *A*. Each monovalued attribute is modeled as a function ($\rightarrow$) from v_A to the type of the attribute. A key is translated into a total injective function ($\rightarrowtail$). An optional monovalued association, involving two classes *C* and *D*, is translated into a partial function ($\nrightarrow$) between v_C to v_D. In addition, a set of basic operations is automatically derived for each class and association. These operations include the insertion and deletion of objects or links and attribute modifications. After generating B specifications, the class diagram is updated by associating each element with its B counterpart. Figure 4 represents association *Loan* completed with the generated B specifications. This figure shows the documentation field of *Loan* filled by its B static description. Similarly, the B basic operations are declared as operations of this association. These operations are stereotyped with "AG" in order to distinguish them from those defined by users.

Figure 4 shows the precondition and the postcondition (body) of operation *BasicAddLoan* that inserts a new link into association *Loan*. This operation takes as parameters the two instances to be linked and a value of each mandatory attribute of this association. The precondition of this operation consists in specifying the type of each input parameter and checking that the requested video copy is available (*Vi* ∈ *VIDEOCOPY - dom*(*Loan*)). This last precondition is deduced from the monovalued characteristic of association *Loan*. Under this precondition, the operation updates the set of the existing links and the attribute values of the association.

Figure 4. The B translation of association Loan and the updated class diagram

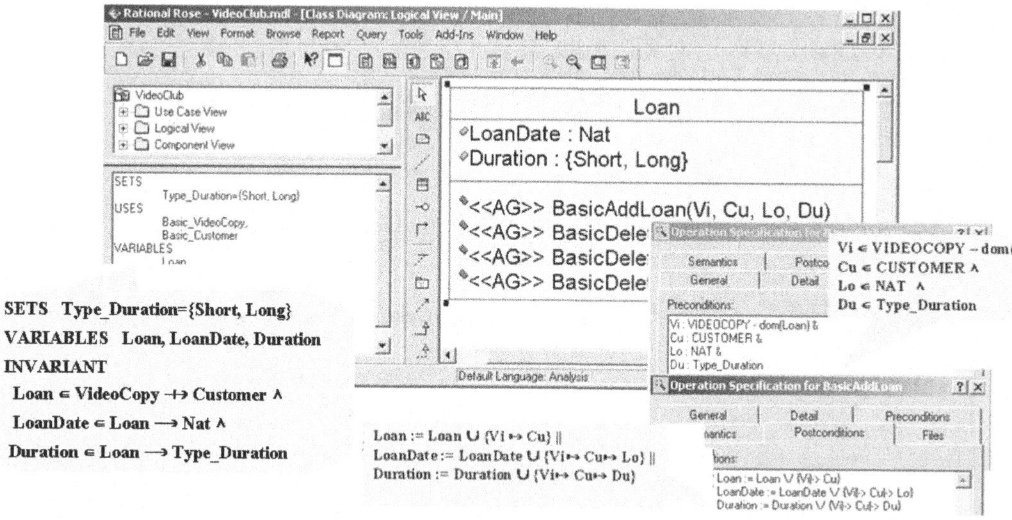

CORRECTNESS OF B SPECIFICATIONS TRANSLATING A CLASS DIAGRAM

In order to ensure the correctness of the specification generated from the *IS-UML* class diagram, a set of proof obligations is automatically calculated by the proof obligations generator (GOP) of AtelierB. These proofs verify that the execution of any operation maintains the invariant. The majority of these proofs (about 90%) are automatically discharged by the automatic prover of AtelierB. The failure of the automatic prover to discharge some of the proofs is mostly due to the lack of rules and/or tactics. Thus, users have to examine each unproved proof to determine the rules to add and the right tactics in order to discharge it. In a general context, B proofs may be of any form, thus finding the missing rules and tactics may be a very difficult activity. Fortunately, the B specifications generated by *UB2SQL* have a well-known form that always gives rise to generic proofs of the same form. This generic form allows us to precisely define the missing rules and tactics, which enable discharge of all generated proofs. For instance, the prover fails to establish the following proof for operation *BasicAddLoan*:

$(Duration \cup \{Vi \mapsto Cu \mapsto Du\}) \in (Loan \cup \{Vi \mapsto Cu\}) \nrightarrow Type\_Duration$[1]

More precisely, the B prover fails to deduce from precondition ($Vi \notin Dom(Loan)$) that ($Vi \mapsto Cu \notin Loan$). So, in order to achieve this proof, we have defined the following B tactic:

$tac\_Add \triangleq (Partial\_Fun \; ; \; Dom\_Prop \; ; \; Axio^{+})^{2}$
where

- *Partial_Fun* is a theory related to partial functions. It contains the following rule:

  $\dfrac{f \in U \nrightarrow V \qquad u \notin dom(f)}{f \cup \{u \mapsto v\} \in U \cup \{u\} \nrightarrow V}$ stating that if

f denotes a partial function, then associating an image with an element, which has no image yet, produces a partial function.

- *Dom_Prop* is a theory expressing properties of operator *domain* (*dom*). It contains the following rule:

  $\dfrac{x \notin dom(f)}{x \mapsto y \notin f}$

stating that to prove that a couple $(x \mapsto y)$ does not belong to a function f, it is sufficient to prove that x does not belong to the domain of f.

- *Axio* is a theory defining the following two obvious rules:

  $\frac{A = B}{A == B}$ and $\frac{binhyp(A)}{A}$.

  The former rewrites each expression A into B in the goal, while the latter enables to discharge goals that are already in the hypothesis. $binhyp(H)$ specifies that H must already be in the hypothesis.

From a practical point of view, a file containing all the defined tactics is created. These tactics are applied, one after the other, on each unproved proof. As this process may be very time consuming, we have related each tactic to a particular form of a proof goal. For instance, by writing (*Pattern*($a \cup b \in c \mapsto\!\!\!\!\!+ d$) & *tac_Add*), we specify that tactic *tac_Add* must be applied on each proof whose goal is of the form ($a \cup b \in c \mapsto\!\!\!\!\!+ d$). To discharge all the interactive proofs, we have defined about 6 tactics and 10 additional rules.

ELABORATION OF DYNAMIC DIAGRAMS AND THEIR B TRANSLATION

Once the class diagram is translated into B specifications, functionalities (behavioral aspects) of the application are described by using state and collaboration diagrams. The aim of these diagrams is to specify the effect of transactions on the objects of the system. The state diagrams we use are similar to those of Harel's Statecharts (Harel, 1987) for which we have defined a particular semantics dedicated to the database domain. In our case, a state diagram describes the changes of state of a single object. Only basic states are considered. The possible states are described by predicates denoting properties that the object must verify. A transition, triggered by an event, may be guarded. To obtain deterministic behavior, we make the assumption that all the guards related to a same event and source state are disjoint. Moreover, to avoid deadlock we assume that when an event occurs at least one of these guards is satisfied. When a transition is fired, one basic operation of the related class or association class may be called. Figure 3 (partially) shows the state diagram of association class *Loan*. We associate with this diagram the following semantics: a loan may either be *long* or *short*. When event *CreateLoan* occurs, if the related customer has made a deposit the loan is created as *long*, otherwise it is *short*. Users are asked to provide the B description of the different states. For instance, the *initial* state is described by ($initial(vc) \triangleq vc \notin dom(Loan)$). The translation into B consists in generating a single operation for each event. Figure 5 depicts the documentation field of the state diagram. This documentation is completed by the B operation translating event *CreateLoan*.

Let us give some explanations about the way whereby each part of this operation is obtained.

1. *Signature*: corresponds exactly to the signature of the related event (same name and same parameters).
2. *Precondition*: the last two conjuncts are derived from the source state of the transitions triggered by the related event. This conjunct includes the predicate of the source state and the disjunction of all the guards associated with the outgoing transitions ($initial(vc) \wedge (Deposit(cu){=}FALSE \vee Deposit(cu){=}TRUE)$). The first three preconditions concern the typing of the parameters and the preconditions of the called operations ($vc \in VIDEOCOPY - dom(Loan) \wedge cu \in CUSTOMER \wedge da \in Nat$). This predicate is automatically inferred from the way these parameters are used in the basic operation calls. From a practical point of view, we proceed as follows. For

Figure 5. The B operation translating an event of a state diagram

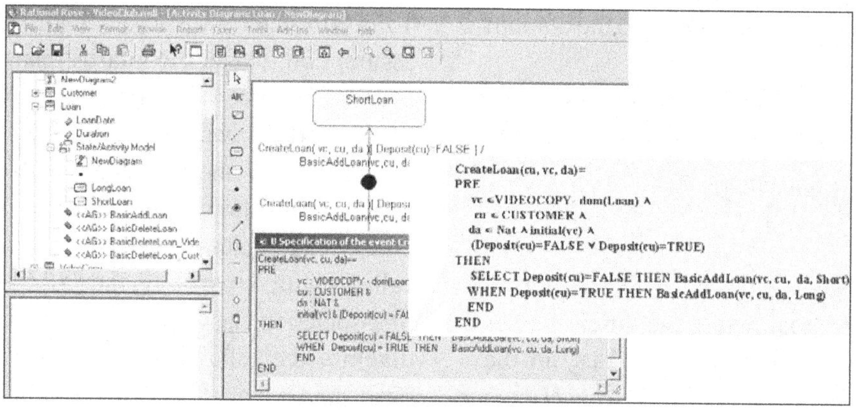

each call $op(EParam_1,...,EParam_n)$ to an operation *op*, whose formal parameters are $FParam_1$, ..., $FParam_n$, we substitute, in the precondition of *op*, each formal parameter by its corresponding actual parameter. Then, the precondition of the operation translating the event denotes the conjunction of all these sub-preconditions. Of course, if an input parameter of an event is not used in an operation call, we cannot infer its type. The error is pointed out by the B type checker.

3. *Postcondition* (*Body*): the set of transitions outgoing from each state is translated by a *SELECT* substitution. Each branch of this substitution is related to a single transition. It is guarded by the guard of the transition, and executes the action specified for it.

In our approach, a collaboration diagram is used to show how the effect of a transaction is decomposed into internal messages sent to each class or association. Figure 6 shows how a collaboration diagram representing the loan of a videocassette to a customer is built.

To make a loan, the following two actions must be performed simultaneously: decrementing the value of attribute *NumFree* of the associated type of the video, and triggering event *CreateLoan*. Note that each message may be guarded by a B predicate that specifies additional conditions for sending the message.

A collaboration diagram is translated into a single B operation whose body consists in simultaneously calling the operations corresponding to the messages (see Figure 6). The typing of the input parameters of the messages is automatically inferred by following the same strategy for state diagrams.

CORRECTNESS OF THE B SPECIFICATIONS TRANSLATING DYNAMIC DIAGRAMS

As for a B specification translating a class diagram, proof obligations are generated for a B specification translating state and collaborations diagrams. Since no additional invariants are derived from these diagrams, these proof obligations mainly concern two points:

1. *Preconditions of the called operations*: for each operation *op* called in an operation *op'* whose precondition is $Prec_{op'}$, a proof obligation checking the precondition $Prec_{op}$ of *op* is generated. This proof obligation is automatically discharged since the precondition $Prec_{op'}$ is obtained by taking the

Figure 6. Editing a collaboration diagram under the Rose environment

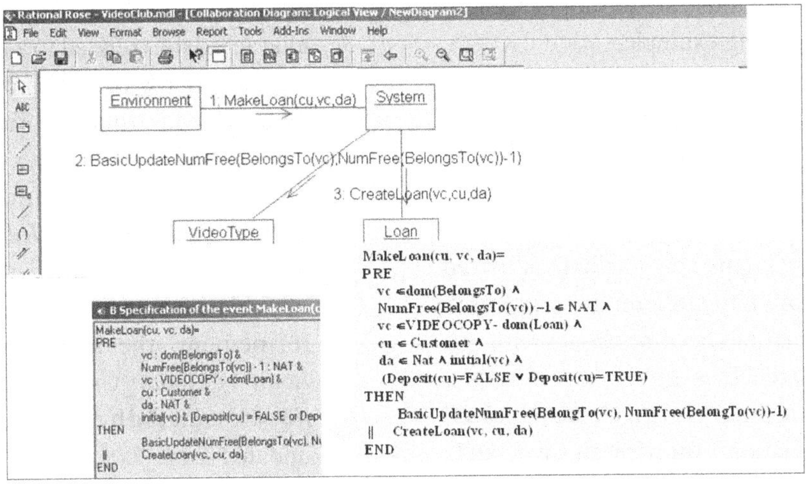

precondition of each called operation into account.

2. *Proofs related to variables read and modified by simultaneous called operations*: such proofs are generated for operations translating collaboration diagrams. Although we have proved that each basic operation, executed separately, establishes its invariant, the simultaneous execution of two (or more) basic operations may violate it. We still need to prove each part of invariants, which depends on variables that are read and modified simultaneously in operations generated from collaboration diagrams. Unfortunately, such invariants can be of any form even for a specific domain, and therefore, we believe that defining tactics to discharge their related proofs constitutes a fully qualified research work. This will be an interesting prospect for our future research.

GENERATION OF A RELATIONAL IMPLEMENTATION

Once the B specifications corresponding to the different *IS-UML* diagrams are generated, they are successively transformed using the B refinement technique, down to a concrete level that is the B representation of a relational database. In this way, coding the B representation into a relational database implementation becomes a straightforward task. Our data structure refinement rules use the algorithm, defined in (Elmasri and Navathe, 2004), that derives a relational schema from a class diagram. The main idea of this algorithm is to reorganize the class diagram into a set of independent classes. So, all elaborated concepts such as inheritance, association class and complex attributes must be transformed. The contribution of our approach is the joint refinement of data and operations (basic operations and transactions). By establishing the refinement proofs, we know the obtained program still satisfies constraints specified at the abstract level. The following subsections illustrate the main steps of our refinement process.

Data Structure Refinement

The goal of this phase is to transform all the UML data concepts that are not possible in the relational model. We have defined a set of formal refinement rules that deals with different concepts such as inheritance and multivalued attributes (Mammar, 2002). Hereafter, we illustrate the application of two rules on a running example:

a. Transformation of association links: an association between classes *C* and *D* with at least one monovalued role (attached for example to class *C*) is replaced by a new attribute in *C*. This new attribute is linked to the key of *D* by a referential constraint. Other associations become classes with two additional attributes linked by referential constraints to the keys of the classes involved in the association. Applying this rule adds two variables *Loan_Vid* and *Loan_Cus* that are linked by referential constraints to attributes *Code* and *CardNo* respectively. Couple (*Loan_Vid*, *Loan_Cus*) constitutes a key for class *Loan*. Since these two added variables are defined on association *Loan*, operation *BasicAddLoan* is refined by adding B substitutions that update these variables.

b. Definition of the database schema: the idea is to gather under a single variable all the characteristics related to a given class. This single variable corresponds to a relational table. By this rule, the functions defined on variable *Loan*: *Loan_Vid*, *Loan_Cus*, *LoanDate* and *Duration* are gathered under the single variable *Table_Loan*, which is defined as the cartesian product of the variables defined on *Loan*. Similarly by refinement, the substitutions updating *Loan_Vid*, *Loan_Cus*, *LoanDate* and *Duration* are replaced by a single substitution that updates *Table_Loan*.

Substitution Refinement

The previous step allows data and basic operations to be refined. The transactions defined in the abstract B specification were only rewritten with respect to the variables introduced during the data refinement. The transactions still contain

Figure 7. The UML representation of a database implementation

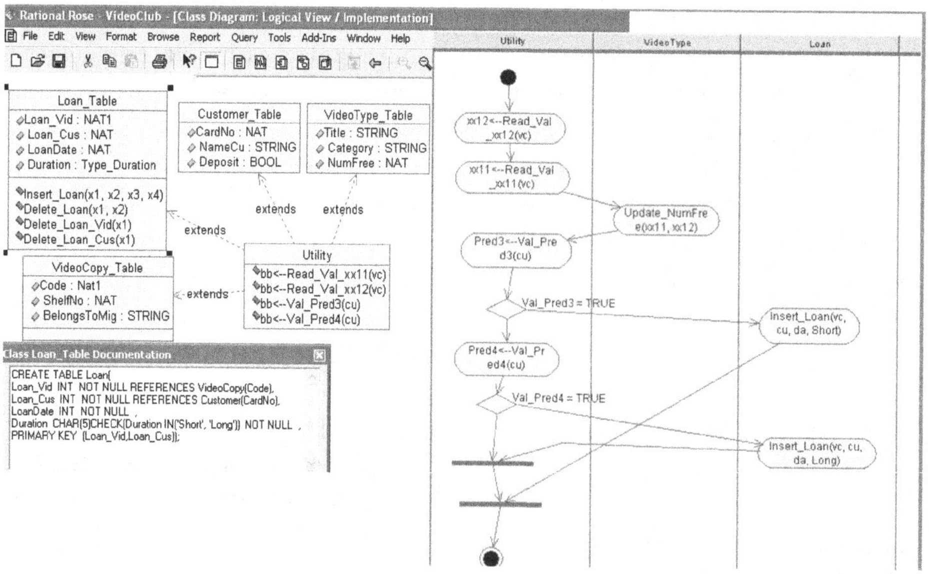

B substitution constructors. The main difficulty concerns the refinement of the parallel constructor. As this constructor is replaced by a sequence one, we have to retrieve the set of modified and read variables for each substitution. After that, another step consists in defining an order among the substitutions of the parallel constructor, such that those modifying the least number of variables are those first executed.

Graphical Representation of a B Relational Implementation

To provide database users with a visual representation of a B relational implementation, the generated database schema is depicted with a new class diagram, while an activity diagram shows how the operation calls are sequenced to achieve the implementation of a transaction. The classes of this new class diagram denote the different tables exhibited by rule (*b*). The attributes of each class correspond to the function names appearing in the cartesian product defining the related table (see rule (*b*)). Its operations correspond to the SQL translation of the basic operations derived in section FROM *IS-UML* DIAGRAMS TO A B SPECIFICATION. For instance, operation *Insert_Loan* is associated with the basic operation *BasicAddLoan*. The document field of each of these classes is filled with the SQL description of the table that it represents. Figure 7 depicts the database schema derived for our example.

It contains four relational tables: one table for each class or multivalued association. The primary key of each table corresponds to the B injective function defined on the variable representing the table. For instance, we infer from rule (*a*) that the couple (*Loan_Vid, Loan_Cus*) is a primary key of table *Loan*. Also, a type check constraint is generated for each attribute whose type corresponds to an enumerated given set (*Duration* field).

Similarly, the activity diagram representing the transaction *MakeLoan* involves three "actors" represented by the swimlanes *Utility* (explained further on), *VideoType* and *Loan*. We have chosen to use activity diagrams for this purpose since such diagrams are well suited for the representation of the transaction's flow. Depicting a transaction by an activity diagram consists in associating with each B substitution or constructor a graphical representation. The activity diagram of Figure 7 is constructed as follows. The filled circle represents the beginning of the transaction, and the filled circle with a border around it represents the termination of the transaction. Each operation call is represented by an activity node and the *IF* constructor by a decision node which is depicted by a diamond. The horizontal bar permits merging of different threads created by a decision node. Activity *Read_Val_X12* (resp. *Read_Val_X11*) returns the value of expression (*NbFree*(*BelongsTo*(*vc*)) - *1*) (resp. (*BelongsTo*(*vc*))). Similarly, activity *Val_Pred3* (resp. *Val_Pred4*) returns the truth value of predicate (*Deposit*(*cu*)=*FALSE*) (resp. (*Deposit*(*cu*)=*TRUE*)). These different activities are included as operations of an additional class called *Utility*, which we add to the class diagram depicting the database schema. Because these operations need to read the attributes of the classes representing the relational tables, *Utility* joins each of these classes using the UML dependency link with stereotype *extends*.

Refinement Proofs

To ensure correctness of the refinement process, we have established the validity of each refinement rule. The refinement process gives rise to about 200 refinement proofs. Proving the refinement of a substitution *S* by a substitution *T* consists in: 1) proving that if *S* terminates then *T* terminates, as well; 2) the execution of *S* and *T* yields the same result. With AtelierB (version 3.5), 70% of these proofs have been automatically discharged, but this concerns only the easiest proofs related to the first condition. The remaining proofs are rather hard and often very tedious to achieve. Fortunately, the generic feature of the refinement rules makes it possible to define proof tactics, like those defined in the section *Correctness of B Specifications Translating a Class Diagram*, which enable automation of the refinement proofs. This means that, once the proof of a generic refinement rule has been achieved, it is possible to reuse it in all the instantiations of the rule (Mammar and Laleau, 2003). To discharge all the interactive refinement proofs, we have defined about 30 tactics and 40 additional rules.

Similarly, to prove the refinement of transactions, we have studied and defined sufficient conditions that allow us to reuse the basic operation refinement proofs. We also pointed out that in the database domain these conditions most often hold. Hence, the proof of the transaction refinement has been largely automated (Mammar and Laleau, 2003).

DISCUSSION

Benefits and Limitations of the Tool

Translating *IS-UML* diagrams into B specifications assigns a formal semantics to them. This helps users remove the ambiguities and make up for the lack of semantics of the UML diagrams. The formal generation of relational implementations from B specifications allows the development of database programs that satisfy all the constraints specified on the data. Moreover, we have shown that the B code corresponding to the implementation of a transaction is, in most cases, longer than its abstract specification, which hides all the implementation concerns introduced by our refinement rules (Mammar and Laleau, 2005). Hence, automating these two development phases frees engineers from tedious and error-prone tasks. Indeed, the development by hand of the running example has taken about one month. Using *UB2SQL*, this task really becomes like a push-button activity (less than 10 seconds). Table 1 gives some statistics about the effort that users should make if they had to handwrite the complete B specification. We have chosen to quantify this effort in terms of the number of lines of the B specification, and the number of interactive proofs to be achieved. *num_att* denotes the number of attributes of a class or an association. *num_states* and *Event* represent respectively the number of states and the set of events of a state diagram. *num_trans*(*ev*) represents the number of transitions associated with a given event *ev*. Similarly, *num_messages* represents the number of messages appearing in a given collaboration diagram and *num_conj* denotes the number of conjuncts, in invariants, that depend on variables which are read and modified simultaneously in the B operations corresponding to collaboration diagrams. For instance, number 20 for a class corresponds to the definition of the name of the B machine associated with it, its abstract set, its variable, its invariant, its initialization, and the different clauses corresponding to the operations that add and suppress instances. Similarly,

Table 1. Experimental results

UMLelement \ Abstract B specification	Number of lines	Number of interactive proofs
Class	$20 + 9 \times num\_att$	$2 \times num\_att$
Association	$22 + 9 \times num\_att$	$3 + 2 \times num\_att$
State diagram	$3 + num\_states + \Sigma_{ev \in Event}(4 + 2 \times num\_trans(ev))$	0
Collaboration diagram	$2 + num\_messages$	num_conj

number 9 corresponds to the variable defining an attribute, its typing and initialization, the substitutions and precondition added to the operations on its class, and the operation updating the value of the attribute. In addition to the results given in Table 1, which are applicable regardless of the considered case study, the refinement of the running example requires handwriting more than 300 lines of B code and establishing 39 interactive and difficult proofs.

On the other hand, it is important to consider the usefulness of UML diagrams for the elaboration of a B model. Converting a class diagram into a B specification gives the complete state: all the variables of the formal model. As we have mentioned in the introduction section, the main difficulty for elaborating a B specification lies in finding appropriate abstractions. In the database domain, designers are accustomed to constructing data models. A state diagram provides a different view of operations of a class, compared to the list of operations of a B machine. It describes ordering constraints between operations that cannot be straightforwardly expressed in B.

From a verification point of view, the tool can be further improved. Using AtelierB, only the safety properties can be verified. Indeed, B method is devoted to develop systems that, when they run, are guaranteed to produce correct results. However, it would be interesting to verify some other kinds of property, such as liveness properties. For instance, we would like to check that the predicate of a source state is not always false (unreachable state). For verifying this kind of property, we think that other provers and/or model checkers should be investigated (Leuschel and Butler, 2003).

Main Problems Encountered During the Construction of UB2SQL

This section reports on the main problems that we faced during the building of *UB2SQL*. These problems can be summarized in four points:

1. *Relevance of information returned by the Rose's APIs*: the form of the information returned by the Rose's APIs does not always meet our requirements. Consequently, the received information often needs appropriate processing in order to be able to make use of it. For state diagrams, for instance, the provided APIs permit only to obtain their transitions. Because our translation rules are defined on events by transforming them into B operations (built on the actions labeling its related transitions), we have been obliged to rearrange the set of transitions into a hashtable-like structure which associates each event with its related transitions.
2. *Calculation of preconditions*: applying the approach described in the previous section to calculate the preconditions of operations derived from state and collaboration diagrams, may produce some redundant conjuncts. Consequently, simplification rules must be applied. Indeed, let us show how the precondition *P* of operation *CreateLoan* (see Figure 5) is obtained:

- From the call to operation *BasicAddLoan(cu, vc, da, Short)*, we infer the following predicate: $P_1 \triangleq vc \in VIDEOCOPY - dom(Loan) \wedge cu \in CUSTOMER \wedge da \in Nat$. We can see that only the parts related to the actual parameters are kept, while $Short \in Type\_Duration$ is removed.
- From the call to operation *BasicAddLoan(cu, vc, da, Long)*, we infer the following predicate: $P_2 \triangleq \mathrm{vc} \in VIDEOCOPY - dom(Loan) \wedge cu \in CUSTOMER \wedge da \in Nat$.

As $P \triangleq (P_1 \wedge P_2)$, we can write $(P \triangleq (vc \in VIDEOCOPY - dom(Loan) \wedge \mathrm{cu} \in CUSTOMER \wedge \mathrm{da} \in \mathrm{Nat} \wedge vc \in VIDEOCOPY - dom(Loan) \wedge cu \in CUSTOMER \wedge da \in Nat))$. In order to simplify this predicate, we have to define a set of rewriting rules in the form of $\frac{A}{B = C}$. Such a rule means that if the antecedent

A is true, then *B* can be rewritten to *C*. To simplify the predicate *P* we have to apply the rule

$$\frac{}{(A \wedge A) = A}.$$

3. *Huge amount of information needed by refinement rules*: the Ocaml functions implementing our refinement rules have a great number of parameters. Some refinement rules need not only the invariant of the first abstract level, but also all those derived by the previous refinement rules. As this information is defined in various B components, they must be passed on as parameters to the Ocaml functions implementing these rules. Such a huge number of parameters may be very stack consuming, especially that these functions are often recursive.
4. *Visual representation of nested "If-Then-Else-End" substitutions*: in the current version of *UB2SQL*, the representation of nested *If-Then-Else-End* substitutions is somewhat unsuitable. In Figure 7 for instance, it would be interesting to replace the sub-diagram from activity *Pred_Pred4*, to the horizontal bar by one "composite" activity (nested activity) associated with the sub-diagram. This would allow us to take into account modularization and reuse it. We have considered such a possibility, however, Rose does not support nested activities.

Table 2. Comparison of the different tools

Criteria \ Tools	FuZe	Roz	ArgoUML+B	UML2B	U2B	Z2UML
Graphical notations	Fusion	UML	UML	UML	UML	UML
Development environment	Paradigm Plus	ROSE	ArgoUML	Objecteering	ROSE	ROSE
Class diagram	+	+	+	+	+	+
UML elements for which operations are generated	classes	classes	-	classes associations	classes	classes associations
State diagrams	-	-	+	+	+	-
Collaboration diagrams	-	-	-	+	-	-
OCL expressions	-	-	-	+	-	-
Formal language	Z	Z	B	B	B	Z
Code generation	-	-	-	-	-	-

Comparison with other Similar Tools

The last decade has witnessed a great number of approaches deriving formal notations from graphical ones (Marcano and Levy, 2002; Ledang and Souquières, 2002; Treharne, 2002; Dupuy et al., 2000; Hall, 1990; Kim and Carrington, 1999; Edmond, 1995; Gunther et al., 1993; Qian, 1993). This section reports on the most representative approaches supported by tools. For a detailed description of the other approaches and a comparison with our own see Mammar (2002). *UML2B* partially reuses *UB2SQL*, in the context of the Lutin project, for translating OCL expressions into B specifications (Marcano and Levy, 2002). *RoZ* is a tool generating Z specifications from UML class diagrams edited under the Rose CASE tool (Dupuy et al., 2000). Contrary to *UB2SQL*, basic operations are generated only for classes. Operations on associations are not supported. Moreover, behavioral diagrams are not considered. A tool similar to *RoZ*, called *FuZe*, has been developed by Bruel and France (Bruel and France, 1996). This tool deals with Fusion class diagrams edited under the *Paradigm Plus* environment. Snoock and Ledang have both developed tools, called *U2B* (Snook and Butler, 2006) and *ArgoUML+B* (Ledang et al., 2003), similar to our own. The former generates B specification files from class and state/transition diagrams, and only the insert operation is generated for associations. Operations on attributes are not considered. Moreover, the considered domain (being reactive systems) and the semantics attached to UML diagrams are different from ours. The *ArgoUML+B* tool uses the *ArgoUML* environment for editing UML diagrams. The automation is restricted to class and state/transition diagrams. Let us remark that none of these tools include generation of code. In (Sun, Dong, Liu, and Wang, 2001), projection techniques and tools mapping UML (in the XMI format) to Object-Z (in the XML format) have been presented. This approach corresponds to the last step of our development: the UML class and activity diagrams describing the database schema and the B implementation of transactions. Table 2 presents a comparison of these tools based on nine representative criteria (minus "-" means that the concept is not supported). Recently, a number of research works investigate the reverse approach: deriving graphical views from formal notations (Idani, Ledru, and Bert, 2005; Chen and Miao, 2004). The derived graphical representations are mainly used as additional documentation that helps system's stakeholders, who are not necessarily expert in formal methods. Tools supporting such approaches, like B2UML (Tatibouet, Hammad, and Voisinet, 2002), are in the primary stages of development.

CONCLUSION AND FUTURE WORK

This paper reports on our experience developing a tool named, *UB2SQL*, that supports a formal approach based on UML and B formal method for the design and implementation of database applications. This approach includes two main phases: 1) translating UML diagrams into B specifications; 2) refining the obtained B specifications into a B representation of a relational implementation. In addition to benefits mentioned in the previous section, to our knowledge, *UB2SQL* is the first tool that covers the different phases of the development process. *UB2SQL* liberates engineers from several tedious tasks. It also allows software engineers to learn the formal notations and the rules implemented in the tools without needing to learn the theoretical background behind them. We have experimented with our approach on academic examples (much more complex than the one presented here) and on student projects, and promising results have been obtained. Also, it is planned to use this tool in the context of the EDEMOI [3] (Ledru, 2003) project that aims at investigating the integration of semi-formal methods (UML) and formal ones (B, Z, etc.) for modeling and verifying airport security properties.

Another interesting and important aspect when developing trustworthy information systems concerns integrity constraints that should always be maintained. The present paper only considers the constraints that can be described graphically using UML notation. Nevertheless, some complex business rules need to define integrity constraints that cannot be expressed using UML. For this reason, we directly specify them as B invariant properties that are simply added to the generated B specification. However, the generated operations may violate such B invariants. This is why we have defined in (Mammar, 2006) a formal approach to identify preconditions that take this kind of constraint into account. The key idea is the definition of rewriting and simplification rules that we apply to the B invariants in order to deduce the weakest precondition of a given operation such that its execution maintains it. A next step in our development activities is then to make UB2SQL evolve to support the automatic calculation of preconditions that permit to re-establish different B invariants.

REFERENCES

Abrial, J. R. (1996). *The B-Book: Assigning Programs to Meanings.* Cambridge University Press.

B-core. (1996). *B-Toolkit Release 3.2. Manual.* Oxford, U.K.

Barros, R. S. M. (1998). On the Formal Specification and Derivation of Relational Database Applications. *Electronic Notes in Theoretical Computer Science*, Volume 14.

Bernard, E., Legeard, B., Luck, X. & Peureux, F. (2004). Generation of test sequences from formal specifications: GSM11-11 standard case study. *International Journal of Software Practice and Experience* 34(10).

Bruel, J.M. & France, R. B. (1996). A Formal Object-oriented CASE Tool for the Development of Complex Systems'. *7th European Workshop on Next Generation of Case Tools.*

Chailloux, E. Manoury, P. & Pagano, B. (2000). *Développement d'Applications avec Objectif Caml.* France. O'REILLY.

Chen, Y. & Miao, H. (2004). From an Abstract Object-Z Specification to UML Diagram. *Journal of Information & Computational Science*, 1(2).

Clearsy. (2003). *Atelier B, Manuel de Référence* [Online]. Available: http://www.atelierb.societe.com.

Clearsy. (2004). http://www.b4free.com/.

Dupuy, S., Ledru, Y. & Chabre-Peccoud, M. (2000). An Overview of RoZ: A Tool for Integrating UML and Z Specifications. In: B. Wangler and L. Bergman (Eds.), *12th International Conference Advanced Information Systems Engineering (*pp. 417–430*)*, Vol. 1789 of *LNCS*, Springer-Verlag.

Edmond, D. (1995). Refining Database Systems. In: J.P. Bowen and M.G. Hinchey (Eds.), *The Z Formal Specification Notation* (pp. 25–44), Vol. 967 of *LNCS*, Springer-Verlag.

Elmasri, R. & Navathe, S. (2004). *Fundamental of Database Systems.* Addison-Wesley, 4th *edition.*

Gunther, T., Schewe, K. D. & Wetzel, I. (1993). On the Derivation of Executable Database Programs from Formal Specifications. In: J. C. P. Woodcock & P. G. Larsen (Eds.), *Industrial-Strength Formal Methods, First International Symposium of Formal Methods Europe* (pp. 351–366), Vol. 670 of *LNCS*, Springer-Verlag.

Hall, A. (1990). Using Z as a Specification Calculus for Object-Oriented Systems. In: D. Bjõrner, C. A. R. Hoare & H. Langmaack (Eds.). *VDM'90: 3rd International Conference, Kiel, Germany* (pp. 290-318), Vol. 428 of *LNCS*, Springer-Verlag.

Hammad, A., Tatibouet, B., Voisinet, J.C. & Weiping, W. (2002). From a B Specification to UML Statechart Diagrams. In: C. George & H. Miao (Eds.), *4th International Conference on Formal Engineering Methods* (pp. 511–522), Vol. 2495 of *LNCS*, Springer-Verlag.

Harel, D. (1987). Statecharts: A Visual Formalism for Complex Systems. *Science of Computer Programming*, 8(3), 231–274.

Idani, A., Ledru, Y. & Bert, D. (2005). Derivation of UML Class Diagrams as Static Views of Formal B Developments. In K. K. Lau & R. Banach (Eds.), 7th *International Conference on Formal Engineering Methods* (37-51). Vol. 3785 of *LNCS*, Springer-Verlag.

Jones, C. (1990). *Systematic Software Development using VDM.* Prentice Hall.

Kim, S. & Carrington, D. (1999). Formalizing the UML class diagram using OBJECT-Z. In: R. France & B. Rumpe (Eds.), *The Unified Modeling Language. Beyond the Standard. Second International Conference* (pp. 83–98). Vol. 1723 of *LNCS*, Springer-Verlag.

Laleau, R. (2000). On the Interest of Combining UML with the B Formal Method for the Specification of Database Applications. *2nd International Conference on Enterprise Information Systems* (pp. 56–63). Available: http://www.univ-paris12.fr/lacl/laleau/.

Laleau, R. & Mammar, A. (2000a). A Generic Process to Refine a B Specification into a Relational Database Implementation. In: J. P. Bowen, S. Dunne, A. Galloway and S. King (Eds.), *First International Conference of B and Z Users on Formal Specification and Development in Z and B* (pp. 22–41). Vol. 1878 of LNCS, Springer-Verlag.

Laleau, R. & Mammar, A. (2000b). An Overview of a Method and its Support Tool for Generating B Specifications from UML Notations. *Fifteenth IEEE International Conference on Automated Software Engineering* (pp. 269–272). IEEE Computer Society.

Laleau, R. & Polack, F. (2001a). A Rigorous Metamodel for UML Static Conceptual Modeling of Information Systems. In: K. R. Dittrich, A. Geppert & A. C. Norrie (Eds.). *13th International Conference on Advanced Information Systems Engineering* (pp. 402–416). Vol. 2068 of LNCS, Springer-Verlag.

Laleau, R. & Polack, F. (2001b). Specification of Integrity-Preserving Operations in Information Systems by Using a Formal UML-based Language. *Information & Software Technology* 43(12), 693–704.

Ledang, H., Souquieres, J. & Charles, S. (2003). ArgoUML+B : Un Outil de Transformation Systématique de Spécifications UML vers B. In: J.M. Jézéquel, (Ed.). *Approches Formelles dans l'Assistance au Développement de Logiciels* (pp. 3-18).

Ledang, H. & Souquires, J.(2002). Contributions for Modeling UML State-Charts in B. In: M. J. Butler, L. Petre & K. Sere (Eds). *Third International Conference on Integrated Formal Methods* (pp. 109-127). Vol. 2335 of LNCS, Springer-Verlag.

Ledru, Y. (2003). http://www-lsr.imag.fr/EDEMOI/

Leuschel, M & Butler, M. J. (2003). ProB: A model checker for B. In: K. Araki, S. Gnesi & D. Mandrioli (Eds.). *12th International FME Symposium* (pp. 855–874), Vol. 2805 of *LNCS*, Springer-Verlag.

Mammar, A. (2002). *Un Environnement Formel pour le Développement d'Applications Bases de Données*. Unpublished PhD thesis, CEDRIC Laboratory, Paris, France. Available: http://se2c.uni.lu/users/AM.

Mammar, A. & Laleau, R. (2003). Design of an Automatic Prover Dedicated to the Refinement of Database Applications. In: K. Araki, S. Gnesi & D. Mandrioli (Eds). *12th International Formal Methods Europe Symposium (*pp. 834–854*)*. Vol. 2805 of *LNCS*, Springer-Verlag.

Mammar, A. & Laleau, R. (2005). *From a B Formal Specification to an Executable Code: Application to the Relational Database Domain. Information & Software Technology Journal*. 48(4), 253-279.

Mammar, A. (2006). A systematic approach to generate B preconditions: application to the database domain. Technical Report, Telecom Sud-Paris, 2006. Submitted to the SOSYM Journal.

Marcano, R. & Levy, N. (2002). Transformation rules of OCL Constraints into B Formal Expressions. In: J. Jurjens, M. V. Cengarle, E. B. Fernandez, B. Rumpe, & R. Sandner (Eds.), *Critical Systems Development with UML. Proceedings of the UML'02 workshop* (pp. 155–162).

OMG. (2003). *Unified Modeling Language Specification, Version* 1.5.

Qian, X. (1993). The Deductive Synthesis of Database Transactions. *ACM Transactions on Database Systems* 18(4), 626–677.

Rational (2003). http://www.rational.com

Siau, K. & Cao, Q. (2001). Unified Modeling Language – A Complexity Analysis. *Journal of Database Management*, 12 (1), pp. 26-34.

Siau, K. & Lee, L. (2004). Are Use Case and Class Diagrams Complementary in Requirements Analysis? -- An Experimental Study on Use Case and Class Diagrams in UML," *Requirements Engineering*, 9(4), pp. 229-237.

Siau, K., Erickson, J. & Lee, L. (2005). Theoretical versus Practical Complexity: The Case of UML. *Journal of Database Management*, 16(3), pp. 40-57.

Snook, C. & Butler, M. (2001). Using a Graphical Design Tool for Formal Specification. In: G. Kadoda (Ed.), *13th Annual Workshop of the Psychology of Programming Interest Group* (pp. 311-321). *Available: http://www.ppig.org/papers/13th-snook.pdf.*

Snook, C. & Harrison, R. (2006). UML-B: Formal modelling and design aided by UML. *ACM Transactions on Software Engineering and Methodology, 15*(1), pp. 92-122.

Spivey, J. (1992). *The Z Notation: A Reference Manual*. International Prentice-Hall.

Sun, J., Dong, J. S., Liu, J. & Wang, H. (2001). Object-Z web environment and projections to UML. *10th international conference on World Wide Web (*pp. 725–734*)*. ACM Press.

Tatibouet, B., Hammad, A. &. Voisinet, J.C. (2002). From an abstract B specification to UML class diagrams. *2nd IEEE International Symposium on Signal Processing and Information Technology* (pp. 5–10).

Treharne, H. (2002). Supplementing a UML Development Process with B. In: L.H. Eriksson & P.A. Lindsay (Eds.), *FME2002: International Symposium Formal Methods Europe* (pp. 568-586). Vol. 2391 of LNCS, Springer-Verlag.

ENDNOTES

1. Duration is a total function, but AtelierB decomposes it as a partial function whose domain is equal to Loan.
2. (r1; r2) means that the rule r1 is applied first, and then the rule r2 is applied. r+ means that the rule (or an ordered set of rules) is applied as many times as possible.
3. The EDEMOI project is supported by the French National Action Concertée Incitative ``Sécurité Informatique'': http://www-lsr.imag.fr/EDEMOI/.

Section III
Queries and Data Analysis

Chapter VIII
Using Decision Trees to Predict Crime Reporting

Juliette Gutierrez
Claremont Graduate University, USA

Gondy Leroy
Claremont Graduate University, USA

ABSTRACT

Crime reports are used to find criminals, prevent further violations, identify problems causing crimes and allocate government resources. Unfortunately, many crimes go unreported. The National Crime Victimization Survey (NCVS) comprises data about incidents, victims, suspects and if the incident was reported or not. Current research using the NCVS is limited to statistical techniques resulting in a limited 'view' of the data. Our goal is to use decision trees to predict when crime is reported or not. We compare decision trees that are built based on domain knowledge with those created with three variable selection methods. We conclude that using decision trees leads to the discovery of several new variables to research further.

INTRODUCTION

The financial loss due to violent and personal crimes in 2004 was $15.85 billion (Sedgwick, 2006) and 57.5% of these crimes were not reported to the police (BJS, 2005). Other costs of unreported crimes include counseling costs, alarms, electronic surveillance equipment and indirect costs such as insurance and taxes (Sedgwick, 2006). An ongoing nationwide survey has been in use since 1973 in order to better understand both reported and unreported crimes. The National Crime Victimization Survey (NCVS) is used to gather data on injury, theft, damage, the amount of lost work and other characteristics of the incident, victim and suspect. One of the goals of the NCVS is to understand the quantity of crimes and crime types that are not reported to the police (BJS, 2005). Each year, 45,000 households are interviewed about past incidents where they were the victim and the NCVS is the main source of data on the characteristics of criminal victimizations (NACJD, 2006). In addition, it also describes crime types not reported to law enforcement and the characteristics of violent offenders (NACJD, 2006).

The NCVS classifies each incident as a personal or property crime. Personal crimes include rape, sexual attack, robbery, assault and purse snatching. Property crimes include burglary, theft and vandalism. For example in 2005, 51% of personal crimes and 59% of property crimes were not reported (BJS, 2006a). Table 1 shows the large number of personal crimes, by crime type, in 2005 and whether or not they were reported. There were a significant percentage of crimes that are not reported.

According to statistics from the Bureau of Justice Statistics (BJS), the criminal justice system does not act in response to many crime incidents because so many crimes are not discovered or reported to the police (BJS, 1967). Our goal is to define new techniques that can help law enforcement evaluate unreported versus reported crime data. Previous research done using the NCVS and descriptive statistics is limited to few variables which show only a limited view of the problem. In contrast, data mining allows for the use of more variables. Moreover, existing work uses descriptive statistics, such as logistic regression or binomial regression, which require a good understanding of these underlying techniques to interpret the outcome. Decision trees, in contrast, reveal which variables are most important and provide an easy to understand overview for users without a data mining background.

Table 1. Number of victimizations, by crime type and whether or not reported (BJS, 2005)

		Percentage Reported		
Crime Type	Number of Victimizations	Yes	No	Unknown
Completed Violence	1,658,660	62	37	1
Attempted/Threatened Violence	3,515,060	41	57	2
Rape/Sexual Assault	191,670	38	62	0
Crimes of Violence	5,365,390	47	51	2
Completed robbery	415,320	61	39	1
Attempted robbery	209,530	36	64	0
Robbery	624,850	52	47	1
Aggravated	1,052,260	62	37	1
Simple	3,304,930	42	55	2
Assault	4,357,190	47	51	2
Completed purse snatching	43,550	51	49	0
Attempted purse snatching	3,260	0	100	0
Pocket picking	180,260	32	67	2
Purse snatching/Pocket picking	227,070	35	64	1

Our objective is using data mining techniques, specifically decision trees, to find variables that influence whether a crime is reported. We focus on personal crimes in order to limit the size of the research dataset and to make the analysis more manageable. We would also expect different types of victim behaviors for property crimes versus personal crimes. Given the large number of variables available in the survey, selective processing using filters and wrappers is necessary to eliminate useless variables. In comparison to the limited number of variables used by descriptive statistics, we believe that many more variables influence the decision to report or not.

This chapter expands on previous work done using decision trees and the NCVS data (Gutierrez & Leroy, 2007) by adding another year of NCVS data. All decision tree models were run using personal crime data from 1992 – 2005. The results were comparable to findings using the 1992 – 2004 NCVS data from previous research.

BACKGROUND

A BJS Special Report states that on average between 1992 and 2000, only 31% of rapes and sexual assault were reported to the police (BJS, 2003). More robberies and assaults were reported: 57% of robberies and 55% of aggravated assaults. A review of current research shows that many variables influence if a crime will be reported. However, most research takes only a few variables into account. These variables are usually selected based on existing theories or assumptions of the researchers and may provide only a partial picture based on only a few variables.

Regression analysis and frequency distributions have been used frequently with the NCVS data to look at chosen variables. Four aspects of an incident, besides the crime type, seem most influential in the decision to report. The first factor, which is also the most researched, is the relationship of the offender to the victim. Violent crime committed by a stranger is more likely to be reported than violent crime committed by non-strangers (BJS, 2003). Felson, et. al., however, (R. Felson, Messner, Hoskin, & Deane, 2002) found that people are just as likely to report domestic assaults, which is one type of violent crime, as they are to report assaults by other people they know. Earlier research by them (Richard B. Felson, Messner, & Hoskin, 1999) included third party reporting data they found that the relationship between the offender and the victim affects third party but not victim reporting. These conclusions are consistent in that it shows no effect on the relationship to victim reporting, but it goes beyond the earlier work by looking at third party reporting. Third parties are people other than the victim such as members of the household or other witnesses. There were two reasons for this effect: 1) third parties are hesitant to report minor assaults and 2) third parties are not likely to witness an assault between people in ongoing personal relationships. In both their studies, they used the NCVS data with frequency distributions and regression analyses.

The age of the victim is the second decisive factor in reporting behavior. Over the years, the BJS reported that older victims, age 65 and older, are more likely than younger victims to report violence and personal theft to the police (BJS, 2000, 2003). Others have found similar results: most crimes against juveniles are not reported (Finkelhor & Ormrod, 2001; Finkelhor & Wolak, 2003). This underreporting is serious since we know that persons age 12 to 19 are the most frequent victims of crime in the United States (BJS, 2006b). Watkins showed with binomial and regression analyses that this inequality in reporting between juveniles and adults could not be accounted for by individual, incident or situational variables (Watkins, 2005).

The third and fourth factors are more recently reported. The third factor is experience with past victimizations. Xie, Pogarsky, et al. (Xie, Pogarsky, Lynch, & McDowall, 2006) used NCVS data from 1998 – 2000 and concluded that an individual was more likely to report a subsequent victimization when prior incidents had been investigated by the police. However, this was only true when the victim reported the incident, not when it was reported by someone else. They also found that whether there was an arrest as a result of past incidents did not effect whether the individual reported a subsequent victimization to the police and also that whether an arrest was made as a result of past incidents with a member of the victim's household did not effect whether the individual reported a subsequent victimization. The fourth, newest factor found in the literature on crime reporting is whether or not the victim is Hispanic. Hispanics are the largest ethnic group in the United States and Rennison showed, using NCVS data from 1993 – 2003, that Hispanics are significantly less likely to report serious violence compared to non-Hispanic whites (Rennison, 2007). However, Hispanics are more likely to report simple assaults than non-Hispanic whites (Rennison, 2007).

Decision trees can provide an alternative way to look at all the variables in the NCVS. Instead of limiting the analysis to a few variables, many variables can be processed together to see what relationships exist. This is different than previous research which uses traditional statistical methods. Data mining methods, specifically decision trees, allow the data to speak for itself and show which variables are most useful in predicting whether a crime has been reported or not.

DECISION TREES

Overview

Data mining helps find patterns in existing data sets. It can be used as a tool for helping to explain the data and make predictions about it. Decision trees are one approach for such predictions. A decision tree is a classifier in the form of a tree where each node in the tree is either a leaf node or a decision node. In Figure 1, we show a partial decision tree. Leaf nodes (rectangles) provide a final classification (REPORT_NO or REPORT_YES) to all data instances that arrive at that node. A decision node (oval) is where a particular variable is tested. In this example, when the value of VICTIM_AGE is greater than 23 the classification will be REPORT_YES meaning that the crime was reported. When the value of VICTIM_AGE is less than or equal to 23 the classification will be REPORT_NO.

Figure 1. Partial decision tree

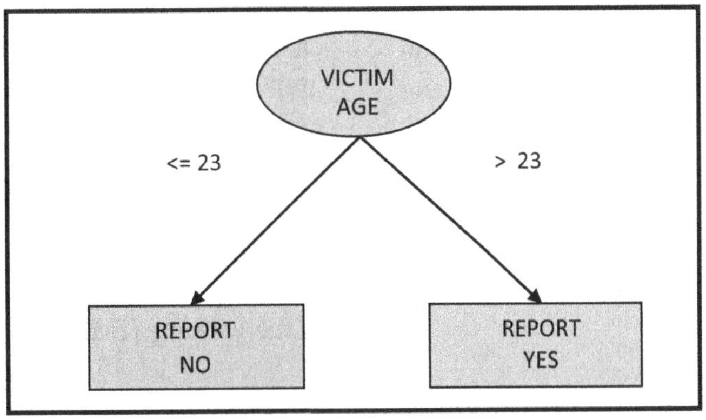

Justification for using Decision Trees

Decision trees have the advantage of being easy to interpret which makes them practical and useful. Quinlan (Quinlan, 1986) states that despite the fact that a decision tree is a simple representation of knowledge, it can still be useful for generating practical solutions to complicated problems. Decision trees make no assumptions about the data which means that the induction algorithms do not rely on any other information other than that which exists in the data. They can handle both categorical and continuous variables. The NCVS data contains both categorical and continuous variables. Furthermore, decision trees are unaffected by insignificant variables since the algorithms are developed to learn which variables are the best to use through the concept of information uncertainty or entropy. As a consequence they indirectly reveal importance of variables: the most important variables are selected first when building a tree.

Although there are many advantages, using decision trees may also have disadvantages. Their main weakness is that they can be unstable which means that variations in the data can cause the induction algorithms to create different decision trees on seemingly similar data. Decision trees also do not work well on small datasets since the induction algorithms learn from the data. In general, a larger dataset helps the algorithms to make better decisions about variables. Larger test samples also allow for more accurate error estimates (Witten & Frank, 2005). Finally, decision trees optimize locally at each level of the tree and so are not good tools to show interactions.

The ID3 algorithm, developed by Quinlan (Quinlan, 1986), uses a divide-and-conquer approach based on entropy to create decision trees. Entropy is a measure of the amount of uncertainty. The algorithms for creating decision trees calculate the information gain for each variable – and so reduce uncertainty – and select the next decision node as that variable that leads to the most information gain or entropy reduction. Several improvements to ID3 which deal with noisy and incomplete data (Quinlan, 1986) produced a practical and influential algorithm for creating decision trees called C4.5 (Witten & Frank, 2005). This is helpful because real-world data, such as that from the NCVS, is unlikely to be entirely accurate and is therefore noisy.

Current Research using Decision Trees

Many other fields of research use data mining techniques and classifiers, such as biology, bioinformatics and medicine. For example, Firouzi et. al. used decision trees to help select patients with inflammatory bowel disease (IBD) who may be at greater risk for developing low bone mineral density (BMD) (Firouzi et al., 2007). The patients smoking habits and use of calcium supplements were shown to be the most important variables in regards to selecting truly affected IBD patients who may require bone densitometry. Huang, Gromiha and Ho (Huang, Gromiha, & Ho, 2007) used interpretable decision trees developed using adaptive boosting to predict protein stability changes. The methods developed in this research showed an accuracy of 82% for discriminating the stabilizing and destabilizing mutant and showed correlation of 0.70 for predicting protein stability changes upon mutations (Huang, Gromiha, & Ho, 2007). Finally, Estrada-Gil et. al. used genetic programming decision trees to predict risk associated genetic variants in common diseases (Estrada-Gil et al., 2007). These researchers comment how common statistical methods are often unable to detect interactions between some of the variants (Estrada-Gil et al., 2007).

ISSUES, CONTROVERSIES, PROBLEMS

Current research is limited to a few statistical techniques resulting in a limited 'view' of the data. Not all variance is explained with these statistical methods so it is important to have different views. Interpreting the outcome of such analyses requires a good background in statistics making it less practical for law enforcement personnel. Visualizations using geographic information systems (GIS) are becoming more popular in law enforcement, but they cannot help answer the question of crime reporting. This research focuses on one alternative, possible solution: decision trees.

SOLUTIONS: PREDICTING CRIME REPORTING WITH DECISION TREES

Overview

We build decision trees to predict when a crime is reported or not. As a first step to make the decision trees smaller, which makes them more practical and useful, we eliminate unnecessary variables. We use 2 methods to eliminate variables: filters and wrappers. Two filters are used and compared: Chi-Squared and Cramer's V Coefficient. One wrapper is used: Forward Selection. We also create a decision tree based on domain knowledge for comparison to our other three methods and to ongoing research using common statistical methods. We conclude by summarizing the results.

Variable Elimination

The primary goal of this phase of research was to pre-process the data to eliminate variables. Many datasets contain too many variables for end users to evaluate. However, only variables that will not contribute to the decision tree can be removed. There are several statistical methods to accomplish. We compare and contrast two fundamentally different methods: filters and wrappers (Witten & Frank, 2005)

Filters

Filters process data independently of the learning algorithm. Variable ranking is a filter process that scores each variable according to a method such as Chi-squared or Cramer's V Coefficient, ranks the output and selects the best, i.e. highest rank , variables (Wang, Parish, Smith, & Vrbsky, 2005).

Chi-squared can be used as a filter-based approach to eliminating variables. It is used widely in research because of the large amount of data which is collected at a nominal level of measurement (Sproull, 1995). Chi-squared tests the null hypothesis that the variables are independent of each other and have no association (Sproull, 1995). It can be useful to find the variables that have a significant association in regard to the target variable (Wang, Parish, Smith, & Vrbsky, 2005). Chi-squared can be calculated by (Becher, Berkhin, & Freeman, 2000):

$$X^2(X,Y) = N_{jq}(P_{jq}-P_jP_q)^2 / (P_jP_q)$$

Where X is the source variable with values j ranging from 1 to J and Y is the target variable with values q ranging from 1 to Q. P represents the distribution. N is the total number of data instances. The outcome indicates whether there is a relationship between the variables.

Cramer's V Coefficient is a measure of the strength of the relationship. It is a well-known normalization of Chi-squared (Becher, Berkhin, & Freeman, 2000). It is similar to Chi-squared in that it measures the level of association between two variables. The values of the Cramer's V Coefficient range from 0 to 1. The higher the V Coefficient of a variable indicates more relevancy to the target variable (Wang, Parish, Smith, & Vrbsky, 2005). The Cramer's V Coefficient can be calculated by (Becher, Berkhin, & Freeman, 2000):

$$V(X,Y) = X^2(X,Y) / (N \min(Q,J) - 1)$$

Wrappers

Wrappers process the data using the evaluation function dependent on the learning algorithm (Wang, Parish, Smith, & Vrbsky, 2005). In order to implement a wrapper it is necessary to know how to search all possible variable subsets, how to assess performance, when to halt the wrapper process and which learning algorithm to use (Guyon & Elisseeff, 2003).

Forward Selection is a wrapper-based approach to eliminating variables. It starts without any variables but adds variables, one at a time into a subset based on evaluation criteria from the learning algorithm, then retests the subset of the variables with the learning algorithm (Witten & Frank, 2005). We used a forward selection process implemented using Weka, an open source Java data mining application (http://www.cs.waikato.ac.nz/ml/weka/). The J48 tree classifier is the C4.5 implementation available in Weka.

Dataset

The NCVS has a large number of variables on the frequency and characteristics of criminal victimizations (NACJD, 2006). The data and the codebook are available to download from http://www.icpsr.umich.edu/NACJD/NCVS/. We used dataset 4469 DS1: 1992-2005 Incident-Level Concatenated File and used all values for the selected variables. No translations were done on any of the variables except for the classification variable (V4399) which was translated to 1 = YES, 2 = NO and all remaining values were translated to MAYBE. In its present state, there are 834 variables. However, the first 2 quarters of 1992 data were deleted from the dataset since there were changes in the survey and the content of the data was inconsistent with all other data and therefore could not be used (USDOJ, 2006). We included all 38,494 rows which includes personal crimes from 1992 to 2005.

Variable Selection Methods

Baseline Variables

For the baseline dataset, we excluded three sets of variables whose information cannot contribute to the victim's decision. The first set consists of linkage and identification variables that are part of the management of the survey data. The second set of variables that are excluded are those that have a direct correlation to V4399 (Reported to Police?) or directly depend on this outcome. The third set of variables were those without a relation to the incident but informative about the NCVS interview.

Filters

We created a Chi-squared filter using an Oracle database with a PL/SQL procedure to calculate the Chi-squared value for each variable in the baseline dataset. The Chi-squared values were written to a table then sorted by the Chi-squared value. The variables with the highest Chi-squared values were selected. We also test the Cramer's V Coefficient filter for comparison to Chi-squared. We wrote an additional PL/SQL procedure to calculate the Cramer's V Coefficient value for each variable in the baseline dataset. The Cramer's V Coefficient values were also written to a table then sorted by the Cramer's V Coefficient. The variables with the highest Cramer's V Coefficient values were selected.

Wrappers

A forward wrapper was implemented to compare against the filter methods. The wrapper was implemented by running each variable in the baseline dataset with V4399 (Reported to Police?) as the classification variable to be predicted. A decision tree was created for each variable and the correctly classified percentage was maintained for each. The variable which created the decision tree with the highest accuracy was selected into a subset of variables to use for the next iteration. The subset of chosen variables was run with all remaining variables in the baseline dataset with V4399 (Reported to Police?) as the variable used for prediction. A decision tree was created with the subset of chosen variables and each remaining variable and the correctly classified percentage was maintained for each variable. The variable with the highest accuracy or correct classifications was selected into the subset of variables to use for the next iteration. This process was iterated until the accuracy of the decision tree started to decline.

The Weka input file was created with data generated from SQL queries that were run against the Oracle database and the required header portion of the file in the ARFF format. Weka (http://www.cs.waikato.ac.nz/ml/weka/) was used to create decision trees and the results were maintained both in Oracle and in Excel. Every classifier run done with Weka used a 10-fold cross validation. The data was then sorted by the accuracy of the resulting decision trees and the variables with the highest accuracy were selected.

Results

In 2005, 57.4% of all crimes were not reported to the police, 41.3% of all crimes were reported and the status of 1.3% of all crimes was not known and not available (BJS, 2006a).

Table 2. Chi-squared variables dataset

Description	Variable	Accuracy (% Correct)
Help From Victim's Agencies?	V4467	57
Incident Occur at Work Site?	V4484	57
Job Located in City/Suburb/Rural Area?	V4483	58
Type of Work Performed at Time of Incident?	V4481	59
Type of Industry at Time of Incident?	V4482	59
Where Did Incident Happen?	V4024	62
Type of Crime Code	V4529	65
Activity at time of incident?	V4478	65
One or more than one Offender?	V4234	65
Any Others Harmed or Robbed?	V4203	65
Total Amount of Medical Expenses?	V4140	66
Know Anything About Any Offenders?	V4235	66
Business Type?	V4481B	66
Medical Care: Emergency Room/Clinic?	V4133	66
Did Actions of Others Help?	V4185	66

Baseline Variables

We excluded 232 variables from the dataset: 32 linkage variables, 77 highly correlated variables and 123 non-incident related variables. The result of this selection process created the baseline dataset for the remainder of the research.

Decision Trees with Chi-Squared Variable Selection (Filter 1)

The variables in Table 2 were selected using Chi-squared on the baseline dataset. These variables had the highest ranked Chi-squared values. We used the top 30 variables with the Weka J48 classifier. Thirty variables were used because of memory and processing limits. The table shows the variables from the resulting decision tree which contained fifteen variables showing that including more variables would not have changed the outcome. Variables that did not add to the accuracy of the tree were eliminated in order to make the tree smaller and easier to use.

V4133, Medical Care: Emergency Room/ Clinic?, is the root node selected with this subset of variables. This means it has the highest information gain, so it is most useful at this stage to predict if crime will be reported or not. The resulting decision tree has an accuracy of 66% with 1,119 leaves. The total size of the tree is 2,237 nodes.

Decision Trees with Cramer's V Variable Selection (Filter 2)

The variables in Table 3 were selected using Cramer's V Coefficient on the baseline dataset. These variables are ranked according to the Cramer's V values with the top value having the highest value. As with the previous filter and so we can compare decision trees, we selected the top 30 variables. The resulting decision tree

Table 3. Cramer's V variables dataset

Description	Variable	Accuracy (% Correct)
Help From Victim's Agencies?	V4467	57
Incident Occur at Work Site?	V4484	57
Job Located in City/Suburb/Rural Area?	V4483	58
Type of Work Performed at Time of Incident?	V4481	59
Type of Industry at Time of Incident?	V4482	59
Anything Damaged?	V4387	61
Where Did Incident Happen?	V4024	63
Type of Crime Code	V4529	66
Activity at Time of Incident?	V4478	66
One or More Than One Offender?	V4234	66
Any Others Harmed or Robbed?	V4203	66
Total Amount of Medical Expenses?	V4140	67
Where was Medical Care Received?	V4128	67
Residue: Medical Care Site?	V4136	67
Reason Time Lost: None?	V4496	67
Business Type?	V4481B	67

contained 16 variables. Including more variables would not have changed the outcome of the decision tree since only 16 of the 30 variables were used in the resulting decision tree. Variables that did not add to the accuracy of the tree were eliminated in order to make the tree smaller and easier to use.

V4496, Reason Time Lost: None, is the root node selected with this subset of variables which means it was the most useful at this level to predict if crime would be reported or not. The resulting decision tree has an accuracy of 67% with 1,084 leaves. The total size of the tree is 2,167 nodes.

Decision Trees with Forward Selection of Variables

All variables in the baseline dataset were processed with the Weka J48 classifier. The 200 variables that made up the decision trees with the highest accuracy were selected to continue with the Forward Selection process due to the manual nature of this processing. In the future, we will automate this process.

The variables in Table 4 were selected using this Forward Selection wrapper. These variables had the highest ranked decision tree accuracy values. V4498, Total Number Days Lost?, is the root node selected with this subset of variables which means that it was most useful in predicting crime reporting at this level. The resulting decision tree has an accuracy of 69% with 872 leaves. The total size of the tree is 1,743 nodes.

Decision Trees with Domain Knowledge Variable Selection

To better compare our results with the ongoing work, we also built a decision tree using the variables reported in the literature. As discussed earlier, there are five factors: crime type (BJS, 2003), the relationship of the offender to the victim

Table 4. Forward selection variables dataset

Description	Variable
Type of Crime Code	V4529
Activity at Time of Incident	V4478
Single Offender: How Did Respondent Know Offender?	V4245
Check B: Attack, Threat, Theft	V3052
Which Best Describes Your Job?	V3074
How Many Times Incident Occurred?	V4016
Total Number Days Lost?	V4498
Help From Victims Agencies?	V4467
Age (Allocated)	V3014
Anything Damaged?	V4387
Covered By Medical Insurance	V4139
Number of Household Members Harmed/Robbed	V4207
Stolen, Attack, Threat: Offender Known	V3044
Thought Crime But Didn't Call Police	V3054
Something Taken? (Allocated)	V4288
Number of Others Harmed or Robbed	V4205

Table 5. Domain knowledge variable selection

Description	Variable
Type of Crime Code	V4529
Age (Allocated)	V3014
Single Offender: How Did Respondent Know Offender?	V4245
How Many Times Incident Occurred?	V4016
Hispanic Origin	V3024

(R. B. Felson, 2002; Richard B. Felson, Messner, & Hoskin, 1999; Rennison & Rand, 2003), the age of the victim (BJS, 2000, 2003; Finkelhor & Ormrod, 2001; Finkelhor & Wolak, 2003; Watkins, 2005), how many times the incident occurred (Xie, Pogarsky, Lynch, & McDowall, 2006) and having a Hispanic origin (Rennison, 2007). We selected variables from the NCVS data that relate to these five factors. This was a subjective process as some research did not list the actual variables from the NCVS survey. We used 5 variables to build the decision tree. After building the tree, variable V3014, Age (Allocated), became the root node selected. The resulting decision tree has an accuracy of 64% with 227 leaves. The total size of the tree is 453 nodes. According to this decision tree, V3014, Age (Allocated) is the predictor of whether or not victims will report a criminal victimization.

Summary of Variable Selection Methods

Table 6 summarizes the results. Each of these methods excludes variables that are used to manage the NCVS dataset. The Forward Selection wrapper process yields the smallest and most accurate decision tree. This tree has about 32% fewer leaves and is smaller overall while being the most accurate. While the Forward Selection process is slower due to the multiple iterations, it does produce a better tree. The tree based on domain knowledge is much smaller due to the smaller number of variables that were used as input. It also has a slightly lower accuracy. The trees created with the Chi-squared and Cramer's V Coefficient filters are the most similar trees with their number of leaves and the size and accuracy of the trees being very comparable. The

Table 6. Summary of variable selection methods

Method	Leaves	Size	Overall Accuracy	Root Node	Description	Accuracy YES	Accuracy NO	Accuracy MAYBE
Chi-squared	1,119	2,237	66%	V4133	Medical Care: Emergency Room/Clinic?	9,473/17,003 = 56%	16,017/20,972 = 76%	22/519 = 4%
Cramer's V	1,084	2,167	67%	V4496	Reason Time Lost: None	9,590/17,003 = 56%	16,217/20,972 = 77%	27/519 = 5%
Forward Selection	872	1,743	69%	V4498	Total Number Days Lost		16,283/20,972 = 75%	24/519 = 4%
Domain Knowledge	227	453	64%	V3014	Age (Allocated)	8,992/17,003 = 53%	15,818/20,972 = 75%	0/519 = 0%

accuracy of these decision trees are comparable to those from research using the smaller NCVS data set, from 1992 to 2004, that we reported earlier (Gutierrez & Leroy, 2007).

If we were to assign the outcome "not reported" to all incidents, our prediction would be 57.4% accurate (baseline). Our decision trees could predict reporting of crime with about 10% more accuracy than the baseline.

RECOMMENDATIONS

The variables that we discovered are different from previous research endeavors. The Forward Selection wrapper method selected V4498, Total Number of Days Lost?, as the root. The two filter methods chose, V4133, Medical Care: Emergency Room/Clinic?, and V4496, Reason Time Lost: None. The wrapper approach provides a different, but equally accurate view of the data compared to the filter approach and compared to the domain knowledge approach. These results are especially interesting as none of the deciding variables were, to our knowledge, used in any prior research to predict crime reporting. Data mining has raised these variables as areas for further research. The area of medical care needs to be carefully researched further since some types of violent crimes require mandatory reporting to the police by healthcare professionals. All of these newly found predictor variables require further research.

Although this first step shows the strength of using decision trees, a shortcoming of our approach is the complexity of these decision trees due to the increased number of variables. With many variables, the size and complexity of the decision tree can easily grow to become unusable and it becomes more difficult for a human expert to interpret.

FUTURE TRENDS

In the future, we will investigate data transformation methods to increase accuracy and reduce the complexity and size of the tree. Preliminary research shows that the addition of data transformations does decrease the complexity and size of the tree and increase the accuracy of the tree significantly. We will also look at other filters and wrappers. Backward elimination is another wrapper method where all variables are brought into the algorithm and then eliminated one at a time. Another path of research would be to analyze property crimes as opposed to personal crimes. Finally, we will integrate such decision trees as tools into a decision support system for law enforcement.

CONCLUSION

Traditional approaches to analyzing the NCVS data have been by descriptive statistics, regression analysis and other common statistical methods. These traditional approaches are limited to a few independent and dependent variables. Our research differs from the traditional approach by using decision trees to analyze the NCVS data. Decision trees allow for multiple variables to be brought into the analysis. The logic to create the decision tree causes the critical variables to be towards the root of the tree and easily ascertained. By definition, the induction algorithm discovers the variables that add the most information gain. We used data mining techniques, specifically decision trees, instead of traditional statistics to predict when crimes are reported. We compared decision trees that were created with variables selected with two filters, Chi-squared and Cramer's V Coefficient, with a forward selection wrapper and with a decision tree based on current domain knowledge. We conclude that using decision trees leads to the discovery of several new variables to research further.

ACKNOWLEDGMENT

The authors would like to acknowledge LAPD Detective Dave McGowan for feedback on initial ideas.

The authors also acknowledge that this research was made possible with support from a Fletcher Jones Grant.

REFERENCES

Becher, J. D., Berkhin, P., & Freeman, E. (2000). *Automating Exploratory Data Analysis for Efficient Data Mining.* Paper presented at the Knowledge Discovery and Data Mining, Boston, MA USA.

BJS. (1967). What is the sequence of events in the criminal justice system? Retrieved October, 2006, from http://www.ojp.usdoj.gov/bjs/flowchart.htm

BJS. (2000). Crimes against Persons Age 65 or Older, 1992 - 1997. Retrieved November, 2006, from http://www.ojp.usdoj.gov/bjs/abstract/cpa6597.htm

BJS. (2003). Reporting Crime to the Police, 1992 -2000. Retrieved November, 2006, from http://www.ojp.usdoj.gov/bjs/abstract/rcp00.htm

BJS. (2005). Percent distribution of victimization, by type of crime and whether of not reported to the police. 2006, from http://www.ojp.usdoj.gov/bjs/pub/pdf/cvus/current/cv0591.pdf

BJS. (2006a). Percent distribution of victimizations, by type of crime and whether or not reported to the police. 2006, from http://www.ojp.usdoj.gov/bjs/pub/pdf/cvus/current/cv0591.pdf

BJS. (2006b, September 10, 2006). Teens and young adults experience the highest rates of violent crime. 2006

Estrada-Gil, J. K., Fernandez-Lopez, J. C., Hernandez-Lemus, E., Silva-Zolezzi, I., Hildalgo-Miranda, A., Jimenez-Sanchez, G., et al. (2007). GPDTI: A Genetic Programming Decision Tree Induction method to find epistatic effects in common complex diseases. *Bioinformatics, 23*(13), 167-174.

Felson, R., Messner, S. F., Hoskin, A. W., & Deane, G. (2002). Reasons for Reporting and Not Reporting Domestic Violence to the Police. *Criminology, 40*(3), 617-650.

Felson, R. B. (2002). *Violence and Gender Reexamined.* Washington D.C.: The American Psychological Association.

Felson, R. B., Messner, S. F., & Hoskin, A. (1999). The Victim-Offender Relationship And Calling The Police in Assaults. *Criminology, 37*(4), 931-947.

Finkelhor, D., & Ormrod, R. K. (2001). Factors in the Underreporting of Crimes Against Juveniles. *Child Maltreatment, 6*(3), 219-229.

Finkelhor, D., & Wolak, J. (2003). Reporting Assaults Against Juveniles to the Police: Barriers and Catalysts. *Journal of Interpersonal Violence, 18*(2), 103-128.

Firouzi, F., Rashidi, M., Hashemi, S., Kangavari, M., Bahari, A., Daryani, N. E., et al. (2007). A decision tree-based approach for determining low bone mineral density in inflammatory bowel disease using WEKA software. *European Journal of Gastroenterology and Hepatology, 19*(12), 1075-1081.

Gutierrez, J., & Leroy, G. (2007, August 9, 2007). *Predicting Crime Reporting with Decision Trees and the National Crime Victimization Survey.* Paper presented at the Americas' Conference on Information Systems, Keystone, CO.

Guyon, I., & Elisseeff, A. (2003). An Introduction to Variable and Feature Selection. *Journal of Machine Learning, 3*, 1157-1182.

Huang, L.-T., Gromiha, M., & Ho, S.-Y. (2007). iPTREE-STAB: interpretable decision tree based method for predicting protein stability changes upon mutations. *Bioinformatics, 23*(10), 1292-1293.

NACJD. (2006). National Crime Victimization Survey Resource Guide. 2006, from http://www.icpsr.umich.edu/NACJD/NCVS/

Quinlan, J. R. (1986). Induction of Decision Trees. *Machine Learning, 1*(1), 81 - 106.

Rennison, C. M. (2007). Reporting to the Police by Hispanic Victims of Violence. *Violence and Victims, 22.*

Sedgwick, J. (2006). The Cost of Crime: Understanding the Financial and Human Impact of Criminal Activity. 2006, from http://www.ojp.usdoj.gov/ocom/testimonies/sedgwick_test_060919.pdf

Sproull, N. L. (1995). *Handbook of Research Methods A Guide for Practitioners and Students in the Social Sciences* (Second ed.). Lanham, MD: The Scarecrow Press, Inc.

USDOJ. (2006). *National Crime Victimization Survey, 1992-2005: Concatenated Incident-Level* Files Codebook. from http://www.icpsr.umich.edu/NACJD/NCVS.

Wang, H., Parish, A., Smith, R. K., & Vrbsky, S. (2005). *Variable Selection and Ranking for Analyzing Automobile Traffic Accident Data.* Paper presented at the 2005 ACM Symposium on Applied Computing.

Watkins, A. M. (2005). Examining the Disparity Between Juvenile and Adult Victims in Notifying the Police: A Study of Mediating Variables. *Journal of Research in Crime and Delinquency, 42*(3), 333 - 353.

Witten, I. H., & Frank, E. (2005). *Data Mining: Practical Machine Learning Tools and Techniques* (Second ed.). San Francisco, CA: Morgan Kaufmann Publishers.

Xie, M., Pogarsky, G., Lynch, J. P., & McDowall, D. (2006). Prior Police Contact and Subsequent Victim Reporting: Results from the NCVS. *Justice Quarterly, 23*(4), 481 - 501.

Chapter IX
A Model for Estimating the Savings from Dimensional vs. Keyword Search

Karen Corral
Boise State University, USA

David Schuff
Temple University, USA

Robert D. St. Louis
Arizona State University, USA

Ozgur Turetken
Ryerson University, Canada

ABSTRACT

Inefficient and ineffective search is widely recognized as a problem for businesses. The shortcomings of keyword searches have been elaborated upon by many authors, and many enhancements to keyword searches have been proposed. To date, however, no one has provided a quantitative model or systematic process for evaluating the savings that accrue from enhanced search procedures. This paper presents a model for estimating the total cost to a company of relying on keyword searches versus a dimensional search approach. The model is based on the Zipf-Mandelbrot law in quantitative linguistics. Our analysis of the model shows that a surprisingly small number of searches are required to justify the cost associated with encoding the metadata necessary to support a dimensional search engine. The results imply that it is cost effective for almost any business organization to implement a dimensional search strategy.

INTRODUCTION

People spend a tremendous amount of time searching for information. One estimate puts the average employee's time at 3-1/2 hours a week for unsuccessful searches (Ultraseek, 2006). For a 1,000 employee company, that works out to $9.7 million a year for just the cost of salary (Ultraseek, 2006). Some estimates put the cost as high as $33 million annually per company when taking into consideration the costs of recreating the information not found (Thompson, 2004). Furthermore, between 60-80% of queries over an intranet (as opposed to the Internet) are for material that the searcher has previously seen (Mukherjee and Mao, 2004).

Keyword search has several well-known problems (for a review, see Blair, 2002), but its advantage over other methods is that once the documents have been saved, there is no additional work that the user has to perform. One alternative to keyword search is dimensional search. Dimensional search eliminates the ambiguity of words (which causes so many of the problems for keyword search) through the use of pre-defined categories (dimensions) to define documents as well as finite sets of possible values for each category. It has been demonstrated that dimensional search reduces the number of irrelevant documents returned in the result set (LaBrie, 2004). However, there is a significant, up-front, time investment that has to be made for dimensional search. In particular, meta-data must be stored about each document, and much of this information must be determined and entered by a human user. So the question becomes, is the increased retrieval accuracy worth the initial cost of categorizing documents?

The content management market was estimated to be over $1 billion in 2003 (Dunwoodie, 2004), and to have grown 9.7% in 2006 (Webster, 2007). Vendors of this software make quite amazing claims about the efficacy of their software, yet for all the money being spent by companies, there has been little academic work done to evaluate these systems. We want to determine the cost, in time, of performing a keyword search versus the cost, in time, of performing a dimensional search, including the initial time-investment. Factors that affect the overall cost of searching include the start-up costs of any content management system, the size of the library (it is much easier to exhaustively search a small library than a large library), the size of the documents in the library (books are more difficult to search than are e-mail messages), and the cost of not finding the document.

While evaluating the best approach to studying this question, we considered a number of research methodologies. A case study approach to this problem, which is largely what IDC, Gartner and other commercial information providers use, would be hampered by a lack of generalizability. Also, attempting to collect data on an employee's search could be considered invasive by the employee. If employees know that their time and actions are being tracked, they might elect to perform searches outside of such data collection, out of concern that the collected data might be used to evaluate their work rather than the content management software. Moreover, drawing data from a survey of content management product users makes comparison of such data difficult as the nature of searches might vary considerably by company as well as by user. And there is the additional concern that users might not have an accurate sense of the time or the effectiveness of their searches.

An experiment would need to consider all the above factors, plus ensure the proper motivation of the users. For these reasons, we elected to use an analytical modeling approach, which allows us to use different values for variables and examine their impact on search cost. From our model we were able to determine the break-even point, in terms of the number of searches, at which dimensional search becomes more cost effective than keyword search. That is, we were able to determine the number of searches an organization must do in order to justify the up-front cost of determining and entering the metadata that is required to support dimensional search.

The rest of this paper is organized as follows. In the next section, we briefly review some of the most important findings in word frequency distributions. After that, we present the basic model for net search cost. We then present a model for estimating the net search cost of keyword searches, followed by a model for estimating the net search cost of dimensional searches. The output of the two models is then compared, followed by a discussion of the implications of the results and possible refinements of the model.

WORD FREQUENCY DISTRIBUTIONS

In 1949, George Zipf published an analysis of the number of different words used and their frequency of occurrence in James Joyce's novel Ulysses. From that, he concluded that $f(r) = k/r^{\alpha}$, where k and α are constants specific to the text, and $\alpha \approx 1$. Zipf demonstrated that this relationship held for Greek and Latin, concluding it held for non-English languages, equally.

Mandelbrot pointed out in 1966 that Zipf's distribution did not adequately approximate the most frequently occurring words when plotted on log-log axes. He adjusted the distribution to $f(r) = k/(1+Cr)^{\alpha}$ where k, C, α are constants specific to the text, and $\alpha \approx 1$. Generally speaking, this resolves the problems associated with function words, or those words which appear very frequently and are usually at a rank lower than 100.

Zipf and Mandelbrot were limited in their analysis by the need to hand count documents to determine the number of times words appeared. In 2001, Montemurro was not constrained by that and was able to analyze very large corpuses. He observed that distributions for very large corpuses consistently began to depart significantly from Zipf's distribution around a rank of 2000-3000. Applying two power-law regimes in a single relationship, as first identified by Tsallis, Montemurro tested $f(r) = 1/([1 - \lambda/\mu + (\lambda/\mu)e^{(q-1)\mu r}]^{1/(q-1)})$, and found that it fits very well even in the low and high rank ranges.

Ha, Sicilia-Garcia, Ming and Smith (2002) analyzed very large corpuses for behavior with two, three, four, and five word combinations as well as the previously studied one word work. In this, they found that Zipf's distribution does hold in English and in Mandarin.

Understanding the distribution of words within documents, and using the findings of these researchers, it is possible to develop a model that estimates the cost of searching with either the keyword method or the dimensional method. That model is presented in the next section.

MODELING NET SEARCH COST

In this section, we develop a basic model that allows us to compare the relative benefits of dimensional search as compared to keyword search. The output from this model is the net search cost (the difference between the dimensional and keyword search) measured in time spent finding a document. We frame the model in terms of cost for several reasons. First, search is a time-consuming activity and therefore every search is an expense to an organization. Second, it is simple (and accurate) to operationalize the cost of search as time – the cost of the technology is trivial compared to the human cost of labor spent locating documents. Third, it simplifies the comparison of alternative solutions since the search method with the lowest cost will be the best choice.

The various methodologies for document search all have two basic components: the initial expense to construct the document store (the costs "now") and the cost of locating documents in the store (the costs "later"). Therefore, we can represent the total search cost as

$$TC = C_{initial} + C_{ongoing}$$

where $C_{initial}$ is the cost to set up the document store and $C_{ongoing}$ represents the cost of the search. The savings from an alternative to keyword search (S) can be represented as follows:

$$S = N(C_{KWS} - C_{ALT})$$

where C_{KWS} is the cost of performing all searches using keyword search, C_{ALT} is the cost of performing all searches using the alternative solution, and N is the number of searches conducted over the life of the system. If $C_{initial}$ is the set up costs associated with the alternative solution, then the net cost of a hypothetical alternative solution to keyword search (NC_{ALT}) can be expressed as:

$$NC_{ALT} = C_{initial} - N(C_{KWS} - C_{ALT})$$

One of the advantages of keyword search is that it indexes the document store automatically, and therefore the initial setup cost is negligible (near zero). The larger the cost difference between keyword search and its alternative, the less the net search cost will be.

There are two components to the cost of search. The first is the time required to read a document and understand whether or not it is relevant to the user's search (C_{SKWS}). The second component is the time cost of missing relevant documents (C_{MKWS}). This is represented as follows:

$$C_{KWS} = C_{SKWS} + C_{MKWS}$$

We make a distinction between two levels of cost associated with determining a document's relevance. On average, it should be easier to "rule out" an irrelevant document than to arrive at the conclusion that it is relevant (this may require reading the entire document). We also consider the time cost associated with missing relevant documents, which we operationalize as the time required to reconstruct the knowledge contained within it.

The parameters for our model are:

$N_D \equiv$ total number of documents in the document store

$N_W \equiv$ total number of words in the document store

$N_{DW} \equiv$ total number of distinct words in the document store

$\overline{N}_W \equiv$ average number of words per document

$\overline{N}_{KW\overline{F}} \equiv$ average number of documents that contain the keyword that has the average frequency

$N_{RD} \equiv$ total number of relevant documents in the document store

$N_{ID} \equiv$ total number of irrelevant documents in the document store

$N_{RR} \equiv$ number of relevant documents returned in a search

$N_{RI} \equiv$ number of irrelevant documents returned in a search

$\overline{T}_{RR} \equiv$ average time required to determine if a returned document is relevant

$\overline{T}_{RI} \equiv$ average time required to determine if a returned document is irrelevant

$\overline{T}_{EN} \equiv$ average time required to encode a new document

$\overline{T}_{RM} \equiv$ average time required to recreate a missed document

$\pi \equiv$ average precision of a search

$\rho \equiv$ average recall of a search

$F_1 \equiv$ frequency of occurrence of word of rank 1 (most frequently occurring word)

$\overline{F} \equiv$ average frequency of a word

Our model draws heavily on Blair's work with the Zipf-Mandelbrot Law (Blair, 2002) regarding the distribution of word frequencies within a document (or collection of documents). From this work, we know

$$N_W = F_1\left(1 + \frac{1}{2} + \frac{1}{3} + \ldots + \frac{1}{F_1}\right)$$

We assume that the frequency of the most frequently occurring word in the document collection is equal to the number of distinct words in the document collection ($F_1 = N_{DW}$). This is equivalent to assuming that $\alpha = 1$ in the Zipf distribution. We can then calculate the average frequency for a word ($\overline{F}$), by substituting the equation for $\overline{N}_W$ into the equation

$$\overline{F} = \frac{N_W}{N_{DW}}$$

which gives us

$$\overline{F} = \frac{F_1\left(1 + \frac{1}{2} + \frac{1}{3} + \ldots + \frac{1}{F_1}\right)}{N_{DW}}$$

This allows us to calculate the average frequency of a word across the entire document collection. However, we also need to be able to calculate how many documents in the collection (on average) contain a particular keyword. We assume a specific keyword is distributed across the documents that contain it according to an isosceles right triangular distribution. Therefore, the average number of documents that contain the keyword with the average frequency ($\overline{F}$) can be found from:

$$\frac{\overline{N}^2_{KW\overline{F}} + \overline{N}_{KW\overline{F}}}{2} = \overline{F}$$

We solve this quadratic equation to find $\overline{N}_{KW\overline{F}}$.

Precision (the ratio of the found documents that are relevant to the total number of documents found) is related to indeterminancy (the number of meanings a particular word has). If a word has only one meaning, then precision should be 100%. If a word has two meanings, and the occurrence of a document with either meaning is equally likely, then precision is 50%. For any given search, the change in indeterminancy is proportional to the change in $\sqrt{\overline{F}}$ as the number of documents increases because the number of meanings a word has is proportional to the number of times it appears in the collection (Zipf, 1965). This can be expressed as

$$N_{RI} = N_{RR} * \left(\sqrt{\overline{F}} - 1\right)$$

Therefore, precision can be expressed as follows:

$$\pi = \frac{N_{RR}}{N_{RR} + N_{RI}} = \frac{N_{RR}}{N_{RR} + N_{RR} * (\sqrt{\overline{F}} - 1)} = \frac{1}{\sqrt{\overline{F}}}$$

For a fixed level of recall (the ratio of relevant documents found to the total number of relevant documents in the collection), this lets us see how the cost of the search increases as the number of documents in the document warehouse increases.

Now that we can determine $\overline{N}_{KW\overline{F}}$ and the precision of a search, we can estimate the cost of a search under varying assumptions. These assumptions include:

- Recall
- Cost of missing a document
- Cost of determining a document is irrelevant
- Cost of determining a document is relevant
- Proportion of relevant documents in collection

In the next two sections, we make these assumptions for keyword and dimensional searches, and estimate the costs for each method.

Keyword Search Costs

Very frequently, business search involves looking for a single document that the searcher knows exists because he/she has seen the document at some previous point in time. This is the most directly comparable scenario for considering keyword and dimensional search. Our model can be extended to any scenario, but we limit it to this one example for this paper.

To begin, solve for N_W using

$$N_W = N_D * \overline{N}_W$$

Solve for F_1 using

$$N_W = F_1\left(1+\frac{1}{2}+\frac{1}{3}+\ldots+\frac{1}{F_1}\right)$$

We assume no fixed costs associated with the keyword search (in other words, the cost of purchase and installation of indexing software is nominal). The relevant variable costs are:

- The average time required to discard an irrelevant document, $\overline{T}_{RI}$
- The average time required to determine that a document is relevant, $\overline{T}_{RR}$
- The average time required to recreate a missed document, $\overline{T}_{RM}$

We assume that it always is possible to recreate a missed document and that there is no cost associated with making a "bad" decision based on the results of the search. Therefore, even in the situation where the document is not recreated (and its knowledge) "lost", a decision made without this information will have no negative business impact.

For this example, we set $\overline{T}_{RI}$ = 30 seconds, $\overline{T}_{RR}$ = 2 minutes, and $\overline{T}_{RM}$ = 8 hours. There is no way to analytically determine recall, so we set recall (ρ) to .9 for the keyword search (a search will return 90% of the relevant documents in the collection). Now we are able to solve

$$\overline{F} = \frac{F_1\left(1+\frac{1}{2}+\frac{1}{3}+\ldots+\frac{1}{F_1}\right)}{N_{DW}}$$

and

$$\frac{\overline{N}^2_{KW\overline{F}} + \overline{N}_{KW\overline{F}}}{2} = \overline{F}$$

for the number of documents that contain the keyword ($\overline{N}_{KW\overline{F}}$) that has the average frequency.

It is unlikely that people will search on only one keyword. Therefore, we assume a typical search uses five keywords, and that the keywords are independently distributed across documents in the collection. We can determine the joint probability that a document contains one, two, three, four, or five of the selected keywords, and use that to determine the total number of documents returned. For five independent events with probabilities P_A, P_B, P_C, P_D, and P_E,

$$\begin{aligned}
P(A \cup B \cup C \cup D \cup E) = {} & P_A + P_B + P_C + P_D + P_E \\
& -(P_{A*}P_B + P_{A*}P_C + P_{A*}P_D + P_{A*}P_E + P_{B*}P_C + P_{B*}P_D + P_{B*}P_E + P_{C*}P_D + P_{C*}P_E + P_{D*}P_E) \\
& +(P_A{*}P_B{*}P_C + P_A{*}P_B{*}P_D + P_A{*}P_B{*}P_E + P_A{*}P_C{*}P_D + P_A{*}P_C{*}P_E + P_A{*}P_D{*}P_E + P_B{*}P_C{*}P_D + P_B{*}P_C{*}P_E + P_B{*}P_D{*}P_E + P_C{*}P_D{*}P_E) \\
& -(P_A{*}P_B{*}P_C{*}P_D + P_A{*}P_B{*}P_C{*}P_E + P_A{*}P_B{*}P_D{*}P_E + P_A{*}P_C{*}P_D{*}P_E + P_B{*}P_C{*}P_D{*}P_E) \\
& + P_A{*}P_B{*}P_C{*}P_D{*}\,P_E
\end{aligned}$$

Since each of the five keywords are similarly distributed across the document collection, we assume

$$P_A = P_B = P_C = P_D = P_E = \frac{\overline{N}_{KW}}{N_D}$$

We know that only one of the returned documents is the document that we seek. The rest are irrelevant documents. Let N_F be the number of found documents:

$$N_F = P(A \cup B \cup C \cup D \cup E) * N_D$$

Therefore, for a single search for single document, the average cost in minutes is the time required to find the target document and discard the irrelevant ones. It is necessary to account for two cases. The first case is where the document is in the result set (90% of the time, as recall = .9), and the second case is where the document was "missed" and is not in the result set (10% of the time):

$$.9 * \left(\overline{T}_{RR} + \overline{T}_{RI} * \left(\frac{N_F - 1}{2} \right) \right) + .1 * (T_{RM} + T_{RI} * N_F)$$

This assumes that on average the document sought is found half way through the search ($\frac{N_F - 1}{2}$) if it was part of the result set. If the document was not part of the result set, the user will search through every document ($\overline{T}_{RI} * N_F$) and then have to recreate it ($\overline{T}_{RM}$).

Dimensional Search Cost

Again we assume there is only one relevant document in the document store, and that the searcher knows the document exists because he/she has seen it at some previous point in time. Solve for N_W using

$$N_W = N_D * \overline{N}_W$$

And solve for F_1 using

$$N_W = F_1 \left(1 + \frac{1}{2} + \frac{1}{3} + \ldots + \frac{1}{F_1} \right)$$

Unlike keyword search, there are fixed costs associated with the dimensional search. These fixed costs are incurred when the documents are assigned the metadata values necessary to establish the dimensions. We assume that the metadata is encoded only once per document and is encoded either by the person that wrote the document or a person that has read the document. We further assume that a system has been set up to enable a person to describe the document using existing dimensions or add a label to existing dimensions. The time to encode a document is thus the time required to determine and select (or type in) the labels for the dimensions used. For this model, we assume that at most five dimensions are used, and the time to encode a document is estimated to be no more than two minutes ($\overline{T}_{EN}$ = 2).

Like the keyword search scenario, relevant costs to this model are:

- The average time required to discard an irrelevant document, $\overline{T}_{RI}$
- The average time required to determine that a document is relevant $\overline{T}_{RR}$,
- The average time required to recreate a missed document, $\overline{T}_{RM}$

We again assume that it always is possible to recreate a missed document, and thus there is no cost associated with making a bad decision. We also assume the same values for $\overline{T}_{RI}$ = 30 seconds, $\overline{T}_{RR}$ = 2 minutes, and $\overline{T}_{RM}$ = 8 hours.

Although we will once again assume a figure for recall, we argue that for the dimensional search the likelihood of not finding the relevant document ($1 - \rho$) decreases by 40%. This is due to the increase in recall that accompanies matching a keyword used in the manual classification of a document instead of relying on word matches within those documents. This is consistent with prior research (LaBrie, 2004). Since we assumed $1 - \rho = .1$ in the keyword search case, we set recall (ρ) to .94 (or 1 – (0.1 * (1– 0.4)) for the dimensional search.

Dimensional search involves the intersection (ANDing) of dimensions. Moreover, it involves the intersection of unambiguous keywords (something that it is impossible to do with a keyword search). Because there is no ambiguity with respect to the keyword, we eliminate responses due to the wrong meaning. This can be adjusted for by assuming that each of the meanings of a keyword appears in the same number of articles, and that only one meaning occurs in a given article. Since the number of meanings is equal to $\sqrt{F}$, and since a specific search is interested in only one of those meanings, this reduces the number of retrieved articles for any keyword by $\left(1-\frac{1}{\sqrt{F}}\right)$ We also can eliminate responses due to over-described terms. If a term is "over-described" it misrepresents the true content of the article. For example, searching for "Unix" could retrieve an article comparing agricultural yields that mentions SAS running on a Unix-based system that was used to analyze the data. Although the article has nothing really to do with Unix systems, the word Unix appears in the article (and therefore matches the keyword search). This is unlikely to occur in a dimensional search scenario because the document would not be classified using the keyword "Unix." We assume 5% of the occurrences of keywords are over-described.

Applying dimensions to a document is to cross-index the document. This differs from keyword searches in that it allows cross-indexing by content (i.e., it adds context to keywords), it allows for a browsable, hierarchical arrangement of the dimensions (i.e., it is based on recognition), and does not require that the classification used in the dimensions appear in text of the article. We assume the five dimensions used are "Keyword," "Subject," "Date," "Author," and (document) "Type." Use of the "Subject" dimension allows for the elimination of keywords with alternative meanings (to the meaning for which the user is searching), and eliminates over-described keywords.

Most documents and articles contain the author and the date. However, they do not contain author and date as dimensions. In other words, if a person's name appears in a document, that document will be returned in a keyword search whether the person was the author, referenced, or just mentioned. Similarly, if a date appears in an article, that article will be returned in a keyword search whether it is the date of publication or simply a date that was mentioned in the article. We were not able to find solid references for the average number of times a person's name appears in an article for which the person is not the author, nor the frequency with which articles contain dates that are not the date on which the article was published. Rather than make an assumption about these attributes, we assume keyword searches handle authors and dates as efficiently as dimensional searches. We recognize that this biases our results against dimensional searches.

Finally, the "type" dimension cannot be represented in keyword searches. The effect of this dimension depends on the composition of the document warehouse. The "type" categories can be very broad or very narrow. For example, the "type" dimension could have only three labels: "email," "document," and "other." These labels could also get quite specific such as "working paper," "white paper," "lessons learned," "academic journal article," "practitioner journal article," "monograph," "book," et cetera. We make the conservative assumption that no "type" category would contain more that one-third of the documents in a document warehouse. We thus assume that the "type" dimension reduces the number of returned documents by two-thirds (it is likely more than this).

To determine the number of documents returned, solve for $\overline{F}$ using:

$$\overline{F} = \frac{F_1\left(1+\frac{1}{2}+\frac{1}{3}+\ldots+\frac{1}{F_1}\right)}{N_{DW}}$$

Then solve for $\overline{N}_{KW\overline{F}}$ using

$$\frac{\overline{N}^2_{KW\overline{F}} + \overline{N}_{KW\overline{F}}}{2} = \overline{F}$$

We assume that the dimensional search also uses five keywords, and that the results are ORed (documents that contain any of the keywords for the "subject" dimension, for instance, would be returned). The number of articles returned for the dimension search is the number of articles returned for the keyword search (N_F) times the "reduction factor" as a result of the improved precision of the dimensional search:

$$N_{FD} = N_F\left(\frac{1}{\sqrt{F}}\right) * .95 * \left(\frac{1}{3}\right)$$

This "reduction factor" ($.95*\left(\frac{1}{3}\right)$) factors in the elimination of $\left(1-\frac{1}{\sqrt{F}}\right)$ of documents with alternative meanings, 5% of documents with the "overdescribed" terms, and the two-thirds of documents that don't match the selected document "type."

We know that only one of the returned documents is the document that we seek. The rest are irrelevant documents. Let N_F be the number of found documents. For a single search for single document, the average cost in minutes is

$$.94*\left(\overline{T}_{RR} + \overline{T}_{RI} * \left(\frac{N_{FD}-1}{2}\right)\right) + .06*(\overline{T}_{RM} + \overline{T}_{RI} * N_{FD})$$

We again assume that on average the sought after document is found halfway through the search.

MODEL RESULTS

We ran a series of scenarios using the models for both methods of search (keyword versus dimensional). In all scenarios, we set the average number of words per document ($\overline{N}_W$) to 3,750. This represents a moderately-sized (12 page) document, and therefore is likely to represent the "average" document in a collection. We also varied the size of the document store from 10,000

Table 1. Eight-hour document reconstruction

Number of Documents	Average Number of words	Time for Key Word Search	Time for Dimensional Search	Total Time to Encode Documents	Savings Per Search	Break Even Number of Searches
10000	3750	57.81510594	30.8197351	20000	26.995371	740.8677629
20000	3750	57.82005148	30.82239347	40000	26.997658	1481.609996
30000	3750	57.82170066	30.82387701	60000	26.997824	2222.40136
40000	3750	57.82252537	30.82489957	80000	26.997626	2963.223529
50000	3750	57.82302024	30.82567626	100000	26.997344	3704.068078
60000	3750	57.82335016	30.82630051	120000	26.99705	4444.930151
70000	3750	57.82358584	30.82682121	140000	26.996765	5185.806594
80000	3750	57.82376259	30.82726712	160000	26.996495	5926.695194
90000	3750	57.82390007	30.82765654	180000	26.996244	6667.594318
100000	3750	57.82401006	30.82800184	200000	26.996008	7408.502708

Table 2. Four-hour document reconstruction

Number of Documents	Average Number of words	Time for Key Word Search	Time for Dimensional Search	Total Time to Encode Documents	Savings Per Search	Break Even Number of Searches
10000	3750	33.81510594	16.4197351	20000	17.395371	1149.731166
20000	3750	33.82005148	16.42239347	40000	17.397658	2299.160034
30000	3750	33.82170066	16.42387701	60000	17.397824	3448.707218
40000	3750	33.82252537	16.42489957	80000	17.397626	4598.328583
50000	3750	33.82302024	16.42567626	100000	17.397344	5748.003842
60000	3750	33.82335016	16.42630051	120000	17.39705	6897.721302
70000	3750	33.82358584	16.42682121	140000	17.396765	8047.473367
80000	3750	33.82376259	16.42726712	160000	17.396495	9197.254713
90000	3750	33.82390007	16.42765654	180000	17.396244	10347.0614
100000	3750	33.82401006	16.42800184	200000	17.396008	11496.89041

Table 3. Zero-hour document reconstruction

Number of Documents	Average Number of words	Time for Key Word Search	Time for Dimensional Search	Total Time to Encode Documents	Savings Per Search	Break Even Number of Searches
10000	3750	9.815105938	2.019735104	20000	7.7953708	2565.625218
20000	3750	9.820051485	2.022393466	40000	7.797658	5129.745355
30000	3750	9.82170066	2.023877007	60000	7.7978237	7694.454591
40000	3750	9.822525371	2.024899571	80000	7.7976258	10259.5331
50000	3750	9.823020238	2.025676264	100000	7.797344	12824.8799
60000	3750	9.823350165	2.026300509	120000	7.7970497	15390.43681
70000	3750	9.823585836	2.02682121	140000	7.7967646	17956.16602
80000	3750	9.823762593	2.027267117	160000	7.7964955	20522.04102
90000	3750	9.823900073	2.027656538	180000	7.7962435	23088.04223
100000	3750	9.824010059	2.02800184	200000	7.7960082	25654.15458

to 100,000 documents (in increments of 10,000) in order to determine how increasing the size of the document store might affect the relative costs of both search methods.

Tables 1, 2, and 3 below summarize the results of our models. We consistently found that the dimensional search took less time than a keyword search. We also calculated the per-search savings using the dimensional search over the keyword search (the variable cost), and the number of searches necessary to break even on the initial expense of encoding the documents for the dimensional store (the fixed cost).To explore the sensitivity of the results to changes in the time required to reconstruct a document if it is not found, we look at reconstruction times of eight, four, and zero hours.

Figure 1 graphs the breakeven points for each of the scenarios.

The breakeven point is surprisingly small, even for the scenario in which there is no cost to

Figure 1. Break even points for three scenarios

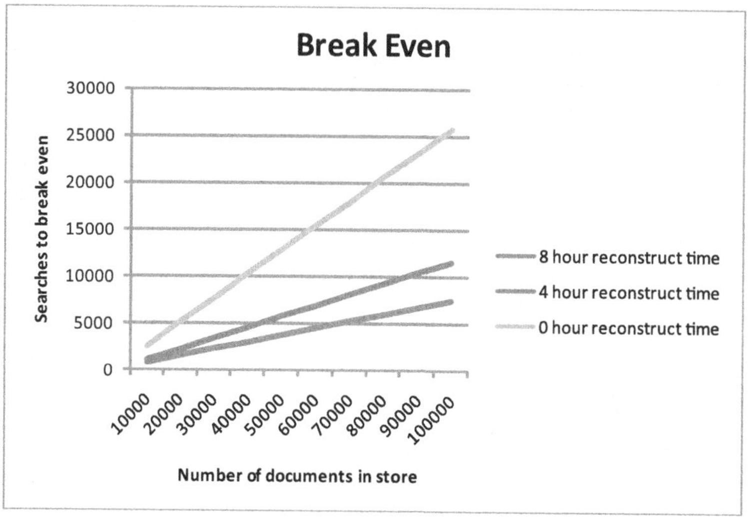

reconstruct the document when it cannot be found. For a firm with 1,000 employees and 100,000 documents in the document store, an average of only 25 searches per employee (25,000 searches) would be required to justify the cost of encoding the metadata required to support dimensional searches. This provides convincing evidence that organizations should strongly consider implementing dimensional document stores. The fact that this technique of classifying and storing documents is not widespread may be due to the complexity in determining its benefits. Our model represents a first effort to provide quantitative evidence regarding the relative efficiency of dimensional search over keyword search.

CONCLUSION AND FURTHER WORK

We believe the results presented in this paper likely *underestimate* the benefits of dimensional search as compared with key word search. Several authors have pointed out that the Zipf-Mandelbrot Law (Montemurro, 2001; Sichel, 1975) does not consistently hold across collections of documents, especially with regard to "unique" words (words with very low frequencies). We know this distribution biases the results in favor of keyword search, especially as document size increases. Therefore, the use of distributions that better approximate the frequencies of the unique words within a document warehouse will almost certainly show even greater savings for dimensional searches. The reason the savings per search are almost constant in Tables 1, 2, and 3 is that average frequency of a keyword does not change as the size of the document warehouse increases. Although the frequency of the most common word goes up dramatically, enough new words with a low frequency also occur, leaving the average frequency of a word unchanged. This is not a characteristic of some of the other distributions that have been proposed in quantitative linguistics.

In the meantime, however, we believe our model is a good first step. It can be used to give organizations a conservative estimate of the benefits of using dimensional search. Any organization can put its own cost estimates in our model and see the benefits. This should greatly enhance the ability of information technology professionals to convince CIOs to invest in improved search methodologies.

REFERENCES

Blair, D. C. (2002). The challenge of commercial document retrieval, Part 1: Major issues, and a framework based on search exhaustivity, determinacy of representation and document collection size. *Information Processing & Management, 38*(2), 273-291.

Dunwoodie, B. (2004, June 19). Gartner Dataquest. As cited in: Column Two: Enterprise Content Management Market Share. [Online]. Available: http://www.steptwo.com.au/columntwo/archives/001304.html.

Ha, L.Q., Sicilia-Garcia, E.I., Ming, J. & Smith, F.J. (2002). Extension of Zipf's Law to Words and Phrases. *Proceedings of 19th International Conference on Computational Linguistics, Vol. 1.* Taipei, Taiwan, (pp. 1-6).

LaBrie, R. C. (2004). The Impact of Alternative Search Mechanisms on the Effectiveness of Knowledge Retrieval. Unpublished doctoral dissertation, Arizona State University, Tempe.

Mandelbrot, B. (1966). Information Theory and Psycholinguistics: A theory of word frequencies. In P.F. Lazarsfeld & N.W. Henry (Eds.), *Readings in Mathematical Social Science* (pp. 350-368). Chicago: Science Research Associates.

Montemurro, M. A. (2001). Beyond the Zipf-Mandelbrot law in quantitative linguistics. *Physica A, 300*(3-4), 567-578

Mukherjee, R. & Mao, J. (2004). Enterprise Search: Tough stuff. *ACM Queue, 2*(2), 37-46.

Sichel, H.S. (1975). On a Distribution Law for Word Frequencies. *Journal of the American Statistical Association, 70*(351), 542-547.

Thompson Scientific. (2004). Strategies for Search, Taxonomy and Classification: Getting just what you need. [Online]. Available: http://i.i.com.com/cnwk.1d/html/itp/ultraseek_MK0759BusinessvConsumerWP_ULT_30-day.pdf.

Ultaseek White Paper. (2006). Business Search vs. Consumer Search: Five differences your company can't afford to ignore. [Online]. Available: http://i.i.com.com/cnwk.1d/html/itp/ultraseek_MK0759BusinessvConsumerWP_ULT_30-day.pdf.

Webster, M. (2007). Worldwide Content Management Software 2007-2011 Forecast: Continued strong growth as market strategies. [Online]. Available: http://www.idc.com/. Document number 206149.

Zipf, G.K. (1965). *Human Behavior and the Principle of Least Effort: An introduction to human ecology.* New York: Hafner.

Chapter X
Integrity Constraint Checking for Multiple XML Databases

Praveen Madiraju
Marquette University, USA

Rajshekhar Sunderraman
Georgia State University, USA

Shamkant B. Navathe
Georgia Institute of Technology, USA

Haibin Wang
Winship Cancer Instutite, USA

ABSTRACT

Global semantic integrity constraints ensure the integrity and consistency of data spanning distributed databases. In this chapter, we discuss a novel representation technique for expressing semantic integrity constraints for XML databases. We also provide the details of XConstraint Checker, a general framework for checking global semantic constraints for XML databases. The framework is augmented with an efficient algorithm for checking these global XML constraints. The algorithm is efficient for three reasons: 1) the algorithm does not require the update statement to be executed before the constraint check is carried out; hence, we avoid any potential problems associated with rollbacks, 2) sub constraint checks are executed in parallel, and 3) most of the processing of algorithm could happen at compile time; hence, we save time spent at run-time. As a proof of concept, we present a prototype of the system implementing the ideas discussed in this paper.

INTRODUCTION

XML (eXtensible Markup Language) has now been adopted as a standard for representation and exchange of data on the web. XML based data exchange occurs in many applications such as finance, health, e-commerce and other application areas. A major goal of a database is to ensure consistency of the data. Integrity constraints are rules which guarantee the consistency of a database. We consider XML constraints in the setting of distributed XML databases. A single update (XUpdate (Tatarinov *et al.*, 2001), (Laux & Martin, 2000)) on one site might cause a global constraint (*global XConstraint*) to be violated. By global XConstraints, we mean global semantic integrity constraints affecting multiple XML databases. We need an approach to check for such constraint violations. In the XML database setting, the majority of the times, users are interested in generating (updating), integrating and exchanging data. So, frequent updates on XML data may cause frequent global constraint violations. *Hence we need an approach that will efficiently and speedily check for such global constraint violations.*

There are two major approaches to this problem. The *first* would be to translate the XML document into relational data using methods such as those found in Shanmugasundaram *et al.* (1999), Chen *et al.* (2003) and Fong and Wong (2004). And then, map the updates and constraints on the XML data to corresponding updates and constraints on the relational data (Chen *et al.*, 2002a). Now the problem of constraint checking on XML data is pushed to the problem of constraint checking on relational data. There are well established models for constraint checking in the relational world. However, this approach suffers from the overhead cost involved in transforming XML data into relational data (Kane, Su & Rundensteiner, 2002). The *second* approach would be to check for constraint violations on the XML data without transforming to relational data. It should be noted that using the *first* approach vs. *second* depends on the application being considered. If the application contains millions of records and if it benefits to use relational database features such as querying, fast indexing, etc., it is worth while to consider the first one otherwise the second approach suffices for a normal sized application. In this chapter, we consider the second approach.

A naïve solution would first update an XML document and then check for constraint violations. If a constraint is violated, we can rollback. However, such a naïve solution suffers from the overhead of time and resources spent on rollback. Also, the update statement is checked against all the constraints with the total new updated database state. However, in an incremental constraint checking strategy (Fan, 2005), (Bouchou *et al.*, 2005), constraints are checked incrementally only on the updated document. Hence, we need an approach that would check for constraint violations before updating the database and therefore obviates the need for rollback situations.

In our constraint checking procedure, constraint violations are checked at compile time, *before* updating the database. Our approach centers on the design of the *XConstraint Checker*. Given an XUpdate (Tatarinov *et al.*, 2001), (Laux & Martin, 2000) statement and a list of global XConstraints, we generate *sub XConstraint* checks corresponding to local sites. Sub XConstraint is an XML constraint, expressed as an XQuery, local to a single site (more details in Section 4). The results gathered from these sub XConstraints determine if the XUpdate statement violates any global XConstraints. Our approach is *efficient*; since we do not require the update statement to be executed before the constraint check is carried out and hence, we avoid any rollback situations. Our approach achieves *speed* as the sub constraint checks can be executed in parallel.

Overview of the System

Figure 1 gives the overview of the system. We propose a three-tier architecture. The server side consists of two or more sites hosting native XML databases. In Figure 1, we show three sites S_1, S_2 and S_3. The client makes an XUpdate request through the middleware. The middleware consists of the *XConstraint Checker* and the XML/DBC (Gardarin *et al.*, 2002) API. We have earlier (Madiraju *et al.*, 2004) introduced our notations for representing XConstraints and proposed an architecture for XConstraint Checker. One of the important modules in XConstraint Checker is the *XConstraint Decomposer* (Madiraju *et al.*, 2006)

Here in this chapter, we (i) give the algorithmic description for the XConstraint Decomposer, (ii) illustrate the algorithm with clear examples, and (iii) implement a prototype system. The XConstraint Decomposer takes as input a global XUpdate and a list of global XConstraints and outputs sub XConstraints to be executed on remote sites.

XML/DBC (Gardarin *et al.*, 2002) is the standard XML XQuery API that facilitates access to XML based data products. The XML/DBC API consists of two API's: 1) The Java API is a JDBC extension to query XML collections using XQuery. 2) The web services API is designed to provide a SOAP style server interface to clients. In our case, XML/DBC API executes sub XConstraints corresponding to remote sites. The XConstraint Checker gathers results obtained from sub XConstraints and makes a decision whether a constraint is violated. Only in the event of no constraint being violated, the XUpdate statement is executed.

The rest of the chapter is organized as follows: In Section 2, we give example XML databases that will be referred to throughout the paper. We also give the syntax of XUpdate language and introduce our notations for defining global XConstraints. In Section 3, we give the internal architecture of the XConstraint Checker. In Section 4, we present the algorithmic description of the XConstraint Decomposer, which decomposes a global XConstraint into a conjunction of sub

Figure 1. Overview of system (Madiraju et al., 2004)

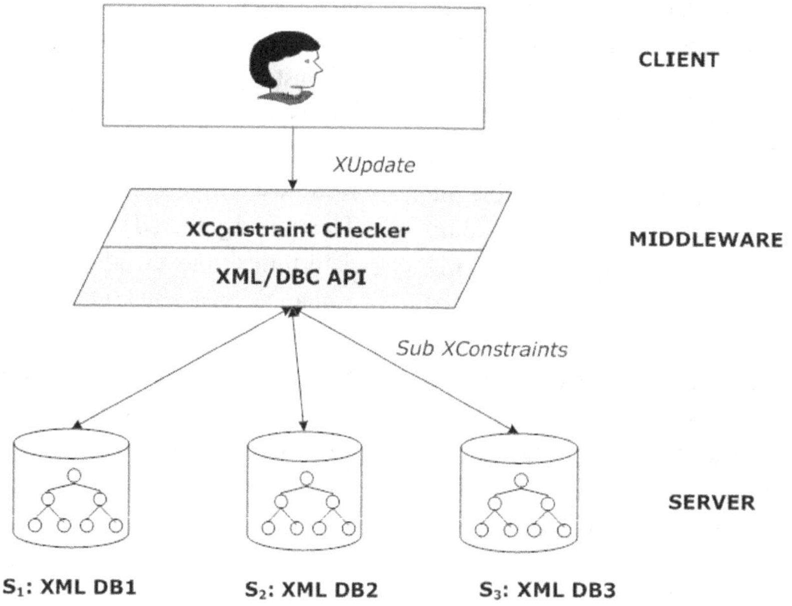

XConstraints. In section 5, we give implementation details. We compare our work with related work in Section 6 and finally offer our conclusions in Section 7.

PRELIMINARIES

Here we give an example healthcare XML database and explain the notations of XUpdate. We also introduce our notation for defining XConstraints.

Example Database

Consider a sample *healthdb.xml* represented in a tree form in Figure 2. Figure 2 gives the logical representation of the HEALTHDB XML databases. Physically, information is distributed across multiple sites:

Site S_1: PATIENT information such as *SSN (primary key)*, *PName* and *HealthPlan* is stored. CASE information with *CaseId (primary key – like a sequence number)*, *SSN*, and *InjuryDate* is also stored.

Site S_2: patient's CLAIM information such as *CaseId (primary key)*, *ClaimDate*, *Amount* and *Type* is recorded.

Site S_3: TREATMENT information such as *CaseId (primary key)*, *DName* (doctor name), *TDate* (Treatment Date), and *Disease* is stored.

Note that a patient can suffer multiple injuries uniquely identified by their *CaseId* at Site S_1, and can also make multiple claims identified by their *CaseId* at site S_2.

XUpdate

XUpdate is the language extension to XQuery to accommodate insert, replace, delete and rename operations. Tatarinov *et al.* (2001) gives the XUpdate language syntax and semantics. For purpose of better presentation, we give brief description and syntax of XUpdate. The syntax of XUpdate is given below.

```
FOR $binding1 IN XPath-expr, ...
LET $binding: = XPath-expr, ...
WHERE predicate1, ...
updateOP, ...
```

Figure 2. Tree representation of healthdb.xml

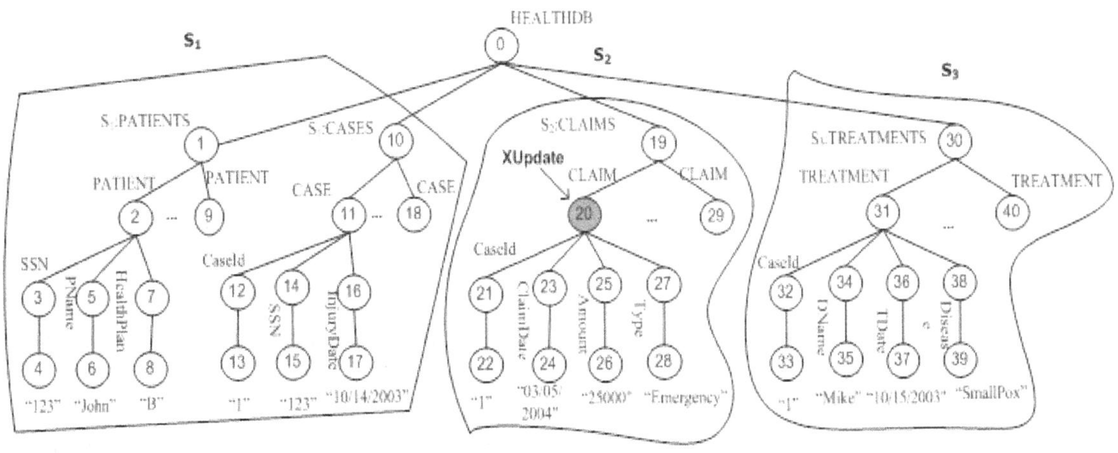

```
where updateOP is defined in EBNF as :

UPDATE $binding { subOP {,subOP}* }

where subOP is defined as :

DELETE $child |
RENAME $child TO name |
INSERT content [BEFORE | AFTER $child]
|
REPLACE $child with $content |
FOR $binding IN XPath-subexpr, ...
    WHERE predicate1, ... updateOP
```

The semantics of the `FOR`, `LET`, `WHERE` clauses (`FLW`) are taken from XQuery, while the `updateOP` clause specifies a sequence of update operations to be executed on the target nodes identified by `FLW` clause. Here, we note that, in our context, the `XPath-expr` from the `FOR` clause can only refer to nodes from a single site, restricting the updates to only a single site. This is a reasonable assumption, as an XUpdate on a single site might cause one or more global XConstraints to be violated and we want to check for such constraint violations at compile time (before the XUpdate is executed). Below, we show a sample XUpdate occurring on the XML tree (node 20) of Figure 2.

```
FOR $cl in document("healthdb.xml")/
HEALTHDB/S2:CLAIMS
UPDATE $cl
{
INSERT <CLAIM>
   <CaseId>1</CaseId>
   <ClaimDate>03/05/2004</ClaimDate>
   <Amount>25000</Amount>
   <Type>Emergency</Type>
</CLAIM>
}
```

For a detailed description of the XUpdate language, readers are referred to Tatarinov *et al.*, (2001) and Laux and Martin (2000). The latest version of XQuery Update facility from the W3C working group can be accessed from Chamberlin *et al.* (2008).

XML Constraint Representation

Semantic integrity constraints can be considered as a general form of assertions. They specify a general condition in the database which needs to be true always. Constraints of this type deal with information in a single state of the world. Throughout the paper, we denote semantic integrity constraints for XML database as *XConstraints*. *GlobalXConstraints* are the constraints spanning multiple XML databases. Here we give the constraint representation for global XConstraints.

A datalog rule (expressed as `HEAD` ← `BODY`) without a `HEAD` clause is referred to as a denial. It is customary to represent integrity constraints in the logic databases as range restricted (safe or allowed) denials.

Definition 2.1: In order to represent global XConstraint in the context of XML database as query evaluation, we consider global XConstraint in the form of range restricted denials (datalog style notation) given below:

$C \leftarrow X_1 \wedge X_2 \wedge, \ldots, X_n$, where *C* is the name of the global XConstraint and each X_i is either an *XML literal* or *Arithmetic literal.* □

We define both XML literal and arithmetic literal below. The definition of XML literal is chiefly inspired by Buneman *et al.* (2001) and Chen *et al.* (2002a). Semantics for representing key constraints for a single XML database are given in Buneman *et al.* (2001) and Chen *et al.* (2002a). We extend their semantics by introducing user defined variables, term paths and XML literals for representing global XConstraints for multiple XML databases.

Definition 2.2: An XML literal is defined as follows:

Xi : (Qi , (Qi' , [Vi1 = ti1 , Vi2 = ti2 ,..., Viki = tiki]))

Using the syntax from (Buneman et al., 2001), (Chen et al., 2002a), Qi , Qi' and ti1, ti2 ,..., tiki are path expressions corresponding to Xi . Vi1, Vi2 ,..., Viki are user defined variables corresponding to ti1, ti2 ,..., tiki . Qi is called the context path, Qi' the target path and ti1, ti2 ,..., tiki are the term paths. Context path Qi identifies the set of context nodes, c and for each c, Vi1, Vi2 ,..., Viki are the set of user defined variables corresponding to the term paths, ti1, ti2 ,..., tiki reachable from c via Qi'. □

Definition 2.3: Arithmetic literal is defined as: expression θ expression, where expression – is a linear expression made of variables occurring in XML literals, integer constants, and the four arithmetic operator +, -, *, /; θ – is a comparison operator (=, <, >, <=, >=, <>). Joins between nodes are expressed either as an equality (=) between two variables in an arithmetic literal or by having the same variable name appear in different XML literals within the same global XConstraint. Note that variables with the same name cannot appear in the same XML literal. □

Now, we are ready to define the satisfiability of a global semantic integrity constraint (global XConstraint), C.

Definition 2.4: An XML tree T is said to satisfy a global integrity constraint (global XConstraint), C, if and only if the conjunction of X1, X2 ,..., Xn evaluates to false □

The motivations behind using our constraint representation and negative semantics for checking the satisfiability of a global semantic integrity constraint are: 1) constraint representation using our approach resembles query evaluation for heterogeneous databases (logic, relational, XML) and hence is very generic due to the inherent logic based approach used in representing the XConstraints. 2) Global XConstraints decomposed using Algorithm 4.1 (Section 4) are much easier using our XConstraint representation, as the sub XConstraints generated are XQueries evaluated against local database and can return a true/false. Hence the overall conjunction (which is also true/false) of sub XConstraints determines the satisfiability of a global XConstraint.

Note that each Q_i ,Q_i', user defined variables and the term paths corresponding to each XML literal - X_i has the site information referred to as S_j and can only refer to a single site. However, a global XConstraint has one or more XML literals and hence can refer to multiple XML databases. In case of Arithmetic literal, *expression θ expression,* the variables in the expression could belong to different sites. If two variables are not the leaf nodes, the equality join among the two variables is similar to the node equality considered in (Buneman *et al.*, 2001).

Example 2.1: Consider two global XConstraints C1 and C2 defined on healthdb.xml. Constraint C1 states that a patient with HealthPlan 'B' diagnosed with 'SmallPox' may not claim more than 40000 dollars. Constraint C2 states that a patient with HealthPlan 'B' may not file a claim of type 'Emergency'.

```
C1:-
  (//S1:PATIENTS,
      (./PATIENT,[ssn=./SSN,healthplan=./
HealthPlan])),
  (//S1:CASES,(./CASE,[caseid=./CaseId,ssn=./
SSN])),
     (//S2:CLAIMS,(./CLAIM,[caseid=./
CaseId,amount=./Amount])),              (//
S3:TREATMENTS,
  (./TREATMENT,[caseid=./CaseId,disease=./
Disease])),
 healthplan = 'B',disease = 'SmallPox',amount
> 40000.
C2:-
```

```
(//S1:PATIENTS,
    (./PATIENT,[ssn=./SSN,healthplan=./
healthplan])),
  (//S1:CASES,(./CASE,[caseid=./CaseId,ssn=./
SSN])),
    (//S2:CLAIMS,(./CLAIM,[caseid=./
CaseId,type=./type])),
  healthplan = 'B',type = 'Emergency'.
```

For the example contained in Figure 2, C1 is satisfied, but C2 is violated. C1 is satisfied for the healthdb.xml as one of the arithmetic literals amount (node 25, value = 25000) > 40000 returns false and hence the whole conjunction for C1 evaluates to false. C2 is violated as the conjunction for C2 evaluates to true. Arithmetic literal, healthplan (node 7, value = 'B') = 'B' evaluates to true and similarly, type (node 27, value='Emergency') = 'Emergency' evaluates to true and hence the whole conjunction for C2 evaluates to true.

We also note that keys introduced in (Chen *et al.*, 2002a), can be expressed using our representation. Consider a key constraint, c_3, which states that within the context of PATIENTS, a PATIENT is uniquely identified by SSN. Using the notation of (Chen *et al.*, 2002a), c_3 can be expressed as follows:

```
C3:-  (/HEALTHDB/S1:PATIENTS,(./PATIENT,{./
SSN}))
```

A key constraint such as c_3 could be expressed in our notation (a functional dependency) as two XConstraints:

```
C31:-
(//S1:PATIENTS,(./PATIENT,[ssn=./
SSN,name1=./PName])),
(//S1:PATIENTS,(./PATIENT,[ssn=./
SSN,name2=./PName])),
name1 <> name2.
C32:-
(//S1:PATIENTS,(./PATIENT,[ssn=./SSN,hp1=./
HealthPlan])),
(//S1:PATIENTS,(./PATIENT,[ssn=./SSN,hp2=./
HealthPlan])),
hp1 <> hp2.
```

This has some similarity with the notion of template dependencies (Elmasri & Navathe, 2003), wherein we can represent any general constraints in relations.

XCONSTRAINT CHECKER

We first give the assumptions of the system and then present the detailed architecture of the XConstraint Checker.

Assumptions

XConstraint Checker relies on the fundamental concepts (XConstraint, XUpdate) introduced in Section 2. The assumptions we make for the XConstraint Checker are:

1. A restricted set of XUpdate language is considered without losing the generality of the approach. We permit the following `SubOP`'s: `DELETE $child`, `INSERT content [BEFORE | AFTER $child]` and `REPLACE $child with $content`. The optional `[BEFORE | AFTER $child]` is applicable for an ordered execution model of XML tree. Also, we restrict the updates to *elementary updates*. The elementary update considers: (i) updates occurring only on one single node of an XML tree and (ii) updates with only one `SubOP` at a time. However, note that any update can be equivalently transformed into a set of elementary updates; therefore, we do not lose the generality of the approach.
2. XML constraint representation follows from Section 2.3.

Figure 3. XConstraint checker internal architecture

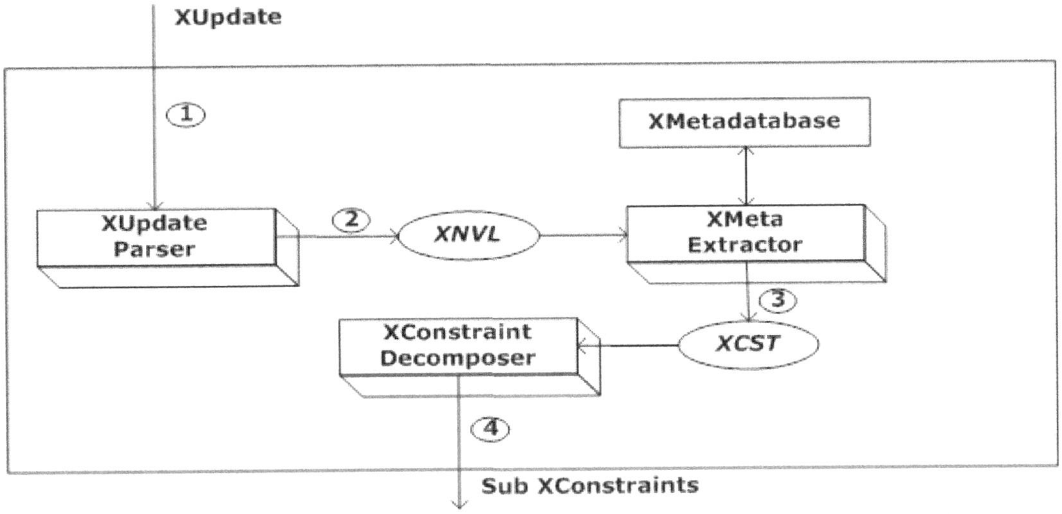

XConstraint Checker Architecture

The internal architecture of the XConstraint Checker is presented in Figure 3. The XConstraint checker interfaces with the rest of the system as shown in Figure 1. The XConstraint Checker consists of the following modules.

- **XUpdate Parser**: parses an XUpdate statement input by the user and identifies the XNode Value List (*XNVL*), involved in the XUpdate.
- **XMetadatabase**: stores and acts as a repository of global XConstraints.
- **XMeta Extractor**: extracts only the global XConstraints being affected by the XUpdate.
- **XConstraint Decomposer**: decomposes a global XConstraint into a set of sub XConstraints to be validated locally on remote sites.

The overall process of constraint checking is explained in the following four steps (see Figure 3).

Step 1

The user issues an XUpdate statement on one of the sites. Figure 4 gives the initial XML database state before the XUpdate statement is executed. For example, user issues an XUpdate statement, XU_1 on site S_2.

```
XU1 =
FOR  $cl  in  document("healthdb.xml")/
HEALTHDB/S2:CLAIMS
UPDATE $cl
{
INSERT <CLAIM>
          <CaseId>1</CaseId>
           <ClaimDate>03/05/2004</Claim-
Date>
          <Amount>25000</Amount>
          <Type>Emergency</Type>
       </CLAIM>
}
```

Figure 5 gives the modified tree representation of the *healthdb.xml*, if the update is successful. The nodes affected by the XUpdate are shown in filled circles.

Figure 4. Tree representation of healthdb.xml before XUpdate

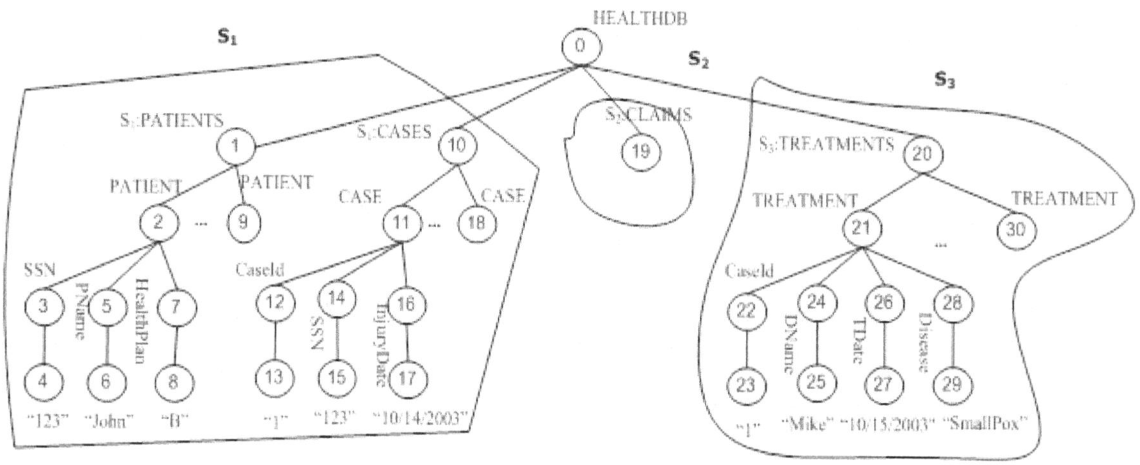

Figure 5. Modified tree representation of healthdb.xml, if XUpdate is successful

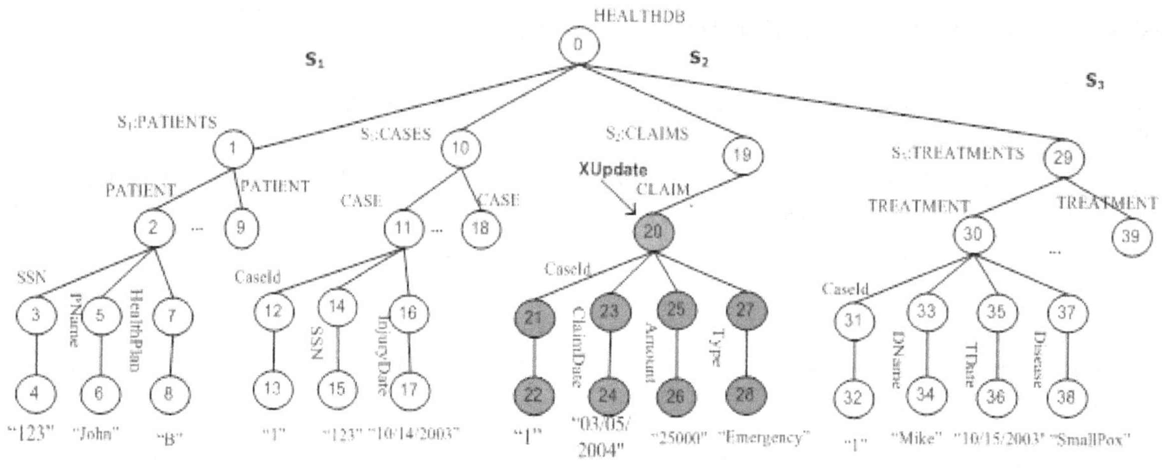

Step 2 (XUpdate Parser)

The XUpdate Parser parses the given XUpdate statement and identifies the XML node being modified. The output from this step is the XML Node Value List (*XNVL*).

XNVL = $N(a_1=v_1,a_2=v_2,\ldots,a_n=v_n)$, where N is the node being updated and is obtained from the `$binding` in the XUpdate syntax, $v_1,v_2,\ldots,v_n$ are the values being updated corresponding to the attributes $a_1,a_2, \ldots ,a_n$. $a_1,a_2, \ldots,a_n$ are either the XML sub elements or XML attributes being updated and are obtained from the `content` of the XUpdate statement (Section 2.2). For the running example,

```
XNVL = {/HEALTHDB/S2:CLAIMS/CLAIM( CaseId
= 1,
        ClaimDate = '03/05/2004', Amount
= 25000,
       Type='Emergency')}
```

Figure 6. XCST

C_i	list(S_j)
C_1	(S_1,S_2,S_3)
C_2	(S_1,S_2)

Step 3 (XMeta Extractor)

Let XU↓ denote the path involved in executing the XUpdate statement, XU on the XML tree T. Similarly, C↓ denotes the path in defining the constraint C. We say that an XUpdate, XU might violate a constraint C if, XU↓ ∩ C↓ is not empty. For the running example, XU_1↓ corresponds to the following nodes: {20,21,22,23,24,25,26,27,28}, C_1↓ matches {3,4,7,8,12,13,14,15,21,22,25,26,31,32,37,38} and C_2↓ matches {3,4,7,8,12,13,14,15,21,22,27,28} (refer to Figure 5). XU_1 ∩ C_1↓ is not empty and XU_1 ∩ C_2 is also not empty; hence, both the constraints might be violated by the update statement. If a global schema or a global DTD is given, we can identify the list of global XConstraints that might be violated by simply consulting the global DTD. The *XMeta Extractor* identifies the list of constraints being affected by the XUpdate and constructs the XConstraint Source Table (*XCST*). *XCST*(C_i) = < C_i, *list*(S_j)>, where C_i is the constraint identifier and *list*(S_j) is the list of sites being affected by C_i. For the running example, *XCST* is given in Figure 6. The XMeta Extractor sends the *XCST* to the XConstraint Decomposer.

Step 4 (XConstraint Decomposer)

The XConstraint Decomposer generates the set of sub XConstraints, C_{ij} on the basis of locality of sites. C_{ij} is the sub XConstraint corresponding to constraint - C_i and site - S_j. We present the algorithmic description of generating C_{ij}'s in the next section. For the running example, C_{11}, C_{12}, C_{13}, C_{21} and C_{22} are generated. The values of the sub XConstraints are also given in the next section.

XCONSTRAINT DECOMPOSER

The basic idea of XConstraint Decomposer (Madiraju *et al.*, 2006) is to decompose a global constraint into a conjunction of sub XConstraints, where each conjunct represents the constraint check as seen from each individual site. Given an XUpdate statement, a brute force approach would be to go ahead and update the XML document and then check for constraint violations. However, we want to be able to check for constraint violations without updating the database. In other words, the XUpdate is carried out only if it is a non constraint violator. Thus, we avoid any potential rollbacks.

Our idea here is to scan through a global XConstraint C_i, XUpdate U and then generate a conjunction of sub XConstraints, C_{ij}'s. The value of each conjunct (each C_{ij}) is either false or true. If the overall value of conjunction is true, constraint C_i is violated (*from Theorem 4.1*).

Algorithm 4.1 gives the constraint decompositions (C_{ij}'s) corresponding to a global constraint C_i and an XUpdate statement involving an insert statement. *Algorithm 4.1* takes as input XML Node Value List, *XNVL* (STEP2, Section 3.2) and XConstraint Source Table - *XCST* (STEP3, Section 3.2) and gives as output the sub XConstraints. *XNVL* (line 1) identifies the node N being inserted with the values v_1...v_n corresponding to attribute names, a_1...a_n (similar to XUpdate syntax). The update is occurring on site S_m. The outer for loop variable *i* (line 4) loops through all the constraints C_1...C_q affected by the XUpdate. The inner for loop variable *j* (line 5) loops through each site < (S_{11},S_{12},...,S_{1n1}),...,(S_{q1},S_{q2},...,S_{qnq})> for each constraint C_i. Inside the for loop (lines 4-28), all the sub constraints C_{ij}'s are generated. X_1...X_r (line 6) denotes vector of user defined variable *v* = path expression *t* in an *XML literal* (Definition 2.2). Q_1.Q_1' (line 8) denotes the conjunction of path expressions Q_1 and Q_1'. A critical feature of the algorithm is the generation of *intermediate*

Algorithm 4.1

```
1: INPUT  : (a) XNVL = $S_m:N(a_1=v_1,a_2=v_2,...,a_n=v_n) on XML tree T
            // Note: insert is occurring on Site S_m
2:    (b) XCST = < <C_1,(S_11,S_12,...,S_1n1)>,...,<C_q,(S_q1,S_q2,...,S_qnq> >
3: OUTPUT: list of sub XConstraints <C_i1,C_i2,...,C_iki> for each C_i affected by XUpdate, XU
4: for each i in {1...q} do
5:   for each j in {1...n_i} do
6:   let S_j:(Q_1,(Q_1',[X_1]) ),..., S_j:(Q_r,(Q_r',[X_r]) ) be XML literals and A be all arithmetic literals
     associated with S_j
7: if (j <> m) then
8:   C_ij = for $var_1 in document("T")Q_1.Q_1',
9:for $var_2 in document("T")Q_2.Q_2', ...,
10:   for $var_r in document("T")Qr.Qr'
11:   where <cond1>
12:   return 1
13: <cond1> is obtained by joining variables with same name appearing in
    XML literals and including any arithmetic conditions
14:else if (j = m) then  /* site where update is occurring */
15:  if (there exists variables in A that do not appear among X_1...X_r) then
16:    for each variable, v in A that do not appear among X_1...X_r do
17:  let k be the site where v appears as one of the XML literals, ( S_k:Q( Q'[X] ) )
18:  IP_ikd = for $v in document ("T")Q.Q'
19:  where <cond2>
20:  return {$v /t_v }
21: t_v is the path expression corresponding to $v in XML literal and <cond 2> is obtained from
   X_1...X_r and X and d is the nth intermediate predicate
22:    end for
23:  end if
24:C_ij = return 1 if (<cond3> and A') else return 0
25:<cond3> is obtained from XNVL and (logical and) X_1...X_r
   A' is A with IP's replacing corresponding variables in A
26:end if
27:  end for
28: end for
```

predicate, *IP* (line 18). *IP*'s are generated only at the site where update is occurring. For each variable that occurs in a different site, we generate *IP*. Conceptually, *IP* denotes information that needs to be shared from a different site; implementation wise, *IP* is an XQuery returning the value of the variable from a different site. IP_{ikd} means the *d*th *intermediate predicate* corresponding to constraint C_i and site S_k.

Theorem 4.1: *The conjunction of sub XConstraints, C_{ij}'s generated from Algorithm 4.1 conclusively determines if an XUpdate statement violates a global XConstraint, C_i.*

Proof sketch:

1. Given an XUpdate statement occurring on site S_m and a global constraint C_i, C_i can be written as conjunction of *XML literals* and *arithmetic literals.* If the whole conjunc-

tion evaluates to *false*, C_i is satisfied (*from Definition 2.4*).

2. Each sub XConstraint C_{ij} needs to achieve the exact same result as the *XML literal* and A*rithmetic literals* corresponding to site S_j.
3. At this point C_{ij} falls in one of the two cases depending on the site S_j :

Case 1: (j <> m) - This is the case where C_{ij} corresponds to a site other than where update is occurring. The generation of C_{ij} in this case involves computing appropriate join conditions and applying arithmetic conditions on *XML literals* and A*rithmetic literals* associated with S_j. Hence C_{ij} naturally achieves the exact same result as the *XML literals* and A*rithmetic literals* associated with S_j.

Case 2: (j = m) - This is the case where C_{ij} corresponds to the site where update is occurring. The generation of C_{ij} in this case consists of two parts. Part 1 consists of information from the same site S_j – trivial case (just like Case 1). Part 2 consists of acquiring information from a different site. For each such variable, a unique *intermediate predicate* is generated. *IP*'s are XQueries that return the values of such variables by computing appropriate joins and arithmetic conditions involved with such variables. Hence, *IP*'s guarantee correct information exchange from a different site. The reason we generate unique *IP*'s is we can either store all the IP's at a global directory such as the XMeta database or we can generate *IP*'s at run time.

From steps 2 and 3 we observe that the conjunction of sub XConstraints C_{ij}'s, entails the global XConstraint, C_i. Hence, if C_i determines whether an XUpdate violates the constraint, then conjunction of its C_{ij}'s also determines if the constraint C_i is violated. In other words, if the whole conjunction of C_i evaluates to false, constraint C_i is not violated, otherwise C_i is violated. □

Example 4.1

We illustrate working of the algorithm on a sample healthdb.xml (refer to Figure 7), when intermediate predicates are not involved. In Figure 7, we show a patient "John" (with SSN – "123") is associated with two CaseId's – 1, 3 and two treatments.

Consider an XUpdate statement, XU_1 occurring on site S_2.

```
XU1 =
FOR $cl in document("healthdb.xml")/
HEALTHDB/S2:CLAIMS
UPDATE $cl
{
INSERT <CLAIM>
          <CaseId>1</CaseId>
            <ClaimDate>03/05/2004</Claim-
Date>
          <Amount>25000</Amount>
          <Type>Emergency</Type>
       </CLAIM>
}
```

Applying STEPS 1-4 from Section 3, we obtain

```
XNVL = {/HEALTHDB/S2:CLAIMS/CLAIM( CaseId = 1,
ClaimDate = '03/05/2004', Amount = 25000,
Type='Emergency')}
CDST (C1) = <C1, (S1, S2, S3)>
where
C1:-
(//S1:PATIENTS,
(./PATIENT,[ssn=./SSN,healthplan=./
HealthPlan])),
(//S1:CASES,(./CASE,[caseid=./CaseId,ssn=./
SSN])),
(//S2:CLAIMS,(./CLAIM,[caseid=./
CaseId,amount=./Amount])),
(//S3:TREATMENTS,
(./TREATMENT,[caseid=./CaseId,disease=./
Disease])),
```

Figure 7. A sample healthdb.xml document

```
                <PName>Clark</PName>
                <HealthPlan>C</HealthPlan>
            </PATIENT>
        </S1_PATIENTS>
        <S1_CASES>
            <CASE>
                <CaseId>1</CaseId>
                <SSN>123</SSN>
                <InjuryDate>10/14/2003</InjuryDate>
            </CASE>
            <CASE>
                <CaseId>2</CaseId>
                <SSN>234</SSN>
                <InjuryDate>06/24/2004</InjuryDate>
            </CASE>
            <CASE>
                <CaseId>3</CaseId>
                <SSN>123</SSN>
                <InjuryDate>10/12/2004</InjuryDate>
            </CASE>
        </S1_CASES>
    <!-- S2 indicates site S2 -->
        <S2_CLAIMS>
            <CLAIM>
                <CaseId>3</CaseId>
                <ClaimDate>11/14/2004</ClaimDate>
                <Amount>40000</Amount>
                <Type>Inpatient</Type>
            </CLAIM>
        </S2_CLAIMS>
        <!-- S3 indicates site S3 -->
        <S3_TREATMENTS>
            <TREATMENT>
                <CaseId>1</CaseId>
                <DName>Mike</DName>
                <TDate>10/15/2003</TDate>
                <Disease>SmallPox</Disease>
            </TREATMENT>
            <TREATMENT>
                <CaseId>3</CaseId>
                <DName>Blake</DName>
                <TDate>10/14/2004</TDate>
                <Disease>LegInjury</Disease>
            </TREATMENT>
        </S3_TREATMENTS>
    </HEALTHDB>
```

healthplan = 'B', disease = 'SmallPox', amount > 40000.

/* C_{11} is generated from Algorithm 4.1 (lines 7-13) */

C_{11} = for $var1 in document("healthdb.xml")//S1_PATIENTS/PATIENT,
    for $var2 in document("healthdb.xml")//S1_CASES/CASE,
    where $var1/SSN = $var2/SSN and $var2/CaseId = 1 and $var1/HealthPlan = "B"
    return 1

/* C_{12} is generated from Algorithm 4.1 (lines 14-26) */

C_{12} = return 1 if {1 = 1 and 25000 > 40000}
    else return 0

```
/* C13 is generated from Algorithm 4.1
(lines 7-13) */
C13 = for $var1 in
    document("healthdb.xml")//
S3_TREATMENTS/TREATMENT
    where $var1/CaseId =
1 and $var1/Disease = "SmallPox"
    return 1
```

So, $C_1 = C_{11} \wedge C_{12} \wedge C_{13}$. In this example, C_{11} = 1(true), C_{12} = 0(false) and C_{13} = 1(true). The conjunction of C_{11}, C_{12} and C_{13} evaluates to *false*. Hence the update statement does not violate constraint C_1 (*from Theorem 4.1*)

```
Similarly,
C21 = for $var1 in document("healthdb.
xml")//S1_PATIENTS/PATIENT,
    for $var2 in document("healthdb.
xml")//S1_CASES/CASE,
    where $var1/SSN = $var2/
SSN and $var2/CaseId = 1 and
    $var1/HealthPlan = "B"
    return 1
C22 = return 1 if {1 = 1 and
"Emergency" = "Emergency"}
else return 0
```

So, $C_2 = C_{21} \wedge C_{22}$. In this example, C_{21} = 1(true), C_{22} = 1(true). The conjunction of C_{21} and C_{22} evaluates to *true*. Hence the update statement violates constraint C_2 (*from Theorem 4.1*). Note that C_2 is defined in Section 2.3.

Example 4.2

Here, we illustrate generation of sub constraints when intermediate predicates are involved. For the example database given in Figure 7, consider C_4, which states "A patient's date of claim may not be earlier than his/her injury date". Constraint C_4 can be expressed as:

```
C4:- (//S1:PATIENTS,(./PATIENT,[ssn=./SSN])),
        (//S1:CASES,
    (./CASE,[caseid=./CaseId,ssn=./
SSN,idate=./InjuryDate])),
    (//S2:CLAIMS,(./CLAIM,[caseid=./
CaseId,cdate=./ClaimDate])),
    cdate<idate.
```

We also assume date arithmetic is available for both XConstraints and sub XConstraints represented as XQueries.

Say, an update statement XU_2 is occurring on site S_2 of the healthdb.xml given in Figure 7.

```
XU2 =
FOR $claim in document ("healthdb.xml")/
HEALTHDB/S2:CLAIMS
UPDATE $claim
{
INSERT <CLAIM>
        <CaseId>1</CaseId>
          <ClaimDate>09/14/2003</Claim-
Date>
        <Amount>25000</Amount>
        <Type>Emergency</Type>
    </CLAIM>
}
Applying STEPS 1-4 from Section 3, we
obtain
XNVL = {/HEALTHDB/S2:CLAIMS/CLAIM( CaseId
= 1,
    ClaimDate = '09/14/2003',Amount =
25000,
    ,Type='Emergency')}
CDST (C4) = <C4, (S1, S2)>
IP411= for $var1 in document("healthdb.
xml")//S1_PATIENTS/PATIENT,
    for $var2 in document("healthdb.
xml")//S1_CASES/CASE,
    where $var1/SSN = $var2/SSN and
$var2/CaseId = 1
    return $var2/InjuryDate
C42 = return 1 if (1 = 1 and (09/14/2003
< IP411) )
```

```
            else return 0
C4 = C42. C42 evaluates to true. Hence,
C4 is violated (from Theorem 4.1).
```

DISCUSSION

Algorithm 4.1 considers elementary XUpdate statements involving an insert statement. The elementary XUpdate statements are statements affecting only one node of an XML tree. We do not consider the issue of transactions. Hence, rollbacks caused by failed transactions can not be avoided.

Here, we make an important observation that an XUpdate statement involving a delete can only violate referential integrity constraints, semantic integrity constraints involving aggregate predicates (sum, max, min, avg and count), state transition and state sequence constraints involving aggregate predicates. It does not violate semantic integrity constraints involving arithmetic predicates considered in this paper. XUpdate statement involving a replace can be modeled as a delete followed by insert. Hence, we have presented a complete model for global semantic integrity constraint checking for XML databases with arithmetic predicates under insert/delete/replace statements.

Let *m* be the number of global constraints, *n* be the number of sites, and *p* be the number of tables at the site where update is occurring. The time complexity of Algorithm 4.1 is *O (m*n)*. If we have a template of possible XUpdate statements, note that all the steps of the algorithm can be carried out at compiling time and we can generate sub constraints for each such template. However, at run time, when an actual XUpdate statement is given, a template match can occur and the corresponding sub constraints, which are already decomposed at compile time, can be executed in parallel at the corresponding sites. Hence, the run time complexity is *O(p)* plus the communication time required for execution at the corresponding sites. If we did not execute sub constraints in parallel, the run time complexity would be *O (m*n)*. Hence, by pushing most of the processing at compile time, we gain efficiency at run time.

Figure 8. XConstraint checker GUI

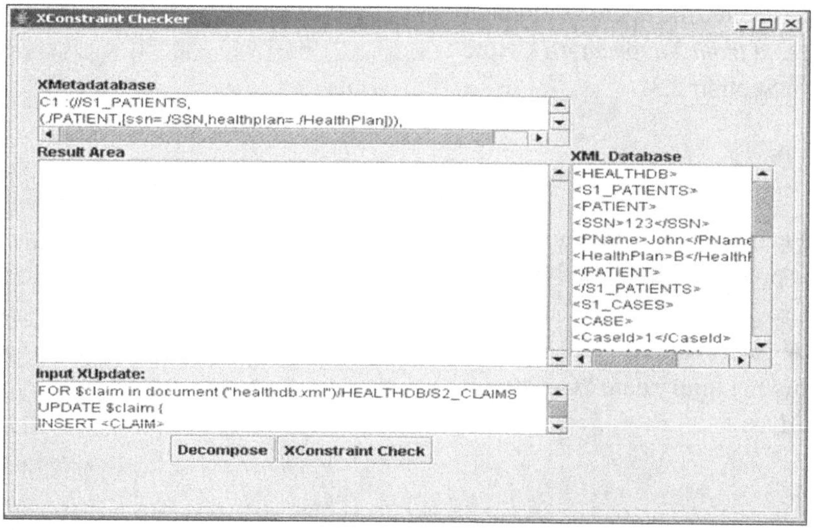

Figure 9. XConstraint checker after decompose

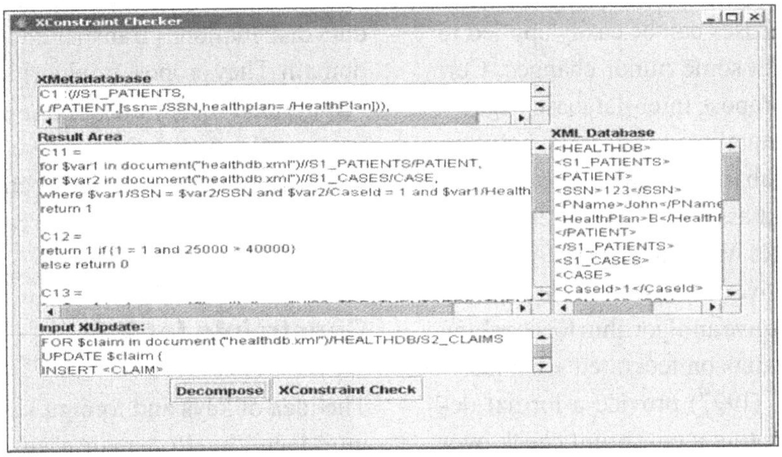

IMPLEMENTATION

The XConstraint Checker architecture and Algorithm 4.1 have been implemented using JDK version 1.3 and the system UI is designed using javax.swing package. A prototype of the system implementation is given in Figure 8. The XMetadatabase panel (top left panel) stores global XConstraints and result area (centre panel) displays the results. The XUpdate panel (lower left panel) allows the user to input XUpdate statements and XML database panel (right most panel) shows the xml files of two or more different sites.

The GUI has two buttons, "Decompose" and "XConstraint Check". When the user clicks "Decompose", sub XConstraints are generated and displayed in the result area panel, shown in Figure 9. The resulting sub XConstraints need to be executed on their corresponding remote XML database sites using the XML/DBC API (Gardarin *et al.*, 2002), when "XConstraint Check" button is clicked. However, for our system implementation, we are not considering the action of XConstraint Check, as we have not seen a working version of the XML/DBC kind of products. We have checked for the validity of the sub XConstraints by executing them on the Galax XQuery interpreter version 0.3.5 (Fernandez & Simeon, 2003) using the sample healthdb.xml file.

RELATED WORK

Our related work section spans three topics: global constraint checking in relational databases, constraints for XML, and constraint checking in XML.

Global Constraint Checking in Relational Databases

Much of the research concerning integrity constraint checking has been done in the area of relational database systems. Grefen & Apers (1993) provide an excellent survey of constraint checking and enforcement methods in relational database systems. Grefen & Widom (1997) give an exhaustive survey of protocols for integrity constraint checking in federated database systems. Gupta & Widom (1993) give approaches for constraint checking in distributed databases at a single site. They show how a class of distributed constraints can be broken down into local update checks. Some of the approaches for distributed databases and federated databases can be easily applied to multidatabases with some minor changes. Ceri & Widom (1993) propose inter-database triggers for maintaining equality constraints between heterogeneous databases. Their approach relies on active rules and assumes a persistent queue facility between sites. Widom & Ceri (1996) mention research on active databases and constraints. Saoudi *et al.* (1996) give an algorithm for checking extensional constraints on federated schemas.

Grufman *et al.* (1997) provide a formal description of distributing a constraint check over a number of databases. They propose that the problem of generating sub constraint from a global constraint is the same as rewriting a predicate calculus expression of the constraint check into a form in which the distribution of the data is respected. The rewritten predicate can be seen as a conjunction of sub constraints, where each sub constraint may be visualized as the constraint check as seen from each individual database. During the process of rewriting the constraint check predicate, they introduce the concept of intermediate predicate. The idea of intermediate predicates used in this paper has been borrowed from them. In their constraint distribution model, an update statement is first carried out and the new database state is checked for constraint violation. If the constraint is violated, the update is rolled back. Our work differs from theirs by giving an algorithm that automatically decomposes a global constraint into a conjunction of sub constraints. Our approach is much more sophisticated, as we check for constraint violations with out actually updating the database. The update is executed only when there are no constraint violations. Hence our algorithm is efficient as there are no problems involved with rollbacks as such. Also, Grufman *et al.* (1997) consider constraint checking in a different context of distributed relational databases.

Ibrahim (2002) proposes a strategy for constraint checking in distributed database where data distribution is transparent to the application domain. They propose an algorithm for transforming a global constraint into a set of equivalent fragment constraints. However, our algorithm coverage is for a different context of multiple XML databases and also we can have different tables on different sites.

Constraints for XML

The idea of keys and foreign keys for XML was introduced in (Buneman *et al.*, 2001), (Chen *et al.*, 2002a). The basic approach is to express constraints using path expressions. We have also studied the constraint representation in distributed databases. In (Gupta & Widom, 1993), a constraint is treated as a query whose result is either false or true. If the query produces false on the database D, D is said to satisfy the constraint. Otherwise, the constraint is violated ((Gupta & Widom, 1993) calls it "panic"). We have extended the approach of (Buneman *et al.*, 2001), (Chen *et al.*, 2002a) with datalog style notations and also used the concepts from (Gupta & Widom, 1993) in representing XConstraints.

Constraint Language in XML, CLiX (Marconi & Nentwich, 2004) is an assertion language based on first order logic and XPath. A survey of different constraint languages proposed in XML can be found in (Fan, 2005). Another approach to representing constraints as active rules in XML has been considered in Bonifati, Ceri, & Paraboschi, 2001), (Rodrigues & Mello, 2007).

Constraint Checking in XML

The area of constraint checking for XML has recently drawn huge attention as evidenced by a plethora of research projects. Research on validating keys for XML can be found in (Benedikt *et al.*, 2003), (Bouchou *et al.*, 2003) and (Chen *et al.*, 2002b). The two major categories of constraint checking for XML are: incremental checking (Abrão et al., 2004), (Balmin et al., 2004) and simplification methods.

Similar to ours, the underlying idea of SAXE (Kane, Su & Rundensteiner, 2002) is to generate constraint check sub queries for a given update statement and a list of constraints. The constraint check sub queries check if the given XUpdate statement violates the consistency of the XML document. The XUpdate statement in SAXE is executed only if it is safe. Hence SAXE avoids any potential rollbacks. SAXE executes only those XUpdates that would preserve the consistency of the XML document with respect to a particular schema. We also take a similar route. However, SAXE does not consider semantic integrity constraint checking for multiple XML databases. Yet, another category of research considers maintaining integrity of XML databases using active rules (Rodrigues & Mello, 2007).

CONCLUSION

Many commercial products have sprung in the last few years which started using latest key technologies in XML such as XQuery. This is evident from the active work being done at W3C working group and the community at large. These commercial applications will use multiple XML database and will need an efficient way to check for global XML constraints. Towards this goal, we have presented the architecture of XConstraint Checker. XConstraint Checker is part of a middleware module, which determines if an XUpdate statement violates any global XConstraints. In a nutshell, we have: (i) introduced a notation for representing XConstraints, (ii) proposed architecture for XConstraint Checker, (iii) formalized an algorithm for XConstraint Decomposer, and (iv) implemented a prototype of the system with the ideas discussed here.

For each global XConstraint that could be violated, multiple sub XConstraints are generated. Hence, we have a large number of sub XConstraints when we consider all the set of global XConstraints. All this process can be done at compiling time. Therefore, efficient ordering of sub XConstraints for executing on remote sites would optimize the constraint checking mechanism. To achieve this, a future research avenue is to incorporate optimization of XML constraint checking process.

REFERENCES

Abrão, M.A., Bouchou, B., Alves, M.H.F., Laurent, D., & Musicante, M. (2004). Incremental Constraint Checking for XML Documents. *Database and XML Technologies: Second International XML Database Symposium (*XSym) Toronto, Canada, August 29-30, LNCS Volume 3186 / 2004

Balmin, A., Papakonstantinou, Y., & Vianu, V.(2004). Incremental Validation of XML Documents. *ACM Transactions on Database Systems*, 29(4):710—751

Benedikt, M., Chan, C.Y., Fan, W., Freire, J. & Rastogi, R. (2003). Capturing both Types and Constraints in Data Integration. *Proceedings of the ACM SIGMOD Conference on Management Of Data*

Bonifati, A., Ceri, S., & Paraboschi, S. (2001). Active Rules for XML: A New Paradigm for E-services. *VLDB Journal* 10(1): 39-47

Bouchou, B., Halfeld-Ferrari-Alves, M. & Musicante, M. (2003). Tree Automata to Verify XML Key Constraints. *International Workshop on the Web and Databases.*

Buneman, P., Davidson, S., Fan, W., Hara, C., & Tan, W. (2001). Keys for XML. *World Wide Web*, pp. 201-210.

Ceri, S., & Widom, J. (1993). Managing Semantic Heterogeneity with Production Rules and Persistent Queues. *Proceedings of the 19th International Conference on Very Large Data Bases,* pp. 108-119.

Chamberlin, D., Florescu, D., Melton, J., Robie, J., & Siméon, J. (2008, February). *XQuery Update Facility 1.0, W3C Working Draft.* [online]. Available : http://www.w3.org/TR/xquery-update-10/

Chen, Y., Davidson, S.B., Hara, C.S., & Zheng, Y. (2003). RRXF: Redundancy Reducing XML Storage in Relations. *Proceedings of the International Conference on Very Large Databases.*

Chen, Y., Davidson, S.B., & Zheng, Y. (2002a). Constraint Preserving XML Storage in Relations. *International Workshop on the Web and Databases.*

Chen, Y., Davidson, S.B., & Zheng, Y. (2002b). XKvalidator: A Constraint Validator for XML. *Proceedings of ACM Conference on Information and Knowledge Management.*

Elmasri, R.A., & Navathe, S.B. (2003). Fundamentals of Database Systems. Addison-Wesley, 4th edition.

Fan, W. (2005). XML Constraints: Specification, Analysis, and Applications. *Proceedings of the 16th International Workshop on Database and Expert Systems Applications*

Fernandez, M., & Siméon, J. (2003) .Growing XQuery. European Conference on Object Oriented Programming (ECOOP).

Fong, J. & Wong, K. (2004). XTOPO: An XML-Based Topology for Information Highway on the Internet. *Journal of Database Management,* 15(3), 18-44.

Gardarin, G., Mensch, A., Tuyet, T., & Smit, D.L.(2002). Integrating Heterogeneous Data Sources with XML and XQuery. *Proceedings of the 13th International Workshop on Database and Expert Systems Applications.*

Grefen, P., & Apers, P. (1993). Integrity Control in Relational Database Systems - An Overview. *Journal of Data and Knowledge Engineering,* 10 (2), pp. 187-223.

Grefen, P. & Widom, J. (1997). Protocols for integrity Constraint Checking in Federated Databases. *International Journal of Distributed and Parallel Databases,* 5(4): 327-355.

Grufman, S., Samson, F., Embury, S.M., Gray, P.M.D., & Risch, T. (1997). Distributing Semantic Constraints Between Heterogeneous Databases. *Proceedings of International Conference on Data Engineering*

Gupta, A., & Widom, J. (1993). Local Verification of Global Integrity Constraints in Distributed Databases. *Proceedings of the ACM SIGMOD Conference on Management of Data.*

Ibrahim, H. (2002). A Strategy for Semantic Integrity Checking in Distributed Databases. *Proceedings of the ninth International Conference on Parallel and Distributed Systems (ICPADS),* pp. 139-144

Kane, B., Su, H. & Rundensteiner, E.A. (2002). Consistently Updating XML Documents using Incremental Constraint Check Queries. *Workshop on Web Information and Data Management (WIDM),* Nov, pp. 1-8.

Laux, A., & Martin, L. (2000). XUpdate Working Draft, 2000, last accessed on August 20, 2004 from http://xmldb-org.sourceforge.net/xupdate/xupdate-wd.html

Marconi, M., & Nentwich, C. (2004). CLiX Language Specification Version 1.0. [online]. last accessed on February 15, 2008 from : http://www.clixml.org/clix/1.0/clix.xml

Madiraju, P., Sunderraman, R. & Navathe, S.B. (2004). Semantic Integrity Constraint Checking for Multiple XML Databases. *Proceedings of 14th Workshop on Information Technology and Systems (WITS 2004),* Washington D.C., December, 2004

Madiraju, P., Sunderraman, S., Navathe, S.B., & Wang, H. (2006). Semantic Integrity Constraint Checking for Multiple XML Databases. *Journal of Database Management,* Vol. 17, No. 4, pp. 1-19

Rodrigues, K. R., & Mello, R.D.S (2007). A Faceted Taxonomy of Semantic Integrity Constraints for the XML Data Model. *Proceedings of 18th International Conference on Database and Expert Systems Applications* (DEXA) pp. 65-74

Saoudi, A., Nachouki, G. & Briand, H. (1996). Checking extensional constraints of federated schemata.. *Proceedings of Seventh International Workshop on Database and Expert Systems Applications,* September, pp. 398-403

Shanmugasundaram, J., Tufte, K., He, G., Zhang, C., DeWitt, D., & Naughton, J. (1999). Relational Databases for Querying XML Documents: Limitations and Opportunities. *Proceedingsof the International Conference on Very Large Databases.*

Tatarinov, I., Ives, Z. G., Halevy, A.Y., & Daniel, S. (2001). Updating XML. *Proceedings of the ACM SIGMOD Conference on Management of Data*

Widom, J., & Ceri, S. (1996). Active Database Systems: Triggers and Rules for Advanced Database Processing. *Morgan Kaufmann, San Francisco, California.*

Chapter XI
Accelerating Multi Dimensional Queries in Data Warehouses

Russel Pears
Auckland University of Technology, New Zealand

Bryan Houliston
Auckland University of Technology, New Zealand

ABSTRACT

Data Warehouses are widely used for supporting decision making. On Line Analytical Processing or OLAP is the main vehicle for querying data warehouses. OLAP operations commonly involve the computation of multidimensional aggregates. The major bottleneck in computing these aggregates is the large volume of data that needs to be processed which in turn leads to prohibitively expensive query execution times. On the other hand, Data Analysts are primarily concerned with discerning trends in the data and thus a system that provides approximate answers in a timely fashion would suit their requirements better. In this chapter we present the Prime Factor scheme, a novel method for compressing data in a warehouse. Our data compression method is based on aggregating data on each dimension of the data warehouse. Extensive experimentation on both real-world and synthetic data have shown that it outperforms the Haar Wavelet scheme with respect to both decoding time and error rate, while maintaining comparable compression ratios (Pears and Houliston, 2007). One encouraging feature is the stability of the error rate when compared to the Haar Wavelet. Although Wavelets have been shown to be effective at compressing data, the approximate answers they provide varies widely, even for identical types of queries on nearly identical values in distinct parts of the data. This problem has been attributed to the thresholding technique used to reduce the size of the encoded data and is an integral part of the Wavelet compression scheme. In contrast the Prime Factor scheme does not rely on thresholding but keeps a smaller version of every data element from the original data and is thus able to achieve a much higher degree of error stability which is important from a Data Analysts point of view.

INTRODUCTION

Data Warehouses are increasingly being used by decision makers to analyze trends in data (Cunningham, Song and Chen, 2006, Elmasri and Navathe, 2003). Thus a marketing analyst is able to track variation in sales income across dimensions such as time period, location, and product on their own or in combination with each other. This analysis requires the processing of multi-dimensional aggregates and group by operations against the underlying data warehouse. Due to the large volumes of data that need to be scanned from secondary storage, such queries, referred to as On Line Analytical Processing (OLAP) queries, can take from minutes to hours in large scale data warehouses (Elmasri, 2003, Oracle 9i).

The standard technique for improving query performance is to build aggregate tables that are targeted at known queries (Triantafillakis, Kanellis, and Martakos 2004; Elmasri, 2003). For example the identification of the top ten selling products can be speeded up by building a summary table that contains the total sales value (in dollar terms) for each of the products sorted in decreasing order of sales value. It would then be a simple matter of querying the summary table and retrieving the first ten rows. The main problem with this approach is the lack of flexibility. If the analyst now chooses to identify the bottom ten products an expensive re-sort would have to be performed to answer this new query. Worse still, if the information is to be tracked by sales location then the summary table would be of no value at all. This problem is symptomatic of a more general one where Database Systems which have been tuned for a particular access pattern perform poorly as changes to such patterns occur over a period of time. In their study (Zhen and Darmont, 2005) showed that database systems which have been optimized through clustering to suit particular query patterns rapidly degrade in performance when such query patterns change in nature.

The limitations in the above approach can be addressed by a data compression scheme that preserves the original structure of the data. The chapter is organized as follows. In the next section we review related work. The next section introduces the Prime Factor Compression (PFC) approach. We then present the algorithms required for encoding and decoding with the PFC approach. The On Line reconstruction of Queries is discussed thereafter. Implementation related issues are then discussed, followed by a performance evaluation of PFC and a comparison with the Haar Wavelet algorithm. We then discuss future trends in optimizing multi-dimensional queries in the light of the results of this research. We conclude with a summary of the main achievements of the research.

BACKGROUND

Previous research has tended to concentrate on computing exact answers to OLAP queries (Ho, and Agrawal, 1997, Wang 2002). Ho describes a method that pre-processes a data cube to give a prefix sum cube. The prefix sum cube is computed by applying the transformation: $P[A_i]=C[A_i]+P[A_{i-1}]$ along each dimension of the data cube, where P denotes the prefix sum cube, C the original data cube, A_i denotes an element in the cube, and i is an index in a range $1..D_i$ (D_i is the size of the dimension D_i). This means that the prefix cube requires the same storage space as the original data cube.

The above approach is efficient for low dimensional data cubes. For high dimensional environments, two major problems exist. Firstly, the number of accesses required is 2^d (Ho *et al*, 1997), which can be prohibitive for large values of d (where d denotes the number of dimensions). Secondly, the storage required to store the prefix sum cube can be excessive. In a typical OLAP environment the data tends to be massive and yet sparse at the same time. The degree of sparsity increases with the number of dimensions (OLAP) and thus the number of non zero cells may be a very small fraction of the prefix sum cube, which by its nature has to be dense for its query processing algorithms to work correctly.

Another exact technique is the Dwarf cube method (Sismannis and Deligiannakis, 2002) which seeks to eliminate structural redundancies and factor them out by coalescing their store. Prefix redundancy arises when the fact table contains a group of tuples having a prefix of redundant values for its dimension attributes. On the other hand, suffix redundancy occurs when groups of tuples contain a suffix of redundant values for its dimension attributes. Elimination of these redundancies has been shown to be effective for dense cubes. Unfortunately, in the case of sparse cubes with a large number of dimensions the size of the fact table can actually increase in size (Sismannis *et al*, 2002), thus providing no gains in storage efficiency.

In contrast to exact methods, approximate methods attempt to strike a good balance between the degree of compression and accuracy. Query performance is enhanced by storing a compact version of the data cube. A histogram based approach was used by (Matias and Vitter, 1998), (Poosala and Gnati, 1999), (Vitter *et al*, 1998), to summarize the data cube. However, histograms too suffer from the curse of high dimensionality, with both space and time complexity increasing exponentially with the number of dimensions (Matias *et al*, 1998).

The Progressive Approximate Aggregate approach (Lazaridis and Mehrotra, 2001) uses a tree structure to speed up the computation of aggregates. Aggregates are computed by identifying tree nodes that intersect the query region and then accumulating their values incrementally. All tree nodes that are fully contained in the query region provide an exact contribution to the query result, whereas nodes that have a partial intersection provide an estimate. This estimation is based on an assumption of spatial uniformity of attribute values across the underlying data cube. In practice this assumption may be invalid as with the case of the real-world data (US Census) that we experimented with in our study. In contrast, our method makes no such assumptions on the shape of the source data distribution. Another issue with the above scheme is that it has a worst case run time performance that is linear in the number of data elements covered by the query, as observed by (Chen and Chen, 2003). This has negative implications for queries that span a large fraction of the underlying data cube, particularly since compression is not utilized to store source data.

Sampling is another approach that has been used to speed up aggregate processing. Essentially, a small random sample of the database is selected and the aggregate is computed on this sample. The sampling operation can be done off-line, whereby the sample is extracted from the database and all queries are run on this single extracted sample. On the other hand, in on-line sampling data is read randomly from the database each time a query is executed and the aggregate computed on the dynamically generated sample (Hellerstein *et al*, 1996). The very nature of sampling makes it very efficient in terms of run time, but its accuracy has been shown to be a limiting factor in its widespread adoption (Vitter and Wang, 1999).

Vitter *et al*, use the wavelet technique to transform the data cube into a compact form. It is essentially a data compression technique that transforms the original data cube into a Wavelet Transform Array (WTA) which is a fraction of the size of the original data cube. In their research Matias *et al* show that wavelets are superior to the histogram based methods, both in terms of accuracy and storage efficiency. Wavelets have also been shown to provide good compression with sparse data cubes, unlike the Dwarf compression method.

Given the wavelet's superior performance over its rivals and the fact that it is an approximate technique, it was an ideal choice for comparison against our Prime Factor scheme which is also approximate in nature. The next section provides a brief overview of the encoding and decoding procedures used in wavelet data compression.

In principle, any data compression scheme can be applied on a data warehouse For example, a 3-dimensional warehouse that tracks sales by time period, location and products can be compressed along all three dimensions and then stored in the form of "chunks" (Sarawagi and Stonebraker, 1994). Chunking is a technique that is used to partition a d-dimensional array into smaller d-dimensional units.

However a high compression ratio is needed to offset the potentially huge secondary storage access times. This effectively ruled out standard compression techniques such as Huffman Coding (Cormack, 1985), LZW and its variants (Lempel and Ziv, 1977; Hunt 1998) as well as Arithmetic Coding (Langdon, 1984). These schemes enable decoding to the original data with 100% accuracy, but suffer from modest compression ratios (Ng and Ravishankar, 1997). On the other hand the trends analysis nature of decision making means that query results do not need to reflect 100% accuracy. For example, during a drill-down query sequence in ad-hoc data mining, initial queries in the sequence usually determine the truly interesting queries and regions of the database. Providing approximate, yet reasonably accurate answers to these initial queries gives users the ability to focus their explorations quickly and effectively, without consuming inordinate amounts of valuable system resources (Hellerstein, Haas and Wang, 1997).

This means that lossy schemes which exhibit relatively high compression and near 100% accuracy would be the ideal solution to achieving acceptable performance for OLAP queries. This chapter investigates and presents the performance of a novel scheme, called Prime Factor Compression (PFC) and compares it against the well known Wavelet approach (Vitter and Wang, 1998; Vitter and Wang 1999, Chakrabarti and Garofalakis, 2000). Recent results have indicated that the Prime Factor Compression scheme outperforms the Wavelet scheme in terms of error stability, maintaining a very low and virtually constant level of accuracy irrespective of the size of the query (Pears and Houliston, 2007). This is in marked contrast to the Wavelet scheme which exhibits large swings in accuracy with varying query size. This problem has been attributed to the thresholding technique used to reduce the size of the encoded data (Garofalakis and Gibbons, 2004) and is an integral part of the Wavelet compression scheme. The Prime Factor scheme, on the other hand does not rely on thresholding but keeps a smaller version of every data element from the original data and is thus able to achieve a much higher degree of error stability which is important from a Data Analysts point of view.

In this chapter we provide a fuller exploration of the PFC scheme, including detailed results on various different types of datasets and a formal evaluation of its performance on sparse data.

Wavelet Data Compression Scheme

The Wavelet scheme compresses by transforming the source data into a representation (the Wavelet Transform Array or WTA) that contains a large number of zero or near-zero values. The transformation uses a series of averaging operations that operate on each pair of neighboring source data elements. In this manner the original data is transformed into a data set (the Level 1 transform set) that contains the averages of pairs of elements from the original data set. The pair-wise averaging process is then applied recursively on the Level 1 transform set. The process continues in this manner until the size of the transformed set is equal to 1. In order to be able to reconstruct the original data the pair-wise differences between neighbors is kept in addition to the average. The WTA array then consists of all pair-wise averages and differences accumulated across all levels.

A thresholding function is then applied on the WTA to remove a large fraction of array elements which are small in value. The thresholding function applies a weighting scheme on the WTA elements as those elements at the higher levels play a more significant role in reconstruction than their counterparts at the lower levels. For details of the wavelet encoding and decoding techniques the reader is referred to (Vitter *et al*, 1999).

Wavelet Decoding

The decoding process reconstructs the original data by using the truncated version of the WTA. The decoding process is best illustrated with the following example. Figure 1 shows how the coefficients of the original array are reconstructed from the WTA (the C coefficients hold the original array while the S coefficients hold the WTA).

Any coefficient C(i) is reconstructed by using its ancestor S coefficients in the path from the root node to itself. Thus for example, C(0) = S(0) +S(1)+S(2) +S(4) and C(1) = S(0)+S(1)+S(2)-S(4).

Consider a scenario where S(4), although relatively large in comparison to S(0), S(1) and S(2), is thresholded out due to its lower weighting, thus leading to inaccuracies in the estimation of C(0) and C(1). This is symptomatic of the general case where the lower level coefficients are significant contributors to the reconstruction process but are thresholded out to make way for their more highly weighted ancestor coefficients. The problem is especially acute in the case of data that is both skewed and have a high degree of variability.

THE PRIME FACTOR SCHEME

In response to the problems associated with wavelets, we present the "Prime factor Scheme". The scheme works broadly on the same lines as the Wavelet technique in the sense that data compression is used to reduce the size of the data cube prior to processing of OLAP queries. OLAP queries are run on the compressed data, which is decoded to yield an approximate answer to the query.

Our encoding scheme uses pre-processing to reduce the degree of variation in the source data which results in better compression. An overview of the encoding process is given in the following section.

Figure 1. Wavelet reconstruction process

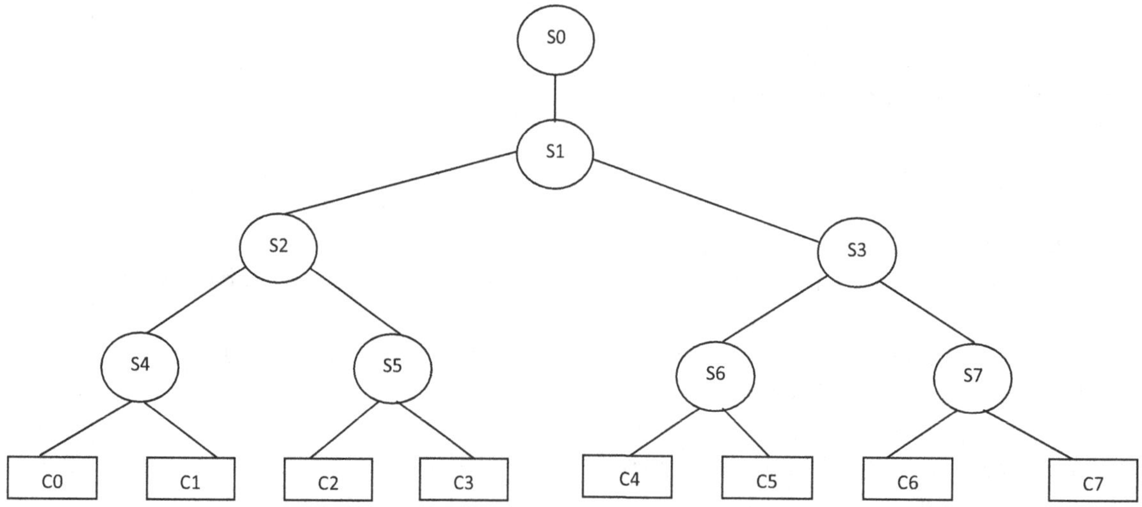

Overview of Prime Factor Encoding Scheme

The data is first scaled using the standard min-max scaling technique . With this technique, any value V in the original cube is transformed into V', where V' =(V-min)*(nmax-nmin)/(max-min)+nmin, where min, max represent the minimum and maximum values respectively in the original data cube; nmin and nmax are the corresponding minimum and maximum values of the scaled set of values. Each scaled value V' is then approximated by its nearest prime number in the scale range [nmin, nmax].

The choice of nmin and nmax influences both the degree of compression and the error rate as we shall show later in the "Experimental Setup" section. The rationale behind the scaling is to induce a higher degree of homogeneity between values by compressing the original scale [min, max] into a smaller scale [nmin, nmax], with nmin $\geq$ min and nmax < max. In doing so, this pre-processing step improves the degree of compression.

The scaled data cube is then partitioned into equal sized chunks. The size of the chunk c represents the number of cells that are enclosed by the chunk. The size of the chunk affects the decoding (query processing) time. Higher values mean fewer chunks need to be decoded, thus reducing the decoding time (see Theorem 3 in the section on "On line Reconstruction of Queries").

Each chunk is encoded by the prime factor encoding algorithm which yields an array containing 2c cells. Although the encoded version has twice the number of cells it is much smaller in size since each cell is very small in numerical value. In fact, our experimental results reveal that the vast majority of values are very small integers (see Figures 13a and 13b in the "Experimental Setup" section). Figure 2 below summarizes the Prime Factor encoding process.

In addition to transforming values to very small integers, the other major benefit of the algorithm is that the integers are highly skewed in value towards zero. For example, on the Census data set (US Census) with a chunk size of 64, over 75% of the values turned out to be zero. These results were also borne out with the synthetic data sets that we tested our scheme on. The source (original) data in some of these data sets were not skewed in nature, showing that the skew was induced, rather than being an inherent feature of the original data.

We exploited the skewed nature of the encoded data by using the Elias variable length coding scheme (Elias, 1975). Elias encoding works by encoding smaller integers in a smaller number of bits, thus further improving the degree of compression.

The next section will describe the details involved in step 3 of the above process, the PFC encoding algorithm.

Figure 2. Overview of the prime factor scheme

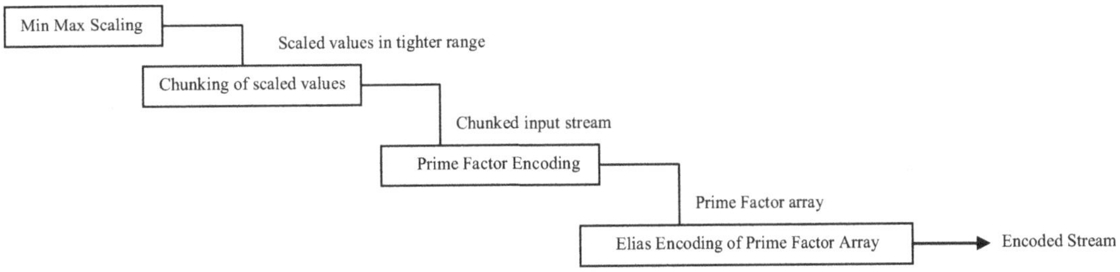

The Prime Factor Encoding Algorithm

The algorithm takes as its input the scaled set of values produced by the min-max scaling technique. For each chunk, every scaled value is converted into the prime number that is closest to it. We refer to each such prime number as a *prime factor*. The algorithm makes use of two operators which we define below. Both operators α and β take as their input a pair of prime factors V_k and V_{k+1}.

Definition 1: The operator α is defined by $\alpha(V_k, V_{k+1})$ = nearest prime $(V_k + V_{k+1} + I(V_{k+1}) - I(V_k))$, where $I(V_{k+1})$, $I(V_k)$ denote the ordinal (index) positions of V_{k+1} and V_k on the prime number scale. The operator takes two primes (V_k, V_{k+1}) adds them together with the difference in index positions between the 2nd prime and the 1st prime and converts the sum obtained to the nearest prime number.

Definition 2: The operator β is defined by $\beta(V_k, V_{k+1})$ = nearest prime$(V_k + V_{k+1})$

The α operator is applied pair-wise across all values (a total of c prime factors) in the chunk. This yields a stream of c/2 prime factors. The α operator is then applied recursively on the processed stream until a single prime factor is obtained. This recursive procedure gives rise to a tree of height $\log_2 c$ where c is the chunk size. We refer to this tree as the *Prime Index Tree.*

In parallel with the construction of the prime index tree we construct another tree, called the *Prime Tree.* The prime tree is constructed in the same manner as its prime index counterpart except that we apply the β operator, instead of the α operator.

We illustrate the construction of the trees with the help of the following example. For the sake of simplicity we take the cube to be of size 4, the chunk size c to be 4 (i.e. we have only one chunk) and the scale range [nmin, nmax] to be [0, 101].

For the prime index tree (Figure 3a), the prime values 37 and 2 at the leaf level are summed as 37+2+I(2)-I(37), which is transformed to its nearest prime number, 29. Similarly 71 and 97 when processed yield the prime number, 173. The node values 29 and 173 in turn yield a root value of 233.

As shown in Figure 3b, the leaf values 37 and 2 when summed and converted into its nearest prime yields a value of 37. Following the same

Figure 3a. The construction of the Prime Index Tree

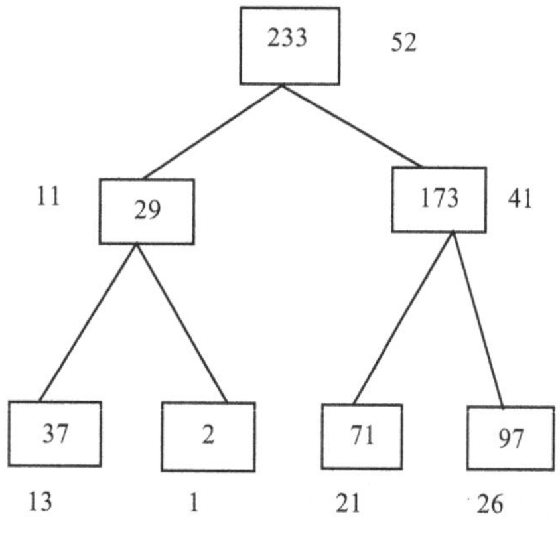

Figure 3b. The construction of the Prime Tree

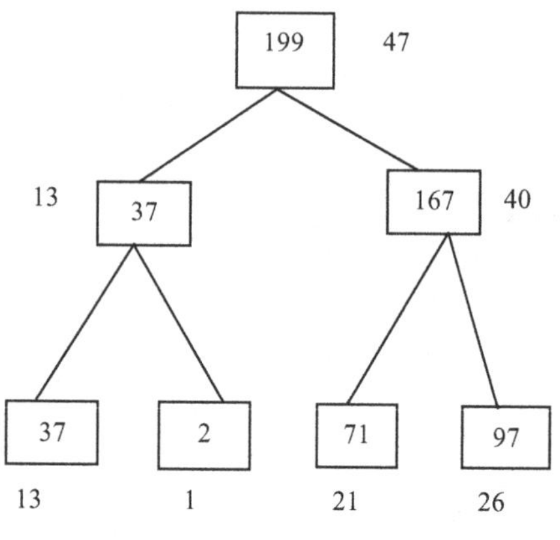

process, we obtain values of 167 and 199 for the remaining nodes.

We annotate each internal node by its corresponding index value. The encoded array E now consists of the differences in index positions across corresponding positions in the two trees. These differences are referred to as *differentials*. For the example above the array turns out to be E = {5, -2, 1}. We also store the index value of each prime tree root separately in another array R. Each chunk gives rise to its own prime tree root, and for the simple example above, since we have only one chunk, this results in a single value {47} for R.

Decoding requires the use of the two arrays E and R. We start with the first value in array R, which is 47, and then add it to the first value in array E which is 5, yielding the value 52. We use 52 as an index into a table of primes (this table has the pseudo prime 0 added to it with index value 0) and extract 233 as the corresponding prime value. We now search for pairs of primes (P1, P2) which satisfy the condition:

$\alpha(P1, P2) = 233$, $\beta(P3, P4) = 199$, $I(P3) = I(P1+2)$ and $I(P4) = I(P2-1)$ --------(1), where P3, P4 are the corresponding nodes to P1, P2 in the prime tree

This search in general would yield a set S of candidate pairs for (P1, P2) rather than a single pair. In order to extract the correct pair, we associate an integer with each internal node of the Prime Index tree which records the ordinal position within the set S which would enable us to descend to the next level of the tree. In this case this integer turns out to be 0 since there is only one pair that satisfies condition (1). These integers are collectively referred to as *offsets*. The complete set of offsets for the tree above is {0, 0, 0}. The complete version of E contains the sequence of differentials followed by the sequence of offsets. Thus for our example we have E = {5,2,-1,0,0,0}. We are now able to decode by descending both trees in parallel and recover the original set of leaf values 37, 2, 71 and 97.

For ease of understanding, the encoding process above has been described for a 1-d dimensional case. The extension to d dimensions follows naturally by encoding along each dimension in sequence. For example, if we have a 2 dimensional cube <D_1, D_2 > we would first construct 2- dimensional chunks. With a chunk size of 16 and the use of equal width across each dimension, each chunk would consist of a 4 by 4 2-d array. We first run the encoding process across dimension D_1. This would yield a 1-dimensional array consisting of 4 prime root values for each chunk. The differentials and offsets that result from this encoding are stored in a temporary cache. The 4 prime root values from encoding on D_1 are then subjected to the encoding process across dimension D_2 to yield the final encoding. The differentials and offsets that result from encoding along D_2 are merged with those from encoding along dimension D_1 to yield the final set of encoded values.

Encoding Performance

The encoding takes place in four steps as given in Figure 2. Steps 1 and 2, involving scaling and chunking can be done together. As data is read it can be scaled on the fly with the chunking process. If the original data is stored in dimension order (D_1, D_2, ...D_d) with the rightmost indices changing more rapidly, then it can be shown the I/O complexity involved in chunking is $O\left(\frac{N}{B}\log_{\frac{M}{B}}\frac{N}{B}\right)$, where M is the available memory size and B is the block size of the underlying database system.

The reader is referred to [Vitter 1999] for a proof. The I/O complexity of steps 3 and 4 is $O\left(\frac{N}{B}\right)$. Thus the I/O complexity is bounded by the $O\left(\frac{N}{B}\log_{\frac{M}{B}}\frac{N}{B}\right)$ term required for the chunking step.

However it should be noted that this only reflects a one time cost in reorganizing the data from dimension order to chunked format. Once this is done, no further chunking is required as updates to values do not affect the chunk structure. Thus the time complexity on a regular basis would be bounded above by $o\left(\frac{N}{B}\right)$. The only exception occurs when the dimensions are reorganized and either grow or shrink as a result. This would require repetition of the chunking step.

The Rationale behind the Prime Factor Scheme

Prime numbers provide us with a natural way of constraining the search space since they are much less dense than ordinary integers. The first 100 positive integers are distributed across only 25 primes. At the same time the primes themselves become less dense as we move up the integer scale (Andrews, 1994). The next 900 positive integers after 100 only contain 143 primes. This means that the prime number encoding technique has good scalability with respect to data value size. From the error point of view the use of primes introduces only small errors as it is possible to find a prime in close neighborhood to any given integer (Andrews, 1994). Theorem 1 below gives the distribution of primes in the general case.

Theorem 1

The number of prime numbers less than or equal to a given number N approaches.

$$\frac{N}{\log_e(N)} \text{ for large N.}$$

Proof: The reader is referred to (Andrews, 1994) for a proof.

Theorem 1 reinforces the observations made above. Firstly, the division by the logarithm term ensures that the primes are less dense that ordinary integers. Secondly, the average gap between a given prime N and its successor is approximately $N/\left(\frac{N}{\log_e N}\right) = \log_e N$. This means that encoding a number N using its nearest prime will result in an absolute error of $\frac{1}{2}\log_e N$ on the average. These properties make prime numbers an attractive building block for encoding numerical data.

The basic idea that we utilize is to convert a stream of primes into a single prime, the Prime Tree root value by a series of pair wise add operations. We then augment the root value with a set of coefficients to enable us to decode. The use of prime numbers enables us to drastically reduce the search space involved in decoding and as a consequence reduce the space required to store the encoded data. As an example consider the prime root value of 29. In order to decode (assuming that we simply use the Prime Tree) to the next level we have to consider just eight combinations (5,23), (23,5), (7,23), (23,7), (11,19), (19,11) , (13, 17) and (17,13). On the other hand if prime numbers were not used as the basis, then we would have a total of 30 combinations to consider – in general, if N were the prime root, then N+1 combinations would have to be tested.

The use of the Prime Index tree in conjunction with the Prime Tree enables us to constrain the search space even further. With the introduction of the former we are able to distinguish between pairs such as (5,23) and (23,5). The pair (5,23) encodes as 31 in the Prime Index tree and 29 in the Prime tree, whereas (23,5) encodes as 23 in the Prime Index tree and 29 in the Prime tree. Apart from this, the other major benefit of growing two trees instead of one is that we can encode taking the differentials between corresponding nodes across the two trees rather than node values themselves. Since the two trees evolve from a common set of leaf values, the α and β operators evaluate to approximately the same values which in turn causes the differentials to be much smaller than the node values themselves (see Figure 13a in the "Experimental Setup" section).

Comparison of the Wavelet and Prime Factor Schemes

The wavelet and prime factor schemes both use the concept of reducing the original data to differentials between progressively increasing sub sets. However one major difference is that that the

Wavelet scheme uses thresholding to drop some of the differentials. As noted before, this makes it unstable with respect to the error rate (Garofalakis and Gibbons, 2004) and this is confirmed by our results which we present later. In contrast, the Prime Factor scheme does not use thresholding but exploits the skew induced by the prime factor transformation to encode the resulting coefficients using an Elias code. This means that *every* value in the original data set is represented in the encoded version which results in much greater stability over the Wavelet scheme.

Another major difference is that the encoded data in the Wavelet scheme are represented as relational tuples in the form $<i_1, i_2, \ldots i_d, c>$ where each i_k (in the range 1 to d) identifies the index position within dimension k in which the surviving coefficient with value c is located. For large values of d, the degree of compression obtained can degrade quite severely as each index takes up additional storage. In contrast, the Prime Factor scheme does not require any such indexes as thresholding is not used and thus we would expect it to have relatively better compression for high dimensionality data.

Figure 4a. Left prefix prime index tree

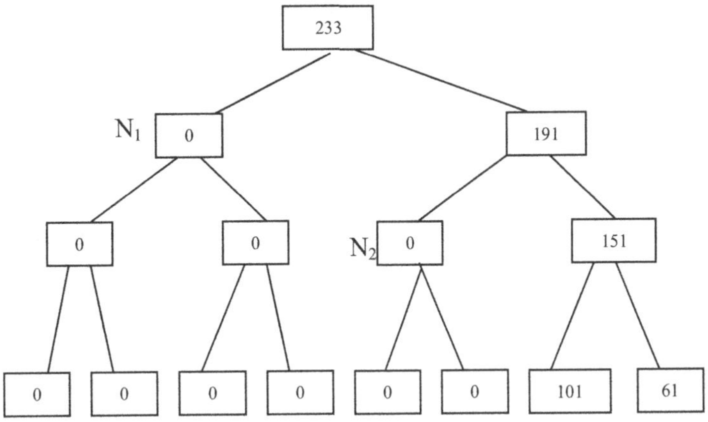

Figure 4b. Left prefix prime tree

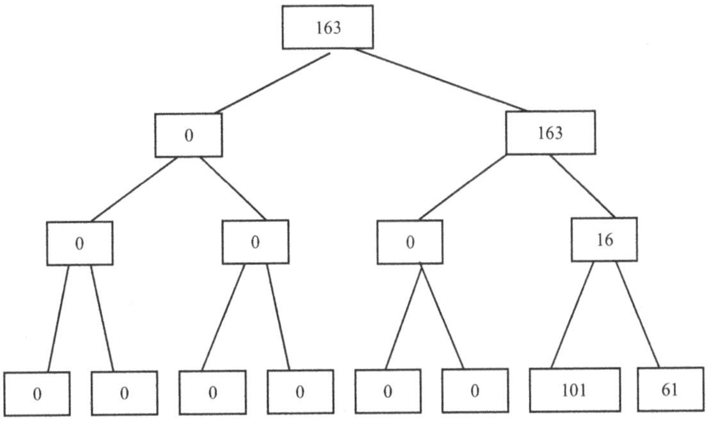

The Prime Factor scheme also copes well in the case of sparse data. All zero values in the original data will scale to 0 with the scaling scheme that we use. Let us consider an example where we have a run of six zero's followed by the primes 101 and 61 in the scaled data set and suppose that we use a chunk size of 8. Since we have extended the prime number set to include the pseudo prime 0, the 0 values encode to 0 and this results in a *left prefix* tree where we have non-zero values preceded by a run of zero values. Figures 4a and 4b show the resulting trees.

Similarly, when the original data stream consists of a sequence of non zero values followed by a run of zero values, we obtain a *right prefix* tree after encoding, where a non zero internal node has a zero valued node as its sibling in each of the Prime Index and Prime trees.

The left and right prefix trees can be "collapsed" and stored compactly as indicated by the following Lemma and Theorem 2.

Lemma 1 *If* $\beta(P_1, P_2) = 0$, *then we must have* $P_1+P_2=0$.

Proof: From the definition of β, we have $\beta(P_1, P_2) = P_1+P_2+s = 0$ -------(1), where s is an integer that rounds the sum of P_1+P_2 to the nearest prime factor. Suppose that $s \neq 0$. We now consider two cases, $s>0$ and $s<0$.

Case 1 $s<0$. Since $s<0$, it follows that $P_1+P_2<1$ -------(2), otherwise, it will be impossible to round the sum of P_1+P_2 to 0. We also have $P_1+P_2\geq 0$ -----(3) since $P_1\geq 0$, $P_2\geq 0$. From (2) and (3) it follows that $P_1+P_2=0$.

Case 2 $s>0$. The proof is similar to Case 1 above.

Since $s>0$, the only way that we can satisfy (1) is for $P_1+P_2\leq 0$ ---(4), in order to have any chance of rounding to 0.

From (3) and (4) it follows that $P_1+P_2=0$.

Theorem 2 *If in a left prefix or right prefix tree a given node encodes to zero, then it follows that the entire sub tree under that node and its associated leaf values must be zero valued.*

Proof: We use the proof by contradiction method as a proof sketch. We start with a pair of leaf nodes having values P_1 and P_2. Suppose that $P_1\neq 0$, $P_2\neq 0$. Foe the prime index tree, we have $\alpha(P_1, P_2) = P_1+P_2+I(P_2)-I(P_1)+r = 0$ ---------(5), where r is an integer that rounds the value of the sum of the preceding terms to the nearest prime factor.

From Lemma 1 we have $P_1+P_2=0$. Substituting this in (5), we have $\alpha(P_1, P_2) = I(P_2)-I(P_1)+r = 0$. Thus $I(P_1)=I(P_2)+r$. Thus, if $r>0$, we have $I(P_1)>I(P_2)$, which in turn means that $P_1>P_2$. With $P_1>P_2$ and $P_1, P_2\geq 0$, we have $P_1+P_2>0$, which leads to a contradiction. Similarly, with $r<0$, we have $P_2>P_1$, which again leads to $P_1+P_2>0$. Thus, in either case, our original assumption of $P_1\neq 0$, $P_2\neq 0$ must be in error and we have $P_1=0$ and $P_2=0$. A similar proof holds for the prime tree.

This means that any node with a value of 0 must give rise to a pair of zero valued child nodes (this is true of both the Prime Index and Prime trees). Each of these zero valued child nodes in turn will yield children who have zero valued. This completes the proof sketch.

We now return to the example in Figures 4a and 4b. In Figure 4a we can collapse the tree by pruning all branches for the sub trees rooted at nodes N_1 and N_2. This means that we only need to store a total of six coefficients, made up of 3 differentials and 3 offsets (as opposed to a total of 14 for the non-sparse case).

Thus it can be seen that the Prime Factor scheme adapts to a sparse data set without the need to keep explicit indexes to keep track of the zero values in the data set.

Encoding Error Rate for the Prime Factor Algorithm

In this section we present a formal analysis for the average relative error involved in decoding with the Prime Factor scheme. Theorem 2 below quantifies this error rate.

Proof Sketch:

Consider the Prime tree given in Figure 5 below with chunk size 8.

Thus it can be seen that a parent node's value is given by the sum of the values of the leaf node values that can be reached by the parent node plus the error terms at the intermediate node levels.

The above result captures the relationship between the error rate, chunk size and scale range. As the chunk size increases, the error rate grows as a log function. This is shown visually in Figure 11b, whereby the average error rate increases sub linearly with respect to increasing chunk size.

ON LINE RECONSTRUCTION OF QUERIES

In this section we examine how multi-dimensional range sum queries are answered with the Prime Factor scheme. These queries are of the form: $\{l_i \le D_i \le h_i | \ l_i, h_i \in \{0,1,\ldots\ldots, |D_i|-1\}, h_i = l_i + \Delta_i\}$, where Δ_i is a positive integer.

We will first derive an expression for the time complexity involved in answering a 1-dimensional query as some of the concepts involved are shared with the general the n-dimensional case.

Answering One Dimensional Range Sum Queries

In this case we need to consider three regions R_1, R_2 and R_3 as shown in Figure 6 below. The query requires the sum of all elements in the 1-dimensional cube which are in the range $[l_1, h_1]$, with $l_1 = 22$ and $h_1 = 690$. The bulk of the query resides in region R_2 (the shaded region) which is aligned with the chunk structure. The sum across this region can be answered very efficiently by taking the sum of the root values for the chunks that span this region, thus avoiding the need for decoding across a large portion of the query. Since each of these values corresponds to the root associated with the Prime tree they are a close approximation to the sum contained within a chunk.

Furthermore, with a large enough chunk size we would expect that the root values comprise a very small fraction of the size of the original cube and thus be either held in memory or stored

Theorem 3 : The average relative error is approximately $\frac{1}{2}\frac{\log_e(C\overline{V})}{\overline{V}}$, where C is the chunk size, and $\overline{V}$ is the average value of an element within a chunk

The value of an internal node, say P_9 is given by $P_9 = P_1 + P_2 + \Delta_{P_2,P_1}$

where Δ is an error term that denotes the approximation to the nearest prime number

Similarly, $P_{10} = P_3 + P_4 + \Delta_{P_4,P_3}$ and $P_{13} = P_9 + P_{10} + \Delta_{P_{10},P_9}$.

Substituting for P_9 and P_{10} in the expression for P_{13} we obtain

$$P_{13} = P_1 + P_2 + P_3 + P_4 + \Delta_{P_2,P_1} + \Delta_{P_4,P_3} + \Delta_{P_{10},P_9}$$

Figure 5. Error Tree for Chunk Size 8

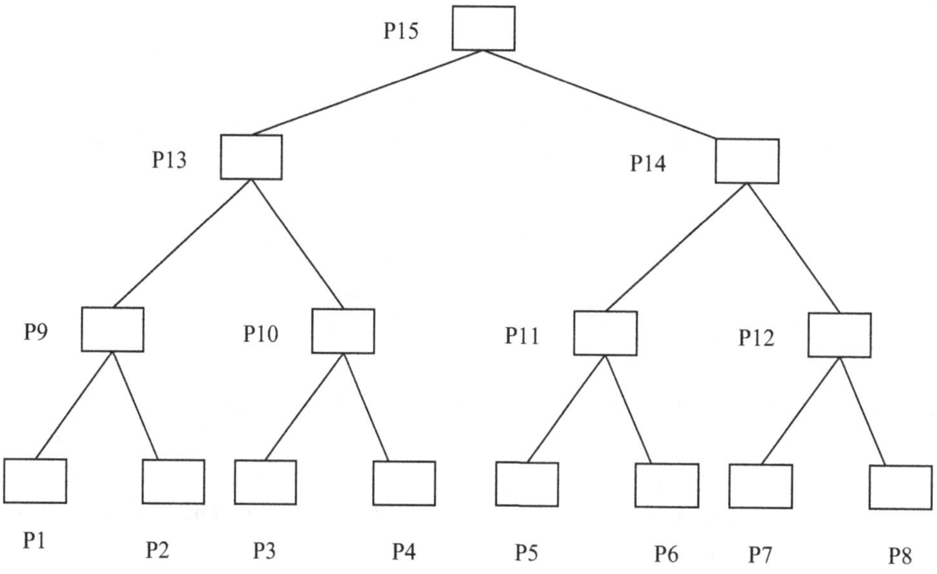

The value of an internal node, say P_9 is given by $P_9 = P_1 + P_2 + \Delta_{P_2, P_1}$
where Δ is an error term that denotes the approximation to the nearest prime number
Similarly, $P_{10} = P_3 + P_4 + \Delta_{P_4, P_3}$ and $P_{13} = P_9 + P_{10} + \Delta_{P_{10}, P_9}$.
Substituting for P_9 and P_{10} in the expression for P_{13} we obtain

$$P_{13} = P_1 + P_2 + P_3 + P_4 + \Delta_{P_2, P_1} + \Delta_{P_4, P_3} + \Delta_{P_{10}, P_9}$$

In general, we have P_{2C-1}, the root node value given by $P_{2C-1} = \sum_{i=1}^{C} P_i + \sum_{i=1}^{C-1} \Delta_{P_{2i, 2i-1}}$

The sum of the values T in the chunk is given by $T = \sum_{i=1}^{C} P_i$

Thus we have $d = P_{2C-1} - T = \sum_{i=1}^{C-1} \Delta_{P_{2i, 2i-1}}$ ----- (1)

From Theorem1, we have the average gap between a prime number P and its next as $\log_e(P)$. This result can be used to estimate the average value of the error coefficient Δ as $\Delta \approx \frac{\log_e(P_{LC} + P_{RC})}{2}$, where P_{LC}, P_{RC} represent the left and right children of a given parent node, the divison by 2 is necessary because the Prime Factor algorithm encodes each value with its nearest prime number.

Put $P_{2i} + P_{2i-1} = K_i T$, where $K_i \leq 1$ for i = 1, 2, …., C - 1

Each error term can now be written as $\Delta_{P_{2i,2i-1}} = \frac{1}{2}\log_e(K_i T)$

Thus from (1) above we have d $\approx \frac{1}{2}\sum_{i=1}^{C-1}\log_e(K_i T) \approx \frac{1}{2}\sum_{i=1}^{C-1}\log_e(K_i) + \frac{1}{2}(C-1)\log_e(T)$

$$\approx \frac{1}{2}\sum_{i=1}^{C-1}(K_i - 1) + \frac{1}{2}(C-1)\log_e(T)$$

using the Taylor series expansion for the log function and taking a first order approximation for $0 \leq K_i \leq 2$.

From the definition of K_i, we have $\sum_{i=1}^{C-1} K_i \approx \log_2(C)$

Since $\log_2(C) << \frac{1}{2}(C-1) << (C-1)\log_e(T)$, we have $d \approx \frac{1}{2}(C-1)\log_e(T)$

The relative error, $\frac{d}{C\overline{V}} \approx \frac{1}{2}\frac{(C-1)}{C}\frac{\log_e(C\overline{V})}{\overline{V}}$. Note : the scaling terms to scale the difference d and the sum $C\overline{V}$ to the original data scale do not need to be considered as they cancel each other off in the numerator and denominator.

Thus d $\approx \frac{1}{2}\frac{\log_e(C\overline{V})}{\overline{V}}$ for large C

on a small number of blocks on secondary storage (with a chunk size of 256 for example, these root values comprise just 1/256 of the number of elements within the original cube). Note that this is true irrespective of the dimensionality of the query or that of the cube.

The only decoding that is necessary is for the two chunks at the "ends" of the query, i.e. regions R_1 and R_3. Thus it can be seen that the chunking has helped to minimize the effort involved in decoding. It is also important to note that the decoding effort is dependent on the dimensionality of the query involved and not on the dimensionality of the cube. For example, for a query such as $[l_3, h_3]$ (say with $l_3 = 22$ and $h_3 = 690$) on dimension 3 of a 5-dimensional cube, the number of chunks to be decoded is still 2 since we only need to consider the one dimensional slice along dimension 3 which is aggregated across dimensions 1, 2, 4 and 5. Again, this observation holds for the general case as well. However, the amount of effort (in terms of the number of chunks to be decoded) involved will depend on the dimensionality of the query as we shall see in the next section.

In the next section we will present an expression for the general case, involving queries on n dimensions.

Figure 6. Decoding and answering a 1 dimensional query

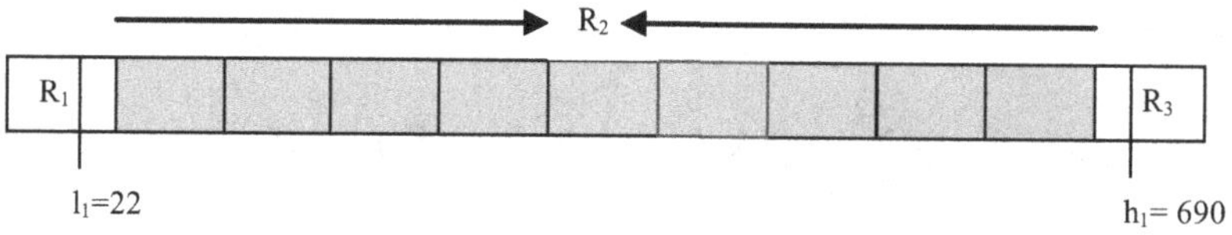

THE N-DIMENSIONAL CASE

Suppose that the query spans n dimensions. On each of these dimensions we can define three regions, the two regions at the ends of the query and the "middle" region which is aligned with the chunk structure. This leads to a total of 3^n regions. Out of these the majority of the query is aligned with the chunk structure in a single contiguous region in n-dimensional space, thus requiring decoding across $3^n - 1$ regions. Each of these regions is on a boundary of the query in n-dimensional space and thus tends to be small in size. Theorem 4 below quantifies the amount of decoding effort involved in the general case.

Theorem 4 *The total number of chunks to be decoded for an n-dimensional query is*

$$\left(\frac{3^n - 2^n - 1}{n}\right)\sum_{i=1}^{n}(d_i - 2) + 2^n \text{ where } d_i = \left\lceil \frac{\ddot{A}_i}{c} \right\rceil$$

Proof Sketch: We will first consider the regions on the "corners" of the cube defined by the query. There are 2^n such corners. Each of these corner regions are contained in exactly one chunk. This leaves a total of $(3^n - 2^n - 1)$ regions, occurring along n dimensions. Each of these regions along dimension i will span $(d_i - 2)$ chunks, since 2 of the total number comprises the corner chunks. Thus the total number of these chunks is $\left(\frac{3^n - 2^n - 1}{n}\right)\sum_{i=1}^{n}(d_i - 2)$. To this number we must add the 2^n corner regions. This completes the proof.

Figures 7a and 7b provide a geometrical explanation for the 2D case. Figure 7a illustrates the region that requires no decoding, and it can be seen that it covers the bulk of the query space. Figure 7b gives a complete breakdown of regions bounded by the query. The region R_7 corresponds to the shaded region in Figure 7a; R_1, R_2, R_3, R_4 represent the four corner regions that each require decoding a single chunk; the regions R_5, R_6, R_8 and R_9 in general span larger regions containing multiple chunks that require decoding.

Theorem 5 *For a given query dimensionality n, the chunking scheme improves decoding efficiency by a minimum factor of*

$$\left(\frac{n}{3^n - 2^n - 1}\right)\frac{\prod_{i=1}^{n} d_i}{\sum_{i=1}^{n} d_i}$$

Proof Sketch: Follows from Theorem 4 above and the fact that an n-dimensional query requires decoding $\prod_{i=1}^{n} d_i$ chunks if aggregate sums (prime tree root values) are not stored at chunk level.

IMPLEMENTATION CONSIDERATIONS

In this section we will provide a brief overview of the implementation of some of the major components of PFC. The system was implemented entirely in Java. We made use of a table of prime numbers (Alfeld) readily available from the Web. All other functionality was custom built.

Figure 7a. The Region aligned with the chunk structure

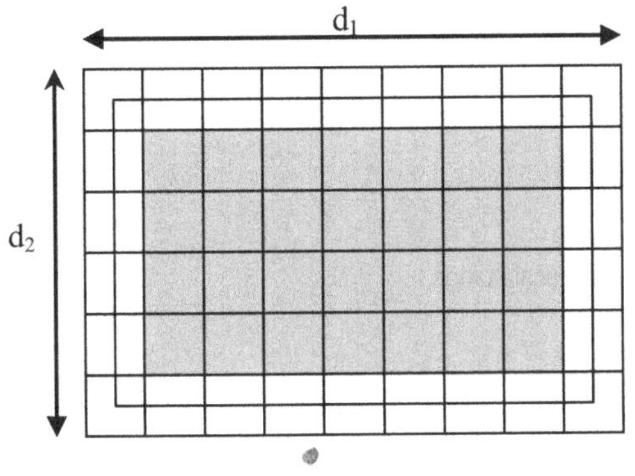

Figure 7b. Regions bounded by a 2-dimensional query

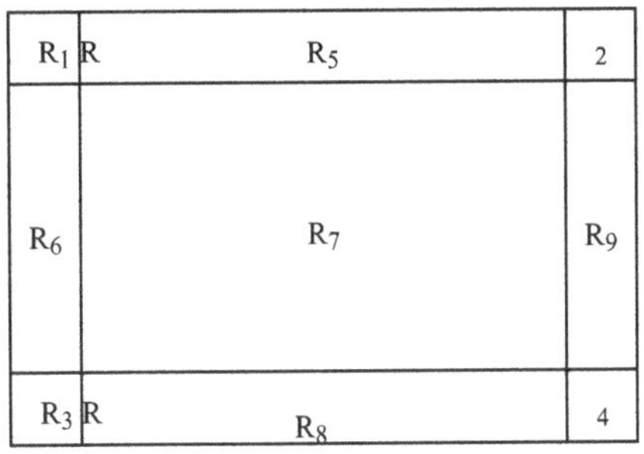

Encoding

The three main functions that were used extensively with respect to encoding were Find_Nearest_Prime(N), Evaluate_Alpha(N, M) and Evaluate_Beta(N, M). The Find_Nearest_Prime(N) function was fairly straightforward to implement as the use of the prime table meant that the complexity of testing for primes was avoided. The other two functions, Evaluate_Alpha(N, M) and Evaluate_Beta(N, M), formed the core of the PFC scheme and were used to build the Prime Index and Prime Trees respectively. These functions essentially took two prime numbers as their arguments and converted their sum to the nearest prime number (the Evaluate_Alpha function also added a component that involved the difference in index positions between the two given primes). Thus these two functions were quite straightforward to implement as well, as they only involved simple computations.

Decoding

With respect to decoding there were two cases to consider. The first case involved chunks that required no recovery of the individual leaf nodes within the chunk. This case covers a large fraction of the chunks involved in a query, as quantified by Theorem 4. For these chunks all that was required was extraction of the prime tree root value and subsequent re-scaling to transform the value back to the original source data scale range.

The second case involved chunks that required actual decoding and this was accomplished through a function, Descend_Prime_Tree(N), that was used to descend one level down the Prime Tree. Basically, this function took a prime number denoting the ancestor node in the corresponding tree as its argument, and then returned a set containing pairs of primes that were candidates for the child nodes. We used a heuristic to speed up the generation of these candidate sets. For a given ancestor node, with prime value N, we extracted the prime number M that is nearest to $\lceil N/2 \rceil$. The pair (M, M) is guaranteed to be a candidate for the Prime Tree child nodes. This pair was used as a starting point for the generation of the rest of the pairs. Figure 8 below illustrates the algorithm used for generating the Prime Tree candidate set.

In order to further speed up the process of decoding we cached the prime pairs for a given integer N. The decoding process benefits from such a cache as prime tree nodes with a given value N are likely to recur many times across different chunks. In such cases, the process of generating prime pairs is reduced to a fast in-memory table lookup. Our experiments show that this cache occupied less than 1% of the storage of the original source data.

Figure 8. Algorithm for generating Candidate Prime Pairs

```
Descend_Prime_Tree (N)
{
   C={};
   M = nearest_prime (⌈N/2⌉)
   C = C ∪ {(M, M)};
   Indx = I(M);                        // the index value of prime M
   U = M;
   L = nearest_prime(P[Indx-1]);       // the largest prime less than M
   while (L ≤ nmin and U ≥ nmax)       // [nmin..nmax] represents the scale range
   {
      V = β(U, L);
      if (V = = N) then
      {
         C = C ∪ {(L, U), (U, L)};
         U = nearest_prime(P[I[U]+1]); // increase upper value in prime pair
      }
      else if (V <N) then
         U = nearest_prime(P[I[U]+1]);  // increase upper value in prime pair
      else L = nearest_prime(P[I[L]-1]);   // decrease lower value in prime pair
   }
}
```

With the compilation of the candidate prime pairs, the decoding process reduces to applying the differential and offset coefficients to descend both trees in parallel to extract the leaf level values, as described earlier in the section on "The Prime Factor Encoding Algorithm".

EXPERIMENTAL SETUP

In this section we describe the experiments we carried out with the Prime Factor and Wavelet schemes. The experimentation could be broadly divided into two main categories:

- A performance comparison between the two schemes,
- An investigation into the performance of the PFC scheme with respect to key parameters

We use two metrics, *Compression Ratio*, and *Relative Error* to quantify the degree of compression and error respectively. The compression ratio (cr) is defined by: cr = encoded data size in bytes/size of original data set in bytes, while the relative error (re) is given by: re = |S-R|/S, where S represents sum of the query on the original (un-encoded) data set, and R is the reconstructed sum after decoding has been carried out with the Prime Factor or Wavelet schemes.

Comparison of the Prime Factor and Wavelet Schemes

In this section we focus on a performance comparison between the Prime Factor and Wavelet schemes on a range of different data sets. We used both real-world data from the (US Census) that was used in (Vitter *et al*, 1998; 1999, Chakrabarti *et al*, 2000) as well as synthetic data sets for this purpose.

The synthetic data sets were modeled on the criteria used in (Ng and Ravishankar, 1997). Two parameters, degree of skew and degree of variation were used in their generation. The degree of skew was taken to be *high* when 70 percent of the data elements were drawn from 30% of the domain value range, with the other 30% of the data drawn from a uniform data distribution in the domain value range. On the other hand, the degree of variation was taken to be *high* when the difference in data element values is more than 100% of the average data element value. When the differences in data element values was no more than 10% of the average data element value, then the data variation was taken to be *low*. Variation in the value of these two parameters gave rise to four different data sets: (No Skew, Low Variance), (High Skew Low Variance), (No Skew, High Variance) and (High Skew, High Variance).

Decoding Time

The first experiment was run on the US Census data and was designed to gain an insight into how the decoding times varied with the size (i.e. the portion of the data that the query retrieved, expressed as a percentage) of the query posed. We used a chunk size of 64 and a scale range of [0..307] for the PFC and a threshold of 7 % for the Wavelet. These parameter settings ensured that the two schemes produced roughly the same degree of compression in order to isolate the effect of encoded file size on the timings. At each value of query size we ran 50 tests, consisting of a batch of 10 for each value of the query dimensionality parameter which ranged from 1 to 5, and the average time was recorded across the 50 runs.

Figure 9 shows that the Prime Factor outperformed the Wavelet scheme in the entire range tested. The two curves start at roughly the same point at the lower end of the size scale, but diverge quite rapidly as the query size increases. The good performance of the Prime Factor scheme can be attributed to two factors.

Firstly, its lower average (taken across the entire range of query size) decoding time per data element was 0.0021 ms versus 0.0057 ms for the Wavelet. In the case of the Prime Factor scheme the information (i.e. the decoding coefficients) necessary for decoding a data element is localized within the chunk that encapsulates it. There is no concept of a single global tree, since each chunk is encoded separately, thus giving rise to a collection of independent trees. This means that chunks can be decoded independently from each other, and only those coefficients belonging to chunks that require decoding need to be examined. On the other hand, the Wavelet scheme encodes using a single tree and thus query processing involves searching through the entire set of wavelet coefficients to determine the contributions made by each individual coefficient (Vitter, 1999).

Secondly, PFC decodes a much smaller number of data elements, as only chunks along the boundaries of a query need to be decoded (as proved by Theorem 5).

Error Rates

In the next set of experiments we compared the two schemes on error rate. As before we varied the query size in steps of 5 in the range 5% to 90% and measured the relative error at each step. For each size value we ran 10 tests, with each test retrieving data from different regions in the data set. For each batch of 10 runs we measured the minimum, maximum and average relative error values (all expressed as percentages) for the PFC (with scale range of [0..307]) and the Wavelet (with thresholding set at 7%).

As can be seen from Tables 1 and 2 for roughly the same compression ratio the two schemes have significantly different error throughout the range tested. The PFC scheme exhibits a small average error rate of around 0.3% right up to the 90% mark (this was true for higher percentages of the query size parameter - up to 99% which we have omitted for reasons of brevity). As Theorem 2 demonstrates

Figure 9. Effect of query size on decoding time

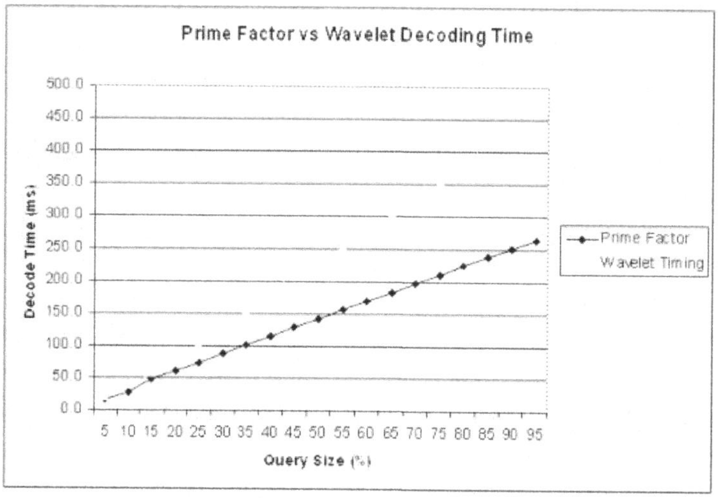

the average error rate for the PFC is essentially dependent on the scale range and the chunk size used and is not a function of query size.

The differential between the average error rates for the two schemes is much higher at the lower end of the query size range (e.g. from 5% to 55%) than at the upper end. At the upper end of the query size range the Wavelet's performance improves as the top level wavelet coefficient representing the overall mean of the data set assumes more importance in reconstruction.

The relative error for the PFC scheme is remarkably stable throughout the query size range. The minimum, average and maximum values are much closer together than its Wavelet counterparts. With the Wavelet scheme we have significant deviations between the minimum and maximum error values in the entire size range. This is in line with previous research (Vitter *et al*, 1999), (Garofalakis *et al*, 2004). In practice error stability is important as this would inspire more confidence in users of the accuracy of results to ad-hoc OLAP queries.

We cross checked these results with the synthetic data sets that we generated and observed the same trends.

Sensitivity of Prime Factor Performance on Key Parameters

We investigated the effects of scale range size and chunk size on performance. We also looked at the distributions of the encoded coefficients in order to gain an insight into whether the Elias code would be an effective representation mechanism. The experiments were conducted on the real world US Census data set.

Effect of Scale Range Size

In this set of experiments we tested the effect of scale range on both compression ratio and accuracy. We kept the lower bound of the scale at 0, and varied the upper bound from 101 to 1009 in approximate steps of 100. Figures 10a and 10b track the effects of this variation on compression ratio and relative error. We measured the relative

Table 1. Comparative compression rates

	Compression Ratio
PF 307	8.05
Wavelet (7%)	7.37

Table 2. Comparative error rates

Query Size (%)	Relative Error (%)					
	Min PFC 307	Min Wavelet	Avg PFC 307	Avg Wavelet	Max PF 307	Max Wavelet
5%	0.104	0.479	0.292	6.046	0.453	15.446
10%	0.151	0.181	0.280	4.738	0.424	16.541
15%	0.172	0.012	0.345	1.932	0.438	5.063
20%	0.144	0.136	0.291	2.210	0.418	5.868
25%	0.167	0.483	0.317	2.994	0.410	5.568
30%	0.211	0.282	0.328	2.275	0.454	4.993
35%	0.230	0.706	0.341	2.785	0.390	5.672
40%	0.249	0.074	0.326	0.934	0.371	5.071
45%	0.263	0.011	0.347	0.728	0.402	1.168
50%	0.286	0.195	0.338	0.559	0.394	1.539
55%	0.326	0.001	0.361	0.535	0.386	1.102
60%	0.305	0.046	0.342	0.351	0.402	0.932
65%	0.311	0.327	0.332	0.524	0.360	0.958
70%	0.315	0.214	0.334	0.635	0.380	1.006
75%	0.321	0.067	0.356	0.515	0.382	0.877
80%	0.317	0.041	0.339	0.382	0.372	0.713
85%	0.314	0.045	0.328	0.349	0.343	0.759
90%	0.320	0.007	0.329	0.206	0.342	0.507

error on queries that randomly picked a 20% sample of the data (in actual fact the relative error was obtained by averaging across 10 runs for each value of the scale range parameter).

As shown in Figure 10a the compression ratio decreases as the scale range widens. It decreases steadily from a maximum of 18.4 at the narrow range of [0..101] and tends to flatten out at wider ranges (i.e. at [0..701] and beyond). At low scale ranges values the data tends to have a low degree of variation in value and this in turn induces a large number of zero or near zero coefficients after encoding. Widening of the scale produces the opposite effect, resulting in relatively low compression.

We would also expect a trade-off between the degree of compression and accuracy. At higher compression ratios the error rate would tend to be higher than at lower degrees of compression. Figure 10b exhibits this trade-off. As the scale widens we see a steady drop in relative error until the scale range value of [0..503] is reached, and thereafter the error continues to drop but at a much lower rate. At the narrow scale ranges the prime factors obtained by rounding off the scaled values tends to produce a much coarser approximation than at the wider scale ranges, and this has the effect of inflating the error at the lower scale ranges.

Effect of Chunk Size

The total size of the root values produced by the chunks is also of interest as this affects the ef-

Figure 10a. Effects on compression ratio

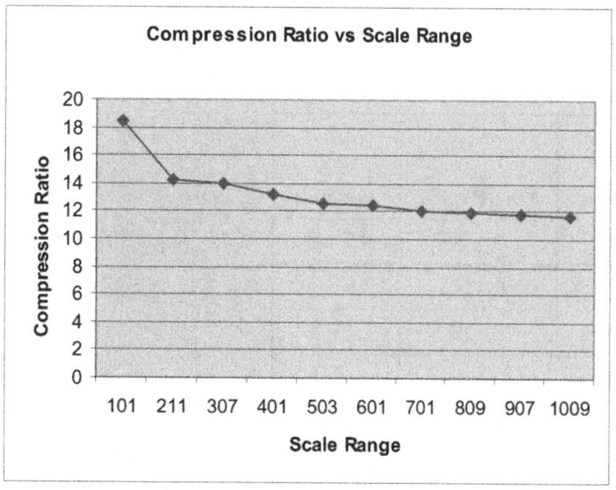

Figure 10b. Effects on relative error

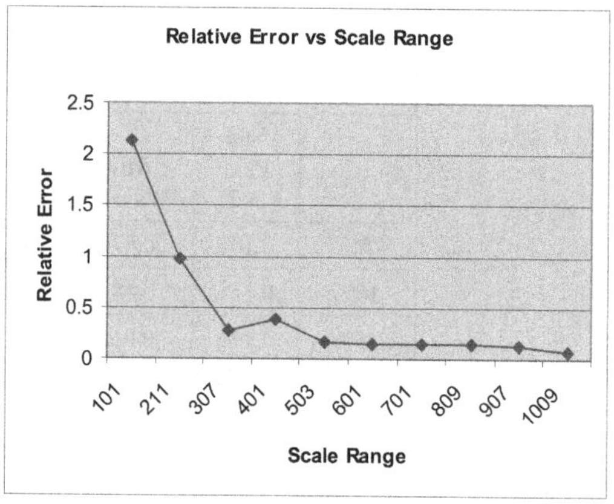

Figure 11a. Effects of chunk size on root file size

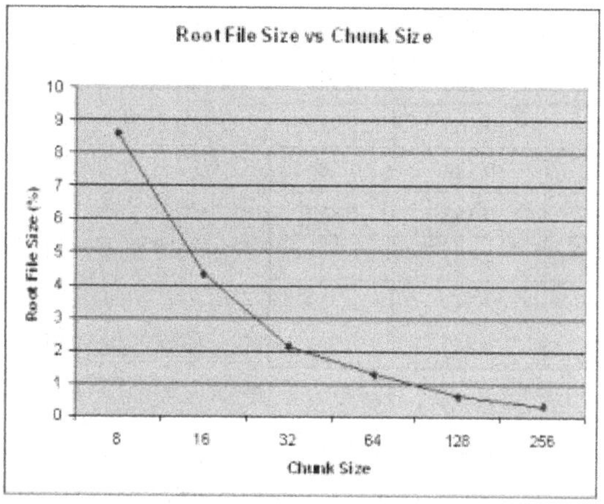

Figure 10a. Effect of chunk size on relative error

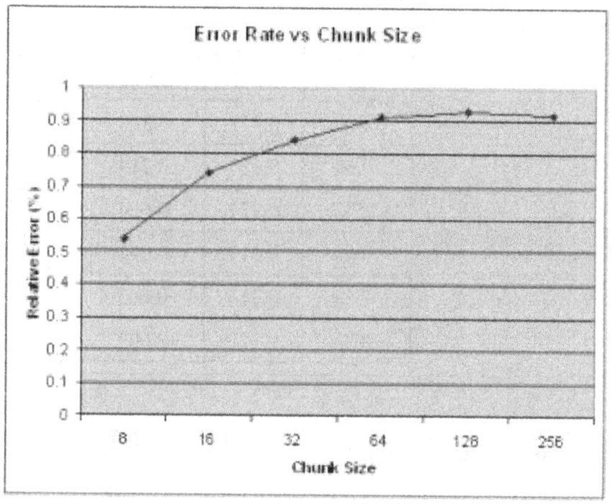

ficiency of decoding. As we saw in earlier in the section on "On Line Reconstruction of Queries" a large portion of the query can be answered by simply summing up the root values produced by the chunks. A smaller root file (used to store the root values of the chunks) size would thus greatly speed up the decoding process. We thus experimented with differing chunk sizes to test the effect on the root file size. We would expect the root file size to decrease monotonically with an increase in chunk size. Figure 11a confirms that this is the case.

However, we also wanted to test whether or not larger chunk sizes have an adverse effect on accuracy. Figure 11b shows that the relative error decreases slightly in the range 256 to 64 and then decreases more rapidly thereafter. Thus we have a basic trade-off between root file size and accuracy. Figure 11b shows that the decrease in the error is not significant until we reach a chunk size of 16 or smaller. Thus from a practical viewpoint a larger chunk size of 256 or 128 would yield a very small root file size (approximately 0.32% of the original data set size for a chunk size of 256) and a reasonable level of accuracy. We repeated

Figure 12a. Simultaneous effects of chunk size and scale range on relative error (Census Data Set)

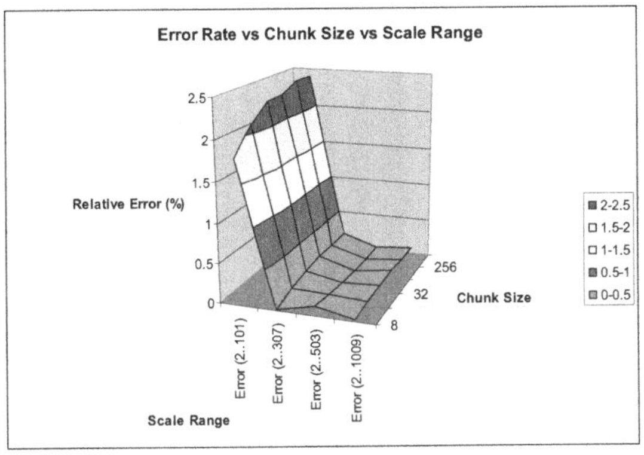

Figure 12b. Simultaneous effects of chunk size and scale range on relative error (High Variance High Skew Data Set)

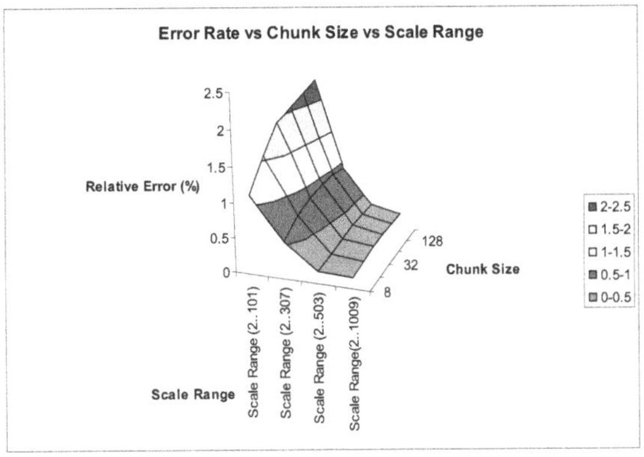

this experiment on different data sets and found a similar trend.

We would thus expect that in most cases that the root file would be small enough to be cached in memory when using a chunk size of 256 or greater.

Having established the effects of the individual effects of chunk size and scale range on the error rate, we next investigated the simultaneous effects of both these parameters on the relative error. The 3D surface plot in Figure 12a clearly illustrates two facts: firstly, the error rate is sensitive to both scale range and chunk size (in accordance with the results presented in Figures 10b and 11b); secondly, the two parameters interact with each other. With larger values of scale range, for example (2..1009), variation in chunk size produces an increase of only 0.05% in the relative error rate, whereas the corresponding increase at the low end of the scale range, (2..101) was 0.6%. Figure 12b shows similar trends for the (High Variance, High Skew) synthetic data set. Results for the other three synthetic data sets had similar behavior.

Effect of Elias Coding on Prime Factor Performance

We next conducted an experiment to test the effect of Elias coding on the coefficients produced by the PFC scheme. We plotted a histogram of the distributions of the differential (we plotted the absolute values, as a differential can take a negative value) and *offset* coefficients to test whether these would be skewed. A high degree of skew would mean that the Elias code would be able to perform better by encoding the most frequent symbols in the smallest number of bits thus improving the compression ratio.

Figures 13a and 13b show that there is a high degree of left skew, i.e. the coefficients tend to be clustered around the smaller values. These results show that a good variable length encoder such as the Elias coder would be successful in further compressing the raw output of the Prime Factor scheme (i.e. the *differential* and *offset* coefficients). This helps to explain the good compression ratios that we obtain from the Prime Factor scheme (see Figure 10a).

Experimentation on Synthetic Data

In order to gain an insight into how the Prime Factor scheme performs with different types of data sets, we generated synthetic data with varying degrees of skew and variability in the data. We adopted the framework provided in (Ng and Ravishankar, 1997) to quantify the skew and data variability parameters as follows:

Figure 13a. Distribution of differentials

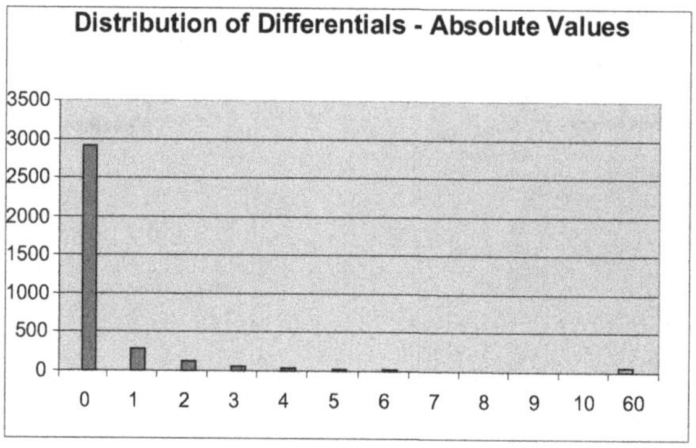

Figure 13b. Distribution of offsets

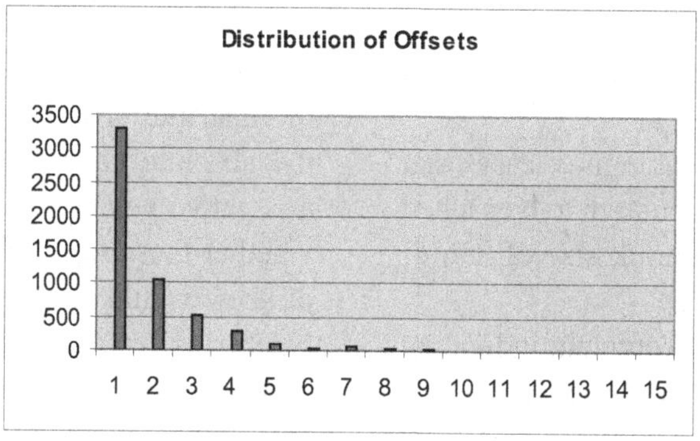

- The data variance is low when the data is spread so that the values are clustered at a distance no more than 10% from the mean value. It is high when the spread is more than 100% from the mean.
- The distribution of values is skewed when 70% of the values were drawn from 30% of the value domain. When values were drawn randomly from the value domain, then no skew was registered.

These two parameters lead to the generation of four types of data sets: Low Variance and no skew, Low Variance with High Skew, High Variance with no skew and finally High Variance with Skew. We ran the Prime Factor and Wavelet schemes on each of these four data sets and measured the compression ratio. For the Prime Factor scheme we used three different scale range settings: [0..101] (i.e. PF 101), [0..307] (PF 307) and [0..1009] (PF 1009).

Table 3 above shows that for the synthetic data, the relationship between width of scale range and compression ratio mirrors what was obtained with the real-world data. The results with respect to respect to Relative Error also exhibit the same trend as with the real-world data with the Prime Factor for scale ranges [0..307] and [0..1009] performing better than the Wavelet for query sizes up to 80%, and maintaining an error rate of less than 0.1% thereafter.

Table 3 also shows other interesting trends. First of all, we can see the effects of data variability on compression. Across both schemes it is clear that a low degree of variability allows for better compression performance. This is consistent

Table 3. Comparative compression ratios

	Low Variance	Low Variance Skew	High Variance	High Variance Skew
PF 101	12.47	17.30	7.77	7.53
PF 307	10.96	12.32	6.45	6.19
PF 1009	8.04	9.76	5.15	4.73
Wavelet	7.49	7.52	7.00	6.73

across all variants of the Prime Factor scheme as well as the Wavelet scheme. At the same time skewness in the data impacts on compression performance, especially with the Prime Factor scheme. In the case of low variability in the data a high degree of skew has a positive effect on compression performance whereas with a higher degree of data variability skew seemed to have the opposite effect. These results are in line with those reported by **Ng and Ravishankar.**

With a low degree of data variability, the data elements are clustered in value space and leads to a higher proportion of encoded coefficients with smaller values which helps both the Prime Factor and Wavelet schemes. The degree of data skew now has a positive effect on the Prime Factor compression performance. The skew amplifies the clustering effect as a large percentage of data elements occur in a small value domain thus making the encoded coefficients smaller in value. On the other hand when the data variability is high the data elements are spread far apart in value space and thus the skew does not increase the inherent level of value clustering in the source data.

FUTURE TRENDS

One of the main issues facing contemporary Database Systems in general and Data Warehouses in particular, is performance. Given that data storage volumes are increasing rapidly and that much of this information is being incorporated into Data Warehouses, it becomes incumbent that an optimization strategy that scales well with storage volume is put in place. Data compression is one of the most important tools that have been used to combat this problem of increasing storage.

In parallel with this we foresee an increasing research effort directed towards answering multi-dimensional queries more efficiently with the use of novel indexing schemes that are tailored to queries that are typically expressed in data warehouses (Albrecht et al 2000). At the same time we also see a sustained interest in caching synopses of multi-dimensional queries (Shim et al, 2004, Park and Lee, 2005, Gemulla et al 2007) so that parts of the cache can be re-used across several such queries. We see the work presented in this chapter as complementing the research effort in such query optimization strategies. Albrecht el al report that cost reductions of up to 60% was obtained with the use of the cache. Data Compression can be used to leverage the benefits of caching synopses of data by reducing the storage size, thereby improving the cost reduction efficiency. The same holds true for indexing structures such as bitmap indexes. Once again, compression can be applied to further improve the cost benefits of using bitmap indexes for aggregate queries.

CONCLUSION

We have demonstrated the effectiveness of the Prime Factor Compression (PFC) scheme in answering OLAP queries against a data warehouse. In this chapter we presented a detailed design of the PFC scheme, and formulated analytic proofs of several aspects of its performance, including optimizations suitable for use with sparse data. We also presented an implementation strategy for encoding and decoding with the PFC scheme. Finally, we conducted a detailed experimental study on both real-world and synthetic data that reinforced some of the theoretical proofs that were derived.

The PFC scheme is able to achieve a very high degree of error stability because it uses information from every source data element (albeit in a condensed form), unlike its Wavelet counterpart. This aspect is important to Data Analysts as the answers to their queries are within a predictable and small margin from the true values.

The scheme as presented here was customized to answer multi-dimensional aggregate queries efficiently through the use of a chunking technique. The chunks stored aggregate sums which removed the need for decoding large sections of the query.

However the basic compression algorithm that we presented can be used in other contexts such as Image data compression. Image data is interesting as pixel values in close proximity tend to be highly clustered in value space and so we would expect to obtain higher data compression ratios than with numeric warehouse data. Another area for future investigation would be to test the effect of replacing the Elias coder with other variable length encoders in the post-processing phase of the PFC encoding scheme.

REFERENCES

Andrews, G. (1994). Number Theory, Dover Publications, New York.

Albrecht J., Bauer A., Deyerling O., Günzel W., Hümmer W., Lehner W., & Schlesinger L. (1999). Management of multidimensional aggregates for Efficient online analytical processing, Proceedings of the International Symposium Proceedings on Database Engineering and Applications, 1999.

Alfeld, P. University of Utah, US, online at http://www.math.utah.edu/~alfeld/math/primelist.html

U.S. Census Bureau. Census bureau databases, online at http://www.census.gov/

Chakrabarti K., & Garofalakis M. (2000). Approximate Query processing Using Wavelets, Proceedings of the 26th VLDB Conference, pp 111-122.

Chen Z., & Chen L., et al. (2003). Recent Progress on Selected Topics in Database Research, J Computer Science & Technology, 18(5), pp 538-552.

Cormack G. (1985). Data Compression on a Database System, Communications of the ACM, 28(12), pp 1336 – 1342.

Cunningham C., Song I., & Chen P. (2006) Data Warehouse Design to Support Customer Relationship Management Analyses, Journal of Database Management, Hershey, 17(2), pp 62-84.

Elias P. (1975). Universal Codeword Sets and Representations of the Integers, IEEE Transactions on Information Theory, 21(2), pp 194-203.

Elmasri R., & Navathe S. (2003). Fundamentals of Database Systems, Addison Wesley.

Garofalakis M., & Gibbons P. (2004). Probabilistic wavelet synopses, ACM Transactions on Database Systems, 29(1), pp 43-90.

Gemulla R., Lehner W., & Haas P.J., (2007), Maintaining bounded-size sample synopses of evolving datasets, VLDB Journal, Special Issue, 2007.

Hellerstein J.M., Haas P.J., & Wang H.J. (1997), Online Aggregation, Proc. of the 1997 ACM SIGMOD Intl. Conf. on Management of Data, pp 171-182.

Ho C., & Agrawal R. (1997). Range Queries in OLAP data cubes, Proceedings of the 1997 ACM SIGMOD Conference on Management of Data, pp 73-88.

Hunt J., Vo K.-P., & Tichy W. F., (1998). Delta algorithms: An empirical analysis. ACM Trans. Softw. Eng. Method. 7, 2, pp 192–214.

Langdon G. (1984). An Introduction to Arithmetic Coding, IBM J. Research and Development, 28(2), pp 135-149.

Lazaridis I., & Mehrotra S. (2001). Progressive Approximate Aggregate Queries with a Multi-Resolution Tree Structure, Proc. of SIGMOD, 2001, pp 401-412.

Lempel A., & Ziv J. (1977). A Universal Algorithm for Sequential Data Compression, IEEE Transactions on Information Theory, 23(3), pp 337-343.

Matias Y., & J Vitter J. (1998). Wavelet-Based Histograms for Selectivity Estimation, Proceedings of the 1998 ACM SIGMOD International Conference on Management of Data, June 1998, pp 448-459.

Ng W., & Ravishankar C. (1997). Block-Oriented Compression Techniques for Large Statistical Databases, IEEE Transactions on Knowledge and Data Engineering, 9(2), pp 314-328.

OLAP Report, online at http://www.olapreport.com/DatabaseExplosion.htm

Oracle 9i. (2005). Oracle Data Warehousing Guide, Oracle Corporation.

Park M., & Lee S. (2005). A Cache Optimized Multidimensional Index in Disk-Based Environments, IEICE Trans. Inf. & Syst, 88(8), 2005.

Pears R., & Houliston B. (2007). Optimization of Aggregate Queries in Data Warehouses, Journal of Database Management, IDEA Group Publishing, USA, 18(1), 2007.

Poosala V., & Gnati V. (1999). Fast Approximate Answers to Aggregate Queries on a Data Cube, Proceedings of 1999 International Conference on Scientific and Statistical Database Management, pp 24-33.

Sarawagi S., & Stonebraker M. (1994). Efficient organization of large multidimensional arrays, Proceedings of the 11th Annual IEEE Conference on Data Engineering, pp 328-336.

Shim J., Song S., Yoo J., & Min Y. (2004). An efficient cache conscious multi-dimensional index structure, Information Processing Letters, 92, pp 133-142, 2004.

Sismannis Y., Deligiannakis A. (2002). Dwarf: shrinking the PetaCube, Proceedings of the 2002 ACM SIGMOD International Conference on Management of Data, pp 464-475.

Triantafillakis A., Kanellis P., & Martakos D.(2004) Data Warehouse Interoperability for the Extended Enterprise, Journal of Database Management, Hershey, 15(3), pp 73-84.

Vitter J., & Wang M. (1998). Data Cube Approximation and Histograms via Wavelets, Proceedings of the Seventh International Conference on Information and Knowledge Management, Washington D.C, pp 96-104.

Vitter J., & Wang M. (1999). Approximate Computation of Multidimensional Aggregates of Sparse Data Using Wavelets, Proceedings of the 1999 ACM SIGMOD International Conference on Management of Data, pp 193-204.

Wang, W., Feng J., Lu H., & J. X. Yu. J. (2002). Condensed Cube: An Effective Approach to Reducing Data Cube Size. In Proc. of ICDE, pages 155-165, San Jose, California, USA, 2002, pp 155-165.

Zhen H., & Darmont J. (2005). Evaluating the Dynamic Behavior of Database Applications, Journal of Database Management, Hershey, 16(2), pp 21-45.

Chapter XII
View Materialization in a Data Cube: Optimization Models and Heuristics

Vikas Agrawal
Fayetteville State University, USA

P. S. Sundararaghavan
The University of Toledo, USA

Mesbah U. Ahmed
The University of Toledo, USA

Udayan Nandkeolyar
The University of Toledo, USA

ABSTRACT

Data warehouse has become an integral part in developing a DSS in any organization. One of the key architectural issues concerning the efficient design of a data warehouse is to determine the "right" number of views to be materialized in order to minimize the query response time experienced by the decision makers in the organization. We consider a bottleneck objective in designing such a materialization scheme which has the effect of guaranteeing a certain level of performance. We examine linear integer programming formulations, and develop heuristics and report on the performance of these heuristics. We also evaluate heuristics reported in the literature for the view materialization problem with a simpler objective.

INTRODUCTION

In today's fast-paced, ever-changing and wants-driven economy, information is seen as a key business resource to gain competitive advantage (Haag, Cummings & McCubbrey, 2005). Effective use of this information requires good decision support systems. Most decision support systems require reliable and elaborate data backbone which needs to be converted into useful information. With the widespread availability and ever-decreasing cost of computers, telecommunications technologies, and Internet access, most businesses have collected a wealth of data. However, that is only the first and easy step. Many firms are becoming data rich but remain information and knowledge poor (Gray & Watson, 1998; Grover, 1998; Han & Kamber, 2001; Nemati, Steiger, Iyer & Herschel, 2002). To alleviate this problem, many corporations have built, or are building, unified decision-support databases called *data warehouses* on which decision makers can carry out their analysis. A data warehouse is a very large data base that integrates information extracted from multiple, independent, heterogeneous data sources into one centralized data repository to support business analysis activities and decision-making tasks.

Business analysts run complex queries over this centralized data repository housed in a data warehouse to gain insights into the vast data and to mine for hidden knowledge. The key to gaining such insight is to design a decision support system which would get the right information to the right person and at the right time which will aid in making quality and often strategic decisions. In order to achieve this objective, design of the data warehouse architecture plays a pivotal role. There are many architectural issues concerning the efficient design of a data warehouse system. Lee, Kim, and Kim (2001) highlighted the importance of metadata for implementing data warehouse. They pointed out that integrating data warehouse with its metadata offers a new opportunity to create a more adaptive information system. Furtado (2006) proposed the concept of node partitioning, a method for parallelism, to improve the performance of a data warehouse system. Huang, Lin, and Deng (2005) proposed an intelligent cache mechanism for a data warehouse system in a mobile environment. They pointed out that because mobile devices can often be disconnected from the host server, and due to the low bandwidth of wireless networks, it is more efficient to store query results from a mobile device in the cache.

Data cube design is one such important aspect of the data warehouse architecture. Data cubes are constructs to store subsets of summarized data by some measures of interest for easy and quick access, and for timely and dynamic updates of these summarized data on an ongoing basis (Chun, Chung & Lee, 2004).

Accessing data from a data cube, if not materialized, can be a time consuming and resource intensive process. A data cube consists of many views with existing interrelated dependencies among themselves (such view is also known as a cuboid or a query). If such a view is stored, it is denoted as a materialized view. The problem of quick and easy access to the data cube may be alleviated by an efficient selection of a set of views to be materialized. Since not all views in a data cube may be materialized due to constraints imposed on the system, selecting the right set of views to materialize is an integral part of the design of data cube and its associated views. An efficient design will dramatically reduce the execution time of decision support queries and hence prove pivotal in delivering competitive advantage.

Many researchers have studied the problem of selecting the "right" set of views to be materialized in a data cube in order to minimize decision support query response time. The problem is generally described as the materialized view selection (MVS) problem, which has the objective of minimizing the access time subject to constraints on either the number of views that may be materialized or the storage space that may be used for materialization of views (Gupta & Mumick, 2005; Harinarayan, Rajaraman & Ullman, 1996, 1999). In this article we have worked on several variants of the MVS problems and have solved these optimally as well as using heuristics. Our specific contributions may be summarized as follows:

- We have presented a linear integer programming formulation for two versions of the MVS problem with a bottleneck objective, which minimizes the maximum weighted access time experienced by any class of users.
- We have developed heuristics for the above two problems and reported on their performance.
- We have also presented linear integer programming formulations for the general MVS problem reported in Harinarayan et al. (1999), and also reported on the performance of their greedy heuristics.

RELATED WORK

Today, virtually every major corporation has built, or is building, unified data warehouses to support business analysis activities and decision-making tasks. According to a report from the market research and consulting firm, the Palo Alto Management Group (Mountain View, CA, www.pamg.com), the market for data warehousing and decision support will grow more than 50% a year to pass $113 billion annually by the year 2002. The study, based on forecast modeling and 375 interviews, also predicted that average data warehouse size will balloon from 272 GB to 6.5 TB, and the number of users accessing data warehouses will soar from 2,200 to nearly 100,000 in the next 3 years. This comes to hundreds of billions of dollars of annual investments in these technologies for the current decade (Hillard, Blecher & O'Donnell, 1999; Walton, Goodhue & Wixom, 2002).

In a typical organization, information is spread over many different multiple, independent, heterogeneous, and remote data sources. Acting as a decision support system, a data warehouse extracts, integrates, and stores the "relevant" information from these data sources into one centralized data repository to support the information needs of knowledge workers and decision makers in the form of online analytical processing (OLAP) (Han & Kamber, 2001).

Business analysts run business queries over this centralized data repository to gain insights into the vast data and to mine for the hidden knowledge. Results of such queries are generally precomputed and stored ahead of time at the data warehouse in the form of materialized views. Such materialization of views reduces the query execution time to minutes or seconds which may otherwise take hours or even days to complete.

For an extension of these concepts and a discussion of the appropriate architecture for harnessing knowledge in a broad sense using knowledge warehouse, where knowledge workers can integrate knowledge that is available in the data warehouses as well those that reside in the minds of knowledge workers, one can refer to Nemati et al. (2002).

While operational databases maintain current transactional information, data warehouses typically maintain information from a historical perspective. Hence, data warehouses tend to be very large and grow over time. Also, users of DSS are more interested in identifying hidden trends rather than looking at individual records in isolation. As a result, decision support queries are much more complex than online transaction processing (OLTP) queries and call for heavy use of aggregations.

The size of the data warehouse and the complexity of queries can cause decision support queries to take a very long time to complete. This delay is unacceptable in most DSS environments as it severely limits the productivity. The usual requirement for most query execution times is only a few seconds or at most a few minutes (Gupta & Mumick, 2005; Harinarayan et al., 1996, 1999).

Many techniques have been discussed in the literature to improve the query response time performance goals. Query optimization and query evaluation techniques can be enhanced to handle the aggregations better (Chaudhuri & Shim, 1994; Gupta, Harinarayan & Quass, 1995). Also, different indexing strategies like bit-mapped indexes and join indexes could be used to handle group-by(s) better (O'Neil & Graefe, 1995).

One method of tackling the demand for RAM space and the need for quick response is to compute the necessary aggregate values more efficiently. Chun et al. (2004) provide an interesting example of a new representation for the prefix sum cube which dramatically reduces storage space as well as update times.

Judicious management of data warehouses can also improve overall performance efficiency and query response time. For a recent successful incorporation of data governance strategies and its impact on data warehouse management in Blue Cross and Blue Shield of North Carolina, please refer to Watson, Fuller, and Ariyachandra (2004).

The focus of our article is to improve access times across users in an egalitarian or prioritized fashion in a data warehouse. A commonly used technique to improve net access time is to materialize (precompute and store) the results of frequently asked queries. But picking the "right" set of views to materialize is a nontrivial task. For example, one may want to materialize a relatively infrequently asked query if it helps in answering many other frequent queries faster. One cannot materialize all the views in a given data cube as such materialization is constrained by the availability of storage space, view maintenance cost, and computational time. On the other extreme, if one does not materialize any view, then business queries have to be run over the source data; a process that would take considerable time leading to intolerable delays. Between these two extremes, one needs to find the optimum number of views to be materialized that will give a reasonably good query response time while satisfying all the constraints. The MVS problem with the objective of minimizing sum of access times has been shown to be NP-Complete (Harinarayan et al., 1999). The bottleneck version, which is the focus of this article, is likely to be difficult to solve optimally as it attempts to minimize the maximum weighted number of pages to be retrieved. Next, we address the literature specifically related to the materialized views.

In the 1980s, materialized views were investigated to speed up the data retrieval process for running queries on views in very large databases (Adiba & Lindsay, 1980). Subsequently, further research studies were reported in view and index maintenance along with comparative evaluations of materialized views on the performance of queries (Blakeley & Martin, 1990; Qian & Wiederhold, 1991; Segev & Fang, 1991).

Gray, Chaudhuri, Bosworth, Layman, Reichart, and Venkatrao (1997) propose the data cube as a relational aggregation operator generalizing group-by, cross-tabs, and subtotals. Harinarayan et al. (1996, 1999) have discussed the major features of the MVS problem elaborately. They have employed a lattice framework to capture the dependencies among views. This lattice framework was then used to develop a greedy algorithm.

Kalnis, Mamoulis, and Papadias (2002) have reported on a randomized local search algorithm to generate the "right" views to materialize; this approach is particularly useful in large dynamic view selection problems where the execution time for solving the materialized view selection problem is critical. Park, Kim, and Lee (2002) assume that the set of materialized views present is given and then ask the question: How do we to rewrite the given OLAP query to make the best use of existing materialized views? They have developed algorithms for the rewrite as well as identifying the materialized views that will best answer the query.

One might wonder whether solutions to these problems have impacted software development in the context of data warehouse. We are aware of applications in SQL Server Analysis Services (Jacobson, 2000) where user input includes disk space available for use in a data warehouse application. The response time is inversely related to allocated disk space. We believe that this and similar work will impact software development in the future. Next we define some variants of the MVS problem.

Problem Definition

Figure 1 presents a data cube and its associated views organized as a lattice in a hypothetical data warehouse. Each node represents a view (i.e., cuboid) and the numbers inside each node represent the number of pages (p) that must be retrieved to respond to the underlying query and the weight (w) that is associated with each view. We are using pages rather than rows as a surrogate for estimating the time it will take to answer the underlying query. This is consistent with the typical database retrieval process where blocks of rows called pages are retrieved during each physical access of the database. The page is then stored in cache or RAM from where rows can be retrieved quickly. Consequently, the number of pages is a better estimator of the time needed to obtain a particular view. The weight (w) of each view is a function of frequency of access and/or the importance of the user accessing the view.

View A (at the root) contains the lowest level of aggregated data, and it is assumed to be materialized. The links in the lattice indicate parent-child relationships. Hence View B, for example, can be obtained from View A by processing 100 pages of data. If View B is materialized, it will contain 50 pages of data, and a query on View B will involve retrieving 50 pages. In general, for a given node, an ancestor node is defined as any node from which the given node may be reached by traversing only directed arrows. A query or a view may be answered by materializing the corresponding view or from any of its materialized ancestor views. For example, obtaining View F from View A will require retrieving 100 pages, while it will require retrieving 50 pages to obtain it from View B, or 70 pages to obtain it from View C. View F cannot be obtained from View

Figure 1. A graphical representation of a data cube with associated views

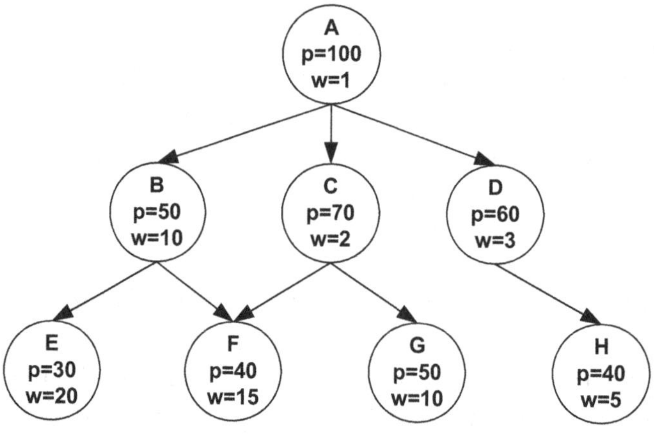

D. However, we would not have to use both Views B and C even if both were materialized in order to obtain View F.

Based upon this type of configuration, we would like to know the specific set of views that should be materialized to achieve some predetermined objectives. One such objective is termed as a bottleneck objective. For the bottleneck version formulated here, the objective is to minimize the maximum weighted number of pages to be retrieved. Minimizing the maximum weighted number of pages to be retrieved attempts to limit the amount of time it will take to obtain any of the views. This is a bottleneck objective as it tries to minimize the maximum value. This measure also takes into account the relative importance (i.e., weight) of the various views. This objective will help to improve the response time of the system. We consider two types of constraints – the total number of views that may be materialized and the total amount of storage space (measured in pages) available to store the materialized views – leading to two formulations. Limiting the number of views that may be materialized is a commonly used constraint and attempts to limit the complexity of the data warehouse design architecture (Harinarayan et al., 1996, 1999). The storage of too many views will make the data warehouse design more complex, and increase the amount of time and effort required to both compute and maintain the various views. In addition, there may be a limit on the amount of space available to store the materialized views. Hence, from a practical point of view, a more realistic constraint might be to compute the storage requirement of the views and limit this to the amount of space available.

General Assumptions Used in MVS Problems

In this article, we have used the following assumptions to define and solve the MVS problems:

a. The cost of constructing a view from its materialized ancestor is a linear function of the number of pages in its materialized ancestor.
b. If view i is materialized, its storage cost will be p_i, where p_i is the number of pages in view i.
c. Whenever a user (or an application) requests a view, the request is always for the entire view and not for any part of it.
d. The views are either stored or created from relational database tables.

Next, we define bottleneck variants of the MVS problem (i.e., Problem 1 and 2) and the traditional MVS problems discussed in the literature (i.e., Problems 3 and 4).

Problem 1

Given a data cube, the list of associated views, weight associated with each view, and the maximum number of views that may be materialized, determine the set of views to be materialized so as to minimize the *maximum* weighted number of pages to be retrieved.

Problem 2

Given a data cube, the list of associated views, weight associated with each view, and the maximum number of pages that can be stored, determine the set of views to be materialized so as to minimize the *maximum* weighted number of pages to be retrieved.

Problem 3

Given a data cube, the list of associated views, weight associated with each view, and the maximum number of views that may be materialized, determine the set of views to be materialized so as to minimize the total weighted number of pages to be retrieved.

Problem 4

Given a data cube, the list of associated views, weight associated with each view, and the maximum number of pages that can be stored, determine the set of views to be materialized so as to minimize the total weighted number of pages to be retrieved.

In the next section, we present the 0-1 Integer Programming models for these problems and how it may be adopted for the conventional MVS problems.

Integer Programming Models for the MVS Problem

In this section, we have developed the integer programming formulations for the bottleneck MVS problem. We present the linear integer programming models LIP 1 and LIP 2, for Problems 1 and 2 respectively.

LIP 1

$$Min{:}Z \qquad (1)$$

Such that:

$$\sum_i x_{ij} = 1, \quad \forall j \qquad (2)$$

$$x_{ij} \leq x_{ii}, \ \forall i \text{ and } i \neq j \qquad (3)$$

$$\sum_i x_{ii} \leq T \qquad (4)$$

$$w_j \sum_i x_{ij} p_{ij} = Z_j, \ \forall j \qquad (5)$$

$$Z \geq Z_j, \ \forall j \qquad (6)$$

$$x_{ij} = 1 \ or \ 0 \qquad (7)$$

Where

$N = \{1, 2, 3, \ldots, T_{total}\}$
$i,j \in N$

$x_{ij} = 1$ *implies that view j is obtained from i and 0 otherwise.*

Specifically, $x_{ii} = 1$ *implies that view i is obtained from i itself meaning that view i is materialized.*

w_j = Weight assigned to view j
p_{ij} = Number of pages associated with view i, if view i is an ancestor of j
= M otherwise (where M assumes a very big value)
T = Maximum number of views that can be materialized
T_{total} = Total number of views present in a given data cube
w_j = Weight of view j
Z_j = Weighted number of pages that must be retrieved to obtain view j
Z = Maximum weighted number of pages that must be retrieved to obtain any of the views in a given data cube

Explanation

We will illustrate the above formulation with the example shown in Figure 1 with the caveat that at most five views may be materialized. The weights and pages associated with the nodes are also given in Figure 1. Our formulation uses the "Big M" approach. We assign an arbitrary high number of pages (for computational purposes, it is assumed to be 10,000 pages for this specific illustration) for obtaining view j from view i when view i is not an ancestor of view j. Hence in Table 1, which presents the number of pages, one would find many 10,000s which correspond to view j that cannot be obtained from view i.

The objective function in (1) minimizes the maximum weighted number of pages to be re-

Table 1. The p_{ij} matrix for Problem 1 defined in Figure 1

i \ j	A	B	C	D	E	F	G	H
A	**100**	**100**	**100**	**100**	**100**	**100**	**100**	**100**
B	10000	**50**	10000	10000	**50**	**50**	10000	10000
C	10000	10000	**70**	10000	10000	**70**	**70**	10000
D	10000	10000	10000	**60**	10000	10000	10000	**60**
E	10000	10000	10000	10000	**30**	10000	10000	10000
F	10000	10000	10000	10000	10000	**40**	10000	10000
G	10000	10000	10000	10000	10000	10000	**50**	10000
H	10000	10000	10000	10000	10000	10000	10000	**40**

trieved to obtain all the views in the given data cube. Equations in (2) ensure that every view in the data cube can be obtained, and each is obtained from exactly one source. This will in general be the most economical view among the views materialized. However, if there are alternate solutions, this view may be any of the views materialized by the solution. Equations in (3) ensure that view *j* can be obtained from view *i* if and only if view *i* is materialized. For example, the cell corresponding to column G and row C in Table 2 can be 1, only if cell corresponding to column C and row C is equal to 1. Equation (4) ensures that a maximum of 'T' views will be materialized that is the sum of the main diagonal elements of Table 2 must be less than or equal to T (for this illustration, T = 5). Equations in (5) compute the weighted number of pages to be retrieved to obtain each view *j*. Equations in (6) ensure that the optimal *Z* is equal to the largest weighted number of pages retrieved. The constraints in (7) define the x_{ij} as binary. If $x_{ij} = 1$, it implies that queries on view *j* is answered using view *i*. Otherwise, $x_{ij} = 0$. $x_{ii} = 1$ implies that view *i* is materialized and $x_{ii} = 0$ implies that it is not materialized.

The optimal solution indicates that Views A, B, E, F, and G should be chosen for materialization to minimize the maximum weighted number of pages to be retrieved. The objective function value for this solution is 600. In addition it tells us that Views C, D, and H should be obtained from View A. This accounts for all of the "T" views (i.e., 5 views) to be materialized.

LIP 2

$$Min{:}Z \quad (8)$$

Such that:

$$\sum_i x_{ij} = 1, \quad \forall j \quad (9)$$

$$x_{ij} \leq x_{ii}, \ \forall i \text{ and } i \neq j \quad (10)$$

$$\sum_i x_{ii} p_{ii} \leq S \quad (11)$$

$$w_j \sum_i x_{ij} p_{ij} = Z_j, \ \forall j \quad (12)$$

$$Z \geq Z_j, \ \forall j \quad (13)$$

$$x_{ij} = 1 \ or \ 0 \quad (14)$$

Where:

$N = \{1, 2, 3, ..., T_{total}\}$
$i, j \in N$

$x_{ij} = 1$ *implies that view j is obtained from i and 0 otherwise.*

Table 2. The x_{ij} solution for Problem 1 defined in Figure 1

i \ j	A	B	C	D	E	F	G	H
A	**1**	0	**1**	**1**	0	0	0	**1**
B	0	**1**	0	0	0	0	0	0
C	0	0	0	0	0	0	0	0
D	0	0	0	0	0	0	0	0
E	0	0	0	0	**1**	0	0	0
F	0	0	0	0	0	**1**	0	0
G	0	0	0	0	0	0	**1**	0
H	0	0	0	0	0	0	0	0

Specifically, x_{ii}= 1 implies that view i is obtained from i itself meaning that view i is materialized.

p_{ij} = Number of pages associated with view *i*, if view *i* is an ancestor of *j*
= *M* otherwise (where *M* assumes a very big value)

S = Maximum number of pages that can be stored

w_j = Weight of view *j*

Z_j = Weighted number of pages that must be retrieved to obtain view *j*

Z = Maximum weighted number of pages that must be retrieved to obtain any of the views in a given data cube

T_{total} = Total number of views present in a given data cube

Explanation

The objective function in (8) minimizes the maximum weighted number of pages to be retrieved to obtain all the views in a given data cube. The constraints are the same as Problem 1, except that equations in (11) ensure that the number of pages stored does not exceed "S," whereas the corresponding constraint (4) in Problem 1 was limiting the number of views that can be materialized.

LIP 3

This denotes the integer programming formulation of the traditional MVS problem which minimizes the total weighted number of pages to be retrieved when the number of views to be materialized is constrained. This objective function is given as follows.

$$Min: \sum_i \sum_j w_j x_{ij} p_{ij} \qquad (15)$$

Constraints are same as (2), (3), and (4) and (7).

LIP 4

This denotes the integer programming formulation of the traditional MVS problem which minimizes the total weighted number of pages to be retrieved when disk space (measured in number of pages) for views to be materialized is constrained. The objective function is same as (15) above and the constraints are given by (9), (10), (11) and (14).

In the next section, we present the heuristic procedures developed for various versions of the MVS problem.

Figure 2. Data cube problem instance (only direct ancestor views are shown)

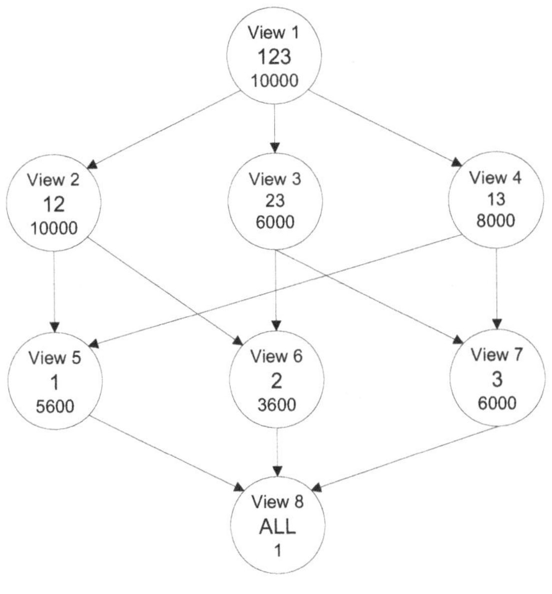

Heuristic Procedures for the MVS Problem

Heuristic When Number of Views to be Materialized is Constrained

Next, we present a heuristic procedure (Heuristic 1) for Problem 1.

Heuristic 1

- **Step 1:** Let k be the maximum number of views that may be materialized. Let $|N|$ denote the cardinality of the set N, where N is the set of all views under consideration, which will initially be all views except the root View A. Let M be the set of views to be materialized. Initially, let $M = \{A\}$ where View A is the root view which is required to be materialized. Let w_j be the weight associated with view j and let p_j be the number of pages required to represent materialization of view j. For each view j, calculate $f_j = w_j$ * (minimum number of pages to be retrieved to answer queries based on view j using only views in the current solution given by set M, which has all materialized views). Let $Z = \text{Max}: f_j$ for $j \in N \cup M$.
- **Step 2:** For each View $j \in N$, calculate Z_j for $j \in N$, where Z_j is the objective function value if view j were to be materialized in addition to all the views in M. Let view $j' \in N$ be such that it maximizes $(Z- Z_j)$ for $j \in N$ and $(Z- Z_j)>0$ breaking ties arbitrarily. If there is no such j', go to *Step 3*. Otherwise, let $M = M \cup j'$, $N = N–j'$. Set $Z= Z_{j'}$. If $|M| = k$ go to *Step 3*, else repeat *Step 2*.
- **Step 3:** Views to be materialized are given by the set M. Z gives the objective function.

Example Demonstrating Heuristic 1

Applying Heuristic 1 to the problem whose data cube and its associated views are given in Figure 1, we get the following:

- **Step 1:** Let $M = \{A\}$ and $N = \{B, C, D, E, F, G, H\}$. Let the set of weights associated with Views A through H be {1, 10, 2, 3, 20, 15, 10, 5}. Initial value of the objective function Z = Max{1*100, 10*100, 2*100, 3*100, 20*100, 15*100, 10*100, 5*100} = 2000.
- **Step 2:** For each node j calculate Z_j. For example, details of the calculation of Z_B corresponding to materializing View B is given by Z_B = Max{1*100, 10*50, 2*100,3*100, 20*50, 15*50, 10*100,5*100} = 1000. Similarly, Z_j for nodes C through H is given by {2000, 2000, 1500, 2000, 2000, 2000}. So j' will be B. So $M = \{A, B\}$. $N = \{C, D, E, F, G, H\}$. Z = 1000.
- <u>**Repeat Step 2:**</u> Calculate Z_j for nodes C through H= {1000, 1000, 1000, 1000, 1000, 1000}. Since there is no such node j that satisfies $(Z - Z_j)>0$ for $j \in N$, we go to *Step 3*.
- **Step 3:** The solution is: $M = \{A, B\}$, and Z = 1000.

Heuristic When Storage Spaces Is Constrained

Below, we present the heuristic procedure (Heuristic 2) for Problem 2.

Heuristic 2

- **Step 1:** Let S be the total storage space available before materializing the root view. Let set N be the set of all views under consideration, which will initially be all views except the root View A. Let M be the set of views to be materialized. Initially, let $M = \{A\}$ where View A is the root view which is required to be materialized and this will be denoted as the current solution. Let Q be the set of views that may not be considered. Initially Q will be empty. Let w_j be the weight associated with view j and let p_j, S_j respectively be the number of pages required, and space required to materialize view j. Let S_M be the space required to materialize all the views in the set M. For each node j, calculate $f_j = w_j$ * (minimum number of pages to be retrieved to answer queries based on view j using only views in the current solution given by set M, which has all materialized views). Let the objective function value $Z = \text{Max}$ (f_j for $j \in N \cup M$).
- **Step 2:** For each view $j \in N - Q$, calculate Z_j, where Z_j is the objective function value if view j were to be materialized in addition to all other views in M. Let view $j' \in N - Q$ be such that it maximizes $(Z - Z_j)$ for $j \in N - Q$ and $(Z - Z_j) > 0$. If there is no such j', go to *Step 4* else go to *Step 3*.
- **Step 3:** If there is such a j' and if $S - S_M - S \geq 0$, then let $M = M \cup j'$, $N = N - j'$. Set $Z = Z_{j'}$. Go to Step 2, breaking ties arbitrarily. If $S - S_M - S < 0$, that implies that there is not enough space left to accommodate view j'. Reset $Q = Q \cup j'$. Go to Step 2.
- **Step 4:** Views to be materialized are given by the set M. Z gives the objective function.

Heuristic 3 and Heuristic 4 for Problems 3 and 4

Effective greedy heuristics have been reported by Harinarayan et al. (1999) for Problems 3 and 4. Comparative analysis of these heuristics against the optimal solutions has not been presented in their article. Since we have developed linear integer programming models for these two problems, we decided to test these heuristics against the optimal solutions (obtained using LIP 3 and LIP 4 respectively). For testing purposes, we label the greedy heuristics presented in Harinarayan et al. (1999) as Heuristic 3 (for Problem 3) and Heuristic 4 (for Problem 4).

In the next section, we discuss and compare the solutions obtained using Heuristics 1 through 4 with the solutions obtained using LIP 1 through 4 for Problems 1 through 4 respectively.

EXPERIMENTAL RESULTS

Problem Generation Scheme

We randomly generated three sets of 10 representative instances of data cubes; one with 32 views (i.e., 5 dimensions and one level), one with 64 views (i.e., 6 dimensions and one level), and the other with 128 views (i.e., 7 dimensions and one level). For a given number of dimensions with a unitary level present in each of these dimensions, the number of views present in a given data cube will be given by 2^n, where n is the number of dimensions. For example, if $n = 3$, the number of views present in a data cube will be $2^3 = 8$ views (or cuboids). The procedure of generating problem instances in the case of three dimensions ($n = 3$) is described below in Figure 2.

The root view is labeled as View 1 and it has data summarized by three dimensions. The nota-

Table 3. Cost comparison between optimal and heuristic solutions for randomly generated problem instances

Heuristics and Problems	Number of Problem Instance Solved	Number of Dimensions	Total Number of Views in the Data Cube	Number of Views to be Materialized	Allowed % of storage space	Range of % Deviation	Avg. of % Deviation	Number of Instances Solved Optimally
	10	5	32	10	n.a.	0 – 8.99	0.89	9
Heuristics 1 to Problem 1	10	6	64	20	n.a	0 – 47.47	8.43	7
	10	7	128	50	n.a.	0 – 52.07	18.08	5
	10	5	32	n.a.	50	0 – 29.41	2.94	9
Heuristics 2 to Problem 2	10	6	64	n.a.	50	0 – 66.67	16.66	5
	10	7	128	n.a.	50	0 – 52.07	24.75	3
	10	5	32	10	n.a.	0 – 0.93	0.18	5
Heuristics 3 to Problem 3	10	6	64	20	n.a.	0 – 0.56	0.15	5
	10	7	128	50	n.a.	0 – 0.16	0.05	5
	10	5	32	n.a.	50	0 – 0.70	0.18	3
Heuristics 4 to Problem 4	10	6	64	n.a.	50	0 – 0.36	0.15	1
	10	7	128	n.a.	50	0.02 – 0.22	0.08	0

tion 123 in the node corresponding to View 1 may be interpreted as if the data have summarized values by its three dimensions, say customer (corresponding to Dimension 1), product (corresponding to Dimension 2), and time of sales (corresponding to Dimension 3). The measure that goes with it may be the dollar value of sales. In the node corresponding to View 2, the notation 12 implies that the data in this node have summarized values by the customer and the product dimensions, but has not been aggregated by the time dimension. The measure corresponding to this view would be total sales for all time periods for a given customer and product

Next we will find all the possible combinations of two dimensions out of these three dimensions. So the possible combinations are View 2 having data aggregated by Dimensions 1 and 2, View 3 having data aggregated by Dimensions 2 and 3, and View 4 having data aggregated by Dimensions 1 and 3 and all of them are answered from the root view View 1. The numbers in the nodes correspond to the number of pages in the respective aggregations. For example, the number 6,000 in the node corresponding to View 3 represents the number of aggregated pages by Dimensions 2 and 3 in that view.

Next level of nodes corresponds to all possible combinations of one dimension out of the three, which results in the View 5, View 6, and View 7. The last view has just one row which will have data summarized across all the dimensions. In order to create numerous problem instances for this study, the following simulation regiment was used. In general, for any child node, the number of pages was obtained by using the formula, UN(0.6,1)*(Min{p_i} $i \in K$) , where K is the set of all immediate ancestors of i. The weight associated with root view was always set to 1. The weights corresponding to all other nodes were generated from UN(1,100). Using this scheme, problems with any number of dimensions can be generated.

In our experiments, we have solved all three randomly generated problem sets (as mentioned above) for two different view materialization constraints (i.e., number of views to be materialized and storage space), each by applying Heuristics 1 through 4 on LIP 1 through 4 respectively. Please note that Heurisitcs 3 and 4 assume equal weight of 1.0 for all views in the data cube.

In addition to the synthetic problem instances generated above, we wanted to test the algorithms on real-world inspired databases. TPCH (http://www.tpc.org/tpch/) is a well-known database used for benchmarking commercial database and data warehouse products. We decided to use this as one of our problem generation platforms. We populated a 1-GB TPCH Benchmark database (referred as TPCH database) to test our heuristics. In this case, the root node of the data cube generated using TPCH database has three dimensions, that is, customer, part, and time dimensions and one measure of interest that is sale. We have considered two levels in each of these dimensions. For example, *customer* data could be grouped by individual customers (C) and by nation (N). Similarly, *part* data could be grouped by individual part (P) and by part type (T), and *time* dimension data could be grouped by month (M) and by year (Y). Number of views (T) in a data cube with given dimensions and levels in those dimensions are given by the formula $T = \prod_{i=1}^{n} (L_i + 1)$, where L_i is the number of levels associated with dimension i,and n is the number of dimensions. This results in 27 views for our TPCH database, as shown in Figure 3 in Appendix I along with the actual number of pages in each view.

We also wanted to test our algorithm on another type of data cube with specific characteristics, such as wider variation in the number pages corresponding to the associated views. We decided to generate another database to accommodate this need. This is referred to as AANS database. The size of this database is roughly 1.5 GB. The daily transactions in this database were created

Table 5. Average computation time in seconds to solve the MVS problem instances

Total Number of Views in the Data Cube	Number of instances solved	Number of Views to be Materialized Constraint		Storage Space Constraint		Numberof Views to be Materialized Constraint		Storage Space Constraint	
		Optimal	Heuristic 1	Optimal	Heuristic 2	Optimal	Heuristic 3	Optimal	Heuristic 4
32	30	3.3	0.1	3.5	0.1	3	0.1	3.2	0.1
64	30	22	0.2	23	0.15	26	0.2	27	0.4
128	30	215	0.1	150	0.1	44	2.5	63	4

randomly from certain predefined probability distributions. We imposed an additional requirement that the number of pages in a descendent view be significantly less than the minimum number of pages in the immediate ancestral views. The dimensions and levels in each dimension were kept the same as the TPCH data cube, which ensured an identical structure. The corresponding data cube with page counts is shown in Figure 4 in Appendix I.

We then solved one set of five problem instances each using LIP 1 and 2 and corresponding Heuristics 1 and 2. The weights corresponding to all other views except the root views, which has a weight equal to one, were generated from UN(1,100) as mentioned earlier. In the next section, we discuss the results of the experimentation.

Results

We solved the linear integer programming models for Problems 1 through 4 using LINGO software. Heuristic solutions were obtained by implementing the heuristics using VB.NET.

Table 3 shows the cost comparison between the optimal solutions and the solutions obtained using heuristics for Problems 1 through 4 respectively. For Problems 1 and 3, the number of views to be materialized was set to 10 for 32-node data cube, 20 for 64-node data cube, and 50 for 128-node data cube. For Problems 2 and 4, the amount of storage space available was set to 50% of the total space (which is the space required if all the views including the root view were materialized).

As observed in Table 3, Heuristic 1 reached the optimal solution in 21 out of 30 instances. In the remaining nine instances, the deviation of the heuristic solution from the respective optimal solution varied between 0 – 8.99% for 32-node problem instances and 0 – 52.07% for 128-node problem instances. The performance of the heuristic may improve with tighter stopping condition, but at a cost of increase in processing time.

Heuristic 2 found the optimal solution in 17 out of 30 instances. In the remaining 13 instances, the deviation of the heuristic solution from the respective optimal solution varied between 0 – 29.41% for 32-node problem instances and between 0 – 52.07% for 128-node problem instances. Furthermore, our experimental evaluation of Problem 1 through 4 points to the fact that the space constrained environment is more demanding on the heuristic, that is, it seems to find the optimal solution in fewer instances. One must note that a space constrained problem is inherently harder to solve since many combinations of views with different cardinality may satisfy the space constraint, and all of these have to be examined as a part of heuristic or optimal solution process.

In case of Heuristic 3, we set the weights equal to 1.0 for all views. We found that Heuristic 3 produces solutions within 1% of the optimal solution in all of the 30 problem instances. Furthermore, Heuristic 3 found the optimal solution for 15 of the 30 problem instances. Based on the size and complexity of problems tested here, Heuristic 3 seems to be a good method for solving Problem 3.

However, it is not possible to generalize this observation for situations where there are more views present in a data cube and perhaps more complex dependencies among those views. Harinarayan et al. (1999) have presented an upper bound to the extent of the error. For situations requiring three views to be materialized (including the base view), this upper bound is 25%.

In case of Heuristic 4, (with weights set to 1.0) again the heuristic solutions are within 1% of the optimal solutions for all 30 problem instances. However, in this case the Heuristic 4 found the optimal solution only in 10% of the number of problem instances as compared to 50% of the number of problem instances solved in case of Problem 3 using Heuristic 3.

Next, we discuss the performance of Heuristics 1 and 2 on problems formulated using real-word inspired databases denoted as TPCH and AANS. Using each database, we created a data cube with 27 nodes using three dimensions and two levels in each dimension. The weights (*w*) associated with views were generated randomly from UN(1,100). The number of views to be materialized was set to five for Problem 1, and the amount of storage space to 55% of the total space for Problem 2. Then we solved five problem instances for each problem type and data cube combination.

Table 4 details these results. In case of Problem 1 using TPCH data cube, Heuristic 1 reached the optimal solution in two out of five problem instances. The deviation between the costs varied between 0% and 24.89% and the average deviation is noted to be 13.42%. In case of Problem 2 using TPCH data cube, Heuristic 2 reached the optimal solution in two out of five problem instances and the deviation between the costs varied between 0% and 63.42%. The average deviation is noted to be 17.67%.

In the case Problem 1 using AANS data cube, Heuristicl reached the optimal solution in two out of five problem instances and the deviation between the costs varied between 0% and 89.68%. The average deviation is noted to be 45.29%. In case of Problem 2 using AANS data cube, Heuristic 2 reached the optimal solution in two out of five problem instances and the deviation between the costs varied between 0% and 37.5%. The average deviation is noted to be 16.85%.

Next, we look at the computation times required for finding the optimal and the heuristic solutions. All problems were solved using laptop computer with Intel Pentium III processor, 996 MHz, and 256 of RAM. Table 5 summarizes the average computation time in seconds for finding the optimal and heuristic solutions for Problems 1 through 4. The instances are same as those described in Table 3. The average time to optimally solve a 32-node problem corresponding to Problem 1 was 3.5 seconds, while average for Heuristic 1 was only 0.1 second. For Problem 1 over a 64-node cube, the average computation time was 22 seconds for the optimizing algorithm, while it just took 0.2 seconds for Heuristic 1. Problem 1 over a 128-Node data cube had an average computation time of 215 seconds for the optimizing algorithm, while it just took 0.1 seconds in case of the Heuristic 1. For 32-node and 64-node data cubes, the computation time averages were of the same order of magnitude for Problems 1 through 4. However, for the 128-node data cube, the computation times for the optimizing algorithm for Problems 2 through 4 were relatively lower than that of Problem 1. However, the average time for Heuristics 2 was about 0.1 second, and for Heuristics 3 and 4 it was 2.5 and 4 seconds respectively. As discussed earlier, the computation time for the optimizing procedure is expected to increase exponentially with problem size and we have the evidence based in Table 5. However, the computation time for the heuristics is only increasing linearly with the problem size for all problem instances and is expected to behave similarly over the wide ranges of problem sizes. Hence, very large problem instances can be effectively solved using these heuristics. In the next section, we conclude this article and suggest future research directions.

CONCLUSION AND FUTURE RESEARCH

Data warehouses are seen as a strategic weapon to gain competitive advantage for businesses. A data warehouse extracts, integrates, and stores the "relevant" information from multiple, independent, and heterogeneous data sources into one centralized data repository to support the information needs of decision makers and knowledge workers in the form of online analytical processing (OLAP). Business analysts run complex business queries over the data stored at the data warehouse to mine the valuable information and identify hidden business trends. Results of such queries are generally precomputed and stored ahead of time at the data warehouse in the form of materialized views. This drastically reduces the query execution time to minutes or seconds which otherwise may take hours or even days to complete.

There are many architectural issues involved in the design of a data warehouse. In this context, selecting the "right" set of views to be materialized in a data cube is a major concern. In this article, we have presented two detailed heuristic procedures for solving two bottleneck versions of the materialized view selection problem. In Heuristic 1, the constraint is the maximum number of views that can be materialized, and in Heuristic 2 the constraint is the total storage space available for materialization of views. We also outlined two more heuristics (i.e., Heuristics 3 and 4) from literature for two more versions of the MVS problem. We presented two novel optimization formulations for the bottleneck problems denoted as Problems 1 and 2. We used the standard optimization formulations for Problems 3 and 4. We used these formulations to solve three sets of 10 randomly generated problem instances each with 32-node, 64-node, and 128-node data cubes. We then compared the costs of optimal solutions with the corresponding costs of heuristic solutions.

In order to use these formulations on a wider set of data cubes, we generated a quasi-commercial database called TPCH, designed by the Transactions Processing Counsel. Based on this benchmark database, we formulated and solved Problems 1 and 2 over a 27-node data cube derived from this database. The heuristics performed well, thus reiterating its role in such problems. We have also used it on another data cube derived from our own database, denoted as AANS. The results were similar, though the range of deviation between heuristic and optimal solutions for Problem 1 was little higher.

Our findings generally indicate that the heuristics used to solve the problem instances of Problems 1 and 3 are effective and find solutions close to optimal very often. Heuristics for Problems 2 and 4 are less effective, and it reflects the inherent additional complexities of the storage space constrained problems. Even though the Problems 1 and 2 are NP-complete, we were able to solve optimally 128-node problem instances of this type within and average of 4 minutes using our formulation. We also found that the computation time for the heuristics is nearly linear with problem size and considerably less than that of the optimal procedures. Hence, even very large problems can be effectively solved using these heuristics. We observe that in general it takes more time to solve problems with the storage space constraint as it puts higher burden on the system to check each possible combination to find the best set of views to materialize for obtaining optimal solution.

A critical application of these models and heuristics may be found in the design of large data warehouse systems, where one could use these models in an online environment to dynamically change the materialization scheme to suit users' objectives at a point in time. For example, during peak times, the objective may be to provide a guaranteed level of weighted service for all users, which may be well served by the bottleneck formulations. During times when there is a significant demand on storage space, the storage space constrained models may find an application.

The heuristics may be improved upon as well as validated against real-world data warehouse systems. One could also analyze the relationship between weights and optimal solutions using sensitivity analysis. One can also focus on how to derive these weights more systematically and assign them to respective views. The optimization models and heuristics presented in this article do not consider the view maintenance cost. Further research can focus on incorporating view maintenance cost in the optimization models and the heuristics presented here and validating these heuristics against the real world data warehouse systems.

REFERENCES

Adiba, M.E., & Lindsay, B. (1980). Database snapshots. In *Proceedings of the 6th International Conference on Very Large Databases* (pp. 86-91), Montreal, Canada.

Blakeley, J.A., & Martin, N.L. (1990). Join index, materialized view, and hybrid hash join: A performance analysis. In *Proceedings of the 6th IEEE Conference on Data Engineering* (pp. 256-263), Los Angeles, California.

Chaudhuri, S., & Shim, K. (1994). Including group-by in query optimization. In *Proceedings of the 20th International Conference on Vary Large* Databases (pp. 354-366), Santiago, Chile.

Chun, S., Chung, C., & Lee, S. (2004). Space-efficient cubes for OLAP range-sum queries. *Decision Support Systems, 37,* 83-102.

Furtado, P. (2006). Node partitioned data warehouses. *Journal of Database Management, 17*(2), 43-61.

Gray, J., Chaudhuri, S., Bosworth, A., Layman, D., Reichart, D., & Venkatrao, M. (1997). Data cube: A relational aggregation operator generalizing group-by, cross-tab, and sub-totals. *Data Mining and Knowledge Discovery, 1*(1), 29-53.

Gray, P., & Watson, H.J. (1998). *Decision support in the data warehouse.* Data Warehousing Institute Series, Prentice Hall.

Grover, R. (1998). *Identification of factors affecting the implementation of data warehouse.* Unpublished doctoral dissertation, Auburn University, Alabama.

Gupta, A., Harinarayan, V., & Quass D. (1995). *Generalized projections: A powerful approach to aggregation.* Paper presented at the 21st International Conference on Very Large Databases (pp. 358-369), Zurich, Switzerland.

Gupta, H., & Mumick, I.S. (2005). Selection of views to materialize in a data warehouse. *IEEE Transaction on Data and Knowledge Engineering, 17*(1), 24-43.

Haag, S., Cummings, M., & McCubbrey, D. (2005). *Management information systems for the information age.* McGraw-Hill Irwin.

Han, J., & Kamber, M. (2001). *Data mining: Concepts and techniques.* San Francisco: Morgan Kaufmann.

Harinarayan, V., Rajaraman, A., & Ullman, J.D. (1996). Implementing data cubes efficiently. In

Proceedings of the ACM-SIGMOD International Conference on Management of Data (pp. 205-216), Montreal, Canada.

Harinarayan, V., Rajaraman, A., & Ullman, J.D. (1999). Implementing data cubes efficiently. In A. Gupta & I. Mumick (Eds.), *Materialized views: Techniques, implementation and applications* (pp. 343-360). MIT Press.

Hillard, R., Blecher, P., & O'Donnell, P.A. (1999). The implications of chaos theory on the management of a data warehouse. In *Proceedings of the 5th conference of the International Society of Decision Support Systems*, Melbourne, Australia

Huang, S.-M., Lin, B., & Deng, Q.-S. (2005). Intelligent cache management for mobile data warehouse. *Journal of Database Management, 16*(2), 46-65.

Jacobson, R. (2000). *Microsoft SQL server 2000 analysis services: Step by step.* Microsoft Press.

Kalnis, P., Mamoulis, N., & Papadias, D. (2002). View selection using randomized search. *Data and Knowledge Engineering, 42*, 89-111.

Lee, H., Kim, T., & Kim, J. (2001). A metadata oriented architecture for building data warehouse. *Journal of Database Management, 12*(4), 15-25.

Nemati, H.R., Steiger, D.M., Iyer, L.S., & Herschel, R.T. (2002). Knowledge warehouse: An architectural integration of knowledge management, decision support artificial intelligence and data warehousing. *Decision Support Systems, 33*, 143-161.

O'Neil, P., & Graefe, G. (1995). Multi-table joins through bitmapped join indices. *SIGMOD Record, 24*(3), 8-11.

Park, C., Kim, M.H., & Lee, Y. (2002). Finding an efficient rewriting of OLAP queries using materialized views in data warehouses. *Decision Support Systems, 32*, 379-399.

Qian, X., & Wiederhold, G. (1991). Incremental recomputation of active relational expressions. *IEEE Transaction on Knowledge and Data Engineering, 3*(3), 227-341.

Segev, A., & Fang, W. (1991). Optimal update policies for distributed materialized views. *Management Science, 37*(7), 851-870.

Watson, H.J., Fuller, C., & Ariyachandra, T. (2004). Data warehouse governance: Best practices at Blue Cross and Blue Shield of North Carolina. *Decision Support Systems, 38*, 435-450.

Walton, H., Goodhue, D.L., & Wixom, B.H. (2002). The benefits of data warehousing: Why some organizations realize exceptional payoffs. *Information & Management, 39*, 491-502.

APPENDIX A.

Figure 3. Data cube lattice with actual number of pages present in each associated cuboid (Source: TPCH Benchmark Database) *

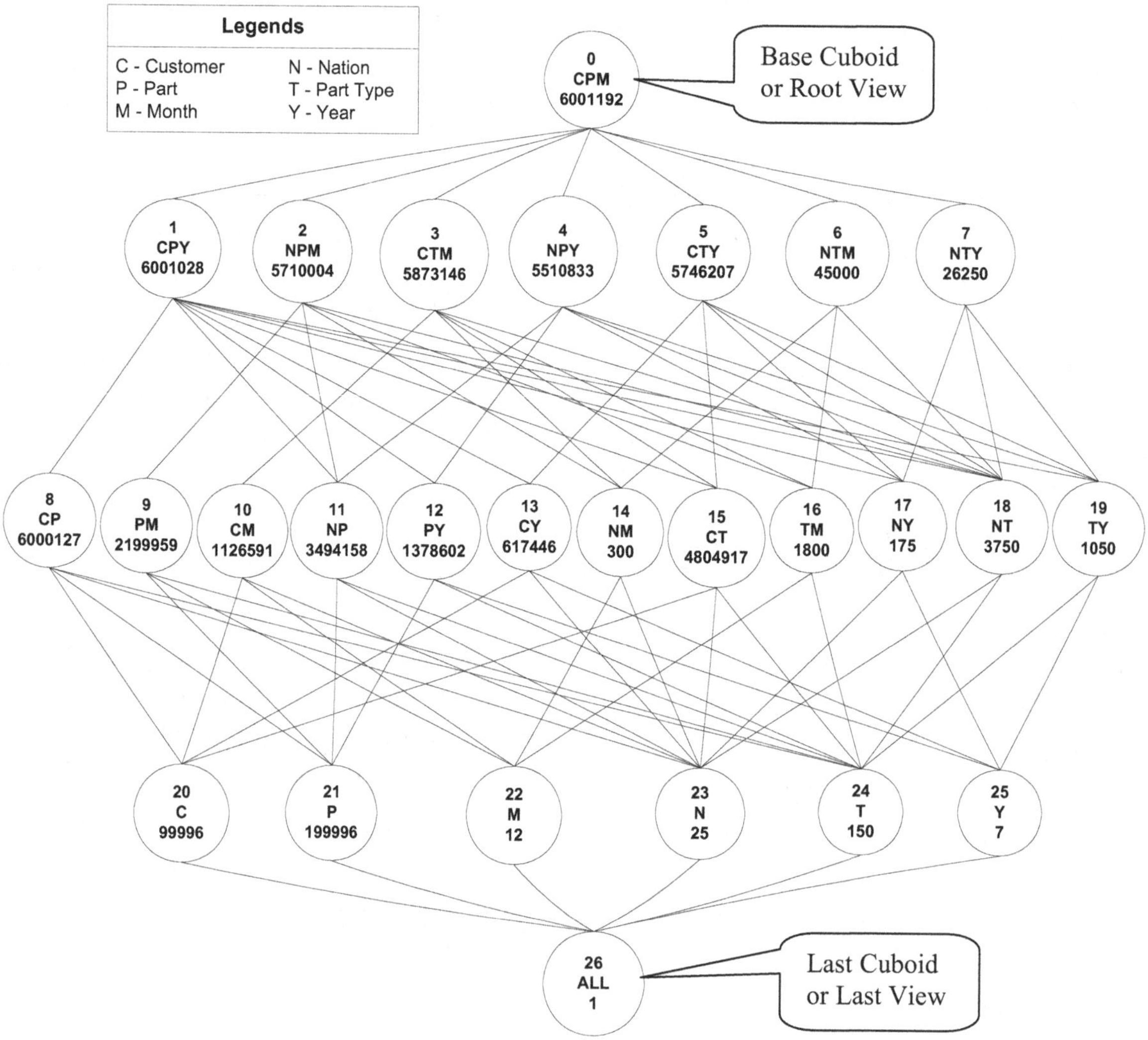

**To keep the diagram simple, some dependencies have not been shown*

*Figure 4. Data cube lattice with actual number of pages present in each associated cuboid (Source: AANS Database)**

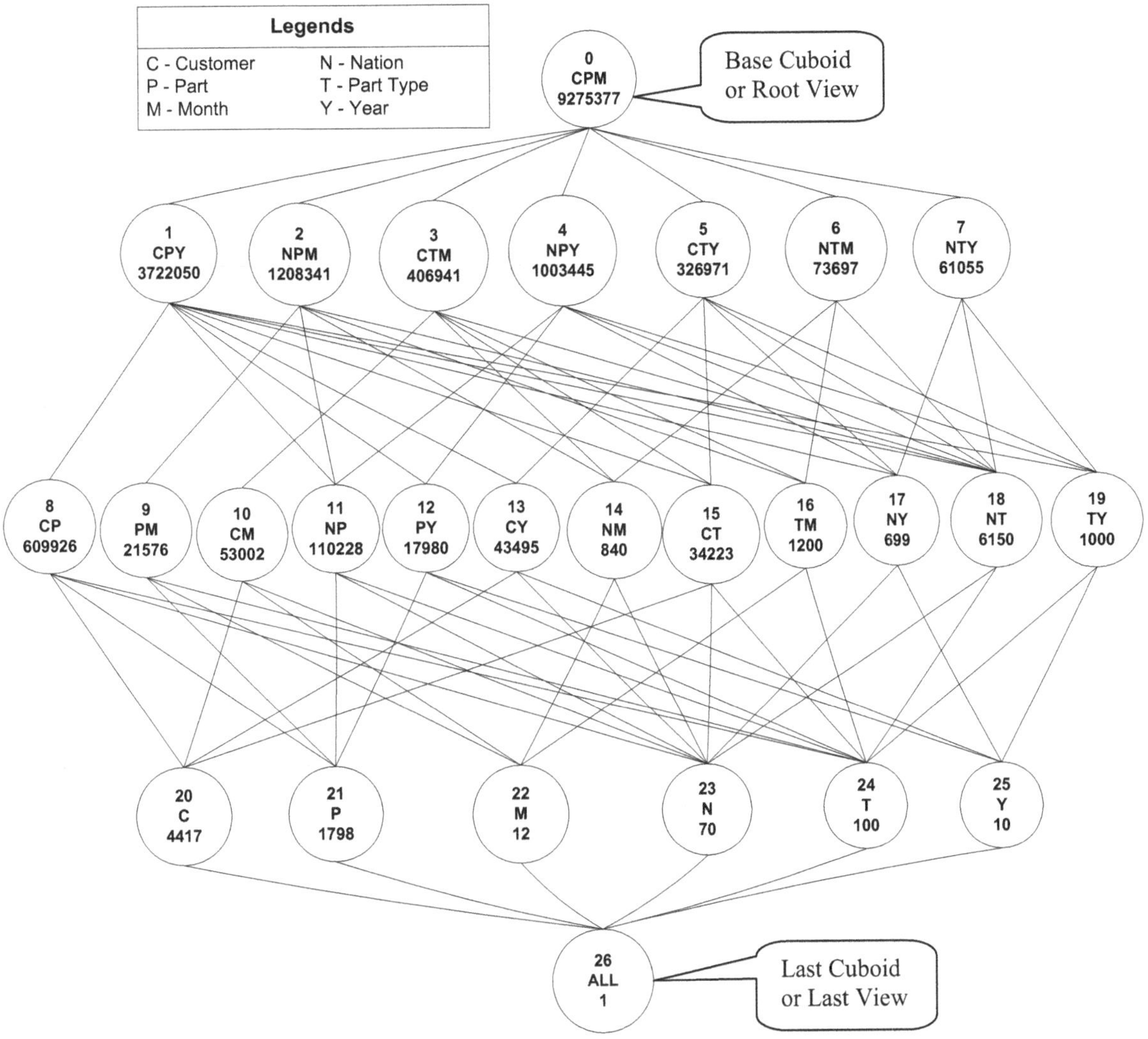

* *To keep the diagram simple, some dependencies have not been shown*

This work was previously published in Journal of Database Management, Vol. 18, Issue 3, edited by K. Siau, pp. 1-20, copyright 2007 by IGI Publishing, formerly known as Idea Group Publishing (an imprint of IGI Global).

Section III
Web and Mobile Commerce

Chapter XIII
WebFINDIT:
Providing Data and Service-Centric Access through a Scalable Middleware

Athman Bouguettaya
CSIRO ICT Center, Australia

Zaki Malik
Virginia Tech, USA

Xumin Liu
Virginia Tech, USA

Abdelmounaam Rezgui
University of Pittsburgh, USA

Lori Korff
Virginia Tech, USA

ABSTRACT

The ubiquity of the World Wide Web facilitates the deployment of highly distributed applications. The emergence of Web databases and applications has introduced new challenges related to their organization, access, integration, and interoperability. We present a dynamic architecture and system for describing, locating, and accessing data from Web databases and applications. We describe a scalable middleware for efficient data and application access that we have built using the available technologies. The resulting system is called WebFINDIT. It is a scalable and uniform infrastructure for accessing heterogeneous and autonomous databases and applications.

INTRODUCTION

The information revolution has led organizations worldwide to rely heavily on numerous databases to conduct their daily business. Because databases usually exist in broad, highly dynamic network-based environments, formally controlling the changes occurring in the information space-such as registering new information sources or eliciting cooperative tasks-poses a challenge. Moreover, the World Wide Web has facilitated access to any database (located virtually anywhere) with a Web interface. These Web-accessible databases, or *Web databases*, provide an elegant solution to store any data content to which a ubiquitous access is needed (Gribble, 2003). However, there is a need to provide users with a uniform, integrated view for querying the content of *multiple* Web databases. In this regard, *interoperability* between disparate systems provides the biggest challenge. To address the interoperability issue, more than a networking infrastructure is needed. The need has therefore arisen for a middleware that transcends all types of heterogeneities and provides users with a uniform view of the content of Web databases (Bouguettaya *et al*, 2006).

Key requirements of an integrative middleware for Web databases includes the ability to provide across the board transparency to allow users to access and manipulate data irrespective of platforms, locations, systems, etc (Bouguettaya *et al*, 2004; Su, 2005). Moreover, flexible tools for information space organization, communication facilities, information discovery, content description, and assembly of data from heterogeneous sources is required. To meet these challenges, we identify three key issues:

- *Locating* relevant information sources. In Web applications, the information space is very large and dynamic. A way must be found to organize that information space in a rational and readily comprehensible manner to facilitate the location of pertinent data.
- *Understanding* the meaning, content, terminology, and usage patterns of the available information sources. Users must be educated about the information of interest and dynamically provided with up-to-date knowledge of database contents. Users must also be instructed as to the appropriate means of linking to information sources.
- *Querying* sources for relevant information items. Once appropriate information sources have been found, users need to be provided with the tools necessary to access and integrate data from these information sources.

To address the above mentioned issues, we have developed a middleware framework for supporting seamless access to Web databases and applications. WebFINDIT integrates a large set of heterogeneous technologies. A key feature of the system is the large spectrum of heterogeneities being supported at all levels, including hardware, operating system, database, and communication middleware. We have presented an easy to use architecture for databases to be accessed over the Web, despite their distributed, autonomous and heterogeneous nature. WebFINDIT provides a scalable and distributed ontological approach for organizing Web databases according to their domains of interest. It also provides a uniform interface to query Web databases and applications as if they are components of a single Web accessible database. We have provided an extensible middleware for querying autonomous Web databases and applications. We have incorporated Web services in our system to provide uniform access to applications. The Web services technology has been developed to assist in the integration and interoperation of isolated, autonomous and heterogeneous sources of information and services. The participants of a Web services system do not have to worry about the operating system, development language environment or the component model used to create or access the services.

The major contribution of the system is providing support for achieving effective and efficient data sharing in a large and dynamic information space. WebFINDIT presents an incremental and self-documenting approach. The system processes a user query in two steps. First, querying metadata for information sources location and semantic exploration. Second, querying selected sources for actual data. WebFINDIT provides support for educating the user about the available information space. The efforts related to registering and advertising the content of information sources are minimized.

The paper is organized as follows. In Section 2, we present a brief overview of the related work. Section 3 provides an example scenario that will be used to explain the architectural approach of WebFINDIT. In Section 4, we present WebFINDIT's design principles. Section 5 provides a detailed description of the architecture of the WebFINDIT system. In Section 6, we explain the implementation concepts of WebFINDIT. In Section 7, we show the results of the performance evaluation experiments of the WebFINDIT system. In Section 8, we conclude and mention some related future research areas.

MOTIVATING SCENARIO

In this section, we discuss a scenario that will be used in the paper to illustrate the different system principles. This scenario is based on a joint project with the Indiana *Family and Social Services Administration* (FSSA) and the US Department of *Health and Human Services* (HHS). The FSSA

Figure 1. Database interactions

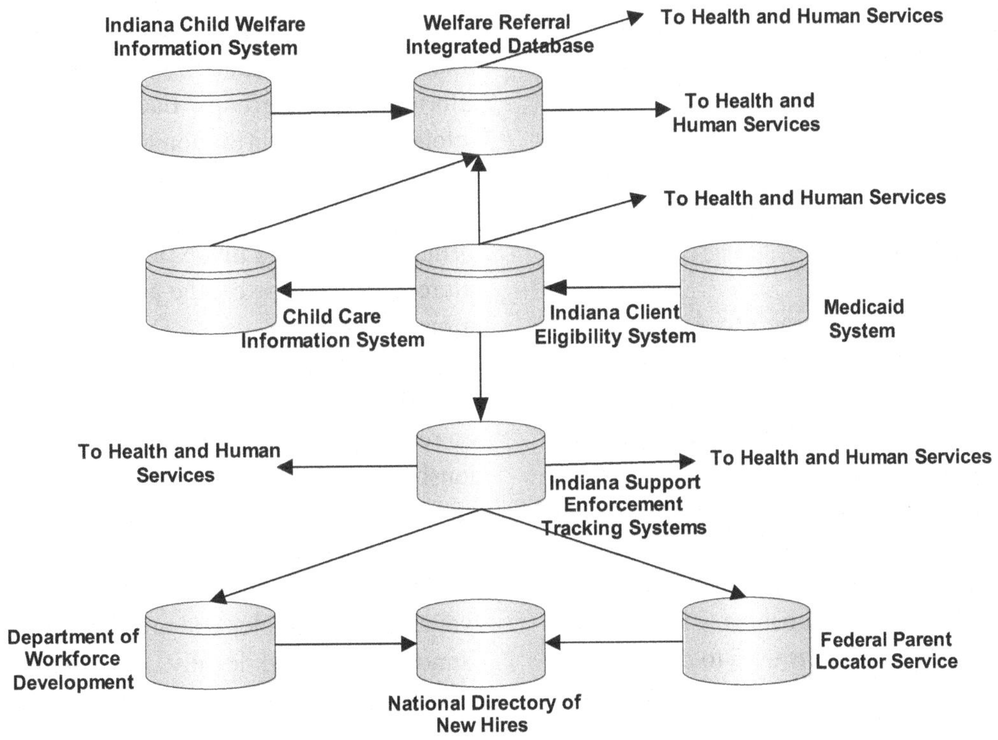

serves families who have issues associated with low income, mental illness, addiction, mental retardation, disability, aging, and children who are at risk for healthy development. These programs interact with their federal counterpart to address issues requiring access to data from other agencies (state and local governments). Federal agencies also need this information for better planning and budgeting. This interaction is also required for reporting and auditing purposes. It is important to note that each program usually maps to a separate information system and each system maps to usually several databases. In that respect, FSSA uses the primary database systems shown in Figure 1.

The current process for collecting social benefits within FSSA is time-consuming and frustrating, as citizens must often visit multiple offices located within and outside their home town. Case officers must use a myriad of applications, manually determining which would satisfy citizens' individual needs, deciding how to access each form, and combining the results returned by different applications. This difficulty in obtaining help hinders many people's ability to become self-dependent. In the following, we show how WebFINDIT facilitates the discovery of data and applications for citizens' needs.

SYSTEM DESIGN

In this section, we examine the design of the WebFINDIT system. We first discuss the way in which we propose to organize the information space. We then discuss our ontological approach to organizing databases. We follow this discussion by examining the inter-ontology relationships and discussing metadata repositories (*co-databases*). Co-databases are used to support the ontologies and inter-ontology relationships. Finally, we present the *documentations* used to describe the content and behavior of the databases. We introduce the concept of agents to dynamically update relationships between ontologies and databases.

Organization of the Information Space

There is a need for a meaningful organization and segmentation of the information space in a dynamic and constantly changing network of Web-accessible databases. Key criteria that have guided our approach are: scalability, design simplicity, and the use of structuring mechanisms based on object-orientation. Users are incrementally and dynamically educated about the available information space without being presented with all available information. We propose a two-level approach to provide participating databases with a flexible means of information sharing.

The two-level approach we suggest in this research corresponds to ontologies and inter-ontology relationships. Ontologies are a means for databases to be *strongly* coupled, whereas the inter-ontology relationships are a means for them to be *loosely* connected. To reduce the overhead of locating information in large networks of databases, the information space is organized as information-type groups. Each group forms an ontology to represent the domain of interest (some portion of the information space) of the related databases. It also provides the terminology for formulating queries involving a specific area of interest. A database can be associated with one or more ontologies.

In this regard, a database may contain information related to many topics. Ontologies are related to each other by inter-ontology relationships. Such a relationship contains only the portions of information that are directly relevant to information exchange among ontologies and databases. They constitute the resources that are available to an ontology to answer requests that cannot be handled locally. Documentation is provided to document the context and behavior of the information sources being advertised. Actual databases are responsible for coding and storing the documentation of the information they are advertising. Documentation consists of a set of context-sensitive demonstrations about the advertised item.

The proposed two-level approach presents an ontology-based integration of data sources. This approach is more suitable than having a global schema due to scalability issues in the context of Web databases. The number of Web databases is expected to be large. A global schema cannot efficiently maintain this information due to heterogeneity issues. Having an ontology-based solution allows semantic operability between the various data sources and provides a common understanding. The ontologies are expected to be initiated by domain experts. However, the maintenance is performed in an automatic manner. In the following sections, we provide a detailed description of our proposed approach.

Ontological Organization of Web Databases

A key feature of the WebFINDIT system is the clustering of Web databases into distributed *ontologies*, which provide abstractions of specific domains of information interest (Fensel *et al* 2001). An ontology may be defined as a set of knowledge terms, including the vocabulary, the semantic interconnections, and some simple rules of inference and logic for some particular topic (Gruber, 1993; Katifori, 2007; Sugumaran and Storey, 2006). Within the WebFINDIT system, an ontology defines taxonomies based on the semantic proximity of concepts (domains of interest) (Bouguettaya, 1999). It also provides domain-specific information for interaction with its participating databases which accelerates information search and allows the sharing of data in a tractable manner.

As new databases join or existing ones drop, new ontologies may form, old ontologies may dissolve, and components of existing ontologies may change. Ontologies and databases are linked together using *inter-ontology relationships*. When a user submits a query which may not be resolvable locally, the system tries to locate other ontologies capable of resolving the query. In order to allow such query "migration", inter-ontology relationships are established between ontologies and databases based on users' needs. These links are therefore dynamically formed based on users' interests.

We have identified nine ontologies in the FSSA/HHS application. Each ontology defines a single information type as either a service or a goal. The nine ontologies are `Low Income`, `At Risk Children`, `Mental Illness and Addiction`, `Finance`, `Mental Retardation Disability`, `Government Agencies`, `Law Enforcement`, `Local Health and Human Services`, and `Medicaid` (see Figure 2). Note that the `Elderly` database, in our example, does not belong to any ontology. An overlap of two ontologies depicts the situation where an information source may store information that is of interest to both ontologies. The inter-ontology relationships are initially determined statically by the ontology administrator. They essentially depict a *functional* relationship that would dynamically change over time. Our proposed architecture supports the dynamic changes in inter-ontology relationship.

Database Schema Interoperability

A major problem in integrating heterogeneous database systems is schema integration. The idea behind schema integration is to present users with one uniform view across individual databases (Chiticariu *et al*, 2007). Often, information may exhibit different behaviors from database to database, even if the data model is the same across all participating databases (Wang & Murphy, 2004). Traditionally, database administrators are responsible for understanding the different schemas and then translating them

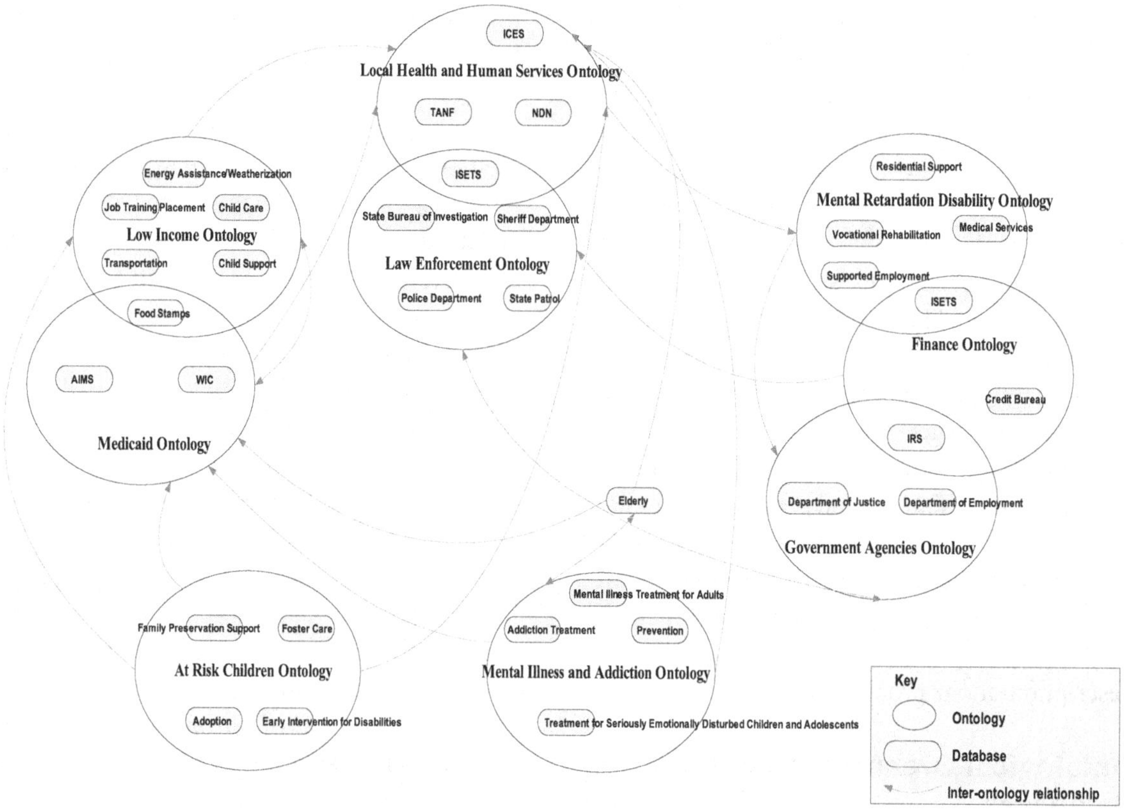

Figure 2. Example of ontologies and inter-ontologies relationships

into the uniform schema utilized by the users. This approach is acceptable when the number of databases is small, as it would be reasonable to assume that enough interaction between designers would solve the problem. However, in the vast and dynamic Internet database environment, such interaction is impractical. For this reason and in addition to recording the information types that represent a database's domains of interest, WebFINDIT *documents* each database so that users can understand the content and behavior of the database. The documentation consists of a set of *demonstrations* that describe each information type and what it offers. A demonstration may be textual or graphical depending on the underlying information being demonstrated. By associating appropriate documentations with each database, WebFINDIT provides a novel approach to educating the user about the information space. In this context, WebFINDIT provides a richer description of the database than most standard schematic integration approaches.

Dynamically Linking Databases and Ontologies

It is important that WebFINDIT allow for an adaptive evolution of the organization of the inherently dynamic information space. The adaptive evolution is necessary to provide support for discovery of *meta-meta data*, *meta- data*, and *data*. To maintain and update the dynamic relationships between ontologies and/or databases, WebFINDIT uses *distributed agents*. They act independently of other system components (Petrie & Bussler, 2003). They monitor the system and user behavior and formulate a strategy for the creation or removal of inter-ontology relationships. It is assumed that the agents are always running. For instance, among agents' tasks is to determine whether a new inter-ontology relationship is needed. This is achieved by monitoring the traffic over inter-ontology relationships and checking whether the destination is final based on users' activity. On the one hand, if an inter-ontology relationship is rarely used, then it is most likely to be stale. The agent would recommend its removal. In what follows, we elaborate on the processes of creating and deleting inter-ontology relationships.

Creating Inter-Ontology Relationships

Figure 3a illustrates a scenario where a new inter-ontology relationship is created. In this scenario, the ontology Mental Illness and Addiction has an outgoing inter-ontology relationship with Medicaid, which in turn has an outgoing inter-ontology relationship with Low Income. During the execution of the system, the monitoring agents discover the following: The majority of users who begin their query session from Mental Illness and Addiction and traverse the inter-ontology relationship between Mental Illness and Addiction and Medicaid do not initiate queries on the ontology Medicaid. Rather, they use the inter-ontology relationship between Medicaid and Low Income to go to the Low Income ontology, where they do initiate queries. In this case, observing that the ontology Medicaid is being used as a bridge between Mental Illness and Addiction and Low Income, the monitoring agents would recommend the creation of a new inter-ontology relationship from Mental Illness and Addiction to Low Income. This would allow users to navigate directly from Mental Illness and Addiction to Low Income and reduce the number of traversed nodes to reach relevant ontologies.

Figure 3. Creation and deletion of inter-ontology relationships

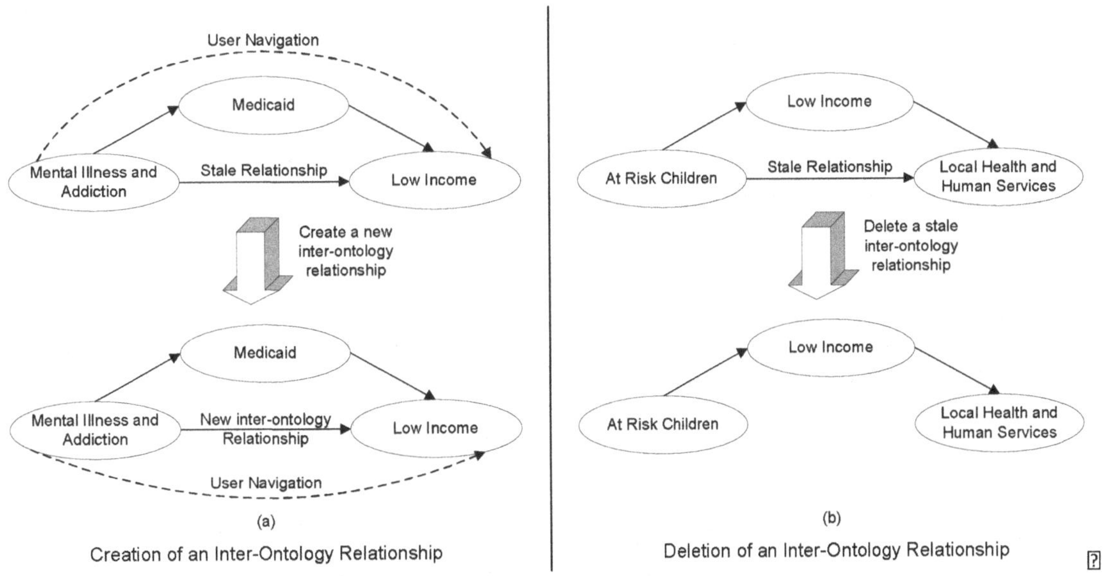

Deleting Inter-Ontology Relationships

If an inter-ontology relationship is rarely used or always leads to a non-relevant ontology, then it is considered to be a *stale* relationship. In this case, a monitoring agent would recommend the deletion of the inter-ontology relationship. Consider the example of Figure 3b. The ontology At Risk Children has an outgoing inter-ontology relationship with the ontology Low Income, which in turn has an outgoing inter-ontology relationship with the ontology Local Health and Human Services. Monitoring agents of these ontologies report the following: The majority of users who navigate directly from At Risk Children to Local Health and Human Services ultimately leave Local Health and Human Services without performing any query. This suggests that the direct link between At Risk Children and Local Health and Human Services is not a useful link. The agents would therefore recommend the deletion of the inter-ontology relationship between At Risk Children and Local Health and Human Services. Local Health and Human Services would still be navigable from At Risk Children via `Low Income`, but the overhead associated with a stale link would have been eliminated.

Ontological Support for Databases

To provide support for distributed ontologies, we introduced the concept of *co-databases.* A co-database is a metadata repository associated with a participating database. Each co-database is an object-oriented database that stores information about the underlying database (e.g., DBMS and query language), the ontology or ontologies to which the database belongs, and any inter-ontology relationships that the database has formed. The ontology administrator is responsible for monitoring the database registration process. Propagation of new database information to member co-databases is performed automatically. The new database would then instantiate the co-database and populate the schema accordingly. The co-database instantiation is based on the template schema defined for the application (see Fig.4). This facilitates the semantic interoperability between different data sources. After the initial definition of a co-database, the maintenance is carried out in an automatic manner and no administrator intervention is required.

Each co-database's schema is composed of two sub-schemas: the first sub-schema represents ontologies and the second represents inter-ontology relationships (Figure 4).

The first sub-schema consists of a tree of classes where each class represents a set of databases that can answer queries about a specialized type of information. The class Ontology Root is the root of this sub-schema. Each sub-class of Ontology Root represents the root of an ontology tree. Each node in that tree represents a specific information type. This hierarchical organization allows for the structuring of ontologies according to specialization relationships. The classes composing the ontology tree support each other in answering queries directed to them. If a user query conforms more closely to the information type of a given sub-class, then the query is forwarded to this sub-class. If no classes are found in the ontology tree to answer the query, then the user either simplifies the query or the query is forwarded to other ontologies (or databases) via inter-ontology relationships.

The class Ontology Root contains generic attributes that are inherited by all classes in the ontology tree. Every sub-class of the class Ontology Root has some specific attributes that describe the domain model of the related set of underlying databases. As shown in our running example, the attribute *Information-type* represents the name of the information-type, "Low Income" for all instances of the class Low Income. The attribute `Synonyms` describes the set of alternative descriptions of each information-type. Each sub-class of the Ontology Root class includes

Figure 4. Co-database template schema in WebFINDIT

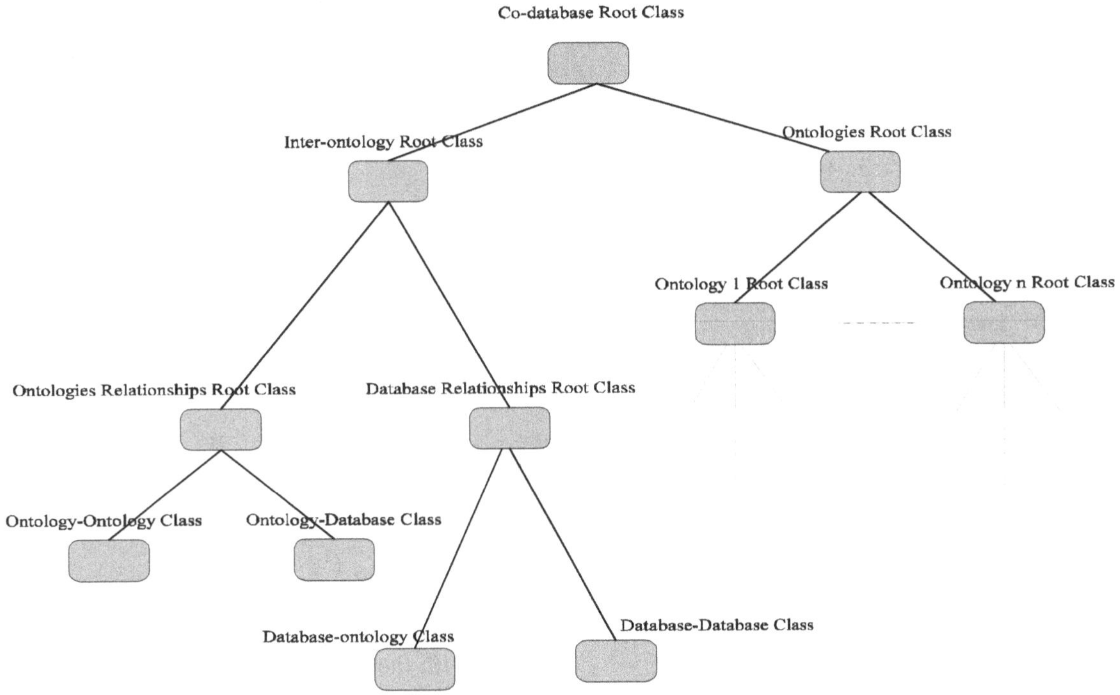

specific attributes that describe the domain model of the related set of underlying databases. These attributes do not necessarily correspond directly to the objects described in any particular database. For example, a subset of the attributes of the class Low Income is:

```
Class Low Income Isa Ontology Root{
attribute string County;
attribute Person Citizens;
attribute set(Provider) Providers;
}
```

The second sub-schema represents inter-ontology relationships. The class Inter-Ontology Root forms the root of the sub-schema. It is organized into two sub-classes: the Ontologies Relationships Root Class, which represents inter-ontology relationships involving the ontology of which the database is member, and the Database Relationships Root Class, which represents relationships involving the database itself. The Ontologies Relationships Root Class consists in turn of two sub-classes: the Ontology-Ontology Class which describes relationships with other ontologies and the Ontology-Database Class which describes relationships with other databases. Similarly, the Database Relationships Root Class consists of two sub-classes: Database-Ontology Class and Database-Database Class.

The class Inter-Ontology Root contains generic attributes that are relevant to all types of inter-ontology relationships. These relationships may be used to answer queries when the local ontology cannot answer them.

Let's assume that in our example (Figure 2) the user queries the ontology Low Income about Mental Retardation Benefits. The use of the synonyms and generalization / specialization relationships fails to answer the user query. However, the ontology Low Income has an inter-ontology relationship with the ontology Mental Retardation Disabilities where the value of the attribute Description is {"*Mental Retardation*"}. It is clear

Figure 5. Case manager interface

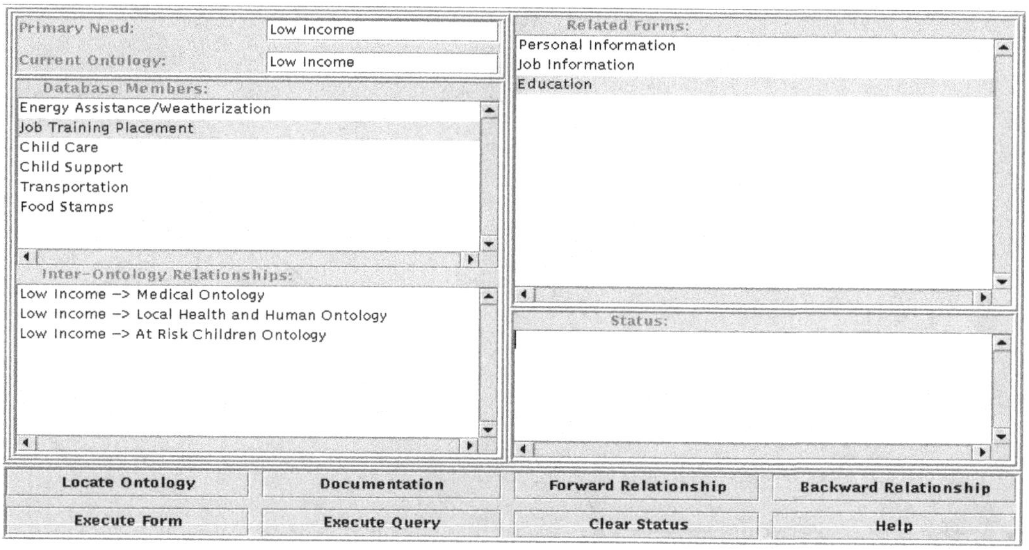

that this inter-ontology relationship provides the answer to the user query.

Application Scenario

When visiting the FSSA, citizens come with specific needs. They may be unemployed, unable to support their families, have children with disability, etc. Using the ontological approach helps case managers notify relevant FSSA services so that the applicants receive all benefits to which they are entitled.

In our scenario, the case manager starts searching for relevant ontologies based on the primary need expressed by the citizen. The system will connect to either the local ontology or alternatively, a remote ontology based on the information implied by the different inter-ontology relationships. Relevance is based on simple matching between the primary need, the information type of the ontology or one of its synonyms. In

Figure 5, we consider a simple case where the primary focus, Low Income, corresponds to the local ontology. All databases and inter-ontology relationships related to the located ontology are displayed. The case manager may be familiarized with the content or behavior of a particular database by requesting its documentation. The system also provides a list of forms for each database. Each form is used to gather information about the citizen in the context of the current database. For example, by selecting the database *Job Training Placement* in the ontology Low Income, three forms may be potentially needed (see Figure 5). Another possibility of our system is to submit queries to a particular database in its native query language.

After filling out all required forms, the case manager may decide to find other relevant ontologies by traversing the different inter-ontology relationships. This provides a flexible mechanism to browse through and discover other databases of potential interest. The case manager can then submit requests for *all* benefits that a citizen is entitled to. Note that not all forms need to be filled out as some may not be relevant depending on the situation of the citizen. Citizens can also use our system to inquire about the status of their pending requests. They are also able to browse the different ontologies and corresponding databases. By providing their social security numbers, citizens can obtain the status of their requests.

Advertising Databases

In the previous section, we described the metadata model used for describing ontologies. In this section, we describe the situation where a new database needs to be added to the system. Database providers will advertise (make available) their databases by making this metadata available in the corresponding co-databases. Initially this process is manual.

The ontology administrator is responsible for monitoring the database registration process. Propagation of new database information to member co-databases is performed automatically. The new database would instantiate the co-database and populates the schema accordingly. Thus, the initial addition process is manual. After the initial definition of a co-database, no administrator intervention is required. Search and maintenance of the databases and ontological relationships are automatic. In this way, databases can be plugged in and out of the WebFINDIT system with minimal changes to the underlying architecture.

The membership of a database to ontologies is materialized by creating an instance of one or many classes in the same or different ontologies. As an illustration on how a database is advertised and linked to its ontologies, consider the Indiana Support Enforcement Tracking System (ISETS) database. The co-database attached to the ISETS database contains information about all related ontologies. As the ISETS is a member of four ontologies (Mental Retardation Disability, Local Health and Human Services, Finance, and Law Enforcement), it stores information about these four ontologies (see Fig. 2). This co-database also contains information about other ontologies and databases that have inter-ontology relationships with these four ontologies and the database itself.

The ISETS database will be made available by providing information about its content, information types, documentation (a file containing multimedia data or a program that plays a product demonstration), access information, which includes its location and wrapper, etc. The database's content is represented by an object-oriented view of the database schema. This view contains the terms of interest available from that database. These terms provide the interface that can be used to query the database. More specifically, this view consists of one or several types containing the exported properties (attributes and functions) and a textual description of these properties. The ISETS database can be advertised in WebFINDIT by using the following statement.

```
Advertise Database IESTS {
Information Types {"Medical and Finance"}
Documentation "http://www.iests.in.us/MF"
Location "dba.iests.in.us"
Wrapper "dba.iests.in.us/WWD-QLOracle"
Interface {ResearchProjects; PatientHistory}
. . .
}
```

The URL, "http://www.iests.in.us/MF" contains the documentation about the ISETS database. It contains any type of presentation accessible through the Web (e.g., a Java applet that plays a video clip). The exported interface contains two types about research and patients which represent the database's view that the provider decides to advertise. For example, the PatientMentalHistory type is defined as follows.

```
Type PatientMentalHistory {
attribute string Patient.Name;
attribute int History.DateRecorded;
function string Description (string Patient.Name, Date History.DateRecorded)
}
```

Note that the textual explanations of the attributes and functions are left out of the description for clarity. Each attribute denotes a relation field, and each function denotes an access routine to the database. The implementation of these features is transparent to the user. For instance, the function Description() denotes the access routine that returns the description of a patient sickness at a given date. In the case of an object-oriented database, an attribute denotes a class attribute and a function denotes either a class method or an access routine.

Using WebFINDIT, users can locate a database, investigate its exported interface, and fetch useful attributes and access functions. The interface of a database can be used to query data stored in this database only after ensuring it is relevant. However, users may sometimes be interested to express queries that require extracting and combining data from multiple databases. In WebFINDIT, querying multiple databases is achieved by using domain attributes of ontology classes. As pointed out before, each subclass of the class OntologyRoot has a set of attributes that describe the domain model of the underlying databases. These attributes can be used to query data stored in the underlying databases.

Ontological Support for Database Applications

The Web is evolving from a set of single isolated application systems into a World wide network of disparate systems interacting with each other. This requires means to represent the semantics of different applications so that they could be automatically understood. This is where ontologies play a crucial role, providing machine processable semantics of applications residing on heterogeneous systems. The development of ontologies is often a cooperative process involving different entities possibly at different locations (e.g., businesses, government agencies). All entities that agree on using a given ontology commit themselves to the concepts and definitions within that ontology (Buhler & Vidal, 2003).

In WebFINDIT, an ontology defined for an application typically consists of a hierarchical description of important concepts in a domain, along with descriptions of the properties of each concept. Formally, an ontology contains a set of concepts (also called classes) which constitutes the core of the ontology (Gruber, 1993). The notion of concept in ontologies is similar to the notion of class in object-oriented programming (Lozano-Tello & Gomez-Perez, 2004). Each concept has a set of properties associated to it. This set describes the different features of the class. Each property has a range (also called type) indicating a restriction on the values that the property can take.

We identify three different types of ontologies in the WebFINDIT system, depending on their generality level: vertical, horizontal, and metadata ontologies. Other types of ontologies such as representational, method and task ontologies also exist (Fensel, 2003) but are out of the scope of our research. Vertical ontologies capture the knowledge valid for a particular domain such as Medicaid, Low Income, and At Risk Children. Horizontal ontologies describe general knowledge that is valid across several domains. They define basic notions and concepts (e.g., time, space) applicable in many technical domains. Metadata ontologies provide concepts that allow the description of other concepts.

Application Scenario

To illustrate the drawbacks of the current system and how WebFINDIT can help, we can examine a typical scenario under the scope of our FSSA example. A pregnant teen, say Mary, goes to an FSSA office to collect social benefits. Mary needs a government-funded health insurance program. She would also like to receive nutritional advice for maintaining an appropriate diet during her pregnancy. Because Mary will not be able to take care of the future newborn, she is also interested in finding a foster family.

Fulfilling all of Mary's needs requires access to services scattered among various agencies. For instance, the case officer, let's call him John, first manually looks up which social programs offer health insurance and food assistance for Mary. Medicaid and WIC (a federally funded food program for Women, Infants, and Children) would be the best candidates. Assuming Medicaid (a health care program for low-income citizens) is locally accessible, John has to connect to the corresponding application and interact with it. However, since WIC is a federal program John has no direct access to the corresponding application. That means Mary must visit another agency, perhaps in a different town, to apply for the benefit.

More difficulties arise when John tries to find a foster family service. Using local resources, he finds no matching program, although Teen Outreach Pregnancy (TOP), an FSSA partner, does offer such services. To complicate things further, each time John connects to an application, he has to make sure that it abides by privacy rules related to the access to and use of sensitive information such as Mary's social security number.

This process of manually researching and accessing individual services is clearly time-consuming. It would be more efficient if John could specify Mary's needs once and address them altogether. He could then seamlessly access all related services through a single access point, perhaps a Pregnancy Benefits service that outsources from WIC,

Medicaid, and TOP regardless of the programs locations or providers. That is exactly what WebFINDIT aims to do. We provide an efficient data and application access middleware. Existing applications are wrapped in modular Web services. This facilitates the use of welfare applications and expeditiously satisfies citizen needs.

Support for Synchronous and Asynchronous Queries

WebFINDIT supports two types of queries: synchronous and asynchronous. Synchronous queries are those where a specific query order is imposed on some or all of the sub-queries. For example, consider a citizen requesting to be admitted at a local health facility. There exist two requirements for obtaining this social benefit: the citizen must have a low income and, if this is the case, then he must not be covered for such an expense by his insurance policy. Assume that queries *Q_1* and *Q_2* check the citizen's income and insurance coverage respectively. Obviously, in this case, *Q_1* must be evaluated first and, if the citizen's income is under the specified threshold then *Q_2* must be evaluated. In practice, the citizen would submit a single request to WebFINDIT. The system then decomposes the request into the two sub-queries *Q_1* and *Q_2*. It then sends *Q_1* and *Q_2* to the ontologies Low Income and Local Health and Human Services respectively. Before the processing of the initial request (to get admitted into a local health facility) can proceed, the system must first receive the answers to the two sub-requests *Q_1* and *Q_2*. In case of a negative answer from either one of the two, the request is declined. Asynchronous queries are those where no query order constraint exists. The citizen's request may be fulfilled in an asynchronous manner, i.e., the result of one query is not dependent on the value of the other. For instance, in the previous example, the sub-requests *Q_1* and *Q_2* may be evaluated asynchronously (for some other social benefit that does not require serial execution).

WEBFINDIT ARCHITECTURE

In this section, we provide a detailed description of WebFINDIT. We first look at the WebFINDIT architecture from a "data access" point of view. Then we present our "application access" infrastructure.

Data Access Architecture

To provide an efficient approach for accessing and manipulating Web databases irrespective of their data models, platforms and locations, we have divided the WebFINDIT data access architecture into seven layers (Figure 6): *interface layer, query layer, transport layer, communication layer, access layer, metadata layer,* and *data layer.* The division into these layers makes the data access architecture modular. The layered approach provides a separation of concerns which allows dealing with the problems described earlier in an efficient manner. In the following, we first briefly present an overview of the data access architecture. We then elaborate on three of its major layers.

- **Interface layer**. This layer provides the users access to WebFINDIT services. It allows users to browse, search, and access ontologies and databases using graphical and text queries. This layer enables users to formulate both SQL and XML queries.
- **Query layer**. This layer processes user queries and locates the data that corresponds to user queries. This layer contains two components: the *Data Locator* and the *Agent Contractor*. The role of these components will be discussed in the upcoming sections.
- **Transport layer**. This layer enables communication between WebFINDIT components. It provides a standard means of sending and receiving messages: the Internet Inter-Orb Protocol (IIOP).
- **Communication layer**. This layer is responsible for interpreting exchanges of

Figure 6. WebFINDIT data access layers

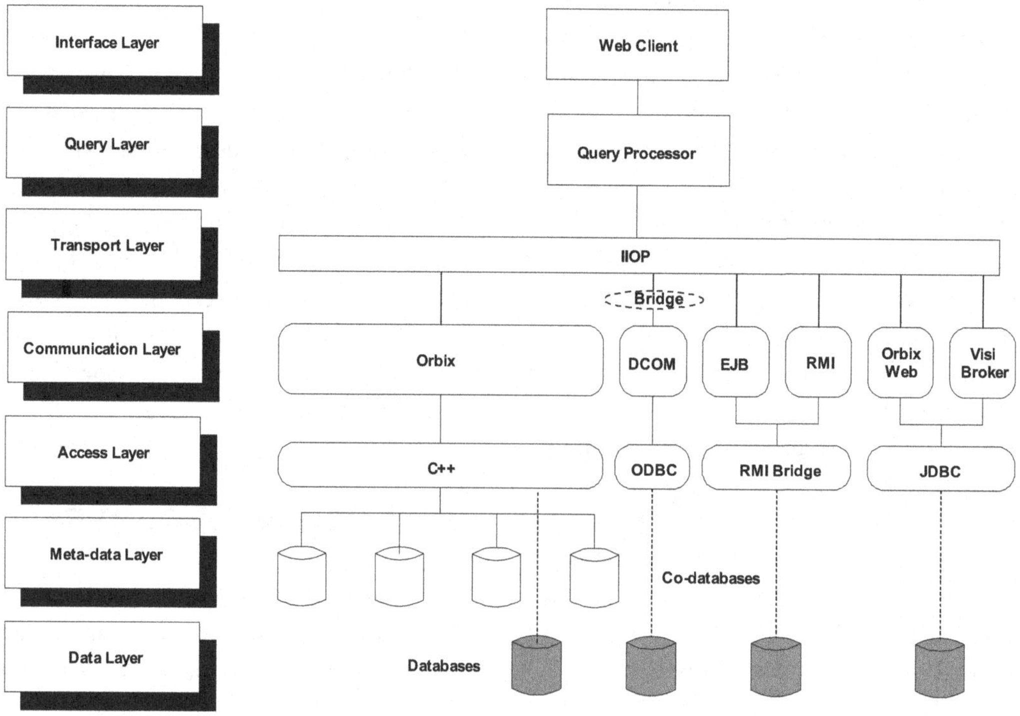

messages between the query processor and the metadata/database servers. This layer consists of a network of communication middleware components, including CORBA, EJB, DCOM, and RMI.

- **Access layer**. This layer allows access to the metadata repositories and the databases. It comprises of a variety of database access methods, including ODBC, JDBC, and an RMI bridge.
- **Metadata layer**. This layer consists of a set of metadata repositories. Each repository stores metadata about its associated database (i.e., location, wrappers, ontologies, etc.) Metadata is stored in object-oriented databases and XML-enabled databases.
- **Data layer**. This layer has two components: databases and wrappers. The current version of WebFINDIT supports relational (mSQL, Oracle, Sybase, DB2, MS SQL Server and Informix) and object oriented databases (ObjectStore). Each wrapper provides access to a specific database server.

In the rest of this section, we provide a more detailed description of WebFINDIT's three most important layers, namely, the communication layer, the access layer, and the data layer.

Communication Layer

WebFINDIT's communication layer enables heterogeneous databases to communicate and share information. It encompasses several communication middleware technologies. These include CORBA, DCOM, EJB, and RMI

CORBA provides mechanisms to support platform heterogeneity, transparent location and implementation of objects, interoperability and communication between software components of a distributed object environment (Henning & Vinoski, 1999). In WebFINDIT, CORBA allows the different databases participating in the system to be encapsulated as CORBA objects, thereby providing a standardized method of communication between databases.

DCOM allows components to communicate across system boundaries. For components to interact, they must adhere to a specific binary structure. The binary structure provides the basis for interoperability between components written in different languages (Wallace, 2001). DCOM is incorporated into the WebFINDIT system to expand the scope of the project to include databases resident in the Windows NT environment.

In EJB, business logic may be encapsulated as a component called an *enterprise bean.* It provides a separation between the business logic and the system-level details. This separation extends Java's "Write Once, Run Anywhere" portability to allow Java server components to run on any EJB-compliant application server (Roman, Ambler, & Jewell, 2003). We installed an EJB Server on a Windows NT machine and placed the corresponding database at a separate UNIX server. This was done to provide a standard vendor-independent interface for a Java application server.

RMI is Java-specific and is therefore able to provide connectivity to any system incorporating a Java Virtual Machine. As a result, RMI is able to pass entire objects as arguments and return values, whereas traditional RPC systems require the decomposition of objects into primitive data types (Pitt & McNiff, 2001). We Extended the WebFINDIT implementation to support an even greater degree of heterogeneity. Coupled with Java Native Interface (JNI) to overcome its lack of multi-language support, RMI proved to be a particularly effective middleware technology.

An established way of facilitating communication between RMI and CORBA is to use RMI-IIOP, a standard which allows Java RMI to interoperate with the CORBA IIOP protocol. By means of RMI-IIOP, RMI clients may invoke CORBA server methods. Similarly, CORBA clients may invoke RMI server methods (Figure 7).

Figure 7. RMI to CORBA invocation via RMI-IIOP

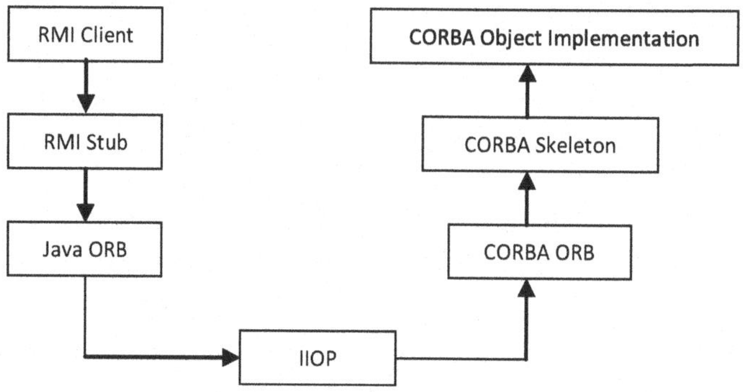

Figure 8. Method Invocation via JNI

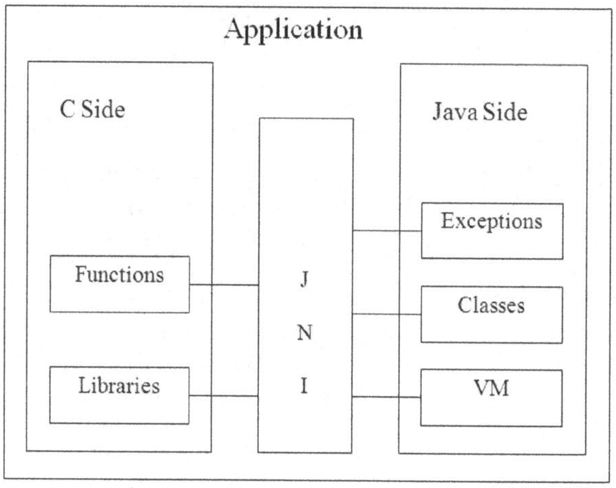

RMI and DCOM are based on Java and C++ respectively. In order to enable communication between RMI and DCOM, it is necessary to find an intermediary technology between Java and C++. In WebFINDIT, we have elected to use the *Java Native Interface* (JNI). JNI allows Java code that runs within a Java Virtual Machine to operate with applications and libraries written in other languages, such as C and C++. In addition, the invocation API allows embedding the Java Virtual Machine into native applications. Figure 8 shows how the JNI ties the C side of an application to Java.

DCOM and CORBA rely on different network protocols (IIOP and Microsoft DCOM protocol) that do not readily interoperate. To enable CORBA and DCOM interoperability in WebFINDIT, we have used an RMI server as a bridge between CORBA and DCOM.

This two-step approach combines the solution described previously for CORBA-RMI and RMI-DCOM interoperability. As depicted in Figure 9, the first step uses an RMI bridge to allow interactions between CORBA and RMI. The second step uses JNI to allow communications between RMI and DCOM.

Access Layer

The WebFINDIT system was intended to allow querying based both on the metadata provided by

Figure 9. Interoperability among distributed object middlewares

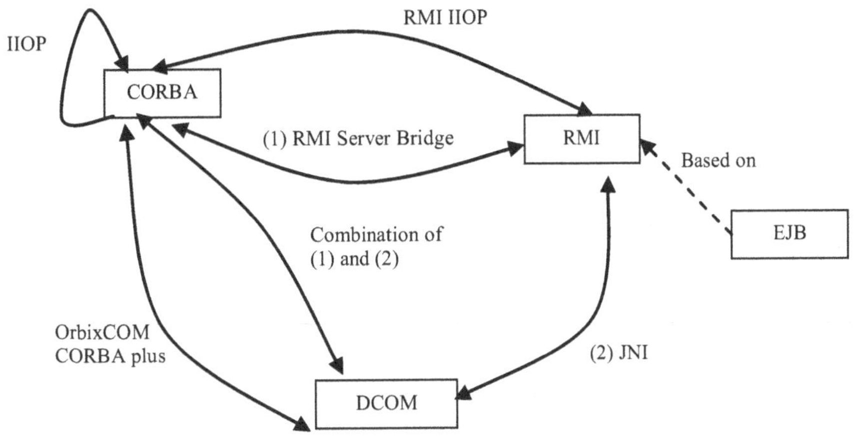

the co-databases and the actual data contained in the databases themselves. Due to the wide variety of database technologies included in the WebFINDIT system, a full spectrum of access methods are required to permit direct querying of database contents. In the following we list various access methods used in WebFINDIT to support querying across the different databases.

JDBC (Java Database Connectivity) is a Java package that provides a generic interface to SQL-based relational databases (Fisher, Ellis, & Bruce, 2003). Most DBMS vendors provide Java interfaces. JDBC is used to access the majority of the WebFINDIT's databases.

JNI (Java Native Interface) is a Java API that allows Java code running within a Java Virtual Machine (VM) to operate with applications and libraries written in other languages, such as C and C++ (Liang, 1999). JNI was employed in forming the RMI/DCOM middleware bridge. By embedding JNI in a wrapper class, additionally defined as both an RMI server and a DCOM client, bi-directional interoperability between RMI and DCOM was achieved.

C++ method invocation allows communication between the server and the C++ interfaced, object-oriented databases. In WebFINDIT, C++ method invocation handles the communication between the Iona's CORBA Orbix C++ server and object-oriented ObjectStore database. C++ method invocation is also used to access all co-databases, which are ObjectStore databases.

ODBC allows a database driver layer between an application and a database management system. This allows access to any ODBC-compatible database from any application (Wood, 1999). In WebFINDIT, ODBC is used to provide access to the Informix database on the Windows NT server.

Data Layer

This layer contains the underlying databases and their wrappers. Several database technologies have been used in the development of WebFINDIT which include DB2 (Zikopolous, Baklarz, deRoos, & Melnyk, 2003), Oracle (Loney & Koch, 2002), Ontos, MS SQL Server, ObjectStore (Software, 2005), UniSQL (IBM, 2005), Sybase (Worden, 2000), Informix (IBM, 2005) and mSQL (Yarger, Reese, & King, 1999)

Each database system has its own characteristics that make it different from the other database systems. It is out of the scope of this paper to explain the functionalities exhibited by these databases. The different types of databases were added to the WebFINDIT system as part of an initiative to expand the system and exhibit database heterogeneity.

WebFINDIT also supports XML at the data layer. To enable existing databases to respond to queries submitted in XML format, we first generated XML documents from the content of the underlying databases. We then modified the co-databases to include an attribute indicating whether their associated databases could accept XML queries. The query processor was also modified to support resolution of XML queries. These modifications included a check to determine whether the target database provides XML query support, methods for submitting XML queries, and methods for interpreting XML query results.

Application Access Architecture

We have incorporated Web services in the WebFINDIT system to provide efficient reuse access to Web applications. In this section, we describe the basic principles of Web services and show how WebFINDIT supports the technology.

Web services are defined in different ways in the literature. A Web service is defined as "a business function made available via the Internet by a service provider and accessible by clients that could be human users or software applications" (Casati & Shan, 2001). It is also defined as "loosely coupled applications using open, cross-platform standards which interoperate across organizational and trust boundaries" (Tsur et al., 2001). The W3C (World Wide Web Consortium) defines a Web service as a "software application identified by a URI (Uniform Resource Identifier), whose interfaces and bindings are capable of being defined, described and discovered by XML artifacts and supports direct interactions with other software applications using XML-based messages via Internet-based protocols" (W3C, 2004). These definitions can be seen as complementary to each other. Each definition emphasizes some part of the basic Web service characteristics (discovery, invocation, etc.). In this section, we define Web services as functionalities that are:

Programmatically accessible: Web services are mainly designed to be invoked by other Web services and applications. They are distributed over the Web and accessible via widely deployed protocols such as HTTP and SMTP. Web services must describe their capabilities to other services including their operations, input and output messages, and the way they can be invoked (Alonso, Casati, Kuno, & Machiraju, 2003).

Loosely coupled: Web services generally communicate with each other by exchanging XML documents (Peltz, 2003). The use of a document-based communication model caters for loosely coupled relationships among Web services. This is in contrast with component based frameworks which use object-based communication, thereby yielding systems where the coupling between components is tight. Additionally, by using HTTP as a communication protocol, Web services enable much more firewall friendly computing than component-based systems. For example, there is no standard port for IIOP, so it normally does not traverse firewalls easily.

Organizing WebFINDIT Services

Interactions among Web services involve three types of participants: service provider, service registry, and service consumer. Service providers are the parties that offer services. In our running example, providers include FSSA bureaus or divisions (for example, the Bureau of Family Resources) as well as external agencies such as the U.S. Department of Health and Human Services. They define descriptions of their services and publish them in the service registry, a searchable repository of service descriptions. Each description contains details about the corresponding service such as its data types, operations, and network location. Service consumers that include citizens and case officers, use a find operation to locate services of interest. The registry returns the description of each relevant service. The consumer uses this description (e.g., network location) to invoke the corresponding Web service. Providers describe the operational features of WebFINDIT services in the Web Services Description Language (WSDL) (W3C, 2005). Each operation has one of four possible modes:

- one-way, in which the service receives a message.
- notification, in which the service sends a message.
- request-response, in which the service receives a message and sends correlated message.
- solicit-response, in which the service sends a message and receives correlated message.

For instance, in our running example, the WIC service offers a request-response operation called checkEligibility. This operation receives a message that includes a citizen's income and family size and returns a message indicating whether the citizen is eligible for `WIC`. WebFINDIT stores WSDL descriptions in a registry based on Universal Description, Discovery and Integration (UDDI) (W3C, 2005). The registration of the Medicaid service, for example, includes the URL for communicating with this service and a pointer to its WSDL description.

WebFINDIT services communicate via SOAP messages. Because SOAP uses XML-based messaging over well-established protocols like HTTP and SMTP, it is platform-independent, but it has a few drawbacks. For one thing, SOAP does not yet meet all the scalability requirements of Web applications. Unlike communication middleware such as CORBA and Java RMI, SOAP encoding rules make it mandatory to include typing information in all SOAP messages. Additionally, SOAP defines only simple data types such as String and Int. Hence, using complex data types may require the XML parser to get the corresponding XML schema definitions from remote locations, which might add processing overhead.

The use of a document-based messaging model in Web services caters for loosely coupled relationships. Additionally, Web services are not statically bound to each other. New partners with relevant features can be discovered and invoked. However, to date, dynamic discovery of Web services takes place mostly at development time (Ran, 2003). Heterogeneous applications (e.g., Java, CORBA objects) may be wrapped and exposed as Web services. For example, the Axis Java2WSDL utility in IBM's Web Services Toolkit enables the generation of WSDL descriptions from Java class files. Iona's Orbix E2A Web Services Integration Platform may be used to create Web services from existing EJBs or CORBA objects. In terms of autonomy, Web services are accessible through published interfaces. Partners interact with Web services without having to be aware of what is happening behind the scene. They are not required to know how the operations provided by the service are internally implemented. Some operations can even be transparently outsourced from third parties.

Composing WebFINDIT Services

A major issue in defining composite services is checking whether Web services can be composed of the outsourced services. For example, it would be difficult to invoke an operation if no mapping exists between the parameters requested by that operation and those transmitted by the client service. To deal with this issue, WebFINDIT defines a set of rules that check composability for services by comparing syntactic (such as operation modes) and semantic (such as domain of interest) features.

Semantic description of Web services is the key to automating customized service delivery. We focus on business process semantics, which describe features related to Web service execution. We use these descriptions to model laws and policies that regulate access to social and welfare services. You can apply semantics to other system descriptions as well—for example, to describe message parameters at the message level or functionality at the operational level. We define a metadata ontology that provides a conceptual template that service providers, such as government agencies, can use to describe their operations. In our approach, the service providers are responsible for describing their operations by assigning values to the operations' attributes, such as their purposes and categories. The service composer, often a case officer like John (in our running example), provides a high-level specification of the desired composition. This specification simply contains the list of operations to be performed, without referring to any existing service. Based on semantic composability rules, WebFINDIT then generates a composition plan that gives the list of outsourced services and how they interact with each other through plugging operations mapping messages, and so forth to achieve the desired composition. Details of all the processes involved in constructing service compositions can be found in (Medjahed and Bouguettaya, 2005).

IMPLEMENTATION

In this section, we describe how WebFINDIT's components are put together to provide an efficient middleware for accessing Web databases. The current implementation of WebFINDIT is deployed on a large cluster of UNIX and Windows machines. Figure 10 shows the type of database that resides at each machine (e.g., only an object-oriented database is stored on Elara). The figure shows a number of health related ontologies (e.g., Low Income and Medicaid residing on the hosts `Saturn` and `Thebe` respectively.) WebFINDIT supports a broad spectrum of heterogeneity. This heterogeneity appears at all levels of the system including hardware, operating system, database, and communication middleware. It supports three types of databases: relational (Oracle, Informix, DB2, and mSQL), object-oriented (ObjectStore), and XML-enabled databases. The databases used to store XML-formatted data are Oracle and DB2. Host operating systems of databases are Unix (Sun Solaris) and Windows NT platforms. Different distributed object middlewares have been used to interconnect databases: three CORBA ORBs (Visibroker, Orbix, and OrbixWeb), two Sun RMI servers, one WebLogic EJB server, and one Microsoft DCOM server.

Consumers access WEBFINDIT via a graphical user interface (GUI) implemented using HTML/Servlet. Figure 10 shows the architecture of the WebFINDIT system with Web services support. Two types of requests are supported by WebFINDIT: querying databases and invoking applications. All requests are received by the WebFINDIT manager. The Request Handler is responsible for routing requests to the Data Locator (DL) or the Service Locator (SL). Data queries are forwarded to the Data Locator. Its role is to educate users about the information space and locate relevant databases. All information necessary to locate databases is stored in co-databases (ObjectStore).

The *Query Processor* handles access to WebFINDIT's databases. It provides access to databases via JDBC for relational databases in UNIX platforms, ODBC for databases on the NT machine, and C++ method invocations for object-oriented databases. The *Query Processor* may also process users' queries formatted as XML documents. In this case, it uses the *Oracle XML-SQL Utility* and *DB2 XML Extender* to access XML-enabled databases. Query results can be returned in either tabular or XML formats. The *Query Processor* also interacts with the *AgentContractor*. The *Agent Contractor* informs monitoring agents (implemented in Voyager 2.0) when users move from one ontology to another.

One monitoring agent is associated with each database ontology. It stores information about destinations of all outgoing and incoming inter-ontology relationships. This information makes it possible for the agents to determine the usefulness of inter-ontology relationships.

All co-databases are implemented using ObjectStore. The use of an object-oriented database was dictated by the hierarchical structure of the co-database schema. We used four CORBA Orbix ORBs to represent the existing ontologies. A fifth ORB was added for co-databases associated with databases that do not belong to any ontology. Each co-database is registered to a given ORB through a CORBA object wrapper. Users can learn about the content of each database by displaying its corresponding documentation in HTML/text, audio, or video formats. Once users have located the database of interest, they can then submit SQL queries. The Query Processor handles these queries by accessing the appropriate database via JDBC gateways. Databases are linked to OrbixWeb or VisiBroker ORBs.

In order to allow for the creation and maintenance of dynamic service links in WebFINDIT, we have chosen to use the Voyager agent-enabled platform. Voyager 2.0 combines the power of autonomous agents and object mobility with dynamic CORBA and RMI compatibility. A new version of Voyager supports simultaneous bi-directional communication with EJB and COM programs. It performs as a universal gateway which can translate messages between non-Voyager systems of different standards. Voyager is also among a very few agent platforms that support full native CORBA, IDL, IIOP and bi-directional IDL/Java conversion.

Figure 10. WebFINDIT implementation

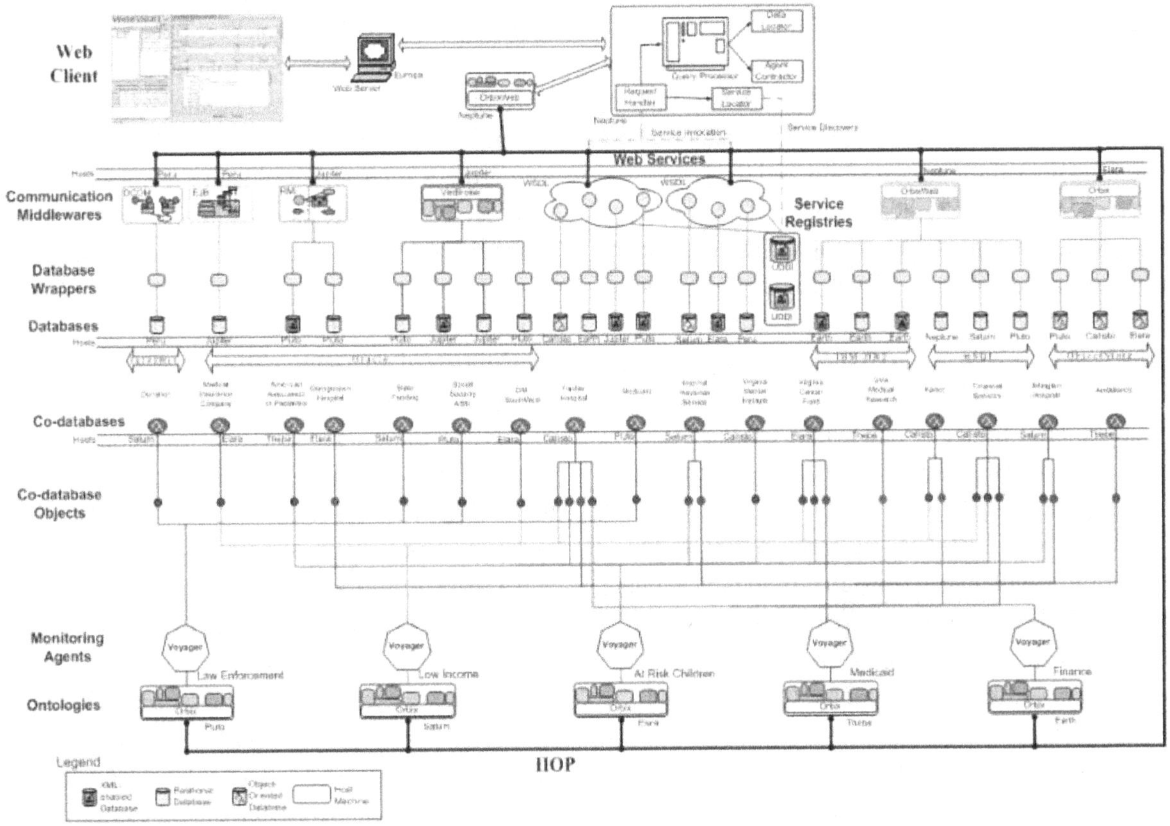

WebFINDIT currently includes several applications implemented in Java. These applications are wrapped by WSDL descriptions. These describe Web services as a set of endpoints operating on messages containing document-oriented information. WSDL descriptions are extensible to allow the description of endpoints and their messages regardless of what message formats or network protocols are used to communicate. Each service accesses a database (Oracle, Informix, DB2, etc.) in the backend to retrieve and/or update the information. We use the IBM's Web Services Toolkit to automatically generate WSDL descriptions from Java class files. WSDL service descriptions are published into a UDDI registry. We adopt Systinet's WASP UDDI Standard 3.1 as our UDDI toolkit. WebFINDIT services are deployed using Apache SOAP 2.2). Apache SOAP provides not only server-side infrastructure for deploying and managing service but also client-side API for invoking those services. Each service has a deployment descriptor. The descriptor includes the unique identifier of the Java class to be invoked, session scope of the class, and operations in the class available for the clients. Each service is deployed using the service management client by providing its descriptor and the URL of the Apache SOAP Servlet rpcrouter. The Service Locator allows the discovery of WSDL descriptions by accessing the UDDI registry. The SL implements UDDI Inquiry Client using WASP UDDI API. Once a service is discovered, its operations are invoked through SOAP Binding Stub which is implemented using Apache SOAP API. The operations are executed by accessing various databases.

WebFINDIT offers an elegant solution to the scalability challenge. Its design provides efficient plug-and-play mechanisms for adding new databases or dropping existing ones with minimal overhead. Adding a new database to WebFINDIT is a 3-step process. In the first step, the database owner would register with an ORB through a template. In the second step, it would connect to WebFINDIT through an API template (e.g., ODBC, JDBC). In the third step, it would create a co-database based on the template described in Figure 4. Prior to filling out the co-database, a negotiation process would have taken place defining the type of relationships this database would have with other databases and ontologies. This 3-level process requires minimal programming effort, thus enabling the scalable expansion of databases in WebFINDIT.

PERFORMANCE EVALUATION

We have performed several experiments to identify the critical points of query execution by determining the time spent in each component of the WebFINDIT system. The WebFINDIT experiments were run with the architecture depicted in Figure 10. The network setting is a 10Mb Ethernet based local area network. Physical databases and co-databases were running on a variety of Sun Sparc stations, including, IPX, Sparc 5, Sparc 10, and Ultra 5 machines. All machines were running Solaris version 2.6. The aim of this set of experiments is to identify the bottlenecks when executing a query. The idea is to measure the time each query spends in the major components of the WebFINDIT system. We identified the following major components: query processor, ORB (co-databases), IIOP, and co-databases.

Compared to other sections of the system, the query spends, on average, a large portion of time in the query processor component (see Figure 11). We believe this is partly caused by the implementation language (Java). Also, the query processor parses each result item into a new CORBA wrapper object. This is usually an expensive operation. We observe that the times (see Figure 11) are almost linearly proportional to the number of items which are wrapped. The time spent in the co-database server objects (Figure 12), is uniform and short. This is because a server object's main task is transforming the arguments

Figure 11. Query processor component elapsed time

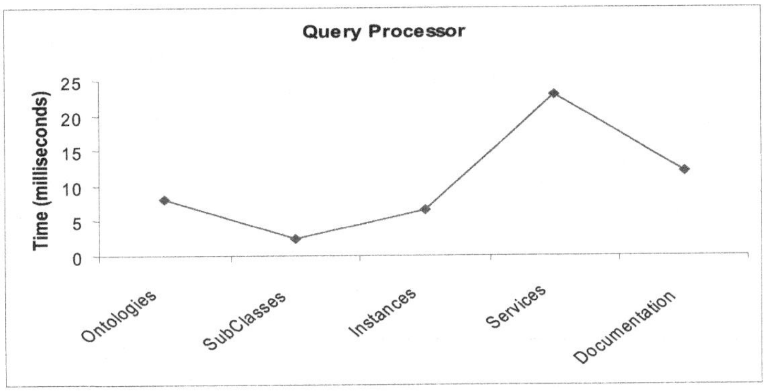

Figure 12. ORB (co-database) component elapsed time

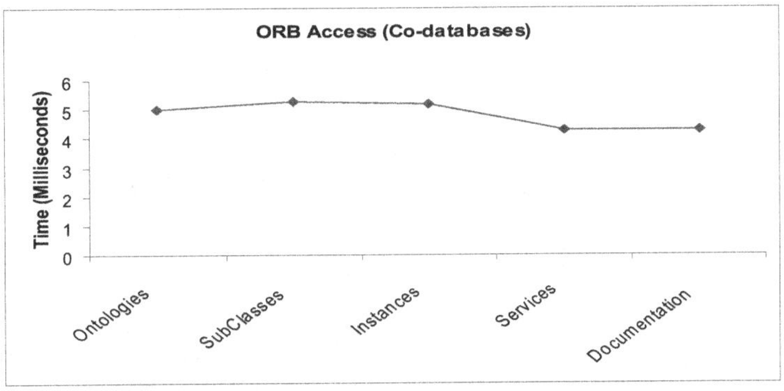

Figure 13. Co-database component elapsed time

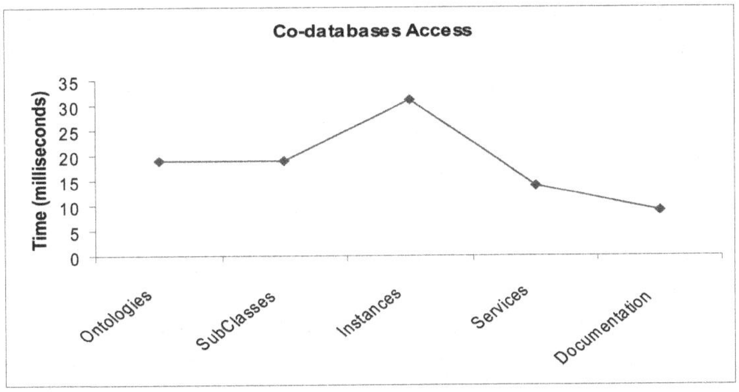

Figure 14. IIOP component elapsed time

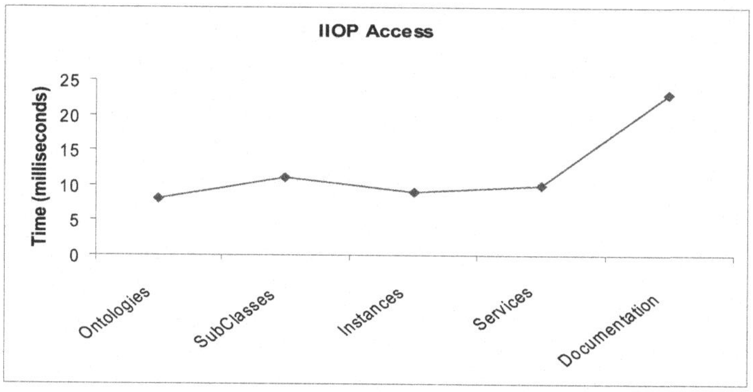

received via IIOP, into a call to the ObjectStore database. Programmatically, this is not a very expensive task.

We also note that the time spent in the ObjectStore database is generally high, compared to times spent in other components (see Figure 13). This is to be expected, as it is here where most of the processing occurs. More specifically, at this point of their evolution, object oriented databases lag behind their relational counterparts in performance.

In particular, the time taken by the instance query class stands out above the others. This result is attributed to the complexity of the query within the ObjectStore database. Not only are the instances of the current class returned, but also those of all its subclasses.

Figure 14 shows the time each query spent traveling the network via IIOP. The only point of note is the exceptional value for the documentation query class. This doubled value can be explained by the fact that this class of query, travels first to the co-database and then on to the actual database. This necessitates two IIOP communications.

The preliminary results show the two most expensive sections of the system are the query processor and the ObjectStore databases. The former because of the performance limitations of its implementation language, and the latter because the internal operation is quite complex. IIOP communication time is also high. However, the protocol itself is unlikely to change, so the efficiency of IIOP communication is likely to remain the same.

RELATED WORK

There is a large body of relevant literature on information extraction, access, and integration. The works most closely related to ours, include *multidatabases* (Wyss and Wyss, 2007), *WWW information retrieval systems* (Kuck and Gnasa, 2007; Bowman, *et al*, 1995; Fernandez *et al*, 1998), system integration (Park & Ram, 2004) and *WWW information brokering systems* (Kashyap, 1998) (Florescu, Levy, & Mendelzon, 1998). The major difference between WebFINDIT's approach and the systems listed above lies in the *goals* and *means* to achieve data and application sharing over the Web. Our approach tries to be all-encompassing in that it attempts to provide a single interface to all Web-accessible databases. WebFINDIT is a system that deals with data and services across heterogeneous sources in an efficient and seamless manner. Our approach features the following concepts for achieving ubiquitous access to Web databases. First, simple access to and advertisement of information sources are key features when querying data and services on the Web. The system processes a user query in two steps: (i) querying meta-data for information sources discovery and exploration, and (ii) querying selected sources for actual data. In the first level, the system provides support for educating the user about the available information space. Second, since scalability is of great importance in the context of Web-based environments, the information space in WebFINDIT is organized in sub-spaces using information type based clustering. This reduces the overhead of locating information and information sources in large information spaces. One of the greatest strengths of our approach is extensibility. Compared to the approaches that use ontologies for information brokering, the addition of new information is simpler in Web-FINDIT. While the mappings between sources and domain models require great efforts in these approaches, our underlying distributed ontology design principles make it easier to construct and manage ontologies. Finally, we provide a seamless Internet-based implementation of the WebFINDIT infrastructure. A few systems closely related to our research are listed below.

The *InfoSleuth* project (Bayardo et al., 1997) (successor of the *Carnot* project (Woelk, Cannata, Huhns, Shen, & Tomlinson, 1993)) presents an approach for information retrieval and processing in a dynamic environment such as the Web. Its functionalities include gathering information from databases and semi-structured sources distributed across the Internet, performing polling and notification for monitoring changes in data, and analyzing gathered information. The InfoSleuth architecture consists of a network of semi-autonomous agents (*user, task, broker, ontology, execution, resource, multi-resource query,* and *monitor agents*), each of which performs some specialized functions. These agents communicate with each other by using the Knowledge Query and Manipulation Language (KQML). Users specify queries over specified ontologies via an applet-based user interface. Although this system provides an architecture that deals with scalable information networks, it does not provide facilities for user education and information space organization. InfoSleuth supports the use of several domain ontologies but does not consider inter-ontology relationships. Thus, it is not clear how a query constructed using one ontology can be converted (if needed) to a query in another ontology.

OBSERVER (Mena, Kashyap, Illarramendi, & Sheth, 1998) is an architecture for information brokering in global information systems. One of the addressed issues is the vocabulary differences across the component systems. OBSERVER features the use of pre-existing domain specific ontologies (ontology servers) to define the terms in each data repository. A data repository may be constituted of several data sources which store the actual data. Each data source has an associated logical schema (a set of entity types and attributes) representing its defined view. A wrapper is responsible for retrieving data from data repositories. Relationships across terms in different ontologies are supported. In addition, OBSERVER performs brokering at the metadata and vocabulary levels. OBSERVER does not provide a straightforward approach for information brokering in defining mappings from the ontologies to the underlying information sources. It should be noted that OBSERVER does not provide facilities to help or train users during query processing.

The TSIMMIS project (The Stanford-IBM Manager of Multiple Information Sources) (Garcia-Molina *et al*, 1997) is a system for integrating heterogeneous information sources that may include both structured and semistructured data. It is based on a mediation architecture and it proposes a new data model, called the Object Exchange Model (OEM), to achieve the integration. OEM is a lightweight object model used to convey information between components. This is a selfdescribing data model where data can be parsed without reference to an external schema. Each object contains its own schema as defined by an identifier, a label (meaning), a type (schema), and a value. A declarative Mediator Specification

Language (MSL) is used as the query language, the specification language for mediators, and the query language for wrappers. TSIMMIS primarily focused on the semiautomatic generation of wrappers and mediators that allows the integration and access to underlying information sources when processing OEM-based queries. Query resolution in TSIMMIS aims to find feasible query plans that respect the limited capabilities of available sources. If these capabilities are not taken into account, plans involving source queries that cannot be answered by the sources may be generated. The TSIMMIS approach provides effective and flexible solutions for data sharing in the context of semistructured sources. However, the issues of information discovery, information space organization, and terminological problems are not tackled.

Automatic service composition has been the focus of several recent Web services projects. *WSMF* (Web Service Modeling Framework) combines the concepts of Web services and ontologies to cater for semantic Web enabled services (Bussler, Fensel, & Maedche, 2002). *WSMF* is still in its early stage. The techniques for the semantic description and composition of Web services are still ongoing. Furthermore, *WSMF* does not address the issue of service composability. Other techniques for composing Web services include *WISE* (Lazcano, Alonso, Schuldt, & Schuler, 2000), *eFlow* (Casati, Ilnicki, Jin, Krishnamoorthy, & Shan, 2000), and *CMI* (Schuster, Georgakopoulos, Cichocki, & Baker, 2000). These techniques generally assume that composers are responsible of checking service composability.

AgFlow (Zeng, Benatallah, Ngu, Dumas, Kalagnanam & Chang 2004.) is a QoS-aware middleware for Web service composition. It uses ontologies to model the component services. The data types follow the XML specification and the message exchange relies on the data flow approach. The orchestration model is specified using statecharts and generated by the programming-based composition scheme. AgFlow defines a QoS model to evaluate Web services from five quality aspects: price, duration, reputation, success execution rate, and availability. Users can specify their preferences by assigning weights to each of these quality parameters. AgFlow proposes two planning strategies, local and global, to select the proper component services. The candidate composition plans are evaluated against an objective function, whereby the optimal plan with the highest objective value can be selected. Users' constraints are also considered during the planning. The global strategy can adapt to the dynamic changes in the service environment. When some component service becomes unavailable or significant changes occurs to its QoS, a re-planning process will be triggered. The re-planning is to enable the composite service to remain optimal in a dynamic environment. The performance of AgFlow is efficient when there are a small number of tasks to be accomplished by the composition. However, as the number of tasks increases, the response time of AgFlow exhibits an exponential growth. This situation becomes even more severe when re-planning is required by the composition.

Several techniques have been proposed to deal with service composability. LARKS defines five techniques for service matchmaking: context matching, profile comparison, similarity matching, signature matching, and constraint matching (Sycara, Klush, and Widoff, 1999). These techniques mostly compare text descriptions, signatures (inputs and outputs), and logical constraints about inputs and outputs. The ATLAS matchmaker defines two methods to compare service capabilities described in DAML-S. The first method compares functional attributes to check whether advertisements support the required type of service or deliver sufficient quality of service. The second compares the functional capabilities of Web services in terms of inputs and outputs. No evaluation study is presented to determine the effectiveness and speed of ATLAS matchmaker.

A pi-calculus model for extending CORBA IDL with protocol descriptions is proposed in (Canal *et al*, 2003). The model is based on the concept of role which allows the specification of the observable behavior of CORBA objects. Techniques for testing the compatibility of behaviors are also presented. Protocol Specifications is another approach for describing object service protocols using finite state machines (Yellin and Strom, 1997). This approach describes both the services offered and required by objects. It also defines techniques that allow components to be checked for protocol compatibility. In contrast to our model, the aforementioned composition techniques deal with objects and components not Web services.

CONCLUSION AND FUTURE DIRECTIONS

In this paper, we presented the WebFINDIT system, a middleware for accessing and querying heterogeneous Web databases and applications. WebFINDIT supports a broad spectrum of heterogeneity. This heterogeneity appears at all levels, including hardware, operating system, database, and communication middleware. A major challenge in developing WebFINDIT was to efficiently and seamlessly integrate these diverse technologies. The WebFINDIT middleware as it exists today represents an elegant and robust solution to the problem of accessing distributed, heterogeneous databases and applications. In the future we intend to conduct experiments regarding application access, i.e., service accessibility, composition and execution. Moreover, there still remain exciting areas of research to be explored in connection with various aspects of the WebFINDIT project. These include: (i) the automatic discovery and maintenance of ontologies, (ii) benchmarking and performance analysis, and (iii) hybrid XML/SQL query processing.

ACKNOWLEDGMENT

This research is partly supported by the National Science Foundation's CNS grant 0627469.

REFERENCES

Alonso, G., Casati, F., Kuno, H., & Machiraju, V. (2003). *Web services: Concepts, architecture, and applications*. Springer Verlag.

Bayardo, R., Bohrer, W., Brice, R., Cichocki, A., Fowler, G., Helal, A., et al. (1997, June). InfoSleuth: Agent-Based Semantic Integration of Information in Open and Dynamic Environments. *In Proceeedings of ACM Sigmod International Conference on Management of Data.* Tucson, Arizona.

Bouguettaya, A. (1999). Introduction to the special issue on ontologies and databases. *International Journal of Distributed and Parallel Databases*, 7 (1).

Bouguettaya, A., Malik, Z., Rezgui, A., & Korff, L. (2006). A Scalable Middleware for Web Databases. *Journal of Database Management*, 17(4): 20-47, October-December.

Bouguettaya, A., Rezgui, A., Medjahed, B., & Ouzzani, M. (2004). Internet computing support for Digital Government. *In: M. P. Singh (Ed.), Practical handbook of internet computing,* Chapman Hall & CRC Press.

Bowman, C., Danzig, P., Schwartz, U. M. M., Hardy, D., & Wessels, D. (1995). *Harvest: A scalable, customizable discovery and access system (Tech. Rep.).* University of Colorado, Boulder.

Buhler, P., & Vidal, J. M. (2003). Semantic Web services as agent behaviors. In: B. Burg et al. (Eds.), *Agentcities: Challenges in open agent environments* (pp. 25-31). Springer-Verlag.

Bussler, C., Fensel, D., & Maedche, A. (2002, December). A conceptual architecture for semantic

Web enabled Web services. *SIGMOD Record*, 31 (4), 24-29.

Canal, C., Fuentes, L., Pimentel, E., Troya, J.M. & Vallecillo, A. , (2003). Adding Roles to CORBA Objects, *IEEE Trans. Software Eng.*, 29(3): 242-260, March.

Casati, F., Ilnicki, S., Jin, L., Krishnamoorthy, V., & Shan, M.-C. (2000, June). Adaptive and dynamic service composition in eFlow. *In CAISE conf. (p. 13-31).* Stockholm, Sweden.

Casati, F., & Shan, M. (2001). Models and languages for describing and discovering e-services (tutorial). *In Proceedings of ACM Sigmod International Conference on Management of Data.* Santa Barbara, Calif., USA.

Chiticariu, L., Hernández, M. A., Kolaitis, P. G., & Popa, L. 2007. Semi-automatic schema integration in Clio. In *Proceedings of the 33rd international Conference on Very Large Data Bases* (Vienna, Austria, September 23 - 27, 2007)

Gruber, T. R., (1993). A translation approach to portable ontologies. *Knowledge Acquisition*, 5(2):199-220.

Fensel, D. (2003). *Ontologies: A silver bullet for knowledge management and electronic commerce.* Springer Verlag.

Fensel, D., Harmelen, F. van, Horrocks, I., McGuinness, D., & Patel-Schneider, P. (2001, March-April). OIL: An ontology infrastructure for the semantic Web. *IEEE Intelligent Systems*, 16(2).

Fernandez, M., Florescu, D., Kang, J., Levy, A., & Suciu, D. (1998, June). Catching the boat with strudel: Experience with a Web-site management system. . *In Proceedings of ACM Sigmod International Conference on Management of Data.* Seattle, Washington, USA.

Fisher, M., Ellis, J., & Bruce, J. (2003). *JDBC API Tutorial and Reference.* Addison-Wesley Pub Co.

Florescu, D., Levy, A., & Mendelzon, A. (1998, September). Database techniques for the World Wide Web: A survey. *In Proceeedings of ACM Sigmod International Conference on Management of Data,* 27(3).

Garcia-Molina, H., Papakonstantinou, Y., Quass, D., Rajaraman, A., Sagiv, Y., Ullman, J., Vassalos, V., & Widom, J., (1997). The TSIMMIS Approach to Mediation: Data Models and Languages J. *Intelligent Information Systems*, 8(2): 117-132.

Gribble, C. (2003, November). *History of the Web: Beginning at CERN.* [Online]. Available: http://www.hitmill.com/internet/webhistory.asp.

Gruber, T. R. (1993). A translation approach to portable ontology specifications. *Knowledge Aquisition,* 5(1), 199-220.

Henning, M., & Vinoski, S. (1999). *Advanced CORBA programming with C++.* Addison-Wesley Publishing Corporation.

IBM. (2005, September). *Informix Tools.* [Online]. Available: http://www-306.ibm.com/software/data/informix/.

IBM. (2005, September). *UniSQL database solutions.* [Online]. Available:http://www.unisql.com.

IBM. (2005, September). *WebSphere.* [Online]. Available:http://www-306.ibm.com/software/websphere.

Kashyap, V. (1998). *Information brokering over heterogeneous digital data: A metadata-based approach,* The State University of New Jersey, New Brunswick, NJ, USA.

Katifori, A., Halatsis, C., Lepouras, G., Vassilakis, C., & Giannopoulou, E. (2007). Ontology visualization methods—a survey. *ACM Comput. Surv.* 39, 4, November.

Kuck, J., & Gnasa, M., (2007). Context-Sensitive Service Discovery Meets Information Retrieval, *Fifth Annual IEEE International Conference on Pervasive Computing and Communications Workshops, 2007. PerCom Workshops '07.*, 601-605, 19-23 March.

Lazcano, A., Alonso, G., Schuldt, H., & Schuler, C. (2000, September). The WISE approach to electronic commerce. *Journal of Computer Systems Science and Engineering*, 15(5), 343-355.

Liang, S. (1999). *Java(TM) Native Interface: Programmer's Guide and Specification*. Addison-Wesley Pub Co.

Loney, K., & Koch, G. (2002). *Oracle9i: The complete reference*. Oracle Press.

Lozano-Tello, A. & Gomez-Perez, A. (2004). ONTOMETRIC: A method to choose the appropriate ontology. *Journal of Database Management*, 15(2), 1-18.

McLeod, D. (1990, December). Report on the workshop on heterogeneous database systems. *SIGMOD record*, 19(4), 23-31.

Medjahed, B., & Bouguettaya, A. (2005). A Multilevel Composability Model for Semantic Web Services. *IEEE Transactions on Knowledge and Data Engineering* (TKDE), 17(7), July.

Mena, E., Kashyap, V., Illarramendi, A., & Sheth, A. (1998, June). Domain specific ontologies for semantic information brokering on the global information infrastructure. *Proceedings of the international conference on formal ontologies in information systems (FOIS'98)*. Trento, Italy.

Microsoft. (2005, September). *.NET.* [Online]. Available: http://www.microsoft.com/net.

Park, J., & Ram, S. (2004). Information systems interoperability: What lies beneath? *ACM Transactions on Information Systems*, 22(4), 595-632.

Peltz, C. (2003, January). *Web services orchestration*. Technical Report, Hewlett Packard.

Petrie, C., & Bussler, C. (2003, July). Service agents and virtual enterprises: A survey. *IEEE Internet Computing,* 7(4).

Pitt, E., & McNiff, K. (2001). *Java(TM) RMI: The remote method invocation guide*. Addison-Wesley Publishing Corporation.

Ran, S. (2003, March). A model for Web services discovery with QOS. *SIGecom Exchanges*, 4(1).

Roman, E., Ambler, S. W., & Jewell, T. (2003). *Mastering enterprise JavaBeans*. John Wiley & Sons.

Schuster, H., Georgakopoulos, D., Cichocki, A., & Baker, D. (2000, June). Modeling and composing service-based and reference process-based multienterprise processes. *CAISE conference*. 247-263, Stockholm, Sweden.

Software, P. (2005, September). *Progress Software: ObjectStore*. [Online]. Available: http://www.objectstore.net/index.ssp.

Su, J. (2005). Web service interactions: analysis and design. *The Fifth International Conference on Computer and Information Technology, CIT 2005*. 21-23 September.

Sugumaran, V. & Storey, V. C. (2006). The role of domain ontologies in database design: An ontology management and conceptual modeling environment. *ACM Trans. Database Syst.* 31, 3, September.

Sycara, K., Klush, M., & Widoff, S., (1999). Dynamic Service Matchmaking among Agents in Open Information Environments, *ACM SIGMOD Record*, 28(1): 47-53, March.

Tsur, S., Abiteboul, S., Agrawal, R., Dayal, U., Klein, J., & Weikum, G. (2001). Are Web services the next revolution in e-commerce? (panel). *Conference on VLDB*. Rome, Italy.

Vaughan-Nichols, S. J. (2002, February). Web Services: beyond the hype. *IEEE Computer,* 35 (2), 18-21

W3C. (2005, September). *Universal Description, Discovery, and Integration (UDDI).* [Online]. Available: http://www.uddi.org

W3C. (2005, September). *Web Services Description Language (WSDL).* [Online]. Available: http://www.w3.org/TR/wsdl

W3C. (2004, February). *Web Services Architecture.*[Online]. Available:http://www.w3.org/TR/ws-arch/.

Wallace, N. (2001). *COM/DCOM blue book: The essential learning guide for component-oriented application development for windows.* The Coriolis Group.

Wang, T.-W. & Murphy, K. (2004). Semantic heterogeneity in multidatabase systems: A review and a proposed meta-data structure. *Journal of Database Management* ,15(2), 71-87.

Woelk, D., Cannata, P., Huhns, M., Shen, W., & Tomlinson, C. (1993, January). Using carnot for enterprise information integration. *Second international conference on parallel and distributed information systems,* 133-136.

Wood, C. (1999). *OLE DB and ODBC Developer's Guide.* John Wiley & Sons.

Worden, D. (2000). *Sybase System 11 Development Handbook.* Morgan Kaufmann.

Wyss, C. M. & Wyss, F. I. (2007). Extending relational query optimization to dynamic schemas for information integration in multidatabases. In *Proceedings of the 2007 ACM SIGMOD international Conference on Management of Data* (Beijing, China, June 11 - 14, 2007). SIGMOD '07. ACM, New York, NY, 473-484.

Yarger, R. J., Reese, G., & King, T. (1999). *MySQL and mSQL.* O'Reilly & Associates.

Yellin, D.M. & Strom, R.E., (1997). Protocol Specifications and Component Adaptors, ACM Trans. *Programming Languages and Systems,* 19(2): 292-233, March.

Zeng, L., Benatallah, B., Ngu, A.H.H., Dumas, M., Kalagnanam, J., & Chang, H. (2004). Qos-aware middleware for web services composition. *IEEE Trans. Softw. Eng.,* 30(5):311-327.

Zikopolous, P. C., Baklarz, G., deRoos, D., & Melnyk, R. B. (2003). *DB2 Version 8: The Official Guide.* IBM Press.

Chapter XIV
Retrieval Optimization for Server-Based Repositories in Location-Based Mobile Commerce

James E. Wyse
Memorial University of Newfoundland, Canada

ABSTRACT

Location-based mobile commerce (LBMC) incorporates location-aware technologies, wire-free connectivity, and server-based repositories of business locations to support the processing of location-referent transactions (LRTs) between businesses and mobile consumers. LRTs are transactions in which the location of a business in relation to a consumer's actual or anticipated location is a material transactional factor. Providing adequate support for LRTs requires the timely resolution of queries bearing transaction-related locational criteria. The research reported here evaluates and extends the author's location-aware method (LAM) of resolving LRT-related queries. The results obtained reveal LAM's query resolution behavior in a variety of simulated LBMC circumstances and confirm the method's potential to improve the timeliness of transactional support to mobile consumers. The article also identifies and evaluates a heuristic useful in maintaining optimal query resolution performance as changes occur in the scale and scope of server-based repositories.

INTRODUCTION

Recent years have witnessed the emergence of transaction-supporting devices directed toward the mobile consumer. Devices range from simple handsets in mobile/cellular phone systems to those involving the convergence of palm-top computing, location-determining technologies, and wireless Internet connectivity. To support applications in location-based mobile commerce (LBMC), such devices must incorporate communication capabilities that permit a significant degree of consumer mobility (Leung and Atypas, 2001; Santami, Leow, Lim, and Goh, 2003) and they must be location-aware. Location-awareness refers to the capability of a device to obtain data about geographical position and then use the data to manipulate information with respect to that position (Butz, Bauss, and Kruger, 2000). Yuan and Zhang (2003) suggest that "location awareness [adds an important] new dimension for value creation" in mobile commerce. Figure 1 illustrates an LBMC context in which location-aware client applications operating on mobile, GPS-enabled, handheld computing devices avail of wireless connectivity to access a variety of Internet-based servers providing information and functionality to support the transactional activities of a mobile consumer.

An essential component in large-scale, location-aware, mobility-supporting applications is a specialized database (repository) of transaction-supporting information (note Figure 1's Locations Repository). Repository content supports the resolution of queries associated with location-referent transactions (LRTs). LRTs are transactions in which the location of a business in relation to a consumer's actual or anticipated location is a material transactional factor. Siau, Lim and Shen (2001) and later Siau and Shen (2003) call for research on improving the processing of transactional queries in circumstances "where users are constantly on the move and few [end user device] computing resources are available" (p. 13). The research reported here responds to this call: it is concerned with the timely process-

Figure 1. Location-based mobile commerce – Configuration of components

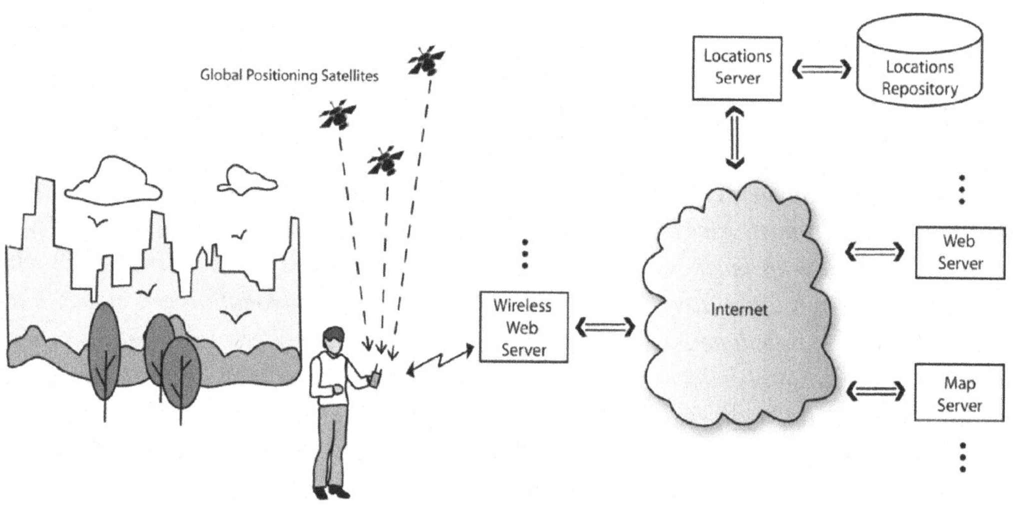

Source: Wyse (2007). © 2007 IEEE, reproduced with permission

ing of queries initiated by location-variant (on the move) consumers operating resource-limited devices that rely on centralized repositories of location-qualified information.

LBMC's emergence has spawned streams of research in areas related to the components shown in Figure 1: mobile consumer location determination (McGuire, Plataniotis, and Venetsanopoulos, 2005; Quintero, 2005; Samaan and Karmouch, 2005), mobile device interface design (Lee and Benbasat, 2004), mobile business application design (Gebauer and Shaw, 2004; Khunger and Riekki, 2005), and mobility-related wireless connectivity (Chao, Tseng, and Wang, 2005; Chou and Shin, 2005, Lin, Juang, and Lin, 2005; Xu, Shen, and Mark, 2005; Yeung and Kwok, 2005; Cinque, Cotroneo, and Russo, 2005). LBMC-related research has also addressed the issue of query resolution in mobile computing environments: Kottkamp and Zukunft (1998) developed and evaluated a mobility aware cost model for location-aware query optimization in the context of mobile user location management; Choy, Kwan, and Hong (2000) proposed a distributed database system architecture to support query processing in mobile geographical applications; Lee and Ke (2001) conducted a cost analysis of strategies for query processing in a mobile commerce environment; Lee, Xu, Zheng, and Lee (2002) and Huang, Lin, and Deng (2005) addressed the validity of query results and the efficiency of query processing through improved mobile device cache management; while Wyse (2003) proposed a location-aware method of repository management to support the processing of LBMC-related transactions. It is last area that is addressed here; this article evaluates and extends the location-aware approach to resolving an important class of LRT-related queries that often arise in the provision of location-based services to mobile consumers.

A synopsis of LAM is provided in Appendix A. The method employs the *linkcell* construct as a means of transforming co-ordinates in geographical space to spatially-oriented table names in relational space. A specialized search method operates on the relational tables to resolve location-referent queries. Results from previous work (Wyse, 2003) suggest that the method significantly improves query resolution performance over that realized from the use of conventional enumerative methods. However, the method's performance was evaluated in limited circumstances (small repository sizes, fixed geographical coverage, minimal business categorization) and the effect on resolution performance of variations in the linkcell's *size* parameter remains unexamined. Wyse (2003) contemplates the existence of a linkcell size that would optimize query resolution performance but offers no approach that would result in its determination.

These contemplations and limitations give rise to four questions to be addressed by the research reported here: (1) Will the method yield resolution performance profiles consistent with those previously observed when greater repository sizes, larger variations in geographical coverage, and richer business categorizations are used? (2) How is linkcell size related to query resolution performance? (3) Is there a specific linkcell size that will optimize query resolution performance? And (4) how might an optimal linkcell size be determined? Before providing results that address these questions some discussion is warranted on the nature of the problem for which LAM is proposed as a solution.

THE REPOSITORY MANAGEMENT PROBLEM

Mobile consumers frequently require information presented in some consumer-centric proximity pattern on the locations of businesses offering products and services in a specified business category. Figure 2 shows a consumer-centric proximity portal constructed by a prototypical mobile client application typifying that used by the mobile consumer in Figure 1. Proximity portals may be provided in response to questions such as *Where is the nearest health food outlet? How far away am I from a golf course? Where am I situated in relation to a medical facility?* Note that the queries arising from such questions must incorporate both a category criterion (e.g., *medical facility*) and a proximity criterion (e.g., *nearest*).

Two distinctions between category criteria and proximity criteria have implications for the management of locational repositories. Firstly, category criteria are invariant with respect to a mobile consumer's location while proximity criteria are not. Nievergelt and Widmayer (1997) recognize the distinction between the two types of criterion and point out its implication for the efficient management of locationalized repositories: "Spatial data differs from all other types of data in important respects. Objects are embedded in ... Euclidean space ... and most queries involve proximity rather than intrinsic properties of the objects to be retrieved. Thus, data structures developed for conventional database systems are unlikely to be efficient"(p. 186). The issue of efficiency is readily seen in the second distinction: category attribute values are patently resident in a repository while proximity attribute values must be derived from the locational attributes of both the consumer and the business offering a consumer-targeted product or service category. Thus, each change in a consumer's geographical position will in general necessitate a redetermination of the values for a business's proximity attribute.

Figure 2. Consumer-centric proximity portal generated by the i-DAR prototype

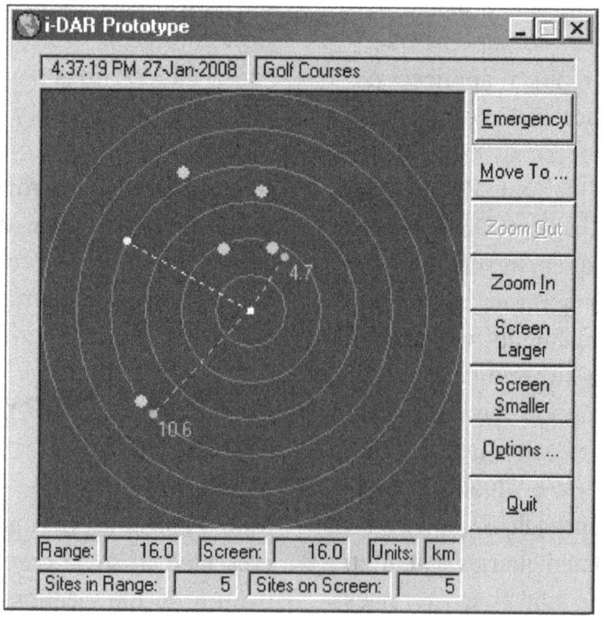

The i-DAR Prototype is a location-aware mobile client application developed by the author to generate consumer-centric proximity portals. The dots appearing on i-DAR's screen represent the geo-positions of businesses in the consumer's proximity. The dots are also hyperlinks to the websites for each location.

The requirement to continually requery a repository and redetermine a consumer-centric proximity pattern places an extensive burden on server-side repository functionality. For a given level of computational capability, continual re-querying and redetermination eventually results in service time degradation as repository sizes increase and/or as the number of consumers increase and/or as consumers more frequently change location. For many location-based services such as those involving publicized business directories, increased repository size (i.e., a richer set of locations from which the mobile consumer may obtain information) would likely attract greater numbers of mobile consumers. In turn, greater numbers of consumers would likely motivate the construction of larger, more richly populated repositories which would then attract even more consumers (Lee, Zhu, and Hu, 2005). Thus, a cycle is created wherein repository sizes will increase and, in the absence of mitigating investments in computational capability, result in degradation of the service times experienced by consumers accessing the repository. Thus, an important challenge facing those who are tasked with managing large-scale locational repositories is one of minimizing the increase (i.e., degradation) in the service times realized by mobile consumers while at same time enriching (i.e., enlarging) the repository available to mobile consumers.

SOLUTION APPROACHES

The nature of queries initiated by mobile consumers (e.g., *Where's the nearest health food outlet?*) suggests that the problem of query resolution is conceptually similar to the nearest neighbor (NN) problem. Formally, NN solutions incorporate constructs and procedures that, when faced with a set P of n points and a query point q, result in $p \in P$ such that for all $p' \in P$ we have $d(p, q) \leq d(p', q)$ where $d(p', q)$ is the distance between p' and q (Cary, 2001). Several works have developed NN solution methods: Arnon, Efrat, Indyk, and Samet (1999), Lee (1999) and Cary (2001) propose solutions from computational geometry while Kuznetsov (2000) proposes a solution based on the space filling curves developed by Sierpinski (1912) and Hilbert (Butz, 1969; Butz, 1971). Gaede and Gunther's (1998) review of point access methods and Chavez et al.'s (2001) examination of proximity searches represent comprehensive surveys of the methods and techniques whose development has been motivated by the inadequacy of conventional methods of resolving proximity queries. The various methods yield solution times that improve upon those realized from naïve enumerative methods; however, solution times are positively related to n, the number of points in the set P, an outcome that is not favorable to mitigating the retrieval time degradation that can be expected with an expanding large-scale repository of locations.

A mapping of the terms of the NN problem to aspects of the problem of managing a repository of locations gives n as the repository size, P as the repository, q as the mobile consumer's location, p as the nearest location in P, and $d(p', q)$ as the proximity attribute needed to resolve the consumer's query. This mapping recognizes the dependency of the proximity attribute on both the consumer's location (q) and the locational attributes contained in the repository for each location, p'. Furthermore, the condition that $d(p, q) \leq d(p', q)$, for all $p' \in P$, implies that new proximity attribute values are required whenever there is any change in the consumer's location (q). This condition in combination with solution times that are positively related to repository size (n) corroborate the assessment that service times associated with mobile consumer access to locational repositories will degrade as repository size is increased.

An important aspect of mitigating service time degradation is the use of a retrieval method not requiring a determination of $d(p', q)$, for all $p' \in P$. In other words, new proximity attribute values should be calculated for as few of the locations in the repository as possible whenever the mobile consumer changes location. The solution methods referenced above take such an approach; however, these methods have solution times that increase, albeit in varying ways, as n increases. The location-aware method examined here also does not require a determination of $d(p', q)$, for all $p' \in P$. As shown by the results in Figure 3, the method avoids this determination to such an extent that it appears capable of producing resultset completion times (RCTs)[1] that are, for practical purposes, invariant with respect to repository size. In contrast, the dependence of the Enumerative Method[2] on the determination of $d(p', q)$, for all $p' \in P$ renders it an unacceptable means of accommodating an expanding large-scale repository.

Although LAM's solution goal is essentially the same as that for other NN solution methods, it does not draw upon that the constructs and procedures of any of these methods. Instead, as seen in Appendix A, LAM relies on the relational approach to data management and the structure of the latitude/longitude convention for designating geographical position to achieve its solution goals. Previous work demonstrated LAM's effectiveness in producing valid NN solutions. In what follows, the method is evaluated in circumstances that extend beyond those of previous work both in scale (much larger repository sizes) and scope (variability of geographical areas and richness of business categorization).

OPTIMAL LINKCELL SIZE DETERMINATION: METHODS AND MEASURES

Appendix A discusses the formulation of the linkcell construct and defines linkcell size. The Appendix also notes that changes in linkcell size result in redistributions of repository locations amongst linkcells, and that these redistributions have a substantial impact on query resolution performance. Wyse's (2003) work used a single

Figure 3. Resultset completion times for enumerative and location-aware methods by repository size

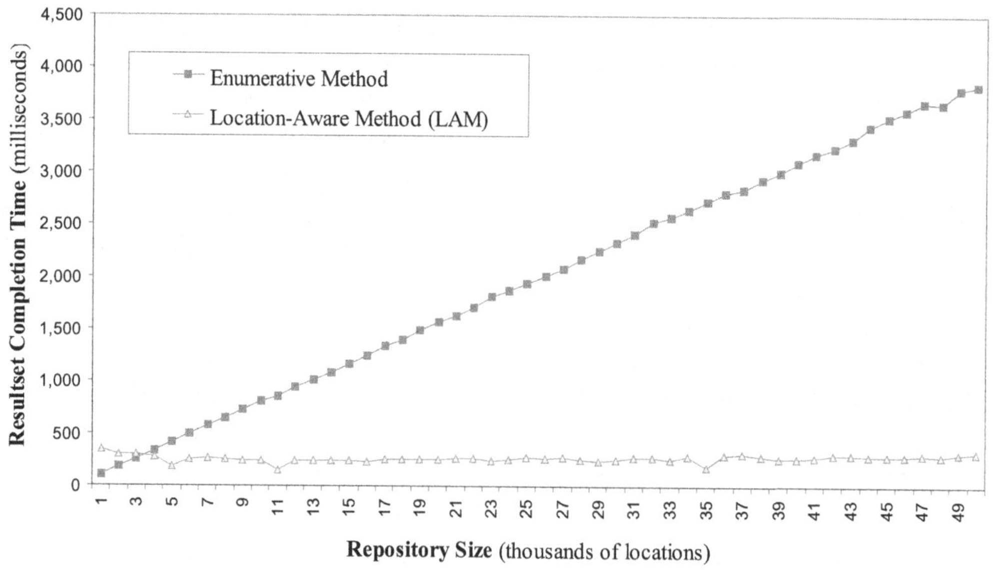

Source: Wyse (2003), p. 135. © Inderscience Publishers, reproduced with permission.

Figure 4. LAM resultset completion times (RCT_L) by Linkcell Size (Repository: 100,000 locations, 100 product-service categories, area N30° to N50° and W070° to W130°)

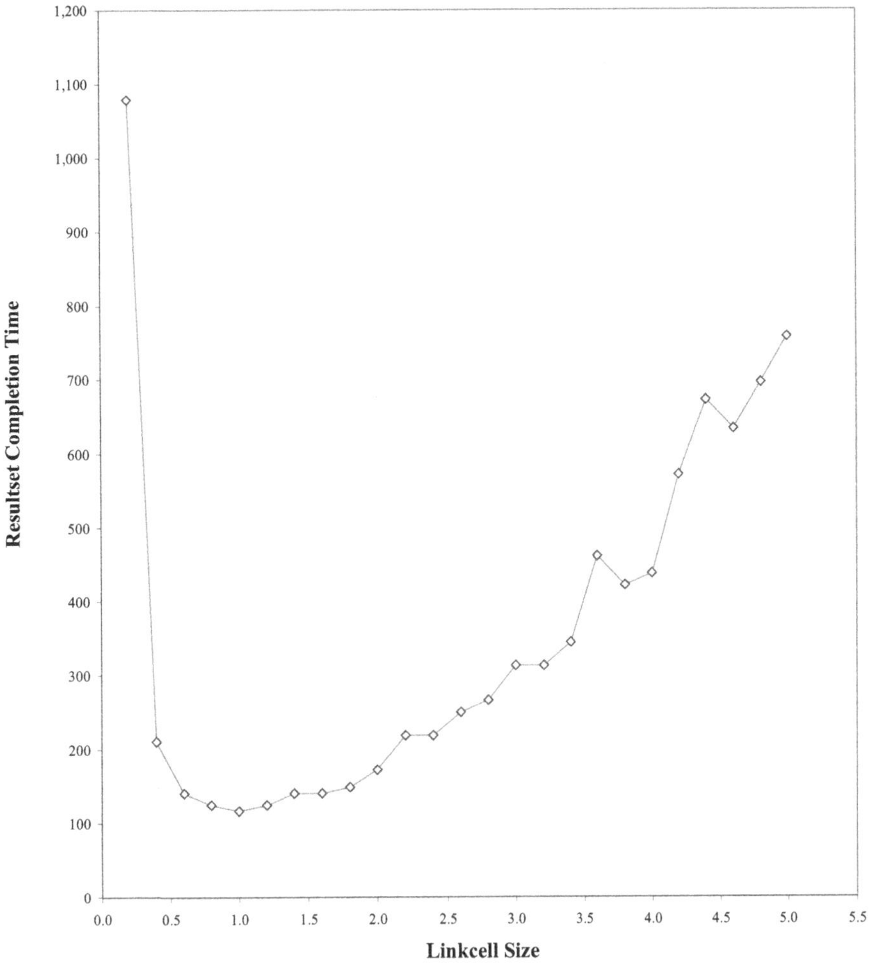

linkcell size (1.0) for all of the various analyses that were conducted; and, beyond noting that other linkcell sizes could be used, the work provides little guidance on optimal linkcell size determination. In preliminary work here, a brute force search method was imposed on a series of simulated repository scenarios as a means of identifying an optimal linkcell size. Figures 4 and 5 show results from two of the many scenarios on which a brute force search was carried out. All scenarios revealed what appeared to be an optimal linkcell size; however, the optimal value was generally not the same across the scenarios. Note that an optimal linkcell size of 1.0 was revealed for the scenario in Figure 4 while an optimal linkcell size of 0.8 was revealed for that in Figure 5. Figure 5 also illustrates that a poorly chosen linkcell size (for example, 5.0) could result not just in RCTs that are far removed from optimal values but also in the complete loss of any performance advantage attributable to LAM.

The methodology used to generate the RCT curves in Figures 4 and 5 is similar to the simulation-based approach used in Wyse's (2003) evaluative work on the location-aware method. Software called the Linkcell Performance Analyzer (LPA) was developed which (1) generates repositories with a specified number of locations

Figure 5. Resultset completion times for location-aware and enumerative methods by linkcell size (Repository: 100,000 locations, 200 business categories, area N35° to N45° and W080° to W110°)

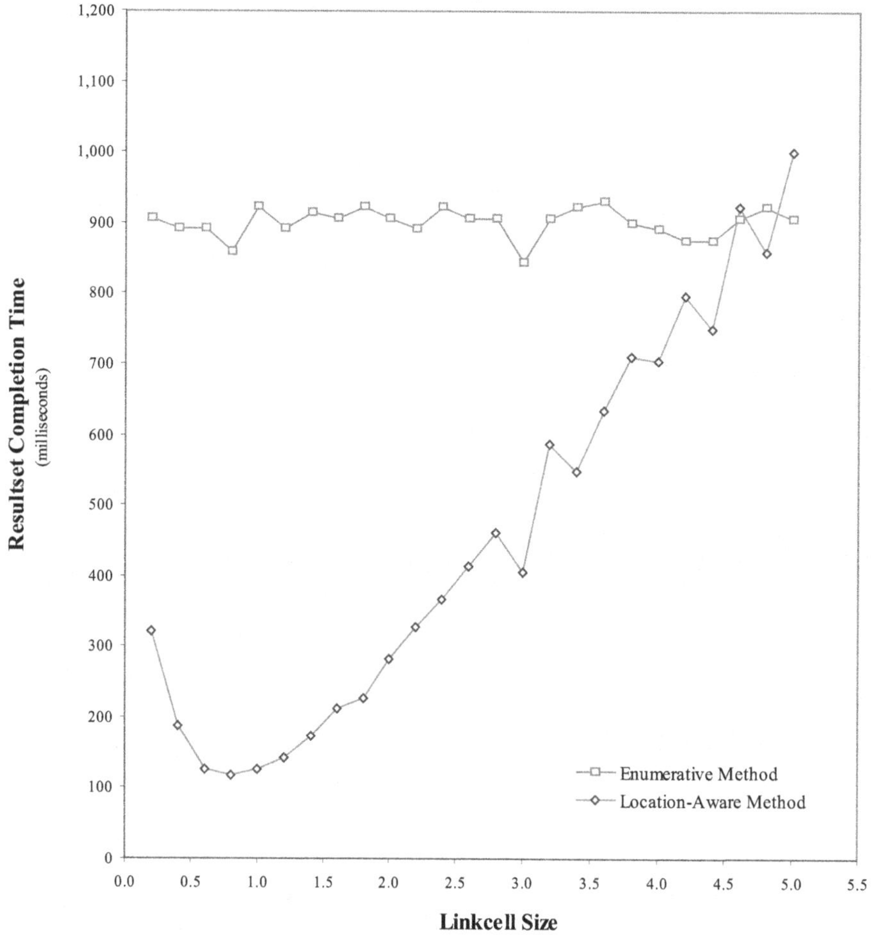

distributed over a specified geographical areas and qualified with respect to a specified set of business categories; (2) creates linkcells from repository locations based on a specified linkcell size; (3) assembles and processes simulated queries bearing randomly assigned category criteria for randomly located consumers; (4) resolves the location-referent queries using both enumerative (E) and location-aware (L) methods; and, (5) determines resultset completion times (RCT_E and RCT_L) for each method. Table 1 provides LPA-generated results associated with the RCT_L values plotted in Figure 4. The first column shows the series of linkcell sizes (from 0.2 to 5.0) for the plot's horizontal axis. Columns 6 through 10 report RCT_L statistics derived from simulated queries originating from 100 randomly chosen consumer locations. All five statistics reveal their lowest resultset completion time values at a linkcell size of 1.0, a result reflected in the plot of RCT_L's 50th percentile values shown in Figure 4.[3]

The results shown in Columns 2, 3, and 4 of Table 1 help to explain why an optimal linkcell size can be expected to exist. Column 2 indicates the maximum number of linkcells that may be created for each linkcell size, a quantity that varies from 30,000 linkcells for a linkcell size of 0.2 down to 48 linkcells for a linkcell size of 5.0. The numbers in Column 2 are the result of allocating the linkcell size along the horizontal and vertical extents that encompass a repository's locations. For a linkcell size of 0.2, these extents potentially result in 30,000 relational tables (linkcells), a number that is the product of 300 linkcell-sized intervals along the repository's horizontal extent (W070° to W130°) and 100 intervals along its vertical extent (N30° to N50°).[4] Not all of the maximum number of relational tables may actually be created. Appendix A's discussion on linkcell creation notes that a relational table corresponding to a linkcell only comes into existence when its name is derived from a location in the repository. Thus, the number of linkcells actually generated from a repository's locations may be less than the maximum potential number of linkcells. Such an outcome is seen in Column 3 where, for a linkcell size of 0.2, only 28,923 of the 30,000 possible linkcells were actually created.

Column 4 reports the mean number of linkcell entries for each linkcell size and is obtained by dividing the total number of repository locations (100,000 in this case) by the number of linkcells

Table 1. Selected repository scenario (100,000 locations, 100 product-service categories, area N30° to N50° and W070° to W130°)

(1) Selected Linkcell Size	(2) Maximum Number of Linkcells	(3) Linkcells Actually Generated	(4) Mean Linkcell Entries	(5) Probability of Linkcell with Targeted Category	RCT_L					(11) Compacted Disk Space (MB)	(12) Repository x-Linkcells Multiple
					(6) Mean	(7) Min	(8) Max	(9) 50th	(10) 90th		
0.2	30,000	28,923	3.5	0.03	1,580	63	8,094	1,079	3,453	358.0	46.6
0.4	7,500	7,500	13.3	0.13	268	16	984	211	516	98.7	12.9
0.6	3,434	3,434	29.1	0.25	182	16	1,047	141	344	49.5	6.4
0.8	1,976	1,976	50.6	0.40	176	16	969	125	328	31.7	4.1
1.0	1,200	1,200	83.3	0.57	144	16	391	117	281	22.4	2.9
1.2	867	867	115.3	0.69	185	16	922	125	373	18.4	2.4
1.4	645	645	155.0	0.79	164	31	531	141	313	17.6	2.3
1.6	546	546	183.2	0.84	165	16	496	141	313	16.2	2.1
1.8	420	420	238.1	0.91	167	16	750	149	281	14.6	1.9
2.0	300	300	333.3	0.96	202	31	969	172	391	13.7	1.8
2.2	290	290	344.8	0.97	231	31	875	219	406	13.4	1.7
2.4	234	234	427.4	0.99	236	31	906	219	422	12.9	1.7
2.6	216	216	463.0	0.99	267	31	656	250	453	12.6	1.6
2.8	176	176	568.2	1.00	296	31	750	266	547	12.2	1.6
3.0	147	147	680.3	1.00	331	31	1,172	313	641	12.1	1.6
3.2	140	140	714.3	1.00	337	31	734	313	594	12.0	1.6
3.4	133	133	751.9	1.00	367	31	1,328	344	578	11.9	1.5
3.6	108	108	925.9	1.00	461	63	1,500	461	797	11.6	1.5
3.8	119	119	840.3	1.00	476	78	1,375	422	895	11.7	1.5
4.0	96	96	1,041.7	1.00	473	31	1,984	438	813	11.5	1.5
4.2	75	75	1,333.3	1.00	585	47	1,703	571	100	11.3	1.5
4.4	90	90	1,111.1	1.00	653	47	2,000	672	1,156	11.5	1.5
4.6	70	70	1,428.6	1.00	696	109	2,500	633	1,156	11.3	1.5
4.8	70	70	1,428.6	1.00	751	78	2,281	696	1,281	11.3	1.5
5.0	48	48	2,083.3	1.00	758	141	1,859	758	1,344	11.0	1.4

(Column 3) created from those locations. Note that small linkcell sizes result in the generation of large numbers of small relational tables while large linkcell sizes result in the generation of small numbers of large relational tables. Consequently, as linkcells initially increase in size, query resolution times will improve because fewer relational tables have to be examined in order to find a location in the targeted category; however, with each increase in size, query resolution times will also degrade because more relational table entries have to be examined in order to find a targeted location. The optimal linkcell size corresponds to the size at which the RCT gains from processing fewer linkcells begin to be overwhelmed by the RCT losses incurred from processing linkcells with greater numbers of linkcell entries. The RCT statistics in Columns 6 through 10 indicate that such gains and losses combine to reveal an optimal linkcell size of 1.0.

The generation of linkcells increases the size of a database containing a repository. Column 11 shows the disk space consumed by the repository for each linkcell size. A size of 0.2 results in the generation of 28,923 linkcells and requires disk storage of approximately 358 MB, an amount of storage almost 47x the 7.7 MB storage amount consumed by the repository without linkcells (referred to as "Repository x-Linkcells" in Column 12). At the other end of the linkcell range, a size of 5.0 results in the generation of 48 linkcells and requires 11.0 MB of storage, or 1.4x as much storage as the repository x-linkcells. At the observed optimum of 1.0, the repository requires 2.9x as much storage. In general, disk storage consumption varied across the scenarios investigated. With respect to the results shown in Figure 5, the optimum requires 2.0x as much storage as repository x-linkcells. Thus, service level performance gains from using LAM come at a repository space cost that may be several multiples of that required when using the enumerative method.

The fifth column of Table 1 reports the probability $P_{TC}(S)$ that a linkcell of size S contains an entry for a location in the category targeted by the mobile consumer. As will be explained below, values for $P_{TC}(S)$ were generated in order to identify optimal linkcell sizes in a more computationally efficient and managerially useable way than brute force identification methods. Formally, the probability that a linkcell contains a location in the targeted category, TC, is given by:

$$P_{TC}(S) = 1 - \left(1 - n_{TC}/N\right)^{N/C_S} \quad \ldots\ (I)$$

where n_{TC} is the number of locations in the repository with category code, TC,

N is total number of locations contained in the repository,

C_S is the number of linkcells of size, S, created from the repository's N locations, and

N/C_S is the mean number of entries per linkcell.

For example, if a mobile consumer initiates a query about the nearest medical facility which has been assigned, for instance, a category code of *C016* then the targeted category TC is *C016*. Referring to Table 1 for a linkcell size of 0.2, we see that $P_{C016}(0.2)$ is 0.03, a value determined from Equation (I).

Equation (I) was formulated as follows:

1. The manner in which linkcells are created, populated, and destroyed (see Appendix A) results in one and only one linkcell entry for each repository location. Thus, the probability that any linkcell entry bears the targeted category code is the ratio of the number of locations in the repository in the targeted category to the total number of locations in the repository in all categories, or n_{TC}/N.
2. Each location is qualified by one and only one category code. Thus, each linkcell en-

try either bears the targeted code or it does not. Consequently, if the probability that a linkcell entry bears TC is n_{TC}/N, then the probability that a linkcell entry does not bear TC is $(1 - n_{TC}/N)$.

3. The probability that none of a linkcell's entries bears the targeted code is given by the product of the probabilities that each linkcell entry does not bear the targeted code, or $(1 - n_{TC}/N)$ x $(1 - n_{TC}/N)$ x .... x $(1 - n_{TC}/N)$, which may be estimated by $(1 - n_{TC}/N)^{N/CS}$.
4. Hence, the probability that at least one of the linkcell entries bears the targeted code is $(1 - (1 - n_{TC}/N)^{N/CS})$, which is the right hand side of Equation (I).

An important assumption underlining Equation (I) is the independence of the probabilities of occurrence of repository entries in the same business category with respect to a given geographical area. Since the repositories used here are generated based on a uniform distribution of locations, the assumption of independent probabilities in this respect is reasonably sound. However, this assumed distribution of locations may not be reflective of the locational behaviour of individual firms in many industrial settings (e.g., fast-food businesses often locate next to other fast-food businesses).

An examination of various repository scenarios indicated the potential usefulness of Equation (I) in identifying optimal linkcell sizes. Instead of starting the search for an optimal linkcell size at some arbitrary point, the search was started at the linkcell size S that results in a value of $P_{TC}(S)$ that is close to 0.5.[5] If we let $S_{0.5}$ denote a linkcell size such that $P_{TC}(S_{0.5}) \cong 0.5$, then for smaller linkcell sizes ($S < S_{0.5}$), a linkcell examined during a LAM search probably does not contain a location in the consumer-targeted category; however, for larger linkcell sizes ($S > S_{0.5}$) an examined linkcell probably does contain a consumer-targeted location. Thus, somewhere in the vicinity of $S_{0.5}$ it starts to become likely that a linkcell contains a consumer-targeted location. Consequently, searches for RCT minima that begin at $S_{0.5}$ are likely to more quickly identify an optimal linkcell size than would a brute force search initiated at an arbitrary linkcell size.

An analysis of selected repository scenarios suggested that searches initiated at a linkcell size of $S_{0.5}$ were effective in quickly identifying optimal linkcell sizes. In the case of the repository scenario associated with Figure 4, Equation (I) yields $S_{0.5} \cong 0.9$ as the starting linkcell size. Recall that the optimal size previously revealed by brute force is 1.0. With respect to repository scenario associated with Figure 5, Equation (I) yields $S_{0.5} \cong 0.7$, a size close to the 0.8 revealed by brute force. Application of Equation (I) in the context of these two and various other repository scenarios indicated its usefulness in improving the efficiency of optimal linkcell size identification. However, the repository scenarios were arbitrarily chosen and the results of their analysis provide only a rough indication of both the existence of linkcell size optima as well as Equation (I)'s managerial usefulness in their identification.

In the following sections, more comprehensive and rigorous assessments of the existence of linkcell optima are reported with respect to variations in (1) repository size, (2) geographical coverage, and (3) business location categorization. A simulation-based methodology was used wherein RCT curves like those seen in Figures 4 and 5 were constructed.

LINKCELL SIZE OPTIMA AND REPOSITORY SIZE VARIABILITY

Figure 6 plots resultset completion times (RCTs) for repositories ranging in size from 20,000 to 500,000 locations. Each point is the 50th percentile of RCTs for 200 queries issued by mobile consumers from randomly selected geographical locations. Table 2 presents linkcell sizes, P_{TC}

Figure 6. Resultset completion times by repository size

(a) RCT_E, "Unmanaged" RCT_L, and "Managed" RCT_L

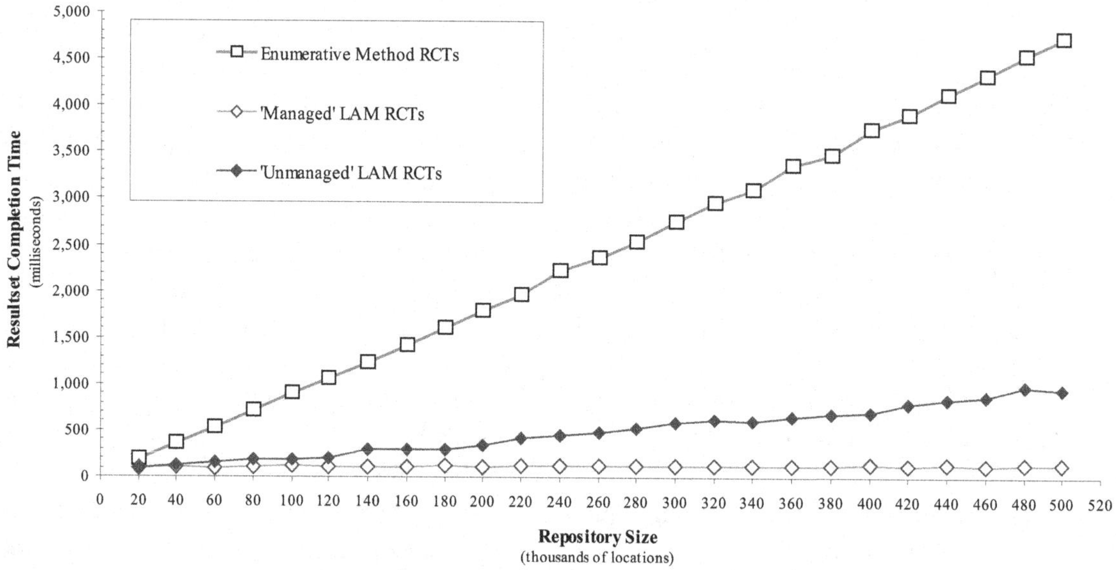

(b) RCT_E and RCT_L at Mean $P_{TC}(S_{OPT})$

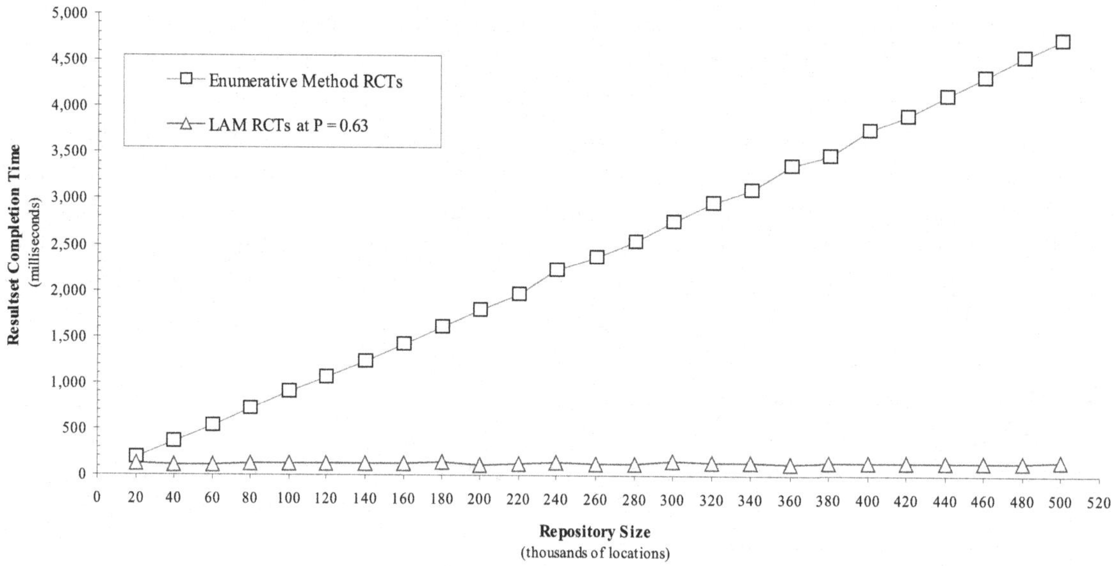

Table 2: Linkcell sizes and resultset completion times by repository size (200 product-service categories, area N30° to N50° and W070° to W130°)

(1) Repository Size (Locations)	(2) $S_{0.5}$ Linkcell Size	(3) Observed S_{OPT} Linkcell Size	(4) $P_{TC}(S_{OPT})$ Prob. linkcell has Targeted Category	(5) RCT_E 50th Percentile	(6) RCT_L 50th Percentile	(7) Linkcell Size at $P_{TC}(S_{OPT})$'s Mean Value	(8) RCT_L for Mean $P_{TC}(S_{OPT})$ Linkcell Size
20,000	3.1	3.3	0.53	187	94	3.9	125
40,000	2.2	2.5	0.65	358	109	2.5	109
60,000	1.7	2.4	0.72	531	94	2.0	109
80,000	1.5	1.4	0.46	723	109	1.9	125
100,000	1.3	1.4	0.54	897	117	1.7	125
120,000	1.3	1.7	0.72	1057	109	1.5	125
140,000	1.1	1.2	0.55	1232	109	1.3	125
160,000	1.1	1.4	0.71	1420	109	1.3	125
180,000	1.0	1.3	0.70	1605	117	1.2	141
200,000	0.9	1.1	0.61	1788	109	1.1	109
220,000	0.9	1.0	0.60	1970	125	1.1	125
240,000	0.9	0.9	0.54	2234	125	1.0	141
260,000	0.8	1.0	0.66	2365	125	1.0	125
280,000	0.8	0.9	0.59	2537	125	0.9	125
300,000	0.8	1.1	0.76	2760	125	0.9	156
320,000	0.7	1.0	0.74	2954	125	0.9	141
340,000	0.7	0.8	0.58	3107	125	0.9	141
360,000	0.7	0.8	0.60	3366	125	0.8	125
380,000	0.7	0.9	0.70	3469	125	0.8	141
400,000	0.7	0.7	0.54	3747	141	0.8	141
420,000	0.6	1.0	0.83	3917	125	0.8	141
440,000	0.6	0.6	0.47	4132	141	0.8	141
460,000	0.6	0.8	0.69	4337	125	0.7	141
480,000	0.6	0.6	0.50	4543	141	0.7	141
500,000	0.6	0.9	0.80	4741	141	0.7	156

values, and RCTs for the repositories associated with Figure 6. The geographical coverage area and the number of category codes remained fixed for all repository sizes. Three RCT curves are shown in Figure 6(a): (1) the RCT_E values plotted in topmost curve (and shown in Column 5 of Table 2) are the result of using enumerative query resolution; (2) the RCT_L values plotted in the bottom curve (and shown in Column 6) are the result of using LAM query resolution and doing so at each repository's observed optimal linkcell size (seen in Column 3); and, (3) the RCT_L values plotted in the middle curve are the result of using LAM query resolution but here the linkcell size is the same for all repository sizes and was set to the observed optimal linkcell size (3.3) for a repository size of 20,000.

The middle curve in Figure 6 reflects a circumstance in which linkcell size is set to its optimal value with respect to some initial repository size and then remains unchanged (unmanaged) as repository growth occurred. The curve indicates that an unmanaged linkcell size results in query resolution time deterioration as a repository grows in size. As seen from the point on the curve for a 500,000-location repository, RCT_L eventually reaches 953ms when linkcell size remains unmanaged (i.e., un-optimized), a query resolution time that is almost 7 times the RCT_L of 141ms for a managed (i.e., optimized) linkcell size. This outcome suggests that in order to continually realize optimal query resolution performance, linkcell size must be adjusted as repository size changes.

The observed optimal linkcell size S_{OPT} was identified as the linkcell size corresponding to the minimum observed RCT. The search for S_{OPT} began at a linkcell size of $S_{0.5}$ (determined from Equation (I)) and then expanded above and below $S_{0.5}$ in increments of 0.1 until a RCT minimum was discernable. Table 2 shows $S_{0.5}$ (Column 2) and the observed optimal linkcell size S_{OPT} (Column 3) for each repository size. Of the 25 repository sizes, $S_{0.5}$ is within 0.3 for 22 of them and never exceeds 0.7 for any of them. Furthermore, for 24 of the 25 repository sizes, $S_{OPT} >= S_{0.5}$, a result consistent with the previously noted implication of Equation (I) that when $S > S_{0.5}$ a linkcell probably contains a location in the targeted category. Column 4 shows values for $P_{TC}(S_{OPT})$, the probability that a linkcell contains a consumer-targeted location at the observed optimal linkcell size. These probability figures are consistent with the expectation that optimal linkcell sizes would rarely be observed at a $P_{TC}(S_{OPT})$ value that is substantially below 0.50.

A comparison of the RCT curves in Figure 6(a) indicates that the methodology used to identify S_{OPT} yields linkcells sizes that result in query resolution performance that is not only superior to the enumerative methodology but also substantively independent of repository size. Although these two outcomes are managerially important, the methodology by which they are realized is likely to be regarded as cumbersome and inconvenient by those tasked with repository management. Thus a simpler method was sought that would be more readily applicable in practical circumstances. In the course of the investigation it was observed that the use of linkcell sizes derived from Equation (I) with $P_{TC}(S)$ set to the mean value of $P_{TC}(S_{OPT})$ resulted in RCT values that, for practical purposes, very closely approximate the minimal RCT values associated with optimal linkcell sizes. The mean of the $P_{TC}(S_{OPT})$ values in Column 4 is 0.63. Column 7 shows the linkcell sizes that result from setting Equation (I) = 0.63 and solving for S. Column 8 presents the RCT values that result from using the linkcell sizes in Column 7. The bottom curve in Figure 6(b) is a plot of Column 8's RCT values. A comparison of Columns 8 and 6, or equivalently, a comparison of the bottom curves in Figures 6(a) and (b) reveals minimal differences in query resolution performance across the examined range of repository sizes. The outcomes associated with $P_{TC}(S) = 0.63$ suggest that it is a practical method of identifying performance-optimizing linkcell sizes, and one with considerable potential to simplify the repository manager's task of linkcell size determination. Furthermore, the method is structured to an extent that it may be readily captured in a software module and made available to the repository manager as an item in the database management toolset (as is the case for the LPA software package mentioned above).

Although this method of linkcell size identification is more convenient and considerably less cumbersome than both the brute force method and the $S_{0.5}$ method, its applicability relies heavily on the validity of setting $P_{TC}(S)$ to the mean value of $P_{TC}(S_{OPT})$ as a basis for estimating optimal linkcell sizes. The next two sections provide further assessments of validity in this respect through examinations of circumstances in which (1) geographical area is varied and (2) differing category code sets are used to qualify the repository's locations. Consistent with the methodological approach used above, optimal linkcell sizes are identified in both cases firstly by the method of constructing RCT curves at successive incremental linkcell sizes in the region of $S_{0.5}$ (i.e., the $S_{0.5}$ method) and secondly by the method of determining linkcell sizes with reference to the mean value of $P_{TC}(S_{OPT})$.

LINKCELL SIZE OPTIMA AND GEOGRAPHICAL AREA VARIABILITY

Figure 7 plots resultset completion times for a 100,000-location repository whose geographical coverage varies over 24 areas of increasing size beginning with an area bounded by N35° to N40° and W095° to W105° (or 5° of latitude by 10° of longitude) and ending with an area bounded by N30° to N50° and W070° to W130° (or 20° of latitude by 60° of longitude). For convenience, the areas are shown in Figure 7 as the simple product of their latitudinal and longitudinal extents (50, 100, …., 1200). Note that, in contrast to the results seen in Figure 6, RCT_E values here are essentially invariant with respect to geographical area. (Changes in area affect the range of values over which the coordinates of locations will vary; however, there is no additional computational burden placed on the enumerative method when different coordinate values are assigned to the same repository locations.)

Three curves are shown in Figure 7(a): (1) the topmost curve is the result of using the enumerative method; (2) the bottom curve is the result of using LAM and doing so for each area's observed optimal linkcell size; and, (3) the middle curve is the result of using LAM with the linkcell size unchanged from the optimal linkcell size (0.3) for the smallest area. Here, as before, unmanaged linkcell sizes result in query resolution time degradation. As seen from the point on the RCT curve for the largest area, RCT_L eventually reaches 672ms when linkcell sizes remain unoptimized, a query resolution time that is more than six times the RCT_L of 109ms for an optimized linkcell size.

The results presented in Figure 7(a) indicate that in the observed range of geographical coverage LAM yields superior levels of query resolution. However, the results also indicate that linkcell size must be appropriately adjusted to maintain this performance as the area of coverage changes. This outcome leads once again to a consideration of how the burden associated with determining linkcell size optima may be lightened by using the method of assigning sizes with reference to the mean value of $P_{TC}(S_{OPT})$. For the 24 areas associated with the results shown in Figure 7, the mean $P_{TC}(S_{OPT})$ is 0.58. The bottom curve in Figure 7(b) shows the RCT_L values that result for each of the 24 areas when S is determined by setting Equation (I) = 0.58. The curve suggests that, as was observed for repository size, the application of this method results in linkcell sizes giving query resolution performance that is approximately the same as the performance realized when linkcell sizes are identified by the more cumbersome $S_{0.5}$-method. Thus, the method of assigning linkcell sizes with reference to the mean value of $P_{TC}(S_{OPT})$ appears to be as useful in the context of variations in geographical area as it is for variations in repository size. Next, the method is assessed with respect to variations in the rate of occurrence of a specific category code.

LINKCELL SIZE OPTIMA AND TARGETED CATEGORY OCCURRENCE RATE VARIABILITY

Figure 8 plots RCTs for variations in targeted category occurrence rate (TCOR) for a 100,000-location repository whose locations are distributed over a fixed geographical area (the largest in Figure 7). TCOR refers to the portion of a repository's locations falling into the category targeted by a mobile consumer's query. The results seen previously in Figures 6 and 7 are based on repositories in which the category attribute for each location was randomly assigned from a set of 200 product-service category codes *{C001, C002, …, C200}*. This, in effect, resulted in the rate with which each category occurs across a repository's locations of 1/200 or, equivalently, a TCOR of 0.005. The RCT values in Figure 8 correspond to TCOR rates that vary from 0.0250 to 0.0011. A TCOR

Figure 7. Resultset completion times by geographical area

(a) RCT_E, "Unmanaged" RCT_L, and "Managed" RCT_L

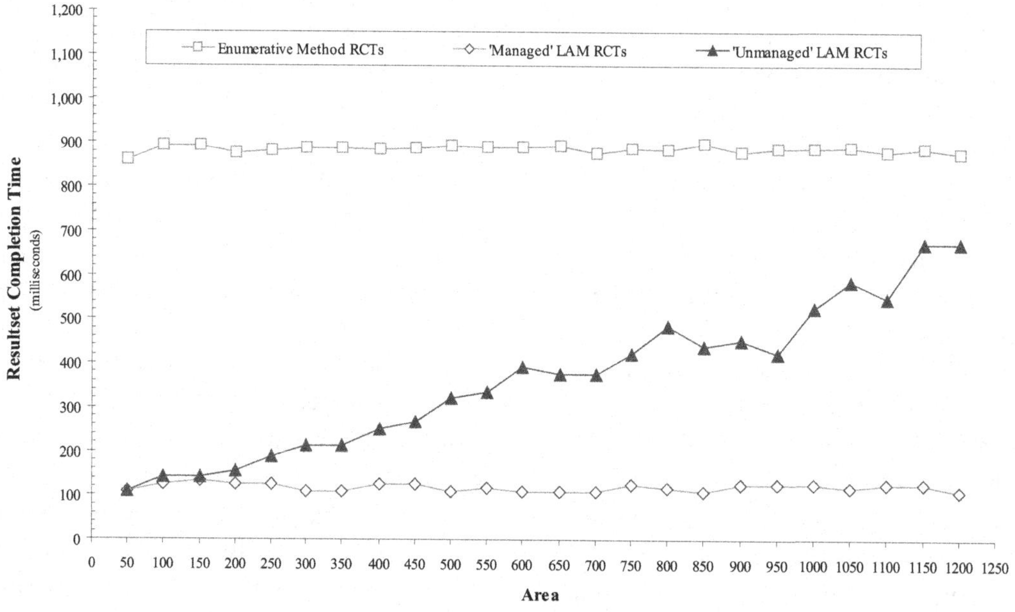

(b) RCT_E and RCT_L at Mean $P_{TC}(S_{OPT})$

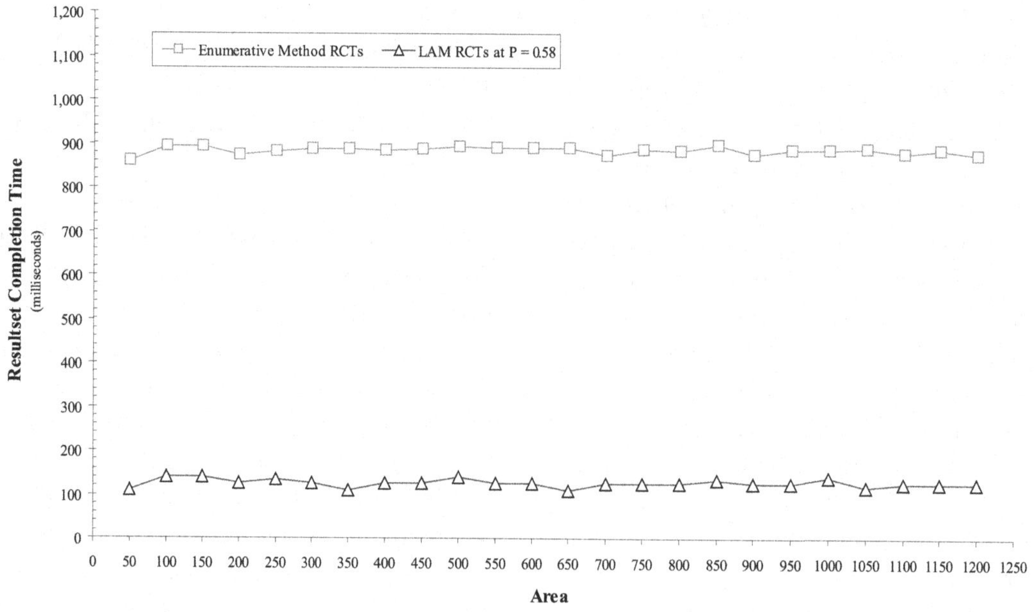

Figure 8. Resultset completion times by targeted category occurrence rate

(a) RCT_E, "Unmanaged" RCT_L, and "Managed" RCT_L

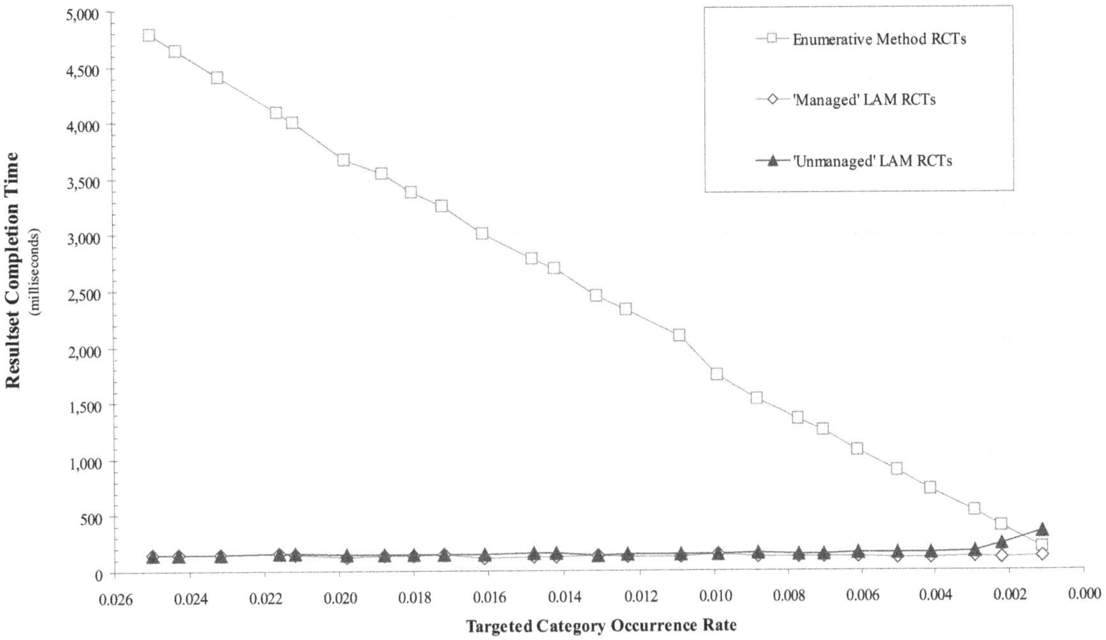

(b) RCT_E and RCT_L at Mean $P_{TC}(S_{OPT})$

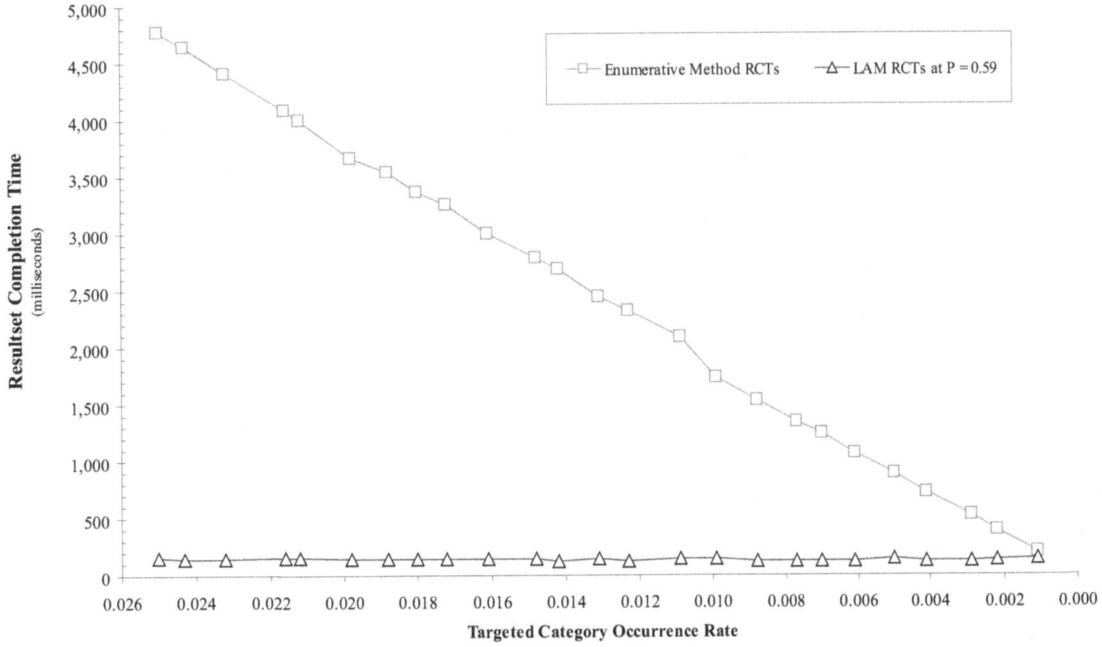

value of 0.250 corresponds to using a set of 40 equally occurring category codes while a TCOR value of 0.0011 corresponds to using a set of 909 equally occurring categories.[6]

Figure 8(a) presents the usual three curves: (1) the topmost curve shows enumerative results, (2) the bottom curve shows optimized LAM results, and (3) the middle curve shows unmanaged LAM results. As before, the third curve reflects a circumstance in which linkcell size is set to an optimal value with respect to some initial TCOR value (0.0250 in this case) and then remains unadjusted (unmanaged) as TCOR changes. It is readily seen that unmanaged linkcell sizes reveal little appreciable effect on query resolution performance except at the smallest TCOR levels. Not until TCOR reaches 0.002 (500 categories) is there a substantive separation of the two curves. The separation attains a managerially significant level in the vicinity of 0.001 (1000 categories) where RCT_L eventually reaches 352 ms, a resolution time that not only exceeds RCT_E but is also 2.5 times the optimized RCT_L value of 141ms.

As with the analyses respecting repository size and geographical area, TCOR-related analysis also considers how the repository manager's burden in identifying optimal linkcell sizes may be lightened by using the method of assigning sizes with reference to the mean value of $P_{TC}(S_{OPT})$. For the 24 TCOR values associated with the results shown in Figure 8, the mean $P_{TC}(S_{OPT})$ is 0.59. The bottom curve in Figure 8(b) shows the RCT_L values that result for each of the 24 TCOR values when S is derived from Equation (I) = 0.59. The curve suggests, as was seen above for repository size and geographical area, that the application of this method produces linkcell sizes resulting in query resolution performance that is approximately the same as the performance realized when linkcell sizes are identified using the $S_{0.5}$-method. Thus, the method of assigning linkcell sizes using the mean value of $P_{TC}(S_{OPT})$ appears to be as valid in the context of TCOR variability as it is in the previous two contexts.

LINKCELL SIZE DETERMINATION IN PRACTICAL OPERATIONAL CIRCUMSTANCES

The results obtained from the mean value approach to estimating optimal linkcell size in all three contexts, along with the observation that the three mean values (0.63, 0.58, and 0.59) are close to their average value of 0.60, suggest that reasonably valid estimates for optimal linkcell sizes may be obtained for practical purposes in a wide range of circumstances on the basis that:

$$P_{TC}(S) = 1 - \left(1 - {n_{TC}}/{N}\right)^{N/C_S} = 0.6 \ldots \quad \text{(II)}$$

The validity of Equation (II)'s use in linkcell size determination was further assessed by revisiting the RCT_L curves with linkcell sizes estimated using Equation (II). Doing so yields query resolution performance profiles that are essentially the same as those shown in Figures 6(b), 7(b), and 8(b). Although the sizes identified using Equation (II) generally differed from those identified by the $S_{0.5}$-method, differences were minimal and the resulting values for S always fell in a range of linkcell sizes associated with a region of minimal RCT values. Regions in this respect may be discerned in Figures 4 and 5. Minimal RCT values are seen in Figure 4 where linkcells vary in size from about 0.8 to 1.2 and in Figure 5 for sizes from about 0.5 to 1.0. These results along with those seen above form the basis for proposing that Equation (II) represents, to this point, a heuristic with considerable potential to assist repository managers in realizing close-to-optimal levels query resolution performance.

FURTHER WORK

Although the major dimensions (repository size, geographical area, and business categorization) associated with repository content are addressed here, there are other operational circumstances where LAM's performance and the methods by which it may be optimized need further assessment. The circumstance where mobile consumers engage in LRTs from locations that are well beyond a repository's geographical boundaries is one where more needs to be known. Preliminary results in this respect suggest that values for $P_{TC}(S) > 0.6$ should be used to identify optimal linkcell sizes. Results also suggest that $P_{TC}(S) \rightarrow 0.6$ as a consumer's location approaches a repository's boundaries. Further work on this circumstance will assess the method's applicability and performance when repositories with highly localized information are used to support the LRTs of remotely located mobile consumers.

The robustness of $P_{TC}(S)$'s application in circumstances that relax the assumption of a uniform distribution of locations requires further examination. Product and service providers of similar type often choose locations in a non-independent, proximal fashion (e.g., law firms in legal districts, fast food services in shopping mall food courts, retail petroleum outlets at highway intersections, etc.). Consequently, pending the outcome of further research in this respect, the use of uniform distributions of locations should be considered an important limitation on the applicability of this study's results.

Finally, work has thus far been primarily concerned with repositories of locations classified using a set of business categories. These multiple category repositories (MCRs) are conceptually similar to business information repositories (e.g., Yellow Pages) wherein a set of categories is used to classify businesses based on their product/service offerings. While such directory-like MCRs are likely to play an important role in *m*-commerce, there are a variety of circumstances in which single category repositories (SCRs) are also likely to find use in supporting the transactional activities of mobile users. SCRs contain locations with no attribute for business category. Examples could include a repository with only cash machines or one consisting exclusively of emergency facilities.

As with MCRs, identifying a performance optimizing linkcell size for SCRs is an important repository management task; however, Equation I provides no assistance here. For any SCR we have $n_{TC} = N$, thus $P_{TC}(S)$ collapses to 1 for all values of S. Although brute force methods could be used, they are as impractical for SCRs as they are for MCRs. Recent research on SCRs has resulted in the development of a tentative formula to assist with linkcell size selection. Here, S is determined with reference to the probability P(S) that a linkcell area in geographical space contains *any* repository location:

$$P(S) = 1 - \left(1 - \pi S^2/4A\right)^N \quad .... \qquad \text{(III)}$$

where A is the entire geographical area covered by repository, S^2 is the area covered by a linkcell, and N is (as before) the total number of repository locations. Preliminary work on SCRs used $P(S) = 0.6$ to estimate an S that maximizes query resolution performance. Figure 9 shows some preliminary results in which SCRs were generated for each of four linkcell size guesses ($S = 0.1$, $S = 0.01$, $S = 0.001$, and $S = 0.0001$) along with SCRs with S determined from $P(S) = 0.6$. Note that the RCT values in Figure 9 are plotted on a log scale, an indication of the considerable differences in performance levels across linkcell sizes. An examination of RCTs for $P(S) = 0.6$ reveals superior levels of query resolution performance; however, at this point in our research on SCRs, the extent to which $P(S) = 0.6$ yields S values that approximate optimal linkcell sizes remains unknown and is an important concern of on-going work.

Figure 9. Resultset query resolution performance for single category repositories

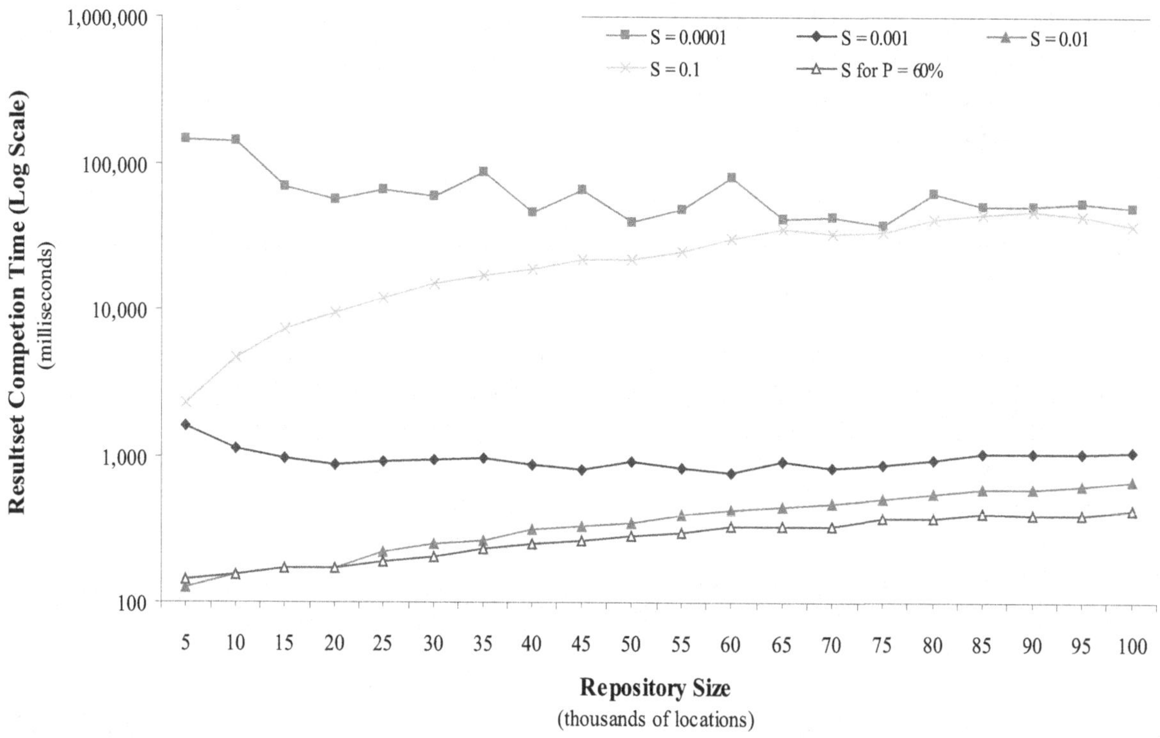

CONCLUSION

Although any application of the research reported here must be done with an appreciation of its limitations, the results obtained address to varying extents the four questions posed at the beginning of this article:

Question (1) concerned the consistency of query resolution performance in the face of greater variability in repository size, geographical coverage, and business categorization. It may be seen from results here that the query resolution performance profiles observed in previous work for an invariant linkcell size are not inconsistent with those observed here. However, the present study's variant linkcell size combined with greater variability in repository sizes, geographical area, and business categorization permitted the observation of appreciable performance degradation in unmanaged circumstances.

Question (2) concerned the relationship of linkcell size and query resolution performance. Results here reveal the varying dominance of two types of retrieval tasks: (i) the processing of relatively large numbers of relational tables containing relatively few entries when linkcell sizes are small, and (ii) the processing of relatively small numbers of relational tables containing relatively more entries when linkcell sizes are large. The interplay of (i) and (ii) consistently produces U-shaped performance curves.

Question (3) concerned the existence of an optimizing linkcell size. The U-shaped relationship between resolution time and size always reveals a distinct minima or narrow region of minima indicative of the existence of a specific linkcell size that could be associated with maximum query resolution performance.

Question (4) concerned the means by which an optimal linkcell size may be determined. This may be done in three ways: (i) by brute force, (ii) by the $S_{0.5}$-method, and (iii) by solving for S such that $P_{TC}(S) = 0.6$. While the first two size determination methods were effective in revealing optimal linkcell sizes, the logistics associated with their application limits their usability in practical settings. The third method is considerably less burdensome to use and results suggest that it is a useful linkcell size determination heuristic.

REFERENCES

Arnon, A., Efrat, A., Indyk, P., & Samet, H. (1999) 'Efficient regular data structures and algorithms for location and proximity problems', *Proceedings of the 40th Annual Symposium on Foundations of Computer Science*, New York (Oct 17-19), 160-170.

Butz, A. R. (1969) 'Convergence with Hilbert's space-filling curve', *Journal of Computer and System Sciences*, 3(May), 128-146.

Butz, A. R. (1971, April) 'Alternative algorithm for Hilbert's space-filling curve', *IEEE Transactions on Computers*, *C-20*, 424-426.

Butz, A., Bauss, J. & Kruger, A. (2000) 'Different views on location awareness', [Downloaded file "awareness.ps" from http://www.coli.uni-sb.de/sfb378/1999-2001/publications/butzetal2000d-de.html, on 16 September 2005], 3 pages.

Cary, M. (2001) 'Towards optimal ε-approximate nearest neighbor algorithms', *Journal of Algorithms*, 41(2), 417-428.

Chao, C-M., Tseng, Y-C., & Wang, L-C. (2005) 'Dynamic bandwidth allocation for multimedia traffic with rate guarantee and fair access in WCDMA systems', *IEEE Transactions on Mobile Computing*, 4(5), 420-429.

Chavez, E., Navarro, G., Baeza-Yates, R. and J. Marroquin. (2001). "Searching in metric spaces." ACM Computing Surveys. 33 (3): 273-321.

Chou, C-T. & Shin, K. (2005) 'An enhanced inter-access point protocol for uniform intra and intersubnet handoffs', *IEEE Transactions on Mobile Computing*, 4(4), 321-334.

Choy, M., Kwan, M-P., & Hong, V. (2000) 'Distributed database design for mobile geographical applications', *Journal of Database Management*, 11(1), 3-15.

Cinque, M., Cotroneo, D. & Russo, S. (2005) 'Achieving all the time, everywhere access in next-generation mobile networks', *ACM SIGMOBILE Mobile Computing and Communications Review*, 9(2), 29-39.

Gaede, V. and O. Gunther. (1998). "Multidimensional Access Methods." ACM Computing Surveys. 30 (2): 170-231.

Gebauer, J. & Shaw, M. (2004) 'Success factors and impacts of mobile business applications: results from a mobile e-procurement study', *International Journal of Electronic Commerce*, 8(3), 19-41.

Huang, S.-M., Lin, B. & Deng, Q.-S. (2005) 'Intelligent cache management for mobile data warehouse systems', *Journal of Database Management*, 16(2), 46-65.

Khungar, S. & Reikki, J. (2005) 'A context based storage system for mobile computing applications', *ACM SIGMOBILE Mobile Computing and Communications Review*, 9(1), 64-68.

Kottkamp, H-E. & Zukunft, O. (1998) 'Location-aware query processing in mobile database systems', *Proceedings of the 1998 ACM Symposium on Applied Computing*, Atlanta, Georgia, United States, (February 27 - March 1), 416-423.

Kuznetsov, V. E. (2000) 'Method for storing map data in a database using space filling curves and a method of searching the database to find objects in a given area and to find objects nearest to a location', United States Patent Number 6,021,406, issued February 1, 2000.

Lee, C. & Ke, C-H. (2001) 'A prediction-based query processing strategy in mobile commerce systems', *Journal of Database Management*, 12(3), 14-26.

Lee, D. (1999) 'Computational geometry II', In: M. Atallah (Ed.), *Algorithms and Theory of Computation Handbook* (pp. 20-1 to 20-31). Boca Raton: CRC Press.

Lee, D., Xu, J., Zheng, B. & Lee, W-C. (2002, July-September) 'Data management in location-dependent information services', *IEEE Pervasive Computing*, 1(3), 65-72.

Lee, D., Zhu, M. & Hu, H. (2005) 'When location-based services meet databases', *Mobile Information Systems*, 1(2), 81-90.

Lee, E. & Benbasat, I. (2004) 'A framework for the study of customer interface design for mobile commerce', *International Journal of Electronic Commerce*, 8(3), 79-102.

Leung, K. & Atypas, J. (2001) 'Improving returns on m-commerce investments', *The Journal of Business Strategy*, 22(5), 12-13.

Lin, H-P., Juang, R-T. & Lin, D-B. (2005) 'Validation of an improved location-based handover algorithm using GSM measurement data', *IEEE Transactions on Mobile Computing*, 4(5), 530-536.

McGuire, M., Plataniotis, K. & Venetsanopoulos, A. (2005) 'Data fusion of power and time measurements for mobile terminal location', *IEEE Transactions on Mobile Computing*, 4(2), 142-153.

Nievergelt, J. & Widmayer, P. (1997) 'Spatial data structures: concepts and design choices', In: M. van Kreveld, J. Nievergelt, T. Roos & P. Widmayer (Eds.), *Algorithmic Foundations of Geographic Information Systems* (pp. 153-197). Berlin: Springer Verlag.

Quintero, A. (2005) 'A User Pattern Learning Strategy for Managing Users' Mobility in UMTS Networks', *IEEE Transactions on Mobile Computing*, 4(6), 552-566.

Samaan, N. & Karmouch, A. (2005) 'A Mobility Prediction Architecture Based on Contextual Knowledge and Spatial Conceptual Maps', *IEEE Transactions on Mobile Computing*, 4(6), 537-551.

Santami, A., Leow, T., Lim, H. & Goh, P. (2003) 'Overcoming barriers to the successful adoption of mobile commerce in Singapore', *International Journal of Mobile Communications*, 1(1/2), 194-231.

Siau, K., Lim, E. & Z. Shen. (2001) 'Mobile commerce: promises, challenges, and research agenda', *Journal of Database Management*, 12(3), 4-13.

Siau, K. & Shen, Z. (2003) 'Mobile communications and mobile services', *International Journal of Mobile Communications*, 1(1/2), 3-14.

Sierpinski, W. (1912) 'Sur une novelle courbe continue qui remplit tout une aire plaine', *Bulletin International De L'Academie Des Sciences de Cracovie*, Ser. A., 462-478.

Wyse, J. (2003) 'Supporting m-commerce transactions incorporating locational attributes: an evaluation of the comparative performance of a location-aware method of locations repository management', *International Journal of Mobile Communications*, 1(1/2), 119-147.

Wyse, James E. (2006) "Data Management for Location-Based Mobile Business Applications: The Location-Aware Linkcell Method." *Proceedings of the Seventh World Congress on the Management of e-Business*, Halifax, Nova Scotia, Canada, (July 13-15): 18 pp.

Wyse, James E. (2007). "Applying location-aware linkcell-based data management to context-aware mobile business services." *Proceedings of the Sixth International Conference on Mobile Busi-*

ness, Toronto, Ontario, Canada, (July 9-11): 8 pages.

Wyse, J. (2008) 'Optimizing server performance for location-aware applications in mobile commerce: The repository's manager's formula.' *International Journal of Wireless and Mobile Computing* (forthcoming).

Xu, L., Shen, X. & Mark, J. (2005) 'Fair resource allocation with guaranteed statistical QoS for multimedia traffic in a wideband CDMA cellular network', *IEEE Transactions on Mobile Computing*, 4(2), 166-177.

Yuan, Y. & Zhang, J. (2003) 'Towards an appropriate business model for m-commerce', *International Journal of Mobile Communications*, 1(1/2), 35-56.

Yeung, M. & Kwok, Y-K. (2005) 'Wireless cache invalidation schemes with link adaptation and downlink traffic', *IEEE Transactions on Mobile Computing*, 4(1), 68-83.

ENDNOTES

1 Resultset Completion (RCT) is the time required to extract a set of repository locations that represents a resolution of a consumer-initiated query.

2 The Enumerative Method (1) selects repository locations in the consumer-targeted category, (2) calculates consumer-relative distances for each of the selected locations, (3) orders the selected locations in ascending order by consumer-relative distance, and (4) presents the first N locations as the resultset resolving the query.

3 Wyse (2003) used mean RCT values as the primary statistic to measure query resolution performance. The work here has chosen to use 50th percentile RCT values as the primary performance measurement statistic, a choice that (1) minimizes the disproportionate impact of the infrequent occurrence of very large query resolution times and (2) is consistent with widely used approaches to measuring and monitoring response time performance of computer-based transaction processing.

4 Formally, the number of linkcells C_S of size S is given by:

$$C_S = \left(\left[\frac{UVL}{S}\right] - \left[\frac{LVL}{S}\right] + 1\right)\left(\left[\frac{LHL}{S}\right] - \left[\frac{RHL}{S}\right] + 1\right)$$

where UVL and LVL represent the upper and lower limits, respectively, of the vertical extent of the geographical area covered by the repository's locations, and LHL and RHL represent the left and right limits, respectively, of the area's horizontal extent. ([ ] ≡ greatest integer.)

5 The phrase "close to" is deliberately used since the integrally valued components of $P_{TC}(S)$, primarily C_S, result in values for $P_{TC}(S)$ that will rarely equal 0.5.

6 Two observations with respect to Figure 8 are worthy of note: (1) query resolution times are measured at unequal TCOR intervals, and (2) RCT_E values decline as TCORs become smaller (i.e., category code sets become larger). With respect to the first observation, the TCOR value of 0.0011 (or 909 equally occurring category codes) resulted when LPA was supplied with a TCOR of 0.0010 (or 1000 equally occurring codes) and then asked to generate a repository in which locations are randomly assigned a category code. This randomized assignment results in realized (or output) TCORs that are close to, but generally different from, supplied (or input) TCORs. Thus, unlike the RCT values seen in Figures 6 and 7, those in Figure 8 do not generally occur at equal intervals. With respect to the second observation, note that increases in the number of category codes will, for a given repository size, result in

fewer repository locations in each category, including the category matching the category criteria on a consumer's query. A consideration of the enumerative method's procedural details (note 2) will reveal that this circumstance results in fewer instances where consumer-relative distances must be determined as well as in smaller resultsets that must be sorted. Thus, as TCORs become smaller, the enumerative method completes its work faster, an outcome reflected in the downward sloping curve for RCT_E.

APPENDIX A: THE LOCATION-AWARE METHOD (LAM)

A synopsis of LAM's fundamental components is given below with respect to (1) the requisite structure of a location-qualified data repository, (2) a formulation of the linkcell construct, (3) the general tasks of linkcell management (creation, modification, and destruction), and (4) the method's linkcell-based retrieval process. A detailed description may be found in Wyse (2003).

Repository Structure: The solution approach assumes that the repository is a relational database table containing a tuple for each repository location minimally consisting of four attributes: (1) a unique identifier for the location, (2) a horizontal coordinate (e.g., the location's longitude), (3) a vertical coordinate (e.g., the location's latitude), and (4) a code that qualifies each location in terms of its product or service offering. Table A1 provides a sample repository segment.

The Linkcell Construct: LAM relies on a set of auxiliary relational tables referred to as *linkcells*. Linkcells contain subsets of repository content and take relational table names derived from the coordinates of repository locations. Figure A1 illustrates the relationship between a repository's locations and its linkcells. Linkcells are generated based on the existence of repository locations within the area

Table A1. Repository segment

Location Identifier	Horizontal Coordinate	Vertical Coordinate	Category Code
•	•	•	•
•	•	•	•
•	•	•	•
L0340	W112.91761	N40.71098	C001
L0341	W089.45995	N49.70451	C007
L0342	W097.81718	N47.78187	C014
L0343	W076.55539	N45.00473	C013
•	•	•	•
•	•	•	•

Figure A1. Locations and linkcells

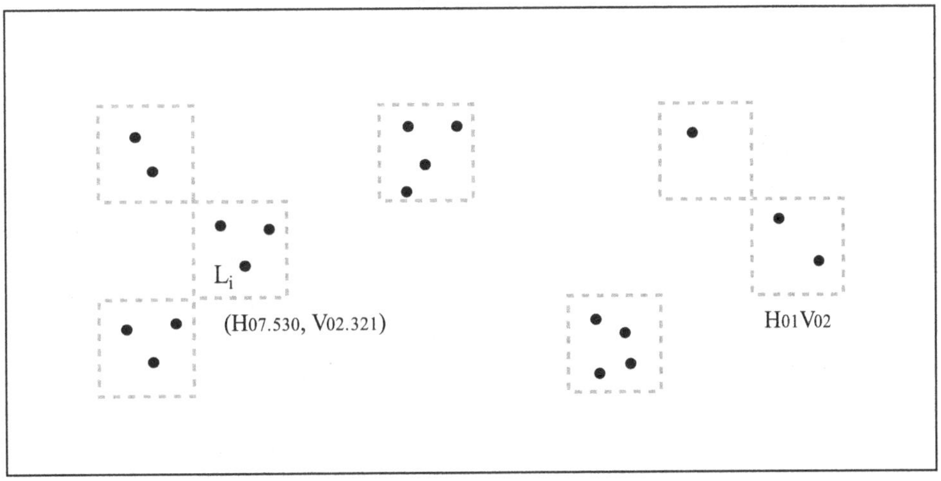

Source: Wyse (2003), p. 125. © 2003 Inderscience Publishers, reproduced with the permission.

Table A2. Linkcells as relational tables

Linkcell: W112N40	
Location Id	Category Code
L0340	C001
L0736	C016
L2043	C010
L2063	C010

Linkcell: W089N49	
Location Id	Category Code
L0341	C007
L4028	C011

Linkcell: W097N47	
Location Id	Category Code
L0342 C	014
L0856 C	006
L1021 C	001
L1326 C	004
L1593 C	006
L2148 C	016

encompassed by the linkcell. A linkcell's name is derived from the coordinates of any location situated within the linkcell. To illustrate how this is accomplished, note L_i's coordinates in Figure A1. Truncating the fractional part of each coordinate yields the linkcell name. Thus, the name for the linkcell containing location L_i is H07V02. The same linkcell name would also be derived from the other two locations contained in the same linkcell.

Formally, a linkcell with the relational table name HNVM will contain all repository locations with horizontal coordinate values HN.0 through HN.999··· and vertical coordinate values VM.0 through VM.999···. Each linkcell, in its relational table form, contains a tuple for each of the repository locations encompassed by the linkcell's boundaries. Linkcells, manifested as relational tables, could appear as shown in Table A2.

Linkcells may be varied in size through coordinate scaling. For example, if L_i's positional coordinates are scaled by 10 (say) from (H07.530, V02.321) to (H075.30, V023.21) then L_i's linkcell name becomes H075V023 and the linkcell now relates to a smaller geographical area. The smaller area consists, in this instance, of vertical and horizontal extents that are 1/10th of the respective extents of the original linkcell. The use of a different linkcell size does not affect the relative positions of a repository's locations; however, using a different linkcell size may result in a redistribution of a repository's locations amongst the linkcells.

Linkcell Creation, Destruction, and Modification: Whenever a location is added to the repository, a linkcell name is derived from the location's horizontal and vertical coordinates. The derived name is used to query the repository about the existence of a corresponding linkcell. If the linkcell exists, the location's identifier and category code are placed in the linkcell. If the linkcell does not exist, it is created using the name derived from the location's coordinates and then the location's identifier and category code are placed in the newly created linkcell. Whenever a location is removed from the repository, a linkcell name is derived from the location's coordinates. Since the location had been previously added to the repository, it is assumed that a linkcell with the derived name already exists. If the location to be removed is the only remaining location in the linkcell, then the linkcell is destroyed. If the linkcell contains other location identifiers, only the attribute tuple for the location to be removed is deleted and the linkcell is not destroyed. Thus, linkcells (manifested as relational tables) are created, destroyed, and modified dynamically based on repository changes.

Retrieval Procedure: The procedure relies on two types of linkcells: (1) the Core Linkcell, and (2) the Cursor Linkcell. The Core Linkcell derives its name using the method described above but not from the coordinates of any repository location; instead, from the coordinates of the consumer's location. The structure of the linkcell construct and its manifestation as a relational table implies that once the Core Linkcell's name is derived, the search procedure is immediately aware of the existence or non-existence of any repository locations in the immediate vicinity of the consumer. Once derived, the Core Linkcell name remains unchanged; however the Cursor Linkcell takes on a sequence of linkcell names that effectively *moves* it in search of other locations in the vicinity of the consumer.

The procedure begins by setting the Cursor Linkcell name to the Core Linkcell name and checking for the existence of a linkcell with the same name as the Cursor Linkcell. If the linkcell exists, its contents are examined for locations with a category code equal to that sought by the query. When a sought-after location is found, its attributes are placed in the query's resultset. The procedure then expands the search area by generating a sequence of Cursor Linkcell names. This is done by systematically changing the numeric sections of the Cursor Linkcell's name using a sequence that pivots the Cursor Linkcell around the Core Linkcell in a clockwise pattern. Whenever the Cursor Linkcell is assigned a new name, it checks for the existence of a linkcell with its currently assigned name. If the linkcell exists then its contents are examined and the actions outlined above are performed resulting in further locations being accumulated in the query resultset. The numbers in parenthesis in Figure A2 indicate the sequence in which relational table names are generated and examined as the Cursor Linkcell moves clockwise. The search area may be further expanded by moving the Cursor Linkcell through additional linkcell layers on the outer periphery of the linkcells previously examined. This outward-spiraling, clockwise-moving process continues until the sought-after number of locations is found.

Figure A2. LAM retrieval procedure - Cursor linkcell naming sequence

(9) H09V03	(2) H08V03	(3) H07V03
(8) H09V02	(1) Core Linkcell H08V02	(4) H07V02
(7) H09V01	(6) H08V01	(5) H07V01

Source: Wyse (2003), p. 128. © 2003 Inderscience Publishers, reproduced with the permission

Chapter XV
Migrating Legacy Information Systems to Web Services Architecture

Shing-Han Li
Tatung University, Taiwan

Shi-Ming Huang
National Chung Cheng University, Taiwan

David C. Yen
Miami University, USA

Cheng-Chun Chang
National Chung Cheng University, Taiwan

ABSTRACT

The lifecycle of information system (IS) became relatively shorter compared with earlier days as a result of information technology (IT) revolution and advancement. It is tremendous difficult for an old architecture to catch up with the dynamic changes occurred in the market. To match with the fast pace of challenges, enterprises have to use the technology/concept of information system reengineering (ISR) to preserve the value of their legacy systems. Consequently, web services-based systems with Service-Oriented Architecture (SOA) are widely accepted as one of the possible solutions for an enterprise information system to retain/keep its old legacy systems. Using this aforementioned architecture, enterprise information systems tend to be more flexible and agile to fit into the capricious business environment, and thus, be easier to integrate with additional applications. In other words, it is indeed an essential requirement for an enterprise to establish such a system to further improve corporation's productivity and operational efficiency. In specific, the requirement is simply to migrate the legacy systems to be SOA architecture. However, it is a trade-off between the value of legacy systems and the compatibility with SOA to decide whether this alternative is a feasible one. The purpose of this manuscript is to propose a migrating solution to convert the architecture of the legacy system into SOA with a systematic approach. This proposed methodology is different from the traditional object-oriented approaches, which migrates the system to have a services-oriented focus without incorporating general objected-oriented (OO) or functional oriented feature. In this study, a case study and information capacity theory were employed to verify/validate that this approach is indeed an effective and a practicable one.

INTRODUTION

Due to the dynamic advancement of information technology (IT), the life cycle of the information system (IS) is greatly reduced to a certain extent. Generally speaking, the traditional legacy information systems possess such undesirable characteristics as latency of information, poor reach, inflexibility, and higher cost of maintenance. Furthermore, the traditional system architectures such as centralized and client/server are frequently incompatible with the requirements and specifications which exist in today's business environment. To be more specific, the legacy information systems have these aforementioned shortcomings, which have prevented the businesses and/or organizations to react/respond dynamically to the rapid challenges as they should. Consequently, enterprises have a strong need to utilize the technology of information system reengineering (ISR) to preserve the value of their legacy systems.

In this situation, enterprises or software companies are always in a dilemma of redeveloping/redesigning their legacy systems to include the newer Web services components (Bouguettaya, Malik, Rezgui, & Korff, 2006; Chen, Zhou, & Zhang, 2006; Kim, Sengupta, Fox, & Dalkilic, 2007). Discarding and redeveloping the existing systems not only wastes the money allocated for software investments, but also causes organizations to lose competitive advantages to meet numerous unanticipated contingencies and/or uncertainties.

Based on prior study (Ommering, 2005), the system migration will be one of the best ways to reengineer a legacy system. Traditionally, there are two approaches available to migrate the legacy system to the Web services architecture (Vanston, 2005). The first approach is the legacy externalization approach. This approach is usually the main alternative available on the current market. It generally uses strategic or pointed forms, along with new types of interface display, to develop the integrated products (such as "Web Scraping"). The other approach is the component encapsulation approach. This is another viable alternative to utilize the component standard technology like Common Object Request Broker Architecture (CORBA) (OMG, 1995; Vinoski, 1997), Component Object Model (COM) (Microsoft, 2007), or Enterprise Java Beans (EJB) (Sun, 2007) to encapsulate the legacy system into the components, and then translate them into a Web Services standard. Ultimately, this second approach is migrated to the component-based and transaction-oriented framework (such as IBM WebSphere and BEA WebLogic) (Liu, Fekete, & Gorton, 2005; Waguespack & Schiano, 2004). Both of the aforementioned approaches may not be a bad way for the legacy system to migrate into the equivalent Web services standards. However, they normally utilize the hard-cording technique to implement the interface with the corresponding standard (Brereton & Budgen, 2000; Kwan & Li, 1999; McArthur, Saiedian, & Zand, 2002). Being a traditional structure program, the system normally has a shorter life cycle and lacks scalability, feasibility, and reusability. Further, it would be much more difficult to maintain in the future. On the other hand, if a company is applying the component encapsulation approach without incorporating appropriate component migrating methods, the system still has these aforementioned shortcomings (Rahayu, Chang, Dillon, & Taniar, 2000). Unfortunately, most alternatives adopted now by enterprises and/or businesses do not use the proper component migrating method.

Many related studies (Erickson, Lyytinen, & Siau, 2005; Fong, Karlapalem, Li, & Kwan, 1999; Gall, Klosch, & Mittermeir, 1995; Kwan & Li, 1999; Sang, Follen, Kim, & Lopez, 2002) have presented methods that can be utilized to systematically reengineer the legacy system into the Object-Oriented (OO) or the distributed system. However, the Web Services architecture by nature is different from a general distributed system. The core concept of Web Service is a Service-Oriented Architecture (SOA) (Huang, Hung, Yen, Li, & Wu, 2006; Stal, 2002). In the SOA environment, resources in a network are made available as an independent service that can be accessed without any knowledge of the underlying platform implementation (Erl, 2005). Web services can certainly rely on a Web-services composition language (WSCL) such as the Business Process Execution Language for Web Services (BPEL4WS) (IBM, BEA Systems, Microsoft, SAP AG, & Siebel Systems, 2002) to transform an existing Web service into a new type of Web service by employing well-defined process modeling constructs (Chen, Hsu, & Mehta, 2003; Curbera, Khalef, Mukhi, Tai & Weerawarana, 2003), enterprise architects believe that SOA can help businesses respond more quickly and cost-effectively to fast-changing market conditions (Sutor, 2006). This style of architecture, in fact, promotes reusability at the macro level (service) rather than the micro levels (objects). By doing so, it can greatly simplify interconnection to and usage of existing IT (legacy) assets (Carroll & Calvo, 2004).

The purpose of this study is to propose a methodology which utilizes the existing data design of an information system to migrate the legacy system to an SOA system. The benefits include the following items: First, this approach has the advantage of reengineering the legacy system to various *system components* from a technical aspect, and use the Web services composition language (WSCL) to translate the existing model into the new Web services architecture. Unlike traditional object-oriented approaches, this proposed methodology migrates the old systems to services-oriented or functional-oriented ones. Additionally, this approach can be employed to develop a system which will be more flexible and adaptable to fit better to the constantly-changing business environment. Furthermore, this proposed approach will no doubt make the conversion process easier to integrate with other additional applications.

The remainder of this article is organized as follows: The second section provides a brief overview of some legacy systems' reengineering and Web services approaches. The proposed legacy system's migrating approach and the implementation of a prototype will be discussed in the third section. The fourth section contains the system implementation using simulation and a real case study. A comparison of the proposed approach with others is provided in the fifth section. Finally, the sixth section concludes this manuscript.

LITERATURE REVIEW

Information Flow for Business Process (IFBP)

Business Process Management (BPM) is one of the basic elements of Web services architecture

(Basu & Kumar, 2002). It can be decomposed of two major phases—process design and diagnosis. The process diagnosis phase will discover an entire picture of the business process for an enterprise, also known as the AS-IS Model. The exploration of AS-IS Model is a very time-consuming and experience-oriented task. As a result, an enterprise has to spend a lot of time and pay huge labor costs during the process diagnosis phase. Besides, it is difficult for the process designers to transform one process model to another equivalent one. There are certain gaps among different process-designing methods. Thus, the study of Shi-Ming Huang and Fu-Yun Yu (2004) investigates a novel methodology for business process discovery based on information flow, called IFBP. This IFBP methodology includes the following three phases: transformation, integration, and conversion phases. The input of IFBP is actually dataflow diagrams (DFD) for the existing information systems. The output is an Event-Driven Process Chain (EPC) diagram for enterprise process flow.

Information System Reengineering

There are several direct and indirect system migrating approaches.

Direct Migration

Sang et al. (2002) presented an approach to integrate legacy applications written in FORTRAN into a distributed object-based framework. FORTRAN codes are modified as little as possible when being decomposed into modules and wrapped as objects. They used object-oriented technique such as C++ objects to encapsulate individual engine components as well as the CORBA, and implement a wrapper generator, which takes the FORTRAN applications as input and generates the C++ wrapper files and interface definition language file.

Serrano, Montes, and Carver (1999) presented a semiautomatic, evolutionary migration methodology that produces an object-based distributed system for legacy systems. They first used ISA (Identification of Subsystems based on Associations), a design recovery and subsystem classification technique to produce a data-cohesive hierarchical subsystem decomposition of the subject system. Second, they adapted the subsystems to develop the object-oriented paradigm. Third, they wrapped up and defined interfaces of the subsystems in order to define components. Finally, middleware technologies for distributed systems were used to implement the communication between components.

Indirect Migration

Gall et al. (1995) proposed an approach, which rearchitect the old procedural software to an object-oriented architecture. The transformation process was developed to identify potential objects in the procedural source codes in order to enable the utilization of object-oriented concepts for future, related software maintenance activities. This approach was not directly performed on the source-code level, but instead, different representations were developed out of the procedural program on higher levels of abstraction (e.g., structure charts, data flow diagrams, entity-relationship diagrams, and application models), which represent different kinds of program information. Additional application-domain knowledge was introduced by human experts to support the program transformation to enable several higher-level decisions during the development process.

Kwan and Li (1999) proposed a methodology to reengineer those previously-developed relational database systems to OO database systems. Their approach is based on the input of: (1) Extended Entity Relationship model (EER) that provides rules for structuring data; (2) Data Dictionary that provides static data semantics; and (3) DFD that provides dynamic data semantics. This approach captures the existing database design, uses knowledge in OO modeling, and then represents them by means of production rules, to guild the pattern extraction algorithm that is applied to perform the data mining process to identify the "data dependency of a process to an object". The existing Data Dictionary, DFD, and EER model are all useful and hence, are needed for capturing the existing database design to recover the hidden dynamic semantics.

Huang et al. (2006) proposed a methodology that focused on how to migrate legacy systems with a well-structured OO analysis to ensure the quality of a reengineered component-based system. This research adopted the well-structured object-oriented analysis to improve the quality of reengineered systems. The result of the reengineered system will be a Web-enabled system. The proposed migration approach discusses how to process a well-structured object-oriented analysis. The research considered the following four factors—(1) multi-value attributes, (2) inheritance relationships, (3) functional dependency, and (4) object behavior to ensure the quality of a reengineered component-based system. Further, their study considered the migration from three aspects—data, process, and user interface to make the applied reengineering process more complete. The comparison of all aforementioned reengineering approaches is shown in Table 1, which is shown below. In this comparison table, it is noted that the approach proposed by Huang et al. (2006) could present a more semantic legacy system with a higher quality of components.

Business Component and Service Component Definition

Business components typically emulate a specific business entity, such as a customer, an order, or an account. When sets of coherent components are linked together, they can inter-operate to accomplish an even higher level of business function (Herzum & Sims, 1998; Jin, Urban, & Dietrich, 2006; Lee, Pipino, Strong, & Wang, 2004; Vi-

Table 1. Comparison of the reengineering approaches

Indicator \ Approach		Sang (2002)	Serrano (1999)	Gall (1995)	Kwan (1999)	Huang (2006)
Proposed Time		2002	1999	1995	1997	2002
Approach		Direct Migration	Direct Migration	Indirect Migration	Indirect Migration	Indirect Migration
How to find objects		codes	codes	ERD	ERD	ERD
How to find methods		codes	Codes	Codes	DFD	DFD
Is component-based		Yes	Yes	No	No	Yes
User Interface Consideration		No	No	No	No	Yes
Quality of Object-Oriented Model	Aggregation Consideration	No	No	No	No	Yes
	Inheritance Consideration	No	No	No	No	Yes
	Object Behavior Consideration	Yes	Yes	Yes	Yes	Yes
	Multi-value attributes consideration	No	No	No	No	Yes

tharana & Jain; 2000; Zhao & Siau, 2007). The scope of a component discussed in this article will include the class and its related interfaces together as a component. By doing so, it can preserve the simple execution function of a component from getting over-complicated. Services are self-describing, open components that can support rapid, low-cost composition of distributed applications (Papazoglou & Georgakopoulos, 2003). Service-Oriented components attempt to fulfill users' requirement. Consequently, the service providers' responsibility is mainly to design/develop the most adaptable service processes and components for different users. The users just enjoy the content and quality of the provided service, but do not care about who the true service provider is and how to acquire the service.

Some definitions of service argue that they can be implemented by components (Sprott, 2002). However, in a complex environment, a service can actually include several components (Perrey & Lycett, 2003). Therefore, this article considers that the service is comprised of a number of system components, which could simultaneously interact and integrate with each other. Enterprise has a tendency to keep distance from the composition of too many small and trivial system components and hence has a strong reservation about the operation and management of each other while applying the services. For this reason, this research defines the service to be composed of system components from the perspective of users' requirements. A service-oriented feature should be an extension of the component-oriented one, and should be aimed at satisfying the user's situation.

MIGRATING METHODOLOGY

By nature, Web services are different from legacy systems in terms of architecture and the degree of coupling. To migrate the system from a tightly-coupled one or from a loosely-coupled one, the best strategy is to apply OO reengineering. It is noted that the complete Web services architecture generally utilizes the Web services composition language (WSCL) to construct the service components. Most available WSCL are designed based on business process. From the business perspective, most approaches available today merely apply business process to represent the legacy system. To this end, this article will perceive that the business process is one of the main elements of Web services. From the above discussion, this research analyzes the legacy system from two aspects: technical and business. This approach, as visualized in Figure 1, is summarized in five subsequent steps. Traditionally the system designers use the tools and techniques such as ERD, DFD, and user interfaces to describe the entire architecture and then design/develop the information system. These aforementioned models have been applied to analyze the business process of the legacy system and then have been reengineered to the corresponding system components. This research reengineers the legacy system to various system components from the technical aspect, analyzes the model of the legacy system to attain the business processes from the business aspect, integrates the system components and the business processes together, and then analyzes the service based on processes. Finally, according to this proposed integrated model, it translates the model to the Web services composition language to build a Web services architecture. The following sections discussed below describe each of the five steps of this proposed approach.

Step 1: Reengineer System Components

To migrate the system to a loosely-coupled architecture, the OO reengineering approach could be utilized. In the comparison table (Table 1) discussed earlier, the Huang et al. (2006) approach could be utilized to represent more semantics of the legacy system with higher-quality components. The Huang et al. (2006) approach, as visualized

Figure 1. Migration methodology

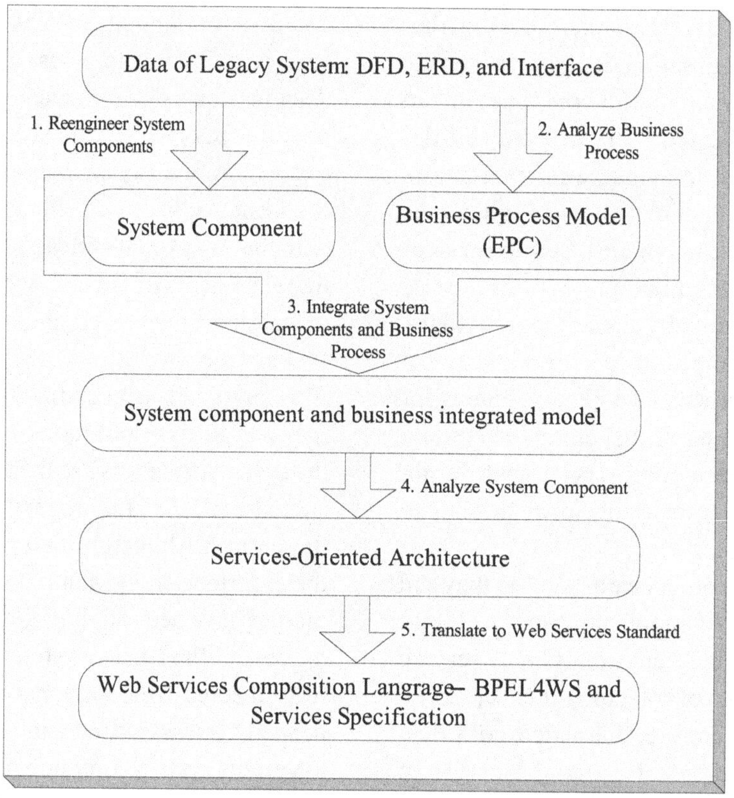

in Figure 2, is summarized in the following five steps. This study extends Huang's methodology to reengineering system components.

The first activity is to employ the model diagrams of a legacy system such as DFD, ERD, and system interface as different inputs. There are two extended rules associated with this step and can be discussed as follows:

- **Extended rule 1:** In step 1 of Huang's approach, the fact represented from the data stores and external entities of a DFD can be translated to classes and attributes. In some cases, the DFD itself may also imply a comprehensive system. For this reason, the DFD can consequently be translated to be a system class.
- **Extended rule 2:** In step 3 of Huang's approach, this article performs a further analysis between the functions and external entities (or data store). When a dataflow is connected between two functions, it actually indicates the directional flow of the arrow from one function to another one. It is very similar to the control flow used in EPC.

In this step, the authors regard every dataflow as a method, especially the dataflow between one function and another. Since the aforementioned data flow implies that the IS controls the flow of data in the system, there should be a corresponding method of a system class. An illustrative example is provided in Figure 3.

After the completion of this step, we can get the output—component specifications.

Figure 2. Object-oriented migration methodology (Source: Huang, Hung, Yen, Li & Wu, 2006)

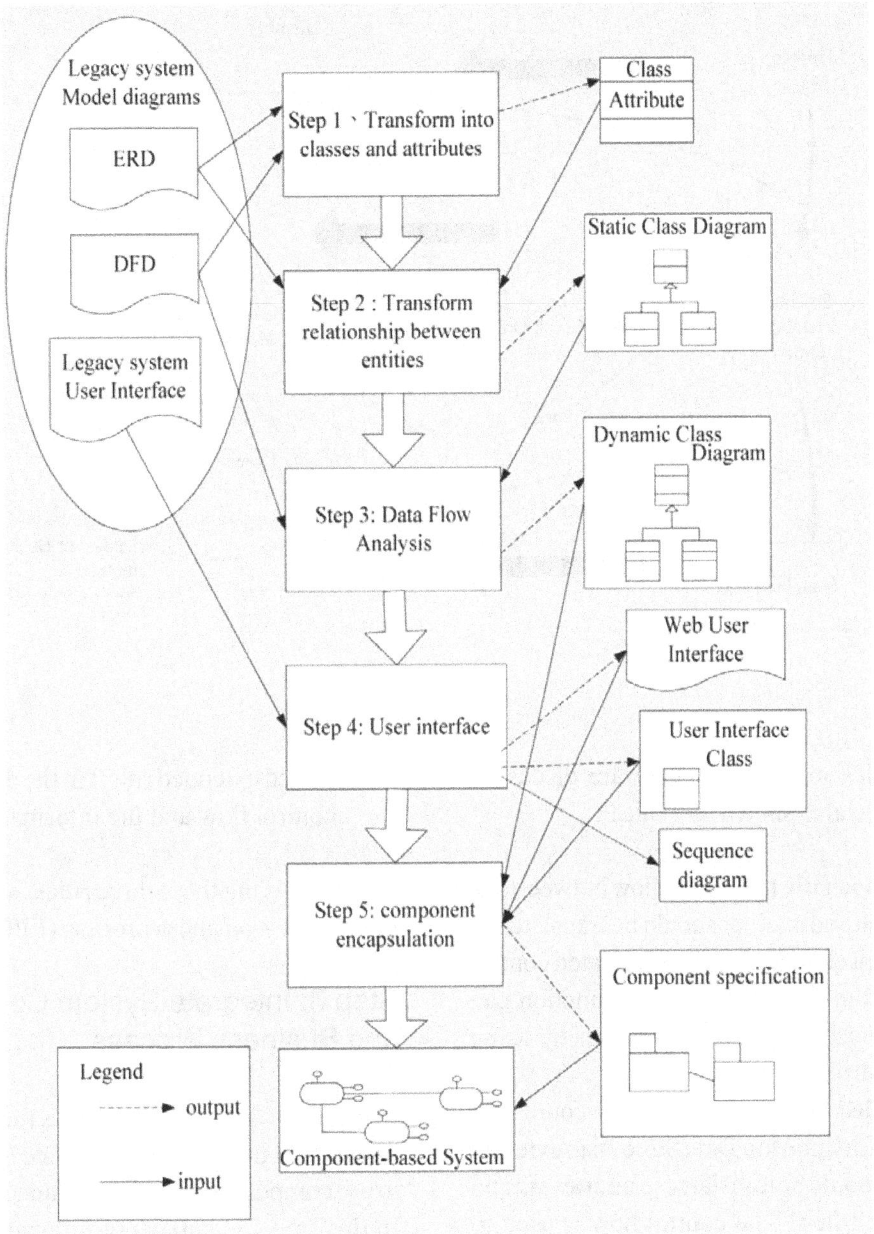

Step 2: Analyze the Business Process

Due to tight integration with the system components in step 1, this study analyzes business process from a system perspective. This step applies and extends the "Information Flow for Business Process" (IFBP) (Huang & Yu, 2004) method to analyze the business process. Table 2 illustrates the idea of this conversion methodology for IFBP.

Again, the first activity is to use DFD of the legacy system as an input. There are three

Figure 3. The DFD is translated into several classes

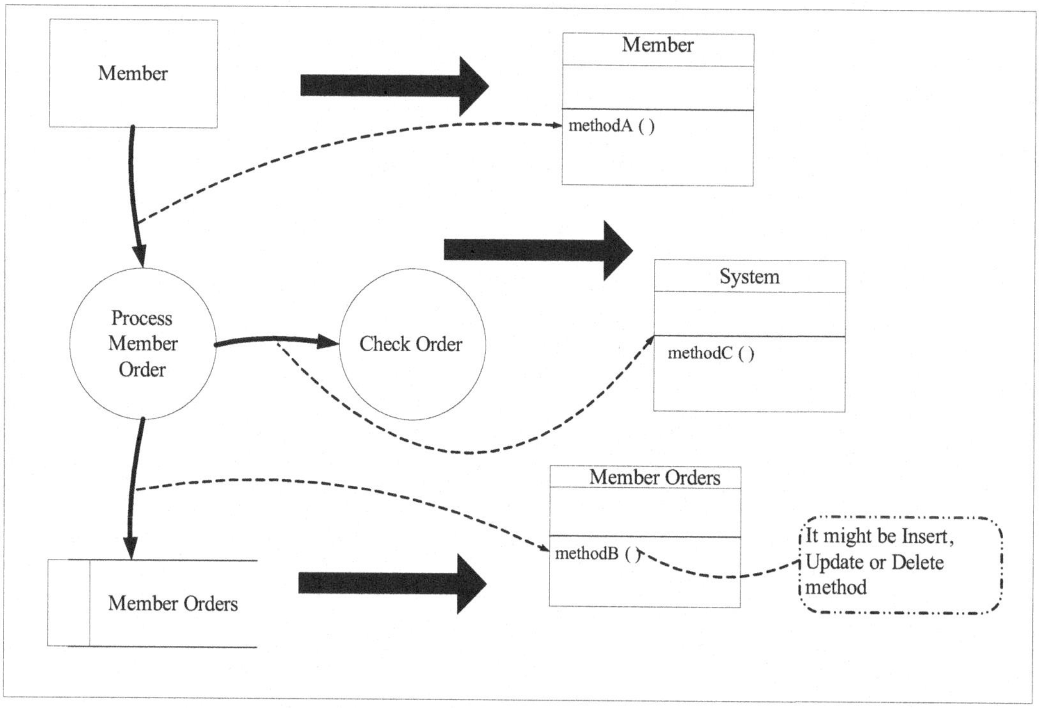

extended rules in this step; they are discussed below and are also shown in Table 3:

- **Extended rule 1:** The dataflow between one function and another should be translated to the event element and the associated control flow of an EPC. Further, the function can be connected with various events by using the control flow.
- **Extended rule 2:** The dataflow connected from a function to a Data Store or an external entity should be translated to be an event and a control flow. The control flow is used to connect the function and the event, and the information flow is employed to connect the function and the external entity.
- **Extended rule 3:** This rule is similar to the extended rule 2. The dataflow connected from a data store or an external entity to a function should be translated to an event and a control flow. It differs from the aforementioned extended rule 2 in the direction of the control flow and the information flow.

By applying these three rules, we can then get the output—business process (EPC).

Step 3: Integrate System Components and Business Process

In this step, this study integrates the system component and business process. The first activity is to use component specification and EPC as inputs. In this step, the authors will integrate processes from their original sources-DFD. The dataflow in DFD is translated to be a method of a class in step 1 and an event in step 2, so that it can be integrated later based on the same source. Afterwards, these aforementioned DFD can be shown in an EPC model, which is noted as the methods of classes. Figure 4 demonstrates the situation to integrate the system components and business processes.

Table 2. The conversion methodology for IFBP

Steps	Description	DFD	EPC
Step 1	DFD(Function) map to EPC(Function)	Function	Function
Step 2	DFD(Data Flow) map to EPC(Event)	Data Flow	Event
Step 3	Using EPC(Control Flow) connect between EPC(Function) and EPC(Event)		Function → Event
Step 4	Using logical symbol (AND, OR, XOR) combine more than one EPC(Event) with EPC(Function)		Function → ∧ → Event 1, Event 2
Step 5	DFD(External Entity) map to EPC(Information Object)	External Entity	Information Object
Step 6	DFD(Data store) map to EPC(File)	Data store	File
Step 7	DFD('Data Flow' connect with 'Data Store') map to EPC(Information flow)	→ Data store	→ File

Finally, in this step, we can get the output—the integrated EPC model.

Step 4: Analyze Services

This study considers that a service is composed of system components from the perspective of the users who are employing the service. First of all, using the integrated EPC model as inputs, this research utilized the integrated EPC model in step 3 to analyze system services from the users' perspective. Enterprises using services to apply the interaction between the external entity and other elements in the EPC model. For simplicity, this study analyzes all possible interactive situations between two entities in the EPC model, and then classifies them into seven possible situations introduced as follows.

- **Situation 1:** There is no entity in the process. Analyzer should use low-level DFD until it locates the interaction between the entities. The analyzer can translate the whole process into a service.

Table 3. The extended rules for IFBP

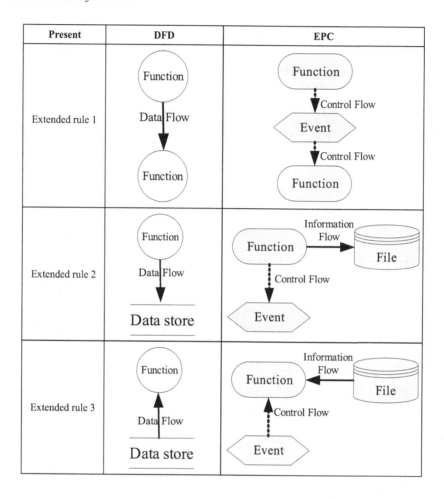

Present	DFD	EPC
Extended rule 1	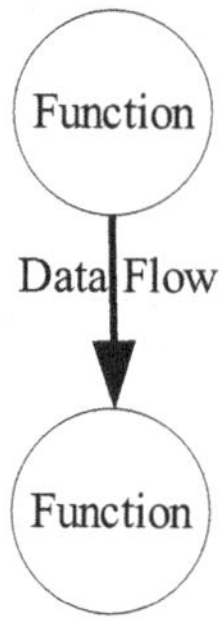	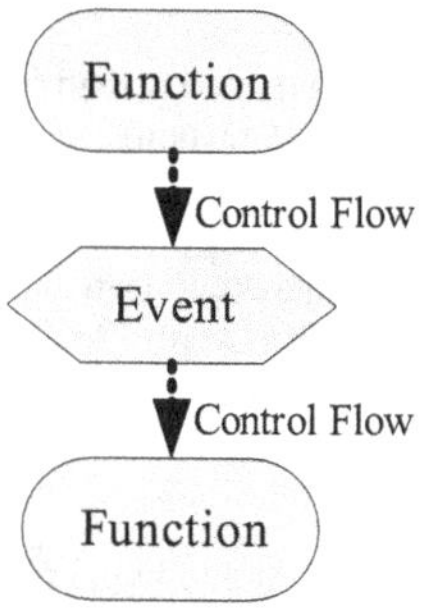
Extended rule 2	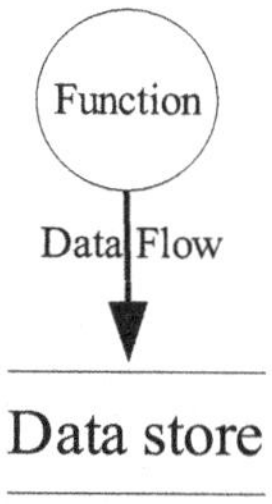	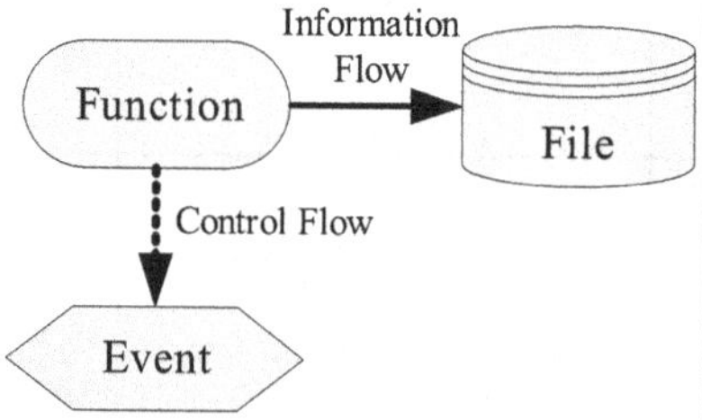
Extended rule 3	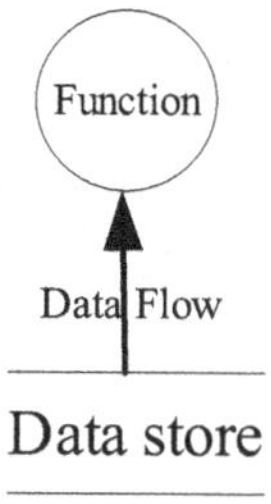	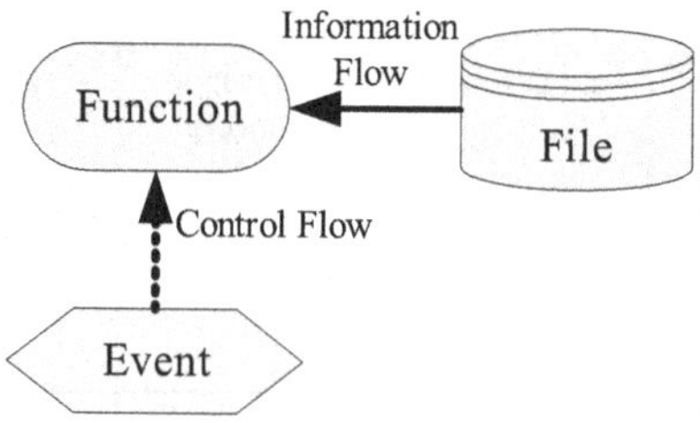

- **Situation 2:** The external entity only inputs information into one function. The analyzer can translate the whole process into a service.
- **Situation 3:** Only one function inputs information to the external entity. Again, the analyzer can translate the whole process into a service.
- **Situation 4:** The external entity inputs information into the process, and then the process outputs information to another external entity. As presented in Figure 5 and Situation 4, the whole process provides the service for A and B, so the analyzer can translate the whole process into a service.
- **Situation 5:** The external entity outputs the process, and then the process inputs information into another external entity. As presented in Figure 5 and Situation 5, A and B are two separate services that do interact with each other.
- **Situation 6:** Two external entities input different functions. As presented in Figure 5 and Situation 6, A and B are two separate services that do not interact with each other.
- **Situation 7:** Two external entities input different functions. As presented in Figure 5 and Situation 7, A and B are two separate services that do not interact with each other. Finally, we can get the outputs - service com-

Figure 4. Integrating the system components and business processes

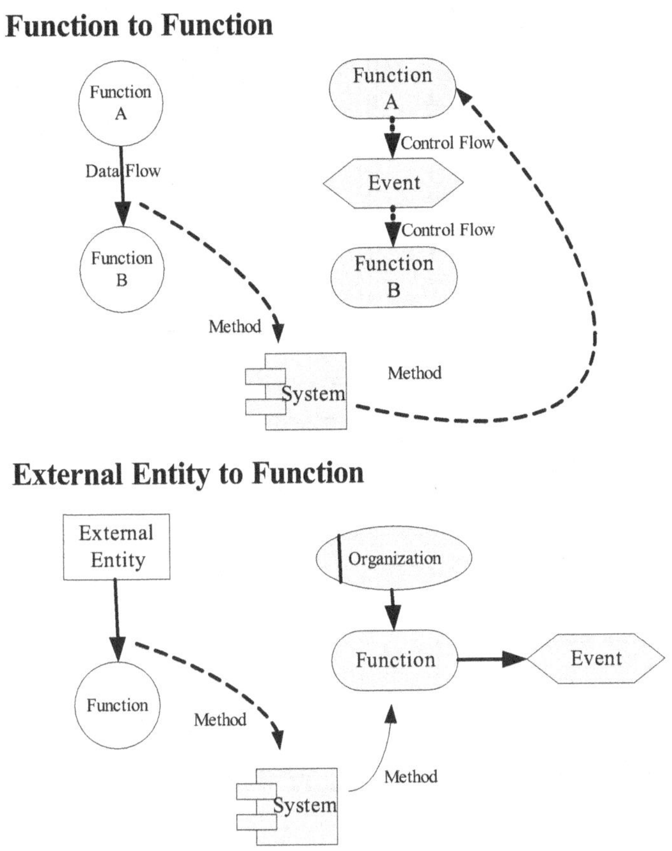

ponent specification and services-oriented EPC model.

After translating the related process to service components, the service components can be presented by the EPC event to repaint the EPC model, as shown in Figure 6.

Step 5: Translate to Web Services Standard

After the EPC model has been built, the services components and the services-oriented process need to be translated into a suitable Web services standard. This study translates it to business process execution language for Web services (BPEL4WS), which is one of the Web services composition languages. The user applies the translated Web services components and BPEL4WS process model to build the Web Service Architecture-based system. In this step, the research does not evaluate which component technology should be used to encapsulate the component, but translates the EPC model to BPEL4WS by using the approach of Huang and Yu (2004). Since a services component includes many associated system components, it is required to encapsulate the system component, process, and interface into a new component.

CASE STUDY

As shown in Figure 7, the Prototype system includes three layers (i.e., Interaction layer, Transla-

Figure 5. Services analysis

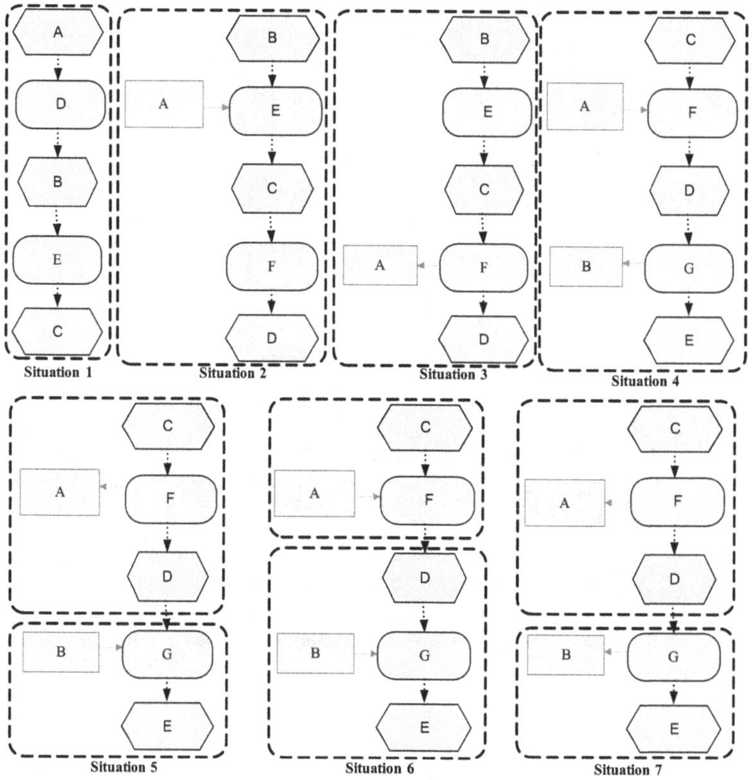

Figure 6. Translation of services to process

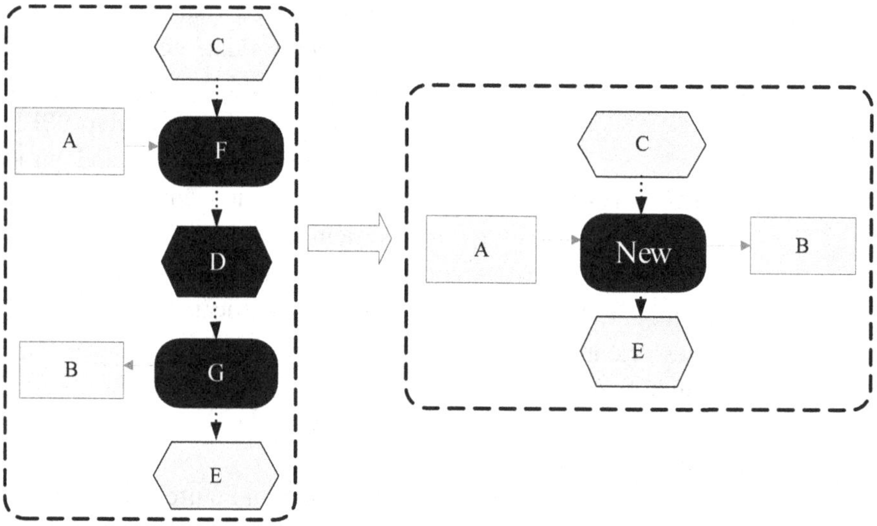

Figure 7. System architecture

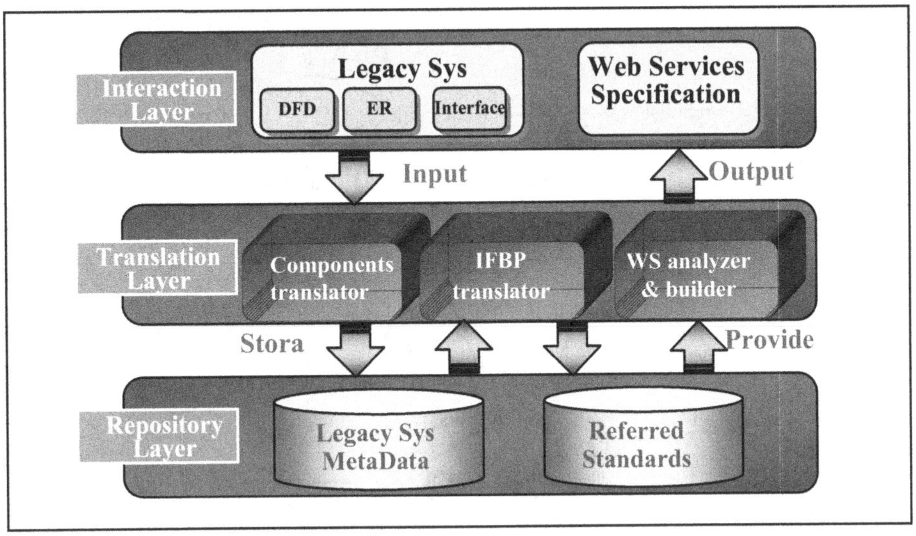

Figure 8. The system snapshot of the prototype

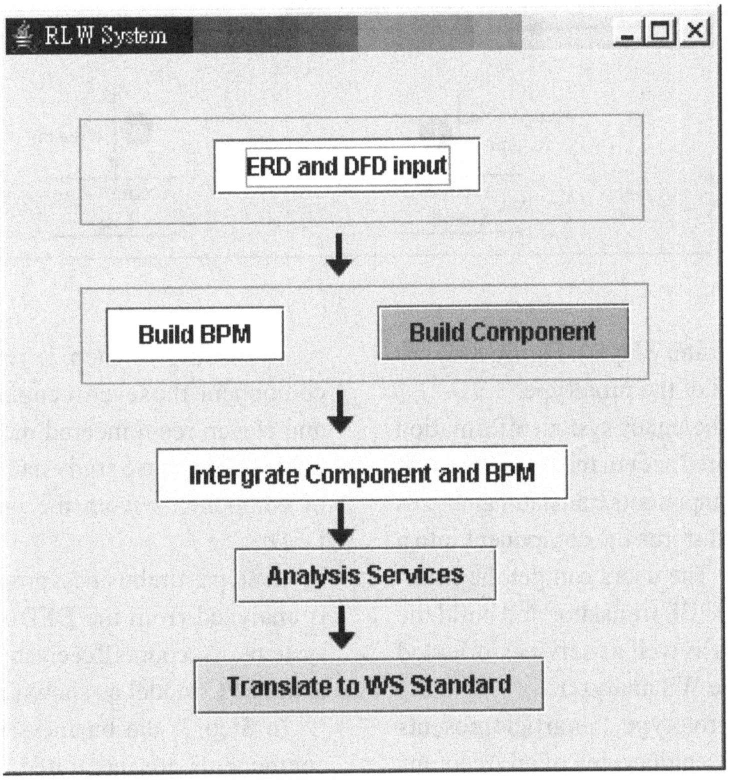

Figure 9. The DFD of accounts receivable system

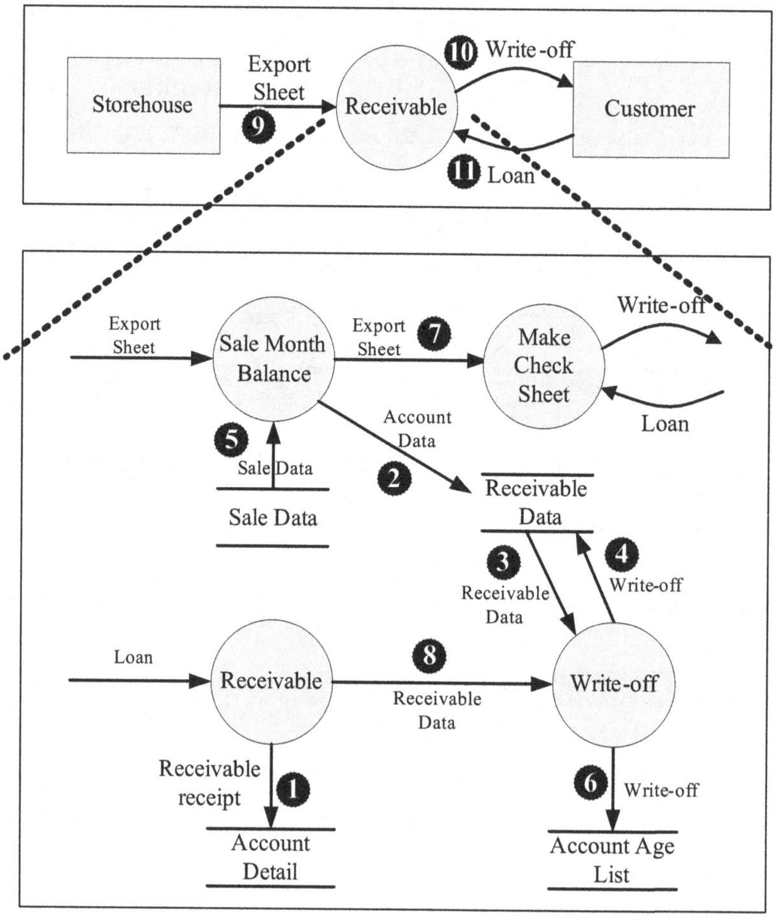

tion layer, and Repository layer). Figure 8 shows the system snapshot of the prototype.

The users input the legacy system information (DFD, ERD, user interface) in the prototype system, and then the components translator analyzes this information and stores the component into a Metadata database. The users can get the information flow by the IFBP translator and build the service components as well as services-oriented process by using the WS analyzer.

To validate this prototype, this article presents a case study of the reengineering of an Accounts Receivable System (ARS). By employing experts' help, the ERD of the database and DFD are described in Figure 9.

According to Step 1, reengineering system component, the seven reengineering components, and eleven reengineered methods are shown on Table 4. This case study named various methods of components from the original data flow of DFD.

In Step 2, the business process of this case study is analyzed from the DFD model of the legacy system—Accounts Receivable System. The output is the EPC model as shown in Figure 10.

In Step 3, the business process and system components are integrated, and the methods of system components are employed onto the business process components. It is shown in Figure 11.

Table 4. Components and methods of ARS

Methods	Sources	Objectives	Type	Components (class)
❶Receivable Receipt	Receivable Data	Account Detail	Insert, Update, Delete	Account Detail
❷Account Data	Sale Month Balance	Receivable Data	Insert, Update, Delete	Receivable Data
❸Receivable Data	Receivable Data	Write-off	Select	Receivable Data
❹Write-off	Write-off	Receivable Data	Insert, Update, Delete	Receivable Data
❺Sale Data	Sale Data	Sale Month Balance	Select	Sale Data
❻Write-off	Write-off	Account Age List	Insert, Update, Delete	Account Age List
❼Export Sheet	Sale Month Balance	Make Check Sheet	Function to Function	ARS
❽Receivable Data	Receivable	Write-off	Function to Function	ARS
❾Export Sheet	Storehouse	Receivable	External Entity to Function	Storehouse
❿Write-off	Receivable	Customer	External Entity to Function	Customer
⓫Loan	Customer	Receivable	External Entity to Function	Customer

In Step 4, the services for the integrated model of this case study were analyzed, and the services-oriented architecture was consequently built. It is shown in Figure 12. The prototype implementation combined seven components and eleven methods into two services, as shown in Figure 13.

In Step 5, services components and services-oriented processes need to be translated into a suitable Web services standard. The users can then edit some information about the services components and translate it into business process execution language for Web services (BPEL4WS). Figure 14 demonstrates the system snapshot of this translation and the result.

In this case study, the legacy accounts receivable system (ARS) is a stand-alone system. In order to provide more flexibility, improve the corporation's productivity, and enhance the capability to fit into the capricious business environment, the Web services architecture is chosen. By using this proposed migration methodology, the original seven components and eleven methods are, in fact, combined into two services. The proposed approach uses component-based technology and builds the system based on business process. For this reason, it is more suitable for business process and management. This study analyzes service components architecture based on user interaction in the business process, so it will be more closely matched with the users' requirements.

CONCLUSION

The advancement of information technology is rapid. It is hard for an old architecture to keep up with the changes in the current market. Enterprises need to use the technology of information system reengineering (ISR) to preserve the value of their existing legacy systems. Currently, a Web services-based system with Service-Oriented Architecture (SOA) is widely adopted as a solution to reengineer enterprise ISs. Using this architecture, the system will be more flexible and adaptable to fit to the dramatically-changing business environment, and hence, make it easier to integrate

Figure 10. The EPC of accounts receivable system

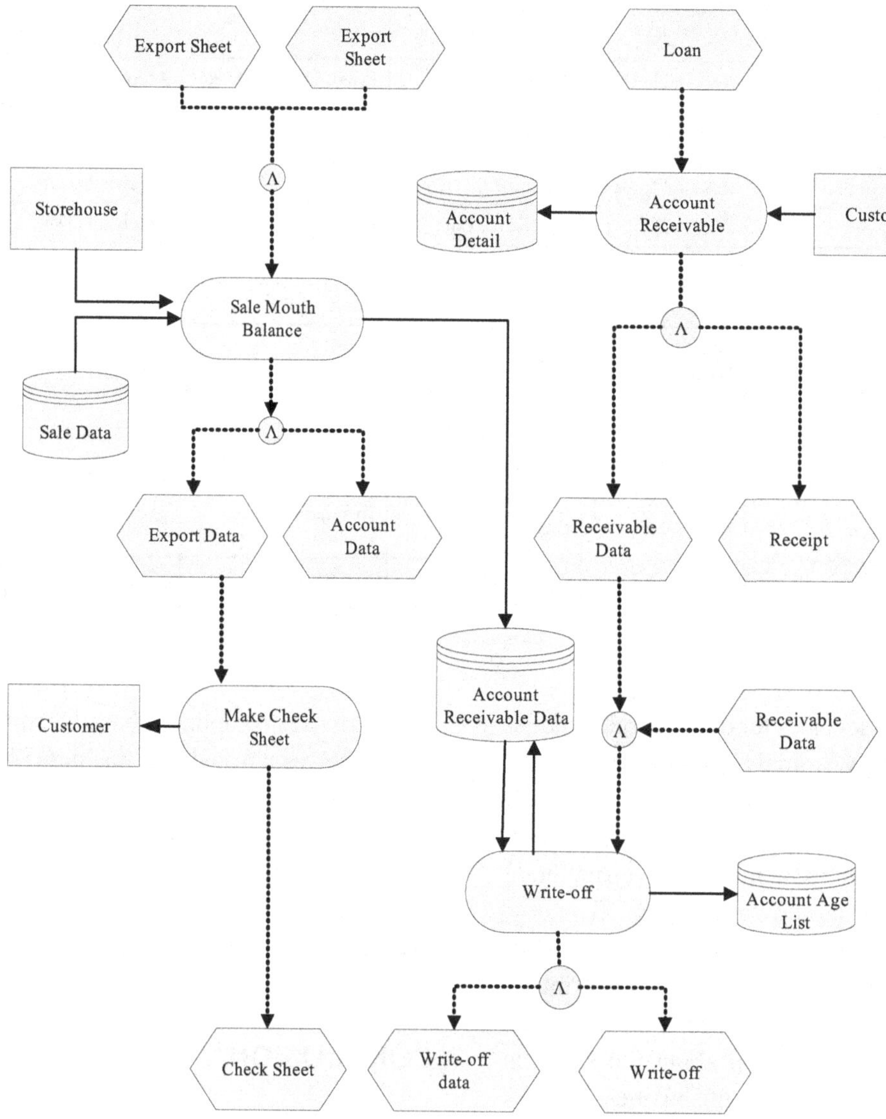

additional applications. Obviously, an enterprise will need to have great synergy to establish such a system. The purpose of this research is to propose a migrating solution to translate the architecture of the legacy system to the SOA with a systematic approach. This methodology is different from traditional object-oriented approaches (see Table 5), which migrates the system to be services-oriented without applying general objected-oriented (OO) or functional oriented features. In this study, the system architecture is implemented according to the prototyping development discussed above.

The contribution of this research can be summarized as follows. First of all, this study uses a systematic approach to explore the service provided by a legacy system. In specific, this research uses a systematic approach to extract business flows from the DFD diagram of a legacy system, and analyzes the service provided by the system from a service perspective. It is indeed a

Figure 11. Integrated model

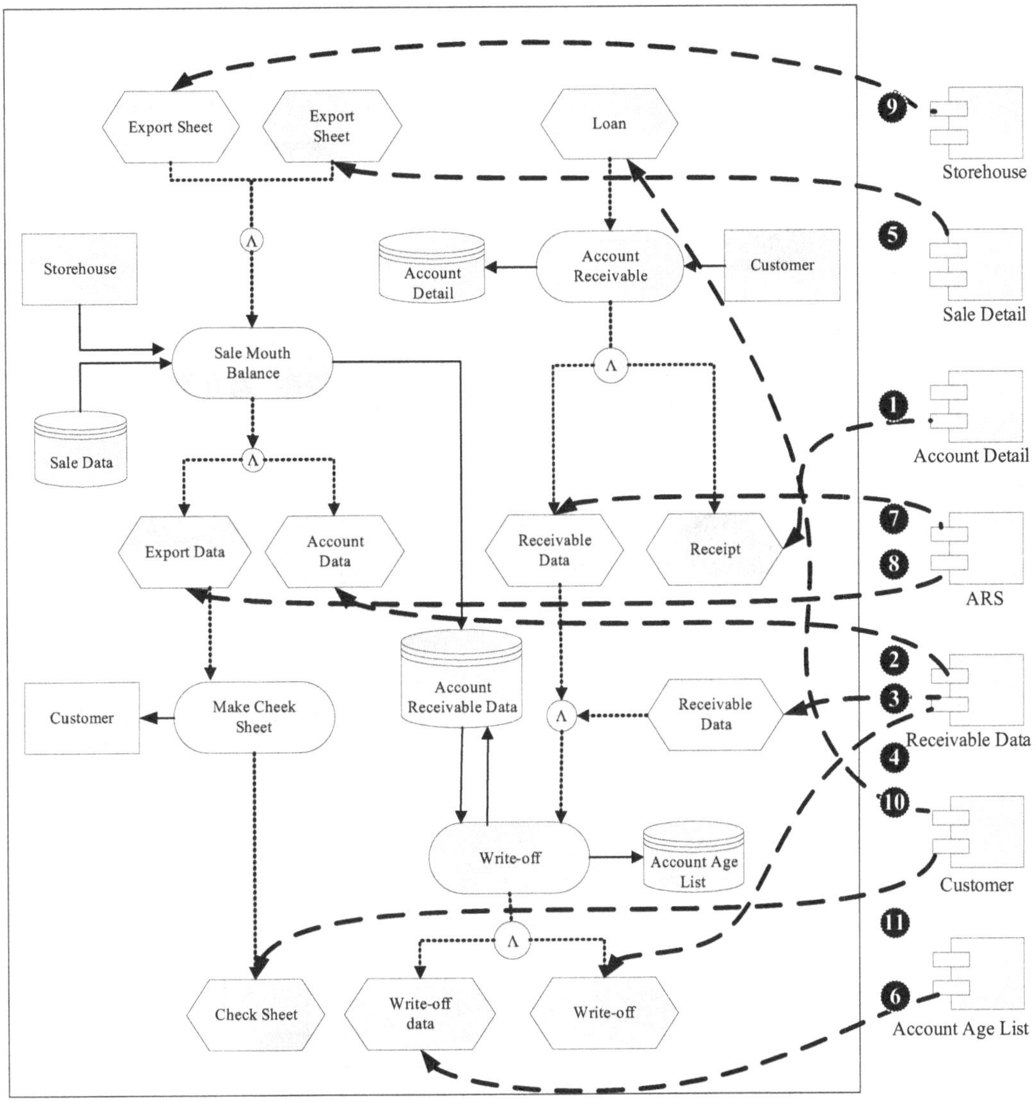

reasonable fit for today's Web Service environment. Second, this study has tightly coupled the analyzed services and the rebuilt components, which will be easily extracted by the legacy system. Consequently, this proposed approach will create a more compact system, which may increase the operational efficiency. Third, the proposed methodology presented in this study can help locate the shared semantic between system components and business processes, and use a systematic method to integrate the system component and business process tightly by carefully analyzing the process. Furthermore, this method can be employed to build a methodology to translate the traditional structured analysis to a corresponding service-oriented framework. This study analyzed the DFD, ERD, and system user interface to develop business processes and system components. In addition, this study analyzed service to construct a systematic approach, which can be utilized to translate the model diagram of a legacy system into a services-oriented EPC

Figure12. Service-oriented model

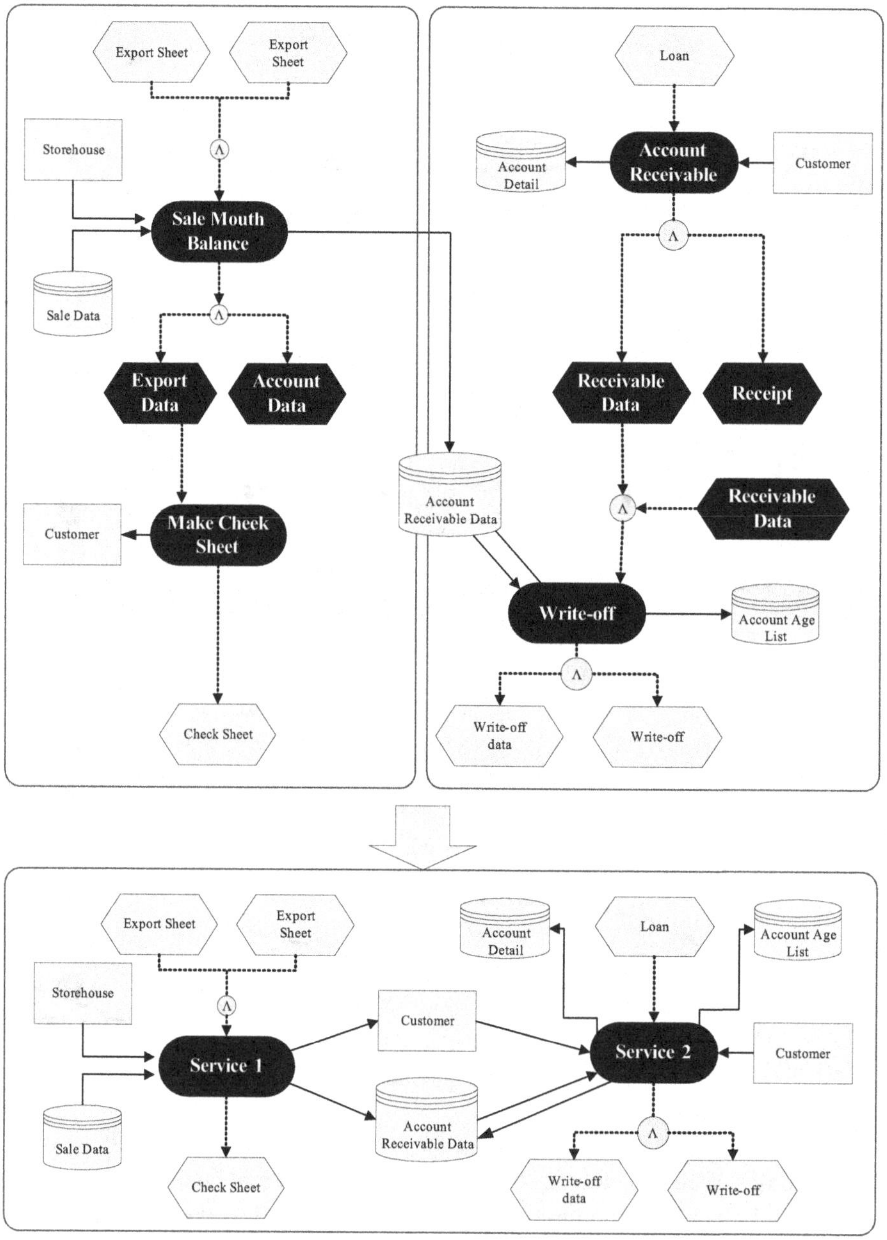

model. The specifications of the Web Service components can be easily built in this case, which in turn can help users to construct Web Service components more efficiently. In addition, the IS reengineering technique can be utilized to build the prototype based on the proposed Web Services framework. To this end, this study built a prototype to validate this proposed methodology. This prototype can guide users to reengineer the legacy system into a Web Service framework. As a result, this research can be a valuable reference for other future studies.

This study adopted a Rule-Based translation methodology, which can be used to improve not

Figure13. Service-oriented model

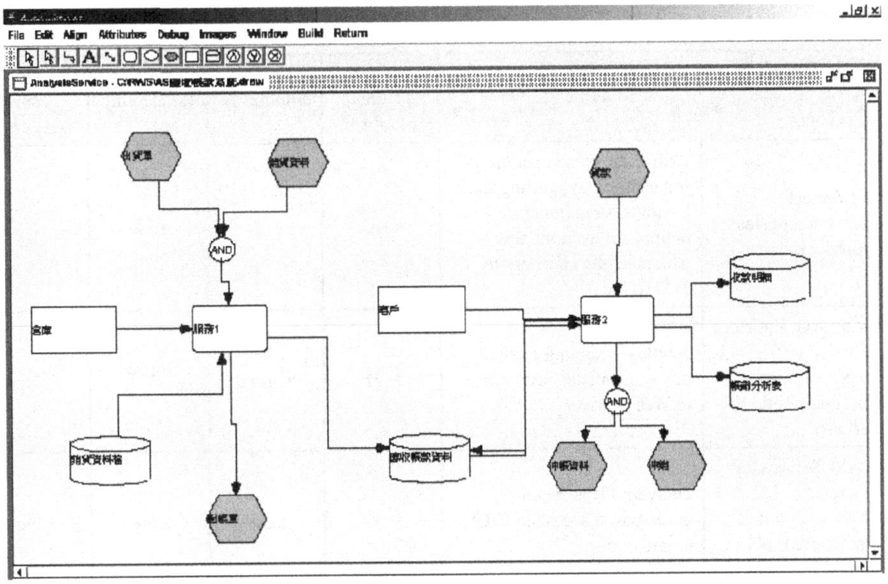

Figure 14. System snapshot of translation to Web services standard

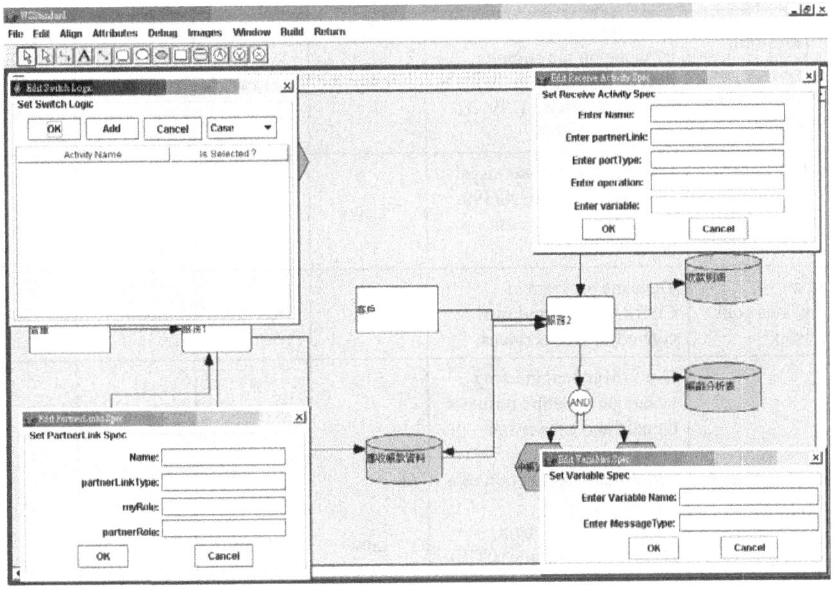

only the quality of the design/development, but also to enhance the correctness of the original data. Some ambiguous or vague wordings presented in the original DFD can definitely influence the quality of a translated process. It is obvious that every phase should be properly revised, so that the output would better fit the actual practice performed in the businesses and/or industries.

In practice, some organizations can either have incomplete DFDs or even have no DFDs to

Table 5. Comparison between the proposed methodology and other similar products and methodologies

Feature / Product/ methodology	Principle	Support different platform	Flexibility	Reusability	Support business process
Cape Connect http://www.capeclear.com/products/	Utilize the screen-scraping technology; getting the legacy system interface definitions as input and generates the appropriate WSDL files	Normal	Low	Low	No
Software AG EntireX http://www.softwareag.com/Corporate/products/entirex/default.asp	Employ wrapping technology translate legacy system to Web services	High	Normal	Normal	No
IBM CICS Transaction Gateway http://www-306.ibm.com/software/htp/cics/ctg/	Delivers J2EE™ standards-based access to CICS applications	Low	Low	Low	No
EXTES Xuras http://www.beacon-it.co.jp/products/pro_serv/eai/xuras/index.shtml	Utilize the wrapping technology to translate legacy system into Web services	High	Normal	Normal	No
GoXML Transform Server http://www.goxml.com/features.php	Integrate business processes by mapping the complex data formats such as EDI, SWIFT, COBOL, CSV, flat text, XML, XBRL	Normal	Low	Low	No
Xbridge Host Data Connect http://www.xbridgesystems.com/	Enhance the Web-services' capabilities of the OS/390 mainframe data access product	Low	Low	Low	No
IONA Orbix http://www.iona.com/products/orbix/	Translate program to COBRA object and then convert to Web services	High	Normal	Normal	No
BALES (Heuvel, Hillegersberg, & Papazoglou, 2002)	Use forward engineering technique to define business domain and use reverse engineering technique to understand the function of a legacy system; use of the Component Definition Language (CDL) to specify both legacy and business objects in order to facilitate a search for matching objects and parameters of Web-services with legacy objects	Low	Low	Low	Yes (only focus on functions reference)

Table 5. continued

This study	Use a systematic approach to explore the service provided by a legacy system, integrate system component and business process, and generates the appropriate WSDL files	High	High	High	Yes (using ERD, DFD, user interface to understand the business process)

perform the system/service design. This study cannot be applied to such organizations. Fortunately, techniques such as IS reverse engineering have gained considerable progress in translating source code to information flow such as DFD (Benedusi, Cimitile, & De Carlini, 1989; Lakhotia, 1995) or translating into ERD diagram from database (Computer Associates, Inc., 2006; SyBase, Inc., 2007).

This study placed focus on the conversion methodology, and paid limited attention to the techniques to develop system components, such as EJB, CORBA, or COM+. Practically, different composition techniques may have different ways to implement the Web Services. To this end, this study lacks any discussion of the different implementation alternatives to design/develop the Web Services.

The proposed methodology is tailored to IS' assistance to various business operations. It works better in situations such as having complicated processes and external transactions. As a result, it does not have sufficient capability in dealing with a simple process or some applications without process. Furthermore, other system programming and firmware that require specific hardware cannot be easily applied with this study.

Future work needs to be done towards a full automatic reengineering process to eliminate the unexpected human factors and/or possible errors. Further study should also be investigated to determine the right component implementation technique. In addition, it is also required to enhance the participation of domain knowledge experts. In the future, additional benefit may include the development of new applications by composing these software components found in the reengineering process in order to accelerate the development time.

ACKNOWLEDGMENT

The National Science Council, Taiwan, under Grant No. NSC95-2524-S-194-004-, has supported the work presented in this article. We greatly appreciate its financial support and encouragement.

REFERENCES

Basu, A., & Kumar, A. (2002). Research commentary: Workflow management issues in e-business. *Information Systems Research, 13*(1), 1-14.

Benedusi, P., Cimitile, A., & De Carlini, U. (1989). A reverse engineering methodology to reconstruct hierarchical data flow diagrams for software maintenance. *Proceedings of the IEEE International Conference on Software Maintenance* (pp. 180-189).

Bouguettaya, A., Malik, Z., Rezgui, A., & Korff, L. (2006). A Scalable Middleware for Web

Databases. *Journal of Database Management, 17*(4), 20-46.

Brereton, P., & Budgen, D. (2000). Component-based systems: A classification of issues. *IEEE Computer, 33*(11), 54-62.

Carroll, N. L., & Calvo, R. A. (2004, July 5). Querying data from distributed heterogeneous database systems through Web services. *Proceedings of the Tenth Australian World Wide Web Conference* (AUSWEB 04). Retrieved from http://ausweb.scu.edu.au/aw04/papers/refereed/carroll/

Chen, Q., Hsu, M., & Mehta, V. (2003). How public conversation management integrated with local business process management. *Proceedings of the IEEE International Conference on E-Commerce, CEC 2003* (pp. 199-206).

Chen, Y., Zhou, L., & Zhang, D. (2006). Ontology-Supported Web Service Composition: An Approach to Service-Oriented Knowledge Management in Corporate Services. *Journal of Database Management, 17*(1), 67-84.

Computer Associates, Inc. (2006, October 6). *AllFusion Erwin Data Modeler.* Retrieved from http://www3.ca.com/Solutions/Product.asp?ID=260

Curbera, F., Khalef, R., Mukhi, N., Tai, S., & Weerawarana, S. (2003, October). The next step in Web services. *Communications of the ACM, 46*(10), 29-34.

Erickson, J., Lyytinen, K., & Siau, K. (2005). Agile Modeling, Agile Software Development, and Extreme Programming: The State of Research. *Journal of Database Management, 16*(4), 88-100.

Erl, T. (2005). Service-oriented architecture: Concepts, technology, and design. Upper Saddle River, NJ: Prentice Hall.

Fong, J., Karlapalem, K., Li, Q., & Kwan, I. (1999). Methodology of schema integration for new database applications: A practitioner's approach. *Journal of Database Management, 10*(1), 3-18.

Gall, H., Klosch, R., & Mittermeir, R. (1995). Object-oriented re-architecturing. *Proceedings of the 5th European Software Engineering Conference (ESEC '95).*

Herzum, P., & Sims, O. (1998). The business component approach. *Proceedings of OOPSLA'98 Business Object Workshop IV.*

Heuvel, W. V. D., Hillegersberg, J. V., & Papazoglou, M. (2002). A methodology to support Web-services development using legacy systems. *IFIP Conference Proceedings; Vol. 231, Proceedings of the IFIP TC8 / WG8.1 Working Conference on Engineering Information Systems in the Internet Context* (pp. 81-103).

Huang, S. M., Hung, S. Y., Yen, D., Li, S. H., & Wu, C. J. (2006). Enterprise application system reengineering: A business component approach. *Journal of Database Management, 17*(3), 66-91.

Huang, S. M., & Yu, F. Y. (2004). IFBP: A methodology for business process discovery based on information flow. *Journal of Information Management, 11*(3), 55-78.

IBM, BEA Systems, Microsoft, SAP AG, & Siebel Systems (2002, July 30). *Business Process Execution Language for Web Services, Version 1.1.* Retrieved from http://www-128.ibm.com/developerworks/library/specification/ws-bpel/

Jin, Y., Urban, S. D., & Dietrich, S. W. (2006). Extending the OBJECTIVE Benchmark for Evaluation of Active Rules in a Distributed Component Integration Environment. *Journal of Database Management, 17*(4), 47-69.

Kim, H. M., Sengupta, A., Fox, M. S., & Dalkilic, M. (2007). A measurement ontology generalizable for emerging domain applications on the semantic

Web. *Journal of Database Management, 18*(1), 20-42.

Kwan, I., & Li, Q. (1999). A hybrid approach to convert relational schema to object-oriented schema. *International Journal of Information Science, 117*, 201–241.

Lakhotia, A. (1995, February). Wolf: A tool to recover dataflow oriented design from source code. *Proceedings of the Fifth Annual Workshop on Systems Reengineering Technology.*

Lee, Y. W., Pipino, L., Strong, D. M., & Wang, R. Y. (2004). Process-embedded data integrity. *Journal of Database Management, 15*(1), 87-103.

Liu, Y., Fekete, A., & Gorton, I. (2005). Design-level performance prediction of component-based applications. *IEEE Transactions on Software Engineering, 31*(11), 928-934.

McArthur, K., Saiedian, H., & Zand, M. (2002). An evaluation of the impact of component–based architectures on software reusability. *Information and Software Technology, 44*(6), 351-359.

Microsoft (2007, April 16). COM: Component object model technologies. Retrieved from http://www.microsoft.com/com/default.mspx

OMG (1995). *Common Object Request Broker Architecture*. Retrieved from http://www.omg.org/gettingstarted/gettingstartedindex.htm

Ommering, R. V. (2005). Software reuse in product populations. *IEEE Transactions on Software Engineering, 31*(7), 537-544,.

Papazoglou, M. P., & Georgakopoulos, D. (2003). Service-oriented computing. *Communications of ACM, 46*, 25-28.

Perrey, R., & Lycett, M. (2003, January). Service-oriented architecture. *Proceedings of the 2003 Symposium on Applications and the Internet Workshops* (pp. 27-31).

Rahayu, J. W., Chang, E., Dillon, T. S., & Taniar, D. (2000). A methodology for transforming inheritance relationships in an object-oriented conceptual model to relational tables. *Information and Software Technology, 42*(8), 571-592.

Sang, J., Follen, G., Kim, C., & Lopez, I. (2002). Development of CORBA-based engineering applications from legacy Fortran programs. *Information and Software Technology, 44*(3), 175-184.

Serrano, M. A., Montes, D. O., & Carver, D. L. (1999). Evolutionary migration of legacy systems to an object-based distributed environment. *Proceedings of the IEEE International Conference on Software Maintenance (ICSM'99)* (pp. 86-95).

Sprott, D. (2002). Service-oriented process matters. *CBDi Forum Newsletter.*

Stal, M. (2002). Web services: Beyond component-based computing association for computing machinery. *Communications of the ACM, 45*(10), 71-77.

Sun - Java EE (2007, April 16). *Enterprise JavaBeans Technology*. Retrieved from http://java.sun.com/products/ejb/

Sutor, B. (2006, May 21). Open standards vs. open source: How to think about software, standards, and service-oriented architecture at the beginning of the 21st century. Retrieved from http://www.sutor.com/newsite/essays/e-OsVsOss.php

SyBase, Inc. (2007, April 16). *Sybase Power Designer Redefining Enterprise Modeling*. Retrieved from http://www.sybase.com/products/enterprisemodeling/powerdesigner

Vanston, M. (2005, August 21). Integrating legacy systems with Web services. *The Meta Group Inc.* Retrieved from http://www.metagroup.com/us/displayArticle.do?oid=32393

Vinoski, S. (1997, February). *CORBA*. Integrating diverse applications within distributed heterogeneous environments. *IEEE Communications Magazine, 14*(2), 46-55.

Vitharana, P., & Jain, H. (2000). Research issues in testing business components. *Information & Management, 37*(6), 297-309.

Waguespack, L., & Schiano, W. T. (2004). Component-based IS architecture. *Information Systems Management, 21*(3), 53-60.

Zhao, L., & Siau, K. (2007). Information mediation using metamodels—An approach using XML and common warehouse metamodel. *Journal of Database Management, 18*(3), 69-82.

This work was previously published in Journal of Database Management, Vol. 18, Issue 4, edited by K. Siau, pp. 1-25, copyright 2007 by IGI Publishing, formerly known as Idea Group Publishing (an imprint of IGI Global).

Section V
Organizations and Structures

Chapter XVI
A Socio-Technical Interpretation of IT Convergence Services:
Applying a Perspective from Actor Network Theory and Complex Adaptive Systems

Myeong Ho Lee
Yonsei University, Korea

Lee Jung-hoon
Yonsei University, Korea

Kwak Jeong Ho
Yonsei University, Korea

ABSTRACT

The trend toward convergence, initiated by advances in ICT, entails the creation of new value chain networks, made up by partnerships between actors in unrelated industries. Such a process of convergence, however, can create a new dimension of network complexity, precipitating dynamic behavior among actors. In this paper we seek to understand how different actors in value chain networks have co-evolved in practice with the development of convergence services. Interpretative case studies on two different converged services in Korea (mobile banking, and One phone services) are undertaken to examine how different actor network adapted in different ways to shape the overall complexity of the converged service. The case study analysis is innovative in being conducted within a combined framework of Complex Adaptive Systems and Actor Network Theory. This synthesis offers a way to characterize the drivers of co-evolutionary behavior, capturing the translation processes undergone by actor networks.

INTRODUCTION

The rapid development of Information and Communication Technology (ICT) and associated rollout of ICT infrastructure places firms in a position where they increasingly offer converged digital services. This concept refers both to new services, infrastructure, or features (ITU, 1996), and the integration of various consumer interfaces (EU, 1997). The trend towards convergence involves both a technological development and a socio-economic process, with firms being impelled to create new Value Chain Networks (VCNs) linking activities in previously unrelated industries. The phenomenon of digital convergence can be approached in various ways. For instance, it can mean the convergence of different networks through an increase in interconnection and interoperability, entailing the convergence of services and markets, of firms and industries, and of regulatory institutions (Ovum, 1999). In such situations, there is both a need and an opportunity for the partners in any convergence to adopt a joint coordinated approach in order to establish more efficient value chains. This perception also captures how, in a modern, networked economy, a firm's success or failure may be dependent on the success of its network, rather than on its inter-functional performance (Archibald, Karabakal, and Karlsson, 1999).

As networks develop and firms form new partnerships, however, the process of digital convergence creates a new dimension of network complexity, precipitating dynamic behavior among actors. In recent years, scholars and practitioners have sought to understand how different actors interact with others in the VCN, as these forms of behavior have co-evolved with the development of converged services. The pragmatic challenge for network participants is no longer to eliminate network complexity or volatility, but rather how best to manage and exploit these phenomena. Although a number of articles have discussed the contexts of digital convergence, the drivers of such forms of network evolution have yet to be theoretically explored from a socio-technical perspective. This paper describes an interpretative case study undertaken to examine the specific adaptations of a VCN in the course of the convergence of digital services. We use a combined framework of Complexity Adaptive Systems (CAS) theory (Axelrod and Cohen, 2000; Anderson, 1999) and Actor Network Theory (ANT) based on Callon and Latour (1981), analyzing the theories' implications for different convergence cases. Further, we classify phenomena of digital convergence into two categories and perform case studies for each category. The proposed framework suggests a possible synthesis between CAS and ANT offering a structured way to characterize the drivers of co-evolutionary behavior

This paper is structured as follows. The next section briefly presents a literature review of ANT and CAS. Each case study domain is introduced descriptively. We then characterize ANT and CAS as tools for capturing the emergent co-evolutionary nature of digital convergence. These considerations lead to the framing of our research design and its application. We analyze two different cases of converged services (Mobile banking, the One phone service) in sections 4, 5 and 6 using ANT. Working through our design specification, we then analyze the two different cases according to the key characteristics of CAS, comparing the findings of the two methodologies. Our conclusion considers how CAS and ANT may be to some extent re-specified for the purpose of examining digital convergence from a socio-technical perspective.

LITERATURE REVIEW

Case Study Domain: Digital Convergence Services

This section defines two different convergence domains 1) within the telecommunications sector;

2) between different industries such as telecommunications and banking.

A typical example of convergence within telecommunications is fixed-mobile convergence. Traditionally, fixed and mobile communications have operated separately. Recently, however, fixed and mobile communications have begun to substitute for and compete with each other, with the expectation being that the two formats will eventually integrate in e.g. personal numbering services, unified messaging services, single billing services and unified portals (Murphy, 2002; Horvath and Maldoom, 2002). The one phone service studied here designates a service in which customers are provided with a single mobile phone for home use on fixed-network tariffs and on the road at mobile prices. In the one-phone service, the service provider attempts to gain a commercial advantage by leveraging its capacity across both fixed-lines and mobile connections. At present, however, problems with data communication are preventing one-phone service from delivering anticipated benefits (Sturder, 2001).

Recent years have also seen a growing trend towards the convergence of between telecommunications and other previously distinct, non-competing industries (Kim, Eun, Kang, and Lee, 2006). Typical examples of this type of convergence involve a wide variety of new services such as RFID (radio frequency identification), home networks, telematics, e-government, e-health, e-learning, m-portals, and so on. The example selected in this paper is Mobile banking (M-Banking). Inter-industry convergence represents both an opportunity and a threat to telecommunications and conventional industry sectors. Faced with market saturation and the prospect of stagnation, the telecommunications industry is now seeking new opportunities through convergence. Inter-industry convergence distinctively requires at least two different providers of entirely different origin (in the case of mobile-payment or banking, for example, typically a communications provider and a conventional retail bank). These partners collaborate in the knowledge they may eventually become competitors in the same marketplace. Inter-industry convergence further poses traditional telecom players the problems of a new set of customers (and customer requirements) and regulations.

This paper's subject domains are delimited in that we do not deal, for instance, with forms of convergence between voice and data communications such as VoIP (Voice over Internet Protocol) and WAP (wireless application protocol)-based services, although these count as examples of convergence within telecommunications sector (see Ono and Aoki, 1998, and Shin, 2006 for treatments of these services).

Actor Network Theory

In recent years, Actor Network Theory (ANT) has been applied in Information Systems (IS) contexts to explore dynamic interactions between people and technology in technologies' acceptance stage (Callon 1986a, 1986b; Callon and Latour, 1981). The theory's originators devised ANT to describe how actors form alliances, enrolling other actors to form socio-technical networks. Networks are described as having a focal actor, who enrols other actors (including technology) translating strategic objectives through four different stages: problematization, interessement, enrolment and mobilization.

One of the attractions of using ANT in a technology management context is ANT's symmetric view of people and technologies, which views technology as potentially an influential factor in shaping dynamic network interactions (Walsham, 1997). In order to achieve some measure of network stability, the focal actor needs to align other actors' diverse behaviors through proposing Obligatory Passage Points (OPP). The theory contributes to understand that heterogeneous networks evolve as they are organized, through formalized processes of translation, to mobilize their resources effectively.

ANT has been applied to technology management in a pragmatic way as researchers have sought to describe IS research domains (see Bloomfield *et al*, 1994; Frohmann, 1995, Vidgen and McMaster, 1996, Linde *et al*, 2001, Allen, 2004, Faraj *et al* , 2004). Detailed ANT applications may be found in Walsham (1997), who offer a brief review of ANT applications in the IS field. Recently, Oh and Lee (2005) analyze the convergence service of M-Banking, illustrating how focal actors inscribe their interests in a given technology. In short, ANT has offered a resourceful framework according to which the micro-level of socio-technical changes may be understood and analyzed as dynamic rather than static. Applying ANT to converging services would show how focal actors use driving forces to inscribe other actors in their purposes. This paper proposes to offer such a description.

Complexity Theory and Complex Adaptive Systems

New technological developments and market demands have precipitated dramatic structural and operational transformation in business, entailing the reconfiguration of whole industries and processes. The VCN is no longer static but may be viewed as an evolving network that dynamically changes over time. Each VCN is comprised of a number of actors representing firms or different levels of organizational entity or function (e.g. marketing, manufacturing, sales) within companies (Lee, 2003). These actors interact with each other to create complex new orders. Research addressing these issues has recently begun to turn to methods developed for the study of emerging complexity across physical, biological and social science (Benbya and McKelvey, 2006). Complexity is typically understood as an emergent property of systems as these comprise a larger number of self-organizing actors interacting in dynamic and non-linear fashion. Complexity theory emphasizes the order and disorder of social systems existing on the edge of chaos and shaped by positive feedback (Dooley, 1997). The concepts and theoretical frameworks proposed in the field of organizational science lent impetus to the design and analysis of organizational dynamics in business and management.

While earlier research has focused on manufacturing complexity, other research works deploy CAS in the context of different IS fields. A number of contributions consider IS development (Benbya and Mckelvey, 2006), information as such (Moser and Law, 2006), large scale system change (Chae and Lanzara, 2006) and information processes (Kallinikos, 2006). Kovas and Uendo (2004) draw an analogy between the properties of Complexity Adaptive Systems (CAS) and information systems design for business. Mufatto and Faldani (2003) and Van Aardt (2004) comparably compare open source software to information systems development, where open source tools represent a bottom-up approach which can eventuate in a robust software design. Kim and Kaplan (2006) use CAS properties to model IS engagement between software systems and business organization.

THE PROPOSED FRAMEWORK AND RESEARCH DESIGN

ANT (dealing with the micro-level of inter-actor interaction) and CAS (describing emergent behavior on a meta- or system level) complement each other as ways of capturing the evolution of forms of networked business collaboration. Kim and Kaplan (2006) have recently proposed a synthesis between CAS and ANT, retaining on the one hand the ability of ANT to understand the creation and maintenance over time of order in socio-technical networks, and on the other CAS to explain the drivers of co-evolutionary behaviors in a more structured and holistic way.

The Properties of CAS in the Converged Service

The first step towards characterizing converged actor networks is to identify features corresponding to CAS properties e.g. shifting patterns of interaction between converging network participants. Holland(1988, 1995), Markovsky (1998) and Benbya and McKelvey (2006) explain that such adaptations of organizational network exhibit many of the attributes or exemplify many of the concepts of complexity theory. These may be categorized as *'Connectivity and Interdependence'*, *'Co-evolution'*, *'Far from equilibrium'*, and *'Self-organization'*. In this section, we explain how these attributes may be brought to bear on real examples in case study analysis.

Connectivity & Interdependence: In a complex network, each actor has its own connectivity and interdependence with other actors; its actions may exert a significant impact on other actors and on its environment. Complex behaviors arise out of the interaction of different actor actions; connectivity also defines the level of inter-relatedness of each actor within a converged service network which has both human and systemic (i.e. IS) features or artifacts. A network's degree of interdependence, or fineness in inter-actor responsiveness, is often determined by the degree of inter-actor connectivity (Axelrod and Cohen, 1999). Intense interconnectivity will create multiple and intricate dependencies throughout a system. In supply chain management literature, the bullwhip effect phenomenon (Lee, Padmanabhan, and Whang, 1997) is a classic example of how interdependence may create unforeseen consequences, as volatility is magnified as orders pass up an interconnected chain. Lower degrees of connectivity, by contrast, create damping effects, reducing responsiveness but minimizing disruption.

This paper understands networks' level of connectivity and interdependence as one aspect of how complex behaviors arise and are managed during the translation process in converging networks. However, some actors within a network will also be affected by other dimensional sources of behavioral change, such as social, cultural, technical, economic, political and global concerns (Axerlod and Cohen, 1999). These sources may be considered as external variables in any network and are themselves drivers of network change. In this paper, we will investigate firstly how each actor has an inter-connection with others, describing different actor roles and relationships of interdependence.

Co-evolution: Another question posed by complexity theory is whether any business network may plausibly be described as an eco-system. Kauffman (1993) uses the terms of biological complexity theory to posit the process of co-evolution as an ongoing development in which every network actor is influenced by the actions of every other. A typical example of a co-evolution process might be a merger between actors. The evolution of one network will conceivably be dependent on the activities of each actor within another network (Dooley, 1997).

This paper examines co-evolutionary processes in converged services in terms of actors' driving forces interacting to create whole eco-systems. Kauffman's concept of hill-climbing (Kauffman, 1993), which this paper adopts, explains the fitness value and the fitness landscape of network ecosystems. In the terms of this concept, every network environment may be thought of as more or less mountainous according to a qualitative measure. For instance, if for a single service, two competing networks have been co-evolved, the distribution of fitness value will be less mountainous, meaning that the service landscape as a whole may be subject to sudden deformation. This may have catastrophic effects on the industry as a whole, and on any given industry actor.

Far from equilibrium: The assumption of traditional systems thinking was that systems were stable or in an equilibrium state. Complex theorists suppose that networks are capable of realignment and change when they arrive at points designated as being 'far from equilibrium' or far from a stable state (Cramer, 1993; Mainzer, 1994). If, for instance, unforeseen events occur within a network, networks may fluctuate over time undergoing ripple effects. These chaos states resolve into stable states when the network finds new orders and a new network structure (Lichtenstein and McKelvey, 2004). When systems are forced to deviate from stable states, actors are able to explore new opportunities, entering into a space of possibilities in which they may find pathways towards creating new patterns of network relationships. During this process, actors may theoretically take separate paths eventuating in different forms of network.

This paper specifically explores actor and network behaviors arising from network deviations from an equilibrium state as a result of converged services being initiated. The idea of 'far from equilibrium state' can be applied to explain the evolution over time of networks reshaped by the emergence of new technologies. This model also allows us to identify new sources of space possibilities and alternative paths for actors towards network solutions.

Self-organization: CAS has also typically deployed a concept of self-organization, understanding that term to describe an actor's robust or proactive reaction to stimuli in performing tasks on the basis of its knowledge and resources (Kauffman, 1993; Holland, 1995). Actors do not simply act in response to their environment, but also exhibit goal-oriented behavior in taking the initiative. Certain changes in actors' internal and

Table 1. Summary of key concepts in ANT

Stage	*Description*
Problematization Stage	External or other triggers changes business landscape and agent's space of opportunity Focal actor(s) seek to exploit potential competitive advantage by organizing partners into new network. Actors are motivated by actor-specific goals and intentions Focal actors designate obligatory passage points (OPPs) binding participants to network configuration of focal agent choice; focal agent allocate partner roles and responsibilities (Callon, 1986) Converging service networks characterized by participants' perception of strong mutual advantage in collaborating
Interessement stage	Networks seeks to stabilize their advantage by consolidating inter-agent patterns of relationships and collaboration Focal agents offer both inducements and threats in bid to enforce participation
Enrolment Stage	Actors proceed to "multilateral negotiation, trials of strength & tricks that accompany the interessements and enable them to succeed" (Callon, 1986, pp211). Focal actors define problems & problem-solving responsibilities to the satisfaction of all participants Detailed actor roles are negotiated
Mobilization Stage	Networks have succeeded in translating business vision; networks attain high degree of inter-dependence (the so-called 'black box') among collaborators, whose space of opportunity is reduced (Latour 1987) Subsequent evolution usually precipitated by external change

external environment may activate goals requiring actors' immediate action.

The Translation Process of the Converged Actor Network

ANT defines four stages in the translation of network participants' business vision, describing the evolution of forms of inter-relationship among partners (e.g. supplier-client relationships, technology transfer and sharing, customer information sharing). Focal actors seek to lead participants through a process in which their space of opportunity is progressively reduced as the network gains traction.

All four translation stages detailed above are described from an evolutionary perspective, as the focal actor acts to support enrolment through the imposition of OPP and leveraging of combined network i.e. all-actor resources to meet ultimate network objectives. A distinguishing feature of ANT is its conceptualization of technology (e.g. one-chip technology in M-Banking) as an actor, with inscribed interests and strategies, on the same footing as human organizational actors. The four-part division of converging processes offered by ANT allows us sensitively to trace networks' developments in ways potentially obscured by systemic or external-perspective descriptions.

Research Design and Application

Despite theoretical differences between ANT and CAS, a synthesis of both theories has the potential to enhance our understanding of network dynamics in a complementary way as shown in figure 1. While ANT as a theoretical framework is concerned with understanding the formation and evolution of networks through translation processes initiated by designated focal actors, the CAS perspective studies the characteristics of network behavior manifest on a systemic level through the co-evolution of actor actions.

In order to get some sense of the possible utility of combining ANT and CAS, we conducted a number of interpretative case study in converged services using the combined framework. Thus this paper's research method took the form of a comparative multiple case study aiming to validate (or otherwise) the proposed framework. Comparable multiple case studies have been widely used to verify certain assumptions or prove certain conditions under a variety of experimental or empirical study conditions (Benbasat, Goldstain,

Figure 1. The proposed framework for analyzing the cases of convergence services

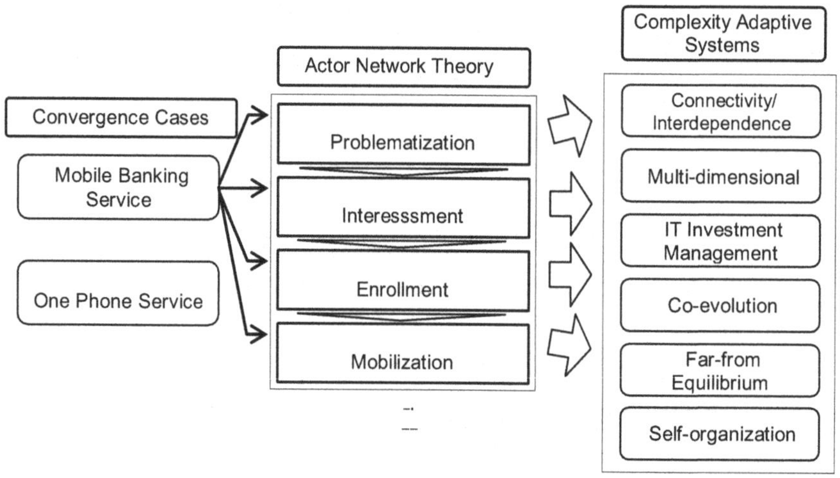

and Mead, 1987). It is accepted that using more than one case study is beneficial in improving the reliability and validity of qualitative studies (Yin, 1984).

In this study, we used multiple cases in subjecting the process oriented methods and properties of converged service networks to analysis, aiming to understand networks' evolution over time, and in so doing, to assess the strengths of each theory. In conducting case study analysis, we collected basic data from media sources in Korea, including business articles and newspapers using a keyword to identify selected cases (e.g. M-Banking). In a parallel way, we also collected information in academic papers and published research institution reports. After transcribing interviews and meetings, we initially analyzed data within the combined conceptual framework of ANT and CAS. The study sought to compensate for the relative paucity of information in each case by conducting semi-structured interviews with participants by email and telephone for each converged service (i.e. M-Banking, the one-phone service). The steps used for this paper were derived from the influential procedures put forward by Eisenhardt (1989) and Yin (1984), and sought throughout to yield a reliable result in terms of its account of the evolution of converged services.

CASE ONE: MOBILE BANKING SERVICE

First Generation of Mobile Banking Service: Web browser based Mobile Banking

Problemization

The focal actor(s) in the case of M-Banking services were Korean mobile carriers who saw an interest in forming a new converged service network in partnership with other actors including commercial banks, mobile phone manufacturers, users and technology as shown in table 2.

The focal actor, SK Telecom, initially acknowledged the banks' strategic interest in extending their networks beyond online banking and voice

Table 2. Networked actors for mobile banking service

Network Actors	*Actor's Role*	*Actor's Name*
Mobile Carriers	Voice and data transmission Internet billing and banking using subscriber information	SK Telecom (The focal actor)
Commercial Banks & Financial Service Providers	Maintaining mobile subscriber's database All relevant banking transaction information including account authorization	Woori, Han-mi Bank, Korean Exchange, Jae-il, Hana, Kyung Nam, Busan, Daegu, securesoft (security) and R2C (platform providers)
Technology	Web browser technology	SK Telecom
Mobile Phone Manufacturing	Manufacturing and supplying the mobile devices	Samsung Electronics, LG Electronics, Motorola
Users	Mobile phone subscribers	
Government & Regulatory Bodies	Mobile banking watch dog and regulatory bodies	Financial Supervisory Service (FSS) Ministry of Information & Communication (MIC)

banking; 'Nemo', SK Telecom's m-banking would benefit banks by extending their coverage to non-territorial areas and creating another sales domain offering significant cost reductions through the specialization of sales channels(Kim, 2003a; Kim, 2003b). The bank actor also realized the marketing benefits of using mobile service providers in expanding their sales channels and affiliating these to converged networks (Kang, 2003). Mobile phone manufacturing actors joined calculating the network would boost demand for their products while imposing relatively light or surmountable technological constraints. Likewise, technology actors were incentivized by the promised further development of new technological capacity. Users stood to benefit from converged services. Lastly, support from the Korean government incentivized participants by promising a large market for m-banking services (MIC, 1999). As the offering was not difficult for other actors to accept, the focal actors in this case found it relatively easy to create a passage point tying all other actors into the particular network determined by their focal initiatives.

Interessement

In this stage, the focal Actor convinces other Actors to adhere to its OPPs so that the actor network achieves a degree of stability. In this instance, the focal Actors allowed banks simply to access their transaction databases, organized in a similar way to fixed-line cable networks, and the mobile manufacturing Actors developed phones supporting M-Banking applications. The focal Actor offered neural application developments, i.e. web-browsers encouraging other Actors to participate in the converging network. Actors were able to join together at the problematization stage in that all clearly saw the benefits of future collaboration. At the same time, the focal Actor consolidated its dominant position by putting in place arrangements standing to entrench its competitive advantage. Banks, for instance, were threatened with a loss of competitive advantage in that they would in future be unable to replicate rival m-banking services without a mobile partner (further, m-banking potentially represented a rival to their traditional bricks-and-mortar offerings). Similarly, mobile phone manufacturers were also constrained in having to use network providers' sales channels. In this instance, in early 2000 the participating mobile phone manufacturer was not able to reject the focal actor's passage point given that the mobile carrier was their primary customer i.e. SK Telecom's major supplier at the time was Samsung Electronics. In short, the focal Actors prevailed upon other Actors to participate in the converged network by offering both positive and negative results of enrolling.

Enrollment

While participant Actors quickly recognized their interest in forming a converged network, during the initial stages of network formation the user Actor's benefits were underplayed, leading to the customer 'being left behind'. In effect, unforeseen technology constraints prohibited the enrolment of user Actors, despite the fact that all network participants had accepted the network passage points. Even though the web-browser technology (virtual machines) were a standard platform, its reliability was not acceptable for user actors, especially in terms of the time taken accessing virtual banking services. The number of service usage was less than 1,200,000 per month in 2004 (National Bank of Korea, 2004). Higher transaction costs were incurred due to long connection times, leading to an incompatibility between what user demands and bank Actors' business-model thresholds (Kim, 2003a). This unexpected constraint fundamentally disrupted the mobilization stage.

Mobilization

First generation M-Banking services, then, was not in success on account of users' difficulties in accepting new technology; this meant that the focal Actor was not able to mobilize networks to the advantage of all network participants.

Second Generation of Mobile Banking Service: IC Chip Based Mobile Banking Actor Networks

Problematization

The initial problem facing participants in any second-generation m-banking service was that a number of previous attempts and virtual architectures (e.g. SMS, WAP) had failed to enrol user actors in mobile banking services (KRNIC, 2005). Nevertheless, the same group of participants had similar interests in forming a converged service network as before. The mobile carriers wanted to grow their subscriber base, while commercial banks wanted to improve operational efficiency through direct marketing. These objectives became possible with the proposition of a new data-based business model using new embedded Integrated Chip (IC) technology. The availability of this technology also brought m-banking to the attention of other actors, and significantly changed the relations of dominance (e.g. as to the identity of the focal actor) around m-banking services. In effect, Kook-min bank, the largest commercial bank, formed a strategic alliance with LG Telecom, the third largest mobile service providers to launch the 'Bank On' service in 2004 (LG Telecom, 2004).

Since the new model envisioned the carriers signing up customers of Kook-min Bank, they did not need to levy either a service charge on users or data transaction fees. The focal actor, Kook-min bank, pursued this second attempt to extend its sales channels since it no longer saw a significant threat to its core banking division from mobile-based operators. At the same time, the bank saw scope for improving customer satisfaction, operational efficiency, and service charge profits through m-services, while maintaining control of user information (Park, 2003). The mobile manufacturer and technology Actors were also able to claim a larger role in second generation m-services, since IC chips required new application features which stood to stimulate future markets. None of these evolutions, though, was so major that it required any significant redefinition of network Actor roles.

Interessement

To compete with LG Telecom's 'Bank On Service', SK Telecom and KTF (the second mobile carrier) launched 'M-Bank' and 'K-Bank' respectively. The focal actors, the commercial banks, retained control over user information by participating in three networks as the only Actor with this cross-market level of data access.

In m-banking, the time-specific emergence of the technology Actor i.e. IC chips might be thought to militate against the emergence of later rival networks to the initial service. However, in the case of the two later entrants (SK Telecom and KTF), the mobile companies spent heavily on advertising in order to ramp up market share. This enabled late-entrant participants to the second and third networks to buy into the focal actor's. Banks could threaten mobile phone companies with their exclusion from m-banking services, which could hinder their subscriber growth and retention, especially as new models came onto the market. As a result, the focal actor was able to enforce its network and the service usage was increasing from 1,199,000 in 2003 to 4,947,000 in 2004 (National Bank of Korea, 2004).

Enrollment

At this stage, most networked actors accepted the focal actor's OPP; some, however, queried the terms of the bank's ownership of information on service users. SK Telecom and KTF continuously claimed that the focal actor wielded a form of monopoly ownership on information, which was also detrimental to the interest of handset manufacturers. Furthermore, bank ownership of information hindered systems' operational efficiency, in that each bank needed a separate embedded IC chip in networked devices serving its own customer base. While IC-enabled m-banking services worked much better than the conventional web browser service, users still wanted an integrated chip mode (Kim, 2004). In short, however much all players had signed up to the banks' OPP, the network they structured was difficult to sustain over any long-run equilibrium.

Mobilization

Even though some potential participants baled at the banks' IC chips, m-banking services were still widely taken up among Korean end-users. It seems that user information has been confirmed as the new network OPP; further, new dimensions of actor networks may come into being with the development of emerging 3G telecommunication technology.

CASE TWO: ONE PHONE SERVICE

One Phone Service-KT

Problematization

The landline service provider, KT, launched 'One Phone Service' firstly to stem the loss of its customers to mobile service providers (SK Telecom, KTF and LG Telecom), further protecting the landline market and creating new business areas (Electronic Times, 2006). Next, KT saw a potential market opportunity in creating a fixed and mobile convergence network utilizing bluetooth (a type of transmission technology) to develop the home networking market. The focal Actor anticipated extending its voice and data services over its developed line network (e.g. PSTN and KORNET: Korean Internet Network) to previously uncovered areas by joining its offer to the provision of its mobile services (KTF). The service was launched in June 2004 with MIC's approval of the fixed line-mobile linkup.

In its inception, the service network comprised mobile carriers, network equipment manufactur-

Table 3. Networked actors for one phone service

Network Actors	*Actor's Role*	*Actor's Name*
One Phone Service Provider	Offering convergence service using fixed line (voice and data) and mobile network of KTF Direct sales service Limited pricing discount	Korean Telecom (the focal actor, KT)
Mobile Carrier	Rent out-door communication network Provide wireless network and contents	KTF (a subsidiary company of KT)
Technology	Bluetooth (Maximum data speed: 56 Kbps)	KT
Mobile Phone and Network Equipment Manufacturers	Manufacturing compatible mobile phones for one phone service Access Point equipment for one phone service including N/W equipments	LG Electronics, Samsung Electronics, Small Mediums Enterprises
Users	One phone service subscribers	
Government & Regulatory Bodies	Governing and regulating one phone service commercializing	MIC

ers and contents providers as shown in the table below.

The focal Actor sought to induce other Actors to participate, including KTF, network equipment manufacturers and content providers. For KTF, the incentive was the opportunity of offering their existing content and wireless services to KT subscribers. For manufacturers, it was new users, and for end-users it was cost and convenience.

However, the focal Actor's plans were scuppered when the government imposed limits on KT in the name of mitigating KT's dominance in the fixed line market. The regulatory authority, therefore, restricted the payment discount that KT could offer mobile capacity participants. In this, the government Actor was critical in that they salami-sliced away many advantages of the converged one phone service (Lee *et al.*, 2004; KTMRL, 2006).

Interessement

KT framed win-win objectives in seeking to induce participation, allowing their immediate strategic partner, KTF, to charge users normal rates when users of the one phone service were outside the Duo Zone. KT further offered manufacturers full equipment inter-operability with their service, seeking to remove technological constraints on actors' participation. The OPP set up by KT was thus the company's fixed line assets, which were thought valuable in a cordless marketplace. Users were imagined to want an integrated service piggybacking on fixed lines, and the government actor neutral as regards developing the actor network.

Enrollment

KT, however, failed to enrol the necessary range of participants when users found that there were no cost advantages to using the combined phone service after the government's regulatory intervention. KT's anticipated cost discounts and driver pricing policy were never carried out, and the network's access points were not compatible with KTF's. In addition, the cost of additional access point equipment for users was not low enough to attract consumer interest. From manufacturers' point of view, the network's slow development did not sufficiently discount R&D costs, stymying the incentive for continuous product improvement. From a technological viewpoint, moreover, the core technology of the one phone service, Bluetooth, had a limited data bandwidth of 56 kbps, making it incompatible with other types of data service offering. In short, the focal Actor's network proposition was rejected by users, as well as other Actors, who found no mutual benefit in developing products for the service. Another critical error on the focal Actor's part was to fail to appreciate the degree to which the user wanted a high speed internet service.

Mobilization

The one phone service did not get so far as the mobilization stage after all other actors rejected the focal actor's definition of mutual business objectives. The KT one phone service was abandoned on March 2006, with KT keeping the business name for strategic purposes and continuing to serve subscribers.

Enjoyment Zone Service

Problematization

While the land operator, KT, invested enormous efforts in offering a one phone service to landline subscribers, LG Telecom, the mobile carrier with the third position in the mobile market, in April 2006 initiated a one phone service for existing and prospective customers known as the 'Enjoyment Zone'. The service was conceived by the focal Actor as tasked with retaining mobile customers,

Table 4. Networked actors for 'Enjoyment Zone' service

Network Actors	*Actor's Role*	*Actor's Name*
'Enjoyment Service' Provider	Fixed and mobile converged service provider No restriction on service price discount by the government actor Used LG Telecom retailer channels	LG Telecom (the focal actor)
Retailer	Providing 'Enjoyment Zone' marketing for subscribers and sales channels	LG Telecom Retailers
Technology	Bluetooth (Used wireless technology for data service)	LG Telecom
Mobile Phone and Network Equipment Manufacturers	Manufacturing compatible mobile phones for 'Enjoyment Zone' Manufacturing N/W Equipments (e.g. Alimi) for the service	LG Electronics; Samsung Electronics; Pantech & Curitel; Small & Medium Enterprises
Users	'Enjoyment Zone' Subscribers	
Government & Regulatory Bodies	'Enjoyment Zone' Subscribers Authorized 'Enjoyment Zone' service for commercialization Regulates fair telecommunications market	Korean Communication Commission (KCC)

protecting its mobile market share against the incursions of primarily land operators i.e. KT's bluetooth based home-networking market, and creating a new market opportunity in combining wire and wireless-based services. The focal Actor (LG Telecom) developed a new technology application 'bluetooth,' offering other Actors (e.g. mobile phone manufacturers, content providers) the opportunity of forming a network by defining detailed collaboration problem.

Table 4 shows the shape of the network at take-up, detailing participant roles.

The focal Actor's initial objective was taken on board by other Actors, meaning that the network was then faced with commercializing a service on a win-win basis, with each participant envisioning an increase in its bottom line. While the one phone service was constrained by government regulations (billing discount) and by technological boundaries, appropriate product development and distribution problems, LG Telecom was not disrupted by any of these factors at this stage.

Interessement

LG Telecom started to build a platform serving mutual objectives among networked participants. Users were signed up on the basis that the home use of cellphones was identical in terms of cost to using landlines. The focal Actor sought to develop relationships between mobile manufacturers, Alami (supporting bluetooth technology) manufacturers, and component and S/W suppliers to provide convergence products through LG Telecom sales branches. LG Telecom's OPPs induced user Actors to subscribe to their mobile service as an alternative to using their land provider at home (Herold Economic, 2006), which threatened mobile manufactures and equipment suppliers by potentially cutting them out of the supply chain. The government Actor imposed no restrictions since LG Telecom's service was not subject to price monitoring in view of LG Telecom's late entry into the mobile carrier market.

Enrollment

User signed up to the network perceiving its cost advantages. The 'Enjoyment Service' model utilized a relatively diverse range of high-quality access equipment ('Alami'), which was priced at a point facilitating mass entry. This enhanced the speed of technology diffusion at the initial stage. LG Electronics, one of LG Telecom's family companies, collaborated closely on product development and invested heavily in advertising. The use of low-bandwidth bluetooth technology was limited to synchronizing with wireless internet networks, LG Telecom instead using its own wireless internet services for connectivity. At this point, land operators argued that the service posed a threat to their offerings, with government subsequently mandating regulatory price increases to ensure a level playing field. Nevertheless, the plan remains for LG Telecom's combined service to make its offer to customers. In short, the network as proposed by the focal Actors succeeded in enrolling consumers and driving a high level of co-investment on the part of network partners.

Mobilization

The focal actor successfully launched the service without the co-evolution of a rival network.

A COMPARATIVE CASE ANALYSIS OF CONVERGENCE SERVICES: CAS PERSPECTIVE

The previous section analyzed two different convergence cases in the terms of ANT; we may now use these preliminary findings in order to capture networks' characteristics from the viewpoint of CAS. Table 5 shows a summary of each network along with the properties of the CASs or network patterns of evolution found in each.

Analysis found that the connectivity and interdependence of all two networks were highly dependent on the designation of the initial OPP. As each network moved towards mobilization, some networks coevolved or split into different competing networks (e.g. m-banking), and some died or sprung into life in response to external factors e.g. the role of the government actor in the one-phone service. Although certain networks were formed by ad-hoc or dyadic supplier relationships between participants and the focal actor, network often deviated from their initial state. The focal actor role in the case of m-banking switched between the mobile carrier and the bank over the question of to information ownership; the one phone service also have two different focal actors (e.g. fixed or mobile line for one phone service) as determined by networks' service scope. Factors such as asset ownership among different industries and differences in envisioned service scope among rival services means that focal actor role will be relatively broadly distributed in converging networks among different industry participants.

Further, we found that the influence of government and regulatory bodies becomes significant when converged networks evolve in a single identifiable industrial domains (e.g. the One Phone Service). Here, the government actor restricted KT's one phone service while passing over LG Telecom's 'Enjoyment Zone'. Besides governmental intervention, the technology actor for each network provided an important driving factor shaping networks configurations and OPPs.

For all two networks, the fitness landscape was initially formed under the impression that stable business relationship and service shapes and scopes would be maintained. In the case of m-banking, this landscape was deformed with the emergence of rival networks, inter-industry linkages and unexpected user thresholds, behavior and expectations as to OPPs. The co-evolution of emerging networks created different orders and

Table 5. Summary of key characteristics of CAS in convergence services

	Mobile Banking	One Phone Service
Connectivity/Interdependence	- The initial OPP was 'm- banking service through web technology'; high costs and cumbersome use meant users rejected the technology - Network connectivity and interdependence with the emergence of two different competing network with different focal actor. - Connectivity for both networks meant inducing other-agent participation. - Two competing net-works were differentiated by ownership of information - The external variable, the government regulation was lighter since government sought to revitalize banking services	- The initial OPP was 'converged service of fixed- and mobile service' proposed by KT (the focal actor) - The initial network connectivity was high though interdependence becomes weaker since the market was not new (all actors have their own market boundary) - Other actors predicted the low demand the service in light of unexpected technology constraints - Network connectivity and interdependence was damaged and other network has emerged led by other mobile carrier - Government restricted the one phone service through limiting pricing discounts and the local calls rate offered by the focal agent. - No restrictive regulation applied to LG Telcom's 'Enjoyment Zone' service on account of LG Telecom's late entry into the market.
Co-evolution	- The fitness landscape was formed as a single actor network but radically altered with emergence of a competing network with a different sector focal agent and different mutual objective - The competing network redistributed the fitness landscape among co-evolving actors; another new fitness landscape may emerge with the launch 3G WCDMA technology	- The fitness landscape was formed by the one phone service became lower as another network emerged - With LG Telecom, the landscape raised as government forbore to impose restrictive regulation. - A new fitness landscape formed with the entry of LG Telecom and its partner actors in offering mobile phone service at home.
Far-from equilibrium	- Each network creates different orders and patterns characterized by both a stable state and some space of possibility to deviance from stable patterns - Conflict emerges with development of competing networks. - The emergence of converged services necessarily induces disturbance - The translation state driven by OPPs failed due to higher user costs at the enrolment stage. - Technological development creates another OPP in the context of a new actor network inititated by a different focal actor - Two different competing networks are also looking at using 3G in m-banking	- The evolved network falls out in a different order, depending on the input of government and user actors - Both network arrive at an equilibrium state, though one has a smaller number of subscribers - The actor network was enables on account of the manufacturer being able to enforce network standards - Price becomes critical issue in determining customer participation and loyalty

continued on following page

Table 5. continued

Self –Organization	- IC based manufacturer provided an innovative product overcoming the first attempt's short-comings - Bank actor formed strategic alliances with LG Telecom using customer information at its disposal - SK Telecom sought to put in place their own forms of network relationships offering different m-banking service. - Both competing network arrived at suboptimal solutions going into the mobilization stage	- Network composition for two networks largely come into being as a result of pre-existent business linkages between subsidiaries of group companies (KTF and LG Electronics). - LGT provided an innovative convergence service and its supply chain network (sales and distribution channel with manufacturing relationship with PR) - Customer actor found it easy to use the conver-gence service.

patterns for each converging service. Equilibrium state became harder to maintain with the emergence of new technology and subsequent transformation of network dimensions (e.g. the focal actor's role or the OPP). Disruption also changes participants' space of possibilities, as it did in m-banking when the emergence of IC chips offered to revive a previously unviable service.

In converging services, each network actor remains adaptive to their external environment. These self-organizing capacities of each actor can induce systemic disequilibrium. The failure of user acceptance deformed m-banking, leading to other networks participants reforming in different strategic alliances overseen by a new focal actor. However close the dyadic relationships between

Figure 2. The driving factor to the converged service network (e.g., One Phone Services)

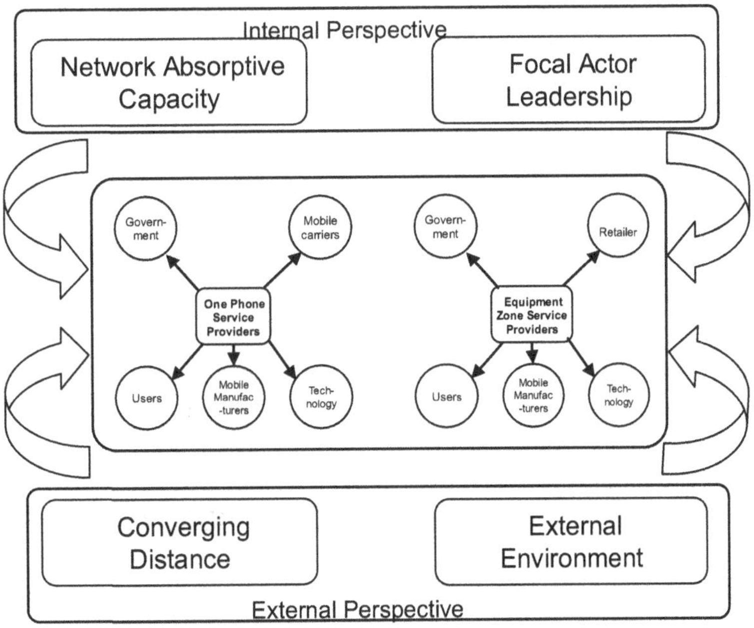

network players and strong the focal actor's leadership, our studies show that converging networks are inherently highly susceptible to change.

DISCUSSION

This comparative case study identified the following driving factors in the evolution of two converging networks (as illustrated in figure 2). Factors may be further categorized as either external or internal.

External Environment

All actor networks were shaped by the emergence of external technology or by the intrusion of external regulatory authority. Translation processes for all networks came to a halt at enrolment, where the networks were alike rejected by their final users (or restricted by the government intervention). The focal Actor and other participants only understood the network's optimal or necessary passage points when services were engaged by final customer Actors, whose requirements were not always anticipated by actor-networks' financial or operational inter-levels.

This state of affairs in all these cases meant that final user acceptance became the critical success factor in networks' stabilization. All converged services, m-banking, one phone service, evolved into two or more competing network services (which appeared either sequentially or simultaneously) due to the time-dimensional emergence of new technology or regulatory intervention.

Converging Distance

Here, we found that actor networks were easier to form and the enrolment of a number of interested Actors facilitated when the so-called converging distance between industries was greater. In contrast, network complexity, causing networks to diverge from states of equilibrium, is greater the closer together the converging networks are. Networks' degree of connectivity depends on the ability of multifunctional or interfacing IT to create synergies between different industries.

Focal Actor Leadership

To a large degree, also, networks' success was a factor of the quality of the leadership exercised by their focal Actor. Focal Actors seek to attract legitimacy to their choice of OPPs, and in certain situations enjoy such an unquestioned position of dominance that they are able to experiment with regard to technologies, passage points and network configurations until a network enrolment level has been attained. This typically describes situations where one Actor has a monopoly or quasi-monopoly advantage (or huge lead in technology).

Network Absorptive Capacity

We also found that the enforcement of network norms is not only secured by focal Actor dominance, but also depends on network absorptive capacity. In other words, the capacity of each actor and its self-organization in responding to any unforeseen events may trigger shifts away from networks' equilibrium state. Different networks will respond in different ways and in different degrees to environmental change; some will respond to competition or new market opportunities quickly, even if readjusting to new circumstances involves breaking network relationships. In converged services particularly, network relationships are likely to take the form of the relatively quick formation and dissolution of supplier partnerships.

CONCLUSION

This paper proposed a combined framework of ANT and CAS for characterizing converged services from a socio-technical perspective. It initially specified ANT and CAS conceptually, defining actors and their network roles with reference to four different processes and evolutionary network characteristics. We then conducted case studies of two different converged services in Korea, Mobile banking, and the One phone service, revealing in each case a high measure of complexity in network structure and evolution. Applying the framework derived four driving factors shaping network evolution in each case: Focal Actor Leadership, Network Absorptive Capacity, Converging Distance and External Environmental Factors. The level of these driving factors determine whether or not networks split, spawning co-evolving rivals. Our conclusion is that ANT is helpful in providing insights into the creation and negotiation of forms of network order over time, while CAS can explain the drivers of co-evolutionary behaviors in a more structured way. This paper aims to contribute to the understanding and management of complex networks in converged services by offering guidance as to the causes of network failure, the deformation of networks' fitness landscape and the emergence of co-evolution. Further work could verify its hypotheses through quantitative modeling of simulations of the two instances of convergence studied.

REFERENCES

Allen, J.P. (2004). Redefining the network: enrollment strategies in the PDA industry, *Information Technology and People*, 17(2), 171-185.

Archibald, G., Karabakal, N. & Karlsson, P. (1999 Winter). Supply chain vs supply chain: using simulation to compete beyond the four walls. [Online]. Available: http://www.wintersim.org/prog99.htm.

Anderson, M. & Karrenman, D. (2000). Complexity theory and organizational science, *Organizational Science*, 10(3), 216-232.

Axelrod, R. & Cohen, M.D. (1999). *Harnessing Complexity: Organizational Implications of a Scientific Frontier.* New York: Basic Books.

Benbasat, I., Goldstain, D.K & Mead, M. (1987). The Case Research Strategy in Studies of Information Systems. *MIS Quarterly*, 11(3), 369-386.

Benbya, H., & McKelvey, B. (2006). Toward a complexity theory of information systems development. *Information Technology and People*, 19(1), 12-34.

Blackman, C. R. (1998). Convergence between telecommunications and other media: How should regulation adapt?. *Telecommunications Policy*, 22(3), 163-170.

Bloomfield, B.P., & Vurdubakis, T. (1994). Boundary disputes: Negotiating the boundary between the technical and the social in the development of IT systems. *Information Technology and People*, 7(1), 9-24.

Callon, M. (1996a). The Sociology of an actor–network: The case of the electric vehicle. In: M. Callon, J. Law, and A. Rip (Eds.), *Mapping the Dynamics of Science and Technology: Sociology of Science in the Real World(*pp.19-34). London: Macmillan.

Callon, M. (1987). Society in the making: The study of technology as a tool for sociological analysis. In: W. E. Bijker, T. P. Hughes, & T. Pinch (Eds.), *The Social Construction of Technological Systems(*pp. 83-103). London: The MIT Press.

Callon, M. (1986b). Some elements of a sociology of translation: Domestication of the scallops and the fishermen of St Brieuc Bay. In: J. Law (Ed.), *Power, Action and Belie(*pp. 197-233). London: Routledge and Kegan Paul.

Callon, M., & Latour, B. (1981). Unscrewing the big leviathan. In: K. Knorr-Cetina & A.V. Cicourel (Eds.), *Advances in Social Theory and Methodology(*pp. 277-303). London: Routledge & Kegan.

Chae, B., & Lanzara, G..F. (2006). Self-destructive dynamics in large-scale techno-change and some ways of counteracting it. *Information Technology and People,* 19(1), pp. 74-97.

Chan-Olmsted & Kang. (2003). Theorizing the strategic architecture of a broadband television industry. *Journal of Media Economics*, 16(1), pp. 3-21.

Cramer, F. (1993). *Chaos and Order.* New York: VCH.

Dooley, K. (1997). A complex adaptive systems model of organization change. *Nonlinear Dynamics, Psychology, & Life Science*, 1(1), pp. 69-97.

Eisenhardt, K.M. (1989). Building theories from case study research. *Academy of Management Review*, 14(4), pp.532-550.

Gap between wired and wireless enlarging. (2006, Oct. 18.). *Electronic Times.*

EC(1997). *Council Directive 97/36/EC of the European Parliament and of the Council of 30 June 1997 amending Directive 89/552/EEC on the coordination of certain provisions laid down by law, regulation or administrative action in Member States concerning the pursuit of television broadcasting activities.* (Official Journal of the European Communities, L202 60, pp.1-25), Brussels, Belgium.

Faraj, S., Kwon, D., & Watts, S. (2004). Contested artifact: Technology sense-making, actor networks, and the shaping of the web browser. *Information Technology and People*, 17(2), pp.186-209.

Frohmann, B.(1995, Jun 7). Taking information policy beyond information science: Applying the actor network theory. [Online]. Available: http://www.cais-acsi.ca/proceedings/1995/frohmann_1995.pdf

LGT, New tariff plan (Enjoyment Zone) raising 0.1 million subscribers. (2006, Oct. 20).. *Herold Economy.*

Holland, J.H. (1988). The global economy as an adaptive system. In Anderson, P.W., Arrow, K.J. and Pines, D. (Eds), *The Economy as an Evolving Complex System (*Vol. 5, pp. 117-24) . Reading: Addison-Wesley.

Holland, J.H. (1995). *Hidden Order.* Reading: Addison-Wesley..

Horvath & Maldoom(2002). Fixed-mobile substitution: a simultaneous equation model with qualitative and limited dependent variables. [Online]. Available: DotEcon Discussion Papers, DP 02/02, WWW.dotecon.com., London. pp.1-25.

ITU (1996), *Regulatory Implications of Telecommunications Convergence.* [Online]. Available: http://www.itu.int/opb/publications.aspx?lang=en&media=electronic&parent=S-GEN-COL6-1996.

Kang, L.H (2003), "Small electronic payment service for collaboration and conflicts between financial and telecommunication industry", Finance Research, Vol. 1, No.2, pp. 136-170.

Kallinikos, J. (2005), "The order of technology: complexity and control in a connected world", Information and Organization, Vol. 15, pp. 185-202.

Kauffman, S. (1993). *The Origins of Order: Self-Organization and Selection in Evolution.* Oxford: Oxford University Press.

Kim, H.S. (2003a). Fair competition analysis of M-commerce development. Research Report 03-16, Seoul: Korea Information Strategy Development Institute(KISDI).

Kim, S. (2003b). Prospect of IC-chip based mobile banking. *Payment and Information Technology,* 15(Nov/Dec.), pp.35-74.

Mobile virtual network operator. (2004, June 14). The Korean Economic Daily.

Kim, S., H. Eun, Y. Kang, & M. Lee (2006). Developing a convergence portfolio matrix for heterogeneous inter-industry convergence. *Telecommunications Review,* 16(1), pp. 82-89.

Kim, R.M., & Kaplan, S.M. (2006). Interpreting socio-technical co-evolution: Applying complex adaptive systems to IS engagement. *Information Technology and People*, 19(1), pp.35-54.

Kovacs, A. & Ueno, H. (2004). Towards complex adaptive information systems. [Online]. Available: http://www.alexander-kovacs.de/kovacs04icita.pdf

KRNIC (2005), *Korean Mobile Year Book.* Seoul: KRNIC.

Krueger, M. (2001). *The Future of M-payments: Business Options and Policy Issues,* Institute for Prospective Technological Studies, Directorate General Joint Research Centre European Commission.

KT Management Research Lab(KTMRL). (2006). *Bundling among telecommunication services in the era of digital convergence*, Seoul: KTMRL.

Lee, H. L., Padmanabhan, V. & Whang, S.J. (1997). Information distortion in a supply chain: The bullwhip effect. *Management Science*, 43(4), pp.546-558.

Lee, J.H. (2003). *The modeling and simulation of dynamic supply chain networks: A multi-agent systems approach*, Unpublished doctoral dissertation, University of Cambridge, Cambridge..

Lee, J.W (2004). One phone service: market trends and forecasting. *ETRI Journal*, 19(2), pp.84-96.

LG Telecom (2004), "Mobile Banking BankOn", LG Telecom Public Relation Department

Lichtenstein, B.B. & McKelvey, B. (2004). Complexity science and computational models of emergent order: What's there? What's missing?. paper presented at the Academy of Management Annual Meeting, New Orleans, LA, August 9.

Linde, A., Linderoth, H., & Raisanen, C.(2003 March 12-13). An actor network theory perspective on IT-projects: A battle of wills. [Online]. Available: http://www.vits.org/konferenser/alois2003/html/6893.pdf.

Mainzer, K. (1994). *Thinking in Complexity.* New York : Springer-Verlag.

Mallat, N., M. Rossi, & V. K. Tuunainen (2004). Mobile banking services. *Communications of the ACM*, 47(5), pp.42-46.

MIC (1999), "Revitalization of the supplement telecommunication service" , [Online]. Available: http://www.mic.go.kr/user.tdf?a=user.board.BoardApp&c=2002&board_id=P_03_01_05&seq=128&ctx=&bad=&isSearch=true&searchVal=□□□□&basic=SUBJECT&npp=15&cp=1&pg=1&mc=P_03_08 (in Korean)

Moser, I., & Law, J. (2006). Fluids or flows? : Information and qualculation in medical practice. *Information Technology & People*, 19(1), pp. 55-73.

Murphy, E.(2002). *The Future of Fixed Mobile Substitution : Choices of Fixed and Mobile Operators*, Analsys.

The Bank of Korea. (2004). Status of mobile payment service in Korea, *Payment Information*, 6, pp. 4 (in Korean)

OECD(2004). The implications of convergence for regulation of electronic communications. [Online]. Available: http://www.oecd.org/dataoecd/56/24/32983964.pdf_

Oh, S. & Lee, H (2005). How technology shapes the actor network of convergence services: A case of mobile banking. Twenty-Sixth International Conference on Information Systems.

Ono, R. & K Aoki. (1998). Convergence and new regulatory frameworks: A comparative study of regulatory approaches to Internet telephony?. *Telecommunications Policy*, 22(10), pp.817-838.

Ovum Report (1999), *Fixed-Mobile Convergence: Service Integration and Substitution*, Ovum

Bank On Service enhancement. (2003, Nov 18). e-daily.

Shin, D. H.(2006). VoIP: A debate over information service or telephone application in US: A new perspective in convergence era. *Telematics and Informatics*, 23(2), pp.57-73.

Studer, B.(2001). Fixed mobile internet convergence(FMIC). *Telematics and Informatics*, 18(2), pp.133-141.

Van Aardt, A. (2004, July 6-9). Open source software development as complex adaptive systems. Proceedings of the 17th Annual Conference of the National Advisory Committee on Computing Qualifications, Christchurch, New Zealand.

Vidgen, R., & McMaster, T. (1996). Black boxes, non-human stakeholders and the translation of IT. In: W.J.Orlikowski, G.. Walsham, M.R.Jones, & J.I.DeGross (Ed.), *Information Technology and Changes in Organizational Work*(pp. 250-271). London: Chapman & Hall.

Walsham, G. (1997). Actor-network theory and IS research: Current status and future prospects. In: A.S.Lee, J.Liebenau, & J.I. DeGross (Ed.), *Information Systems and Qualitative Research* (pp.466-480). London: Chapman & Hall.

Wu. I.(2004). Canada, South Korea, Netherlands and Sweden: regulatory implications of the convergence of telecommunications, broadcasting and Internet services?. *Telecommunications Policy*, 28(1), pp.79-96.

Yin,R.K(1984). Case study research: Design and methods. In: Bickman, L. (Eds.), *Applied Social Research Methods Series* Vol. 5 . Los Angeles: Sage Publication.

Yoffie, D. B.(1997). *Competing in the Age of Digital Convergence*, Boston: Harvard Business School Press.

Zhang, B.(2002). Understanding impact of convergence on broadband industry regulation: a case study of the United States. *Telematics and Informatics*, 19(1), pp. 37-59.

Chapter XVII
Understanding Organizational Transformation from IT Implementations: A Look at Structuration Theory

T. Ariyachandra
Xavier University, USA

L. Dong
Ryerson University, Canada

ABSTRACT

Past evidence suggests that organizational transformation from IT implementations is rare. Data warehousing promises to be one advanced information technology that could produce transformation. Based on the stages of growth theory and adaptive structuration theory (AST), this paper attempts to understand how data warehousing could lead to organizational transformation by studying a data warehouse's growth in an organization. In particular, the benchmark variables for data warehousing stages of growth are examined using adaptive structuration theory to explain organizational transformation that takes account into unique organizational situations.

INTRODUCTION

From its beginnings, MIS has made promises of revolutionary organizational transformation through the use of information technology. Leavitt and Whisler (1958) were among the first MIS scholars to predict that computers would have dramatic impacts on organizations. These promises and predictions motivated management in many organizations to implement IT innovations with the hopes of dramatically affecting organizational performance. Researchers have discovered the evidence of organizational transformation in streamlined organizational business processes, increased decision making, enhanced user skills, improved competitive advantage, and ultimately faster organizational growth (Davenport 2000a; Davenport 2000b; Waston et al. 2002).

The potential benefits reaped through IS implementations usually occur over a sustained time period. Most past IT implementations have been perceived as one-time product implementations producing or enhancing a given business process. In contrast, data warehousing is an advanced information technology perceived more as an IT infrastructure project that has the potential to trigger changes in organizational business processes as it interacts with other sources of organizational structure (DeSanctis et al. 1994). It is perceived more as "a journey, not a destination."

Despite the general impact of advanced information technologies on organizations (Bharadwaj 2000; Oh et al. 2007; Pavlou et al. 2006),, empirical cases demonstrate that different organizations have exhibited different patterns of transformations (Waston et al. 2002). Some have seen improved user skills and increased efficiency, others have seen the revitalization of organizational business processes, and some others have experienced the transformation of organizational culture (e.g., Cooper et al. 2000; Waston et al. 2002). The diversity puzzles practitioners who want to identify and understand organizational transformation due to the introduction of a new information technology, and also challenges researchers as to how to discern distinct transformation patterns for each single organization.

The potential of an IT to evolve and transform business processes in organizations makes it an interesting phenomenon to study. Kotter proposed a prescriptive model for organizational transformation (1995). Recent research has documented the various patterns exhibited by this phenomenon (Cooper et al. 2000; Goodhue et al. 1999; Hayley et al. 1999; Watson et al. 2001). The results of these research efforts present vital information about the complexity, the issues and steps leading to a successful technology adoption and consequent organizational transformation. What is missing is the examination of patterns of organizational transformation through the process of IT implementations.

The purpose of this paper is to demonstrate how examining benchmark variables in stages of growth using adaptive structuration theory can be applied to gain an indepth understanding of organizational transformation that takes into account unique organizational situations. In particular, we intend to answer the following research question "How organizational transformation takes place within the context of data warehouse adoption." By combining aspects of the stages of growth theory with AST, we are able to provide useful insights into transformation patterns that are unique to a single organization.

The paper is structured as follows. We first review the extant literature on IS implementations and innovation adoption. We then present the adaptive structure theory (AST), and apply the theory to capture the intricacies of change in data warehousing at a detailed level and provide reasoning as to why many warehouse implementations show varying patterns of organizational transformation.

THEORETICAL BACKGROUND

Research on Information Systems Implementation

An IS implementation is a complicated process involving the interaction among technology, people, and business processes (Kwon et al. 1987; Leonard-Barton 1988; Lucas et al. 1990; Purvis et al. 2001). Decades of research on information systems implementations have generated an enriched understanding of IS implementations and a wealth of knowledge on success factors for IS implementations.

Information systems implementation is defined as a process whereby target users adapt and accept the innovation, and routinize the technology innovation into their normal working procedures (Kwon et al. 1987). It is an organized change associated with a new system (Lucas 1981). Leonard-Barton (1988) views the change process as a dynamic process of mutual adaptation between an information technology and its environment. The adaptation cycle can be large or small, depending on the magnitude of the misalignments, and may be either beneficial or detrimental. Recent empirical studies have confirmed the mutual adaptation process (Boersma et al. 2005; Soh et al. 2004).

Diverse factors affect the success of IS implementations, including individual factors (e.g., education, job tenure, experience, and role involvement) (e.g., Alavi et al. 1992; Griffith et al. 1996)}, structural factors (e.g., specialization, centralization, and formalization) (e.g., Alavi et al. 1992; Sultan et al. 2000), organizational factors (e.g., size, management support) (e.g., Grover et al. 1993; Sharma et al. 2003), task-related factors (e.g., task uncertainty, autonomy, and responsibility) (e.g., Chengalur-Smith et al. 2000; Sultan et al. 2000), and environmental factors (e.g., heterogeneity, uncertainty, and competition) (e.g., Alavi et al. 1992; Grover et al. 1993).

These studies have revealed the complexity of IS implementations, and provided rich information regarding the implementation processes and factors critical to achieving IS implementation success. However, the extant literature has yet explored how these different factors combined to affect the mutual adaptation process and ultimately organizational transformation.

Research on Innovation Adoption

Organization innovation studies have focused on types of innovations, characteristics of innovations, factors that determine the rate, pattern, and extent of the spread of an innovation among organizations over time (Brancheau et al. 1990; Fichman 2000). The dual-core theory distinguishes two types of innovations— technical and administrative innovations (Daft 1978). A recent study of Swanson extends the dual-core theory by adding IS innovations to the model (Swanson 1994). Depending on the extent of changes in products, services, and production process, innovation studies categorize innovations into radical (those that evoke fundamental changes) and incremental (those that produce a lesser change) (Damanpour et al. 1998; Nord et al. 1987). Aside from organizational structures that facilitate innovation implementation (Duncan 1976), other factors that determine innovation adoption and diffusion include environmental characteristics (e.g., industrial and environmental dynamism), characteristics of innovation (e.g., relative advantage, compatibility, and complexity), organizational characteristics (e.g., organizational structure, financial readiness, and technological readiness), and innovation propagation characteristics (e.g., promotion, pricing, and advertising) (Damanpour 1991; Fichman 2000; Wilson, et al. 1999).

Another theme of innovation studies is the examination of the process through which an innovation is adopted. The most noted is the three-stage model, in which the organizational adoption of an innovation is categorized into three stages: initiation, adoption, and implementation (Pierce et al. 1977; Rogers et al. 1971). The initiation stage involves scanning of organizational problems and opportunities as well as IT solutions. Adoption is a rational and political decision to get organizational backing for implementation of the IT application. Implementation includes development and installation activities designed to ensure that the expected benefits of the innovations are realized. There are other stage models including Nolan's stage model, the evolution of information centers (Magal et al. 1988), integration of business and information systems planning (King et al. 1997), skill requirement changes of systems analysts (Benbasat et al. 1980), and end user computing management (Henderson et al. 1986).

A recent study has defined three stages of growth that follows a "S" curve mark (i.e., initiation, growth, and maturity) (Watson et al. 2001). In the Initiation stage, data warehouse applications are initiated; in the growth state, the applications are diffused within the organization, and in the maturity stage, the applications become fully integrated into the company's operations. Each stage is uniquely identified by a set of characteristics (i.e., benchmarks) (Figure 1), the values of which indicate the most likely theoretical characteristics applicable to each stage of growth (King et al. 1997). Appendix A presents the three stages and the benchmark variables that help identify each stage of data warehousing.

The matrix of benchmark variable values for data warehousing, as they change through the stages, provides a simple guide to understanding a complex phenomenon. For instance, "the impact on user skills and jobs" benchmark variable's evolution through the stages can be described briefly as follows. In the initiation phase, early adopters see a change in the technical skills that they need to perform their jobs. Next, in the growth stage, the early adopters are given lead positions within departments to act as technology diffusion agents. In addition, employee turnover occurs as employees who cannot adjust to the new job and skill requirements leave and the organization acquires technology savvy individuals. Finally, in the maturity stage, the overall organization assimilates the technology. Employees become more specialized in their roles and early adopters become key departmental resources for others

Figure 1. Stages of growth model

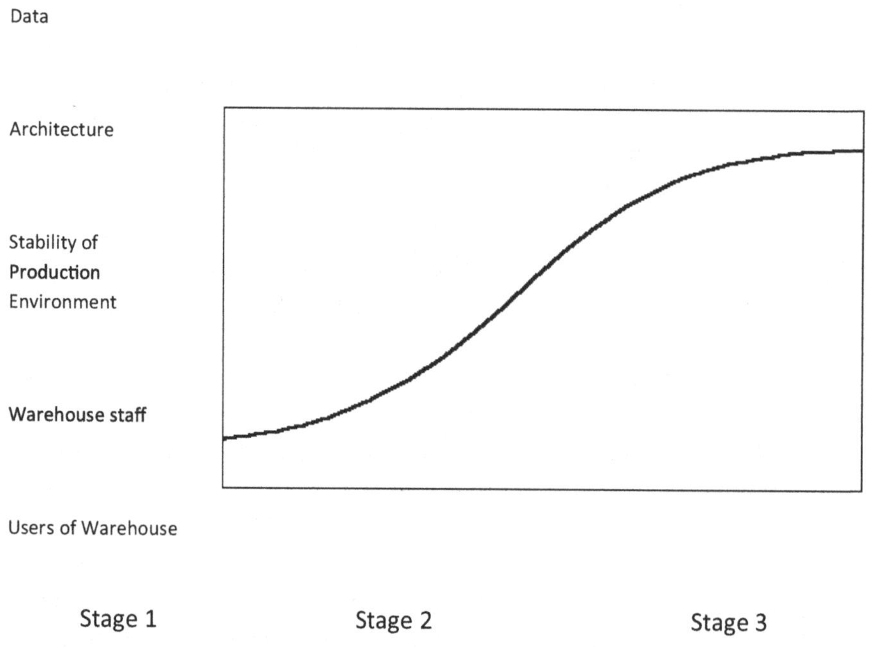

in their business unit. To the manager attempting to understand the effects of data warehouse technology assimilation on the roles and skills of employees, the above information provides, in Nolan's words, "a framework useful for identifying issues and evaluating and controlling the growth of" data warehouses (Gibson et al. 1974).

While intuitively appealing, empirical studies have discovered that actual growth patterns can be inconsistent from the established patterns of growth for a given stage (Benbasat et al, 1984; King et al. 1997). For instance, in stages of growth in data warehousing, not all data warehouse strategy implementations display the benchmark matrix values that define the Maturity stage (Watson et al. 2001). Additionally, in some cases, there was evidence of what appeared to be overlapping and/or switching of benchmark values through the stages.

Accordingly, research on innovation adoption enriches our understanding of different types of innovations, facilitators and inhibitors of innovation adoptions, and stages that organizations grow through the innovation adoption. However, the literature has yet answered why different organizations exhibit different transformation patterns, even through a same information system is adopted. While benchmarks in each stage of growth provide a generalized, broad framework useful for identifying issues and evaluating and controlling the growth of a data warehouse, it does not present an explanation for warehousing efforts that deviate from the benchmark values for each stage. Therefore, to gain a deeper understanding of organizational transformation process evoked by a new information system needs evaluation through the combination of the stages of growth theory and another lens. Adaptive structuration theory provides an appropriate lens to examine the changes in characteristics (i.e., benchmarks variables) at each stage of data warehousing growth.

ADAPTIVE STRUCTURATION THEORY

Orlikowski (1992) was the first to apply the duality of structure concept to IT and propose the concept of duality of IT in organizations. She proposed that IT in organizations have dual states: technology is created and changed by human action and it is also used by humans to accomplish action. The adaptive structuration theory (AST) presented by Desanctis and Poole (1994), extends the work of Orlikowski (1992) further and provides an approach to studying the role of advanced technologies in organizational change by considering the mutual influence of technology and social processes. More specifically, it presents precisely how technology structures can trigger organizational change and vice versa through the analysis of the *complexity* of the technology-action relationship (i.e., analysis of the "cans of worms" as Gibson and Nolan (Gibson et al. 1974)] stated).

The IT structuration as described by AST can help analyze the process of structuration as described from its first appropriation to subsequent actions. It offers a means of looking at different combinations of AST construct values in order to predict the dynamic nature of organizational structure. In Giddens words describing structuration in general,

offers a conceptual scheme that allows one to understand how actors are at the same time the creators of social systems yet created by them...It is an attempt to provide the conceptual means of analyzing the often delicate interlacings of reflexively organized action and institutional constraint (Giddens, 1991, p. 204).

The highlighted phrase emphasizes the central contribution of structuration theory. By enabling one to analyze and understand the 'delicate interlacings of...organized action' the theory provides a platform for understanding how organizational evolution and growth takes place. Thus, structuration, specifically adaptive structuration theory, provides an excellent lens to observe the evolution of information systems innovations within the organization.

In particular, each integral part of the AST model that leads to the recursive process of interaction can be applied to data warehousing implementations. AST can help explain the causation and reasoning behind almost all the benchmark variable values stated in the Data warehousing benchmark variable matrix (Appendix A).

According to the AST model, the structure of an information system, the other sources of structure, such as task and organizational environment and the employee group's internal makeup all affect human interaction with the data warehouse. The manner in which these constructs affect human appropriations with the data warehouse affect outcomes as well as reaffirms and/or changes existing structure. As some existing structures get reaffirmed and other structures emerge through structuration, benchmark variable values (e.g., user skills, routinization) change and provide the reasoning behind the changes in values.

The adaptive structuration theory provides an appropriate lens to understand the finer details of organizational evolution. It can assist in the explanation of the changes in the benchmark variable values through the stages of growth. Anthony Giddens (1984; 1993) work on structuration provides a process-oriented theory that treats organizational structure as both a product of and a constraint on human action. It is a metatheory whose primary goal is to connect human action with structural explanations in social analysis (Riley 1983). To do so, Giddens (1993) introduces the duality of structure that describes the reciprocal relationship between human actors and structure. Thus, structuration can be simply described as the production and reproduction of social systems through the application of generative rules and resources.

Principles of structuration have been applied at the organizational level (Pettigrow 1987; Ranson et al. 1980), at the industry level (Huff et al. 1994)and as an explanation to organizational culture (Riley 1983). Structuration theory provides insights into technology transfer as well (Barley 1986; DeSanctis et al. 1994; Orlikowski et al. 1991).

Before application of AST to attempt to explain benchmark variable data, key facts with regard to structuration theory should be noted. As Giddens stated (1993), structuration is bound by time and space. For example, the varying historical settings within different organizations can lead to the creation of different organizational outcomes from identical technology implementations. Thus, adaptations of AST to the benchmark variable values will vary according to organizational context. As a result, it may not accurately reflect the appropriations process in every organization. However, it does give both researchers and industry alike the opportunity to recognize what aspects of organizational structure and human behavior affect the structuration process. Consequently it provides them an opportunity to predict outcome structures (DeSanctis et al. 1994).

In the following, we are going to apply AST to organizational growth and transformation under the context of data warehousing implementation. Data warehousing is an advanced information technology perceived more as an IT infrastructure project that has the potential to 'trigger changes in organizational business processes as it interacts with other sources of organizational structure' (DeSanctis et al. 1994). As such, data warehousing adoption and growth provides a great vehicle to investigate organizational transformation.

APPLICATION OF THE STAGES OF GROWTH THEORY AND AST TO DATA WAREHOUSING

In this section, we employ a hypothetical case to illustrate how to apply the stages of Growth theory and AST to to explain data warehousing benchmark variable value changes through stages.

Specifically, it can explain some of the possible underpinnings in the impact on user roles and skills benchmark variable previously studied through the lens of stages of growth theory. In the context of Capital X, AST is used to explain the data warehouse's impact on marketing analysts' roles and skills over time and the reasoning behind the impacts (Figure 2).

Capital X is a financial institution, composed of a set of independent units offering different financial products to customers. Each department has established its own conventions on customer interactions, interdepartmental interactions, and legacy system usage. For instance, marketing analysts of different functional units have their own conventions of gathering data from the legacy systems and manually analyzing them.

To increase market share in the financial services industry, upper management issued a directive to build an enterprise wide data warehouse to support an overall customer focus strategy. The project is sponsored by the CIO who hired consultants to construct the enterprise wide data warehouse.

The actual data warehouse implementation took place in two major phases. The first major

Figure 2. Application of AST to capital X marketing analysts [(a) = Early adopter activity and outcomes, (b) = Late adopter activity and outcomes]

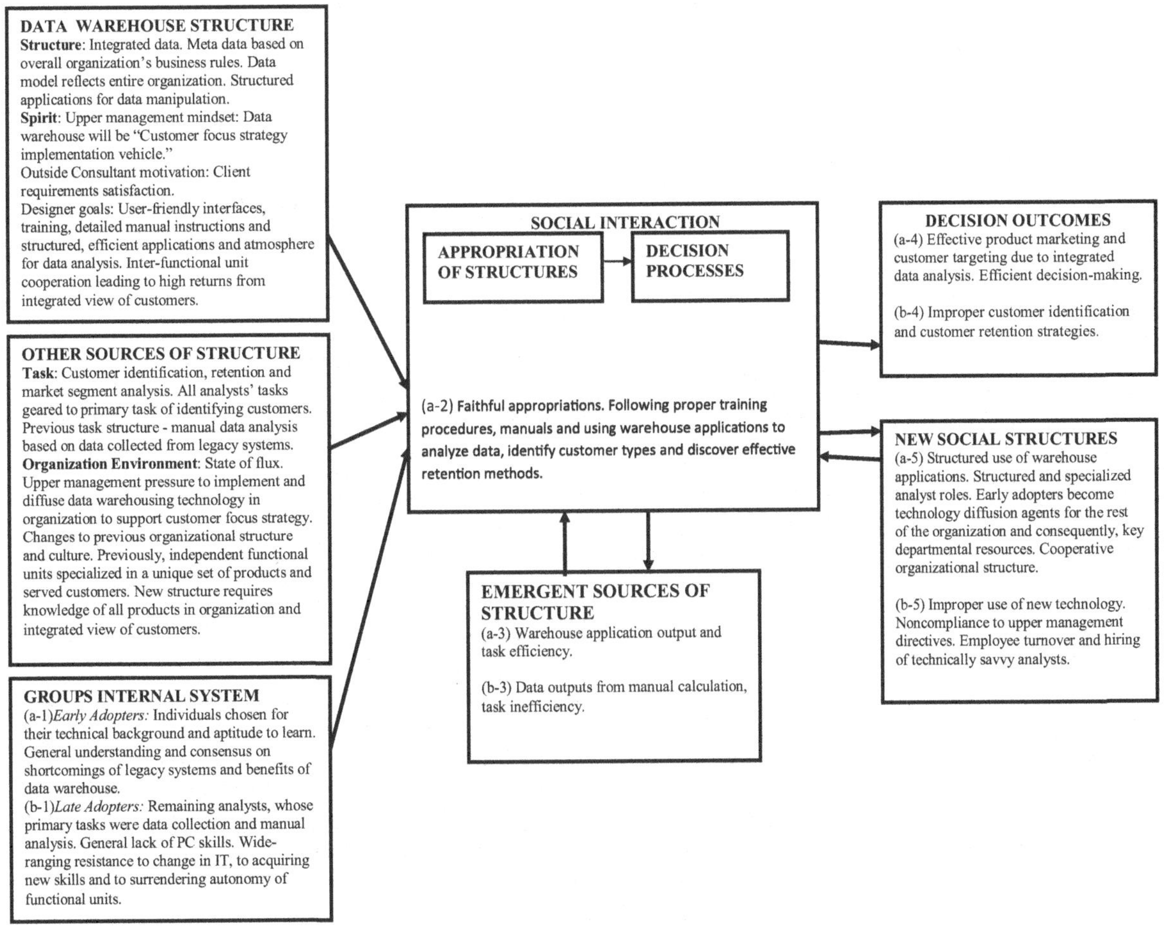

phase, the initiation phase, involved accumulating data from business units, converting the data, and creating the data warehouse. At the conclusion of phase one, the warehouse gave limited functionality to its users to carry out basic marketing analysis tasks. In the second phase, the growth phase, the organization instituted the fully functional enterprise wide data warehouse as a means of collecting, searching, and analyzing information about customers to support the new organizational strategy and diffused it to the entire organization.

During Capital X's first phase, a set of 30 staff members were chosen from various functional units based on their good PC and mainframe skills to be trained as the first adopters of the data warehouse. Despite their different functional unit origins, their technical aptitude and desire to learn a new application characterized the general mindset of this group of early adopters (Figure 2, a-1). They went through the training process with a sense of eagerness; their technical knowledge had them attuned to the faults of the legacy systems and lack of integration. Knowing the intent of upper management, the availability of the consultants and proper training programs, the early adopters began utilizing the system to identify customer segments (Figure 2, a-2). The ease and simplification provided by the warehouse application evidenced by initial output and task efficiency led to continued faithful appropriations of the warehouse (Figure 2, a-3). The early adopters social interactions with the data warehouse resulted in the development of more effective customer retention strategies and other decision outcomes (Figure 2, a-4). Consequently, early adopters began to form an integrated view of the organization and a more structured approach to tasks (Figure 2, a-5). Due to their integral role as early adopters, these marketing analysts first became diffusion agents and gradually key departmental resources for data warehousing applications.

In the second phase, Capital X began diffusing the technology to the remaining marketing analysts within the organization. Although the spirit of the warehouse was further solidified to the late adopters by the actions of the early adopters, their general behavior towards the new technology was resistance (Figure 2, b-1). Their

Table 1. Benchmark variable matrix for the stage of growth for capital X

Benchmark variables	Initiation stage	Growth stage
Data	fragmented data for entire organization	Integrated data across organizational departments
Architecture	Multiple data marts	Multiple data marts
Stability of product environment	Procedures are inconsistent across departments	Standard procedures are not well established
Warehouse staff	In-house personnel are inexperienced	In-house personnel are inexperienced and resistant to the data warehouse
Users	Users do not access the warehouse	Users have access to the warehouse
Impact on users' skills and jobs	Users need to update their knowledge and skills	Users need to realize the benefits of the warehouse
Applications	Identify customer segments	ad hoc access
Costs and Benefits	Task efficiency	The analysis and outcomes lack quality and do not provide the company with the information that promote its customer focused strategy
Organizational impact	Contribute to the development of more effective customer retention strategies and other decision outcomes	Resistors are fired, and people with the right analytical skills need to be hired

technical knowledge and skills were limited. The late adopters had traditionally used the legacy systems for data collection and conducted manual analysis of data (Figure 2, b-2). The senior analysts took leadership in leading the rest of the late adopters to unfaithful appropriations of the data warehouse. As the late adopters were unaware of the inefficiencies of the pervious system and task process, they continued to try to find familiar data elements from the data warehouse to conduct manual analysis (Figure 2, b-3). Upper management had not implemented a monitor and control system to supervise appropriations. Furthermore, as the previous organizational structure provided more autonomy and did not require the structure dictated by the new roles, the late adopters saw no need to change their skills or behavior. As a result, the analysis and outcomes from the late adopter group lacked quality and did not provide Capital X with information that promoted their customer focus strategy (Figure 2, b-4). Furthermore, their unfaithful appropriations led to insubordinate behavior and task completion (Figure 2, b-5). Despite early adopter and management efforts to convert late adopters to use the warehouse faithfully, such structuration was not successful. Consequently, resistors (i.e., senior traditional marketing analysts) were fired, to hire employees with the right analytical skills to utilize the data warehouse applications to its maximum potential. Benchmark variable matrix for the stage of growth for Capital X is listed in Table 1.

As shown in Table 1, some of these benchmark variables are not unique across the initiation and growth stage. Additionally, despite the fact that the data warehouse is fully integrated into Capital X, benchmark variables do not display values defining that the company is in the maturity stage. However, with the structuration perspective, the benchmark variables reveal the duality of structure at play. Initially, the warehouse changed the behavior and structure of task performance of the early adopter and late adopter. Consequently, through knowledge acquisition and power gained through expertise, the early adopter began to change the existing organizational structure taking on the role of training other users and becoming an indispensable resource for his/her business unit. The late adopter that did not faithfully appropriate began to negatively affect the quality of output produced, and tried to establish a deviant behavior structure. As a consequence, the late adopter was replaced preventing the creation of a deviant social structure.

The case of Capital X and the behavior of its marketing analysts present one possible interpretation for the benchmark variable values over time. They also indicate how the interplay of different constructs in the AST model at any given time could change the structural outcomes and the values of the benchmark variables. In order to explore these ideas further, we present initial results from a case study at a manufacturing company that implemented an enterprise data warehouse.

REAL WORLD CASE: LARGE MANUFACTURING COMPANY

We spent time at a large manufacturing company (LMC) gathering information for our study. We interviewed five individuals at the company: one data warehouse manager, data warehouse architect, product team lead, and two power users. The interviews were semi-structured and lasted approximately one and a half hours. The transcribed interviews along with other organizational documents such as memos used to communicate the vision of the data warehouse and data warehouse planning documents were reviewed. Our objective was to understand how user roles and skills were affected during different stages of the data warehouse implementation process. Benchmark variable matrix for the stage of growth for LMC is listed in Table 2.

LMC is a leading producer of consumer products such as food and beverages. It employs over

Table 2. Initial benchmark variable matrix for the stage of growth for LMC

Benchmark variables	Pre – data warehouse	Initiation stage	Growth Stage
Data	Transaction level data residing in various silos across the organization	Integrated transaction level data on several subject areas for all divisions	Transaction level data on multiple subject areas
Architecture	Multiple divisional transaction processing systems and multiple data marts	Potion of enterprise data warehouse as proof of concept	Central data store of data warehouse completed
Stability of product environment	Inconsistent data standards and business rules in different divisions	Enterprise level business rules and data standards begin to emerge.	Enterprise level business rules and data standards are becoming practice
Warehouse staff	In-house personnel skill set limited to existing applications and systems	In-house personnel receiving training from vendors to gain skills	In-house personnel become more experienced and take over operations from consultants
Users	Users integrate data as needed to complete tasks	Early adopters have access to integrated data from the warehouse	Late adopters have access to data from the warehouse
Impact on users' skills and jobs	User skills and knowledge are limited to existing legacy system applications and use	Early adopter training on new BI tools	Late adopter training on new BI tools to create awareness of the power of the data warehouse.
Applications	Predefined report access to decision making	BI applications for past and future trend analysis	BI applications for past and future trend analysis
Costs and Benefits	Ineffective task completion	Time savings from access to integrated data	Excess time spent using work around to new applications
Organizational impact	Inefficient business practices and ineffective decision making	Better decision making through integrated data access	General resistance to new applications and tools and request for old functionality

100, 000 people from across the globe to produce these consumer products under several different brands. It is an information intensive environment requiring fast decision making from employees of all levels globally to ensure successful task completion from product inception to sales/marketing to the end consumer. However, product divisions operated almost as independent companies and information sharing was not the norm in LMC's strong, conservative and antiquated corporate culture. To design and produce more competitive products across the corporation, upper management directed the implementation of an enterprise wide transaction level information system. When delivered, the enterprise data warehouse (EDW) was touted to increase information sharing, create product synergies, and develop effective product design and management practices between product divisions.

The transaction level marketing, sales and customer subject areas for each product division were first loaded to the initial version of the EDW in phase one (i.e., the initiation stage). Approximately 25 percent of the power users across divisions volunteered to be trained and were given access to the EDW and a new suite of BI tools at the end of phase one. These volunteers were technology savvy professionals who were capable of quickly grasping the EDW and new BI tool suite (Figure 3, a-1). Previously, these power users merged data from aggregated internal reports with external data in MS Excel to make decisions on product design and management. If data was required for further analysis, special requests were made to IT to provide the data sets. This typically took time and delayed product design decisions. The EDW provided a comprehensive data source to meet their internal and external data needs using a powerful

Figure 3. Application of AST to LMC's product management [(a) = Early adopter activity and outcomes, (b) = Late adopter activity and outcomes]

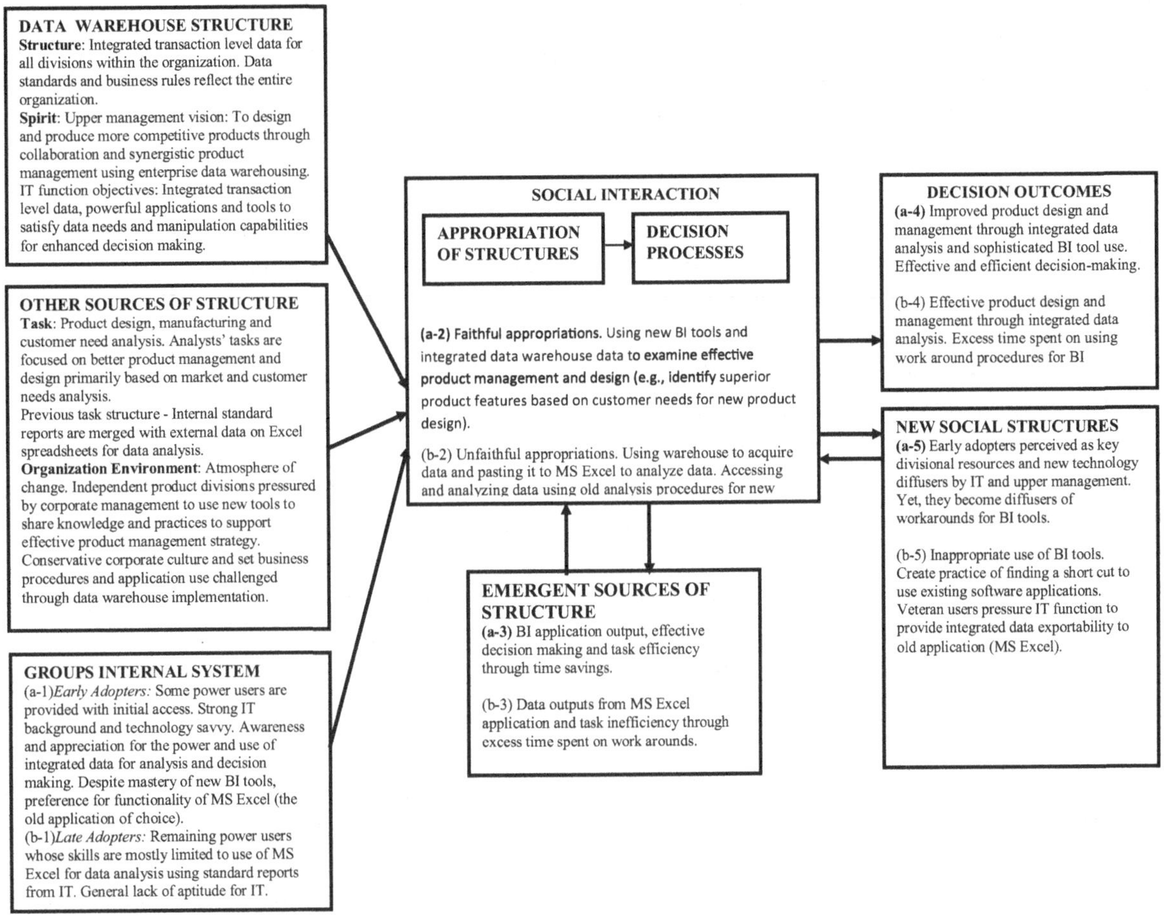

BI tool (Figure 3, a-2). The time savings gained through data integration was welcomed by these early adopters (Figure 3, a-3). However, despite their enthusiasm, one common request made to the data warehousing team for improvement was EDW data exportability to MS Excel. In phase two, when EDW access and the BI tool suite were released to the rest of the power user population in the growth stage, this request/complaint became the key reason for unfaithful appropriations of the new BI tools.

Analytical skills of the remaining power users were heavily dependent on MS Excel, which was the application of choice prior to EDW implementation. Furthermore, power users, due to their strong analytical skills, were generally perceived by others as a group with power within each product division. As a result, LMC experienced a low turnover rate of elite power users. The remaining power users, however, given their limited skill set and power within the organization, expressed strong resistance to using the new BI tool suite (Figure 3, b-1). Instead, they resorted to the familiar MS Excel functionality to analyze the integrated EDW data (Figure 3, b-2). While the output from data analysis was mostly effective, these late adopters spent a considerable amount of time finding ways to export EDW data to MS

Excel. Time better spent analyzing was mostly used for basic data entry (Figure 3, b-3). As a result, decision making was sometimes delayed (Figure 3, b-4). For example, one power user explained that standard decisions that required a week of data analysis required 50 percent more time with the new system as they had to cut and paste data and often do manual data correction prior to analysis. Upon observing the unfaithful appropriations by users in the second phase, the early adopters renewed their request for data exportability to Excel. As the request did not receive due attention[a], the early adopters became advocates for the workarounds and unfaithful appropriations (Figure 3, a-5). As an early adopter described, "when our need fell on deaf ears, we started showing the others easy ways to use the data in Excel. It is just an easier and familiar tool. It gets the job done. We just need IT to deliver what we want to create the reports we want."

Consequently, the data warehousing team's effort to encourage faithful appropriations of the BI tool suite was fruitless. The structuration that emerged during the growth stage of the data warehouse was an ineffective use of the data warehouse and its BI application. The transformation that the organization expected did not emerge. Recognizing that LMC's culture is not amenable to change, the data warehousing team is investigating reengaging the vendor consultants to provide users with the requested functionality.

From pre-data warehouse stage to the growth stage, benchmark variables reveal a rising trend that a central data store of data warehouse is being established and enterprise level business rules and data standards is becoming a norm. Warehouse staff have become more experienced with the new data warehouse system and been able to extract data from the system to conduct analyses. However, the benchmark variable Costs and Benefits and Organizational Impact discern inefficiency and resistance that do not bode well with the rising trend. The summary of benchmark variables for LMC is presented in Table 2.

DISCUSSIONS AND CONCLUSION

The study is a first step in the process of attempting to understand the data warehouse's capacity to transform an organization when aligned with strategy. However, this study is limited in that we apply a hypothetical example and the initials findings of a case study to illustrate the merit of our perspective. In order to get an accurate understanding of the appropriations process in interactions and the structures that emerge, an intensive ethnographic type study of the organizational data warehousing growth would be necessary.

The primary contribution of this paper is that we combine the stages of growth theory and AST to explain how benchmark variables for data warehousing stages of growth change over time. This is a first step in the process of studying organizational transformation as it takes place when aligned with an advanced IT technology such as data warehousing. In particular, we demonstrate, through a case analysis, the growth and transformation that take place due to a data warehouse implementation. It goes beyond giving a list of features presented by the benchmark variable matrix. Thus, structuration provides a deeper understanding of why some values exist for a benchmark variable in one given stage as well as how some values differ in a a given stage. Furthermore, it confirms Nolan's words that transformation and changes in an organization takes place in the form of a fluid process (Gibson et al. 1974). This fluid process is explained through the ever-changing nature of structure in structuration theory. Structuration theory explains the process of evolution (i.e., stages of growth) at a deeper level with arbitrary break points which practitioner could call stages. Structuration enables industrialists and academicians alike to understand what occurs as the data warehouse grows and how the stages will progress.

The paper also brings another reality to light. Depending on their inputs to the system – technology structure, other sources of technology, and group internal system – the appropriations that take place and the decision outcomes that result will change. Simultaneously, organizational structure will also change. Thus, AST identifies three key aspects of organizations, which may dictate how organizational transformation may occur that organizations should pay attention to. For instance, the fact that one of those aspects is group internal systems, (i.e., human actors and human behavior) speaks volumes of the predictability of AST or structuration. It illustrated with LMC, group internal systems indicate that as long as human beings play a role in organizations, organizational transformation can never be accurately predicted. However, what this theory provides is a means of identifying telltale signs stating the direction structure is changing and progressing.

Further explanation of concepts revealed in this paper requires study of organizational growth and change in an industry setting. Desanctic and Poole (1994) presents a method of studying organizational transformation through different levels of analysis –micro, global and institutional. Data need to be gathered from all sources of social structures including users, warehouse staff, top managers, consultants, and customers. Qualitative data analysis techniques can be applied (Eisenhardt 1989; Miles et al. 1994; Orlikowski 1996). Further study along this line of research may lead to the discovery of different types of appropriations and emerging structures that would enable both industry and academe to deal with and understand uncertainty in organizations and more effectively pursue business goals.

REFERENCES

Alavi, M., and Joachimsthaler, E.A. "Revisiting DSS Implementation Research: A Meta-Analysis of the literature and Suggestions for Researchers," *MIS Quarterly* (16:1), 1992, pp 95-116.

Barley, S.R. "Technology as An Occasion for Structuring: Evidence from Observations of CT Scanners and the Social Order of Radiology Departments," *Administrative Science Quarterly* (31:1), 1986, pp 78-108.

Benbasat, I., Dexter, A.S., and Mantha, R.W. "Impact of Organizational Maturity on Information Systems Skills," *Communications of the ACM* (27:5), 1980, pp 476-485.

Bharadwaj, A.S. "A Resource-based Perspective on Information Technology Capability and Firm Performance," *MIS Quarterly* (24:1), 2000, pp 169-198.

Boersma, K., and Kingma, S. "From Means to Ends: The Transformation of ERP in a Manufacturing Company," *Journal of Strategic Information Systems* (24:2), 2005, pp 197-219.

Brancheau, J.C., and Wetherbe, J.C. "The Adoption of Spreadsheet Software: Testing Innovation Diffusion Theory in the Context of End-user Computing," *Information Systems Research* (1:2), 1990, pp 115-143.

Chengalur-Smith, I., and Duchessi, P. "Client-server Implementation: Some Management Pointers," *IEEE Transaction on Engineering Management* (47:1), 2000, pp 127-145.

Cooper, B.L., Watson, H.J., Wixom, B., and Goodhue, D.L. "Data Warehousing Supports Corporate Strategy at First American Corporation," *MIS Quarterly* (24:4), 2000, pp 547-568.

Daft, R.L. "A Dual-core Model of Organizational Innovation," *Academy of Management Journal* (21:2), 1978, pp 193-210.

Damanpour, F., and Gopalakrishnan, S. "Theories of Organizational Structure and Innovation Adoption: The Role of Environmental Change," *Journal of Engineering and Technology Management* (15:1), 1998, pp 1-24.

Davenport, T.H. "The Future of Enterprise System-enabled Organizations," *Information Systems Frontiers* (2:2), 2000a, pp 163-180.

Davenport, T.H. *Mission Critical: Realizing The Promise of Enterprise Systems* Harvard Business School Press, Boston, Massachusetts, 2000b.

DeSanctis, G., and Poole, M.S. "Capturing the Complexity in Advanced Technology: Adaptive Structuration Model," *Organization Science* (5:2), 1994, pp 121-147.

Duncan, R.B. "The Ambidextrous Organizations: Designing Dual Structures for Innovation," in: *The Management of Organization: Strategy and Implementation,* R.H. Kilmann, L.R. Pondy and D.P. Slevin (eds.), North-Holland, New York, 1976, pp. 167-188.

Eisenhardt, K.M. "Building Theories from Case Study Research," *Academy of Management Review* (14:4), 1989, pp 532-550.

Fichman, R.G. "The Diffusion and Assimilation of Information Technology Innovations," in: *Framing The Domains of IT Management: Projecting the Future. Through The Past,* R.W. Zmud and M.F. Price (eds.), Pinnaflex Educational Resources, Inc., Cincinnati, Ohio, 2000, pp. 105-127.

Gibson, C.F., and Nolan, R.L. "Managing the Four Stages of EDP Growth," *Harvard Business Review* (40:1), 1974, pp 76-88.

Giddens, A. *The Constitution of Society: Outline of the Theory of Structure* University of California Press, Berkeley, CA, 1984.

Giddens, A. *Problems of Action and Structure* Stanford University Press, 1993.

Goodhue, D.L., Wixom, B., and Waston, H.J. "Data Warehousing and Organizational Change at the IRS: Increasing Compliance Without Taxpayer Audits," in: *Annals of Cases on Information Technology Applications and Management in Organizations*, Idea Group Publishing, Hershey, Pennsylvania, 1999.

Griffith, T.L., and Northcraft, G.B. "Cognitive Elements in the Implementation of New Technology: Can Less Information Provide More Benefits?" *MIS Quarterly* (20:1), 1996, pp 99-110.

Grover, V., and Goslar, M.D. "The Initiation, Adoption, and Implementation of Telecommunications Technologies in U.S. Organizations," *Journal of Management Information Systems* (10:1), 1993, pp 141-163.

Hayley, B.J., Watson, H.J., and Goodhue, D.L. "The Benefits of Data Warehousing at Whirlpool," in: *Annals of Cases on Information Technology Applications and Management in Organizations,* Idea Group Publishing, Hershey, Pennslyvania, 1999.

Henderson, J.C., and Treacy, M.E. "Managing End User Computing for Competitive Advantage," *Sloan Management Review* (50:4), 1986, pp 37-46.

Huff, A., Stimpert, L., and Huff, J. "Enterpreneural Activity and Industry Structuring," *Organization Science* (3:3), 1994, pp 398-427.

King, J.L., and Teo, T.S.H. "Integration between Business Planning and Information Systems Planning: Validating Stage Hypothesis," *Decision Sciences* (28:2), 1997, pp 279-309.

Kotter, J.P. "Leading Changes: Why Transformation Efforts Fail," *Harvard Business Review* (73:2), 1995, pp 59-67.

Kwon, T.H., and Zmud, R.W. "Unifying the Fragmented Models of Information Systems Implementation," in: *Critical Issues in Information Systems Research,* B.R. Hirschheim (ed.), John Wiley and Sons Ltd., New York, 1987, pp. 227-252.

Leavitt, H.J., and Whisler, T.L. "Management in the 1980's," *Harvard Business Review* (36:6), 1958, pp 41-48.

Leonard-Barton, D. "Implementing as Mutual Adaptation of Technology and Organization," *Research Policy* (17:5), 1988, pp 251-267.

Lucas, H.C. *Implementation: The Key to Successful Information Systems* Columbia University Press, New York, 1981, pp. x, 208 ill. 224 cm.

Lucas, H.C., Jr., Ginzberg, M.J., and Schultz, R.L. *Information Systems Implementation: Testing A Structural Model* Ablex Publishing Corporation, Norwood, New Jersey, 1990.

Magal, S.R., Carr, H.H., and Waston, H.J. "Critical Success Factors for Information Center Managers," *MIS Quarterly* (12:3), 1988, pp 413-425.

Miles, M.B., and Huberman, A.M. *Qualitative Data Analysis: An Expanded Sourcebook* SAGE Publications Inc., Thousand Oaks, California, 1994.

Nord, W.R., and Tucker, S. *Implementing Routine and Radical Innovation* Lexington Books, Lexington, M.A., 1987.

Oh, W., and Pinsonneault, A. "On the Assessment of the Strategic Value of Information Technologies: Conceptual and Analytical Approaches," *MIS Quarterly* (31:2), 2007, pp 239-265.

Orlikowski, W.J. "The Duality of Technology: Rethinking the Concept of Technology in Organizations," *Organization Science* (3:3), 1992, pp 398-427.

Orlikowski, W.J. "Improvising Organizational Transformation Over time: A Situated Perspective," *Information Systems Research* (7:1), 1996, pp 63-92.

Orlikowski, W.J., and Robey, D. "Information Technology and the Structuring of Organizations," *Information Systems Research* (2:2), 1991, pp 143-169.

Pavlou, P.A., and Sawy, O.A.E. "From IT Leveraging Competence to Competitive Advantage in Turbulent Environment: The Case of New Product Development," *Information Systems Research* (17:3), 2006, pp 198-227.

Pettigrow, A.M. "Context and Action in the Transformation of the Firm," *Journal of Management Studies* (24:6), 1987, pp 649-670.

Pierce, J.L., and Delbecq, A. "Organization Structure, Individual Attributes and Innovation," *Academy of Management Review* (2:1), 1977, pp 27-37.

Purvis, R.L., Sambamurthy, V., and Zmud, R.W. "The Assimilation of Knowledge Platforms in Organizations: An Empirical Investigation," *Organization Science* (12:2), 2001, pp 117-135.

Ranson, S., Hinings, G., and Greenwood, R. "The Structure of Organizational Structures," *Administrative Science Quarterly* (25:1), 1980, pp 1-17.

Riley, P. "A Structurationist Account of Political Culture," *Administrative Science Quarterly* (28:3), 1983, pp 414-437.

Rogers, E.M., and Shoemaker, E.F. *Communications of Innovations* Free Press, New York, NY, 1971.

Sharma, R., and Yetton, P. "The Contingent Effects of Management Support and Task Independence on Successful Information Systems Implementation," *MIS Quarterly* (27:4), 2003, pp 533-555.

Soh, C., and Sia, S.K. "An Institutional Perspective on Sources of ERP Package-organization Misalignments," *Journal of Strategic Information Systems* (13:4), 2004, pp 375-397.

Sultan, F., and Chan, L. "The Adoption of New Technology: The Case of Object-oriented Computing in Software Companies," *IEEE Transaction on Engineering Management* (47:1), 2000, pp 106 -126.

Swanson, E.B. "Information systems innovation among organizations," *Management Science* (40:9), 1994, pp 1069-1092.

Waston, H.J., Goodhue, D.L., and Wixom, B. "The Benefits of Data Warehousing: Why Some Organizations Realize Exceptional Payoffs," *Information & Management* (39:6), 2002, pp 491-502.

Watson, H.J., Ariyachandra, T., and Matyska, R. "Data Warehousing Stages of Growth," *Information Systems Management* (18:3), 2001, pp 42-50.

ENDNOTE

[a] The data warehouse team did not have the skill set and were unwilling to customize the vendor BI tool suite to add MS Excel functionality.

APPENDIX A

The Benchmark Variable Matrix for the Stages of Growth in Data Warehousing Adopted from Watson et al. (2001)

Benchmark variables	Initiation stage	Growth stage	Maturity stage
Data	Limited amount for a single or few subject areas	Data for multiple subject areas	Enterprise wide data, well integrated and for multiple time periods
Architecture	A single data mart	Multiple data marts	A data warehouse with dependent data marts
Stability of the production environment	Procedures are ad hoc and evolving	Procedures are not well established	Procedures are routinized and documented
Warehouse staff	In-house personnel inexperienced; consultants are frequently used	In-house personnel have gained experience and consultants are not heavily relied on	In-house personnel are experienced; the staff has well-defined roles and responsibilities
Users	Analysts in the business unit served by the data mart	Users from all of the business units are served by the data marts, diverse in their information needs and computer skills	Users from throughout the organization access the warehouse; suppliers and customers may have access to the warehouse data
Impact of users' skills and jobs	Some users may not have the skills or inclination for the more analytical jobs	More users experience changes in the skills they need in order to perform their jobs	Users throughout the organization need improved computer skills in order to perform their jobs
Applications	Reports are predefined and ad hoc queries, backward looking to what has already occurred	Reports and predefined queries, more analysis of why things occurred and "what-if" analyses for future scenarios	Reports, redefined queries and ad hoc queries, DSS and EIS; data mining provides predictive modeling capabilities; integration with operational systems
Costs and benefits	Costs are moderate; benefits include time savings new and improved information and improved decision making	Benefits include time savings, new and better information and improved decision making, the benefits exceed the costs for the first time	Benefits include time saving, new and better information, improved decision making, redesigned business processes and support for corporate objectives; high ROI may be realized
Organizational impact	Operational and tactical in a few business units	Operational and tactical in additional business units	Organization wide and often strategic as well as operation and tactical

Chapter XVIII
Social Network Structures in Open Source Software Development Teams

Yuan Long
Colorado State University–Pueblo, USA

Keng Siau
University of Nebraska–Lincoln, USA

ABSTRACT

Drawing on social network theories and previous studies, this research examines the dynamics of social network structures in Open Source Software (OSS) teams. Three projects were selected from SourceForge.net in terms of their similarities as well as their differences. Monthly data were extracted from the bug tracking systems in order to achieve a longitudinal view of the interaction pattern of each project. Social network analysis was used to generate the indices of social structure. The finding suggests that the interaction pattern of OSS projects evolves from a single hub at the beginning to a core/periphery model as the projects move forward.

INTRODUCTION

The information system development arena has seen many revolutions and evolutions. We have witnessed the movement from structured development to object-oriented (OO) development. Modeling methods, such as data flow diagram and entity relationship diagram, are facing new

OO modeling languages, such as the unified modeling language (UML) (see Siau & Cao, 2001; Siau, Erickson, & Lee, 2005; Siau & Loo, 2006) and OO methodologies, such as unified process (UP). The latest development includes agile modeling (see Erickson, Lyytinen, & Siau, 2005), extreme programming, and OSS development. While many of these changes are related to systems development paradigms, methodologies, methods, and techniques, the phenomenon of OSS development entails a different structure for software development teams.

Unlike conventional software projects, the participants of OSS projects are volunteers. They are self-selected based on their interests and capability to contribute to the projects (Raymond, 2000). In addition, the developers of OSS projects are distributed all around the world. They communicate and collaborate with each other through the Internet, using e-mails or discussion boards. Therefore, effective and efficient communication and collaboration are critical to OSS success. However, little empirical research has been conducted to study the underlying interaction pattern of OSS teams, especially the dynamics of the social network structures in OSS development teams. To fill this gap, this study examines the evolvement of social structure in OSS teams. The study contributes to the enhancement of the understanding of OSS development, and provides foundation for future studies to analyze the antecedents and consequences of social networks in the OSS context.

The remainder of the paper is structured as follows. First, prior studies on social network structures in OSS teams are reviewed. Second, theories related to social structure and social network theory are discussed. Third, the research methodology is presented, and the research results are reported. Next, discussions of the results, the limitations, and the implications are provided. The paper concludes with suggestions for future research.

LITERATURE REVIEW

The phenomenon of OSS development has attracted considerable attention from both practitioners and researchers in diverse fields, such as computer science, social psychology, organization, and management. Because of the multifaceted nature of OSS, researchers have investigated OSS phenomenon from varied perspectives. For example, focusing on technical perspective, researchers studied issues such as OSS development methodology (e.g., Jørgensen, 2001) and coding quality (e.g., Stamelos, Angelis, Oikonomu, & Bleris, 2002). Based on social psychology, researchers investigated individual motivation (e.g., Hann, Robert, & Slaughter, 2004), new developers (Von Krogh, Spaeth, & Lakhani 2003), the social network (e.g., Madey, Freeh, & Tynan, 2002), and the social structure (e.g., Crowston & Howison, 2005). In terms of organizational and managerial perspective, researchers examined knowledge innovation (e.g., Hemetsberger 2004; Lee & Cole 2003, Von Hippel & von Krogh, 2003) and the governance mechanism (e.g., Sagers 2004).

An OSS development team is essentially a virtual organization in which participants interact and collaborate with each other through the Internet. Compared to conventional organizations, the structure of virtual organizations is decentralized, flat, and nonhierarchical (Ahuja & Carley 1999). However, some researchers challenge the belief (e.g., Crowston & Howison 2005; Gacek & Arief, 2004;; Mockus, Fielding, & Herbsleb, 2000; Mockus, Fielding, & Herbsleb, 2002; Moon & Sproull, 2000). They argue that the social structure of OSS projects is hierarchical rather than flat, like a tree (Gacek & Arief, 2004) or an onion (Crowston & Howison, 2005). The social structure of OSS teams directly influences the collaboration and the decision-making process and further affects the overall performance of the teams as well as individuals' perception of belonging and satisfaction. Therefore, one wonders what form of social structure might be present in the OSS development and what type of structure will emerge—centralized or decentralized, hierarchical or nonhierarchical, onion-like or tree-like, or a combination of the above depending on certain specific situations?

A social network, as stated by Krebs and Holley (2004), is generally built in four phases, each with its own distinct topology (as shown in Figure 1).

1. scattered clusters,
2. single hub-and-spoke,
3. multihub small-world network, and
4. core/periphery.

Most organizations start from isolated and distributed clusters (Krebs & Holley, 2004). Then an active leader emerges and takes responsibility for building a network that will connect the separate clusters. However, this single-hub topology is fragile. With more participants entering the group, the leader changes his/her role to a facilitator and helps to build multiple hubs, which is stage three. The core/periphery model, the last stage, is the most stable structure. In the core/periphery model, the network core encompasses key group members who are strongly connected to each other, while the periphery contains members who are usually weakly connected to each other as well as to the core members. With the general network building phases in mind, one can argue that OSS projects may follow the same four stages (i.e., scattered clusters, single hub-and-spoke, multihub small-world network, and core/periphery model). But is

Figure 1. Four phases of social structures (from Krebs and Holley 2004)

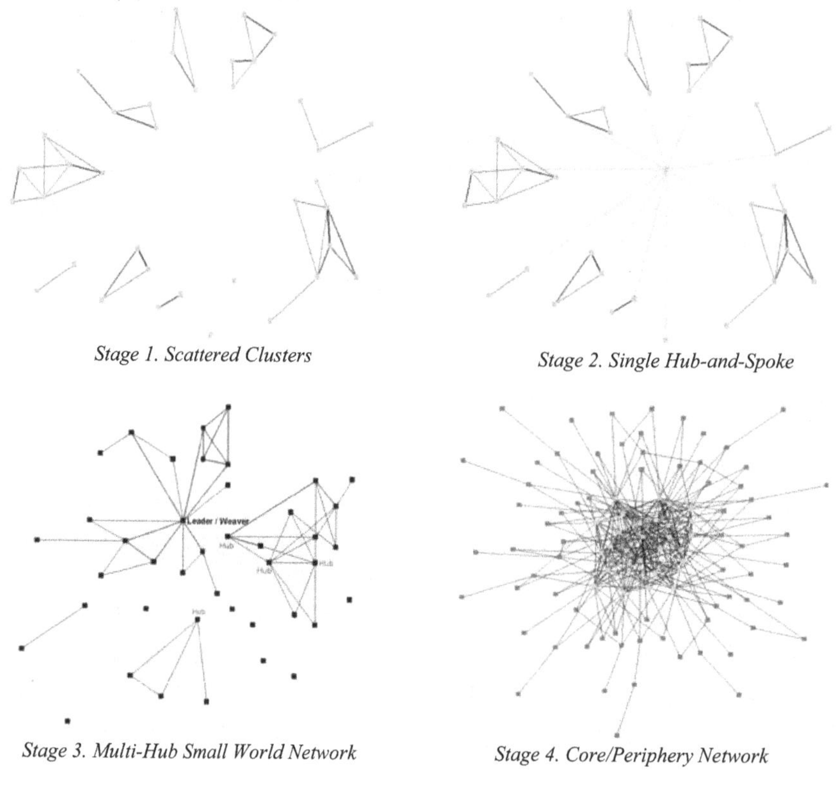

that true for OSS projects? How does the social structure of OSS teams evolve over time?

Our research addresses the following two questions:

1. What is the social structure of OSS teams?
2. How does the social structure evolve over time?

THEORETICAL FOUNDATION

Social Structure and Social Interaction

Social structure, as suggested by Schaefer and Lamm (1998), refers to the way in which society is organized into predictable relationships. Social structure can be considered in terms of three aspects—actors, their actions, and their interactions. The social actor is a relatively static concept addressing issues such as roles, positions, and statuses. Individual actors are embedded in the social environment and, therefore, their actions are largely influenced by the connections between each other. Social interaction is generally regarded as the way in which people respond to one another. These interaction patterns are to some extent independent of individuals. They exert a force that shapes both behavior (i.e., actions) and identity (i.e., actors) (Schaefer & Lamm, 1998).

Research on social interaction focuses on how individuals actually communicate with each other in group settings. These studies address issues such as the interaction patterns, the underlying rules guiding interaction, the reasons accounting for the way people interact, and the impacts of the interaction patterns on the individual behavior and the group performance. These issues begin by questioning what might be the interaction pattern in a specific social setting and that addresses our research question—understanding social interaction of OSS project teams.

Social Network Theory

Social network theory focuses on studying actors as well as their relationships in specific social settings. Network theory is analogous to systems theory and complexity theory. It is an interdisciplinary theory stemming from multiple traditional fields, including psychology, which addresses individuals' perception of social structure; anthropology, which emphasizes social relationships; and mathematics, which provides algorithms (Scott, 2000).

Based on the view of social network, the world is composed of actors (also called nodes) and ties between them. The ties can represent either a specific relationship (such as friendship and kinship) between a pair of actors or define a particular action which an actor performs. Different kinds of ties specify different networks and are typically assumed to function differently. For example, the ties in a family network are distinctive from those in a working network, and the centrality in the "who loves whom" network obviously has different meaning than the centrality in the "who hates whom" network.

Social network theory is based on the intuitive notion that the social interaction patterns are essential to the individuals who reflect them. Network theorists believe that how individuals behave largely depends on how they interact with others and how they are tied to a social network. Furthermore, besides individual behavior, network theorists believe that the success or failure of societies and organizations often depends on the internal interaction pattern (Freeman, 2004).

Besides the theoretical essence, social network theory is also characterized as a distinctive methodology encompassing techniques for data collection, statistical analysis, and visual representation. This approach is usually called social network analysis and will be discussed in the research methodology section. This paper draws on the social network theory to study the interaction pattern of OSS development project.

RESEARCH METHODOLOGY

Social Network Analysis

Social network analysis is used in our study to investigate the interaction pattern of the OSS development process. Social network analysis focuses on uncovering the interaction pattern of interdependent individuals (Freeman, 2004). Through a structural analysis of a social network diagram, a map depicting actors as well as the ties that connect them, social network analysis can reveal the patterns of relationships and the relative position of individuals in a specific social setting. This approach has been effectively used in organizational research, social support, mental health, and the diffusion of information (Freeman, 2004).

Social network analysis is used in our study for two primary reasons. First, the purpose of social network analysis fits our research objective. Social network analysis aims to analyze the relationship among a set of actors instead of their internal attributes. Our research aims to reveal the interaction pattern of OSS project teams. Therefore, social network analysis is helpful in answering our research questions.

Second, the rich interactive data extracted from OSS projects presents a "gold mine" for social network analysis. Social network analysis is grounded in the systematic analysis of empirical data. However, there is usually a lack of convenient and objective resources from which to draw the links (i.e., relationships) among actors. Most OSS projects have online mailing lists, forums, and tracking systems that are open to public, thus providing a rich set of longitudinal data. Based on these public data, researchers are able to capture input data sets for social network analysis.

Longitudinal Data

Because we are interested in studying how the interaction pattern of OSS projects evolves over time, cross-sectional observations of interaction networks are not sufficient. Cross-sectional observations of social networks are snapshots of interactions at a point in time and cannot provide traceable history, thus limiting the usefulness of the results. On the other hand, longitudinal observations offer more promise for understanding the social network structure and its evolvement. In this study, we extracted longitudinal data on OSS projects.

Case Selection

OSS projects were selected from the SourceForge[1], which is the world's largest Web site hosting OSS projects. SourceForge provides free tools and services to facilitate OSS development. At the time of the study, it hosted a total of 99,730 OSS projects and involved 1,066,589 registered users (This data was retrieved on May 4, 2005). Although a few big OSS projects have their own Web sites (such as Linux), SourceForge serves as the most popular data resource for OSS researchers.

Following the idea of theoretical sampling (Glaser & Strauss, 1967), three OSS projects were selected from SourceForge in terms of their similarities and differences. Theoretical sampling requires theoretical relevance and purposes (Orlikowski, 1993). In terms of relevance, the selection ensures that the interaction pattern of OSS projects over time is kept similar. Therefore, the projects that are selected have to satisfy two requirements. First, the projects must have considerable interaction among members during the development process. All three projects had more than 10 developers, and the number of bugs reported was more than 1,000. Second, since we are interested in the interaction over time, the projects must have a relatively long life. In our case, all three projects were at least three years old.

In addition to similarities, differences are sought among cases because the study aims to study interaction patterns of various OSS projects. Therefore, the three projects differ on

Table 1. Summary of three projects

		Net-SNMP	Compiere ERP + CRM	J-boss
Description		Net-SNMP allows system and network managers to monitor and manage hosts and network devices.	Compiere is a smart ERP+CRM solution covering all major business areas—especially for small-medium enterprises.	JBoss is a leading open source Java application server. After Linux and Apache, it is the third major open source project to receive widespread adoption by corporate IT.
Similarities	Bug reports (more than 1,000 bugs)	1,361	1,695	2,296
	Development duration (more than 3 years)	55 months (registered on 10/2000)	47 months (registered on 6/2001)	50 months (registered on 3/2001)
Differences	Software type	Internet, network management	Enterprise: ERP+CRM	J2EE-based middleware
	Group size (number of developers)	Small (14)	Median (44)	Large (75)
	Intended audience	Developers, system administrators	Business	Developers, system administrators

several project characteristics, such as project size, project type, and intended audience. These differences enable us to make useful contrasts during data analysis.

The Table 1 summarizes the three projects with a brief description.

Data Collection and Analysis

Social network analysis can be divided into the following three stages (Borgatti, 2002).

1. Data collection. In this stage, researchers collect data, using surveys and questionnaires, or from documents and other data resources, and generate input data sets for social network analysis.
2. Statistical analysis. Based on mathematics algorithms, this stage generates network indices concerning group structure (such as centralization and density) as well as individual cohesion (such as centrality and bridges).
3. Visual representation. This stage employs network diagrams to show the interaction structure as well as the position of specific actors.

First is the data collection. The data were collected in April 2005 from SourceForge.net. Data were extracted from the bug tracking system of each project. We chose the bug tracking system as the primary data resource for three reasons. First, open source software is characterized as peer review of open codes. Raymond (1998) proposed the "Linus' law" in his well-known essay *The Cathedral and the Bazaar*— "Given enough eyeballs, all bugs are shallow." Therefore, the bug system can be viewed as the representative of open source spirit. Second, compared to other development activities, such as patch posting and feature request, the bug-fixing process is the most active procedure to illustrate the close collaboration between developers and users as well as among developers themselves. Finally,

Figure 2. An example of the social matrix for an OSS project

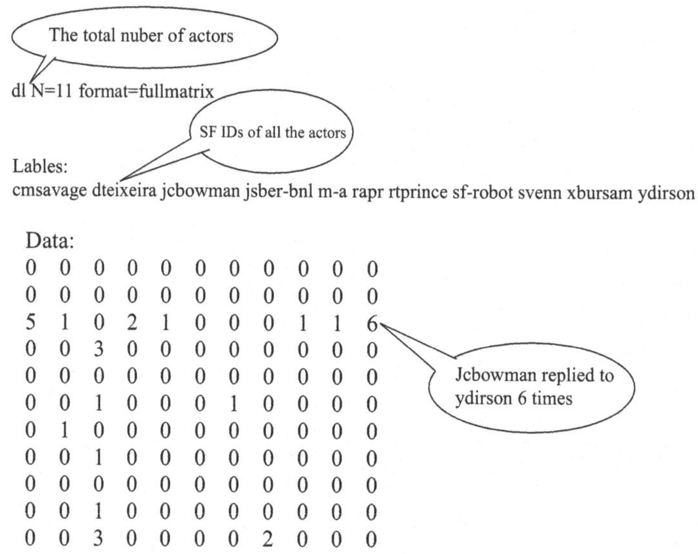
The total nuber of actors
dl N=11 format=fullmatrix
SF IDs of all the actors
Lables:
cmsavage dteixeira jcbowman jsber-bnl m-a rapr rtprince sf-robot svenn xbursam ydirson
Data:
0 0 0 0 0 0 0 0 0 0 0
0 0 0 0 0 0 0 0 0 0 0
5 1 0 2 1 0 0 0 1 1 6
0 0 3 0 0 0 0 0 0 0 0
0 0 0 0 0 0 0 0 0 0 0
0 0 1 0 0 0 1 0 0 0 0
0 1 0 0 0 0 0 0 0 0 0
0 0 1 0 0 0 0 0 0 0 0
0 0 0 0 0 0 0 0 0 0 0
0 0 1 0 0 0 0 0 0 0 0
0 0 3 0 0 0 0 2 0 0 0
Jcbowman replied to ydirson 6 times

the bug tracking system provides rich data that record the interactive process.

A Web spider program, which is based on the work of Crowston and Howison (2005) with necessary revision, was used to download the bug tracking Web pages from the project Web site. After that, a Web parsing program was developed to analyze the Web pages. The interaction data was extracted from the bug tracking Web pages month-by-month, starting from the date the project was registered until the date the data was downloaded for this study. The output of this stage is a social matrix describing the interaction among users. Figure 2 shows an example of such a social matrix for an OSS project. In the matrix, each row or column represents a distinctive participant, which is identified by a unique SourceForge user identity. The values of cells indicate the degree of the interaction between each pair of participants, which is counted by the amounts of messages that participant A (i.e., row A) replied to participant B (i.e., column B).

Second is the statistical analysis. Our study focuses on two important and distinctive properties of network structure—group centralization and core/periphery fitness. Ucinet, which was developed by Borgatti, Everett, and Freeman (2002), was used to calculate these two properties.

Group centralization, as suggested by Wasserman and Faust (1994), refers to the extent to which a network revolves around a single center. A typical case of centralized structure is a "star" network. Group centralization can be viewed as a rough measure of inequity between individual actors, and the variability and dispersion of the interaction pattern.

The other property is core/periphery fitness. It measures the extent to which the network is close to a perfect core/periphery structure. The core/periphery structure depicts a dense, connected group surrounded by a sparse, unconnected periphery. The opposite structure is clique, which represents a structure of multiple subgroups, each with its own core and peripheries (Borgatti, 2002).

Finally is the visual representation. We used Ucinet (Borgatti et al., 2002) to draw the interaction networks for each of the three projects.

Table 2. Three snapshots for each project

		Net-SNMP	Compiere	JBoss
Group centralization (%)	1st.	9.420	15.624	4.931
	2nd.	3.071	2.294	4.45
	3rd.	2.316	1.288	4.12
Core/periphery fitness	1st.	0.674	0.774	0.485
	2nd.	0.654	0.796	0.477
	3rd.	0.651	0.765	0.501
Density	1st.	0.0235	0.0584	0.0073
	2nd.	0.0109	0.0610	0.0039
	3rd.	0.0072	0.0571	0.0026
Average distance	1st.	2.546	2.711	3.438
	2nd.	2.794	2.302	3.281
	3rd.	2.917	2.278	3.239
Distance-based cohesion	1st.	0.181	0.198	0.118
	2nd.	0.143	0.253	0.147
	3rd.	0.141	0.279	0.136

RESEARCH RESULTS

Snapshots of the Three Projects

Monthly data were extracted from the bug tracking system of each project. To illustrate the trend of interaction pattern, we provide three snapshots for each project (see Figures 3-5)[2].

Table 2 summarizes the relevant network characteristics of each project. In addition to the group centralization and core/periphery fitness, we also report other network characteristics, such as density, average distance, and distance-based cohesion. Density depicts how "close" the network looks, and it is a recommended measure of group cohesion (Blau, 1977; Wasserman & Faust 1994). The value of density ranges from 0 to 1. Average distance refers to average distance between all pairs of nodes (Borgatti, 2002). Distance-based cohesion takes on values between 0 and 1—the larger the values, the greater the cohesiveness.

Looking at the statistical results and the network plots, we can observe the following.

First, the evolvement of interaction patterns of the three projects reveals a general trend. As shown in the network plots (i.e., Figures 3-5), the interaction pattern develops from a centralized one with a single (sometimes dual) hub with several distributed nodes, to a core/periphery structure that has a core (a group of core developers) together with several hangers-on (periphery). Intense interactions exist within the core (among several core developers) and between each core member and his/her periphery. However, only loose relationships exist among peripheries. This pattern suggests a layer structure (i.e., core with its periphery) instead of a complete flat one with equal positions across all the members.

Second, although the interaction patterns of the three projects share some commonalities, their exact shapes are different. The shape of Net-SNMP (as shown in Figure 3) is more like a typical core/

Figure 3. Interaction patterns of Net-SNMP

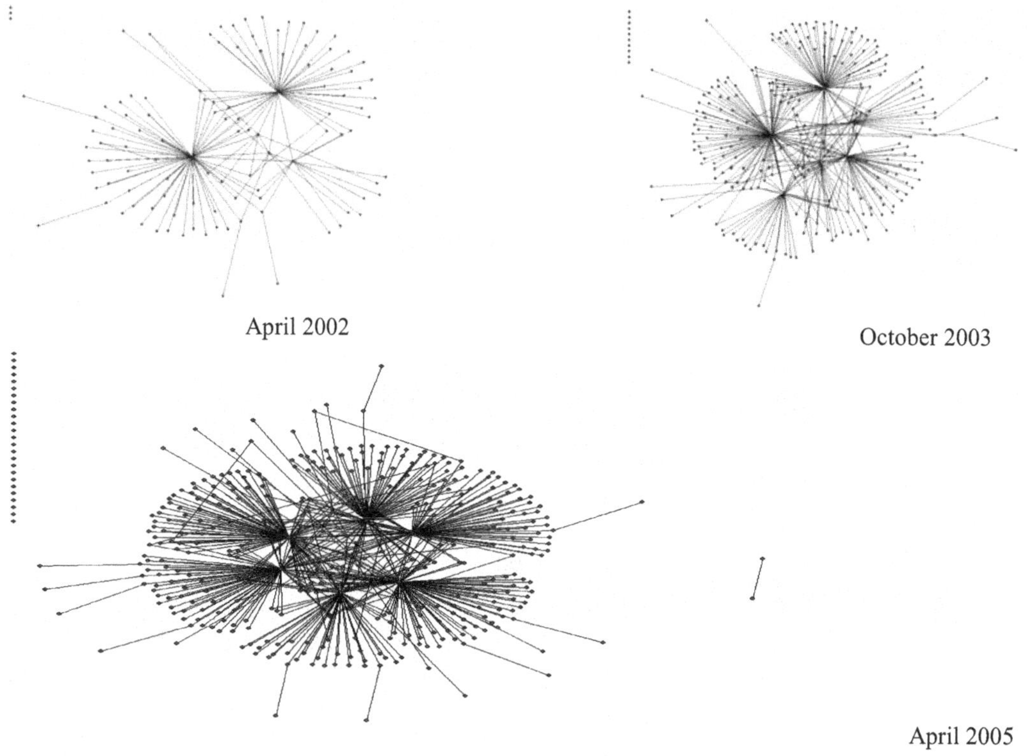

periphery compared to the other two. Compiere (as shown in Figure 4) keeps two cores, and the shape looks like a dumbbell. Jboss (as shown in Figure 5), which is the largest project among the three, maintains a more complex structure that shows multiple layers instead of just one core with the rest as peripheries (e.g., Net-SNMP)

Third, as time goes by, the group centralization decreases across the three projects, showing a trend that moves from a centralized structure to a decentralized structure irrespective of project sizes (The three projects with different project sizes are shown in Table 1), project types, and intended audience.

Fourth, the indices of core/periphery fitness of each project fluctuate slightly but maintain a relatively high value (larger than 0.5 on average). However, no observable trend was found across projects.

Fifth, since each project has a relatively large group (i.e., more than 100 actors including all the registered users), the values of density are relatively low with little variation. Therefore, density is not appropriate for comparing the projects.

From the snapshots, we observed the following trend. First, the OSS interaction network evolves into a core/periphery structure. Second, group centralization decreases over time. Third, core/periphery fitness stays relatively stable. To verify our observations, we used longitudinal data generated from the bug tracking systems to analyze the evolvement of interaction pattern (discussed in the following section).

Group Centralization and Core/Periphery Fitness

Table 3 shows the values of both group centralization and core/periphery fitness over time based on

Figure 4. Interaction patterns of compiere CRM+ERP

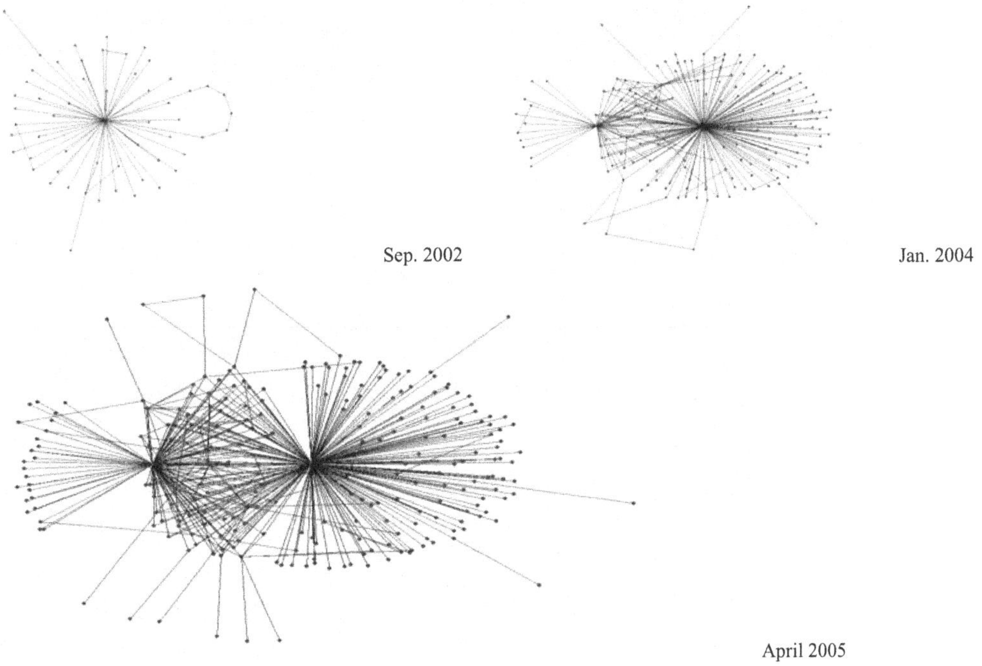

Figure 5. Interaction patterns of JBoss

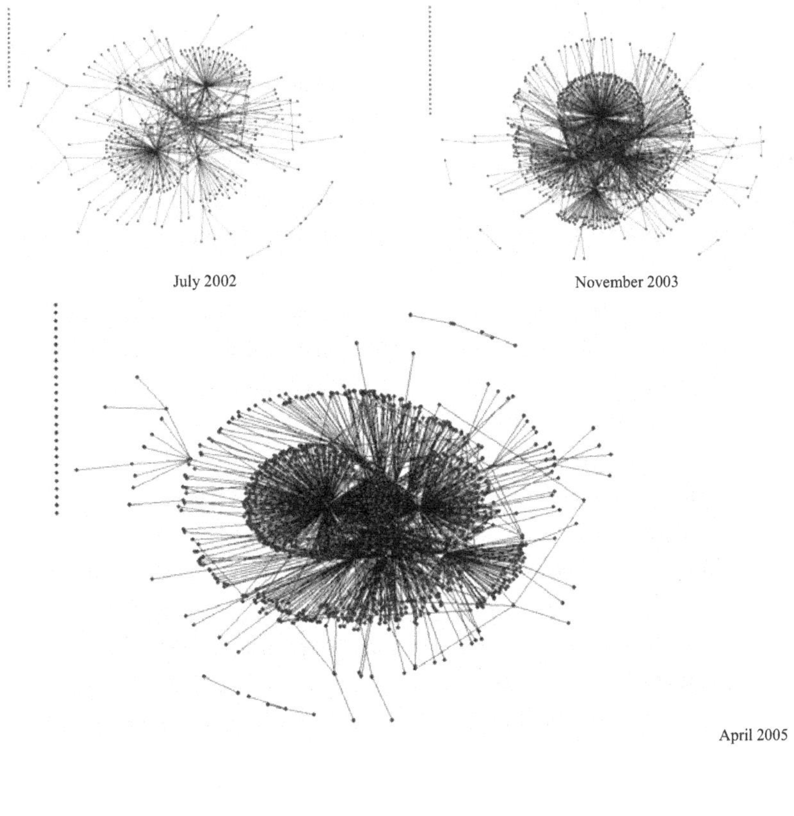

Table 3. Group centralization and core/periphery fitness based on longitudinal data

	Group centralization	Core/periphery fitness
Net-SNMP		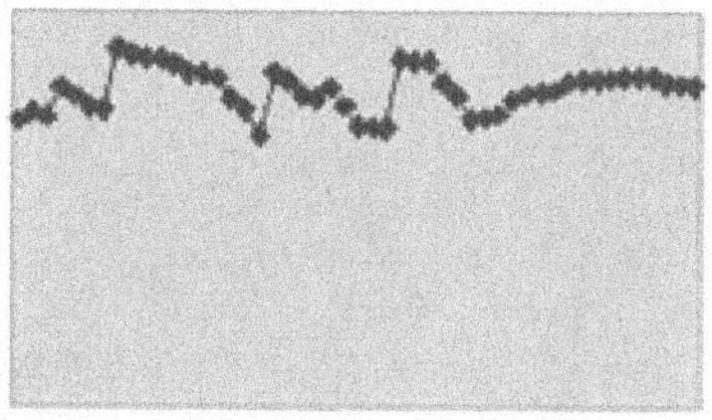
Compiere	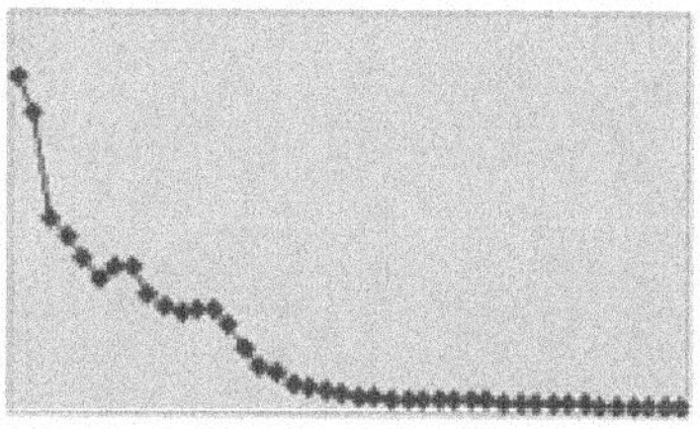	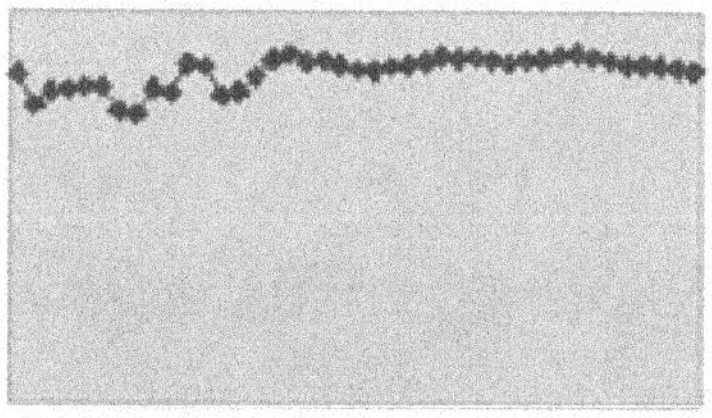
JBoss	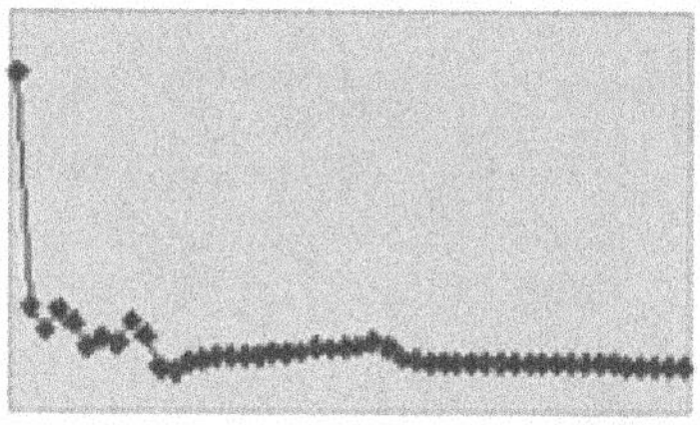	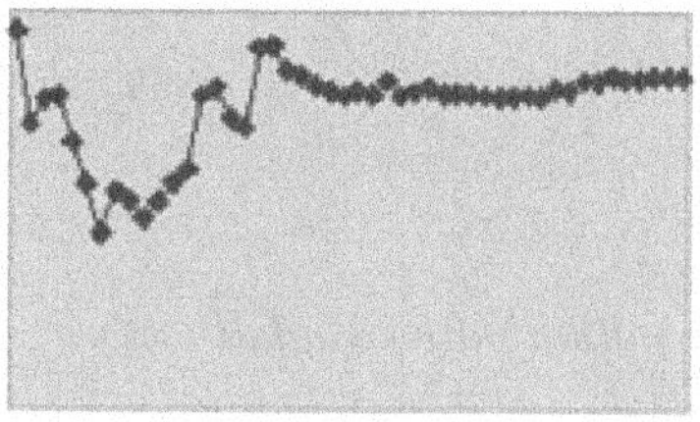

the monthly interaction data. For each figure, the Y-axis indicates the social structure indices (i.e., group centralization or core/periphery fitness), and the X-axis reflects the time dimension.

Two primary observations can be made based on the statistical analysis.

First, the group centralization shows a decreasing trend across the three projects. This observation indicates that as OSS projects progress, the social network structure evolves from centralized to decentralized and then stabilizes. Also, the three figures suggest no substantial differences in the trend among the three projects.

Second, the core/periphery index is maintained at a relatively stable level for each project over time. In addition, the average fitness value stays relatively high for each project (larger than 0.5), indicating a closeness to a perfect core/periphery structure.

Besides a holistic view of network structure for OSS projects, the results also reveal other interesting findings. For example, by examining the core members over time, we found a relatively stable core for each project. The cores are usually project developers and administrators. This observation further demonstrates the existence of strong and stable core as well as loose hangers-on in OSS projects.

DISCUSSION

This research uses the longitudinal data of three OSS projects selected from SourceForge to study the social network structures of OSS teams. The purpose of this study is to investigate the evolvement of interaction patterns of OSS project teams.

The research results suggest a decrease of group centralization over time and a tendency of core/periphery structure in OSS project teams.

The network plots (as shown in Figures 3-5) indicate a layer structure instead of a flat one as suggested by earlier literature. The interaction pattern evolves from a single hub to a core/periphery structure. As the number of participants increases, a core with only one person (who may be the starter/initiator of the project) cannot satisfy the increasing requirements of development and communication. Therefore, other developers or active users join the core to serve as key members of the project. This results in a more stable structure, and the project is less dependent on a single leader.

With the growth of a software project, more people are attracted to the project. The original leader may not be able to solve all the technical problems encountered in the development process. Each key member has his/her specialty, is responsible for solving relevant problems, and has his/her own periphery in the network plot. Although there are multiple peripheries in the project, collaboration among key members in the project is vital. This phenomenon of distribution and collaboration can be viewed as a critical success factor of OSS development. And the evolvement is vividly demonstrated in our social network analysis.

In a way, the social structure of OSS projects is both centralized and decentralized. On one hand, it is centralized in the sense that there is a core that consists of key members. These key members are responsible for various issues encountered during the development process. On the other hand, it is decentralized in the sense that the decision or communication core is not concentrated on one or two members but a group of key members.

Like any other research, this research has its share of limitations. First, the cases were only selected from SourceForge.net. Although SourceForge is the world's largest Web site hosting open source software, there are also some other similar Web sites. Therefore, the total number of OSS projects in SourceForge cannot be viewed as the whole population. However, as we argued before, SourceForge is probably the best data collection site for this research.

Second, the bug tracking system was chosen as our data resource. The selection of bug tracking system as our research setting and data resource may have had an effect on the outcome and results. Besides the bug tracking forum, there are other forums that also provide space for participants to communicate with one another, such as mailing lists and feature requests. However, as we highlighted earlier, the bug systems are the most active forum, providing rich interaction data. The bug tracking systems also represent the spirit of open source software development. Examining the interaction data from other forums can be one of our research extensions in the future.

Third, because our research objective is to investigate interaction pattern, we chose projects that have a relatively large number of developers, a large number of bug reports, and relatively long history. Although we tried to involve different types of projects (i.e., different project sizes, project types, and intended audience), these three cases may not be representatives of OSS projects, for example, small projects with only one or two developers and few interactions. Increasing the sample size and including various types of OSS projects is one of our future research directions.

IMPLICATIONS AND CONCLUSION

This paper examines the interaction patterns of OSS teams. The research findings suggest that the interaction structure starts from a single hub and evolves to a core/periphery model. We argue that the social structure of OSS teams is both centralized and decentralized. It is centralized in the sense that there exists a relatively stable core that consists of a group of key developers. It is also decentralized because of distributed decision making among key developers and the broad collaboration between developers and users as well as among developers themselves.

The paper presents the evolvement of the social structure of OSS projects from a longitudinal perspective. It also provides empirical evidence of the change of interaction patterns from a single hub to a core/periphery model. Moreover, the paper utilizes social network analysis as the research method. This approach has been shown in this research as an effective tool in analyzing the social structure in OSS teams.

Social structure is an important variable for understanding social phenomenon. Open source software, with its open and unique nature, attracts researchers to ask a series of questions. For example, how do participants of OSS projects interact and collaborate with each other? What factors facilitate the interaction and the collaboration? And further, how does the collaboration affect project performance of OSS teams? Social network analysis is a good approach to investigate these questions. This research represents a pioneering effort in this direction.

REFERENCES

Ahuja, M., & Carley, K. (1999). Network structure in virtual organizations. *Organization Science, 10*(6), 741-747.

Blau, P. M. (1977). *Inequity and heterogeneity.* New York: Free Press.

Borgatti, S. (2002). *Basic social network concepts.* Retrieved from http://www.analytictech.com/networks/basic%20concepts%202002.pdf

Borgatti, S. P., Everett, M. G., & Freeman, L. C. (2002). Ucinet for Windows: Software for social network analysis. Harvard, MA: Analytic Technologies.

Crowston, K., & Howison, J. (2005). The social structure of free and open source software development. *First Monday, 10*(2).

Erickson, J., Lyytinen, K., & Siau, K. (2005). Agile modeling, agile software development, and extreme programming: The state of research. *Journal of Database Management, 16*(4), 88-100.

*Freeman, L. C. (*2004). *The development of social network analysis: A study in the sociology of science.* Vancouver, Canada: Empirical Press.

Gacek, C., & Arief, B. (2004). The many meanings of open source. *IEEE Software, 21*(1), 34-40.

Glaser, B. G., & Strauss, Anselm L., (1967). *The Discovery of Grounded Theory: Strategies for Qualitative Research*, Chicago, Aldine Publishing Company

Hann, H., Robert, J., & Slaughter, S. (2004). Why developers participate in open source software projects: An empirical investigation. In *Twenty-Fifth International Conference on Information Systems*, (pp. 821-830). Washington, DC: .

Hemetsberger, A. (2004). Sharing and creating knowledge in open-source communities: The case of KDE. *The Fifth European Conference on Organizational Knowledge, Learning, and Capabilities in Innsbruck, Austria.*

Jørgensen, N. (2001). Putting it all in a trunk: Incremental software development in the freeBSD open source project. *Information Systems Journal, 11,* 321-336.

Krebs, V., & Holley, J. (2004). *Building sustainable communities through network building.* Retrieved from http://www.orgnet.com/BuildingNetworks.pdf

Lee, G. K., & Cole, R. E. (2003). From a firm-based to a community-based model of knowledge creation: The case of the Linux kernel development. *Organization Science, 14*(6), 633-649.

Madey, G., Freeh, V., & Tynan R. (2002). The open source software development phenomenon: An analysis based on social network theory (AMCIS2002). Dallas, TX.

Mockus, A., Fielding, R. T., & Herbsleb, J. D. (2000). A case study of open source software development: The Apache server. ICSE 2000.

Mockus, A., Fielding, R. T., & Herbsleb, J. D. (2002). Two case studies of open source software development: Apache and Mozilla. *ACM Transactions on Software Engineering and Methodology, 11*(3), 309–346.

Moon, J. Y., & Sproull, L. (2000). Essence of distributed work: The case of Linux kernel. *First Monday, 5*(11).

Orlikowski, W. J. (1993). CASE tools as organizational change: investigating incremental and radical changes in systems development. *MIS Quarterly, 17*(3), 309-340.

Raymond, E. S. (1998). The cathedral and the bazaar. *First Monday, 3(3)*, Retrieved January , 2005, from http://www.catb.org/~esr/writings/cathedral-bazaar/cathedral-bazaar/

Sagers, G. W. (2004). The influence of network governance factors on success in open source software development projects. In *Twenty-Fifth International Conference on Information Systems* (pp. 427-438). Washington, DC:

Schaefer, R. T., & Lamm, R. P. (1998). *Sociology* (6th ed.). McGraw-Hill.

Scott, J. (2000). *Social network analysis. A handbook* (2nd ed.). London: SAGE Publications.

Siau, K., & Cao, Q. (2001). Unified modeling language—A complexity analysis. *Journal of Database Management, 12*(1), 26-34.

Siau, K., Erickson, J., & Lee, L. (2005). Theoretical versus practical complexity: The case of UML. *Journal of Database Management, 16*(3), 40-57.

Siau, K., & Loo, P. (2006). Identifying difficulties in learning UML. *Information Systems Management, 23*(3), 43-51.

Stamelos, I., Angelis, L., Oikonomu, A., & Bleris, G. L. (2002). Code quality analysis in open-source software development. *Information Systems Journal, 12*(1), 43-60.

Von Hippel, E., & Von Krogh, G. (2003). Open source software and the „private-collective" innovation model: Issues for organization science. *Organization Science, 14,* 209-223.

Von Krogh, G., Spaeth, S., & Lakhani, K. R. (2003). Community, joining, and specialization in open source software innovation: A case study. *Research Policy, 32*(7), 1217-1241.

Wasserman, S., & Faust, K., (1994). *Social Network Analysis: Methods and Applications.* New York: Cambridge University Press.

ENDNOTE

1. The Web address for SourceForge is www.sourceforge.net.
2. The three time stamps for Net-SNMP are 4/2002, 10/2003 and 4/2005; for Compiere are 9/2002, 1/2004 and 4/2005; and for Jboss are 7/2002, 11/2003 and 4/2005.

This work was previously published in Journal of Database Management, Vol. 18, Issue 2, edited by K. Siau, pp. 25-40, copyright 2007 by IGI Publishing, formerly known as Idea Group Publishing (an imprint of IGI Global).

Chapter XIX
Design of a Data Model for Social Network Applications

Susanta Mitra
International Institute of Information Technology, Kolkata, India

Aditya Bagchi
Indian Statistical Institute, Kolkata, India

A.K. Bandyopadhyay
Jadavpur University, Kolkata, India

ABSTRACT

A social network defines the structure of a social community like an organization or institution, covering its members and their inter-relationships. Social relationships among the members of a community can be of different types like friendship, kinship, professional, academic etc. Traditionally, a social network is represented by a directed graph. Analysis of graph structure representing a social network is done by the sociologists to study a community. Hardly any effort has been made to design a data model to store and retrieve a social network related data. In this paper, an object-relational graph data model has been proposed for modeling a social network. The objective is to illustrate the power of this generic model to represent the common structural and node-based properties of different social network applications. A novel multi-paradigm architecture has been proposed to efficiently manage the system. New structural operators have been defined in the paper and the application of these operators has been illustrated through query examples. The completeness and the minimality of the operators have also been shown.

INTRODUCTION

A social network is a social structure between actors (individuals, organizations, or other social entities) and indicates the ways in which they are connected through various social relationships like friendships, kinships, professional, academic, and so forth. Usually, a social network may represent a network of acquaintance between people; a club and its members; a city or village community; a research group communicating over the Internet; or a group of people communicating with each other through e-mail messages. Recently, the World Wide Web or just Web, as it is popularly known, has played a major role in the formation of communities (*cyber communities or Web communities*) where the members or people from different parts of the globe can join a community with common interest. For example, members of an IEEE society communicating with each other through e-mail may form a Web community. Social network applications include the traditional social network applications as studied by the social scientists Hanneman (2001), Holland and Leinhardt (1979), and Leinhardt (1977); network of acquaintances or referral system as proposed in Yu and Singh (2003) and Kuatz, Selman, and Shah (1997); and finally the Web community (Hanneman, 2001; Newman, 2003). Incidentally, in a referral system, each actor in the social community provides a set of links to its acquaintances that in turn become members of the community. In the same way, these new actors bring their acquaintances to the community again. Thus, the social network keeps on growing. This view of social network has given rise to different commercial applications like LinkedIn.com (http://www.LinkedIn.com), Ryze.com (http://www.Ryze.com), Tribe.net (http://www.Tribe.com), and so forth. For example, a commercial referral network on the Web may offer employment services, where actors provide information like *qualification, experience,* and so forth. Similarly, another referral network may offer matrimonial services, where actors provide information like *age, marital-status, sex, monthly earnings,* and so forth.

Social networks can have a few or many actors, and one or more kinds of relations between pairs of actors. For example, two houses of a village community may be connected to each other because of a family relationship yielding a *kinship* relation or they may communicate for lending or borrowing money generating an *economic* relationship. Two actors of a social network may even be connected by more than one relation. For example, an actor i may refer to another actor j, since they belong to the same professional area (e.g., computer scientist), and at the same time they may also be connected by another relation like the same hobby (e.g., playing baseball).

To build a useful understanding of a social network, a complete and rigorous description of a pattern of social relationships is a necessary starting point for analysis. This pattern of relationships between the actors can be better understood through mathematical or formal representation, like graphs. Therefore, a social network is represented as a directed graph or digraph. In this graph, each member of a social community (people or other entities embedded in a social context) is considered as a node, and communication (collaboration, interaction, or influence) from one member of the community to another member is represented by a directed edge. In order to understand the social properties and behavior of a community, social scientists analyze the corresponding digraph. The number of nodes in social network applications can be very few representing a small circle of friends or very large representing a Web community. This graphical representation is useful for the study and analysis of a social network. In addition, each social network will also have some node-related information depending on the application area or the type of social community the network is representing. For example, in a village community, each node may represent a household in the village with data relevant to such houses.

In the 1970s Leinhardt (1977) first proposed the idea of representing a social community by a digraph. Later, this idea became popular among other research workers like, network designers, Web-service application developers, and e-learning modelers. It gave rise to a rapid proliferation of research work in the area of social network analysis. A graph representing a social network has certain basic structural properties, which distinguishes it from other type of networks or graphs. This type of graph is meant to study the nature of a real life social community and its structural changes over time. These properties are useful for analysis of a social network. It may even be used for structural comparison between two social networks that in turn represents comparison between two social communities. Some of the notable properties are connectedness between actors; reachability between a source and a target actor; reciprocity or pair-wise connection between actors with bi-directional links; centrality of actors or the important actors having high degree or more connections; and finally, the division of actors into sub-structures or cliques or strongly connected components (SCC). The cycles present in a social network may even be nested (Rao & Bandyopadhyay 1987 and Rao et al., 1998). The formal definition of these structural properties will be provided later. The division of actors into cliques or sub-groups can be a very important factor for understanding a social structure, particularly the degree of cohesiveness in a community. The number, size, and connections among the sub-groups in a network are useful in understanding how the network, as a whole, is likely to behave. Social scientists, through network analysis, focus attention on how solidarity and connection of large social structures can be built out of smaller groups. These basic structural properties are common in different social network applications including Web and referral systems.

The graph representing a social network has some additional structural properties not present in other graph-based systems, like biological networks, geographical information systems, and so forth.. When some new members join a social community like, new immigrants to a village or new members of a club, they may not have any connection with any other member of the community. Thus, these members of the community would give rise to *isolated nodes* when mapped on to the corresponding social network. The percentage of isolated nodes in a community is an important parameter of study for a social scientist. Once again, all members of a community may not have contact with all other members. As a result, the community may form separate sub-groups. Members within a sub-group will have connection among them, whereas, members of two different sub-groups will remain isolated from each other. When mapped on to the graph representing a social network, these sub-groups would generate isolated sub-graphs.

Motivation

Discussions made so far indicate that social scientists make rigorous computation on the node-based and structural information of a graph representing a social network. For each such computation, entire graph-related (both node-based and structural) data need to be accessed. Since a social network may give rise to a graph of thousands of nodes and edges, accessing the entire graph each time will contribute significantly to the overall computation time. Moreover, some social network-related applications try to search for interesting patterns on the existing data (both node-based and structural) (Chen, Gupta, & Kurul, 2005). Such social network-related applications are quite common in Web-based mining (Chakraborty, 2004). Overall computation time can be reduced to a great extent if the structure-based and node-based selection and searching can be done efficiently. In order to make it effective, the relevant information for both nodes and links along with common built-in structures like sub-graphs, cycles, paths, and so forth may be computed and stored a priori. If any application needs a particular type of computation quite often, such information can also be pre-computed and stored. In short, instead of starting from raw node and edge-related data for each type of analysis, some storage and selective retrieval facility should be provided for social network applications involving large graphs. So, a data model needs to be designed primarily for social network applications. This research effort intends to build up a comprehensive data model that can be a useful tool for the structural, node-based, and composite analysis of different social network applications. An object-relational data model named Social Network System (SONSYS) has already been proposed for this purpose (Bagchi, Mitra, & Bandyopadhyay, 2003; Mitra, Bagchi, & Bandyopadhyay, 2006). The initial data model proposed in (Bagchi et al., 2003) has represented a traditional social network application involving a village community. The more recent publication (Mitra et al., 2006), on the other hand, considers a Web community as a social network and develops a data model for the corresponding Web graph. The present article provides a generic object-relational data model to cover basic structural properties common to different social network applications. The need for pre-processing of a graph representing a social network has been explained along with the justification for different proposed structural operators. A four-tier, multi-paradigm architecture for analyzing and querying a social network has also been proposed.

Sociologists also use category systems to describe "social positions" or "social roles" of actors. Members of one category may have similar types of relations with members of another category. This categorization is based on the attributes of the members. For example, "Santhal, an Indian tribe, aged 40-60 years are likely to have higher income compared to other tribes." It indicates a group of people who are demographically similar and share certain node-based attributes (tribal ancestry, biological age, and income). Social scientists may also need to formulate composite queries (involving both node-based and structural information) to find relations (e.g., kinship, monetary, etc.) among the nodes of one category (e.g., "Santhal" tribe in a village) with that of another category (e.g.. "Pal" tribe in a village). This process of categorization of data may ultimately gives rise to categorization hierarchy. This hierarchy may be used to build index structure for faster access to node-based data. The present article has proposed such a facility as well. Though considerable work has been done for designing a graph-based data model in the area of tourism (Amann & Scholl, 1992), biological pathways (Newman, 2003), and so forth, hardly any data model is known to exist that provides the facility to study both the structural as well as node-based properties of a social network. The main motivation behind the current research effort is to meet this requirement.

Based on the previous discussions, the proposed data model will support the following type of queries on a social network:

- query on node-based information only;
- graph pattern matching on the communication structure of the social network;
- index-based search using the category hierarchy of the nodes; and
- composite queries exploiting the aforementioned facilities.

The present article, however, designs the data model of a social network for a time frame under which the node and edge structures are assumed to be unaltered. Thus, the proposed system considers a snapshot of the evolutionary process and creates a database for it. The network evolution will be part of future research efforts.

The Related Work section provides information on the related works. The section on Data Model discusses the salient features of the data model, and the Multi-Paradigm Architecture section describes a multi-paradigm architecture for querying the network system. The section on Query Operators deals with the query operators and the Query Examples section provides a few relevant queries. Finally, the section on Conclusion and Future Works provides the conclusion and the scopes for future work.

RELATED WORK

Several proposals have been made from the last decade to model data organized as graphs and define algebra and languages to query such graph structures. However, these models have mainly considered path-based queries or direct search of nodes and edges. Query facilities for complex structures like cycles or nested cycles have not been considered. On the other hand, a social network deals with many complex structures that define the nature and properties of a social community. Social scientists even use these structural properties to distinguish between two similar communities (say, social structures of two villages). Different structures and sub-structures required in a social network will be discussed in the subsequent sections. This is an area where the present data model significantly differs from the graph models proposed so far.

Moreover, most of these models tend to pre-compute the paths required for query. No doubt, this approach reduces query processing time, but such effort is not possible for a large graph involving thousands of nodes. As a result, the well-known graph models do work well for a small set of nodes and edges only. The data model proposed in this article strikes a balance. By a process called *path normalization* (Bhanu Teja, 2005), some paths and sub-paths are pre-computed and the others are computed during query processing. The detail of path normalization has been communicated else where (Bhanu Teja, Mitra, Bagchi, & Bandyopadhyay, in press) and so cannot be elaborated here to avoid duplicate submission. The present article mainly covers the data model, multi-tier architecture, and the use of structural operators. Some seminal works on graph data model have now been discussed so that the relevance and efficacy of the proposed data model can be appreciated later.

Gutiérrez, Pucheral, Steffen, and Thévenin (1994) provide a functional definition of graphs that allows graph implementation independent of its physical organizations like relational or object oriented file systems. This model provides the facility to dynamically compute the paths during the graph traversals. However, for large networks like transportation networks, this computation of paths at run time will make the query processing considerably slow.

The graph data model, Gram, as proposed in Amann and Scholl (1992), is a hypertext graph model used for tourism application. The query language provides two structures *walk* and *hyperwalk* for graph traversal. Walk is an alternating sequence of nodes and edges. A hyperwalk is basically a combination of walks. Gram model supports good traversal facility with walk/hyperwalk-based operators. Walks and hyperwalks are mostly pre-computed. According to the authors, the system works well for about a dozen nodes.

Consens and Mendelzon (1990) proposed a model, GraphLog that supports a visual query system where both data and queries are visualized as graphs. It provides an environment for browsing, displaying, and editing graphs. Later in Pardaens, Peelman, and Tanaca (1995) the authors have proposed a model, G-Log, providing a facility to map a relational model to graph. A declarative query language G has also been provided. However, according to the authors the expressive power of the language needs to be increased. The work is mostly theoretical. Hardly any effort has been taken for implementation of these proposals or their applications to real–life, graph-based systems.

Guting (1994) is an important work for explicit representation of graphs within a general database environment with a smooth integration into a standard object-oriented modeling and querying environment. This model is suitable for spatially embedded networks like public transport. However, no complete query language has been described formally. For complex queries, the query structure can become confusing as the queries are to be expressed in several steps.

Another important research work by Sheng, Özsoyoglu, and Özsoyoglu (1999) proposes an object-oriented graph data model and the corresponding query language, GOQL. It is an effort to design a multimedia data model with the help of graphs. Here also, the authors have ultimately proposed a system where paths are pre-computed. This model has however been implemented and used for real-life applications. The authors admit that the system works efficiently for about 50 nodes. Therefore, the model may not be suitable for large graphs.

An initial work for studying the Web graph with several hundred millions of nodes (html pages) and billions of directed edges (hyperlinks) has been discussed in Kleinberg, Kumar, Raghavan, Rajagopalan, & Tomkins (1999). Here an algorithm was proposed for automatic community discovery. The hyperlinks represent a source of a few sociological information. However, this application deals with one time data-mining-based analysis and does not provide a database platform for serving queries.

Raghavan and Garcia-Molina (2003) have proposed an S-node representation scheme that combines graph compression with support for complex queries and local graph navigation for massive Web graphs. However, only a few specific observed properties of the Web graph could be exploited by this representation scheme. So, the system is designed to serve a set of dedicated queries. It is not a generic graph-based data model.

Thus, it is apparent from the previous discussion that none of the earlier research and development efforts have proposed any generic data model that can be used for different graph-based applications. In addition, a social network needs to cover many different structural components that are not present in other application areas. Since none of the earlier proposals could cover them, a new effort, as proposed in the current article, is needed.

DATA MODEL

The graph representing a social network is composed of two subsystems; a structural subsystem and node-based subsystem. The two subsystems are discussed separately in the following subsections. A generic object-relational (OR) data model for the social network applications is proposed here. Since node-based data is dependent on the application area modeled by the social network, this article has considered a village community as a running example to explain the data model here. As a matter of fact, this research effort is the outcome of the requirements generated in a real-life social survey done at some remote tribal villages of India by the sociological research unit of the Indian Statistical Institute (Rao et al., 1998).

Structural Subsystem

In order to understand the structural subsystem a sample social network has been considered. The network is shown in Figure 1.

Although a few nodes and edges have been considered here, the explanation will soon show that even this small graph covers all the structural peculiarities of a social network. Such structural peculiarities commonly found in different social communities are well explained in Newman (2003 and Hanneman (2001). This network consists of the following structural components:

Figure 1. Sample social network

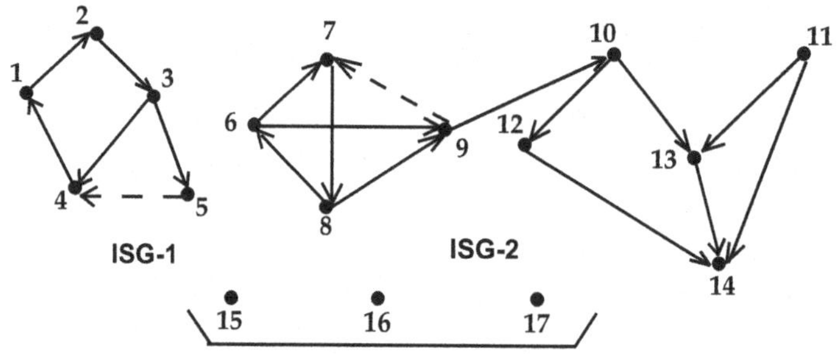

- **Isolated subgraph (ISG):** An isolated subgraph is a graph such that, if a graph G(V,E) has two isolated subgraphs G'(V',E') and G''(V'',E''), then $V' \subseteq V$, $V'' \subseteq V$ but $V' \cap V'' = \phi$ and also $E' \subseteq E$, $E'' \subseteq E$ but $E' \cap E'' = \phi$.

In a community, all members may not have contact with each other, giving rise to isolated subgraphs. The sample social network of Figure 1 has two isolated subgraphs, (1-2-3-4-5) and (6-7-8-9-10-11-12-13-14).

- **Isolated nodes:** Any node v in a directed graph G(V.E), where $v \in V$, has two properties Ind as the in-degree and Oud as the out-degree. In-degree provides the number of edges incident to v and out-degree is the number of nodes going out of v. A node v is an isolated node, if Ind. v = 0 and also Oud. v = 0.

In Figure 1, nodes 15, 16, and 17 are the isolated nodes:

- **Strongly-connected-component (SCC):** An SCC is a maximal subgraph of a directed graph such that for every pair of nodes v_1, v_2 in the subgraph, there is a directed path from v_1 to v_2 and also a directed path from v_2 to v_1.

If there exists an operator $R(v_1, v_2)$, such that $R(v_1, v_2)$ =True if node v_2 is reachable from node v_1, that is, there exists a path from node v_1 to node v_2, then subgraph G'(V',E') of graph G(V,E) is a SCC, if $R(v_1, v_2)$ = True and also $R(v_2, v_1)$ = True, where $(v_1, v_2) \in V'$.

This definition indicates that a reachability operator *R* will be required in order to check the existence of paths between any two nodes of a graph. Detail discussion will be made in the section on query operators.

The sample social network in Figure 1 has two edge types shown by farm and chain lines. In ISG-1, node sequence (1-2-3-4-1) represents a SCC when same edge types are considered, whereas (1-2-3-5-4-1) is a SCC with different edge types:

- **Cycle:** If the sequence of nodes defining a path of a graph starts and ends at the same node and includes other nodes at most once, then that path is a cycle. If in a graph G(V,E), $(v_0, v_1, \ldots\ldots\ldots, v_n)$ be a node sequence defining a path P in G such that $(v_0, v_1, \ldots\ldots\ldots, v_n) \in V$ and $v_0 = v_n$, then P is a cycle.

Figure 1 shows many cycles. ISG-1 has cycles, (1-2-3-5-4-1), (1-2-3-4-1), (3-5-4-3), and (3-4-3). ISG-2 has cycles, (6-7-8-6), and (7-8-9-7). In the previous examples, all the cycles have been considered irrespective of the variation in edge types.

The cycles may even be nested. In ISG-1 of Figure 1, cycle (3-4-3), is nested within the cycle (1-2-3-4-1) and (3-5-4-3). Again, (1-2-3-4-1) and (3-5-4-3) are nested within (1-2-3-5-4-1):

- **Reciprocal edge:** A cycle having only two nodes is a reciprocal edge. So, a reciprocal edge $(v_1, v_2) \in V$ has directed edge from v_1 to v_2 and also from v_2 to v_1. A reciprocal edge is the smallest size cycle.

For example, cycle (3-4-3) in Figure 1 is a reciprocal edge:

- **Nested cycle:** If there exists two cycles $C_i (V_i, E_i)$ and $C_j (V_j, E_j)$ in graph G(V,E), then C_i is a cycle nested within C_j that is, $C_i \subseteq C_j$ if $V_i \subseteq V_j$ and $E_i \subseteq E_j$.
- **Hyper-node:** In a nested-cycle structure, the largest or the outermost cycle is defined as a hyper-node. For a graph G(V,E), if there exists a nested cycle structure with a set of cycles such that, $\{C_1 \supseteq C_2 \supseteq \ldots \supseteq C_n)\}$ where C_i is a cycle in G, then C_1 is the hyper-node corresponding to the nested cycle structure. So, a hyper-node represents a SCC.

The cycle detection and fusion algorithm as used in SONSYS, is an iterative process where each cycle as and when detected, is fused to a hyper-node till no such cycle is found that is nested within any other cycle. So, the hyper-nodes finally found at the end of the fusion process are the fused SCC present in the original graph.

In the nested cycle structure of ISG-1 in Figure 1, since all cycles are nested within the largest cycle (1-2-3-5-4-1), so (1-2-3-5-4-1) is the hyper-node here:

- **Homogeneous hyper-node:** If in a hyper-node all the edge types are same, then it is a homogeneous hyper-node. Let, $\{C_1 \supseteq C_2 \supseteq \ldots \supseteq C_n)\}$ be a nested cycle structure in a graph G(V,E) where, C_i is a cycle in G. Now C_1 will be a homogeneous hyper-node if for any pair of edges, $(v_i, v_j) \in C_1$ and $(v_r, v_s) \in C_1$, (v_i, v_j).edge type = (v_r, v_s).edge type.

In ISG-1 of Figure 1, (1-2-3-4-1) is a homogeneous hyper-node:

- **Heterogeneous hyper-node:** In a heterogeneous hyper-node all the edge types need not be same.

In ISG-1 of Figure 1, (1-2-3-5-4-1) is a heterogeneous hyper-node.

Though by definition, a hyper-node is the largest cycle in a nested cycle structure, the hyper-nodes themselves can also be nested. Since in a homogeneous hyper-node all the edges must be of same type, this hyper-node may be nested within another larger cycle formed by edges of different types resulting in a heterogeneous hyper-node. So, a homogeneous hyper-node may be nested within a heterogeneous hyper-node.

In ISG-1 of Figure 1, (1-2-3-4-1) is a homogeneous hyper-node, which is nested within the heterogeneous hyper-node (1-2-3-5-4-1). Since the edge (5,4) is of different type, it is not considered in forming the homogeneous hyper-node (1-2-3-4-1). However this edge is considered in the heterogeneous hyper-node (1-2-3-5-4-1).

Hyper-Node Based Compression

The present article has suggested a compression method based on hyper-nodes. Since a hyper-node is a relevant structure of study for the social scientists as a measure of cohesiveness of a society (Dorogovtsev & Mendes, 2003; Rao et al., 1998), it needs to be captured and stored separately. Thus, for object-relational schema design, hyper-node of a graph will be a separate object data type besides node and edge objects. For compression, a hyper-node is fused to a single node and its structural details are encapsulated within the corresponding object instance covering both the nodes and edges within it. Detail discussion of such object structure will be made in the structural schema design.

Compression based on homogeneous hyper-nodes: Considering the aforementioned principle of compression the sample social net in Figure 1 is augmented to Figure 2 considering homogeneous hyper-nodes only. Nodes within a hyper-node H may be connected to other nodes and hyper-nodes outside H. After H is fused to a single node as part of graph compression process, all these edges external to H but connected to its different nodes will now be connected directly to H.

In homogeneous hyper-node (1-2-3-4-1) of ISG-1 in Figure 1, node 3 and 4 are connected to the external node 5 by edges (3,5) and (5,4). After the hyper-node is fused to H-1 in Figure 2, node 5 is now connected to H-1 by edges (H-1, 5) and (5, H-1) in the augmented graph.

In ISG-2 of Figure 1, homogeneous hyper-node (6-7-8-6) is fused to H-2 in Figure 2. Before compression, nodes 6,7 and 8 of H-2 were connected to node 9 by edges (6,9), (8,9) and (9,7). After fusion, in Figure 2, these three edges are (H-2, 9), (H-2, 9), and (9, H-2). Now, the edges (6,9) and (8,9) in the original graph are of same edge type and they are both mapped as edges (H-2, 9) and (H-2, 9) in the augmented graph. The compression process will fuse these two identical edges of same type and direction to a single edge He-1 defined as hyper-edge. So, the hyper-edge He-1 covers the edge-set {(6,9), (8,9)}. Similar to hyper-node, hyper-edge will also be treated as an object data type in the object-relational schema:

- **Hyper-edge:** If any node p outside a hyper-node H is connected to more than one node belonging to H with same edge type and in the same direction, all such edges will be fused to only one edge as a hyper-edge. This hyper-edge will now connect p to H. A hyper-edge may connect a hyper-node with a node or another hyper-node.

Compression based on heterogeneous hyper-nodes: The compression process so far, has considered fusion of homogeneous hyper-nodes only. However in Figure 1, both ISG-1 and ISG-2 can be further compressed if cycles formed by different edge types are also considered and such cycles are also fused to form heterogeneous hyper-nodes. After such compression, the final augmented form of the original graph is shown in Figure 3. As can be seen in Figure 2, the homogeneous hyper-node H-1 and node 5 formed a cycle with two edges of different types. Similarly, homogeneous hyper-node H-2 and node 9 formed a cycle with hyper-edge He-1 and another edge of different edge types. So, fusion process creates heterogeneous hyper-nodes H-3 and H-4 as shown in Figure 3.

Figure 2. Augmented social network

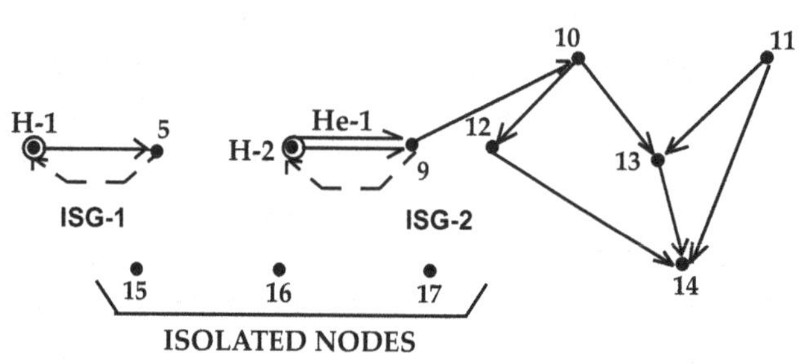

Figure 3. Final augmentation

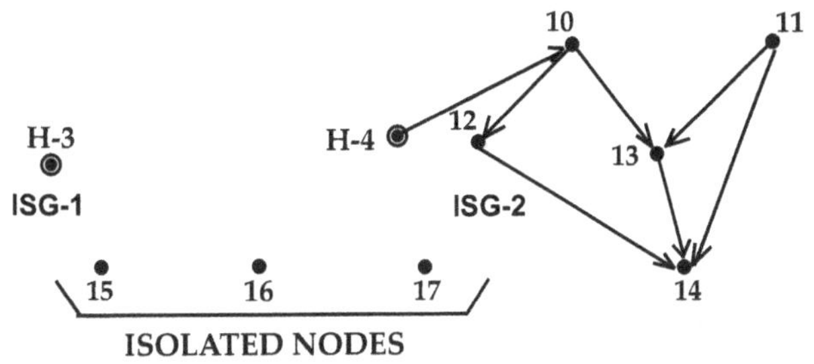

It is found that after the final augmentation, the original graph turns into a directed acyclic graph (DAG).

Initial condition: In the process of fusion, all hyper-structures (hyper-nodes and hyper-edges) are stored separately in the object-relational framework. Details of such object structures are given in the section on structural schema. It helps in generating the original digraph back from the fused DAG.

Lemma 1: Hyper-node and hyper-edge based compression turns a digraph to a DAG.

Proof :

Let, $u_1 \rightarrow u_2$ represents a path between nodes u_1 to u_2, where $u_1, u_2 \in G$.

As given in the *Structural Subsystem* section, by definition, any hyper-node H_i in graph G(V,E) is a fused SCC. So, there cannot exist any cycle C_i in G such that $C_i \supseteq H_i$. If in G there exists, $H_i \rightarrow v$ or $H_i \rightarrow H_j$ where H_i and H_j are any two hyper-nodes in G and v is any node in G, then as a result of fusion, there cannot exist any path $H_j \rightarrow H_i$ or $v \rightarrow H_i$ in G.

Hence the augmented graph generated after fusion is acyclic or the original digraph gets converted to a DAG.

Lemma 2: Conversion to DAG from original digraph is connectivity invariant.

Proof :

Let G = (V, E) be the original digraph and nodes u,v,x $\in$ G, and H be any hyper-node in the augmented DAG, $G' = (V', E')$ i.e. $H \in G'$.

Let u,v $\in$ H and x $\notin$H and also in G, there exists paths $u \rightarrow x$ and $v \rightarrow x$.

To prove the invariance of connectivity it is sufficient to prove that original connections i.e. $u \rightarrow x$ and $v \rightarrow x$ should remain unaltered if H is connected to x by a path i.e. $H \rightarrow x$ in G'.

Let the path $u \rightarrow x$ exists but the path $v \rightarrow x$ does not exist in G'.

Now, since $u \in H$, $v \in H$ so, $u \rightarrow v$, $v \rightarrow u$.

Again, $v \rightarrow u$ and $u \rightarrow x$ implies $v \rightarrow x$.

This contradicts the assumption that the path $v \rightarrow x$ does not exist in G'.

Similarly, if there exists paths $x \rightarrow u$ and $x \rightarrow v$ in G, it can be shown that connections remain unaltered in G', if x is connected to H by a path i.e. $x \rightarrow H$.

Hence, the conversion to DAG from original digraph is connectivity invariant.

According to the *initial condition* given previously, paths $u \rightarrow x$ and $v \rightarrow x$ are present in G while G' will have only $H \rightarrow x$. Original paths can be retrieved from the underlined object structures retained for the hyper-nodes:

- **Path:** A path in a graph is an alternate sequence of nodes and edges. It is usually from a source to a sink, where any source is a node with in-degree zero and any sink is a node with out-degree zero.

So, a path cannot start from or end to a member node of an SCC, since such node can neither be a source nor a sink. However, if a path is searched from one such node to any other node of the graph outside the SCC, many paths may unnecessarily be derived. Let an SCC S has N nodes. By definition of SCC, all such nodes of S are reachable from each other. Let q be a node outside S that has an incoming edge from only one member node p of S. Now, a path detection algorithm searching for paths between any member node of S to q, ignoring the SCC structure, may enumerate to a maximum of (N-1)! paths just for the internal connections of the SCC.

Again, according to the node compression mechanism, a SCC is fused to a hyper-node. So, S becomes a hyper-node and the edge (p,q) from internal node p to external node q with respect to S maps to an edge (S,q) in the compressed graph and there will be only one path from S to q instead of a maximum of (N-1)! paths.

Effect of compression on paths: As discussed in Lemma 2, compression process of a digraph as described in this article and the consequent transformation to DAG is connectivity invariant. Salient features of the compression process are:

- Compressed graph is a DAG and a path detection algorithm will not encounter any cycle.
- Hyper-nodes and hyper-edges are stored as separate object instances under proper object types in an object-relational schema and there by, their internal structures are not visible to the compressed graph.
- As a result of the compression process, a path in the compressed graph will be formed by simple nodes or hyper-nodes and simple edges or hyper-edges.
- Structure and length of paths will change when transformed from original to compressed graph. However, a path query should return the actual sequence of nodes belonging to the original graph before compression.

Limitation of compression process: A path detection algorithm, when executed on a graph, returns paths that are either pre-computed or generated at run time containing simple nodes and edges. However, when such algorithm is executed on the compressed graph as proposed in this article, the paths may have hyper-nodes and hyper-edges within it. So, the path detection algorithm needs additional steps to break the encapsulation of those structures (hyper-nodes and hyper-edges) to get the paths involving simple nodes and edges belonging to the original graph. It is, therefore, apparent that execution time is more for path detection in the compressed graph.

In order to alleviate such problem, in the SONSYS system, some paths and sub-paths are pre-computed and stored while others are generated at run time. This process has been termed as path normalization (Bhanu Teja et al., in press). The algorithmic detail of this process is not within the scope of this article. Moreover, an efficient DAG search algorithm and corresponding engine has recently been developed that improves the search process quite significantly (Chen et. al., 2005).

Advantage of compression process: As a result of the compression process, SONSYS gives rise to a two-level graph structure. The top level provides the compressed graph with the hyper-structures, whereas the lower level has the original graph. The hyper-structures are stored separately and the constituent nodes and edges resident at the lower level are accessed only if a query requires them. The object-relational model helps in making such access. In other words, only the compressed DAG is initially loaded to the memory, and if needed, the details of any hyper-structure are accessed from the disk.

A research group at Stanford University has also proposed a two-level representation scheme called S-node representation (Raghavan & Garcia-Molina, 2003) in order to compress and store a large Web graph. Here, a top-level graph is connected with a lower-level graph through pointers. The top-level graph serves the role of an index structure, allowing the members of the lower-level graph to be quickly located. The top-level compressed graph resides in the main memory and the required nodes and edges of lower-level graphs are loaded from disk into memory as and when necessary during the query processing. However, S-node scheme is not a generic, graph-based data model and can represent only a few specific observed properties of the Web graph. So, the system is designed to serve a set of dedicated queries. On the other hand, SONSYS is a generic data model that can represent all important graph structures related to a social network and can efficiently handle composite queries by exploiting the aforementioned techniques.

Structural Schema

The SONSYS system, designed as an OR model admits the following type structures:

- **Atomic types:** An atomic type is standard and represents basic types like integer, float, string, and Boolean.
- **Structured types:** A structured (or collection) type is also standard and contains sets, bags, sequences, multi-sets, and so forth. It also contains record type defined as the product of other structured or atomic types.
- **Constructed types:** A constructed type supports more complex types like cycle, hyper-node, hyper-edge, path, and so forth. Constructed types are also defined as the product of other structured or atomic types. These are implemented as abstract data types (ADT).
- **Object:** An object type contains an object identifier and a number of object properties conforming to any of the types described previously.

The relevant object types for compressed graph and original graph of the structural subsystem are shown next:

Graph

```
(
type : ADT;
graph_id : string;
ISGs : TABLE OF REF ISG;
    isolated_nodes : TABLE OF REF Node;
member functions :
no_of_ISG  returns integer,
no_of_isolated_nodes  returns  integer,
    and  other member functions;
    )
ISG
(
type : ADT;
ISG_id : string;
homogeneous_hyper_nodes : TABLE OF REF Homogeneous_hyper_node;
heterogeneous_hyper_nodes : TABLE OF REF Heterogeneous_hyper_node;
hyper_edges : TABLE OF REF Hyper_edge;
nodes : TABLE OF REF Node;
edges : TABLE OF REF Edge;
paths : TABLE OF REF Path;
member functions :
isg_size returns no_of_nodes as integer,
no_of_ heterogeneous_hyper_nodes returns integer,
no_of_ homogeneous_hyper_nodes returns integer,
max_homogeneous_hyper_node_size returns
no_of_nodes as integer,
max_path_length returns no_of_nodes as integer,
and other member functions
)
```

Homogeneous_hyper_node

```
(
type : ADT;
homogeneous_hyper_node_id : string;
homogeneous_hyper_node_edge_type : string;
// since all edges within a homogeneous_hyper_node are of same type, inclusion of homogeneous_hyper_node_edge_type is useful to process queries searching for homogeneous_ hyper_nodes of specific edge_type //
cycles : TABLE OF REF Cycle;
nodes : TABLE OF REF Node;
edges : TABLE OF REF Edge;
member functions :
homogeneous_hyper_node_size returns no_of_nodes as integer,
and other member functions
```

)

Heterogeneous_hyper_node

(
type : ADT;
heterogeneous_hyper_node_id : string;
homogeneous_hyper_nodes : TABLE OF REF Homogeneous_hyper_node;
hyper_edges : TABLE OF REF Hyper_edge;
cycles : TABLE OF REF Cycle;
nodes : TABLE OF REF Node;
edges : TABLE OF REF Edge;
member functions :
heterogeneous_hyper_node_size returns no_of_nodes as integer,
and other member functions
)

Hyper_edge

(
type : set of edges;
hyper_edge_id : string;
start_node : REF Heterogeneous_hyper_node or Homogeneous_hyper_node or Node;
end_node : REF Heterogeneous_hyper_node or Homogeneous_hyper_node or Node;
hyper_edge_type : string;
// since all edges within a hyper-edge are of same type, inclusion of hyper_edge_type is useful to process queries searching for hyper_edges of specific edge_type //
hyper_edge_members : TABLE OF REF Edge;
member functions :
hyper_edge_size returns no_of_edges as integer,
and other member functions
)

Cycle

(
type : ADT;
cycle_id : string;
nodes : TABLE OF REF Node;
edges : TABLE OF REF Edge;
member functions :
cycle_size returns no_of_nodes as integer,
and other member functions
)

Path

(
type : sequence_of_nodes;
path_id : string;
path_start_node : REF Heterogeneous_hyper_node or Homogeneous_hyper_node or Node;
path_end_node : REF Heterogeneous_hyper_node or Homogeneous_hyper_node or Node;
path_edgelist : TABLE OF REF Hyper_edge or Edge;
member functions :
path_length returns no_of_nodes as integer,
// no_of_nodes refers to the total number of heterogeneous_hyper_nodes, homogeneous_hyper_nodes as well as nodes belonging to the path //
and other member functions
)

Edge

(
type : sequence of nodes;
edge_id : string;
edge_type : string;
start_node : REF Node;
end_node : REF Node;
// edge is a sequence of nodes of length 2
)

Node

(
type : object;
node_id : string;
in_degree : integer;
out_degree : integer;
node_type : string;
// the system defines four types of nodes; isolated, source, sink, communicator
)

In node objects, node-type has been added for the convenience of structure-based computations. Node-type *source* has in-degree zero; *sink* has out-degree zero; *isolated* node has both in-degree and out-degree equal to zero; and *communicator* has both in-degree and out-degree greater than zero. In Figure 1, node 11 is a source, node 14 is a sink, node 15, 16, and 17 are isolated and the rest are of communicator type. This classification of nodes is advantageous for structural computations. Only communicator type nodes will be members of a cycle. So, any cycle detection algorithm can do an initial pruning of the node list and will not consider any other type of node. Similarly, any path detection algorithm will always start from a source node and terminate at a sink. All nodes in between must be of communicator type. These considerations significantly improve the performances of *the relevant algorithms* in a large graph.

The type structure described previously should have been preceded by <*create type*> for each object type. Just for the sake of convenience of representation, the corresponding type has been included within each type structure like, (type : ADT in **Graph**). This deviation from norm is deliberate. The IDs included in the type structures are also the system supplied object IDs and not user specified. They have been shown for the convenience of representation only.

It is evident from the structural schema that it supports complex objects. For example, a hyper-node object can have cycle objects within it and each of these cycles can have edge objects. Hierarchical relationship among object types can be explained in Backus-Naur Form (BNF). For example:

<digraph> : : = <ISG> <isolated node>
<ISG> : : = <hyper-node> <hyper-edge> <path> | < hyper-node> <path> | <hyper-node> | <path>
Also,,
<cycle> : : = <edge> <edge> | <edge> <cycle>
<edge> : : = <node> <node>

Such a hierarchy can itself be represented as a DAG as shown in Figure 4. This DAG structure helps in easy and efficient access of any ancestor (e.g., parent hyper-node of a cycle) or all ancestors (e.g., digraph, ISG, and hyper-node of a cycle), any or all descendants (e.g., cycles belonging to a hyper-node or nodes belonging to a cycle), common descendants (e.g., nodes belonging to more than one cycle), and so forth. It is evident from the discussion that for structural query processing appropriate operators will be needed to search for ancestors and descendants.

Node-Based Subsystem

Similar to structural subsystem, a social network needs to represent the node-based information as well. However, unlike the structural subsystem, the node-based data does not have any generic structure but it is application dependent. This article has considered a large tribal village as a social community. The corresponding node-based schema consists of three object types; *Household, Plot,* and *Crop. Household* object contains data related to village households, *Plot* contains detail of different plot of lands owned by each household, and *Crop* contains detail of crops grown.

Node-Based Schema

The object types for the node-based schema are:

Figure 4. Complex structural object hierarchy

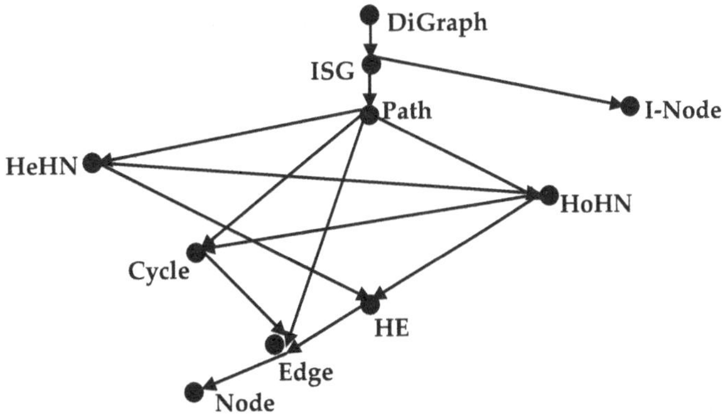

Legend: *ISG - Isolated Sub-graph, I-Node - Isolated node, HeHN- Heterogeneous Hyper-node, HoHN – Homogeneous Hyper-node, HE- Hyper-edge.*

Household
(
type : object;
node_id : string; // unique identifier representing household, same as node_id of structural schema
village_name : string; // name of the village
house_no : integer; // house number
tribe : string; // the tribal identity of a house
monthly_income : integer; // total monthly income of the household
profession : string; // profession of the head of a household
no_of_members : integer; // number of members in a house
plots : REF Plot; // plot of lands owned by a household, referring to 'Plot' type object
member functions :
find income_group returns string,
// categorization of households by income_group (low, medium or high) has been discussed later
and other member functions
)

Plot
(
type : object;
plot_no : string; // unique identifier representing a plot of land
land_type : string; // type of land
area : float; // area of land
cropping_practice : string; // mono-cropping, multi-cropping etc.
crops : REF Crop; // information on crops cultivated on a plot; referring to 'Crop' type object
member functions
)

Crop
(
type : object;
cropping_season :string; // season during which crop has been cultivated
year : integer; // production year of the crop
crop_type : string; // type of crop cultivated
production : float; // amount of production
member functions
)

Node Categorization

Based upon the sociological analysis pattern it has been observed that there are certain attributes on which the queries are made frequently, ***tribe*** in *Household* is such an attribute. Domain of each of these important attributes can be partitioned into categories based on the domain values. For example, *tribe* can be categorized by the name of different tribes like, *Santhal*, *Pal,* and so forth. Categorization can also be made by grouping of domain values. For example, attribute *monthly_income* in *Household* can be used for categorization of household instances into different income groups; *low, medium,* or *high.* This process of categorization leads to a semantic hierarchy of objects. In the parlance of object orientation, it offers a class hierarchy. A sample node categorization hierarchy for the tribal village is shown in Figure 5.

This hierarchy can be used as an index structure for query processing. Value-based indexing is quite common in query processing. For example, since an individual tribe name will generate equality predicates, hashing is the common method for indexing. On the other hand, search on income group will give rise to range queries and would therefore be processed by tree indexing (usually B^+ tree). Since for value-based indexing common methods have been followed, detail discussion in this area has deliberately been avoided. Justification of such practice is quite apparent. As SONSYS system is based on object-relational model, the underlying relational structure would automatically provide standard value-based indexing methods.

MULTI-PARADIGM ARCHITECTURE

Classical approach of database design involves a three-layer architecture; physical, conceptual, and view. However, design of a graph data model in SONSYS system gives rise to a four-tier architecture. Preprocessing of the original digraph to a DAG justifies the existence of an additional tier. Since the compressed graph representing a social network provides the social properties of the corresponding community, the object-relational schema is developed on the compressed graph using the structural components like, hyper-nodes, hyper-

Figure 5. Sample node categorization hierarchy

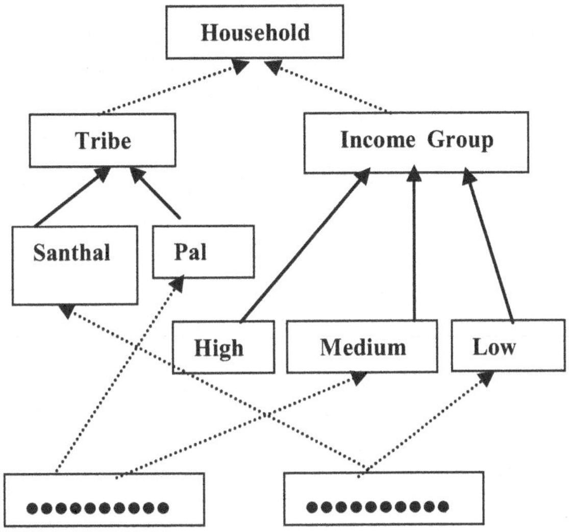

edges, and so forth. Thus the four-tier architecture provides an integrated framework to compress, model, store, and retrieve digraph-related data for social network application. Any query posed on this DAG through a user interface percolates down the architecture to the underlying relational framework of the original graph present in the object-relational model. The basic advantage of this architecture is that it not only focuses on the structural part of the network data but also on the content and semantic part of the node-based data. This architecture helps to formulate and process complex queries based on these two types of data. This process of combining the two subsystems (structural and node-based) in complex queries is a "multi-paradigm querying approach," a term borrowed from Wen, Li, Ma, and Zhang (2003). Since this approach is based on four-tier architecture of SONSYS, it has also been termed as *multi-paradigm architecture*. The earlier efforts on graph data models did not consider this type of multi-tier approach. The four-tier architecture is shown in Figure 6.

The salient features of different tiers are:

- **Network tier:** As the lowest tier, it provides the basic connectivity in the form of relational tables to specify the digraph representing a given social network. It also maintains the necessary tables for the node-based data depending on the application for which the proposed model has been used.
- **Analytical tier:** This tier analyses the given social network to generate different metrics required by the social scientists. Necessary preprocessing including compression of the digraph to a DAG is done at this layer. Since the SONSYS system is modeled as an object-relational schema, outcome of this tier will be two comprehensive lists relating the nodes and edges to different structural components generated by preprocessing.

Nodelist (node_id, in_degree, out_degree, ISG_id, cycle_id, hyper_node_id, node_type)

Edgelist (edge_id, edge_type, start_node, end_node, cycle_id, hyper_node_id, hyper_edge_id)

Justification of these underlying relations will be made in the section on query operators.

- **Retrieval tier:** The key components of this tier are structural, node-based subsystems, and a query engine. Each of the two subsystems provides their own retrieval methods and uses the corresponding schemas to handle the two categories of queries. Each subsystem has its own file structures, data structures, and indexing mechanisms to support its queries.

- **Conceptual tier:** This tier involves two schemas corresponding to structural and node-based subsystems. These schemas can function independently to process queries. So the query processor can take one of the three possible approaches to process a composite query:
    - First, search for relevant nodes using value-based predicates from node-based schema. Using the nodes found, make structural search to answer the original query.
    - First, make structural navigation to find the relevant structural components and then search the node-based schema to satisfy value-based predicates present in the original query.
    - Break the original query into structure-based and node-based sub-queries. Independently search in two subsystems. Mediate the answers from two sub-queries to get the final result.

Choice of an approach will be dependent on the type of query. Breaking into two separate schemas has a distinct advantage. If a query involves node-based schema only, the four-tier system will process it without accessing the structural subsystem at all. This approach is significantly different from the earlier efforts on graph data model design. Relevant query examples in the *Query Examples* section will explain the previous query processing approaches:

- **User interface:** It accepts the queries from the users, does syntactic check, and passes them to the corresponding schemas for query processing. It is also responsible for returning the final result of the query back to the user. To provide accurate and fast response to the queries, conceptual and logical interfaces similar to those mentioned in Siau, Chan, and Wei (2004) and Siau, Chan, and Wei (1995) can be developed. The user interface is still under development.

QUERY OPERATORS

Queries in the SONSYS system can be classified as structural and node-based types. Irrespective of the strategy of evaluation of a composite query, as described in the *concept tier* of the section on multi-paradigm architecture, the two subsystems would either work separately or in tandem. A set

Figure 6. Four-tier multi-paradigm architecture

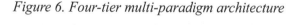

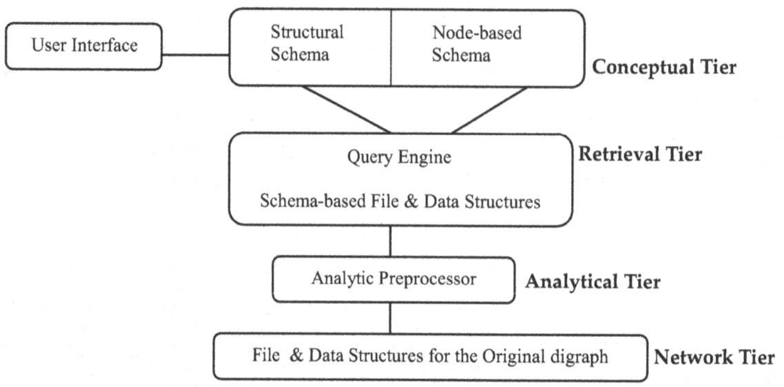

of operators has been defined in SONSYS system and the algebraic specification of the queries can be made using these operators. There are two sets of operators corresponding to the node-based and structural subsystems. Operators for the node-based subsystem follow the standard ODMG specification whereas new operators have been defined for the structural subsystem. However, standard selection (σ) and projection operators have been extended to apply on the graph structure. Operators in the structural subsystem are divided into two groups; *fundamental* operators and *derived* operators. An operator is said to be a fundamental operator if it cannot be expressed in terms of any other operator. A derived operator, on the other hand, can be expressed in terms of one or more fundamental operators. Relevance of each operator has been explained with its definition.

Fundamental Operators

Ancestor. Ancestor or Containment ($\subset$) operator finds all the structures that are ancestor to a referenced structure as defined in complex structural object hierarchy of Figure 4 in the section on structural schema.

For referencing a node and for navigating a DAG structure, SONSYS has followed the methods of Agarwal, Borgida, and Jagadish (1989) and Christophides, Scholl, and Tourtonis (2003). Similar to their propup(S-1), an operator $\Uparrow$ (S-1) has been defined that recursively propagates upwards following the complex structural object hierarchy of Figure 4 and returns all the object ids of the ancestors of referenced structure S-1 till the original digraph. Relevance of Ancestor operator has already been highlighted in the *Structural Schema* section. So by definition:

$$\subset (S\text{-}1) = \{o\text{-}id \mid o\text{-}id \in \subset (S\text{-}1) \cup \Uparrow (S\text{-}1)\}$$

For example, the ancestor operation on cycle (3-4-3) (in Figure 1) represented by C-1(say) gives hyper-nodes H-1, H-3, then ISG-1 and the original digraph (G) as the result set. In other words, $\subset$ (C-1) = {H-1, H-3, ISG-1, G}.

Descendant. Descendant ($\supset$) operator finds all the structures that are descendant to a referenced structure as defined in complex structural object hierarchy of Figure 4 in the section on structural schema.

Similar to propdesc(S-2) operator of (Agarwal et al., 1989; Christophides et al., 2003), an operator $\Downarrow$ (S-2) has been defined that recursively propagates downwards following the complex structural object hierarchy of Figure 4 and returns all the object IDs of the descendants of referenced structure S-2 till the leaves (nodes of original digraph). The relevance of Descendant operator has already been highlighted in the *Structural Schema* section. So by definition:

$$\supset (S\text{-}2) = \{o\text{-}id \mid o\text{-}id \in \supset (S\text{-}2) \cup \Downarrow (S\text{-}2)\}$$

- is usually from a source to a sink, where any source is a node with in-degree zero and any sink is a node with out-degree zero.

For example, in Figure 1, the descendant operation on cycle (3-4-3) represented by C-1 (say), returns edges (3,4) and (4,3) and nodes 3,4 as the result set. In other words, $\supset$ (C-1) = {(3,4), (4,3), 3, 4}.

Path. Path (ρ) operator returns all possible paths from a source node, where a source is a node with in-degree zero. Enumeration of a path needs a recursion process that navigates from one edge to the other, recursively adding them in a sequence to form a path. Agarwal (1987) and IMPRESS (1993) have proposed a recursion operator α over a relation R containing the edges of a graph and Δ is an attribute of α(R) contains a set of edges forming a path. Exploiting this process, SONSYS defines a similar operator over any digraph G for enumerating paths from any source node s as:

$\rho(s) = \{ p \mid p \in \prod_{\Delta} (\sigma_{from = S} (\alpha(G)))\}$

where, p indicates any path object.

For example, for graph in Figure 1 through Figure 3, ρ(H-2) would return 2 paths, {(H-2, 9), (9,10), (10,12), (12,14)} and {(H-2, 9), (9,10), (10,13), (13,14)}.

Derived Operators

Common_Ancestor. Common_Ancestor (℘) operator finds all the ancestors that are common between two structures.

Let S-1 and S-2 be two structures then the operation can be defined as:

$S\text{-}1 \wp S\text{-}2 = \{o\text{-}id \mid o\text{-}id \in (\subset (S\text{-}1)) \cap (\subset (S\text{-}2))\}$

For example, for graph in Figure 1 through Figure 3, the common ancestors of nodes 3 and 4 are cycle (3-4-3), H-1, H-3, ISG-1, and G. So, 3℘4 = {cycle(3-4-3), H-1, H-3, ISG-1, G}.

Common_Descendant. Common_Descendant (ϒ) operator finds all the descendants that are common between two structures.

Let S-1 and S-2 be two structures then the operation can be defined as

$S\text{-}1 \ \Upsilon \ S\text{-}2 = \{o\text{-}id \mid o\text{-}id \in (\supset (S\text{-}1)) \cap (\supset (S\text{-}2))\}$

For example, for graph in Figure 1, the common descendants of cycle (3-4-3) and cycle (1-2-3-4-1) are edge (3,4) and nodes 3 and 4. So, ((3-4-3) ϒ (1-2-3-4-1)) = {(3,4), 3, 4}.

Among fundamental operators, Ancestor or Descendent operator for a reference structure provides all the ancestors or descendents of such a structure. For a selective subset of ancestors or descendents, additional selection operator with appropriate predicates may be used. Any structural operator defined for such purpose will definitely be a derived operator. Accordingly, Belongs_to (β) and Membership (μ) operators have been defined.

Belongs_To. Belongs_To (β) operator finds all structures of a particular type that are ancestors to a specified structure. Finding all ancestors of a referenced structure, if a particular type of ancestor is selected, it will give rise to Belongs_To operation. So, the operation can be defined as:

$\beta(S\text{-}1, S\text{-}2) = \sigma_{\ o\text{-}type = S\text{-}2} (\subset (S\text{-}1))$

Here, among all ancestors of structure S-1, only ancestor type S-2 is selected. Considering the complex structural object hierarchy of Figure 4, Belongs_To operation, for example, can find all cycles that contain a particular edge. Here S-1 is edge and S-2 is of type cycle, shown as the required object type (o-type) in the selection predicate. In Figure 1, edge (7,8) belongs to cycles (6-7-8) and (7-8-9).

Membership. Membership (μ) operator finds all structures of a particular type that are descendents to a specified structure. Finding all descendents of a referenced structure, if a particular type of descendent is selected, it will give rise to Membership operation. So, the operation can be defined as:

$\mu \ (S\text{-}1, S\text{-}2) = \sigma_{\ o\text{-}type = S\text{-}1} (\supset (S\text{-}2))$

Here, among all descendents of structure S-2, only descendent type S-1 is selected. Considering the complex structural object hierarchy of Figure 4, Membership operation, for example, can find all edges that are members of a particular cycle. Here S-2 is cycle and S-1 is of type edge, shown as the required object type (o-type) in the selection predicate.

For example, for graph in Figure 1 through Figure 3, μ (node, H-3) returns 4 nodes 1,2,3,4,5. Similarly, μ (edge, H-3) returns seven edges (1,2), (2,3), (3,4), (4,3), (4,1), (3,5), (5,4).

Enumeration. Enumeration operator (E) returns all possible sub-paths between any two nodes. If the concerned nodes are source and sink, then as per the definition of path, all simple paths will be obtained. The process of enumeration is similar to the enumeration of path as discussed earlier.

SONSYS defines an enumeration operator over any digraph G for enumerating paths from any source node s to any target node t as:

$$E\,(s,t) = \{\, p \mid p \in \prod_{\Delta} (\sigma_{from = s,\ to = t}(\alpha(G)))\}$$

where, p indicates any path object. Connotation of α and Δ are same as defined in path operator among fundamental operators.

For example, in Figure 1, $E(10,14)$ would return two sub-paths, {(10,13), (13,14)} and {(10,12), (12,14)}.

Reachability. Reachability operator ($\mathscr{R}$) is a Boolean operator that returns true if a node is reachable from a specified node. As discussed in the section on hyper-node-based compression, a path is usually defined from a source to a sink, where any source is a node with in-degree zero and any sink is a node with out-degree zero. So, in order to find whether a node y is reachable from another node x, the system should verify whether there exists any path that passes through both x and y where x appears before y in the node sequence. However, enumeration of paths between x and y is not necessary to ensure reachability. Agarwal et al. (1989) has defined a node encoding scheme where each node i is associated with a node number i_n, where i_n indicates the number of the node i. Each node is also associated with an interval of node numbers $[s_n, t_n]$. The interval indicates that node number range for nodes s to t (both s_n and t_n included) are reachable from i. This node-numbering scheme is quite popular even in the recent works on graph searching algorithms (Chen et al., 2005) and it has been used in SONSYS as well.

If s_n covers $[p_n, q_n]$, then the condition that the node t is reachable from node s is:

$$\mathscr{R}\,(s,t) = \begin{cases} \text{true}, & \text{if } p_n \le t_n \le q_n \\ \text{false}, & \text{otherwise} \end{cases}$$

For example, in Figure 1 $\mathscr{R}(10,14)$ will return true but $\mathscr{R}(9,8)$ will return false.

Incompatible query specification. Fundamental and derived operators defined in the SONSYS system have either one or two arguments. The two arguments appearing in an operator may have to be specified in a particular order. For example, $\beta(n_i, \text{cycle})$ will search for all cycle type ancestors of node n_i. On the other hand, $\beta(\text{cycle}, n_i)$ will be a wrong specification of query for Belongs_To operation. Such incompatible query specification will give rise to an error. Similar error will occur for Reachability and Membership operators. Arguments in Common_Ancestor and Common_Descendent operators are not order specific. Enumeration operator, however, will either return the required sub-paths or a null set.

Completeness of Query Operators

The operator set available for structural queries should be such that all structural objects are retrievable both at the compressed DAG level (Figure 3) as well as at the original graph level (Figure 1). It is also necessary to ensure that the different structural objects can be accessed using the complex structural object hierarchy of Figure 4. Completeness of operators would ensure that the aforementioned retrievability and accessibility conditions for all structural objects of a given social network are fulfilled. Minimality, on the other hand, would prove that all the structural operators defined are essential and the absence of any of them will not ensure the aforementioned conditions of completeness. Discussion on operators has shown that derived operators are basically an extension of the fundamental operators when used in conjunction with extended selection and projection operations borrowed from relational algebra. So, it is sufficient to show the fundamental operators to be complete and minimal.

Definition 1. Structural hierarchy: A structural hierarchy H = <S, E, R> is a triple where S is a *finite set of structural objects, E is a finite set of edges, and R = S X S, is a finite set of structural relationships.*

H follows the complex structural object hierarchy (as in Figure 4). All structural object types like hyper-node, hyper-edge, path, cycle, and so forth are within *S*. In a graph (compressed or original) representing a social network, two structural objects are related either as ancestor-descendent or by edge-connectivity (lying on the same path). Both the relationships are members of *R*, that is, *R* covers all possible relationships between any two structural object sets.

Definition 2. Operation: An operation is a function that maps one set of structural objects to another set of structural objects ensuring a relationship between the two sets that is a member of R.

In an operation ζ ($S\text{-}1 \rightarrow S\text{-}2$), $S\text{-}1 \subseteq S$, $S\text{-}2 \subseteq S$. and $r = S\text{-}1 \; X \; S\text{-}2$ where, $r \in R$.

Any operation between two sets of structural objects ensures a unique relationship between the two sets.

Definition 3. Operation set: An operation set $\Re$ *is a collection of operations where,* $\forall (r \in R)$, $\exists (\zeta \in \Re)$ *such that:*

$\Re = \{\zeta \mid \zeta (S\text{-}1 \rightarrow S\text{-}2), S\text{-}1 \subseteq S, S\text{-}2 \subseteq S.$ and $r = S\text{-}1 \; X \; S\text{-}2$ where, $r \in R\}$

Lemma 3 (Completeness): The operation set $\Re$ *is complete.*

Proof: Completeness of operations should ensure that all structural objects according to complex structural object hierarchy are retrievable and any two structural objects that are connected on the graph (compressed or original) are reachable where the graph represents a social network. Since by definition of operation set $\Re$., for each member $r \in R$, there exists an operation $\zeta \in \Re$, the Lemma directly follows.

As a matter of fact, structural relationship set *R* has only two members; ancestor-descendent and edge-connectivity. On the other hand, operation set $\Re$. (for fundamental operators only) has three members; Ancestor, Descendent, and Path to cover the retrieval of all structural objects.

Lemma 4 (Minimality): The operation set $\Re$ *is minimal.*

Proof: It is assumed that the set $\Re$ is not minimal. Then $\Re$ is equivalent to the set $\Re$ - <ζ > for $\zeta \in \Re$. Then ζ can be deleted from $\Re$. From the definition of operation, an operation between two sets of structural objects ensures a unique relationship between the two sets. So, deletion of any operation ζ will cause loss of a relationship between two sets of structural objects related by ζ. Hence ζ cannot be deleted from $\Re$ and set $\Re$ is minimal.

QUERY EXAMPLES

This subsection considers a few sample queries covering the query types discussed in the section on query operators. A brief explanation is given for each of these queries.

Node-Based Query

Example-1: List the Santhal households having a monthly income less than Rs.10000 and number of members in the house is greater than five.

σ_θ **(Household)**

where, θ = (monthly_income <10000 $\wedge$ no_of_members >5 $\wedge$ tribe ='Santhal').

σ is the selection operator similar to the equivalent operator available in the relational algebra.

Structural Query:

Example-2: Find the number of ISGs in the village community (original digraph) whose size is greater than five (number of nodes).

$\mathbf{count}(\sigma_{ISG.ISG\_size > 5}\,(\Pi_{ISG}\,\mathbf{(Graph)}))$

Since an ISG may contain hyper-nodes, the member function ISG.ISG_size would generate sub-queries to break the nesting of hyper-nodes in succession till the node level, in order to get the count of member nodes in each such hyper-nodes. Aggregation of these counts will provide the actual count of nodes in the ISG.

The example social network in Figure 2 contains two ISGs; ISG-1 and ISG-2. Breaking of hyper-nodes to the node level shows that ISG-1 does not satisfy the query condition. Only ISG-2 satisfies the query and hence the count is one.

Example-3: Find the number of ways a Santhal household s and a Pal household p can reach the household c belonging to the chief of Mondal tribe.

$E\,((\sigma_{tribe = \text{'Santhal'} \wedge node\_id = \text{'s'}}\,\mathbf{(Household)}), (\sigma_{tribe = \text{'Mondal'} \wedge node\_id = \text{'c'}}\,\mathbf{(Household)}) \cup E\,((\sigma_{tribe = \text{'Pal'} \wedge node\_id = \text{'p'}}\,\mathbf{(Household)}), (\sigma_{tribe = \text{'Mondal'} \wedge node\_id = \text{'c'}}\,\mathbf{(Household)})$

Here the enumeration operator is used to find one set of paths for reaching the node object c from the node object s and another set of paths for reaching the node object c from the node object p. The union of these two sets of paths gives the total number of paths or ways for reaching the chief.

Composite Query:

Example-4: Find the list of Santhal households that consult the Village-Doctor as well as the City-Doctor for any ailment in the family.

$\Pi_{house\_no}(\sigma_{\theta}\,\mathbf{(Household)})$

where θ = (tribe='Santhal' $\wedge\ \mathcal{R}((\sigma_{tribe = \text{'Santhal'}}$ (Household)), $(\sigma_{profession = \text{'Village-Doctor'}}$ (Household))) $\wedge\ \mathcal{R}((\sigma_{tribe = \text{'Santhal'}}$ (Household)), $(\sigma_{profession = \text{'City-Doctor'}}$ (Household))))

Here the reachability operator $\mathcal{R}$ is used, first to find the node objects representing households of Village-Doctor and City-Doctor that are reachable from the node objects representing Santhal households. The house number attribute is then obtained from the selected nodes. For the execution of the reachability operator, the node-ids assigned by the system are extracted from the relevant node objects.

Example-5: Find the list of the Santhal Households who form kinship groups of size greater than or equal to five.

$\mu\mathbf{(node,}(\sigma_{\theta}(\Pi_{ISG}\mathbf{(Graph)}))) \cap (\sigma_{tribe=\text{'Santhal'}}\mathbf{(Household)})$

where, θ = (homogeneous_hyper_node_size $\geq 5 \wedge$ homogeneous_hyper_node_edge_type = 'kinship')

Here, "kinship" is a particular value of the attribute 'homogeneous_hyper_node_edge_type'. Though not apparent from the algebraic expression, the query processor would first identify the relevant nodes from the graph and then would intersect this node set with the node list obtained from the node-based data. The intersection would be done on the node-ids provided by the system.

CONCLUSION AND FUTURE WORKS

This article ventures to develop a data model for a social network. As defined in Wikipedia, a social network is a social structure between actors, mostly individuals or organizations and indicates the ways in which they are connected through various social familiarities ranging from casual acquaintance to close familial bonds. The formal representation of a social network is a digraph that contains structural as well as node-based information. Since the users make queries covering both the structure and the node-based data, a data model is needed to handle such composite queries. In the *Related Works* section, the authors have shown that earlier works on graph data model mainly concentrated on structure-related data and could handle very small graphs. However, a social network can have hundreds of nodes and edges. Moreover, it contains special structures that are relevant to social scientists in understanding a community. So, the data model proposed in this article has considered the graph in two different stages. In one stage it has proposed a structural pre-processing and compression of the graph representing a social network. This process evolves a few structural elements relevant to the study of a social network. These structures have been stored separately as hyper structures allowing direct queries on them. The compressed graph becomes a DAG on which other structural queries can be addressed. The structural equivalence of the original graph and the compressed DAG has been established through suitable lemmas.

Now, considering the structural- and node-based data together, an object-relational model has been proposed. It has two separate subsystems for structural and node-based operations. These two subsystems can work independently or in tandem. Suitable structural operators have been developed and their relevance has also been established. Query examples have been supplied to illustrate the use of the data model over a tribal village community.

The article has concentrated on explaining the techniques for handling large graphs. Pre-processing and compression of such graph and querying on such compressed graphs have been given the importance. A formal way of proposing an object-relational data model as discussed in Siau (1999); Siau and Cao (2001); Siau and Loo (2006); Siau and Lee (2004); and Siau, Erickson, and Lee (2005) has not been considered. Such treatments will be considered in future.

For improved user-database interaction, a suitable user interface is required where users can have better understanding of the database system for creating efficient queries. A user feedback system and user interaction in the conceptual level as proposed in Siau et al (1995); Chan, Wei, and Siau (1997); Chan, Siau, and Wei (1998); and Siau et al. (2004) will be followed in developing the user interface in the future.

Another important area that has to be addressed in the future is the temporal variation of social relationships. As discussed earlier, a social network represents a real-life social community. Now a community is not a static phenomenon. New members may join and old members may leave. Moreover, relations among the members may also change over time. So the number of nodes and the edges connecting them in a social network will also change over time. This evolution of social network is a complex process and it depends upon the properties of the application area under consideration. Though many social network-based analysis under such evolutionary processes have already been done (Liben-Nowell & Kleinberg, 2003; Newman, 2003; Jin, Girvan, & Newman, 2001), no known work of data modeling and query processing has been done on the evolution of social network.

SONSYS system provides a two-level graph structure with the compressed DAG at the top level and the original graph at the lower level. Only comparable work in this respect is the S-node representation scheme as proposed by a research group at Stanford University in Raghavan and Garcia-Molina (2003). It has also proposed a two-level representation scheme in order to compress and store a large Web graph. Here, a top-level graph is connected with a lower-level graph through pointers. In this scheme, a Web graph is represented in terms of a set of smaller directed graphs, each of which encodes the interconnections within a small subset of pages. A top-level directed graph, consisting of "supernodes" and "superedges," contains pointers to these lower-level graphs. By exploiting empirically observed properties of Web graphs to guide the grouping of pages into supernodes and using compressed encodings for the lower-level directed graphs. So in S-node representation, formation of supernodes and superedges are application specific, whereas in SONSYS the compression to hyper-structures is absolutely dependent on the graph structure and independent of any application for which it is formed. Application-specific information is in the nodes for which a separate node-based subsystem has been provided in SONSYS. So, the S-node scheme can represent only a few specific observed properties of the Web graph and is designed to serve a set of dedicated queries. On the other hand, SONSYS is a generic data model that can represent all important graph structures related to a social network and can efficiently handle composite queries by exploiting both node-based and structural information.

REFERENCES

Agrawal, R. (1987). Alpha: An extension of relational algebra to express a class of recursive queries. In *Proceedings of the IEEE 3rd International Conference. Data Engineering*, (pp. 580-590).

Agrawal, R., Borgida, A., & Jagadish, H. V. (1989). Efficient management of transitive relationships in large data and knowledge bases. In *Proceedings of the ACM-SIGMOD*, (pp. 253-262).

Amann, B., & Scholl, M. (1992). Gram: A graph data model and query languages. *ACM Conference. On Hypertext*, 201-211.

Bagchi, A., Mitra, S., & Bandyopadhyay, A. K. (2003). SONSYS—A system to model a social network. *Sixth International Conference on Information Technology*, (pp. 371-374).

Bhanu Teja, C. (2005). *Processing of path queries on trees and DAGs*. M.Tech. Dissertation Report, Indian Statistical Institute.

Bhanu Teja, C., Mitra, S., Bagchi, A., & Bandyopadhyay, A. K. (in press). Pre-processing and path normalization of a Web graph used as a social network. *Journal of Digital Information Management*.

Chakraborty, S. (2004). *Web mining*. Elsevier.

Chan, H., Siau, K., & Wei, K. (1998). The effect of data model, system and task characteristics on user query performance—An empirical study. *The DATA BASE for Advances in Information Systems, 29*(1), 31-49.

Chan, H., Wei, K., & Siau, K. (1997). A system for query comprehension. *Information and Software Technology, 39,* 141-148.

Chen, L., Gupta, A., & Kurul, E. M. (2005). Efficient algorithms for pattern matching on directed acyclic graphs. In *Proceedings of the IEEE ICDE*, (pp. 384-395).

Christophides, V., Scholl, M., & Tourtonis, S. (2003). On labeling schemes for the semantic Web. *World Wide Web Conference (WWW)*, 544-555.

Consens, M. P., & Mendelzon, A. O. (1990). GraphLog: A visual formalism for real life recursion. *ACM PODS*, 404-416.

Dorogovtsev, S. N., & Mendes, J. F. F. (2003). *Evolution of networks: From biological nets to the Internet and WWW*. UK: Oxford University Press.

Gutiérrez, A., Pucheral, P., Steffen, H., & Thévenin, J. M. (1994). Database graph views: A practical model to manage persistent graphs. *Twentieth VLDB Conference*.

Guting, R. (1994). *GraphDB: A Data Model and Query Language for Graphs in Databases. Proc. VLDB.*

Hanneman, R. A. (2001). *Introduction to social network method.* Online textbook.

Holland, P. W., & Leinhardt, S. (1979). *Perspectives on social network research.* Academic Press.

IMPRESS. (1993). *IMPRESS, specification of graph views and graph operators* (Esprit project n° 6355), (Tech. Rep. No. W7-005-R75).

Jin, E. M., Girvan, M., & Newman, M. E. J. (2001). The structure of growing social networks. *Phys. Rev.* E 64, 046132.

Kautz, H., Selman, B., & Shah, M. (1997). The hidden Web. *AI Magazine, 18*(2), 27-36.

Kleinberg, M. J., Kumar, R., Raghavan, P., Rajagopalan, S., & Tomkins, S. A. (1999). Web as a graph: Measurements, models and methods. In *Proceedings of the International Conference on combinatorics and computing*, (pp. 1-18).

Leinhardt, S. (1977). *Social networks: A developing paradigm.* Academic Press.

Liben-Nowell, D., & Kleinberg, J. (2003). The link prediction problem for social networks. In *Proceedings of the ACM CIKM.*

Mitra, S., Bagchi, A., & Bandyopadhyay, A. K. (2006). A data model for a Web graph used as a social network. In *Proceedings of the 1st International Conference on Emerging Applications of Information Technology,* (pp. 23-26).

Newman, M. (2003). The structure and function of complex networks. *SIAM Review, 45,* 167-256.

Pardaens, J., Peelman, P., & Tanaca, L. (1995). G-Log: A graph-based query language. *IEEE Knowledge & data Engineering, 7*(3), 436-453.

Raghavan, S., & Garcia-Molina, H. (2003). Representing Web graphs. In *Proceedings of the IEEE International Conference on Data Engineering.*

Rao, A. R., & Bandyopadhyay, S. (1987). Measures of reciprocity in a social network. *Sankhya: The Indian Journal of Statistics, Series A, 49,* 141-188.

Rao, A. R., Bandyopadhyay, S., Sinha, B. K., Bagchi, A., Jana, R., Chaudhuri, A., et al. (1998). *Changing social relations—Social network approach* (Technical Report). Survey Research and Data Analysis Center, Indian Statistical Institute.

Rosenthal, A., Heiler, S., Dayal, U., & Manola, F. (1986). Traversal recursion: A practical approach to supporting recursive applications. In *Proceedings of the ACM-SIGMOD,* (pp. 166-176).

Sheng, L., Özsoyoglu, M. Z., & Özsoyoglu, G. (1999). A graph query language and its query processing. *ICDE.*

Siau, K. (1999). Information modeling and method engineering: A psychological perspective. *Journal of Database Management, 10*(4), 44-50.

Siau, K., & Cao, Q. (2001). Unified modeling language (UML)—A complexity analysis. *Journal of Database Management, 12*(1), 26-34.

Siau, K., Chan, H., & Wei, K. (1995). The effects of conceptual and logical interfaces on visual query performance of end users. In *Proceedings of the Sixteenth International Conference on Information Systems*, (pp. 225-235).

Siau, K., Chan, H., & Wei, K. (2004). Effects of query complexity and learning on novice user query performance with conceptual and logical database interfaces. *IEEE Transactions on Systems, Man and Cybernetics, 34*(2), 276-281.

Siau, K., Erickson, J., & Lee, L. (2005). Theoretical vs. practical complexity: The case of UML. *Journal of Database Management, 16*(3), 40-57.

Siau, K., & Lee, L. (2004). Are use case and class diagrams complimentary in requirements analysis? An experimental study on use case and class diagrams in UML. *Requirements Engineering, 9*(4), 229-237.

Siau, K., & Loo, P. (2006). Identifying difficulties in learning UML. *Information Systems Management, 23*(3), 43-51.

Wen, J. R., Li, Q., Ma, W. Y., & Zhang, H. J. (2003). A multi-paradigm querying approach for a generic multimedia database management system. *SIGMOD Record, 32*(1), 26-34.

Yu, B., & Singh, M. P. (2003). Searching social networks. In *Proceedings of the ACM International Joint Conference on Autonomous Agents and Multiagent Systems (AAMAS).*

This work was previously published in Journal of Database Management, Vol. 18, Issue 4, edited by K. Siau, pp. 51-79, copyright 2007 by IGI Publishing, formerly known as Idea Group Publishing (an imprint of IGI Global).

Compilation of References

Abrão, M.A., Bouchou, B., Alves, M.H.F., Laurent, D., & Musicante, M. (2004). Incremental Constraint Checking for XML Documents. *Database and XML Technologies: Second International XML Database Symposium (*XSym) Toronto, Canada, August 29-30, LNCS Volume 3186 / 2004

Abrial, J. R. (1996). *The B-Book: Assigning Programs to Meanings.* Cambridge University Press.

Adiba, M.E., & Lindsay, B. (1980). Database snapshots. In *Proceedings of the 6th International Conference on Very Large Databases* (pp. 86-91), Montreal, Canada.

Agarwal, R., & Sambamurthy, V. (2002). Principles and Models for Organizing IT Function. *MIS Quarterly Executive, 1*(1), 1-16.

Agrawal, R. (1987). Alpha: An extension of relational algebra to express a class of recursive queries. In *Proceedings of the IEEE 3rd International Conference. Data Engineering,* (pp. 580-590).

Agrawal, R., Borgida, A., & Jagadish, H. V. (1989). Efficient management of transitive relationships in large data and knowledge bases. In *Proceedings of the ACM-SIGMOD,* (pp. 253-262).

Ahuja, M., & Carley, K. (1999). Network structure in virtual organizations. *Organization Science, 10*(6), 741-747.

Alavi, M., and Joachimsthaler, E.A. "Revisiting DSS Implementation Research: A Meta-Analysis of the literature and Suggestions for Researchers," *MIS Quarterly* (16:1), 1992, pp 95-116.

Albrecht J., Bauer A., Deyerling O., Günzel W., Hümmer W., Lehner W., & Schlesinger L. (1999). Management of multidimensional aggregates for Efficient online analytical processing, Proceedings of the International Symposium Proceedings on Database Engineering and Applications, 1999.

Aleman-Meza, B., Halaschek-Wiener, C., Arpinar, I. B., Ramakrishnan, C., & Sheth, A. P. (2005). Ranking complex relationships on the Semantic Web. *IEEE Internet Computing*, 37-44.

Alfeld, P. University of Utah, US, online at http://www.math.utah.edu/~alfeld/math/primelist.html

Allen, J. F. (1983). Maintaining knowledge about temporal intervals. *Communications of the ACM, 26*(11), 832-843.

Allen, J.P. (2004). Redefining the network: enrollment strategies in the PDA industry, *Information Technology and People*, 17(2), 171-185.

Alonso, G., Casati, F., Kuno, H., & Machiraju, V. (2003). *Web services: Concepts, architecture, and applications.* Springer Verlag.

Alter, S., and Browne, G. "A Broad View of Systems Analysis and Design: Implications for Research," Communications of the Association for Information Systems (15), 2005, pp. 981-999.

Amann, B., & Scholl, M. (1992). Gram: A graph data model and query languages. *ACM Conference. On Hypertext*, 201-211.

Anderson, M. & Karrenman, D. (2000). Complexity theory and organizational science, *Organizational Science*, 10(3), 216-232.

Andrews, G. (1994). Number Theory, Dover Publications, New York.

Archibald, G., Karabakal, N. & Karlsson, P. (1999 Winter). Supply chain vs supply chain: using simulation to compete beyond the four walls. [Online]. Available: http://www.wintersim.org/prog99.htm.

Argyris, C. (1977). Double Loop Learning in Organizations. *Harvard Business Review, 55*(5), 115-125.

Argyris, C. (1996). Unrecognized Defenses of Scholars: Impact on Theory and Research. *Organization Science, 7*(1), 79-87.

Argyris, C. (2003). A Life Full of Learning. *Organization Studies, 24*(7), 1178-1192.

Argyris, C., & Schon, D. A. (1978). *Organizational Learning: A Theory of Action Perspective*. Reading, MA: Addison-Wesley.

Arnon, A., Efrat, A., Indyk, P., & Samet, H. (1999) 'Efficient regular data structures and algorithms for location and proximity problems', *Proceedings of the 40th Annual Symposium on Foundations of Computer Science*, New York (Oct 17-19), 160-170.

Arthur, J. B., & Aiman-Smith, L. (2001). Gainsharing and Organizational Learning: An Analysis of Employee Suggestions Over Time. *Academy of Management Journal, 44*(4), 737-754.

Ashburner, M., Ball, C., Blake, J., Botstein, D., Butler, H., Cherry, J., et al. (2000). Gene ontology: Tool for the unification of biology. *National Genetics, 25*, 25-29.

Attie, A. D. (2003). The new industrialized approach to biology. *Cell Biology Education, 2*, 150-151.

Axelrod, R. & Cohen, M.D. (1999). *Harnessing Complexity: Organizational Implications of a Scientific Frontier.* New York: Basic Books.

Bagchi, A., Mitra, S., & Bandyopadhyay, A. K. (2003). SONSYS—A system to model a social network. *Sixth International Conference on Information Technology, (*pp. 371-374).

Balijepally, V., Mahapatra, R., & Nerur, S. (2004). *Social Capital: A Theoretical Lens for IS Research.* Paper presented at the Tenth Americas Conference on Information Systems, New York, NY.

Balmin, A., Papakonstantinou, Y., & Vianu, V.(2004). Incremental Validation of XML Documents. *ACM Transactions on Database Systems*, 29(4):710—751

Bank On Service enhancement. (2003, Nov 18). e-daily.

Barki, H., Rivard, S., and Talbot, J. "An Integrative Contingency Model of Software Project Risk Management," Journal of Management Information Systems (17:4), 2001, pp. 37-69.

Barley, S.R. "Technology as An Occasion for Structuring: Evidence from Observations of CT Scanners and the Social Order of Radiology Departments," *Administrative Science Quarterly* (31:1), 1986, pp 78-108.

Barros, R. S. M. (1998). On the Formal Specification and Derivation of Relational Database Applications. *Electronic Notes in Theoretical Computer Science*, Volume 14.

Basili, V. and Turner, A. "Iterative Enhancement: A Practical Technique for Software Development," IEEE Transactions on Software Development (1:4), December 1975, pp. 390 – 396.

Basu, A., & Kumar, A. (2002). Research commentary: Workflow management issues in e-business. *Information Systems Research, 13*(1), 1-14.

Batini, C., Lenzerini, M., & Navathe, S. (1986). A comparative analysis of methodologies for database schema integration. *ACM Computing Surveys, 18*(4), 323-364.

Bayardo, R., Bohrer, W., Brice, R., Cichocki, A., Fowler, G., Helal, A., et al. (1997, June). InfoSleuth: Agent-Based Semantic Integration of Information in Open and Dynamic Environments. *In Proceeedings of ACM Sigmod International Conference on Management of Data.* Tucson, Arizona.

B-core. (1996). *B-Toolkit Release 3.2. Manual.* Oxford, U.K.

Becher, J. D., Berkhin, P., & Freeman, E. (2000). *Automating Exploratory Data Analysis for Efficient Data Mining.* Paper presented at the Knowledge Discovery and Data Mining, Boston, MA USA.

Bechhofer, S., Goble, C., & Horrocks, I. (2001, July 30-August 1). *DAML+OIL Is not Enough.* Paper presented at the First Semantic Web Working Symposium (SWWS-01), Stanford, CA.

Beck, K. Extreme Programming Explained, Boston, Massachusetts: Addison-Wesley, 2000.

Beck, K. and Andres, C. Extreme Programming Explained: Embrace Change, Second Edition. Boston, Massachusetts: Addison-Wesley, 2004.

Benbasat, I., Dexter, A. S., & Mantha, R. W. (1980). Impact of Organizational Maturity on Information System Skill Needs. *MIS Quarterly, 4*(1), 21-34.

Benbasat, I., Dexter, A.S., and Mantha, R.W. "Impact of Organizational Maturity on Information Systems Skills," *Communications of the ACM* (27:5), 1980, pp 476-485.

Benbasat, I., Goldstain, D.K & Mead, M. (1987). The Case Research Strategy in Studies of Information Systems. *MIS Quarterly*, 11(3), 369-386.

Benbya, H., & McKelvey, B. (2006). Toward a complexity theory of information systems development. *Information Technology and People*, 19(1), 12-34.

Benedikt, M., Chan, C.Y., Fan, W., Freire, J. & Rastogi, R. (2003). Capturing both Types and Constraints in Data Integration. *Proceedings of the ACM SIGMOD Conference on Management Of Data*

Benedusi, P., Cimitile, A., & De Carlini, U. (1989). A reverse engineering methodology to reconstruct hierarchical data flow diagrams for software maintenance. *Proceedings of the IEEE International Conference on Software Maintenance* (pp. 180-189).

Bensaou, M., and Venkatraman, N. "Configurations of Interorganizational Relationships: A Comparison between US and Japanese Automakers," Management Science (41:9), 1995, pp. 1471-1492.

Bernard, E., Legeard, B., Luck, X. & Peureux, F. (2004). Generation of test sequences from formal specifications: GSM11-11 standard case study. *International Journal of Software Practice and Experience* 34(10).

Berners-Lee, T., Hendler, J., & Lassila, O. (2001). The Semantic Web. *Scientific American, 284*(5), 34-43.

Bhanu Teja, C. (2005). *Processing of path queries on trees and DAGs.* M.Tech. Dissertation Report, Indian Statistical Institute.

Bhanu Teja, C., Mitra, S., Bagchi, A., & Bandyopadhyay, A. K. (in press). Pre-processing and path normalization of a Web graph used as a social network. *Journal of Digital Information Management.*

Bharadwaj, A.S. "A Resource-based Perspective on Information Technology Capability and Firm Performance," *MIS Quarterly* (24:1), 2000, pp 169-198.

Biggerstaff, T.J, Perlis, A. J., (ed) (1989) *Software Reusability Concepts and Models, Volume I and II*, ACM Press Frontier Series, Addison Wesley.

BJS. (1967). What is the sequence of events in the criminal justice system? Retrieved October, 2006, from http://www.ojp.usdoj.gov/bjs/flowchart.htm

BJS. (2000). Crimes against Persons Age 65 or Older, 1992 - 1997. Retrieved November, 2006, from http://www.ojp.usdoj.gov/bjs/abstract/cpa6597.htm

BJS. (2003). Reporting Crime to the Police, 1992 -2000. Retrieved November, 2006, from http://www.ojp.usdoj.gov/bjs/abstract/rcp00.htm

BJS. (2005). Percent distribution of victimization, by type of crime and whether of not reported to the police. 2006, from http://www.ojp.usdoj.gov/bjs/pub/pdf/cvus/current/cv0591.pdf

BJS. (2006). Percent distribution of victimizations, by type of crime and whether or not reported to the police. 2006, from http://www.ojp.usdoj.gov/bjs/pub/pdf/cvus/current/cv0591.pdf

BJS. (2006, September 10, 2006). Teens and young adults experience the highest rates of violent crime. 2006

Blackman, C. R. (1998). Convergence between telecommunications and other media: How should regulation adapt?. *Telecommunications Policy*, 22(3), 163-170.

Blair, D. C. (2002). The challenge of commercial document retrieval, Part 1: Major issues, and a framework based on search exhaustivity, determinacy of representation and document collection size. *Information Processing & Management, 38*(2), 273-291.

Blake, M. B., & Gomaa, H. (2005). Agent-oriented compositional approaches to services-based cross-organizational workflow. *Decision Support Systems, 40*(1), 31-50.

Blakeley, J.A., & Martin, N.L. (1990). Join index, materialized view, and hybrid hash join: A performance analysis. In *Proceedings of the 6th IEEE Conference on Data Engineering* (pp. 256-263), Los Angeles, California.

Blau, P. M. (1977). *Inequity and heterogeneity.* New York: Free Press.

Bloomfield, B.P., & Vurdubakis, T. (1994). Boundary disputes: Negotiating the boundary between the technical and the social in the development of IT systems. *Information Technology and People*, 7(1), 9-24.

Boehm, B. "A Spiral Model of Software Development and Enhancement," ACM SIGSOFT Software Engineering Notes (11:4), August 1986, pp. 14 – 24.

Boehm, B., & Turner, R. (2004). *Balancing Agility and Discipline: A Guide to the Perplexed.* Boston, MA: Addison-Wesley.

Boersma, K., and Kingma, S. "From Means to Ends: The Transformation of ERP in a Manufacturing Company," *Journal of Strategic Information Systems* (24:2), 2005, pp 197-219.

Bonifati, A., Ceri, S., & Paraboschi, S. (2001). Active Rules for XML: A New Paradigm for E-services. *VLDB Journal* 10(1): 39-47

Borgatti, S. (2002). *Basic social network concepts.* Retrieved from http://www.analytictech.com/networks/basic%20concepts%202002.pdf

Borgatti, S. P., Everett, M. G., & Freeman, L. C. (2002). Ucinet for Windows: Software for social network analysis. Harvard, MA: Analytic Technologies.

Bostrom, R. and Thomas, B. "Achieving Excellence in Communications: A Key to Developing Complete, Accurate, and Shared Information Requirements", Special Interest Group on Computer Personnel Research Annual Conference, Charlottesville, VA, 1983.

Bouchou, B., Halfeld-Ferrari-Alves, M. & Musicante, M. (2003). Tree Automata to Verify XML Key Constraints. *International Workshop on the Web and Databases.*

Bouguettaya, A. (1999). Introduction to the special issue on ontologies and databases. *International Journal of Distributed and Parallel Databases*, 7 (1).

Bouguettaya, A., Malik, Z., Rezgui, A., & Korff, L. (2006). A Scalable Middleware for Web Databases. *Journal of Database Management, 17*(4), 20-46.

Bouguettaya, A., Rezgui, A., Medjahed, B., & Ouzzani, M. (2004). Internet computing support for Digital Government. *In: M. P. Singh (Ed.), Practical handbook of internet computing,* Chapman Hall & CRC Press.

Bourdieu, P. (1986). The Forms of Capital. In J. G. Richardson (Ed.), *Handbook of Theory and Research for the Sociology of Education* (pp. 241-258). New York: Greenwood.

Bowers, S., & Ludäscher, B. (2004). *An ontology-driven framework for data transformation in scientific workflows.* Paper presented at the International Workshop on Data Integration in the Life Sciences (DILS'04), Leipzig, Germany.

Bowers, S., Lin, K., & Ludascher, B. (2004). *On integrating scientific resources through semantic registration.* Paper presented at the Scientific and Statistical Database Management.

Bowman, C., Danzig, P., Schwartz, U. M. M., Hardy, D., & Wessels, D. (1995). *Harvest: A scalable, customizable discovery and access system (Tech. Rep.)*. University of Colorado, Boulder.

Brancheau, J.C., and Wetherbe, J.C. "The Adoption of Spreadsheet Software: Testing Innovation Diffusion Theory in the Context of End-user Computing," *Information Systems Research* (1:2), 1990, pp 115-143.

Brereton, P., & Budgen, D. (2000). Component-based systems: A classification of issues. *IEEE Computer, 33*(11), 54-62.

Brilhante, V., & Robertson, D. (2001). Metadata-Supported Automated Ecological Modelling. In C. Rautenstrauch (Ed.), *Environmental information systems in industry and public administration.* Hershey, PA: Idea Group Publishing.

Brown, J. S., & Duguid, P. (1991). Organizational Learning and Communities-of-Practice: Toward a Unified View of Working, Learning, and Innovation. *Organization Science, 2*(1), 40-57.

Browne, G., and Pitts, M. "Stopping Rule Use During Information Search in Design Problems," Organizational Behavior and Human Decision Processes (95:2), 2004, pp. 208–224.

Browne, G., and Ramesh, V. "Improving Information Requirements Determination: A Cognitive Perspective," Information and Management (39:8), 2002, pp. 625-645.

Browne, G., and Rogich, M. "An Empirical Investigation of User Requirements Elicitation: Comparing the Effectiveness of Prompting Techniques," Journal of Management Information Systems (17:4), 2001, pp. 223-249.

Bruel, J.M. & France, R. B. (1996). A Formal Object-oriented CASE Tool for the Development of Complex Systems'. *7th European Workshop on Next Generation of Case Tools.*

Buchanan, B.G. et al. Constructing an Expert System, in F. Hayes-Roth, D.A. Waterman, and D.B. Lenat, eds., Building Expert Systems, Reading, MA: Addison-Wesley, 1983.

Buhler, P., & Vidal, J. M. (2003). Semantic Web services as agent behaviors. In: B. Burg et al. (Eds.), *Agentcities: Challenges in open agent environments* (pp. 25-31). Springer-Verlag.

Buneman, P., Davidson, S., Fan, W., Hara, C., & Tan, W. (2001). Keys for XML. *World Wide Web*, pp. 201-210.

Bunge, M. (1974). *Treatise on basic philosophy: Vol.1: Sense and reference.* Boston: D. Reidel Publishing.

Bunge, M. (1977). *Treatise on basic philosophy: Vol. 3: Ontology I: The furniture of the world.* Boston: D. Reidel Publishing.

Bunge, M. (1979). *Treatise on basic philosophy: Vol. 4: Ontology II: a world of systems.* Boston: D. Reidel Publishing.

Burns, R., and Dennis, A. "Selecting the Appropriate Application Development Methodology," ACM SIGMIS Database (17:1), 1985, pp. 19-23.

Burt, R. S. (1997). The Contingent Value of Social Capital. *Administrative Science Quarterly, 42*(2), 339-365.

Bussler, C., Fensel, D., & Maedche, A. (2002, December). A conceptual architecture for semantic Web enabled Web services. *SIGMOD Record*, 31 (4), 24-29.

Butz, A. R. (1969) 'Convergence with Hilbert's space-filling curve', *Journal of Computer and System Sciences*, 3(May), 128-146.

Butz, A. R. (1971, April) 'Alternative algorithm for Hilbert's space-filling curve', *IEEE Transactions on Computers, C-20*, 424-426.

Butz, A., Bauss, J. & Kruger, A. (2000) 'Different views on location awareness', [Downloaded file "awareness.ps" from http://www.coli.uni-sb.de/sfb378/1999-2001/publications/butzetal2000d-de.html, on 16 September 2005], 3 pages.

Byrd, T., Cossick, K., and Zmud, R. "A Synthesis of Research on Requirements Analysis and Knowledge

Acquisition Techniques," MIS Quarterly (16:1), 1992, pp. 117-138.

C3 Team. Chrysler Goes to "Extremes". *Distributed Computing*, (October 1998), 24 – 28.

Callon, M. (1986b). Some elements of a sociology of translation: Domestication of the scallops and the fishermen of St Brieuc Bay. In: J. Law (Ed.), *Power, Action and Belie(*pp. 197-233). London: Routledge and Kegan Paul.

Callon, M. (1987). Society in the making: The study of technology as a tool for sociological analysis. In: W. E. Bijker, T. P. Hughes, & T. Pinch (Eds.), *The Social Construction of Technological Systems(*pp. 83-103). London: The MIT Press.

Callon, M. (1996a). The Sociology of an actor–network: The case of the electric vehicle. In: M. Callon, J. Law, and A. Rip (Eds.), *Mapping the Dynamics of Science and Technology: Sociology of Science in the Real World(*pp.19-34). London: Macmillan.

Callon, M., & Latour, B. (1981). Unscrewing the big leviathan. In: K. Knorr-Cetina & A.V. Cicourel (Eds.), *Advances in Social Theory and Methodology(*pp. 277-303). London: Routledge & Kegan.

Campbell, A. E., & Shapiro, S. C. (1995). *Ontological mediation: An overview.* Paper presented at the IJCAI Workshop on Basic Ontological Issues in Knowledge Sharing.

Canal, C., Fuentes, L., Pimentel, E., Troya, J.M. & Vallecillo, A. , (2003). Adding Roles to CORBA Objects, *IEEE Trans. Software Eng.*, 29(3): 242-260, March.

Carroll, N. L., & Calvo, R. A. (2004, July 5). Querying data from distributed heterogeneous database systems through Web services. *Proceedings of the Tenth Australian World Wide Web Conference* (AUSWEB 04). Retrieved from http://ausweb.scu.edu.au/aw04/papers/refereed/carroll/

Cary, M. (2001) 'Towards optimal ε-approximate nearest neighbor algorithms', *Journal of Algorithms*, 41(2), 417-428.

Casati, F., & Shan, M. (2001). Models and languages for describing and discovering e-services (tutorial). *In Proceedings of ACM Sigmod International Conference on Management of Data.* Santa Barbara, Calif., USA.

Casati, F., Ilnicki, S., Jin, L., Krishnamoorthy, V., & Shan, M.-C. (2000, June). Adaptive and dynamic service composition in eFlow. *In CAISE conf. (p. 13-31).* Stockholm, Sweden.

Ceri, S., & Widom, J. (1993). Managing Semantic Heterogeneity with Production Rules and Persistent Queues. *Proceedings of the 19th International Conference on Very Large Data Bases,* pp. 108-119.

Chae, B., & Lanzara, G..F. (2006). Self-destructive dynamics in large-scale techno-change and some ways of counteracting it. *Information Technology and People,* 19(1), pp. 74-97.

Chailloux, E. Manoury, P. & Pagano, B. (2000). *Développement d'Applications avec Objectif Caml.* France. O'REILLY.

Chakrabarti K., & Garofalakis M. (2000). Approximate Query processing Using Wavelets, Proceedings of the 26th VLDB Conference, pp 111-122.

Chakraborty, S. (2004). *Web mining.* Elsevier.

Chamberlin, D., Florescu, D., Melton, J., Robie, J., & Siméon, J. (2008, February). *XQuery Update*

Chan, H., Siau, K., & Wei, K. (1998). The effect of data model, system and task characteristics on user query performance—An empirical study. *The DATA BASE for Advances in Information Systems, 29*(1), 31-49.

Chan, H., Wei, K., & Siau, K. (1997). A system for query comprehension. *Information and Software Technology, 39,* 141-148.

Chan, S. and Lammers, T. Reusing Distributed Object Domain Framework, 5th Intl. Conf. on Software Reuse, June 2-5, 1998, Victoria, BC, pp. 216-223.

Chang, A. "Work Time Model for Engineers", Journal of Construction Engineering Management (127:2), 2001, pp. 163-172.

Chang, A. and Chiu, S-H. "Nature of Engineering Consulting Projects", Journal of Management in Engineering (21:4), 2005, pp. 179-188.

Chang, A. and Ibbs, W. "System Model for Analyzing Design Productivity", Journal of Management in Engineering (22:1), 2006, pp. 27-34.

Chang, A., and Tien, C. "Quantifying Uncertainty and Equivocality in Engineering Projects," Construction Management & Economics (24:2), 2006, pp. 171-184.

Chang, K. C.-C., He, B., & Zhang, Z. (2005). *Toward large scale integration: Building a MetaQuerier over databases on the Web.* Paper presented at the CIDR.

Chan-Olmsted & Kang. (2003). Theorizing the strategic architecture of a broadband television industry. *Journal of Media Economics*, 16(1), pp. 3-21.

Chao, C-M., Tseng, Y-C., & Wang, L-C. (2005) 'Dynamic bandwidth allocation for multimedia traffic with rate guarantee and fair access in WCDMA systems', *IEEE Transactions on Mobile Computing*, 4(5), 420-429.

Chaudhuri, S., & Shim, K. (1994). Including group-by in query optimization. In *Proceedings of the 20th International Conference on Vary Large* Databases (pp. 354-366), Santiago, Chile.

Chavez, E., Navarro, G., Baeza-Yates, R. and J. Marroquin. (2001). "Searching in metric spaces." ACM Computing Surveys. 33 (3): 273-321.

Chen Z., & Chen L., et al. (2003). Recent Progress on Selected Topics in Database Research, J Computer Science & Technology, 18(5), pp 538-552.

Chen, L., Gupta, A., & Kurul, E. M. (2005). Efficient algorithms for pattern matching on directed acyclic graphs. In *Proceedings of the IEEE ICDE*, (pp. 384-395).

Chen, Q., Hsu, M., & Mehta, V. (2003). How public conversation management integrated with local business process management. *Proceedings of the IEEE International Conference on E-Commerce, CEC 2003* (pp. 199-206).

Chen, Y. & Miao, H. (2004). From an Abstract Object-Z Specification to UML Diagram. *Journal of Information & Computational Science*, 1(2).

Chen, Y., Davidson, S.B., & Zheng, Y. (2002). Constraint Preserving XML Storage in Relations. *International Workshop on the Web and Databases.*

Chen, Y., Davidson, S.B., & Zheng, Y. (2002). XKvalidator: A Constraint Validator for XML. *Proceedings of ACM Conference on Information and Knowledge Management.*

Chen, Y., Davidson, S.B., Hara, C.S., & Zheng, Y. (2003). RRXF: Redundancy Reducing XML Storage in Relations. *Proceedings of the International Conference on Very Large Databases.*

Chen, Y., Zhou, L., & Zhang, D. (2006). Ontology-Supported Web Service Composition: An Approach to Service-Oriented Knowledge Management in Corporate Services. *Journal of Database Management, 17*(1), 67-84.

Chen, Y., Zhou, L., & Zhang, D. (2006). Ontology-supported Web service composition: An approach to service-oriented knowledge management in corporate services. *Journal of Database Management, 17*(1), 67-84.

Chengalur-Smith, I., and Duchessi, P. "Client-server Implementation: Some Management Pointers," *IEEE Transaction on Engineering Management* (47:1), 2000, pp 127-145.

Chiticariu, L., Hernández, M. A., Kolaitis, P. G., & Popa, L. 2007. Semi-automatic schema integration in Clio. In *Proceedings of the 33rd international Conference on Very Large Data Bases* (Vienna, Austria, September 23 - 27, 2007)

Chou, C-T. & Shin, K. (2005) 'An enhanced inter-access point protocol for uniform intra and intersubnet handoffs', *IEEE Transactions on Mobile Computing*, 4(4), 321-334.

Choy, M., Kwan, M-P., & Hong, V. (2000) 'Distributed database design for mobile geographical applications', *Journal of Database Management*, 11(1), 3-15.

Christophides, V., Scholl, M., & Tourtonis, S. (2003). On labeling schemes for the semantic Web. *World Wide Web Conference (WWW)*, 544-555.

Chui, C. K., & Lian, J. (1996). A study of orthonormal multiwavelets. *Applied Numerical Mathematics: Transactions of IMACS, 20*(3), 273-298.

Chun, S., Chung, C., & Lee, S. (2004). Space-efficient cubes for OLAP range-sum queries. *Decision Support Systems, 37*, 83-102.

Cinque, M., Cotroneo, D. & Russo, S. (2005) 'Achieving all the time, everywhere access in next-generation mobile networks', *ACM SIGMOBILE Mobile Computing and Communications Review*, 9(2), 29-39.

Clayton, R., Rugaber, S., Taylor, L., and Wills, L. "A Case Study of Domain-Based Program Understanding" in Proceedings of the International Workshop on Program Comprehension, Dearborn, Michigan, May 1997.

Clearsy. (2003). *Atelier B, Manuel de Référence* [Online]. Available: http://www.atelierb.societe.com.

Clearsy. (2004). http://www.b4free.com/.

Coleman, D.M., Ash, D., Lowther, B., and Oman, P.W. "Using Metrics to Evaluate Software System Maintainability," Computer (27:8), August 1994, pp. 44-49.

Coleman, J. S. (1988). Social Capital in the Creation of Human Capital. *American Journal of Sociology, 94*, S95-S120.

Collins, H. M. (1993). The Structure of Knowledge. *Social Research, 60*(1), 95-116.

Computer Associates, Inc. (2006, October 6). *AllFusion Erwin Data Modeler*. Retrieved from http://www3.ca.com/Solutions/Product.asp?ID=260

Consens, M. P., & Mendelzon, A. O. (1990). GraphLog: A visual formalism for real life recursion. *ACM PODS*, 404-416.

Cooper, B.L., Watson, H.J., Wixom, B., and Goodhue, D.L. "Data Warehousing Supports Corporate Strategy at First American Corporation," *MIS Quarterly* (24:4), 2000, pp 547-568.

Cormack G. (1985). Data Compression on a Database System, Communications of the ACM, 28(12), pp 1336 – 1342.

Coughlan, J., and Macredie, R. "Effective Communication in Requirements Elicitation: A Comparison of Methodologies," Requirements Engineering (7), 2002, pp. 47-60.

Cramer, F. (1993). *Chaos and Order*. New York: VCH.

Crossan, M. M., Lane, H. W., & White, R. E. (1999). An Organization Learning Framework: From Intuition to Institution. *Academy of Management Review, 24*(3), 522-537.

Crowston, K., & Howison, J. (2005). The social structure of free and open source software development. *First Monday, 10*(2).

Cunningham C., Song I., & Chen P. (2006) Data Warehouse Design to Support Customer Relationship Management Analyses, Journal of Database Management, Hershey, 17(2), pp 62-84.

Curbera, F., Khalef, R., Mukhi, N., Tai, S., & Weerawarana, S. (2003, October). The next step in Web services. *Communications of the ACM, 46*(10), 29-34.

Daft, R. and Weick, K. "Toward a model of organizations as interpretation systems", Academy of Management Review (9:2), 1984, pp. 284-295.

Daft, R., and Lengel, R. "Organizational Information Requirements, Media Richness and Structural Design," Management Science (32:5), 1986, pp. 554-571.

Daft, R., and Macintosh, N. "A Tentative Exploration into the Amount and Equivocality of Information Processing in Organizational Work Units," Administrative Science Quarterly (26:2), 1981, pp. 207-224.

Daft, R.L. "A Dual-core Model of Organizational Innovation," *Academy of Management Journal* (21:2), 1978, pp 193-210.

Damanpour, F., and Gopalakrishnan, S. "Theories of Organizational Structure and Innovation Adoption: The

Role of Environmental Change," *Journal of Engineering and Technology Management* (15:1), 1998, pp 1-24.

Daubechies, I. (1992). *Ten lectures on wavelets.* Capital City Press.

Davenport, T.H. "The Future of Enterprise System-enabled Organizations," *Information Systems Frontiers* (2:2), 2000a, pp 163-180.

Davenport, T.H. *Mission Critical: Realizing The Promise of Enterprise Systems* Harvard Business School Press, Boston, Massachusetts, 2000b.

Davies, J., Duke, A., & Stonkus, A. (2002). *OntoShare: Using ontologies for knowledge sharing.* Paper presented at the Semantic Web Workshop of the WWW Conference, Hawaii, HI.

Davis, G. "Strategies for Information Requirements Determination," IBM Systems Journal (21:1), 1982, pp. 4-30.

DeHondt, G. and Brandyberry, A. "Programming in the eXtreme: Critical Characteristics of Agile Implementations," e-Informatica Software Engineering Journal (1:1), February 2007, pp. 43-58.

DeSanctis, G., and Poole, M.S. "Capturing the Complexity in Advanced Technology: Adaptive Structuration Model," *Organization Science* (5:2), 1994, pp 121-147.

Dispensa, J. M., & Brulle, R. J. (2003). The Sprawling Frontier: Politics of Watershed Management. *Submitted to Rural Sociology.*

Doan, A., Domingos, P., & Halevy, A. Y. (2003). Learning to match the schemas of data sources: A multistrategy approach. *Machine Learning, 50*(3), 279-301.

Dooley, K. (1997). A complex adaptive systems model of organization change. *Nonlinear Dynamics, Psychology, & Life Science*, 1(1), pp. 69-97.

Dorogovtsev, S. N., & Mendes, J. F. F. (2003). *Evolution of networks: From biological nets to the Internet and WWW.* UK: Oxford University Press.

Due, R. "The Economics of Component-Based Development," Information Systems Management (17:1), Winter 2000, pp. 92-95.

Duggan, D. J., Chen, M., Meltzer, P., & Trent, J. (1999). Expression profiling using cDNA microarrays. *Nature Genetics, 21,* 10-14.

Duggan, E. "Generating Systems Requirements with Facilitated Group Techniques," Human-Computer Interaction (18), 2003, pp. 373-394.

Duncan, R. B., & Weiss, A. (1979). Organizational Learning: Implications for Organizational Design. In B. M. Staw (Ed.), *Research in Organizational Behavior* (Vol. 1, pp. 75-123). Greenwich, CT: JAI Press.

Duncan, R.B. "The Ambidextrous Organizations: Designing Dual Structures for Innovation," in: *The Management of Organization: Strategy and Implementation,* R.H. Kilmann, L.R. Pondy and D.P. Slevin (eds.), North-Holland, New York, 1976, pp. 167-188.

Dunwoodie, B. (2004, June 19). Gartner Dataquest. As cited in: Column Two: Enterprise Content Management Market Share. [Online]. Available: http://www.steptwo.com.au/columntwo/archives/001304.html.

Dupuy, S., Ledru, Y. & Chabre-Peccoud, M. (2000). An Overview of RoZ: A Tool for Integrating UML and Z Specifications. In: B. Wangler and L. Bergman (Eds.), *12th International Conference Advanced Information Systems Engineering (*pp. 417–430*),* Vol. 1789 of *LNCS*, Springer-Verlag.

EC(1997). *Council Directive 97/36/EC of the European Parliament and of the Council of 30 June 1997 amending Directive 89/552/EEC on the coordination of certain provisions laid down by law, regulation or administrative action in Member States concerning the pursuit of television broadcasting activities.* (Official Journal of the European Communities, L202 60, pp.1-25), Brussels, Belgium.

Edmond, D. (1995). Refining Database Systems. In: J.P. Bowen and M.G. Hinchey (Eds.), *The Z Formal*

Specification Notation (pp. 25–44), Vol. 967 of *LNCS*, Springer-Verlag.

Egelhoff, W. "Information-processing theory and the multinational corporation", in *Organization Theory and the Multinational Corporation*, 2nd edition, Ghoshal, S. and Westney, E. editors, 2005.

Eisenhardt, K.M. (1989). Building theories from case study research. *Academy of Management Review*, 14(4), pp.532-550.

Eisenhardt, K.M. "Building Theories from Case Study Research," *Academy of Management Review* (14:4), 1989, pp 532-550.

Elias P. (1975). Universal Codeword Sets and Representations of the Integers, IEEE Transactions on Information Theory, 21(2), pp 194-203.

Elmasri R., & Navathe S. (2003). Fundamentals of Database Systems, Addison Wesley.

Elmasri, R. & Navathe, S. (2004). *Fundamental of Database Systems.* Addison-Wesley, 4th *edition.*

EML. *Ecological Metadata Language.* http://knb.ecoinformatics.org/software/eml/

Erickson, J., Lyytinen, K., & Siau, K. (2005). Agile modeling, agile software development, and extreme programming: The state of research. *Journal of Database Management, 16*(4), 88-100.

Erl, T. (2005). Service-oriented architecture: Concepts, technology, and design. Upper Saddle River, NJ: Prentice Hall.

Estrada-Gil, J. K., Fernandez-Lopez, J. C., Hernandez-Lemus, E., Silva-Zolezzi, I., Hildalgo-Miranda, A., Jimenez-Sanchez, G., et al. (2007). GPDTI: A Genetic Programming Decision Tree Induction method to find epistatic effects in common complex diseases. *Bioinformatics, 23*(13), 167-174.

Evermann, J., & Wand, Y. (2001, November 27-30). *Towards ontologically based semantics for UML constructs.* Paper presented at the 20th International Conference on Conceptual Modeling, Yokohama, Japan.

Facility 1.0, W3C Working Draft. [online]. Available : http://www.w3.org/TR/xquery-update-10/

Fan, W. (2005). XML Constraints: Specification, Analysis, and Applications. *Proceedings of the 16th International Workshop on Database and Expert Systems Applications*

Fankhauser, P., Kracker, M., & Neuhold, E. J. (1991). Semantic vs. structural resemblance of classes. *SIGMOD Record, 20*(4), 59-63.

Faraj, S., Kwon, D., & Watts, S. (2004). Contested artifact: Technology sense-making, actor networks, and the shaping of the web browser. *Information Technology and People*, 17(2), pp.186-209.

Fazlollahi, B., and Tanniru, M. "Selecting a Requirement Determination Methodology-Contingency Approach Revisited," Information and Management (21:5), 1991, pp. 291-303.

Felson, R. B. (2002). *Violence and Gender Re-examined.* Washington D.C.: The American Psychological Association.

Felson, R. B., Messner, S. F., & Hoskin, A. (1999). The Victim-Offender Relationship And Calling The Police in Assaults. *Criminology, 37*(4), 931-947.

Felson, R., Messner, S. F., Hoskin, A. W., & Deane, G. (2002). Reasons for Reporting and Not Reporting Domestic Violence to the Police. *Criminology, 40*(3), 617-650.

Fensel, D. (2003). *Ontologies: A silver bullet for knowledge management and electronic commerce.* Springer Verlag.

Fensel, D., Harmelen, F. van, Horrocks, I., McGuinness, D., & Patel-Schneider, P. (2001, March-April). OIL: An ontology infrastructure for the semantic Web. *IEEE Intelligent Systems*, 16(2).

Fenton, N. E. (1994). Software measurement: a necessary scientific basis. *IEEE Transactions on Software Engineering, 20*(3), 199-206.

Fernandez, M., & Siméon, J. (2003) .Growing XQuery. European Conference on Object Oriented Programming (ECOOP).

Fernandez, M., Florescu, D., Kang, J., Levy, A., & Suciu, D. (1998, June). Catching the boat with strudel: Experience with a Web-site management system. . *In Proceedings of ACM Sigmod International Conference on Management of Data*. Seattle, Washington, USA.

Fettke, P., & Loos, P. (2003). *Ontological evaluation of reference models using the Bunge-Wand-Weber model.* Paper presented at the Ninth Americas Conference on Information Systems, Tampa, FL.

Fichman, R.G. "The Diffusion and Assimilation of Information Technology Innovations," in: *Framing The Domains of IT Management: Projecting the Future. Through The Past,* R.W. Zmud and M.F. Price (eds.), Pinnaflex Educational Resources, Inc., Cincinnati, Ohio, 2000, pp. 105-127.

Fikes, R., & Farquhar, A. (1999). Distributed repositories of highly expressive reusable ontologies. *IEEE Intelligent Systems, 14*(2), 73-79.

Finkelhor, D., & Ormrod, R. K. (2001). Factors in the Underreporting of Crimes Against Juveniles. *Child Maltreatment, 6*(3), 219-229.

Finkelhor, D., & Wolak, J. (2003). Reporting Assaults Against Juveniles to the Police: Barriers and Catalysts. *Journal of Interpersonal Violence, 18*(2), 103-128.

Finkelstein, L. (1984). A review of the fundamental concepts of measurement. *Measurement, 2*(1), 25-34.

Fiol, C. M., & Lyles, M., A. (1985). Organizational Learning. *Academy of Management Review, 10*(4), 803-813.

Firouzi, F., Rashidi, M., Hashemi, S., Kangavari, M., Bahari, A., Daryani, N. E., et al. (2007). A decision tree-based approach for determining low bone mineral density in inflammatory bowel disease using WEKA software. *European Journal of Gastroenterology and Hepatology, 19*(12), 1075-1081.

Fisher, M., Ellis, J., & Bruce, J. (2003). *JDBC API Tutorial and Reference.* Addison-Wesley Pub Co.

Florescu, D., Levy, A., & Mendelzon, A. (1998, September). Database techniques for the World Wide Web: A survey. *In Proceeedings of ACM Sigmod International Conference on Management of Data,* 27(3).

Fong, J. & Wong, K. (2004). XTOPO: An XML-Based Topology for Information Highway on the Internet. *Journal of Database Management*, 15(3), 18-44.

Fong, J., Karlapalem, K., Li, Q., & Kwan, I. (1999). Methodology of schema integration for new database applications: A practitioner's approach. *Journal of Database Management, 10*(1), 3-18.

Fowler, M. Analysis Patterns: Reusable Object Models, Massachusetts, Addison-Wesley, 1997.

Fowler, M. Refactoring: Improving the Design of Existing Programs, Addison-Wesley, 1999.

Fox, M. S. (1992). The TOVE project, towards a common sense model of the enterprise. In C. Petrie (Ed.), *Enterprise integration*. Cambridge, MA: MIT Press.

Fox, M. S., & Gruninger, M. (1998). Enterprise modelling. *AI Magazine, 19*(3), 109-121.

Franklin, S., & Graesser, A. (1996). *Is it an agent, or just a program? A taxonomy for autonomous agents.* Paper presented at the Third International Workshop on Agent Theories, Architectures, and Languages.

*Freeman, L. C. (*2004). *The development of social network analysis: A study in the sociology of science.* Vancouver, Canada: Empirical Press.

Friedman, M., Levy, A., & Millstein, T. (1999). *Navigational plans for data integration.* Paper presented at the AAAI/IAAI.

Frohmann, B.(1995, Jun 7). Taking information policy beyond information science: Applying the actor network theory. [Online]. Available: http://www.cais-acsi.ca/proceedings/1995/frohmann_1995.pdf

Furtado, P. (2006). Node partitioned data warehouses. *Journal of Database Management, 17*(2), 43-61.

Gacek, C., & Arief, B. (2004). The many meanings of open source. *IEEE Software, 21*(1), 34-40.

Gaede, V. and O. Gunther. (1998). "Multidimensional Access Methods." ACM Computing Surveys. 30 (2): 170-231.

Galbraith, J. "Organization design: an information processing view", Interfaces (4:3), 1974, pp. 28-36.

Galbraith, J. *Organization Design.* Addison-Wesley, Reading, MA, 1977.

Gall, H., Klosch, R., & Mittermeir, R. (1995). Object-oriented re-architecturing. *Proceedings of the 5th European Software Engineering Conference (ESEC '95).*

Gandon, F. (2001, October 22-24). *Engineering an ontology for a multi-agents corporate memory system.* Paper presented at the ISMICK 2001 Eighth International Symposium on the Management of Industrial and Corporate Knowledge, Université de Technologie de Compiègne, France.

Gandon, F. L., & Sadeh, N. M. (2004). Semantic Web technologies to reconcile privacy and context awareness. *Journal of Web Semantics, 1*(3), 241-260.

Gap between wired and wireless enlarging. (2006, Oct. 18.). *Electronic Times.*

Garcia-Molina, H., Papakonstantinou, Y., Quass, D., Rajaraman, A., Sagiv, Y., Ullman, J., Vassalos, V., & Widom, J., (1997). The TSIMMIS Approach to Mediation: Data Models and Languages J. *Intelligent Information Systems*, 8(2): 117-132.

Gardarin, G., Mensch, A., Tuyet, T., & Smit, D.L.(2002). Integrating Heterogeneous Data Sources with XML and XQuery. *Proceedings of the 13th International Workshop on Database and Expert Systems Applications.*

Garofalakis M., & Gibbons P. (2004). Probabilistic wavelet synopses, ACM Transactions on Database Systems, 29(1), pp 43-90.

Gebauer, J. & Shaw, M. (2004) 'Success factors and impacts of mobile business applications: results from a mobile e-procurement study', *International Journal of Electronic Commerce*, 8(3), 19-41.

Gemulla R., Lehner W., & Haas P.J., (2007), Maintaining bounded-size sample synopses of evolving datasets, VLDB Journal, Special Issue, 2007.

Georgakopoulos, D., Karabatis, G., & Gantimahapatruni, S. (1997). Specification and management of interdependent data in operational systems and data warehouses. *Distributed and Parallel Databases, An International Journal, 5*(2), 121-166.

Gibson, C.F., and Nolan, R.L. "Managing the Four Stages of EDP Growth," *Harvard Business Review* (40:1), 1974, pp 76-88.

Giddens, A. *Problems of Action and Structure* Stanford University Press, 1993.

Giddens, A. *The Constitution of Society: Outline of the Theory of Structure* University of California Press, Berkeley, CA, 1984.

Gilb, T. (1987). *Principles of Software Engineering Management.* Reading, MA: Addison-Wesley.

Girardi, M.R. and Ibrahim, B. "Using English to Retrieve Software," Journal of Systems and Software (30:3), September 1995, pp. 249-270.

Glaser, B. G., & Strauss, Anselm L., (1967). *The Discovery of Grounded Theory: Strategies for Qualitative Research*, Chicago, Aldine Publishing Company

Goh, C. H., Bressan, S., Madnick, S., & Siegel, M. (1999). Context interchange: New features and formalisms for the intelligent integration of information. *ACM Transactions on Information Systems, 17*(3), 270-293.

Goodhue, D.L., Wixom, B., and Waston, H.J. "Data Warehousing and Organizational Change at the IRS: Increasing Compliance Without Taxpayer Audits," in: *Annals of Cases on Information Technology Applications and Management in Organizations*, Idea Group Publishing, Hershey, Pennsylvania, 1999.

Goswami, J. C., & Chan, A. K. (1999). *Fundamentals of wavelets: Theory, algorithms and applications*: John Wiley.

Grady, J. O. (1993). *System requirements analysis*: McGraw-Hill Inc.

Grant, R. M. (1996). Prospering in Dynamically-competitive Environments: Organizational Capability as Knowledge Integration. *Organization Science, 7*(4), 375.

Grant, R. M. (1996). Toward a Knowledge-Based Theory of the Firm. *Strategic Management Journal, 17*, 109-122.

Gray, J., Chaudhuri, S., Bosworth, A., Layman, D., Reichart, D., & Venkatrao, M. (1997). Data cube: A relational aggregation operator generalizing group-by, cross-tab, and sub-totals. *Data Mining and Knowledge Discovery, 1*(1), 29-53.

Gray, P., & Watson, H.J. (1998). *Decision support in the data warehouse.* Data Warehousing Institute Series, Prentice Hall.

Green, G. I. (1989). Perceived Importance of Systems Analysts' Job Skills, Roles, and Non-Salary Incentives. *MIS Quarterly, 13*(13), 2.

Green, P., & Rosemann, M. (2000). Integrated process modeling: an ontological evaluation. *Information Systems, 25*(2), 73-87.

Green, P., & Rosemann, M. (2004). Applying ontologies to business and systems modelling techniques and perspectives: Lessons learned. *Journal of Database Management, 15*(2), 105-117.

Grefen, P. & Widom, J. (1997). Protocols for integrity Constraint Checking in Federated Databases. *International Journal of Distributed and Parallel Databases,* 5(4): 327-355.

Grefen, P., & Apers, P. (1993). Integrity Control in Relational Database Systems - An Overview. *Journal of Data and Knowledge Engineering,* 10 (2), pp. 187-223.

Gribble, C. (2003, November). *History of the Web: Beginning at CERN.* [Online]. Available: http://www.hitmill.com/internet/webhistory.asp.

Griffith, T.L., and Northcraft, G.B. "Cognitive Elements in the Implementation of New Technology: Can Less Information Provide More Benefits?" *MIS Quarterly* (20:1), 1996, pp 99-110.

Grover, R. (1998). *Identification of factors affecting the implementation of data warehouse.* Unpublished doctoral dissertation, Auburn University, Alabama.

Grover, V., and Goslar, M.D. "The Initiation, Adoption, and Implementation of Telecommunications Technologies in U.S. Organizations," *Journal of Management Information Systems* (10:1), 1993, pp 141-163.

Gruber, T. R. (1993). A translation approach to portable ontology specifications. *Knowledge Aquisition,* 5(1), 199-220.

Gruber, T. R. (1993, March). *Towards principles for the design of pntologies used for knowledge sharing.* Paper presented at the International Workshop on Formal Ontology, Padova, Italy.

Gruber, T. R., & Olsen, G. R. (1994). *An ontology for engineering mathematics.* Paper presented at the Fourth International Conference on Principles of Knowledge Representation and Reasoning, Bonn, Germany.

Grufman, S., Samson, F., Embury, S.M., Gray, P.M.D., & Risch, T. (1997). Distributing Semantic Constraints Between Heterogeneous Databases. *Proceedings of International Conference on Data Engineering*

Gruninger, M., & Fox, M. S. (1995). *Methodology for the design and evaluation of ontologies.* Paper presented at the Workshop on Basic Ontological Issues in Knowledge Sharing, IJCAI-95, Montreal, Canada.

Guimaraes, T. "Managing Application Program Maintenance Expenditure," Communications of the ACM (26:10), October 1983, pp. 739-746.

Guinan, P., and Bostrom, R. "Development of Computer-Based Information Systems: A Communication Framework," The DATA BASE for Advances in Information Systems (17:3), 1986, pp. 3-16.

Gunther, T., Schewe, K. D. & Wetzel, I. (1993). On the Derivation of Executable Database Programs from Formal Specifications. In: J. C. P. Woodcock & P. G. Larsen (Eds.), *Industrial-Strength Formal Methods, First International Symposium of Formal Methods Europe* (pp. 351–366), Vol. 670 of *LNCS*, Springer-Verlag.

Gupta, A., & Widom, J. (1993). Local Verification of Global Integrity Constraints in Distributed Databases. *Proceedings of the ACM SIGMOD Conference on Management of Data.*

Gupta, A., Harinarayan, V., & Quass D. (1995). *Generalized projections: A powerful approach to aggregation.* Paper presented at the 21st International Conference on Very Large Databases (pp. 358-369), Zurich, Switzerland.

Gupta, H., & Mumick, I.S. (2005). Selection of views to materialize in a data warehouse. *IEEE Transaction on Data and Knowledge Engineering, 17*(1), 24-43.

Gutiérrez, A., Pucheral, P., Steffen, H., & Thévenin, J. M. (1994). Database graph views: A practical model to manage persistent graphs. *Twentieth VLDB Conference.*

Gutierrez, J., & Leroy, G. (2007, August 9, 2007). *Predicting Crime Reporting with Decision Trees and the National Crime Victimization Survey.* Paper presented at the Americas' Conference on Information Systems, Keystone, CO.

Guting, R. (1994). *GraphDB: A Data Model and Query Language for Graphs in Databases. Proc.VLDB.*

Guyon, I., & Elisseeff, A. (2003). An Introduction to Variable and Feature Selection. *Journal of Machine Learning, 3*, 1157-1182.

Ha, L.Q., Sicilia-Garcia, E.I., Ming, J. & Smith, F.J. (2002). Extension of Zipf's Law to Words and Phrases. *Proceedings of 19th International Conference on Computational Linguistics, Vol. 1.* Taipei, Taiwan, (pp. 1-6).

Haag, S., Cummings, M., & McCubbrey, D. (2005). *Management information systems for the information age.* McGraw-Hill Irwin.

Halevy, A. Y., Ives, Z. G., Suciu, D., & Tatarinov, I. (2003). *Schema mediation in peer data management systems.* Paper presented at the ICDE.

Hall, A.(1990). Using Z as a Specification Calculus for Object-Oriented Systems. In: D. Bjõrner, C. A. R. Hoare & H. Langmaack (Eds.). *VDM'90: 3rd International Conference, Kiel, Germany* (pp. 290-318), Vol. 428 of *LNCS*, Springer-Verlag.

Hammad, A., Tatibouet, B., Voisinet, J.C. & Weiping, W. (2002). From a B Specification to UML Statechart Diagrams. In: C. George & H. Miao (Eds.), *4th International Conference on Formal Engineering Methods (*pp. 511–522*)*, Vol. 2495 of *LNCS*, Springer-Verlag.

Han, J. (1998). *Towards on-line analytical mining in large databases.* Paper presented at the ACM SIGMOD.

Han, J., & Kamber, M. (2000). *Data Mining: Concepts and Techniques*: Morgan Kaufmann.

Han, J., & Kamber, M. (2001). *Data mining: Concepts and techniques.* San Francisco: Morgan Kaufmann.

Han, J., Chee, S., & Chiang, J. (1998). *Issues for on-line analytical mining of data warehouses.* Paper presented at the Proceedings of 1998 SIGMOD'96 Workshop on Research Issues on Data Mining and Knowledge Discovery DMKD, Seattle, Washington.

Hann, H., Robert, J., & Slaughter, S. (2004). Why developers participate in open source software projects: An empirical investigation. In *Twenty-Fifth International Conference on Information Systems*, (pp. 821-830). Washington, DC: .

Hannay, J. E., Sjoberg, D. I. K., & Dyba, T. (2007). A Systematic Review of Theory Use in Software Engineering Experiments. *IEEE Transactions on Software Engineering, 33*(2), 87-107.

Hanneman, R. A. (2001). *Introduction to social network method.* Online textbook.

Harel, D. (1987). Statecharts: A Visual Formalism for Complex Systems. *Science of Computer Programming,* 8(3), 231–274.

Harinarayan, V., Rajaraman, A., & Ullman, J.D. (1996). Implementing data cubes efficiently. In *Proceedings of the ACM-SIGMOD International Conference on Management of Data* (pp. 205-216), Montreal, Canada.

Harinarayan, V., Rajaraman, A., & Ullman, J.D. (1999). Implementing data cubes efficiently. In A. Gupta & I. Mumick (Eds.), *Materialized views: Techniques, implementation and applications* (pp. 343-360). MIT Press.

Hayes, P. J. (1985). Naive physics I: Ontology for liquids. In J. Hobbs & B. Moore (Eds.), *Theories of the commonsense world* (pp. 71-89). Ablex Publishing Corp.

Hayley, B.J., Watson, H.J., and Goodhue, D.L. "The Benefits of Data Warehousing at Whirlpool," in: *Annals of Cases on Information Technology Applications and Management in Organizations*, Idea Group Publishing, Hershey, Pennslyvania, 1999.

Heflin, J. (2000, April 3, 2000). Measurement ontology 1.0 (draft). Retrieved August 15, 2004, from http://www.cs.umd.edu/projects/plus/SHOE/onts/measure1.0.html

Hellerstein J.M., Haas P.J., & Wang H.J. (1997), Online Aggregation, Proc. of the 1997 ACM SIGMOD Intl. Conf. on Management of Data, pp 171-182.

Hemetsberger, A. (2004). Sharing and creating knowledge in open-source communities: The case of KDE. *The Fifth European Conference on Organizational Knowledge, Learning, and Capabilities in Innsbruck, Austria.*

Henderson, J.C., and Treacy, M.E. "Managing End User Computing for Competitive Advantage," *Sloan Management Review* (50:4), 1986, pp 37-46.

Henning, M., & Vinoski, S. (1999). *Advanced CORBA programming with C++*. Addison-Wesley Publishing Corporation.

Herzum, P., & Sims, O. (1998). The business component approach. *Proceedings of OOPSLA'98 Business Object Workshop IV.*

Heuvel, W. V. D., Hillegersberg, J. V., & Papazoglou, M. (2002). A methodology to support Web-services development using legacy systems. *IFIP Conference Proceedings; Vol. 231, Proceedings of the IFIP TC8 / WG8.1 Working Conference on Engineering Information Systems in the Internet Context* (pp. 81-103).

Hewett, M., Oliver, D. E., Rubin, D. L., Easton, K. L., Stuart, J. M., Altman, R. B., *et al.* (2002). PharmGKB: the pharmaco-genetics knowledge base. *Nucleic Acids Research, 30*(1), 163-165.

Hickey, A., and Davis, A. "A Tale of Two Ontologies: The Basis for Systems Analysis Technique Selection," Proceedings of the Ninth Americas Conference on Information Systems), 2003.

Hickey, A., and Davis, A. "A Unified Model of Requirements Elicitation," Journal of Management Information Systems (20:4), 2004, pp. 65-84.

Highsmith, J. (2003). Agile Project Management: Principles and Tools. *Agile Project Management Advisory Service, 4*(2), 37.

Highsmith, Jim. Agile Software Development Ecosystems. Boston, Massachusetts: Addison-Wesley, 2002.

Hillard, R., Blecher, P., & O'Donnell, P.A. (1999). The implications of chaos theory on the management of a data warehouse. In *Proceedings of the 5th conference of the International Society of Decision Support Systems*, Melbourne, Australia

Ho C., & Agrawal R. (1997). Range Queries in OLAP data cubes, Proceedings of the 1997 ACM SIGMOD Conference on Management of Data, pp 73-88.

Hoffer, J., George, J., and Valacich, J. Modern Systems Analysis and Design. Boston, Massachusetts: Addison-Wesley, 1998.

Holland, J.H. (1988). The global economy as an adaptive system. In Anderson, P.W., Arrow, K.J. and Pines, D. (Eds), *The Economy as an Evolving Complex System (*Vol. 5, pp. 117-24) . Reading: Addison-Wesley.

Holland, J.H. (1995). *Hidden Order.* Reading: Addison-Wesley..

Holland, P. W., & Leinhardt, S. (1979). *Perspectives on social network research.* Academic Press.

Horvath & Maldoom(2002). Fixed-mobile substitution: a simultaneous equation model with qualitative and limited dependent variables. [Online]. Available: DotEcon Discussion Papers, DP 02/02, WWW.dotecon.com., London. pp.1-25.

Huang, L.-T., Gromiha, M., & Ho, S.-Y. (2007). iP-TREE-STAB: interpretable decision tree based method for predicting protein stability changes upon mutations. *Bioinformatics, 23*(10), 1292-1293.

Huang, S. M., & Yu, F. Y. (2004). IFBP: A methodology for business process discovery based on information flow. *Journal of Information Management, 11*(3), 55-78.

Huang, S. M., Hung, S. Y., Yen, D., Li, S. H., & Wu, C. J. (2006). Enterprise application system reengineering: A business component approach. *Journal of Database Management, 17*(3), 66-91.

Huang, S.-M., Lin, B., & Deng, Q.-S. (2005). Intelligent cache management for mobile data warehouse. *Journal of Database Management, 16*(2), 46-65.

Huber, G. P. (1991). Organizational Learning: The Contributing Processes and the Literatures. *Organization Science, 2*(1), 88-115.

Huff, A., Stimpert, L., and Huff, J. "Enterpreneural Activity and Industry Structuring," *Organization Science* (3:3), 1994, pp 398-427.

Huhns, M. N., & Singh, M. P. (1998). Workflow agent. *IEEE Internet Computing, 2*(4), 94-96.

Huhns, M. N., & Stephens, L. M. (2001). Automating supply chains. *IEEE Internet Computing, 5*(4), 90 -93.

Hunt J., Vo K.-P., & Tichy W. F., (1998). Delta algorithms: An empirical analysis. ACM Trans. Softw. Eng. Method. 7, 2, pp 192–214.

Hyperion. The Hyperion Project. http://www.cs.toronto.edu/db/hyperion/

IBM, BEA Systems, Microsoft, SAP AG, & Siebel Systems (2002, July 30). *Business Process Execution Language for Web Services, Version 1.1.* Retrieved from http://www-128.ibm.com/developerworks/library/specification/ws-bpel/

IBM. (2005, September). *Informix Tools.* [Online]. Available: http://www-306.ibm.com/software/data/informix/.

IBM. (2005, September). *UniSQL database solutions.* [Online]. Available:http://www.unisql.com.

IBM. (2005, September). *WebSphere.* [Online]. Available: http://www-306.ibm.com/software/websphere.

Ibrahim, H. (2002). A Strategy for Semantic Integrity Checking in Distributed Databases. *Proceedings of the ninth International Conference on Parallel and Distributed Systems (ICPADS),* pp. 139-144

Idani, A., Ledru, Y. & Bert, D. (2005). Derivation of UML Class Diagrams as Static Views of Formal B Developments. In K. K. Lau & R. Banach (Eds.), 7th *International Conference on Formal Engineering Methods* (37-51). Vol. 3785 of *LNCS*, Springer-Verlag.

IMPRESS. (1993). *IMPRESS, specification of graph views and graph operators* (Esprit project n°6355), (Tech. Rep. No. W7-005-R75).

ITU (1996), *Regulatory Implications of Telecommunications Convergence.* [Online]. Available: http://www.itu.int/opb/publications.aspx?lang=en&media=electronic&parent=S-GEN-COL6-1996.

Iversen, J., Mathiassen, L. and Nielsen. "Managing Risk in Software Process Improvement: An Action Research Approach", MIS Quarterly (28:3), 2004, pp. 395-433.

Jacobson, R. (2000). *Microsoft SQL server 2000 analysis services: Step by step.* Microsoft Press.

Jain, H., & Zhao, H. (2004). *Federating heterogeneous information systems using Web services and ontologies.* Paper presented at the Tenth Americas Conference on Information Systems, New York.

Jennings, N. R., Faratin, P., Johnson, M. J., Norman, T. J., O'Brien, P., & Wiegand, M. E. (1996). Agent-based business process management. *International Journal of Cooperative Information Systems, 2 & 3*, 105-130.

Jennings, N. R., Norman, T. J., Faratin, P., P. O'Brien, & Odgers, B. (2000). Autonomous agents for business process management. *Journal of Applied Artificial Intelligence, 14*(2), 145-189.

Jin, E. M., Girvan, M., & Newman, M. E. J. (2001). The structure of growing social networks. *Phys. Rev.* E 64, 046132.

Jin, Y., Urban, S. D., & Dietrich, S. W. (2006). Extending the OBJECTIVE Benchmark for Evaluation of Active Rules in a Distributed Component Integration Environment. *Journal of Database Management, 17*(4), 47-69.

Johnson, L., and Johnson, N. "Knowledge Elicitation Involving Teachback Interviewing," In Knowledge Acquisition for Expert Systems, A. Kidd (ed.) Plenum Press, New York, NY, 1987, pp. 91-108.

Jones, C. (1990). *Systematic Software Development using VDM.* Prentice Hall.

Jørgensen, N. (2001). Putting it all in a trunk: Incremental software development in the freeBSD open source project. *Information Systems Journal, 11,* 321-336.

Kalfoglou, Y., & Schorlemmer, M. (2003). Ontology mapping: The state of the art. *Knowledge Engineering Review, 18*(1), 1-31.

Kallinikos, J. (2005), "The order of technology: complexity and control in a connected world", Information and Organization, Vol. 15, pp. 185-202.

Kalnis, P., Mamoulis, N., & Papadias, D. (2002). View selection using randomized search. *Data and Knowledge Engineering, 42*, 89-111.

Kane, B., Su, H. & Rundensteiner, E.A. (2002). Consistently Updating XML Documents using Incremental Constraint Check Queries. *Workshop on Web Information and Data Management (WIDM)*, Nov, pp. 1-8.

Kang, L.H (2003), "Small electronic payment service for collaboration and conflicts between financial and telecommunication industry", Finance Research, Vol. 1, No.2, pp. 136-170.

Karabatis, G., Rusinkiewicz, M., & Sheth, A. (1999). Interdependent database systems. In *Management of Heterogeneous and Autonomous Database Systems* (pp. 217-252). San Francisco, CA: Morgan-Kaufmann.

Kashyap, V. (1998). *Information brokering over heterogeneous digital data: A metadata-based approach*, The State University of New Jersey, New Brunswick, NJ, USA.

Katifori, A., Halatsis, C., Lepouras, G., Vassilakis, C., & Giannopoulou, E. (2007). Ontology visualization methods—a survey. *ACM Comput. Surv.* 39, 4, November.

Kauffman, S. (1993). *The Origins of Order: Self-Organization and Selection in Evolution.* Oxford: Oxford University Press.

Kautz, H., Selman, B., & Shah, M. (1997). The hidden Web. *AI Magazine, 18*(2), 27-36.

Keller, R. "Technology-Information Processing Fit and the Performance of R&D Project Groups: A Test of Contingency Theory," The Academy of Management Journal (37:1), 1994, pp. 167-179.

Khatri, V., Ram, S., & Snodgrass, R. T. (2004). Augmenting a conceptual model with geospatiotemporal annotations. *IEEE Transactions on Knowledge and Data Engineering, 16*(11), 1324-1338.

Khungar, S. & Reikki, J. (2005) 'A context based storage system for mobile computing applications', *ACM SIGMOBILE Mobile Computing and Communications Review*, 9(1), 64-68.

Kiely, D. "The Component Edge," Informationweek, No. 677, April 13, 1998, pp. 1A-6A.

Kim, H. M. (1999). *Representing and reasoning about quality using enterprise models.* Unpublished PhD thesis, Department of Industrial Engineering, University of Toronto, Toronto, Ontario, Canada.

Kim, H. M. (2002, January 7-10). *XML-hoo!: A prototype application for intelligent query of XML documents using domain-specific ontologies.* Paper presented at the 35th

Annual Hawaii International Conference on Systems Science (HICSS-35), Hawaii, HI.

Kim, H. M., & Fox, M. S. (2002, January 4-7). *Using enterprise reference models for automated ISO 9000 compliance evaluation.* Paper presented at the 35th Hawaii International Conference on Systems Science (HICSS), Big Island, HI.

Kim, H. M., Fox, M. S., & Grüninger, M. (1999). An ontology for quality management: Enabling quality problem identification and tracing. *BT Technology Journal, 17*(4), 131-139.

Kim, H. M., Sengupta, A., Fox, M. S., & Dalkilic, M. (2007). A measurement ontology generalizable for emerging domain applications on the semantic Web. *Journal of Database Management, 18*(1), 20-42.

Kim, H.S. (2003a). Fair competition analysis of M-commerce development. Research Report 03-16, Seoul: Korea Information Strategy Development Institute(KISDI).

Kim, R.M., & Kaplan, S.M. (2006). Interpreting sociotechnical co-evolution: Applying complex adaptive systems to IS engagement. *Information Technology and People*, 19(1), pp.35-54.

Kim, S. & Carrington, D. (1999). Formalizing the UML class diagram using OBJECT-Z. In: R. France & B. Rumpe (Eds.), *The Unified Modeling Language. Beyond the Standard. Second International Conference* (pp. 83–98). Vol. 1723 of *LNCS*, Springer-Verlag.

Kim, S. (2003b). Prospect of IC-chip based mobile banking. *Payment and Information Technology,* 15(Nov/Dec.), pp.35-74.

Kim, S., H. Eun, Y. Kang, & M. Lee (2006). Developing a convergence portfolio matrix for heterogeneous inter-industry convergence. *Telecommunications Review,* 16(1), pp. 82-89.

Kim, Y. and Stohr, E.A. "Software Reuse: Survey and Research Directions," Journal of Management Information Systems: JMIS (14:4), Spring 1998, pp. 113-147.

Kimball, R. (2002). *The data warehouse toolkit* (2nd ed.).

King, J.L., and Teo, T.S.H. "Integration between Business Planning and Information Systems Planning: Validating Stage Hypothesis," *Decision Sciences* (28:2), 1997, pp 279-309.

Kishore, R., Sharman, R., & Ramesh, R. (2004). Computational ontologies and information systems I: Foundations. *Communications of the Association for Information Systems, 14*(8), 158-183.

Kishore, R., Zhang, H., & Ramesh, R. (2004). A helix-spindle model for ontological engineering. *Communications of the ACM, 47*(2), 69-75.

Kishore, R., Zhang, H., & Ramesh, R. (Forthcoming). Enterprise integration using the agent paradigm: foundations of multiagent-based integrative business information systems. *Decision Support Systems.*

Kleinberg, M. J., Kumar, R., Raghavan, P., Rajagopalan, S., & Tomkins, S. A. (1999). Web as a graph: Measurements, models and methods. In *Proceedings of the International Conference on combinatorics and computing,* (pp. 1-18).

Klischewski, A. R., & Jeenicke, M. (2004). *Semantic Web technologies for information management within e-government services.* Paper presented at the 37th Annual Hawaii International Conference on System Sciences (HICSS'04), Big Island, HI.

Kogut, B., & Zander, U. (1992). Knowledge of the Firm, Combinative Capabilities, and the Replication of Technology. *Organization Science, 3*(3), 383.

Kotter, J.P. "Leading Changes: Why Transformation Efforts Fail," *Harvard Business Review* (73:2), 1995, pp 59-67.

Kottkamp, H-E. & Zukunft, O. (1998) 'Location-aware query processing in mobile database systems', *Proceedings of the 1998 ACM Symposium on Applied Computing,* Atlanta, Georgia, United States, (February 27 - March 1), 416-423.

Kovacs, A. & Ueno, H. (2004). Towards complex adaptive information systems. [Online]. Available: http://www.alexander-kovacs.de/kovacs04icita.pdf

Krebs, V., & Holley, J. (2004). *Building sustainable communities through network building.* Retrieved from http://www.orgnet.com/BuildingNetworks.pdf

KRNIC (2005), *Korean Mobile Year Book.* Seoul: KRNIC.

Krueger, M. (2001). *The Future of M-payments: Business Options and Policy Issues,* Institute for Prospective Technological Studies, Directorate General Joint Research Centre European Commission.

KT Management Research Lab(KTMRL). (2006). *Bundling among telecommunication services in the era of digital convergence,* Seoul: KTMRL.

Kuck, J., & Gnasa, M., (2007). Context-Sensitive Service Discovery Meets Information Retrieval, *Fifth Annual IEEE International Conference on Pervasive Computing and Communications Workshops, 2007. PerCom Workshops '07.,* 601-605, 19-23 March.

Kuipers, B. J. (1986). Qualitative simulation. *Artificial Intelligence, 29*(3), 289-338.

Kumar, N., Gangopadhyay, A., & Karabatis, G. (in press). Supporting mobile decision making with association rules and multi-layered caching. *Decision Support Systems.*

Kuznetsov, V. E. (2000) 'Method for storing map data in a database using space filling curves and a method of searching the database to find objects in a given area and to find objects nearest to a location', United States Patent Number 6,021,406, issued February 1, 2000.

Kwan, I., & Li, Q. (1999). A hybrid approach to convert relational schema to object-oriented schema. *International Journal of Information Science, 117,* 201–241.

Kwon, T.H., and Zmud, R.W. "Unifying the Fragmented Models of Information Systems Implementation," in: *Critical Issues in Information Systems Research,* B.R. Hirschheim (ed.), John Wiley and Sons Ltd., New York, 1987, pp. 227-252.

LaBrie, R. C. (2004). The Impact of Alternative Search Mechanisms on the Effectiveness of Knowledge Retrieval. Unpublished doctoral dissertation, Arizona State University, Tempe.

Lakhotia, A. (1995, February). Wolf: A tool to recover dataflow oriented design from source code. *Proceedings of the Fifth Annual Workshop on Systems Reengineering Technology.*

Laleau, R. & Mammar, A. (2000). A Generic Process to Refine a B Specification into a Relational Database Implementation. In: J. P. Bowen, S. Dunne, A. Galloway and S. King (Eds.), *First International Conference of B and Z Users on Formal Specification and Development in Z and B* (pp. 22–41). Vol. 1878 of LNCS, Springer-Verlag.

Laleau, R. & Mammar, A. (2000). An Overview of a Method and its Support Tool for Generating B Specifications from UML Notations. *Fifteenth IEEE International Conference on Automated Software Engineering* (pp. 269–272). IEEE Computer Society.

Laleau, R. & Polack, F. (2001). A Rigorous Metamodel for UML Static Conceptual Modeling of Information Systems. In: K. R. Dittrich, A. Geppert & A. C. Norrie (Eds.). *13th International Conference on Advanced Information Systems Engineering* (pp. 402–416). Vol. 2068 of LNCS, Springer-Verlag.

Laleau, R. & Polack, F. (2001). Specification of Integrity-Preserving Operations in Information Systems by Using a Formal UML-based Language. *Information & Software Technology* 43(12), 693–704.

Laleau, R. (2000). On the Interest of Combining UML with the B Formal Method for the Specification of Database Applications. *2nd International Conference on Enterprise Information Systems* (pp. 56–63). Available: http://www.univ-paris12.fr/lacl/laleau/.

Lam, A. (2000). Tacit Knowledge, Organizational Learning and Societal Institutions: An Integrated Framework. *Organization Studies, 21*(3), 487.

Lamping, J., Rao, R., & Pirolli, P. (1995). *A Focus+Context Technique Based on Hyperbolic Geometry for Visualizing Large Hierarchies.* Paper presented at the Proceedings ACM Conference Human Factors in Computing Systems.

Langdon G. (1984). An Introduction to Arithmetic Coding, IBM J. Research and Development, 28(2), pp 135-149.

Laux, A., & Martin, L. (2000). XUpdate Working Draft, 2000, last accessed on August 20, 2004 from http://xmldb-org.sourceforge.net/xupdate/xupdate-wd.html

Lawrence, P. and Lorsch, J. *Organization and Environment.* Irwin. Homewood, IL, 1969.

Lazaridis I., & Mehrotra S. (2001). Progressive Approximate Aggregate Queries with a MultiResolution Tree Structure, Proc. of SIGMOD, 2001, pp 401-412.

Lazcano, A., Alonso, G., Schuldt, H., & Schuler, C. (2000, September). The WISE approach to electronic commerce. *Journal of Computer Systems Science and Engineering*, 15(5), 343-355.

Leavitt, H.J., and Whisler, T.L. "Management in the 1980's," *Harvard Business Review* (36:6), 1958, pp 41-48.

Ledang, H. & Souquires, J.(2002). Contributions for Modeling UML State-Charts in B. In: M. J. Butler, L. Petre & K. Sere (Eds). *Third International Conference on Integrated Formal Methods* (pp. 109-127). Vol. 2335 of LNCS, Springer-Verlag.

Ledang, H., Souquieres, J. & Charles, S. (2003). ArgoUML+B : Un Outil de Transformation Systématique de Spécifications UML vers B. In: J.M. Jézéquel, (Ed.). *Approches Formelles dans l'Assistance au Développement de Logiciels (*pp. 3-18).

Ledru, Y. (2003). http://www-lsr.imag.fr/EDEMOI/

Lee, C. & Ke, C-H. (2001) 'A prediction-based query processing strategy in mobile commerce systems', *Journal of Database Management*, 12(3), 14-26.

Lee, D. (1999) 'Computational geometry II', In: M. Atallah (Ed.), *Algorithms and Theory of Computation Handbook* (pp. 20-1 to 20-31). Boca Raton: CRC Press.

Lee, D., Xu, J., Zheng, B. & Lee, W-C. (2002, July-September) 'Data management in location-dependent information services', *IEEE Pervasive Computing*, 1(3), 65-72.

Lee, D., Zhu, M. & Hu, H. (2005) 'When location-based services meet databases', *Mobile Information Systems*, 1(2), 81-90.

Lee, E. & Benbasat, I. (2004) 'A framework for the study of customer interface design for mobile commerce', *International Journal of Electronic Commerce*, 8(3), 79-102.

Lee, G. K., & Cole, R. E. (2003). From a firm-based to a community-based model of knowledge creation: The case of the Linux kernel development. *Organization Science, 14*(6), 633-649.

Lee, H. L., Padmanabhan, V. & Whang, S.J. (1997). Information distortion in a supply chain: The bullwhip effect. *Management Science*, 43(4), pp.546-558.

Lee, H., Kim, T., & Kim, J. (2001). A metadata oriented architecture for building data warehouse. *Journal of Database Management, 12*(4), 15-25.

Lee, J. C. "Embracing Agile Development of Usable Software Systems," CHI 2006, April 22 – 27, 2006, Montreal, Quebec, Canada, pp. 1767 – 1770.

Lee, J.H. (2003). *The modeling and simulation of dynamic supply chain networks: A multi-agent systems approach*, Unpublished doctoral dissertation, University of Cambridge, Cambridge..

Lee, J.W (2004). One phone service: market trends and forecasting. *ETRI Journal*, 19(2), pp.84-96.

Lee, Y. W., Pipino, L., Strong, D. M., & Wang, R. Y. (2004). Process-embedded data integrity. *Journal of Database Management, 15*(1), 87-103.

Leinhardt, S. (1977). *Social networks: A developing paradigm.* Academic Press.

Lempel A., & Ziv J. (1977). A Universal Algorithm for Sequential Data Compression, IEEE Transactions on Information Theory, 23(3), pp 337-343.

Lenat, D. B. (1995). CYC: A large-scale investment in knowledge infrastructure. *Communications of the ACM, 38*(11), 33-38.

Leonard-Barton, D. "Implementing as Mutual Adaptation of Technology and Organization," *Research Policy* (17:5), 1988, pp 251-267.

Lesk, A. M. (2005). *Databasse annotation in molecular biology, principles and practice*: John Wiley & Sons Ltd.

Leung, K. & Atypas, J. (2001) 'Improving returns on m-commerce investments', *The Journal of Business Strategy*, 22(5), 12-13.

Leuschel, M & Butler, M. J. (2003). ProB: A model checker for B. In: K. Araki, S. Gnesi & D. Mandrioli (Eds.). *12th International FME Symposium* (pp. 855–874), Vol. 2805 of *LNCS*, Springer-Verlag.

Levy, A. Y., Rajaraman, A., & Ordille, J. J. (1996). *Querying heterogeneous information sources using source descriptions.* Paper presented at the VLDB.

LG Telecom (2004), "Mobile Banking BankOn", LG Telecom Public Relation Department

LGT, New tariff plan (Enjoyment Zone) raising 0.1 million subscribers. (2006, Oct. 20).. *Herold Economy.*

Liang, S. (1999). *Java(TM) Native Interface: Programmer's Guide and Specification.* Addison-Wesley Pub Co.

Liben-Nowell, D., & Kleinberg, J. (2003). The link prediction problem for social networks. In *Proceedings of the ACM CIKM.*

Lichtenstein, B.B. & McKelvey, B. (2004). Complexity science and computational models of emergent order: What's there? What's missing?. paper presented at the Academy of Management Annual Meeting, New Orleans, LA, August 9.

Lientz, B.P. and Swanson, E.B. Software Maintenance Management: A Study of the Maintenance of Computer Application Software in 487 Data Processing Organizations. Addison-Wesley, 1980.

Lim, W.C. "Effects of Reuse on Quality, Productivity, and Economics," IEEE Software (11:5), September 1994, pp. 23-30.

Lin, F. R., Tan, G. W., & Shaw, M. J. (1999). Multiagent enterprise modeling. *Journal of Organizational Computing and Electronic Commerce, 9*(1), 7-32.

Lin, H-P., Juang, R-T. & Lin, D-B. (2005) 'Validation of an improved location-based handover algorithm using GSM measurement data', *IEEE Transactions on Mobile Computing*, 4(5), 530-536.

Lindblom, C. E. (1987). Alternatives to Validity: Some Thoughts Suggested by Campbell's Guidelines. *Knowledge Creation, Diffusion, Utilization, 8*, 509-520.

Linde, A., Linderoth, H., & Raisanen, C.(2003 March 12-13). An actor network theory perspective on IT-projects: A battle of wills. [Online]. Available: http://www.vits.org/konferenser/alois2003/html/6893.pdf.

Lindstrom, Lowell, Jeffries, Ron. "Extreme Programming and Agile Development Methodologies," Information Systems Management (21:3), Summer 2004, pp. 41 – 52.

Liu, Y., Fekete, A., & Gorton, I. (2005). Design-level performance prediction of component-based applications. *IEEE Transactions on Software Engineering, 31*(11), 928-934.

Loney, K., & Koch, G. (2002). *Oracle9i: The complete reference.* Oracle Press.

Lozano-Tello, A. & Gomez-Perez, A. (2004). ONTOMETRIC: A method to choose the appropriate ontology. *Journal of Database Management*, 15(2), 1-18.

Lucas, H.C. *Implementation: The Key to Successful Information Systems* Columbia University Press, New York, 1981, pp. x, 208 ill. 224 cm.

Lucas, H.C., Jr., Ginzberg, M.J., and Schultz, R.L. *Information Systems Implementation: Testing A Structural Model* Ablex Publishing Corporation, Norwood, New Jersey, 1990.

Madey, G., Freeh, V., & Tynan R. (2002). The open source software development phenomenon: An analysis based on social network theory (AMCIS2002). Dallas, TX.

Madiraju, P., Sunderraman, R. & Navathe, S.B. (2004). Semantic Integrity Constraint Checking for Multiple XML Databases. *Proceedings of 14th Workshop on Information Technology and Systems (WITS 2004),* Washington D.C., December, 2004

Madiraju, P., Sunderraman, S., Navathe, S.B., & Wang, H. (2006). Semantic Integrity Constraint Checking for Multiple XML Databases. *Journal ofDatabase Management*, Vol. 17, No. 4, pp. 1-19

Magal, S.R., Carr, H.H., and Waston, H.J. "Critical Success Factors for Information Center Managers," *MIS Quarterly* (12:3), 1988, pp 413-425.

Maiden, N., and Hare, M. "Problem Domain Categories in Requirements Engineering," International Journal of Human-Computer Studies (49:3), 1998, pp. 281-304.

Maiden, N., and Rugg, G. "ACRE: Selecting Methods for Requirements Acquisition," Software Engineering Journal (11:3), 1996, pp. 183-192.

Mainzer, K. (1994). *Thinking in Complexity.* New York : Springer-Verlag.

Mallat, N., M. Rossi, & V. K. Tuunainen (2004). Mobile banking services. *Communications of the ACM*, 47(5), pp.42-46.

Mallat, S. G. (1989). A theory for multiresolution signal decomposition: The wavelet representation. *IEEE Transactions on Pattern Analysis and Machine Intelligence, 11*, 674-693.

Mammar, A. & Laleau, R. (2003). Design of an Automatic Prover Dedicated to the Refinement of Database Applications. In: K. Araki, S. Gnesi & D. Mandrioli (Eds). *12th International Formal Methods Europe Symposium (*pp. 834–854*).* Vol. 2805 of *LNCS*, Springer-Verlag.

Mammar, A. & Laleau, R. (2005). *From a B Formal Specification to an Executable Code: Application to the Relational Database Domain. Information & Software Technology Journal.* 48(4), 253-279.

Mammar, A. (2002). *Un Environnement Formel pour le Développement d'Applications Bases de Données.* Unpublished PhD thesis, CEDRIC Laboratory, Paris, France. Available: http://se2c.uni.lu/users/AM.

Mammar, A. (2006). A systematic approach to generate B preconditions: application to the database domain. Technical Report, Telecom SudParis, 2006. Submitted to the SOSYM Journal.

Mandelbrot, B. (1966). Information Theory and Psycholinguistics: A theory of word frequencies. In P.F. Lazarsfeld & N.W. Henry (Eds.), *Readings in Mathematical Social Science* (pp. 350-368). Chicago: Science Research Associates.

Marakas, G., and Elam, J. "Semantic Structuring in Analyst Acquisition and Representation of Facts in Requirements Analysis," Information Systems Research (9:1), 1998, pp. 37-63.

Marcano, R. & Levy, N. (2002). Transformation rules of OCL Constraints into B Formal Expressions. In: J. Jurjens, M. V. Cengarle, E. B. Fernandez, B. Rumpe, & R. Sandner (Eds.), *Critical Systems Development with UML. Proceedings of the UML'02 workshop* (pp. 155–162).

March, S. and Allen, G. "Challenges in Requirements Engineering: A Research Agenda for Conceptual Modeling", Science of Design – Design Requirements Workshop. Cleveland, OH, 2007.

March, S. and Smith, G. "Design and Natural Science Research on Information Technology", Decision Support Systems (15), 1995, pp. 251-266.

Marconi, M., & Nentwich, C. (2004). CLiX Language Specification Version 1.0. [online]. last accessed on February 15, 2008 from : http://www.clixml.org/clix/1.0/clix.xml

Mars, N. J. I. (1993, March 10-13). *An ontology of measurement units.* Paper presented at the International Workshop on Formal Ontologies in Conceptual Analysis and Knowledge Representation, Padova, Italy.

Massey, B. S. (1971). *Units, dimensional analysis, and physical similarity.* London: Van Nostrom Reinhold.

Masterman, M. (1961). Semantic message detection for machine translation, using an interlingua. *NPL*, pp. 438-475.

Mathiassen, L., Saarinen, T., Tuunanen, T. and Rossi, M. "A Contingency Model for Requirements Development", Journal of the Association of Information Systems (8:11), 2007, pp. 569-597.

Matias Y., & J Vitter J. (1998). Wavelet-Based Histograms for Selectivity Estimation, Proceedings of the 1998 ACM SIGMOD International Conference on Management of Data, June 1998, pp 448-459.

Matias, Y., Vitter, J. S., & Wang, M. (1998). *Wavelet-based histograms for selectivity estimation.* Paper presented at the ACM SIGMOD.

McArthur, K., Saiedian, H., & Zand, M. (2002). An evaluation of the impact of component–based architectures on software reusability. *Information and Software Technology, 44*(6), 351-359.

McCarthy, J., & Hayes, P. J. (1969). Some philosophical problems from the standpoint of AI. In B. Meltzer & D. Michie (Eds.), *Machine intelligence* (Vol. 4, pp. 463-501). Edinburgh, UK: Edinburgh University Press.

McGuinness, D. L., & van Harmelen, F. (2003). *OWL Web Ontology Language overview* (No. CR-owl-features-20030818). W3C.

McGuire, M., Plataniotis, K. & Venetsanopoulos, A. (2005) 'Data fusion of power and time measurements for mobile terminal location', *IEEE Transactions on Mobile Computing*, 4(2), 142-153.

McLeod, D. (1990, December). Report on the workshop on heterogeneous database systems. *SIGMOD record*, 19(4), 23-31.

Medjahed, B., & Bouguettaya, A. (2005). A Multilevel Composability Model for Semantic Web Services. *IEEE Transactions on Knowledge and Data Engineering* (TKDE), 17(7), July.

Meekel, J., Horton, T., France, R., Mellone, C., and Dalvi, S. "From Domain Models to Architecture Frameworks," Software Engineering Notes (22:3), May 1997, pp. 75-80.

Mena, E., Kashyap, V., Illarramendi, A., & Sheth, A. (1998, June). Domain specific ontologies for semantic information brokering on the global information infrastructure. *Proceedings of the international conference on formal ontologies in information systems (FOIS'98).* Trento, Italy.

Mens, T. and Tourwe, T. "A Survey of Software Refactoring," IEEE Transactions on Software Engineering (30:2), February 2004, pp. 126-139.

MIC (1999), "Revitalization of the supplement telecommunication service" , [Online]. Available: http://www.mic.go.kr/user.tdf?a=user.board.BoardApp&c=2002&board_id=P_03_01_05&seq=128&ctx=&bad=&isSearch=true&searchVal=□□□□&basic=SUBJECT&npp=15&cp=1&pg=1&mc=P_03_08 (in Korean)

Microsoft (2007, April 16). COM: Component object model technologies. Retrieved from http://www.microsoft.com/com/default.mspx

Microsoft. (2005, September). *.NET.* [Online]. Available: http://www.microsoft.com/net.

Miles, M.B., and Huberman, A.M. *Qualitative Data Analysis: An Expanded Sourcebook* SAGE Publications Inc., Thousand Oaks, California, 1994.

Mili, A., Mili, R., and Mittermeir, R.T., "A Survey of Software Reuse Libraries," Annals of Software Engineering (5), January 1998, pp. 349-414.

Miller, R. J., Hernandez, M. A., Haas, L. M., Yan, L., Ho, C. T. H., Fagin, R., et al. (2001). The clio project: managing heterogeneity. *SIGMOD Record, 30*(1).

Milton, K. S., & Kazmierczak, E. (2004). An ontology of data modelling languages: A study using a common-sense realistic ontology. *Journal of Database Management, 15*(2), 19-38.

Milton, S. K., & Kazmierczak, E. (2004). An ontology of data modelling languages: A study using a common-sense realistic ontology. *Journal of Database Management, 15*(2), 19-38.

Mitchell, T. M. (1997). *Machine learning*: McGraw-Hill.

Mitra, S., Bagchi, A., & Bandyopadhyay, A. K. (2006). A data model for a Web graph used as a social network. In *Proceedings of the 1st International Conference on Emerging Applications of Information Technology,* (pp. 23-26).

Mobile virtual network operator. (2004, June 14). The Korean Economic Daily.

Mockus, A., Fielding, R. T., & Herbsleb, J. D. (2000). A case study of open source software development: The Apache server. ICSE 2000.

Mockus, A., Fielding, R. T., & Herbsleb, J. D. (2002). Two case studies of open source software development: Apache and Mozilla. *ACM Transactions on Software Engineering and Methodology, 11*(3), 309–346.

Montemurro, M. A. (2001). Beyond the Zipf-Mandelbrot law in quantitative linguistics. *Physica A, 300*(3-4), 567-578

Montezemi, A., and Conrath, D. "The Use of Cognitive Mapping for Information Requirement Analysis," MIS Quarterly (10:1), 1986, pp. 45-56.

Moon, J. Y., & Sproull, L. (2000). Essence of distributed work: The case of Linux kernel. *First Monday, 5*(11).

Moran, P., & Ghoshal, S. (1996). Value Creation of Firms. In J. B. Keys & L. N. Dosier (Eds.), *Academy of Management Best Paper Proceedings* (pp. 41-45).

Morgan, G. Images of Organization, San Francisco, California: Berrett-Koehler Publishers, Inc., 1998.

Moser, I., & Law, J. (2006). Fluids or flows? : Information and qualculation in medical practice. I*nformation Technology & People*, 19(1), pp. 55-73.

Mount, D. W. (2004). *Bioinformatics sequence and genome analysis*. Cold Spring Harbor, New York: Cold Spring Harbor Laboratory Press.

Mukherjee, R. & Mao, J. (2004). Enterprise Search: Tough stuff. *ACM Queue, 2*(2), 37-46.

Murphy, E.(2002). *The Future of Fixed Mobile Substitution : Choices of Fixed and Mobile Operators*, Analsys.

Mylopoulos, J. (1992). Conceptual modeling and telos. In P. Locuopoulos & R. Zicari (Eds.), *Conceptual modeling, databases and cases*. New York: John Wiley & Sons.

NACJD. (2006). National Crime Victimization Survey Resource Guide. 2006, from http://www.icpsr.umich.edu/NACJD/NCVS/

Nahapiet, J., & Ghoshal, S. (1998). Social Capital, Intellectual Capital, and the Organizational Advantage. *Academy of Management Review, 23*(2), 242-266.

Nambisan, S., Agarwal, R., & Tanniru, M. (1999). Organizational Mechanisms for Enhancing User Innovation in Information Technology. *MIS Quarterly, 23*(3), 365-395.

Narens, L. (1985). *Abstract measurement theory*. Cambridge, MA: MIT Press.

Naumann, I., Davis, G., and McKeen, I. "Determining Information System Requirements: A Contingency Method for Selection of a Requirements Assurance Strategy," The Journal of Systems and Software (1), 1980, pp. 273-281.

Nemati, H.R., Steiger, D.M., Iyer, L.S., & Herschel, R.T. (2002). Knowledge warehouse: An architectural integration of knowledge management, decision support artificial intelligence and data warehousing. *Decision Support Systems, 33*, 143-161.

Nerur, S., & Balijepally, V. (2007). Theoretical Reflections on Agile Development Methodologies. *Communications of the ACM, 50*(3), 79-83.

Nerur, S., Mahapatra, R., & Mangalaraj, G. (2005). Challenges of Migrating to Agile Methodologies. *Communications of the ACM, 48*(5), 73-78.

Newman, M. (2003). The structure and function of complex networks. *SIAM Review, 45*, 167-256.

Ng W., & Ravishankar C. (1997). Block-Oriented Compression Techniques for Large Statistical Databases, IEEE Transactions on Knowledge and Data Engineering, 9(2), pp 314-328.

Nidumolu, S. "The Effect of Coordination and Uncertainty on Software Project Performance: Residual Performance Risk as an Intervening Variable," Information Systems Research (6:3), 1995, pp. 191-219.

Nievergelt, J. & Widmayer, P. (1997) 'Spatial data structures: concepts and design choices', In: M. van Kreveld, J. Nievergelt, T. Roos & P. Widmayer (Eds.), *Algorithmic Foundations of Geographic Information Systems* (pp. 153-197). Berlin: Springer Verlag.

Nonaka, I. (1994). Dynamic Theory of Organizational Knowledge Creation. *Organization Science, 5*(1), 14-37.

Nord, R. L., and Tomayko, J. E. "Software Architecture-Centric Methods and Agile Development," IEEE Software (23:2), March/April 2006, pp. 47 – 53.

Nord, W.R., and Tucker, S. *Implementing Routine and Radical Innovation* Lexington Books, Lexington, M.A., 1987.

Novak, G. S., Jr. (1995). Conversion of units of measurement. *IEEE Transactions on Software Engineering, 21*(8), 651-661.

Noy, N. F., & Hafner, C. D. (1997). The state of the art in ontology sesign: A survey and comparative review. *AI Magazine, 18*(3), 53-74.

Nozick, L. K., Turnquist, M. A., Jones, D. A., Davis, J. R., & Lawton, C. R. (2004). *Assessing the Performance of Interdependent Infrastructures and Optimizing Investments.* Paper presented at the 37th Annual Hawaii International Conference on System Sciences, Big Island, HI.

O'Neil, P., & Graefe, G. (1995). Multi-table joins through bitmapped join indices. *SIGMOD Record, 24*(3), 8-11.

Odell, J. (2002). Objects and agents compared. *Journal of Object Technology, 1*(1), 41-53.

OECD(2004). The implications of convergence for regulation of electronic communications. [Online]. Available: http://www.oecd.org/dataoecd/56/24/32983964.pdf.

Oh, H., Labianca, G., & Chung, M.-H. (2006). A Multilevel Model of Group Social Capital. *Academy of Management Review, 31*(3), 569-582.

Oh, S. & Lee, H (2005). How technology shapes the actor network of convergence services: A case of mobile banking. Twenty-Sixth International Conference on Information Systems.

Oh, W., and Pinsonneault, A. "On the Assessment of the Strategic Value of Information Technologies: Conceptual and Analytical Approaches," *MIS Quarterly* (31:2), 2007, pp 239-265.

OLAP Report, online at http://www.olapreport.com/DatabaseExplosion.htm

OMG (1995). *Common Object Request Broker Architecture.* Retrieved from http://www.omg.org/gettingstarted/gettingstartedindex.htm

OMG. (2003). *Unified Modeling Language Specification, Version* 1.5.

Ommering, R. V. (2005). Software reuse in product populations. *IEEE Transactions on Software Engineering, 31*(7), 537-544,.

Ono, R. & K Aoki. (1998). Convergence and new regulatory frameworks: A comparative study of regulatory approaches to Internet telephony?. *Telecommunications Policy*, 22(10), pp.817-838.

Opdahl, A. L., & Henderson-Sellers, B. (2004). A Template for defining enterprise modelling constructs. *Journal of Database Management, 15*(2), 39-73.

Opdyke, W.F. "Refactoring: A Program Restructuring Aid in Designing Object-Oriented Application Frameworks," PhD Thesis, Univ. of Illinois at Urbana-Champaign, 1992.

Oracle 9i. (2005). Oracle Data Warehousing Guide, Oracle Corporation.

Orlikowski, W. J. (1993). CASE tools as organizational change: investigating incremental and radical changes in systems development. *MIS Quarterly, 17*(3), 309-340.

Orlikowski, W.J. "Improvising Organizational Transformation Over time: A Situated Perspective," *Information Systems Research* (7:1), 1996, pp 63-92.

Orlikowski, W.J. "The Duality of Technology: Rethinking the Concept of Technology in Organizations," *Organization Science* (3:3), 1992, pp 398-427.

Orlikowski, W.J., and Robey, D. "Information Technology and the Structuring of Organizations," *Information Systems Research* (2:2), 1991, pp 143-169.

ORS. *Open Research System.* http://www.orspublic.org

Ouksel, A., & Sheth, A. P. (1999). Special issue on semantic interoperability in global information systems. *SIGMOD Record, 28*(1).

Ovum Report (1999), *Fixed-Mobile Convergence: Service Integration and Substitution*, Ovum

Pan, J. Y. C., & Tenenbaum, J. M. (1991). An intelligent agent framework for enterprise integration. *IEEE Transactions on Systems, man, and cybernetics, 21*(6), 1391-1991.

Papakonstantinou, Y., Garcia-Molina, H., & Ullman, J. (1996). *Medmaker: A mediation system based on declarative specifications.* Paper presented at the ICDE.

Papazoglou, M. P., & Georgakopoulos, D. (2003). Service-oriented computing. *Communications of ACM, 46*, 25-28.

Pardaens, J., Peelman, P., & Tanaca, L. (1995). G-Log: A graph-based query language. *IEEE Knowledge & data Engineering, 7*(3), 436-453.

Park M., & Lee S. (2005). A Cache Optimized Multidimensional Index in Disk-Based Environments, IEICE Trans. Inf. & Syst, 88(8), 2005.

Park, C., Kim, M.H., & Lee, Y. (2002). Finding an efficient rewriting of OLAP queries using materialized views in data warehouses. *Decision Support Systems, 32*, 379-399.

Park, J., & Ram, S. (2004). Information systems interoperability: What lies beneath? *ACM Transactions on Information Systems*, 22(4), 595-632.

Parsons, J., & Wand, Y. (1997). Using objects in system analysis. *Communications of the ACM, 40*(12), 104-110.

Pavlou, P.A., and Sawy, O.A.E. "From IT Leveraging Competence to Competitive Advantage in Turbulent Environment: The Case of New Product Development," *Information Systems Research* (17:3), 2006, pp 198-227.

Pears R., & Houliston B. (2007). Optimization of Aggregate Queries in Data Warehouses, Journal of Database Management, IDEA Group Publishing, USA, 18(1), 2007.

Pease, A., & Niles, I. (2002). IEEE standard upper ontology: A progress report. *Knowledge Engineering Review, 17*, 65-70.

Peltz, C. (2003, January). *Web services orchestration.* Technical Report, Hewlett Packard.

Percival, D. B., & Walden, A. T. (2000). *Wavelet methods for time series analysis.* Cambridge University Press.

Perrey, R., & Lycett, M. (2003, January). Service-oriented architecture. *Proceedings of the 2003 Symposium on Applications and the Internet Workshops* (pp. 27-31).

Petrie, C., & Bussler, C. (2003, July). Service agents and virtual enterprises: A survey. *IEEE Internet Computing*, 7(4).

Pettigrow, A.M. "Context and Action in the Transformation of the Firm," *Journal of Management Studies* (24:6), 1987, pp 649-670.

Pierce, J.L., and Delbecq, A. "Organization Structure, Individual Attributes and Innovation," *Academy of Management Review* (2:1), 1977, pp 27-37.

Pitt, E., & McNiff, K. (2001). *Java(TM) RMI: The remote method invocation guide.* Addison-Wesley Publishing Corporation.

Pitts, M. and Browne, G. "Stopping Behavior of Systems Analysts During Information Requirements Elicitation", Journal of Management Information Systems (21:1), 2004, pp. 203-226.

Pohl, K. "The Three Dimensions of Requirements Engineering", Information Systems (19:3), 1994, pp. 243-258.

Polanyi, M. (1966). *The Tacit Dimension*. New York: Anchor Day Books.

Poosala V., & Gnati V. (1999). Fast Approximate Answers to Aggregate Queries on a Data Cube, Proceedings of 1999 International Conference on Scientific and Statistical Database Management, pp 24-33.

Premkumar, G., Ramamurthy, K., and Saunders, C. "Information Processing View of Organizations: An Exploratory Examination of Fit in the Context of Interorganizational Relationships," Journal of Management Information Systems (22:1), 2003, pp. 257-298.

Prieto-Diaz, R. Domain Analysis for Reusability. In Domain Analysis and Software Systems Modeling, Prieto-Diaz, P., Arango, G. (eds), IEEE Computer Society Press, 1991, pp. 63-69.

Purvis, R.L., Sambamurthy, V., and Zmud, R.W. "The Assimilation of Knowledge Platforms in Organizations: An Empirical Investigation," *Organization Science* (12:2), 2001, pp 117-135.

Putnam, R. D. (1993). The Prosperous Community: Social Capital and Public Life. *American Prospect, 13*, 35-42.

Qian, X. (1993). The Deductive Synthesis of Database Transactions. *ACM Transactions on Database Systems* 18(4), 626–677.

Qian, X., & Wiederhold, G. (1991). Incremental recomputation of active relational expressions. *IEEE Transaction on Knowledge and Data Engineering, 3*(3), 227-341.

Quinlan, J. R. (1986). Induction of Decision Trees. *Machine Learning, 1*(1), 81 - 106.

Quintero, A. (2005) 'A User Pattern Learning Strategy for Managing Users' Mobility in UMTS Networks', *IEEE Transactions on Mobile Computing*, 4(6), 552-566.

Raghavan, S., & Garcia-Molina, H. (2003). Representing Web graphs. In *Proceedings of the IEEE International Conference on Data Engineering.*

Rahayu, J. W., Chang, E., Dillon, T. S., & Taniar, D. (2000). A methodology for transforming inheritance relationships in an object-oriented conceptual model to relational tables. *Information and Software Technology, 42*(8), 571-592.

Rahm, E., & Bernstein, P. A. (2001). A survey of approaches to automatic schema matching. *VLDB Journal, 10*(4).

Ram, S., & Park, J. (2004). Semantic conflict resolution ontology (SCROL): An ontology for detecting and resolving data and schema-level semantic conflicts. *IEEE Transactions on Knowledge and Data Engineering, 16*(2), 189-202.

Ram, S., & Wei, W. (2004). *Modeling the semantics of 3D protein structures.* Paper presented at the ER 2004, Shanghai, China.

Ram, S., Khatri, V., Zhang, L., & Zeng, D. (2001). *GeoCosm: A semantics-based approach for information integration of geospatial data.* Paper presented at the Proceedings of the Workshop on Data Semantics in Web Information Systems (DASWIS2001), Yokohama, Japan.

Ram, S., Park, J., & Hwang, Y. (2002). *CREAM: A mediator based environment for modeling and accessing distributed information on the Web.* Paper presented at the British National Conference on Databases (BNCOD).

Ramesh, B., Cao, L., Mohan, K. and Xu, P. "Can Distributed Software Development Be Agile ?," Communications of the ACM (49:10), October 2006, pp. 41 – 46.

Ran, S. (2003, March). A model for Web services discovery with QOS. *SIGecom Exchanges*, 4(1).

Ranson, S., Hinings, G., and Greenwood, R. "The Structure of Organizational Structures," *Administrative Science Quarterly* (25:1), 1980, pp 1-17.

Rao, A. R., & Bandyopadhyay, S. (1987). Measures of reciprocity in a social network. *Sankhya: The Indian Journal of Statistics, Series A, 49,* 141-188.

Rao, A. R., Bandyopadhyay, S., Sinha, B. K., Bagchi, A., Jana, R., Chaudhuri, A., et al. (1998). *Changing social relations—Social network approach* (Technical Report). Survey Research and Data Analysis Center, Indian Statistical Institute.

Ratbe, D., King, W., and Kim, Y. "The Fit Between Project Characteristics and Application Development Methodologies: A Contingency Approach," Journal of Computer Information Systems, 2000, pp. 26-33.

Rational (2003). http://www.rational.com

Ravichandran, T. "Organizational Assimilation of Complex Technologies: An Empirical Study of Component-Based Software Development," IEEE Transaction on Engineering Management, (52:2), 2005, pp. 249 – 268.

Raymond, E. S. (1998). The cathedral and the bazaar. *First Monday, 3(3),* Retrieved January , 2005, from http://www.catb.org/~esr/writings/cathedral-bazaar/cathedral-bazaar/

Reich, B. H., & Benbasat, I. (2000). Factors that Influence the Social Dimension of Alignment between Business and Information Technology Objectives. [Article]. *MIS Quarterly, 24*(1), 81.

Reiger, C., & Grinberg, M. (1977). *The declarative representation and procedural simulations of causality in physical mechanisms.* Paper presented at the Joint Conference on Artificial Intelligence.

Rennison, C. M. (2007). Reporting to the Police by Hispanic Victims of Violence. *Violence and Victims, 22.*

Retz-Schmidt, G. (1988). Various views on spatial prepositions. *AI Magazine, 9*(2), 95-105.

Rice, J. A. (1994). *Mathematical statistics and data analysis.* Duxbury Press.

Rice, R. "Task Analyzability, Use of New Media, and Effectiveness: A Multi-Site Exploration of Media Richness", Organization Science (3:4), 1992, pp. 475-500.

Riley, P. "A Structurationist Account of Political Culture," *Administrative Science Quarterly* (28:3), 1983, pp 414-437.

Roberts, F. (1979). *Measurement theory with applications to decision making, utility and the social sciences.* Reading, MA: Addison-Wesley.

Rockart, J. "Chief Executives Define their Own Data Needs," Harvard Business Review (57:2), 1979, pp. 81-93.

Rodrigues, K. R., & Mello, R.D.S (2007). A Faceted Taxonomy of Semantic Integrity Constraints for the XML Data Model. *Proceedings of 18th International Conference on Database and Expert Systems Applications* (DEXA) pp. 65-74

Rodriguez-Gianolli, P., Garzetti, M., Jiang, L., Kementsietsidis, A., Kiringa, I., Masud, M., Miller, R., & Mylopoulos, J. (2005). Data Sharing in the Hyperion Peer Database System. In *Proceedings of the International Conference on Very Large Databases (VLDB).*

Rogers, E.M., and Shoemaker, E.F. *Communications of Innovations* Free Press, New York, NY, 1971.

Roman, E., Ambler, S. W., & Jewell, T. (2003). *Mastering enterprise JavaBeans.* John Wiley & Sons.

Ronco, L., Grossel, M., Zimmer, M., & Socash, T. (2003). *Modules in emerging fields. Vol 4: Genomics and proteomics.*

Rosenthal, A., Heiler, S., Dayal, U., & Manola, F. (1986). Traversal recursion: A practical approach to supporting recursive applications. In *Proceedings of the ACM-SIGMOD, (*pp. 166-176).

Rusinkiewicz, M., Sheth, A., & Karabatis, G. (1991). Specifying interdatabase dependencies in a multidatabase environment. *IEEE Computer, 24*(12), 46-53.

Sagers, G. W. (2004). The influence of network governance factors on success in open source software development projects. In *Twenty-Fifth International Conference on Information Systems* (pp. 427-438). Washington, DC:

Salam, A. F., Singh, R., & Iyer, L. (2005). Intelligent infomediary-based eMarketplaces: agents in eSupply chains. *Communications of the ACM.*

Samaan, N. & Karmouch, A. (2005) 'A Mobility Prediction Architecture Based on Contextual Knowledge and Spatial Conceptual Maps', *IEEE Transactions on Mobile Computing*, 4(6), 537-551.

Sang, J., Follen, G., Kim, C., & Lopez, I. (2002). Development of CORBA-based engineering applications from legacy Fortran programs. *Information and Software Technology, 44*(3), 175-184.

Santami, A., Leow, T., Lim, H. & Goh, P. (2003) 'Overcoming barriers to the successful adoption of mobile commerce in Singapore', *International Journal of Mobile Communications*, 1(1/2), 194-231.

Saoudi, A., Nachouki, G. & Briand, H. (1996). Checking extensional constraints of federated schemata.. *Proceedings of Seventh International Workshop on Database and Expert Systems Applications,* September, pp. 398-403

SAP-AG. (1995). *SAP R/3 system: Quality management* (No. 4.6). Neurottstrasse 16, 69190 Walldorf, Germany: SAP AG.

Sarawagi S., & Stonebraker M. (1994). Efficient organization of large multidimensional arrays, Proceedings of the 11th Annual IEEE Conference on Data Engineering, pp 328-336.

Sarawagi, S., Agrawal, R., & Megiddo, N. (1998). *Discovery-driven exploration of OLAP data cubes.* Paper presented at the International Conference on Extending Database Technology.

Schaefer, R. T., & Lamm, R. P. (1998). *Sociology* (6th ed.). McGraw-Hill.

Scheaffer, R. L., & McClave, J. T. (1982). *Statistics for engineers.* Boston, MA: PWS Publishers.

Scheer, A. W. (1999). *ARIS-Business Process Modeling.* Berlin: Springer.

Schlenoff, C., Balakirsky, S., Uschold, M., Provine, R., & Smith, S. (2003). Using ontologies to aid navigation planning in autonomous vehicles. *The knowledge engineering review, 18*, 243-255.

Schmidt, R., Lyytinen, K., Keil, M., and Cule, P. "Identifying Software Project Risks: An International Delphi Study," Journal of Management Information Systems (17:4), 2001, pp. 5-36.

Schuster, H., Georgakopoulos, D., Cichocki, A., & Baker, D. (2000, June). Modeling and composing service-based and reference process-based multienterprise processes. *CAISE conference.* 247-263, Stockholm, Sweden.

Scott, J. (2000). *Social network analysis. A handbook* (2nd ed.). London: SAGE Publications.

Sedgwick, J. (2006). The Cost of Crime: Understanding the Financial and Human Impact of Criminal Activity. 2006, from http://www.ojp.usdoj.gov/ocom/testimonies/sedgwick_test_060919.pdf

SEEK. *The Science Environment for Ecological Knowledge.* http://seek.ecoinformatics.org

Segev, A., & Fang, W. (1991). Optimal update policies for distributed materialized views. *Management Science, 37*(7), 851-870.

Senge, P. M. (1990). The Leader's New Work: Building Learning Organizations. *Sloan Management Review, 32*(1), 7.

Serrano, M. A., Montes, D. O., & Carver, D. L. (1999). Evolutionary migration of legacy systems to an object-based distributed environment. *Proceedings of the IEEE International Conference on Software Maintenance (ICSM'99)* (pp. 86-95).

Shanmugasundaram, J., Tufte, K., He, G., Zhang, C., DeWitt, D., & Naughton, J. (1999). Relational Databases for Querying XML Documents: Limitations and Opportunities. *Proceedingsof the International Conference on Very Large Databases.*

Sharma, R., and Yetton, P. "The Contingent Effects of Management Support and Task Independence on Successful Information Systems Implementation," *MIS Quarterly* (27:4), 2003, pp 533-555.

Sheng, L., Özsoyoglu, M. Z., & Özsoyoglu, G. (1999). A graph query language and its query processing. *ICDE*.

Sherif, K. and Vinze, A. A Qualitative Model for Barriers to Software Reuse Adoption. In P. De and J.I. DeGross (Eds.), Proceedings of 20th Internal Conference on Information Systems, Charlotte, North Carolina, December 13-15, 1999.

Sheth, A., & Karabatis, G. (1993, May). *Multidatabase Interdependencies in Industry.* Paper presented at the ACM SIGMOD, Washington DC.

Sheth, A., Aleman-Meza, B., Arpinar, I. B., Bertram, C., Warke, Y., Ramakrishanan, C., et al. (2004). Semantic association identification and knowledge discovery for national security applications. *Journal of Database Management, 16*(1).

Sheth, A., Arpinar, I. B., & Kashyap, V. (2003). Relationships at the heart of Semantic Web: Modeling, discovering, and exploiting complex semantic relationships. In M. Nikravesh, B. Azvin, R. Yager & L. A. Zadeh (Eds.), *Enhancing the power of the Internet studies in fuzziness and soft computing.* Springer-Verlag.

Sheth, A., Bertram, C., Avant, D., Hammond, B., Kochut, K., & Warke, Y. (2002). Managing semantic content for the web. *IEEE Internet Computing, 6*(4), 80-87.

Shim J., Song S., Yoo J., & Min Y. (2004). An efficient cache conscious multi-dimensional index structure, Information Processing Letters, 92, pp 133-142, 2004.

Shin, D. H.(2006). VoIP: A debate over information service or telephone application in US: A new perspective in convergence era. *Telematics and Informatics*, 23(2), pp.57-73.

Siau, K. & Cao, Q. (2001). Unified Modeling Language – A Complexity Analysis. *Journal of Database Management*, 12 (1), pp. 26-34.

Siau, K. & Lee, L. (2004). Are Use Case and Class Diagrams Complementary in Requirements Analysis? -- An Experimental Study on Use Case and Class Diagrams in UML," *Requirements Engineering*, 9(4), pp. 229-237.

Siau, K. & Shen, Z. (2003) 'Mobile communications and mobile services', *International Journal of Mobile Communications*, 1(1/2), 3-14.

Siau, K. (1999). Information modeling and method engineering: A psychological perspective. *Journal of Database Management, 10*(4), 44-50.

Siau, K., & Cao, Q. (2001). Unified modeling language (UML)—A complexity analysis. *Journal of Database Management, 12*(1), 26-34.

Siau, K., & Cao, Q. (2001). Unified modeling language—A complexity analysis. *Journal of Database Management, 12*(1), 26-34.

Siau, K., & Lee, L. (2004). Are use case and class diagrams complimentary in requirements analysis? An experimental study on use case and class diagrams in UML. *Requirements Engineering, 9*(4), 229-237.

Siau, K., & Loo, P. (2006). Identifying difficulties in learning UML. *Information Systems Management, 23*(3), 43-51.

Siau, K., Chan, H., & Wei, K. (1995). The effects of conceptual and logical interfaces on visual query performance of end users. In *Proceedings of the Sixteenth International Conference on Information Systems*, (pp. 225-235).

Siau, K., Chan, H., & Wei, K. (2004). Effects of query complexity and learning on novice user query performance with conceptual and logical database interfaces. *IEEE Transactions on Systems, Man and Cybernetics, 34*(2), 276-281.

Siau, K., Erickson, J., & Lee, L. (2005). Theoretical vs. practical complexity: The case of UML. *Journal of Database Management, 16*(3), 40-57.

Siau, K., Lim, E. & Z. Shen. (2001) 'Mobile commerce: promises, challenges, and research agenda', *Journal of Database Management*, 12(3), 4-13.

Sichel, H.S. (1975). On a Distribution Law for Word Frequencies. *Journal of the American Statistical Association, 70*(351), 542-547.

Sierpinski, W. (1912) 'Sur une novelle courbe continue qui remplit tout une aire plaine', *Bulletin International De L'Academie Des Sciences de Cracovie*, Ser. A., 462-478.

Sikora, R., & Shaw, M. (2002). Multi agent enterprise modeling. In C. Holsapple, V. Jacob & H. R. Rao (Eds.), *Business modeling: A multidisciplinary approach essays in honor of Andrew B. Whinston* (pp. 169-185). Kluwer Academic Press.

Simon, H. "The New Science of Management Decision", in *The Shape of Automation for Men and Management*, Harper & Row. New York, NY, 1965, pp. 57-79.

Sismannis Y., Deligiannakis A. (2002). Dwarf: shrinking the PetaCube, Proceedings of the 2002 ACM SIGMOD International Conference on Management of Data, pp 464-475.

Smith, J. R., Li, C.-S., & Jhingran, A. (2004). A wavelet framework for adapting data cube views for OLAP. *IEEE Transactions on Knowledge and Data Engineering, 16*(5), 552-565.

Snook, C. & Butler, M. (2001). Using a Graphical Design Tool for Formal Specification. In: G. Kadoda (Ed.), *13th Annual Workshop of the Psychology of Programming Interest Group* (pp. 311-321). *Available: http://www.ppig.org/papers/13th-snook.pdf.*

Snook, C. & Harrison, R. (2001). Practitioners Views on the Use of Formal Methods: An Industrial Survey by Structured Interview. *Information and Software Technology* 43(4), 219–283.

Software, P. (2005, September). *Progress Software: ObjectStore.* [Online]. Available: http://www.objectstore.net/index.ssp.

Soh, C., and Sia, S.K. "An Institutional Perspective on Sources of ERP Package-organization Misalignments," *Journal of Strategic Information Systems* (13:4), 2004, pp 375-397.

Spender, J. C. (1996a). Making Knowledge the Basis of a Dynamic Theory of the Firm. *Strategic Management Journal, 17*(S2), 45-62.

Spender, J. C. (1996b). Organizational knowledge, learning and memory: three concepts in search of a theory. *Journal of Organizational Change Management, 9*(1), 63.

Spivey, J. (1992). *The Z Notation: a Reference Manual.* International Prentice-Hall.

Sprott, D. (2002). Service-oriented process matters. *CBDi Forum Newsletter.*

Sprott, D. "Componentizing the Enterprise Application Packages," Communications of the ACM (43:4), April 2000, pp. 63-69.

Sproull, N. L. (1995). *Handbook of Research Methods A Guide for Practitioners and Students in the Social Sciences* (Second ed.). Lanham, MD: The Scarecrow Press, Inc.

Stal, M. (2002). Web services: Beyond component-based computing association for computing machinery. *Communications of the ACM, 45*(10), 71-77.

Stamelos, I., Angelis, L., Oikonomu, A., & Bleris, G. L. (2002). Code quality analysis in open-source software development. *Information Systems Journal, 12*(1), 43-60.

Stevens, R., Goble, C. A., & Bechhofer, S. (2000). Ontology-based knowledge representation for bioinformatics. *Briefings in Bioinformatics, 1*(4), 398-414.

Stevens, R., Goble, C., Horrocks, I., & Bechhofer, S. (2002). Building a bioinformatics ontology using OIL. *IEEE Transactions on Information Technology in Biomedicine, 6*(2), 135-141.

Stoeckert Jr., C. J., & Parkinson, H. (2004). The MGED ontology: A framework for describing functional genomics experiments. *Comparative and Functional Genomics, 4*(1), 127-132.

Stollnitz, E. J., Derose, T. D., & Salesin, D. H. (1996). *Wavelets for Computer Graphics Theory and Applications*: Morgan Kaufmann Publishers.

Studer, B.(2001). Fixed mobile internet convergence(FMIC). *Telematics and Informatics*, 18(2), pp.133-141.

Su, J. (2005). Web service interactions: analysis and design. *The Fifth International Conference on Computer and Information Technology, CIT 2005.* 21-23 September.

Sugumaran, V. & Storey, V. C. (2006). The role of domain ontologies in database design: An ontology management and conceptual modeling environment. *ACM Trans. Database Syst.* 31, 3, September.

Sugumaran, V., Park, S., and Kang, K., "Software Product Line Engineering," Communications of the ACM (49:12), December 2006, pp. 28 - 32.

Sugumaran, V., Tanniru, M., and Storey, V.C., "A Domain Model for Supporting Reuse in Systems Analysis," Communications of the ACM (43:11es), Nov. 2000, pp. 312 - 322.

Sultan, F., and Chan, L. "The Adoption of New Technology: The Case of Object-oriented Computing in Software Companies," *IEEE Transaction on Engineering Management* (47:1), 2000, pp 106 -126.

Sun - Java EE (2007, April 16). *Enterprise JavaBeans Technology.* Retrieved from http://java.sun.com/products/ejb/

Sun, J., Dong, J. S., Liu, J. & Wang, H. (2001). Object-Z web environment and projections to UML. *10th international conference on World Wide Web (*pp. 725–734*).* ACM Press.

Sutor, B. (2006, May 21). Open standards vs. open source: How to think about software, standards, and service-oriented architecture at the beginning of the 21st century. Retrieved from http://www.sutor.com/newsite/essays/e-OsVsOss.php

Swaminathan, J. M., Smith, S. F., & Sadeh, N. M. (1998). Modeling supply chain dynamics: a multiagent approach. *Decision Sciences, 29*(3), 607-632.

Swanson, E.B. "Information systems innovation among organizations," *Management Science* (40:9), 1994, pp 1069-1092.

SyBase, Inc. (2007, April 16). *Sybase Power Designer Redefining Enterprise Modeling.* Retrieved from http://www.sybase.com/products/enterprisemodeling/powerdesigner

Sycara, K., Klush, M., & Widoff, S., (1999). Dynamic Service Matchmaking among Agents in Open Information Environments, *ACM SIGMOD Record*, 28(1): 47-53, March.

Szyperski, C. Component Software: Beyond Object-Oriented Programming, Addison-Wesley, 1998.

Szyperski, C.A. "Emerging component software technologies - a strategic comparison," *Software - Concepts and Tools* (19:1) 1998, pp 2-10.

Taggart Jr, W., and Tharp, M. "A Survey of Information Requirements Analysis Techniques," ACM Computing Surveys (9:4), 1977, pp. 273-290.

Takagaki, K., & Wand, Y. (1991). An object-oriented information systems model based on ontology. In F. V. Assche, B. Moulin & C. Rolland (Eds.), *Object oriented approach in information systems* (pp. 275-296). North, Holland: Elsevier Science.

Tatarinov, I., & Halevy, A. Y. (2004). *Efficient Query Reformulation in Peer-Data Management Systems.* Paper presented at the SIGMOD.

Tatarinov, I., Ives, Z. G., Halevy, A.Y., & Daniel, S. (2001). Updating XML. *Proceedings of the ACM SIGMOD Conference on Management of Data*

Tatibouet, B., Hammad, A. &. Voisinet, J.C. (2002). From an abstract B specification to UML class diagrams. *2nd IEEE International Symposium on Signal Processing and Information Technology* (pp. 5–10).

The Bank of Korea. (2004). Status of mobile payment service in Korea, *Payment Information*, 6, pp. 4 (in Korean)

Thompson Scientific. (2004). Strategies for Search, Taxonomy and Classification: Getting just what you need. [Online]. Available: http://i.i.com.com/cnwk.1d/html/itp/ultraseek_MK0759BusinessvConsumerWP_ULT_30-day.pdf.

Todd, P., McKeen, J. D., & Gallupe, R. B. (1995). The Evolution of IS Job Skills: A Content Analysis of IS Job Advertisements from 1970 to 1990. *MIS Quarterly, 19*(1), 1-27.

TopicMap.*XML Topic Maps (XTM) 1.0* http://www.topicmaps.org/xtm/

Treharne, H. (2002). Supplementing a UML Development Process with B. In: L.H. Eriksson & P.A. Lindsay (Eds.), *FME2002: International Symposium Formal Methods Europe* (pp. 568-586). Vol. 2391 of LNCS, Springer-Verlag.

Triantafillakis A., Kanellis P., & Martakos D.(2004) Data Warehouse Interoperability for the Extended Enterprise, Journal of Database Management, Hershey, 15(3), pp 73-84.

Tsumaki, T., and Tamai, T. "A Framework for Matching Requirements Engineering Techniques to Project Characteristics and Situation Changes," Proceedings of SREP (5), 2005, pp. 44-58.

Tsur, S., Abiteboul, S., Agrawal, R., Dayal, U., Klein, J., & Weikum, G. (2001). Are Web services the next revolution in e-commerce? (panel). *Conference on VLDB*. Rome, Italy.

Turk, D., France, R., and Rumpe, B. "Assumptions Underlying Agile Software Development Processes," Journal of Database Management (16:4), October - December 2005, pp. 62 – 87.

Tushman, M. and Nadler, D. "Information processing as an integrating concept in organizational design", Academy of Management Review (3:3), 1978, pp. 613-624.

Tushman, M.L. "Technical Communication in R & D Laboratories: The Impact of Project Work Characteristics," The Academy of Management Journal (21:4), 1978, pp. 624-645.

U.S. Census Bureau. Census bureau databases, online at http://www.census.gov/

UDDI. *Universal description, discovery and integration.* http://www.uddi.org

Ultaseek White Paper. (2006). Business Search vs. Consumer Search: Five differences your company can't afford to ignore. [Online]. Available: http://i.i.com.com/cnwk.1d/html/itp/ultraseek_MK0759Businessv-ConsumerWP_ULT_30-day.pdf.

Uschold, M., & Gruninger, M. (1996). Ontologies: Principles, methods and applications. *Knowledge Engineering Review, 11*(2), 93-136.

USDOJ. (2006). *National Crime Victimization Survey, 1992-2005: Concatenated Incident-Level* Files Codebook. from http://www.icpsr.umich.edu/NACJD/NCVS.

Valusek, J., and Fryback, D. "Information Requirements Determination: Obstacles Within, Among and Between Participants," Proceedings of the International Conference on Information Systems), 1985, pp. 103-111.

Van Aardt, A. (2004, July 6-9). Open source software development as complex adaptive systems. Proceedings of the 17th Annual Conference of the National Advisory Committee on Computing Qualifications, Christchurch, New Zealand.

Van de Ven, A., and Delbecq, A. "A Task Contingent Model of Work-Unit Structure," Administrative Science Quarterly (19:2), 1974, pp. 183-197.

Van Den Bosch, F. A. J., Volberda, H. W., & De Boer, M. (1999). Coevolution of Firm Absorptive Capacity and Knowledge Environment: Organizational Forms and Combinative Capabilities. [Article]. *Organization Science, 10*(5), 551.

Vanston, M. (2005, August 21). Integrating legacy systems with Web services. *The Meta Group Inc.* Retrieved from http://www.metagroup.com/us/displayArticle.do?oid=32393

Vaughan-Nichols, S. J. (2002, February). Web Services: beyond the hype. *IEEE Computer,* 35 (2), 18-21

Vidgen, R., & McMaster, T. (1996). Black boxes, non-human stakeholders and the translation of IT. In: W.J.Orlikowski, G.. Walsham, M.R.Jones, & J.I.DeGross (Ed.), *Information Technology and Changes in Organizational Work*(pp. 250-271). London: Chapman & Hall.

Vinoski, S. (1997, February). *CORBA*. Integrating diverse applications within distributed heterogeneous environments. *IEEE Communications Magazine, 14*(2), 46-55.

Visser, M. A. X. (2007). Duetero-Learning in Organizations: A Review and a Reformulation. *Academy of Management Review, 32*(2), 659-667.

Vitharana, P. and Jain, H. "Research Issues in Testing Business Components," Information & Management (37:6), September 2000, pp. 297-309.

Vitharana, P., & Jain, H. (2000). Research issues in testing business components. *Information & Management, 37*(6), 297-309.

Vitter J., & Wang M. (1998). Data Cube Approximation and Histograms via Wavelets, Proceedings of the Seventh International Conference on Information and Knowledge Management, Washington D.C, pp 96-104.

Vitter J., & Wang M. (1999). Approximate Computation of Multidimensional Aggregates of Sparse Data Using Wavelets, Proceedings of the 1999 ACM SIGMOD International Conference on Management of Data, pp 193-204.

Vitter, J. S., & Wang, M. (1999). *Approximate computation of multidimensional aggregates of sparse data using wavelets.* Paper presented at the ACM SIGMOD.

Vitter, J. S., Wang, M., & Iyer, B. (1998). *Data Cube Approximation and Histograms via Wavelets.* Paper presented at the 7th CIKM.

Von Hippel, E., & Von Krogh, G. (2003). Open source software and the „private-collective" innovation model: Issues for organization science. *Organization Science, 14,* 209-223.

Von Krogh, G., Spaeth, S., & Lakhani, K. R. (2003). Community, joining, and specialization in open source software innovation: A case study. *Research Policy, 32*(7), 1217-1241.

W3C. (2004, February). *Web Services Architecture*.[Online]. Available:http://www.w3.org/TR/ws-arch/.

W3C. (2005, September). *Universal Description, Discovery, and Integration (UDDI).* [Online]. Available: http://www.uddi.org

W3C. (2005, September). *Web Services Description Language (WSDL).* [Online]. Available: http://www.w3.org/TR/wsdl

W3C. Semantic Web. http://www.w3.org/2001/sw/

Waguespack, L., & Schiano, W. T. (2004). Component-based IS architecture. *Information Systems Management, 21*(3), 53-60.

Wallace, L., Keil, M., and Rai, A. "How Software Project Risk Affects Project Performance: An Investigation of the Dimensions of Risk and an Exploratory Model," Decision Sciences (35:2), 2004, pp. 289-321.

Wallace, N. (2001). *COM/DCOM blue book: The essential learning guide for component-oriented application development for windows.* The Coriolis Group.

Walsham, G. (1997). Actor-network theory and IS research: Current status and future prospects. In: A.S.Lee, J.Liebenau, & J.I. DeGross (Ed.), *Information Systems and Qualitative Research* (pp.466-480). London: Chapman & Hall.

Walton, H., Goodhue, D.L., & Wixom, B.H. (2002). The benefits of data warehousing: Why some organizations realize exceptional payoffs. *Information & Management, 39*, 491-502.

Wand, Y. (1996). Ontology as a foundation for meta-modelling and method engineering. *Information and Software Technology, 38*, 281-287.

Wand, Y., & Weber, R. (1989). An ontological evaluation of systems analysis and design methods. In E. D. Falkenberg & P. Lindgreen (Eds.), *Information system concepts: An in-depth analysis* (pp. 79-107). Amsterdam: North-Holland.

Wand, Y., & Weber, R. (1990). An ontological model of an information system. *IEEE Transactions on Software Engineering, 16*(11), 1282-1292.

Wand, Y., & Weber, R. (1993). On the ontological expressiveness of information systems analysis and design grammars. *Journal of Information Systems, 3*(4), 217-237.

Wand, Y., & Weber, R. (2002). Research commentary: information systems and conceptual modeling - a research agenda. *Information Systems Research, 13*(4), 363-376.

Wand, Y., & Weber, R. (2004). Reflection: ontology in information systems. *Journal of Database Management, 15*(2), iii-vi.

Wand, Y., Monarchi, D. E., Parsons, J., & Woo, C. C. (1995). Theoretical foundations for conceptual modeling in information systems development. *Decision Support Systems, 15*, 285-304.

Wand, Y., Storey, V. C., & Weber, R. (2000). An ontological analysis of the relationship construct in conceptual modeling. *ACM Transactions on Database Systems, 24*(4), 494-528.

Wang, H., Parish, A., Smith, R. K., & Vrbsky, S. (2005). *Variable Selection and Ranking for Analyzing Automobile Traffic Accident Data.* Paper presented at the 2005 ACM Symposium on Applied Computing.

Wang, T.-W. & Murphy, K. (2004). Semantic heterogeneity in multidatabase systems: A review and a proposed meta-data structure. *Journal of Database Management* ,15(2), 71-87.

Wang, W., Feng J., Lu H., & J. X. Yu. J. (2002). Condensed Cube: An Effective Approach to Reducing Data Cube Size. In Proc. of ICDE, pages 155-165, San Jose, California, USA, 2002, pp 155-165.

Wasserman, S., & Faust, K., (1994). *Social Network Analysis: Methods and Applications.* New York: Cambridge University Press.

Waston, H.J., Goodhue, D.L., and Wixom, B. "The Benefits of Data Warehousing: Why Some Organizations Realize Exceptional Payoffs," *Information & Management* (39:6), 2002, pp 491-502.

Watkins, A. M. (2005). Examining the Disparity Between Juvenile and Adult Victims in Notifying the Police: A Study of Mediating Variables. *Journal of Research in Crime and Delinquency, 42*(3), 333 - 353.

Watson, H.J., Ariyachandra, T., and Matyska, R. "Data Warehousing Stages of Growth," *Information Systems Management* (18:3), 2001, pp 42-50.

Watson, H.J., Fuller, C., & Ariyachandra, T. (2004). Data warehouse governance: Best practices at Blue Cross and Blue Shield of North Carolina. *Decision Support Systems, 38*, 435-450.

Weber, R. (2003). Conceptual modelling and ontology: Possibilities and pitfalls. *Journal of Database Management, 14*(3), 1-20.

Weber, R., & Zhang, Y. (1996). An analytical evaluation NIAM's grammar for conceptual schema diagrams. *Information Systems Journal, 6*(2), 147-170.

Webster, M. (2007). Worldwide Content Management Software 2007-2011 Forecast: Continued strong growth as market strategies. [Online]. Available: http://www.idc.com/. Document number 206149.

Weick, K. *The Social Psychology of Organizing*, Addison-Wesley. Reading, MA, 1979.

Weigand, H., & Heuvel, W. J. v. d. (2002). Cross-organizational workflow integration using contracts. *Decision Support Systems, 33*, 247-265.

Wen, J. R., Li, Q., Ma, W. Y., & Zhang, H. J. (2003). A multi-paradigm querying approach for a generic multimedia database management system. *SIGMOD Record, 32*(1), 26-34.

Widom, J., & Ceri, S. (1996). Active Database Systems: Triggers and Rules for Advanced Database Processing. *Morgan Kaufmann, San Francisco, California.*

Witten, I. H., & Frank, E. (2005). *Data Mining: Practical Machine Learning Tools and Techniques* (Second ed.). San Francisco, CA: Morgan Kaufmann Publishers.

Woelk, D., Cannata, P., Huhns, M., Shen, W., & Tomlinson, C. (1993, January). Using carnot for enterprise information integration. *Second international conference on parallel and distributed information systems,* 133-136.

Wood, C. (1999). *OLE DB and ODBC Developer's Guide.* John Wiley & Sons.

Wooldridge, M. (2002). *An introduction to multiagent systems.* West Sussex, UK: John Wiley & Sons, Ltd.

Worden, D. (2000). *Sybase System 11 Development Handbook.* Morgan Kaufmann.

Wroe, C., Stevens, R., Goble, C., & Ashburner, M. (2003). A methodology to migrate the gene ontology to a description logic environment using DAML+OIL. *Pacific Symposium on Biocomputing, 8*, 624-635.

Wu. I.(2004). Canada, South Korea, Netherlands and Sweden: regulatory implications of the convergence of telecommunications, broadcasting and Internet services?. *Telecommunications Policy*, 28(1), pp.79-96.

Wyse, J. (2003) 'Supporting m-commerce transactions incorporating locational attributes: an evaluation of the comparative performance of a location-aware method of locations repository management', *International Journal of Mobile Communications*, 1(1/2), 119-147.

Wyse, J. (2008) 'Optimizing server performance for location-aware applications in mobile commerce: The repository's manager's formula.' *International Journal of Wireless and Mobile Computing* (forthcoming).

Wyse, James E. (2007). "Applying location-aware linkcell-based data management to context-aware mobile business services." *Proceedings of the Sixth International Conference on Mobile Business,* Toronto, Ontario, Canada, (July 9-11): 8 pages.

Wyse, James E. (2006) "Data Management for Location-Based Mobile Business Applications: The Location-Aware Linkcell Method." *Proceedings of the Seventh World Congress on the Management of e-Business,* Halifax, Nova Scotia, Canada, (July 13-15): 18 pp.

Wyss, C. M. & Wyss, F. I. (2007). Extending relational query optimization to dynamic schemas for information integration in multidatabases. In *Proceedings of the 2007 ACM SIGMOD international Conference on Management of Data* (Beijing, China, June 11 - 14, 2007). SIGMOD '07. ACM, New York, NY, 473-484.

Xie, M., Pogarsky, G., Lynch, J. P., & McDowall, D. (2006). Prior Police Contact and Subsequent Victim Reporting: Results from the NCVS. *Justice Quarterly, 23*(4), 481 - 501.

Xu, L., Shen, X. & Mark, J. (2005) 'Fair resource allocation with guaranteed statistical QoS for multimedia traffic in a wideband CDMA cellular network', *IEEE Transactions on Mobile Computing*, 4(2), 166-177.

Yadav, S. "Determining an Organization's Information Requirements: A State of the Art Survey," The DATA BASE for Advances in Information Systems (14:3), 1983, pp. 3-20.

Yarger, R. J., Reese, G., & King, T. (1999). *MySQL and mSQL.* O'Reilly & Associates.

Ye, F., & Agarwal, R. (2003). *Strategic Information Technology Partnerships in Outsourcing as a Distinctive Source of Information Technology Value: A Social Capital Perspective.* Paper presented at the Twenty-Fourth International Conference on Information Systems, Seattle, WA.

Yellin, D.M. & Strom, R.E., (1997). Protocol Specifications and Component Adaptors, ACM Trans. *Programming Languages and Systems*, 19(2): 292-233, March.

Yeung, M. & Kwok, Y-K. (2005) 'Wireless cache invalidation schemes with link adaptation and downlink traffic', *IEEE Transactions on Mobile Computing*, 4(1), 68-83.

Yin, R.K (1984). Case study research: Design and methods. In: Bickman, L. (Eds.), *Applied Social Research Methods Series* Vol. 5 . Los Angeles: Sage Publication.

Yoffie, D. B.(1997). *Competing in the Age of Digital Convergence*, Boston: Harvard Business School Press.

Yu, B., & Singh, M. P. (2003). Searching social networks. In *Proceedings of the ACM International Joint Conference on Autonomous Agents and Multiagent Systems (AAMAS)*.

Yuan, Y. & Zhang, J. (2003) 'Towards an appropriate business model for m-commerce', *International Journal of Mobile Communications*, 1(1/2), 35-56.

Zeng, L., Benatallah, B., Ngu, A.H.H., Dumas, M., Kalagnanam, J., & Chang, H. (2004). Qos-aware middleware for web services composition. *IEEE Trans. Softw. Eng.*, 30(5):311-327.

Zhang, B.(2002). Understanding impact of convergence on broadband industry regulation: a case study of the United States. *Telematics and Informatics*, 19(1), pp. 37-59.

Zhang, H., Kishore, R., Sharman, R., & Ramesh, R. (2004). *The GRITIKA ontology for modeling e-service applications: formal specification and illustration.* Paper presented at the 37th Hawaii International Conference on System Sciences (HICSS-37), Big Island, Hawaii.

Zhang, H., Kishore, R., Sharman, R., & Ramesh, R. (2005). MibML: A conceptual modeling grammar for integrative business information systems using the agent metaphor (Working Paper). New York: State University of New York at Buffalo, School of Management.

Zhao, H., & Ram, S. (2002). *Applying classification techniques in semantic integration of heterogeneous data sources.* Paper presented at the Eighth Americas Conference on Information Systems, Dallas, TX.

Zhao, H., & Ram, S. (2004). Clustering schema elements for semantic integration of heterogeneous data sources. *Journal of Database Management, 15*(4), 88-106.

Zhao, L., & Siau, K. (2007). Information mediation using metamodels—An approach using XML and common warehouse metamodel. *Journal of Database Management, 18*(3), 69-82.

Zhen H., & Darmont J. (2005). Evaluating the Dynamic Behavior of Database Applications, Journal of Database Management, Hershey, 16(2), pp 21-45.

Zikopolous, P. C., Baklarz, G., deRoos, D., & Melnyk, R. B. (2003). *DB2 Version 8: The Official Guide.* IBM Press.

Zipf, G.K. (1965). *Human Behavior and the Principle of Least Effort: An introduction to human ecology.* New York: Hafner.

Zmud, R., Anthony, W., and Stair, R. "The Use of Mental Imagery to Facilitate Information Identification in Requirements Analysis," Journal of Management Information Systems (9:4), 1993, pp. 175-191.

About the Contributors

Keng Siau is the E. J. Faulkner professor of management information systems (MIS) at the University of Nebraska, Lincoln (UNL). He is the director of the UNL-IBM Global Innovation Hub, editor-in-chief of the *Journal of Database Management*, and co-editor-in-chief of the Advances in Database Research series. He received his PhD degree from the University of British Columbia (UBC), where he majored in management information systems and minored in cognitive psychology. Dr. Siau has over 200 academic publications. His research has been funded by NSF, IBM, and other IT organizations. Professor Siau has received numerous research, teaching, and service awards. His latest award is the International Federation for Information Processing (IFIP) Outstanding Service Award in 2006.

John Erickson is an assistant professor in the College of Business Administration at the University of Nebraska at Omaha. His research interests include UML, software complexity and systems analysis and design issues. He has published in journals such as the *CACM*, *JDM*, and in conferences such as AMICIS, ICIS WITS, EMMSAD, and CAiSE. He has also co-authored several book chapters.

* * *

Miguel I. Aguirre-Urreta is currently an instructor at the School of Accountancy and MIS, DePaul University, and a doctoral candidate in information systems at the School of Business, University of Kansas. He earned an MBA from Indiana University and a public accounting degree from the University of Buenos Aires, Argentina. His research focuses on the adoption of technology by organizations, the theory and processes underlying requirements determination, and the individual performance effects associated with the use of information technology. His work has been published in *The Data Base for Advances on Information Systems*, as well as various national and international conferences.

VenuGopal Balijepally is an assistant professor of MIS in the College of Business at Prairie View A&M University, Texas. He received his PhD in information systems from the University of Texas at Arlington and Post Graduate Diploma in Management (MBA) from the Management Development Institute, Gurgaon, India. His research interests include software development, social capital of IS teams, knowledge management and IT management. His research is published or forthcoming in MIS Quarterly, Communications of the ACM, Communications of the AIS and various conference proceedings such as the AMCIS, HICSS and the DSI.

Athman Bouguettaya is on the computer science faculty at Virginia Tech. He is also the director of the E-Commerce and E-Government Research Lab at Virginia Tech. He received his PhD in computer science from the University of Colorado at Boulder in 1992. He is on the editorial boards of the *Distributed and Parallel Databases Journal* and the *International Journal of Cooperative Information Systems*. He guest co-edited a special issue of the IEEE Internet Computing on Database Technology on the Web. He served as the program co-chair of the IEEE RIDE Workshop on Web Services for E-Commerce and E-Government (RIDE-WS-ECEG'04). He served on numerous conference program committees. He is the author of more than 80 publications. His current research interests are in Web databases and Web services focusing on e-government and e-commerce. He is a senior member of the IEEE.

Karen Corral is an assistant professor in the Department of Information Technology and Supply Chain Management, College of Business and Economics, Boise State University. She holds a BA in English from the University of Michigan, an MS in computer information systems from Arizona State University, and a PhD in business administration from Arizona State University. Her research interests are in the area of data and knowledge management as related to decision support. Her work has been published in journals such as *Communications of the ACM*, *Information Systems Frontiers*, and *Decision Support Systems*.

Gerald DeHondt is an assistant professor in the School of Computing and Information Systems at Grand Valley State University. Prior to his current role, he worked for Compuware Corporation providing consulting services to Fortune 500 companies. While at Compuware, he held increasingly responsible positions as a programmer/analyst, quality assurance manager, network architect, enterprise architect, and most recently as a project manager guiding delivery of high-value projects. He has taught courses at the Graduate and Undergraduate level in Web development, network architecture, information security, management information systems, systems analysis and design, and project management. His research interests include extreme programming and the offshoring of systems development. He has a number of journal publications and has presented his research at various national conferences, including the Decision Sciences Institute (DSI) and the Americas Conference on Information Systems (AMCIS).

Bryan Houliston has a bachelor's degree in commerce and a master's degree in IT. His postgraduate research was primarily on wireless and mobile technology, culminating in a dissertation on the application of RFID technology in hospitals. In between his degrees Bryan spent 10 years as a professional software developer, a role to which he has now returned. He is now a candidate in the doctoral programme at the School of Computing and Mathematical Sciences, Auckland University of Technology. He is a member of the ACM and the New Zealand Computer Society.

Lori Korff received a master's degree in information systems at Virginia Tech in 2004. Her research interests include Web databases and information systems.

Régine Laleau is professor at the University Paris12 and member of the LACL research laboratory (http://www.univ-paris12.fr/lacl/) since 2003. As associate professor and a member of the CEDRIC-CNAM laboratory, she obtained an habilitation thesis in 2002. Her current research interests include the use of formal methods for the analysis and design of databases applications, the combination of graphical and formal notations, and the combination of state-based and event-based specifications for information systems.

Gondy Leroy is assistant professor in the School of Information Systems and Technology and on the Extended Faculty for Applied Women's Studies at Claremont Graduate University in California. She received a combined BS and MS degree in cognitive psychology from the Catholic University of Leuven in Belgium (1996), and an MS (1999) and PhD (2003) in management information systems from the University of Arizona. In 2003 and 2006, she was a visiting scholar at the National Library of Medicine. Her research interests are in the design of algorithms and systems that include natural language processing, text mining, and HCI with a focus on healthcare and e-government. Her research has been funded by the National Institutes of Health, the National Science Foundation, and Microsoft Research, among others.

Xumin Liu is a PhD candidate with the Department of Computer Science at Virginia Tech. Her current research interests include change management, ontologies, service oriented enterprises, Internet databases, and Web services. Her PhD dissertation focuses on using ontologies as an efficient tool to manage top-down changes in a service oriented enterprise. Xumin has published several papers in international conferences and journals, including IEEE ICWS, WebDG, CollaborateCom, Very Large Database Journal, and Journal of Software. She got her Master Degree in computer science from Jinan University, China. She is a member of the IEEE and the ACM.

Praveen Madiraju is an assistant professor in the Department of Mathematics, Statistics, and Computer Science at Marquette University, Milwaukee, Wisconsin, USA. He received his MS and PhD in computer science from Georgia State University in 2001 and 2005, respectively. His research interests include databases, XML databases, mobile agents, and middlewares for mobile devices.

Amel Mammar is an associate professor at Télécom & Management SudParis since December 2007. Currently her main research and development activities concern the use of different testing methods (active and passive) to detect software vulnerabilities. She is also working on modeling and validating security policies in general. She received the PhD in computer sciences from the Conservatoire National des Arts et Métiers (CNAM), France, in 2002. Between October 2003 and April-2006, she was senior researcher in LASSY laboratory (http: lassy.uni.lu) where she worked on the coupling of formal and semi-formal methods for the development and the verification of e-business and data-intensive applications. Before joining Télécom & Management SudParis, she was senior engineer at ClearSy which specialized in Safety Critical Systems. During this experience she worked on a proof-based approach to the formal verification of computerized interlocking systems.

RadhaKanta Mahapatra is associate professor of information systems at the University of Texas at Arlington. He holds a PhD in information systems from Texas A&M University. His research interests include software development methodologies, knowledge management, data mining, web-based end-user training, and IT management. His research publications appear in such journals as *MIS Quarterly, Communications of the ACM, Decision Support Systems, Information & Management, Database for Advances in Information Systems, Communications of the AIS, Journal of Database Management, Journal of Computer Information Systems* and *International Journal of Production Research.* He received the Distinguished Research Publication Award and the Distinguished Professional Publication Award from the College of Business Administration of the University of Texas at Arlington.

Zaki Malik received an MS in computer science at Virginia Tech. He is currently a PhD candidate in computer science at Virginia Tech. His research interests include databases, Web services and reputation systems. He is a member of the IEEE and the ACM.

George M. Marakas is a professor of information systems at the University of Kansas. Professor Marakas' research has appeared in many prestigious academic journals including *Information Systems Research*, *Management Science*, *International Journal of Human-Computer Studies*, *Journal of the Association for Information Systems*, and the *European Journal of Information Systems*. In addition, Dr. Marakas is the author of five best selling textbooks in the field of information systems.

Shamkant B. Navathe is a professor at the College of Computing, Georgia Institute of Technology, Atlanta, USA. He has published over 130 refereed papers in database research; his important contributions are in database modeling, database conversion, database design, conceptual clustering, distributed database allocation, and database integration. Dr. Navathe is an author of the book *Fundamentals of Database Systems* with R. Elmasri (Addison Wesley, 4th ed., 2004) which is currently the leading database textbook worldwide. He has worked with IBM and Siemens in their research divisions and has been a consultant to various companies including Digital, CCA, HP and Equifax. He was the program co-chair for many prestigious conferences such as SIGMOD, VLDB, and others. He has been associate editor of many ranked journals, such as *ACM Computing Surveys*, and *IEEE Transactions on Knowledge and Data Engineering*. His current research interests span human genome data management, intelligent information retrieval, text mining, security risk modeling in information systems, engineering data management, and mobile as well as peer-to-peer information processing. Dr. Navathe holds a PhD from the University of Michigan in 1976.

Sridhar Nerur is associate professor of information systems at the University of Texas at Arlington. He received his PhD from the University of Texas at Arlington. His research interests include software development, citation analysis, reuse, maintenance, and philosophical aspects of systems development. He has published in the *MIS Quarterly*, *Strategic Management Journal*, *Communications of the ACM*, *Database for Advances in Information Systems*, *Communications of the AIS*, *Information Systems Management*, *Information Management & Computer Security* and in various conference proceedings. He is an associate editor of the *European Journal of Information Systems*.

Russel Pears (PhD, Cardiff University UK) is a senior lecturer and director of the doctoral programme at the School of Computing and Mathematical Sciences , Auckland University of Technology, New Zealand. Currently he is involved in a number of research projects in data mining, including constraint-based association rule mining, contextual query search and mining high speed data streams. He has published in a number of refereed international conferences and journals in the areas of database management systems, data warehousing and data mining.

Abdelmounaam Rezgui received his MS in computer science from Purdue University. He is currently a PhD candidate in the Department of Computer Science, Virginia Tech. His current research interest is cross-layer design and optimization of sensor-actuator networks. He has published several papers in international conferences and journals, including *IEEE ICDE*, *International Journal of Digital Libraries*, *IEEE Internet Computing*, and *IEEE Security and Privacy*.

David Schuff is assistant professor of management information systems in the Fox School of Business and Management at Temple University. He holds a BA in economics from the University of Pittsburgh, an MBA from Villanova University, an MS in information management from Arizona State University, and a PhD in business administration from Arizona State University. His research interests include the strategic use of information systems, the assessment of total cost of ownership in large networked organizations, and data warehousing. His work has been published in journals such as *Decision Support Systems*, *Information & Management*, *Communications of the ACM*, and *Information Systems Journal*.

Robert D. St. Louis is a professor in the Information Systems Department at the W. P. Carey School of Business. He received his AB degree from Rockhurst College, and his MS and PhD degrees from Purdue University. His research and teaching interests are in the areas of forecasting, data mining, and decision support systems. His work has been published in a variety of journals, including the *Academy of Management Journal*, *Decision Support Systems*, *Journal of Econometrics*, *Communications in Statistics*, and *Communications of the ACM*.

Vijayan Sugumaran is professor of MIS at Oakland University, Rochester, Michigan. His research interests are in the areas of agile and component based software development, ontologies and Semantic Web, intelligent agent and multi-agent systems. He has published over 100 peer-reviewed articles in journals, conferences, and books. He has edited four books and serves on the editorial boards of seven journals. His most recent publications have appeared in *Information Systems Research*, *ACM Transactions on Database Systems*, *IEEE Transactions on Engineering Management*, and *Communications of the ACM*. Dr. Sugumaran is the editor-in-chief of the *International Journal of Intelligent Information Technologies*. He co-chairs the Intelligent Agent and Multi-Agent Systems in Business mini-track for Americas Conference on Information Systems (AMCIS 1999 - 2008). Recently, he served as the program co-chair for the 13th International Conference on Applications of Natural Language to Information Systems (NLDB 2008).

Rajshekhar Sunderraman is an associate professor of computer science at Georgia State University in Atlanta, Georgia. Professor Sunderraman received his PhD in computer science from Iowa State University and has been teaching for more than 15 years. He has published Oracle programming books, which are widely used in many universities in their database courses. His most recent book is titled Oracle 9i Programming: A Primer, published by Addison Wesley, 2004. He has published numerous articles on a wide range of topics, including deductive databases and logic programming; incompleteness, inconsistency, and negation in databases; deductive and object-oriented databases; Web access to databases; and semi-structured data on the Web.

Ozgur Turetken is an associate professor at the Ted Rogers School of IT Management, and a member of the Institute for Innovation and Technology Management at Ryerson University. He holds a BS in electrical and electronics engineering, an MBA (both from Middle East Technical University – Ankara, Turkey), and a PhD (Oklahoma State University). His research interests are in human computer interaction with an emphasis on information organization and presentation, and decision support systems with an emphasis on quantitative modeling. His previous work has appeared in *ACM Database*, *Communications of the ACM*, *Decision Support Systems*, *IEEE Computer*, *Information & Management*, *Information Systems Frontiers*, and several international conferences such as ICIS, ECIS, and AMCIS.

Haibin Wang received his PhD from the Department of Computer Science at Georgia State University in 2005. Currently, he is a research scientist in Winship Cancer Institute at Emory University. His main research areas include uncertainty management in biomedical database, cancer informatics, Semantic Web and Grid computing. He has published one monograph and over 10 papers in international journals and conferences.

James E. (Jim) Wyse is a professor with the Faculty of Business Administration at Memorial University of Newfoundland where he teaches graduate and undergraduate courses in various information systems areas: information technology management, systems analysis and design, electronic commerce, relational database management, and web-based applications development. His research interests include mobile commerce and location-based systems. Articles on his research appear in the *International Journal of Electronic Commerce*, *Journal of Database Management*, *International Journal of Mobile Communications*, and *Journal of Systems Management* and in conference proceedings such as the International Conference on Mobile Business and the World Congress on the Management of e-Business. His professional experience includes software development, systems construction, and project management. His PhD was completed at The University of Western Ontario's Ivey School of Business. His professional qualifications include a CDP (Certified Data Processor) from the Institute for Certification of Computer Professionals and an ISP (Information Systems Professional) from the Canadian Information Processing Society.

Index

F

G

H

I

K

L

M

N

O

P

Q

R

S

T

U

V

W

X

Z